D1067508

KARL MARX
FREDERICK ENGELS

COLLECTED WORKS

VOLUME

6

KARL MARX
FREDERICK ENGELS

COLLECTED WORKS

LAWRENCE & WISHART

LONDON

KARL MARX
FREDERICK ENGELS

Volume
6

MARX AND ENGELS: 1845-48

1976

LAWRENCE & WISHART

LONDON

This volume has been prepared jointly by Lawrence & Wishart Ltd., London, International Publishers Co. Inc., New York, and Progress Publishers, Moscow, in collaboration with the Institute of Marxism-Leninism, Moscow.

Editorial commissions:

GREAT BRITAIN: Jack Cohen, Maurice Cornforth, Maurice Dobb, E. J. Hobsbawm, James Klugmann, Margaret Mynatt.

USA: James S. Allen, Philip S. Foner, Dirk J. Struik, William W. Weinstone.

USSR: for Progress Publishers—N. P. Karmanova, V. N. Pavlov, M. K. Shcheglova, T. Y. Solovyova, Y. V. Torsuyev; for the Institute of Marxism-Leninism—P. N. Fedoseyev, L. I. Golman, A. I. Malysh, A. G. Yegorov, V. Y. Zevin.

ISBN 0 85315 312 4

First printing 1976

Printed in the Union of Soviet Socialist Republics in 1975

Contents

KARL MARX AND FREDERICK ENGELS
WORKS
Autumn 1845-March 1848

FROM THE PREPARATORY MATERIALS

APPENDICES

NOTES AND INDEXES

ILLUSTRATIONS

TRANSLATORS:

JACK COHEN: Articles 1, 14, 30, 34, 41, 54

MICHAEL HUDSON: Article 12

CATHERINE JUDELSON: Appendix 4

JONATHAN KEMP: Articles 27, 28, 35, 38, 42, 57, 61, 63

FRIDA KNIGHT: Articles 48, 49, 51, 62, Appendices 6, 15-18, 20, 23, 24

HUGH RODWELL: Articles 6, 11, 13, 17, 19, 20, 39, 40, 55, 56, 58, 59

BARBARA RUHEMANN: Article 43, From the Preparatory Materials 1-5, Appendices 1-3, 7-11, 13, 14, 19, 21, 22

CHRISTOPHER UPWARD: Articles 4, 18, 22, 25

Preface

Volume 6 of the *Collected Works* of Marx and Engels covers the period between the autumn of 1845 and March 1848, when the bourgeois-democratic revolutions in Europe were maturing, and the contents reflect the manifold theoretical studies and practical activities of Marx and Engels undertaken on the eve of the revolutions of 1848-49. In these activities Marx and Engels were mainly concerned with completing their working out of the general theoretical foundations of Marxism as the ideology of the working class, with taking the first steps towards the creation of a proletarian party based on the principles of scientific communism and proletarian internationalism, and with drawing up the programme and tactical platform of the international working-class movement. It was in this period that Marx and Engels founded the first international proletarian organisation—the Communist League, and produced Marxism's first programmatic statement—the *Manifesto of the Communist Party*.

The volume begins with an article by Engels, "The Festival of Nations in London", in which the principles of proletarian internationalism are set forth in print for the first time. Here Engels stressed that "the proletarians in all countries have one and the same interest, one and the same enemy", that "only the proletarians can destroy nationality, only the awakening proletariat can bring about fraternisation between the different nations" (see this volume, p. 6).

The idea of international proletarian solidarity is also expressed in the "Address of the German Democratic Communists of Brussels to Mr. Feargus O'Connor", a declaration of the German Communists' support for the British working men who had joined forces in the

Chartist Association which was effectively the first party of the working class. It was written for the Brussels Communist Correspondence Committee, which Marx and Engels had initiated at the beginning of 1846 to promote unity of ideas and organisation among the leading figures of the proletarian and socialist movement.

Of great importance among surviving papers of the Brussels Communist Correspondence Committee is the "Circular Against Kriege", a criticism of German "true socialism". Here Marx and Engels firmly opposed the views of the "true socialist" Kriege, who was at this time active in the United States. He was substituting a sentimental theory of universal love for communist ideas, and seeking at the same time to present the American democratic movement for agrarian reform, the progressive significance of which Marx and Engels fully recognised, as a struggle for the communist transformation of society. The "Circular" showed that there was no point in trying to give socialist doctrines a religious colouring and that the communist world outlook was incompatible with religion.

On a more general plane, the "Circular Against Kriege" was also a blow against the views of Weitling and his supporters, who advocated egalitarian utopian communism. Similar in many ways to the beliefs of the "true socialists", these views increased the ideological confusion among the working class and encouraged sectarian and dogmatic attitudes.

Marx's "Declaration Against Karl Grün", Engels' unfinished "The Constitutional Question in Germany", his essays "German Socialism in Verse and Prose", and some other works, are also devoted to the criticism of "true socialism". In "The Constitutional Question in Germany" Engels takes issue with "true socialist" political views. He shows that, by ignoring the supremacy of the absolutist system in Germany and opposing progressive bourgeois reforms, the "true socialists" were playing into the hands of the absolutist feudal circles and acting in profound contradiction to the interests of the working people. After a searching analysis of the social and political situation in Germany Engels outlines the revolutionary tactics of the proletariat in the approaching bourgeois revolution, emphasising that the working class has an interest in the consistent realisation of the aims of such a revolution.

In his essays "German Socialism in Verse and Prose" Engels then criticises the aesthetic ideals of "true socialism", as represented in the poetry and literary criticism of its supporters (the poet Karl Beck, the literary historian Karl Grün, and others). He censures their characteristically sentimental, merely philanthropic themes, their petty-bourgeois tastes and illusions and philistine moralising.

Progressive writers and poets should, he declares, bring to their readers the advanced ideas of their time and acclaim not a "cowardly petty-bourgeois wretchedness", but a "proud, threatening, and revolutionary proletarian" (see this volume, p. 235). Here Engels arrives, too, at important principles of Marxist aesthetics and criteria for the appreciation of works of art. In contrast to Grün's extremely naive and thoroughly petty-bourgeois attitude to the work of such a great writer as Goethe, Engels shows that the critic's task is always to reveal the link between the writer's social environment and his world outlook and thoroughly to investigate its contradictions. He must be able to distinguish between elements of genuine artistic and social value in the work and those which express only a narrowness of outlook on the writer's part.

One of the most important theoretical works of Marxism—Marx's *The Poverty of Philosophy. Answer to the "Philosophy of Poverty" by M. Proudhon*—belongs to this period. Aimed against the growing trend of Proudhonism—a trend which was later to acquire considerable influence in the working-class movement and which Marx and his associates fought for decades—this book was compiled to meet the contemporary needs of the revolutionary struggle and to help make the proletariat theoretically and ideologically independent of the petty bourgeoisie.

The Poverty of Philosophy was prompted by the publication of Proudhon's *Système des contradictions économiques, ou Philosophie de la misère.* Marx saw in Proudhon's ideas the embodiment of a petty-bourgeois mentality, the inconsistency and utopianism permeating the outlook of a class which seeks at once to escape from the disastrous consequences of capitalist development and to preserve the economic foundation of the system—private ownership of the means of production and wage labour. Criticism of Proudhon's views was therefore fundamental for establishing among the workers a true understanding of the revolutionary aims of proletarian struggle and for exposing any attempts to replace these aims with the utopian reformist idea of adapting the capitalist system to the interests of the working people.

Marx's *Poverty of Philosophy* is one of the first works of mature Marxism. Besides criticising Proudhon, Marx expounds his own philosophical and economic views. Here, therefore, in print for the first time (though still in a somewhat polemical form) were formulated the scientific principles of historical materialism which Marx and Engels had worked out mainly in the process of writing *The German Ideology. The Poverty of Philosophy* was Marx's public début as an economist. It is the first published work to outline the fundamental propositions of Marx's economic theory which form the point of departure of Marxist political economy. Marx himself wrote in 1880: "...This book contains in embryo what after a labour of twenty years became the theory that was developed in *Capital*." *The Poverty of Philosophy* also enunciates a number of basic propositions about the working-class movement and its tactics.

Marx first of all shows the weakness of Proudhon's basic approach. He had attempted to apply Hegelian dialectics to political economy with no understanding of what dialectics really means. In Proudhon, dialectics is reduced to the artificial construction of contradictions. He accepted basic facts of economic production and exchange as given and unalterable, and then put forward the utopian idea that their "bad" side could be eliminated, while preserving their "good" side. In this way, he thought, the capitalist system could be "purified" of all those consequences of its development that were inimical to the small producer—competition, concentration of production, the domination of big, particularly banking, capital, and so on. Marx stresses that Proudhon "has nothing of Hegel's dialectics but the language" (see this volume, p. 168), and remains in practice a metaphysician. He shows that Proudhon adopts the idealist form of Hegel's theory of contradictions and deprives it of its rational elements.

Marx contrasts his own interpretation of the materialist character of dialectics to Hegel's idealist interpretation, drawing a clear line of distinction between his own scientific method and the Hegelian method.

In *The Poverty of Philosophy* Marx expressed the essence of the materialist understanding of history in a clear and concise formula: "Social relations are closely bound up with productive forces. In acquiring new productive forces men change their mode of production; and in changing their mode of production, in changing the way of earning their living, they change all their social relations. The hand-mill gives you society with the feudal lord; the steam-mill, society with the industrial capitalist" (see this volume, p. 166). Defining the meaning of the term "productive forces", Marx states that it embraces not only the instruments of production but also the workmen themselves, and he thus arrives at the important proposition that "... the greatest productive power is the revolutionary class itself" (see this volume, p. 211).

In the course of his studies in political economy from 1845 to 1846 Marx had demonstrated the utopianism of the attempts of the English Ricardian socialists—Bray, Thompson and others—to deduce a socialist system from the postulates of classical political economy, particularly, from the labour theory of value. In *The Poverty of Philosophy* he showed that Proudhon was repeating and aggravating this mistake by regarding the economic categories of bourgeois society as the foundation on which to build a new, "just" social order. Unlike the English socialists, however, whose goal was the radical transformation of society on socialist principles, Proudhon sought merely to save the small private producer.

The Poverty of Philosophy describes English classical political economy in its most characteristic aspects and shows the important part it played in the development of economic thought. At the same time, although the criticism of the classical economists is not complete, it shows its weaknesses. Even in this work, however, Marx is already basing his study of economic life on entirely new premises, fundamentally different from those of the classical economists. In contrast to Smith, Ricardo and other bourgeois economists who assumed the eternal and immutable nature of the economic laws of capitalism, Marx argues that the laws of bourgeois production are transient in character, just as the laws of the pre-capitalist social-economic formations were transient. There will inevitably come a time, he wrote, when the laws of bourgeois production will be superseded because the very system of bourgeois relations will disappear from the face of the earth.

In his polemic with Proudhon and the bourgeois economists Marx took a new standpoint in analysing such categories of political economy as value, money, rent, and such economic phenomena as the division of labour and application of machinery, competition and monopoly. Here he still employs as in other economic works of this period (specifically, in the manuscript published in this volume under the title of "Wages") concepts borrowed from the classical economists—"labour as a commodity", "value of labour" and "price of labour"—but he gives these concepts a new meaning which discloses the underlying exploitation in the relations between capital and wage labour. In contrast to Ricardo, who regarded labour as a commodity the same as any other, Marx sees it as a commodity of a special kind, the purchase and use of which leads to the enrichment of the capitalist and a worsening in the position of the owner of this commodity—the worker. Marx formulates, as yet in a general, rudimentary form, the universal law of capitalist accumulation. Under capitalism, he writes, "in the selfsame relations in which wealth is produced, poverty is produced also" (see this volume, p. 176). In *The Poverty of Philosophy* Marx singles out the industrial proletariat that came into being in the process of the development of machine production as the real social force destined to resolve the contradictions of bourgeois society by its revolutionary transformation.

Marx refuted Proudhon's contention that strikes and trade union organisation are of no use to the workers. He showed that the economic struggle, strikes and workers' combinations were essential for the unity and revolutionary education of the proletarian masses. *The Poverty of Philosophy* expresses the profound idea that the awareness of the fundamental contradiction between its own interests and the continuation of the capitalist system, which the proletariat acquires as an organised movement develops, plays a decisive role in converting it from a mass that is "already a class as against capital, but not yet for itself", into "a class for itself" (see this volume, p. 211). Here Marx also formulates one of the most important tactical principles of the revolutionary proletarian movement—the unity of economic and political struggle and the decisive role of the political struggle for the emancipation of the proletariat.

In the period leading up to the revolutions of 1848 Marx and Engels were extremely active as proletarian journalists, reacting to all contemporary events, especially those of a revolutionary nature. This volume includes a large number of their articles and reports published in the working-class and democratic press of the time, particularly in the *Deutsche-Brusseler-Zeitung*, which under their influence became the unofficial organ of the Communist League. The chief aim of Marx and Engels' writing for the press in this period was to explain to the working class its role and tasks in the imminent bourgeois revolution, to prepare the proletarian party that was beginning to take shape for the forthcoming battles, to spread the new revolutionary proletarian world outlook and to defend scientific communism from the attacks of its enemies.

Continuing his contributions to the Chartist *Northern Star*, which he had begun in 1843, Engels wrote regular articles about the maturing revolutionary situation in Germany ("The State of Germany", "Violation of the Prussian Constitution", etc.) and the imminent revolutionary crisis in France ("Government and Opposition in France", "The Decline and Approaching Fall of Guizot.—Position of the French Bourgeoisie", "The Reform Movement in France", etc.). In October 1847 he made contact with the French democrats and socialists associated with the newspaper *La Réforme*, and became an active contributor. He sent the paper a series of articles on the Chartist movement in England ("The Agrarian Programme of the Chartists", "The Chartist Banquet in Connection with the Elections of 1847", etc.), and translated and published with commentaries the major Chartist documents, reports of Chartist meetings, and so on. His contributions also included several articles on the national liberation movement in Ireland ("The Commercial Crisis in England.—The Chartist Movement.—Ireland", "The Coercion Bill for Ireland and the Chartists"). At the same time the *Deutsche-Brüsseler-Zeitung* published articles, mainly by Engels, on the revolutionary events in Switzerland, Italy, Germany, Austria and Denmark ("The Civil War in Switzerland", "The Movements of 1847", "Three New Constitutions", etc.), Engels' article "Revolution in Paris" was a response to the events of February 1848 in France.

The publication of these articles and reports helped to strengthen the international ties between the proletarian and democratic circles of the European countries and to evolve a common platform for the revolutionary forces. The same purpose was served by Marx and Engels' work in the Brussels Democratic Association, their friendly contacts with the London society of Fraternal Democrats, their growing ties with the leaders of Chartism, and their speeches at international meetings and conferences—as a number of the articles included in this volume bear witness (e.g. Marx's article "The *Débat social* of February 6 on the Democratic Association" and Engels' report "The Anniversary of the Polish Revolution of 1830"), and likewise the documents published in the Appendices.

Many of the articles in this volume announce important propositions of the theory of Marxism and the tactics of proletarian revolutionary struggle. Prominent among these is the article "The Communism of the *Rheinischer Beobachter*", which was aimed against the supporters of feudal socialism and their attempts to attribute a special social mission to the Prussian monarchy. This article gave the German working class a clear orientation in a situation of mounting revolution.

To the moderate and conciliatory councils of the liberal opposition Marx counterposed the revolutionary overthrow of the absolute monarchy and drew up a programme of revolutionary-democratic reforms. The victory of the bourgeois revolution, he declared, would make it easier for the working class to achieve its own class aims. "The rule of the bourgeoisie does not only place quite new weapons in the hands of the proletariat for the struggle *against* the bourgeoisie, but ... it also secures for it a quite different status, the status of a recognised party" (see this volume, p. 222).

The idea that the working class should take an active part in the bourgeois-democratic revolution was further developed in the polemic that Marx and Engels conducted with the German democrat Karl Heinzen, who expressed the hostility to communism of a whole group of German radical journalists. Engels' articles "The Communists and Karl Heinzen" and Marx's work "Moralising Criticism and Critical Morality" provide striking examples of how to answer anti-communism and expose its slanders of Communists.

In reply to Heinzen's accusation that the Communists split the democratic camp, Marx and Engels demonstrate that, although their ultimate aims go far beyond establishing bourgeois-democratic freedoms, the Communists' immediate aim is to win democracy, and in this struggle they make common cause with the democrats.

In what Marx and Engels wrote against Heinzen we find a draft of the proposition that the working class must lead the revolutionary movement. In contrast to Heinzen, who assigned the leading role in the impending revolution to the peasantry and urban petty bourgeoisie, Engels argued that not the peasantry but "the industrial proletariat of the towns has become the vanguard of all modern democracy; the urban petty bourgeoisie and still more the peasants depend on its initiative completely" (see this volume, p. 295).

Marx and Engels regarded the bourgeois-democratic revolution as merely an intermediate stage in the proletariat's revolutionary struggle. The proletarians, Marx wrote, "can and must accept the *bourgeois revolution* as a precondition for the *workers' revolution*" (this volume, p. 333). With the victory of the democratic revolution the proletariat is confronted with the task of "becoming a power, in the first place a revolutionary power" in order to carry the struggle against the bourgeoisie itself to its ultimate conclusion (see this volume, p. 319). Thus in their polemic with Heinzen Marx and Engels approached the idea of uninterrupted revolution and regarded the working class' conquest of political power as its next stage. Here we have the first published formulation of the idea of the dictatorship of the proletariat as an instrument for the revolutionary reconstruction of society.

In "Moralising Criticism and Critical Morality" Marx laid the groundwork for the theory of the dialectical interrelationship between the economic basis and the political superstructure. It is not political power, he stressed, that determines property relations, as the bourgeois and petty-bourgeois democrats imagine, but, on the contrary, the character of political power itself depends on historically formed production relations (property relations) and the class structure of society thus created. At the same time, Marx points out that political power is an active factor in social life. In the hands of the rising class it accelerates progressive development; in the hands of the obsolete class it acts as a powerful brake on progress. The revolutionary supplanting of the old political superstructure is therefore an essential condition for the victory of the new social system.

Articles by Engels published in this volume—"The 'Satisfied' Majority...", "Louis Blanc's Speech at the Dijon Banquet", and Marx's "Remarks on the Article by M. Adolphe Bartels"—like the articles against Heinzen, show that while opposing sectarian isolation from the democratic movement and advocating an alliance with the democrats, Marx and Engels sought to build the relations between the proletarian party and the democratic organisations on a principled basis. They refused to condone democratic mistakes and illusions. Engels, in particular, spoke out against the *Réforme* party leaders on issues where their platform was unacceptable to the Communists—their notion of the special cosmopolitan role of France in world history and their nationalistic claims that French democracy should hold a leading position in the international democratic movement. "The union of the democrats of different nations does not exclude mutual criticism," Engels wrote. "It is impossible without such criticism. Without criticism there is no understanding and consequently no union" (this volume, p. 409).

Marx and Engels' criticisms of the bourgeois free traders, for whom free trade was to become a blessing for the proletariat and a panacea for all social ills, provide a striking example of their struggle against ideology hostile to the working class. In the materials relating to the international congress of economists in Brussels, and in Marx's "Speech on the Question of Free Trade", the theory of free trade and its rival bourgeois economic system of protectionism are alike subjected to scientific criticism and given a specifically historical evaluation. In the conditions of the 1840s, Marx gave preference to the free-trade system as the more progressive of the two. "We are for Free Trade, because by Free Trade all economical laws, with their most astounding contradictions, will act upon a larger scale, upon a greater extent of territory, upon the territory of the whole earth; and because from the uniting of all these contradictions into a single group, where they stand face to face, will result the struggle which will itself eventuate in the emancipation of the proletarians" (see this volume, p. 290).

Marx and Engels paid great attention to national liberation movements. They realised the importance of the emancipation struggles of the oppressed peoples in the imminent bourgeois-democratic revolution, and in their articles "The Beginning of the End in Austria" and "A Word to the *Riforma*" and in their speeches at public meetings to mark the anniversaries of the Polish uprisings of 1830 and 1846, they sought to provide the working class with a thoroughly argued position on the question of nationalities. Marx and Engels were emphatic that the proletariat must give full support to the national liberation movement of the oppressed peoples and urged proletarian groups to ally themselves with the revolutionary-democratic wings of the national movements. They saw the guarantee of success for the latter in a combination of the struggle for national liberation with the demand for deep-going internal revolutionary-democratic changes.

"A nation cannot become free," Engels wrote, "and at the same time continue to oppress other nations" (this volume, p. 389). He and Marx stressed that the nationalities question could be finally solved only after the proletariat's victory over the bourgeoisie, whose domination inevitably leads to the intensification of national antagonisms and colonial oppression. The proletarian revolution, they declared, is "the signal of liberation for all oppressed nations" (this volume, p. 388).

Some of the judgments and conclusions reached by Marx and Engels in their articles and reports were still of a preliminary character and sometimes one-sided; they reflected the level of Marxist thought at the time and were later supplemented or clarified in the light of new historical experience and a more profound and comprehensive study of the subject. In their later works, for example, Marx and Engels gave a different, positive interpretation of the role of the peasant movements in the Middle Ages, as compared with what we find in the article "The Communists and Karl Heinzen". They also arrived at a rather different estimate of the struggle of the Swiss against Austrian domination in the 14th and 15th centuries, and the character and results of the war waged by the USA against Mexico in 1846-48, and so on.

The material in this volume shows the work of Marx and Engels as organisers and leaders of the Communist League and, above all, enables us to trace the stages in their working out of the programme and organisational principles of the League.

This volume contains the "Draft of a Communist Confession of Faith", written by Engels for the First Congress of the Communist League (June 1847), Engels' manuscript of the *Principles of Communism* (October 1847) and the *Manifesto of the Communist Party*, written by Marx and Engels on the instructions of the Second Congress held at the end of November and beginning of December 1847. The Appendices to the volume contain two versions of the Rules of the Communist League, which Marx and Engels took part in compiling, and also other documents of the League, to which they contributed in some degree or other.

The "Draft of a Communist Confession of Faith" (the so-called "Credo") which was discovered only in 1968, is the first version of the Marxist programme for the working-class movement. It defines the aims of the Communists and describes the proletariat as the class destined to bring about the socialist revolution. Engels shows that the communist transformation of society depends on historical conditions and the laws of history, maps its paths and indicates the tasks of the working class after its conquest of political power in the conditions of the transitional period from capitalism to the new communist system. This document expresses some profound thoughts concerning the elimination of national differences and the overcoming of religious prejudices in the society of the future.

The programmatic document the *Principles of Communism*, which is written on a broader, more comprehensive theoretical basis, was in effect the original draft of the *Communist Manifesto*. Verifying the formulations and deepening the arguments, Engels introduces a number of points that were absent from the "Draft of a Communist Confession of Faith" and substantially revises many of its propositions (for example, the description of the transitional period). He also defines communism as the theory of the emancipation of the proletariat, reveals the historical preconditions for the rise and development of the working-class movement and formulates its goals. The goal of the proletarian revolution, he writes, "absolutely necessitates a completely new organisation of society, in which industrial production is no longer directed by individual factory owners, competing one against the other, but by the whole of society according to a fixed plan and according to the needs of all" (see this volume, p. 347).

In the *Principles of Communism* the answer to the question of the possible ways of abolishing capitalist private property is more clearly worded than in the "Draft of a Communist Confession of Faith". In contrast to the advocates of peaceful reforms (Cabet, Proudhon and the "true socialists"), and also the Blanquists, who thought communism could be established by means of conspiratorial action on the part of a select group of revolutionaries, Engels argues the necessity for a deep-going proletarian revolution carried out by the masses of the working people—a revolution which in the historical conditions obtaining at the time could be carried out only by force. At the same time Engels stressed that if there arose anywhere or at any stage of development a real possibility of achieving the revolutionary abolition of private property by peaceful means, "the

Communists certainly would be the last to resist it" (this volume, p. 349).

The *Principles of Communism* touches upon the possibility of the victory of a communist revolution in one country. In reply to this question Engels developed the conception of revolution already expounded in *The German Ideology*. He indicated that the proletarian revolution could not be victorious in one country alone, but must take place more or less simultaneously in the developed capitalist countries. "It is a worldwide revolution and will therefore be worldwide in scope" (see this volume, p. 352). These notions of the forthcoming revolutionary process corresponded to the level of capitalist development that had been reached in those days. In the ensuing historical period, however, the transition to imperialism made the development of the capitalist countries far more uneven. Lenin, who shared the general basic conceptions of Marx and Engels in the theory of world communist revolution, reached the fundamentally different conclusion that socialism could be victorious at first in a few capitalist countries or even in one alone.

The description of communist society figures prominently in the *Principles of Communism*. With considerable scientific prevision Engels threw light on many important aspects of the future system and the changes that would ensue in production and consumption, in social relations and social consciousness.

The summit of Marx and Engels' creative work before the 1848 revolution is the *Manifesto of the Communist Party*, the first programmatic document of the international proletarian movement. It was the first document to expound the fundamentals of the Marxist outlook in a comprehensive and systematic form that reflected the essential unity of all the components of Marx's teaching. "With the clarity and brilliance of genius," Lenin wrote of the *Manifesto*, "this work outlines a new world-conception, consistent materialism, which also embraces the realm of social life; dialectics, as the most comprehensive and profound doctrine of development; the theory of the class struggle and of the world-historic revolutionary role of the proletariat—the creator of a new, communist society" (V. I. Lenin, *Collected Works*, Vol. 21, p. 48).

The *Manifesto of the Communist Party* armed the proletariat by proclaiming the scientific proof of the inevitability of the collapse of capitalism and the triumph of the proletarian revolution. "But not only has the bourgeoisie," states the *Manifesto*, "forged the weapons that bring death to itself; it has also called into existence the men who are to wield those weapons—the modern working class—the proletarians" (this volume, p. 490). Having demonstrated the role of the class struggle in history, Marx and Engels went on to argue that the proletariat was the most revolutionary of all classes known in history, the class whose world-historic role was to perform a mission of liberation in the interests of the whole of toiling humanity by ridding society for ever of all oppression and exploitation.

The cornerstone of the *Manifesto* is the idea of the dictatorship of the proletariat—of a proletarian government which is democratic by its very nature, expresses the interests of the great majority of the people and relies on their support. Although they do not as yet use the term "dictatorship of the proletariat", Marx and Engels show how the proletarian state is needed in order to eliminate the exploiting classes, abolish the conditions for the existence of classes in general and ensure the final victory of the social relations of a classless society.

The *Manifesto* described and predicted more fully the features of the future communist system outlined in the *Principles of Communism*—the abolition of all exploitation of man by man, of war, of social and national oppression, and of colonial enslavement; the true burgeoning of material production, the powerful development of the productive forces for the full and all-round satisfaction of the material and spiritual needs of all members of society; the elimination of the antithesis between mental and physical work and between town and country; genuine freedom of the individual, equality of women, and unity of personal and social interests. Marx and Engels emphasise that communism cannot be established all at once. It can be achieved only through the gradual transformation of the old society into the new, so that the proletarian state must carry out a number of measures that prepare the ground for this transformation. While presenting a programme of these measures, they do not treat them as self-sufficient; the specific conditions of the building of the new society would inevitably lead to their being amended.

The *Manifesto* lays the foundations of the Marxist conception of the proletarian party as the organiser and leader of the working class and outlines the fundamentals of its tactics. The setting up of such a party, Marx and Engels stress, is absolutely essential if the proletariat is to win political power and bring about the socialist transformation of society. To perform its role as the vanguard of the proletariat, the party must be able to subordinate the immediate aims of the proletarian movement to its ultimate aims, maintain the unity of the national and international tasks of the proletariat, and support every revolutionary and progressive trend.

Of fundamental importance is the section of the *Communist*

Manifesto which examines would-be socialist trends alien to the scientific outlook of the working class—feudal, Christian, petty-bourgeois and bourgeois socialism. Revealing the class roots of these trends in bourgeois society, Marx and Engels showed the working class and its party how to recognise the anti-revolutionary direction of socialist theories that could lead the working class off the right path and how to combat and overcome them. In their analysis of the teaching of the great utopian socialists, however, they pointed to its rational as well as its weak, anti-scientific sides, and warned against sectarian and dogmatic interpretations of the socialist ideological legacy.

The communist movement must always be international in character, the *Manifesto* declared, and emphasised the tremendous importance of achieving unity of views and actions among the proletarians of various countries, the importance of international proletarian solidarity. In their great slogan "Working Men of All Countries, Unite!" Marx and Engels expressed for their own time and for the times to come the community of the class interests and aims of the workers of the whole world, the idea of proletarian internationalism as the principle of the international communist movement.

The publication of the *Communist Manifesto* (February 1848) signified that the process of the formation of Marxism as an integrated revolutionary world outlook was basically complete.

In the section of the volume headed "From the Preparatory Materials" the reader will find, among other documents, the draft plan for Section III of the *Manifesto* and the only extant page of the rough manuscript of the *Manifesto*. Appearing in English for the first time, they serve as an illustration of how Marx worked on the structure and text of this work.

Besides the already mentioned documents on Marx's and Engels' activities in the Communist League and the Brussels Democratic Association, the Appendices also contain reports of their speeches at international meetings and conferences in London and Brussels, and biographical documents, including papers that illustrate the police action taken against Marx and other German revolutionaries.

* * *

A substantial portion of the works published in this volume appear in English translation for the first time. These include the "Circular Against Kriege" by Marx and Engels, "The Constitutional Question in Germany" and "German Socialism in Verse and Prose" by Engels, the text of an undelivered speech by Marx at the congress of economists in Brussels, the articles by Engels "The Communists and Karl Heinzen", a number of his articles about the Chartist movement in England published in *La Réforme*, documents in the section "From the Preparatory Materials" and the bulk of the material in the Appendices. Information concerning complete or partial publication in earlier English translations of the works included in this volume is provided in the notes. In the present volume these works are published in new or thoroughly revised and amended translations. The translations from the French are noted at the end of each work, where it is also indicated which texts were originally written in English.

The present edition notes more fully than was done in previous publications discrepancies between the authorised translations of certain works ("Speech on the Question of Free Trade", *Manifesto of the Communist Party*) and the texts of these works in the language of the original.

The volume was compiled and the preface and notes written by Vera Morozova and edited by Lev Golman (CC CPSU Institute of Marxism-Leninism). The name index and the indices of quoted and mentioned literature and of periodicals were prepared by Irina Shikanyan (CC CPSU Institute of Marxism-Leninism), and the subject index by Marlen Arzumanov and Boris Gusev.

The translations were made by Jack Cohen, Michael Hudson, Catherine Judelson, Jonathan Kemp, Frida Knight, Hugh Rodwell, Barbara Ruhemann, Christopher Upward and edited by Robert Daglish, Richard Dixon, W. L. Guttsman, Frida Knight, Margaret Mynatt, and Alick West.

The volume was prepared for the press by the editors Natalia Karmanova, Margarita Lopukhina and Galina Sandalneva for Progress Publishers, and Vladimir Mosolov, scientific editor for the Institute of Marxism-Leninism, Moscow.

KARL MARX
and
FREDERICK ENGELS

WORKS

Autumn 1845-March 1848

Frederick Engels

THE FESTIVAL OF NATIONS IN LONDON

(TO CELEBRATE THE ESTABLISHMENT OF THE FRENCH REPUBLIC, SEPTEMBER 22, 1792)[1]

"What do the nations matter to us? What does the French Republic matter to us? Did we not long ago grasp the notion of nations and did we not determine the place of each of them; did we not assign to the Germans the sphere of theory, to the French that of politics, and to the English that of civil society? And the more so the French Republic! What is there to celebrate about a stage of development which has long been superseded, which has abolished itself as a result of its own consequences! If you want to give us some information about England it would be better if you described the latest phase that the socialist principle has reached there; tell us if one-sided English socialism still does not recognise how far it is below our principled heights and how it can claim to be only a *phase* [Ein Moment] and an obsolete one at that!"

Keep calm, dear Germany. The nations and the French Republic matter a great deal to us.

The fraternisation of nations, as it is now being carried out everywhere by the extreme proletarian party in contrast to the old instinctive national egoism and to the hypocritical private-egotistical cosmopolitanism of free trade, is worth more than all the German theories of true socialism put together.

The fraternisation of nations under the banner of *modern democracy,* as it began from the French Revolution and developed into French communism and English Chartism, shows that the masses and their representatives know better than the German theoreticians how things stand.

"But this has nothing whatever to do with what we are discussing. Who is talking about fraternisation, *as it...,* etc., about democracy, *as it...,* etc.? We are talking about the fraternisation of nations in and for itself, about *the* fraternisation of nations, about Democracy, about democracy pure and simple, about democracy *as such*. Have you completely forgotten your Hegel?"

"We are not Romans, we smoke tobacco."[a] We are not talking about the anti-nationalist movement *now* developing in the *world*, we are talking about the abrogation of nationalities through the medium of pure thought—assisted by fantasy in the absence of facts—happening in our *head*. We are not talking about *real* democracy which the whole of Europe is hastening to embrace and which is a quite special democracy, different from all previous democracies. We are talking about a quite different democracy which represents the mean between Greek, Roman, American and French democracy, in short about the *concept* of democracy. We are not talking about the *things* which belong to the nineteenth century, and which are bad and ephemeral, but about categories which are eternal and which existed before "the mountains were brought forth". Briefly, we are not discussing what is being talked about but something quite different.

To sum up: when English people, French people and those Germans who take part in the practical movement but are not theoreticians nowadays talk about democracy and the fraternisation of nations, this should not be understood simply in a political sense. Such fantasies still exist only among the German theoreticians and a few foreigners who don't count. In reality these words now have a social meaning in which the political meaning is dissolved. The Revolution itself was something quite different from a struggle for this or that form of State, as people in Germany still quite frequently imagine that it was. The connection of most insurrections of that time with famine, the significance which the provisioning of the capital and the distribution of supplies assumed already from 1789 onwards, the maximum, the laws against buying up food supplies, the battle cry of the revolutionary armies—"*Guerre aux palais, paix aux chaumières*"[b]—the testimony of the Carmagnole[2] according to which Republicans must have *du pain*[c] as well as *du fer*[d] and *du coeur*[e]—and a hundred other obvious superficialities already prove, without any more detailed investigation of the facts, how greatly democracy differed at that time from a mere political organisation. As it is it is well known that the Constitution of 1793 and the terror

---

[a] Heinrich Heine, "Zur Beruhigung".—*Ed.*
[b] War to the palaces, peace to the cottages.—*Ed.*
[c] Bread.—*Ed.*
[d] Arms.—*Ed.*
[e] Heart (courage).—*Ed.*

originated with the party which derived its support from the insurgent proletariat, that Robespierre's overthrow signified the victory of the bourgeoisie over the proletariat, that Babeuf's conspiracy for equality revealed the final consequences of the democracy of '93—insofar as these were at all possible at that time.[3] The French Revolution was a social movement from beginning to end, and after it a purely political democracy became a complete absurdity.

Democracy nowadays is communism. Any other democracy can only still exist in the heads of theoretical visionaries who are not concerned with real events, in whose view it is not the men and the circumstances that develop the principles but the principles develop of themselves. Democracy has become the proletarian principle, the principle of the masses. The masses may be more or less clear about this, the only correct meaning of democracy, but all have at least an obscure feeling that social equality of rights is implicit in democracy. The democratic masses can be safely included in any calculation of the strength of the communist forces. And if the proletarian parties of the different nations unite they will be quite right to inscribe the word "Democracy" on their banners, since, except for those who do not count, all European democrats in 1846 are more or less Communists at heart.

Despite the fact of the French Republic having been "superseded", the Communists of all countries are fully justified in celebrating it. Firstly, all the nations which were stupid enough to let themselves be used to fight against the Revolution have owed the French a public apology ever since they realised what a *sottise*[a] they committed out of loyalty; secondly, the whole European social movement today is only the second act of the revolution, only the preparation for the *dénouement* of the drama which began in Paris in 1789, and now has the whole of Europe for its stage; thirdly, it is time, in our cowardly, selfish, beggarly, bourgeois epoch, to remember those great years when a whole people all at once threw aside all cowardice, selfishness and beggarliness, when there were men courageous enough to defy the law, who shrank from nothing and whose iron energy ensured that from May 31, 1793 to July 26, 1794[4] not a single coward, petty shopkeeper or stockjobber, in short, not a single bourgeois dared show his face in the whole of France. It is really necessary at a time when European peace is held together by a Rothschild, when a cousin Köchlin screams about protective tariffs, and a Cobden

---

[a] Stupidity.—*Ed.*

about free trade, and when a Diergardt preaches the salvation of sinful humanity through associations for raising up the working classes[5]—in truth it is necessary to remember Marat and Danton, Saint-Just and Babeuf, and the joy over victories at Jemappes and Fleurus.[6] If that mighty epoch, these iron characters, did not still tower over our mercenary world, then humanity must indeed despair and throw itself into the arms of a cousin Köchlin, a Cobden or a Diergardt.

Finally, fraternisation between nations has today, more than ever, a purely social significance. The fantasies about a European Republic, perpetual peace under political organisation, have become just as ridiculous as the phrases about uniting the nations under the aegis of universal free trade, and while all such chimerical sentimentalities become completely irrelevant, the proletarians of all nations, without too much ceremony, are already *really* beginning *to fraternise* under the banner of communist democracy. And the proletarians are the only ones who are really able to do this; for the bourgeoisie in each country has its own special interests, and since these interests are the most important to it, it can never transcend nationality; and the few theoreticians achieve nothing with all their fine "principles" because they simply allow these contradictory interests—like everything else—to continue to exist and can do nothing but talk. But the proletarians in all countries have one and the same interest, one and the same enemy, and one and the same struggle. The great mass of proletarians are, by their very nature, free from national prejudices and their whole disposition and movement is essentially humanitarian, anti-nationalist. Only the proletarians can destroy nationality, only the awakening proletariat can bring about fraternisation between the different nations.

The following facts will confirm everything I have just said.

On August 10, 1845, a similar festival was held in London to celebrate a triple anniversary—that of the revolution of 1792, the proclamation of the Constitution of 1793, and the founding of the "Democratic Association" by the most radical wing of the English movement of 1838-39.[7]

This most radical wing consisted of Chartists, proletarians as might be expected, but people who clearly grasped the aim of the Chartist movement and strove to speed it up. While the great mass of the Chartists was still concerned at that time only with the transfer of state power to the working class, and few had the time to reflect on the use of this power, the members of this Association, which played an important role in the agitation of that time, were unanimous in this:—they were first of all republicans, and moreover, republicans who put forward as their creed the Constitution of '93, rejected all ties with the bourgeoisie, even with the petty bourgeoisie, and defended the principle that the oppressed have the right to use the same means against their oppressors as the latter use against them. But this was not all; they were not only republicans but Communists, and irreligious Communists at that. The Association's collapse followed that of the revolutionary agitation of 1838-39; but its effectiveness was not wasted and it greatly contributed to stimulating the energy of the Chartist movement and to developing its latent communist elements. Communist as well as cosmopolitan[8] principles were already voiced at this festival of August 10; *social* as well as political equality were demanded and a toast to the democrats of all nations was taken up with enthusiasm.

Efforts to bring together the radicals of different nations had already been made earlier in London. These attempts failed, partly because of divisions among the English democrats and the foreigners' ignorance of them, partly because of differences of principle between the party leaders of different nations. The obstacle to all unification, due to difference of nationality, is so great that even foreigners who had lived in London for years, no matter how much they sympathised with English democracy, knew little or nothing about the movement going on before their eyes, or of the real state of affairs, confused the radical bourgeois with the radical proletarians and wished to bring the most confirmed enemies together at the same meeting. The English were led to similar mistakes, partly because of this and partly because of national mistrust, mistakes all the more easily made since the success of such a discussion inevitably depended on the greater or lesser agreement amongst a few top committee members who were rarely personally acquainted. These individuals had been most unfortunately selected on the previous occasions and consequently the matter had soon lapsed again. But the need for such fraternisation was too pressing. Every attempt that failed acted as a spur to new efforts. When some of the democratic spokesmen in London grew weary of the matter others took their places. Last August new approaches were made, which this time were not fruitless,[9] and a celebration on September 22, organised by other people, was used tc proclaim publicly the alliance of democrats of all nations living in London.

Englishmen, Frenchmen, Germans, Italians, Spaniards, Poles and Swiss came together at this meeting. Hungary and Turkey, too, were represented by one-man contingents. The three greatest nations of civilised Europe—the English, German and French—provided the speakers and were very worthily represented. The Chairman was, of course, an Englishman, *Thomas Cooper* "the Chartist" who served nearly two years in prison for his part in the insurrection of 1842[10] and while in gaol wrote an epic poem[a] in the style of *Childe Harold* which is highly praised by the English critics. The main English speaker of the evening was *George Julian Harney*, co-editor of *The Northern Star* for the past two years. *The Northern Star* is the Chartist paper established in 1837 by O'Connor, which has become in every way one of the best journals in Europe since it has been under the joint editorship of J. Hobson and Harney. I only know a few small Paris workers' papers such as the *Union* which can compare with it. Harney himself is a true proletarian who has been in the movement since his youth, one of the chief members of the Democratic Association of 1838-39 already mentioned (he presided at the Festival of August 10), and, with Hobson, undoubtedly one of the best English writers, a fact which I hope to demonstrate to the Germans some day. Harney is perfectly clear about the aim of the European movement and completely *à la hauteur des principes*[b] although he knows nothing about the German theories of true socialism. The main credit for the organisation of this cosmopolitan festival was his; he was tireless in bringing the various nationalities together, in removing misunderstandings and in overcoming personal differences.

The toast proposed by Harney was:

"The solemn memory of the honest and virtuous French Republicans of 1792: may that equality which they desired, and for which they lived, laboured, and died, have a speedy resurrection in France, and extend its reign throughout Europe."

Harney, who was received with cheers, again and again renewed, said:

"There was a time, [Mr. Chairman,] when the holding of such a celebration as this would have subjected the parties assembled not only to the scorn, the sneers, the abuse, and the persecution of the privileged orders, but also to the violence of the ignorant and misguided people, who were led by their rulers and priests to regard the French Revolution as something terrible and hellish, to be looked back upon with horror, and spoken of with execration. [Hear, hear.] Most present will remember that not long ago, whenever a demand was made in this country for the repeal of any bad law, or the enactment of any good one, forthwith the howl of 'Jacobinism!' was raised [by the opponents of all progress]. Whether it was proposed to reform the Parliament, reduce taxation, educate the people, or do anything else that at all savoured of progress, the 'French Revolution', 'Reign of Terror', and all the rest of the raw-head and bloody-bones phantasmagoria were sure to be brought out and duly exhibited to frighten the big babies in breeches, who as yet had not learned to think for themselves.

---

[a] Th. Cooper, *The Purgatory of Suicides.*—*Ed.*

[b] Abreast of principles.—*Ed.*

(Laughter and cheers.) That time is past; still, I question whether we have yet learned to read aright the history of that great revolution. It would be very easy for me in responding to this toast to mouth a few clap-trap sentiments about liberty, equality, the rights of man, the coalition of the European kings, and the doings of Pitt and Brunswick. I might dilate on all these topics, and possibly might win applause for what would probably pass muster as an exceedingly liberal speech. I might do all this, and yet very conveniently for myself shirk the grand question. The grand question, it appears to me, the solution of which the French Revolution had for its mission, was the *destruction of inequality*, and the establishment of institutions which should guarantee to the French people that happiness which the masses are, and ever have been strangers to. [Cheers.] Now, tried by this test, we have comparatively little difficulty in arriving at a fair estimate of the men who figured on the stage of the revolution. Take Lafayette, for instance, as a specimen of the Constitutionalists; and he, perhaps, is the most honest and best man of the whole party. Few men have enjoyed more popularity than Lafayette. In his youth we find him leaving his country, and generously embarking in the American struggle against English tyranny. The great work of American liberation being accomplished, he returned to France, and shortly afterwards we find him one of the foremost men in the revolution which now commenced in his own country. Again, in his old age, we see him the most popular man in France, called, after the 'three days',[11] to the veritable dictatorship, and unmaking and making kings with a single word. Lafayette enjoyed, throughout Europe and America, a greater popularity than perhaps any other man of his time; and that popularity he would have deserved, if his conduct had been consistent with his first acts in the revolution. But Lafayette was never the friend of equality. (Hear, hear.) True, at the outset, he gave up his feudal privileges, and renounced his title—and thus far he did well. Placed at the head of the popular force, the idol of the middle class, and commanding the affection of even the working class, he was for a time regarded as the champion of the revolution. But he halted when he should have advanced. The working men soon found out that all that the destruction of the Bastille and the abolition of feudal privileges had accomplished, was the curbing of the power of the king[a] and the aristocracy, and *increasing the power of the middle class.* But the people were not content with this—they demanded liberty and rights for themselves (cheers)—*they wanted what we want—a veritable equality.* (Loud cheers.) When Lafayette saw this, he turned Conservative, and was a revolutionist no longer. It was he who proposed the adoption of martial law, to authorise the shooting and sabring of the people, in the event of any tumult, at a time, too, when the people were suffering under absolute famine; and under this martial law, Lafayette himself superintended the butchery of the people when [they] assembled in the Champ de Mars, on the 17th of July, 1791, to petition the Assembly against the reinvestiture of the king with supreme power, after his shameful flight to Varennes. Subsequently Lafayette dared to menace Paris with his sword, and proposed to shut up the public clubs by armed violence. After the 10th of August[12] he strove to excite the soldiers under his command to march against Paris, but they, better patriots than he was, refused, and he then fled, and renounced the revolution. Yet Lafayette was perhaps the best man of all the Constitutionalists, but neither he nor his party come within the compass of our toast, for they were not even republicans in name. They professed to recognise the sovereignty of the people, at the same time that they divided the citizens into active and inactive, confining to the payers of direct taxes, whom they called active citizens, the right of the suffrage. In short, Lafayette and the Constitutionalists were mere Whigs, but little, if anything, better than the men who humbugged us with the Reform

[a] Louis XVI.—*Ed.*

Bill. (Cheers.) Next come the Girondists; and this is the party generally upheld as the 'honest and virtuous republicans', but I must differ with those who hold that opinion. It is impossible to refuse them the tribute of our admiration for their talents; the eloquence which distinguished the leaders of this party, accompanied in some instances by stern integrity, as in the case of Roland; by heroic devotion, as in the case of Madame Roland; and by fiery enthusiasm, as in the case of Barbaroux [....] And we cannot, at least I speak for myself — I cannot read of the shocking and untimely end of a Madame Roland, or the philosopher Condorcet, without intense emotion. Still the Girondists were not the men to whom the people could look to rescue them from social slavery. That there were good men amongst the Girondists, cannot be doubted — that they were honest to their own convictions, may be admitted. That many of them were ignorant rather than guilty, may be charitably believed, though to believe this we must believe it only of those who perished; for were we to judge of the party by those who survived what is commonly called the 'reign of terror', we should be forced to the conclusion that a baser gang never existed. These survivors of that party aided in destroying the constitution of '93, established the aristocratical constitution of '95, conspired with the other aristocratic factions to exterminate the real Republicans, and finally helped to place France under the tyranny of the military usurper Napoleon. (Hear, hear.) The eloquence of the Girondists has been highly lauded; but we stern and uncompromising Democrats cannot consent to admire them simply because they were eloquent. Indeed, if we were to do so, we should award the highest honours to the corrupt and aristocratical Mirabeau. When the people, rising for liberty, bursting the shackles of fourteen hundred years' slavery, abandoned their homes to combat against the domestic conspirator, and the foreign invader, they required something more than the eloquent speeches and fine woven theories of the Girondists to sustain them. 'Bread, steel, and equality', was the demand of the people. (Cheers.) Bread for their famishing families, steel with which to beat back the cohorts of the surrounding despots, and equality as the end of their labours and the reward of their sacrifices. (Great cheering.) The Girondists, however, regarded the people, to quote the words of Thomas Carlyle, as mere 'explosive masses to blow up bastilles with'[a] — to be used as tools and treated as slaves. They hesitated between Royalism and Democracy, vainly hoping to cheat eternal justice by a compromise.... They fell, and their fall was merited. The men of energy trampled them down — the people swept them away. Of the several sections of the party of the Mountain, I shall only say that I find none of them but Robespierre and his friends worthy of any commendation. (Great cheering.) The greater number of the Mountainists were brigands, who, only anxious to obtain for themselves the spoils of the Revolution, cared nothing for the people by whose toil, suffering, and courage the revolution had been achieved. These desperadoes, using the language of the friends of equality, and for a time siding with them against the Constitutionalists and the Girondists, so soon as they had acquired power, exhibited themselves in their true characters, and henceforth stood the avowed and deadly enemies of equality. By this faction Robespierre was overthrown and assassinated, and Saint-Just, Couthon, and all the leading friends of that incorruptible legislator were doomed to death. Not content with destroying the friends of equality, the assassins loaded their names with the most infamous calumnies, hesitating not to charge upon their victims the very crimes which they themselves had committed. I know it is unfashionable[b] as yet to regard Robespierre in any other light than as a monster [hear, hear]: but I believe the day is coming when a very different view will be taken of the character of that extraordinary

[a] Th. Carlyle, *The French Revolution: a History.* In three volumes, Vol. III.— *Ed.*

[b] The word "unfashionable" is given in English in the original.— *Ed.*

man. [Great cheering.] I would not deify Robespierre; I do not hold him up as having been all-perfect; but to me he appears to have been one of the very few leading characters of the Revolution who saw what were the means necessary to adopt to extirpate political and social wrong. I have no time to comment on the characters of the indomitable Marat, and that magnificent embodiment of republican chivalry St. Just. Nor have I time to speak of the excellent legislative measures that characterised the energetic rule of Robespierre. I have said the day will come when justice will be done to his name. (Cheers.) ... But, to me, the best proof of the real character of Robespierre, is to be found in the universal regret felt for his loss by the honest democrats who survived him—by those too amongst them, who, mistaking his intentions, had been seduced into favouring his destruction, but who, when too late, bitterly rued their folly. Babeuf was one of these, the originator of the famous conspiracy known by his name. That conspiracy had for its object the establishment of a veritable republic, *in which the selfishness of individualism should be known no more*—(cheers); *in which, private property and money, the foundation and root of all wrong and evil, should cease to be*—(cheers); and in which the happiness of all should be based upon *the common labour and equal enjoyments of all.* (Great cheering.) These glorious men pursued their glorious object to the death. Babeuf and Darthé sealed their belief with their blood, and Buonarroti, through years of imprisonment, penury and old age, persevered to the last in his advocacy of the great principles which we this night dare to vindicate. Nor should I omit mention of those heroic deputies Romme, Soubrany, Duroy, Duquesnoy and their compatriots, who, condemned to death by the traitor aristocrats of the Convention, heroically slew themselves in front of, and in contempt of their assassins, performing this self-tragedy with a single blade which they passed from hand to hand. So much for the first part of our toast. The second part demands but a few words from me, as it will be best spoken by the French patriots who are present. That the principles of equality will have a glorious resurrection, I cannot doubt; indeed, that resurrection they have already had, not merely in the shape of Republicanism, but Communism, for communist societies, I believe, cover France at the present day; but that I leave to my friend Dr. Fontaine and his fellow-countrymen to speak of. I rejoice much that those worthy patriots are here. They will witness tonight proofs of the absurdity of the tirades uttered against the English people by the war-party of France.[13] (Cheers.) We repudiate these national antipathies. We loathe and scorn those barbarous clap-traps, 'natural enemies', 'hereditary foe'[a] and 'national glory'. (Loud cheers.) We denounce all wars, except those into which nations may be forced against domestic oppressors or hostile invaders. (Applause). More than that, *we repudiate the word 'foreigner'—it shall exist not in our democratic vocabulary.* (Great cheering.) We may belong to the English, or French, or Italian, or German section of the European family, but Young Europe is our common designation, and under its banner we march against tyranny and inequality." (Long, enthusiastic applause.)

After a German Communist[b] had sung the *Marseillaise, Wilhelm Weitling* proposed the second toast:

"Young Europe. Repudiating the jealousies and national antipathies of the past, may the Democrats of all nations unite in a fraternal phalanx for the destruction of tyranny, and the universal triumph of equality."

Weitling, who was received with great enthusiasm, read the following speech, since he does not speak fluent English:

[a] The words "hereditary foe" were added by Engels.—*Ed.*
[b] Joseph Moll.—*Ed.*

"Friends! This meeting is a testimony of that common feeling which warms every man's breast, the feeling of universal brotherhood. Yes! Though we are educated to differ one from the other in the use of sounds as the natural means to express and communicate this inner feeling to each other, though the exchange of this feeling is hindered by the differences of language, though thousands of prejudices are united and directed by our common adversaries rather to oppose than to promote a better understanding, an universal brotherhood; yet, notwithstanding all these obstacles, that strong, charitable, and salutary feeling cannot be extinguished. (Cheers.) That feeling that attracts the sufferer to his fellow-sufferer, the struggler for a better state of things to his fellow-struggler. (Cheers.) Those also were our fellow-strugglers whose revolution we this night commemorate; they also were animated by the same sympathies which bring us together, and which possibly may lead us to a similar, and let me hope, a more successful struggle. (Loud cheers.) In times of movement, when the privileges of our native adversaries run great risk, they cunningly try to lead our prejudices over the frontiers of our national fatherland, representing to us that the people there are opposed to our common interest. What a trick! What a fraud! But, reflecting coolly on the matter, we know very well that our nearest enemies are amongst ourselves in the midst of us. (Hear, hear, and cheers.) It is not the exterior enemy we have to fear; that poor enemy is dealt with like us; like us he is compelled to work for thousands of good-for-nothing fellows; like us he takes up arms against any human society because he is forced to do so by hunger, by law, or excited by his passions, nourished by ignorance [...]. National rulers represent our brethren as cruel and rapacious; but who are more rapacious than they who govern us to be instructed in the art of war, who for their own privileges excite and conduct us to war? (Cheers.) Is it really our common interest that necessitates war? Is it the interest of sheep to be led by wolves to fight against sheep likewise led by wolves? (Loud cheers.) They are themselves our most rapacious enemies; they have taken from us all that is ours, to dissipate it in pleasures and debauchery. (Applause.) They take from us what is ours, since all they use is produced by us and ought to pertain to those who produce it, and to their wives and children, their aged and their sick. (Loud cheers.) But see how by their cunning manoeuvres all is stolen from us, and accumulated for a crew of idle consumers. (Cheers.) Is it possible then to be more robbed by a foreign enemy than by our own home enemies? Is it possible then that the people can be more murdered by them than by our cruel money-men, who rob us by their stock-jobbing, money dealing and speculating; by their currency and bankruptcy, by their monopolies, church and land rents, who by all these means rob us of the necessaries of life, and cause the death of millions of our working fellow brethren, to whom they leave not even potatoes enough to live upon. (Great cheering.) Is it not, therefore, clear enough that those who are all by money and nothing without it, are really the enemies of the working people in all countries, and that there are amongst men no other enemies of the human race than the enemies of the labouring and working people. (Cheers.) Is it possible then that we could be more stolen from, and murdered in a time of political war, than we are now, in a so-called state of peace? National prejudices, bloodshed, and robberies are then encouraged by us only for the sake of military glory! What has our interest to gain from such stupid glory? (Cheers.) What in fact have we to do with it, when our interest and our better feelings are opposed to it? (Cheers.) Must we not at all times pay the costs? (Applause.) Must we not work and bleed for it? (Renewed applause.) What interest can we have in all such bloodshed and land robberies, except profiting by such occasions for turning around against the robbery and murder—breeding aristocracy in all nations? (Enthusiastic cheering.) It is only this aristocracy—always this aristocracy—that systematically robs and murders. The poor people, led by them, are but their forced and ignorant instruments chosen from amongst every nation—those the most filled with national prejudices, those wishing to see all nations overpowered by their own nation. But bring them here into this meeting, and they will understand each other, and shake hands with each other.... If before a battle the advocates of liberty and love were permitted to address the ranks of their brethren, there would be no slaughter; on the contrary, there would be a friendly meeting like ours. O! could we but have in a battle-field such a meeting, we should have soon done with all those blood and marrow sucking interests who now oppress and plunder us! (Great cheering.) Such, friends, are the sentiments of that universal feeling whose warmth, concentrated in the focus of universal brotherhood, kindles a fire of enthusiasm which will soon entirely melt away the hindering ice-mountains of prejudices which have too long kept brethren asunder." (Mr. Weitling resumed his seat amid long continued cheering.)

Dr. *Berrier-Fontaine*, an old Republican who during the first years of bourgeois rule played a role in the *Société des droits de l'homme* in Paris, was involved in the trial of April 1834,[14] escaped with the rest of the accused from Sainte Pélagie in 1835 (see Louis Blanc's *Geschichte der 10 Jahre*[a]), and later progressed with the further development of the revolutionary party in France and had friendly contact with Père Cabet, rose to speak after Weitling. He was greeted with stormy applause and said:

"Citizens! My speech must be necessarily brief, as I cannot speak very good English. It gives me pleasure I cannot express to find the English Democrats meeting to commemorate the French Republic. I respond most heartily to the noble sentiments of Mr. Julian Harney. I assure you that the French people do not look upon the English people as their enemies. If some of the French journalists write against the English Government, they do not write against the English people. The Government of England is hateful throughout Europe, because it is the government of the English aristocracy, and not the English people. (Cheers.) The French Democrats, so far from being the enemies of the English people, really desire to fraternise with them. (Loud cheers.) The Republicans of France did not fight for France only, but for all mankind; they wished to establish equality, and extend its blessings throughout the world. (Great applause.) They regarded all mankind as brethren, and warred only against the aristocracies of other nations. (Cheers.) I can assure you, citizens, the principles of equality *have* sprung into renewed life. Communism is advancing with giant strides throughout France. Communist associations are extending all over that country, and I hope that we shall soon see a grand confederation of the Citizen Democrats of all nations, to make Republican Communism triumphant through the whole length and breadth of Europe." (Dr. Fontaine resumed his seat amidst long-protracted cheers.)

After the toast to Young Europe had been taken with "three roof and rafter-ringing shouts" and "one cheer more", further toasts were proposed to Thomas Paine, to the fallen Democrats of all countries, and to those of England, Scotland and Ireland, to the deported Chartists Frost, Williams, Jones and Ellis, to O'Connor, Duncombe and the other propagandists of the Charter and finally three cheers for *The Northern Star*. Democratic songs in all languages

---

[a] The reference is to the German translation of L. Blanc, *Histoire de dix ans. 1830-1840.—Ed.*

were sung (I can only find no mention of German songs), and the Festival was brought to an end in the most fraternal atmosphere.

Here was a meeting of more than a thousand democrats of nearly all the European nations who had united to celebrate an event seemingly completely alien to communism—the foundation of the French Republic. No special arrangements had been made to attract a particular kind of audience; there was nothing to indicate that anything would be expressed other than what the London Chartists understood by democracy. We can therefore certainly assume that the majority of the meeting represented the mass of the London Chartist proletarians fairly well. And this meeting accepted communist principles, the word communism itself, with unanimous enthusiasm. The Chartist meeting was a communist festival and, as the English themselves admit, "the kind of enthusiasm which prevailed that evening has not been seen in London for years".

Am I right when I say that democracy nowadays is communism?

Written at the end of 1845

First published in the journal *Rheinische Jahrbücher zur gesellschaftlichen Reform* Bd. II, 1846

Printed according to the journal

Published in full in English for the first time

The Northern Star,
AND NATIONAL TRADES' JOURNAL.
VOL. VIII. NO. 415. LONDON, SATURDAY, OCTOBER 25, 1845. PRICE FIVEPENCE or Five Shillings and Sixpence per Quarter

Frederick Engels

THE STATE OF GERMANY

LETTER I

TO THE EDITOR OF *THE NORTHERN STAR*

[*The Northern Star* No. 415, October 25, 1845]

Dear Sir,—In compliance with your wish, I commence by this letter a series of articles on the present state of my native country. In order to make my opinions on the subject plainly understood, and to justify the same as being well founded, I shall have to trace with a few words the history of Germany from the event which shook modern society to its very foundation—I mean to say, from the French Revolution.

Old Germany was at that time known by the name of *The Holy Roman Empire*,[15] and consisted of God knows how many little states, kingdoms, electorates, dukedoms, arch and grand dukedoms, principalities, counties, baronies, and free Imperial cities—every one independent of the other, and only subjected to the power (if there was any, which however, for hundreds of years, had not been the case) of the Emperor and Diet. The independence of these little states went so far, that in every war with "the arch-enemy" (France, of course), there was a part of them allied to the French king, and in open war with their own Emperor. The Diet, consisting of the deputations from all these little states, under the presidency of the Imperial one, being intended to check the power of the Emperor, was always assembled without ever coming to any, even the most insignificant, results. They killed their time with the most futile questions of ceremony, whether the embassy of Baron so-and-so (consisting, perhaps, of the tutor of his son and an old livery-servant, or worn-out game-keeper) ought to have precedency before the embassy of Baron so-and-so—or whether the deputy from one Imperial city ought to salute the deputy of another without waiting for his salute, etc. Then there were so many hundreds of thousands of little privileges, mostly burthensome to the privileged themselves, but which were considered as points of honour, and, therefore, quarrelled about with the utmost obstinacy. This and similar important things took up so much of the time of the wise Diet, that this honourable assembly had not a minute to spare for discussing the weal of the empire. In consequence of this, the greatest possible disorder and confusion was the order of the day. The empire, divided within itself in time of war as well as peace, passed through a series of internal wars from the time of the Reformation down to 1789, in every one of which France was allied to the party opposed to the weak and easily vanquished party of the Emperor, and took, of course, its lion's share in the plunder—first, Burgundy; then the three bishoprics, Metz, Toul, and Verdun; then the rest of Lorraine; then parts of Flanders and Alsace—were in this manner separated from the Holy Roman Empire and united to France. Thus Switzerland was allowed to become independent from the empire; thus Belgium was made over to the Spaniards by legacy of Charles V; and all these countries fared better after their separation from Germany. To this progressive external ruin of the empire, was joined the greatest possible internal confusion. Every little prince was a blood-sucking, arbitrary despot to his subjects. The empire never cared about the internal concerns of any states except by forming a court of law (Imperial Court Chamber at Wetzlar[16]) for attending to suits of subjects against their superiors, but that precious court attended so well to these actions, that not one of them has ever been heard of as having been settled. It is almost incredible what cruelties and arbitrary acts were committed by the haughty princes towards their subjects. These princes, living for pleasure and debauchery only, allowed every despotic power to their ministers and government officers, who were thus permitted, without any risk of punishment, to trample into the dust the unfortunate people, on this condition only, that they filled their master's treasury and procured him an inexhaustible supply of female beauty for his harem. The nobility, too, such as were not independent but under the dominion of some king, bishop, or prince, used to treat the people with greater contempt than they bestowed upon dogs, and squeezed as much money as they possibly could out of the labour of their serfs—for servitude was quite a common thing, then, in Germany. Nor was there any sign of liberty in those emphatically, so-called, free Imperial cities; for here a burgomaster and self-elected senate, offices which, in the course of centuries, had become as hereditary as the Imperial crown, ruled with greater tyranny still. Nothing can equal the infamous conduct of these petty-bourgeois aristocrats of the towns, and, indeed, it would not be believed that such was the state of Germany fifty years ago, if it was not in the memory still of many who remember that time, and if it was not confirmed by a hundred authorities. And the people! What did *they* say to this state of things? What did they do? Why, the middle classes, the money-loving bourgeois, found, in this continued confusion, a source of wealth; they knew that they could catch the most fish in the troubled waters; they suffered themselves to be oppressed and insulted because they could take a revenge upon their enemies worthy of themselves; *they avenged their wrongs by cheating their oppressors.* United to the people, they might have overthrown the old dominions and refounded the empire, just as the English middle classes had partly done from 1640 to 1688, and as the French bourgeois were then about to do. But, no, the German middle classes had not that energy, never pretended to that courage; they knew Germany to be nothing but a dunghill, but they were comfortable in the dung because they were dung themselves, and were kept warm by the dung about them. And the working people were not worse off than they are now, except the peasantry, who were mostly serfs, and could do nothing without the assistance of the towns, hired armies being always quartered on them, who threatened to stifle in blood every attempt at revolt.

Such was the state of Germany towards the end of the last century. It was all over one living mass of putrefaction and repulsive decay. Nobody felt himself at ease. The trade, commerce, industry, and agriculture of the country were reduced to almost nothing; peasantry, tradesmen and manufacturers felt the double pressure of a blood-sucking government and bad trade; the nobility and princes found that their incomes, in spite of the squeezing of their inferiors, could not be made to keep pace with their increasing expenditure; everything was wrong, and a general uneasiness prevailed throughout the country. No education, no means of operating upon the minds of the masses, no free press, no public spirit, not even an extended commerce with other countries—nothing but meanness and selfishness—a mean, sneaking, miserable shopkeeping spirit pervading the whole people. Everything worn out, crumbling down, going fast to ruin, and not even the slightest hope of a beneficial change, not even so much strength in the nation as might have sufficed for carrying away the putrid corpses of dead institutions.

The only hope for the better was seen in the country's literature. This shameful political and social age was at the same time the great age of German literature. About 1750 all the master-spirits of Germany were born, the poets Goethe and Schiller, the philosophers Kant and Fichte, and, hardly twenty years later, the last great German metaphysician,[17] Hegel. Every remarkable work of this time breathes a spirit of defiance, and rebellion against the whole of German society as it then existed. Goethe wrote *Goetz von Berlichingen,* a dramatic homage to the memory of a rebel. Schiller, the *Robbers,* celebrating a generous young man, who declares open war against all society. But these were their juvenile productions; when they grew older they lost all hope; Goethe restrained himself to satire of the keenest order, and Schiller would have despaired if it had not been for the refuge which science, and particularly the great history of ancient Greece and Rome, afforded to him. These, too, may be taken as examples of the rest. Even the best and strongest minds of the nation gave up all hope as to the future of their country.

All at once, like a thunderbolt, the French Revolution struck into this chaos, called Germany. The effect was tremendous. The people, too little instructed, too much absorbed in the ancient habit of being tyrannised over, remained unmoved. But all the middle classes, and the better part of the nobility, gave one shout of joyful assent to the national assembly and the people of France. Not one of all the hundreds of thousands of existing German poets failed to sing the glory of the French people. But this enthusiasm was of the German sort, it was merely metaphysical, it was only meant to apply to the theories of the French revolutionists. As soon as theories were shuffled into the background by the weight and bulk of facts; as soon as the French court and the French people could in practice no longer agree, notwithstanding their theoretical union, by the theoretical constitution of 1791; as soon as the people asserted their sovereignty *practically* by the "10th of August": and when, moreover, theory was entirely made silent on the 3lst of May, 1793,[18] by the putting down of the Girondists—then this enthusiasm of Germany was converted into a fanatic hatred against the revolution. Of course this enthusiasm was meant to apply to such actions only as the night of the 4th of August, 1789, when the nobility resigned their privileges,[19] but the good Germans never thought of such actions having consequences in practice widely differing from those inferences which benevolent theorists might draw. The Germans never meant to approve of these consequences, which were rather serious and unpleasant to many parties, as we all know well. So the whole mass, who in the beginning had been enthusiastic friends to the revolution, now became its greatest opponents, and getting, of course, the most distorted news from Paris by the servile German press, preferred their old quiet holy Roman dunghill to the tremendous activity of a people who threw off vigorously the chains of slavery, and flung defiance to the faces of all despots, aristocrats, and priests.

But the days of the Holy Roman Empire were numbered. The French revolutionary armies walked straight into the very heart of Germany, made the Rhine the frontier of France, and preached liberty and equality everywhere. They drove away by shoals noblemen, bishops, and abbots, and all those little princes that for so long a time had played in history the part of dolls. They effected a clearing, as if they were settlers advancing in the backwoods of the American Far West; the antediluvian forest of "Christian-Germanic" society disappeared before their victorious course, like clouds before the rising sun. And when the energetic Napoleon took the revolutionary work into his own hands, when he identified the revolution with himself; that same revolution which after the ninth Thermidor 1794[20] had been stifled by the money-loving middle classes, when he, the democracy with "a single head", as a French author termed him, poured his armies again and again over Germany, "Christian-Germanic" society was finally destroyed. Napoleon was not that arbitrary despot to Germany which he is said to have been by his enemies; Napoleon was in Germany the representative of the revolution, the propagator of its principles, the destroyer of old feudal society. Of course he proceeded despotically, but not even half as despotically as the deputies from the Convention would have done, and really did, wherever they came; not half so much so as the princes and nobles used to do whom he sent a-begging. Napoleon applied the *reign of terror*, which had done its work in France, *to other countries, in the shape of war*—and this "reign of terror" was sadly wanted in Germany. Napoleon dissolved the Holy Roman Empire, and reduced the number of little states in Germany by forming large ones. He brought his code of laws with himself into the conquered countries, a code infinitely superior to all existing ones, and recognising equality in principle. He forced the Germans, who had lived hitherto for *private interests* only, to work at the carrying out of a great idea of some overwhelming public interest. But that was just what aroused the Germans against him. He offended the peasantry by the very same measures that relieved them from the oppression of feudalism, because he struck at the roots of their prejudices and ancient habits. He offended the middle classes by the very means that laid the foundation of German manufacturing industry: the prohibition of all English goods and the war with England[21] was the cause of their beginning to manufacture for themselves, but, at the same time, it made coffee and sugar, tobacco and snuff, very dear; and this, of course, was sufficient to arouse the indignation of the German patriotic shopkeepers. Besides, they were not the people to understand any of the great plans of Napoleon. They cursed him because he led their children away into wars, got up by the money of the English aristocracy and middle classes; and hailed as friends those same classes of Englishmen who were the real cause of the wars, who *profited* by those wars, and who duped their German instruments not only during, but also after the war. They cursed him, because they desired to remain confined to their old, miserable sort of life, where they had nothing but their own little interest to attend to, because they desired to have nothing to do with great ideas and public interest. And at last, when Napoleon's army had been destroyed in Russia, they took that opportunity of shaking off the iron yoke of the great conqueror.

The "glorious liberation war" of 1813-14 and 15, the "most glorious period of German history", etc., as it has been called, was a piece of insanity such as will drive the blood into the cheeks of every honest and intelligent German for some time to come.[22] True, there was great enthusiasm then, but who were these enthusiasts? Firstly, the peasantry, the most stupid set of people in existence, who, clinging to feudal prejudices, burst forth in masses, ready to die rather than cease to obey those whom they, their fathers and grandfathers, had called their masters; and submitted to be trampled on and horse-whipped by. Then the students and young men generally, who considered this war as a war of principle, nay, as a war of religion; because not only they believed themselves called upon to fight for the principle of legitimacy, called their nationality, but also for the Holy Trinity and existence of God; in all poems, pamphlets, and addresses of that time, the French are held up as the representatives of atheism, infidelity, and wickedness, and the Germans as those of religion, piety, and righteousness. Thirdly, some more enlightened men, who mixed up with these ideas some notions about "liberty", "constitutions", and a "free press"; but these were by far the minority. And fourthly, the sons of tradesmen, merchants, speculators, etc., who fought for the right of buying in the cheapest market, and of drinking coffee without the admixture of chicory; of course, disguising their aims under the expressions of the enthusiasm of the day, "liberty", "great German people", "national independence", and so forth. These were the men, who, with the assistance of the Russians, English and Spaniards, beat Napoleon.

In my next letter I shall proceed to the history of Germany since the fall of Napoleon. Let me only add, in qualification of the opinion above given of this extraordinary man, that the longer he reigned, the more he deserved his ultimate fate. His ascending the throne I will not reproach him with; the power of the middle classes in France, who never cared about public interests, provided their private ones went on favourably, and the apathy of the people, who saw no ultimate benefit [for] themselves from the revolution, and were only to be roused to the enthusiasm of war, permitted no other course; but that he associated with the old anti-revolutionary dynasties by marrying the Austrian Emperor's daughter,[a] that he, instead of destroying every vestige of Old Europe, rather sought to compromise with it—that he aimed at the honour of being the first among the European monarchs, and therefore assimilated his court as much as possible to theirs—that was his great fault. He descended to the level of other monarchs—he sought the honour of being their equal—he bowed to the principle of legitimacy—and it was a matter of course, then, that the legitimists kicked the usurper out of their company.

I am, sir, yours respectfully,

Your German Correspondent

October 15th, 1845

LETTER II

TO THE EDITOR OF *THE NORTHERN STAR*

[*The Northern Star* No. 417, November 8, 1845]

Dear Sir,—Having in my first letter described the state of Germany before and during the French Revolution, as well as during the reign of Napoleon; having related how the great conqueror was overthrown, and by what parties, I now resume the thread of my narrative to show what Germany made of herself after this "glorious restoration" of national independence.

The view I took of all these events was diametrically opposed to that in which they generally are represented; but my view is, to a letter, confirmed by the events of the following period of German history. Had the war against Napoleon really been a war of liberty against despotism, the consequence would have been, that all those nations which Napoleon had subdued, would, after his downfall, have proclaimed the principles and enjoyed the blessings of equality. But quite the contrary was the case. With England, the war had been commenced by the frightened aristocracy, and supported by the

[a] Marie Louise.—*Ed.*

moneyocracy, who found a source of immense profit in the repeated loans, and the swelling of the National Debt; in the opportunity afforded them to enter into the South American markets, to cram them with their own manufactures, and to conquer such French, Spanish and Dutch colonies as they thought proper, for the better filling of their purses; to make "Britannia rule the waves" [a] despotic, that they might harass to their heart's pleasure the trade of any other nation, whose competition threatened to endanger the progress of their own enrichment; and lastly, to assert their right of making enormous profits, by providing the European markets, in opposition to Napoleon's continental system. Such were the *real* causes of the long war on the part of those classes in whose hands the Government of England was then deposited; and as to the pretext, that the fundamental principles of the English Constitution were endangered by the French Revolution, it only shows what a precious piece of workmanship this "perfection of human reason" must have been. As to Spain, the war had commenced in defence of the principle of legitimate succession, and of the inquisitorial despotism of the priesthood. The principles of the constitution of 1812 [23] were introduced later, in order to give the people some inducement to continue the struggle, being *themselves* of French origin. Italy never was opposed to Napoleon, having received nothing but benefits from his hands, and having to thank him for her very existence as a nation. The same was the case with Poland. What Germany was indebted for to Napoleon I have related in my first letter.

By all and each of the victorious powers the downfall of Napoleon was considered as the *destruction of the French Revolution*, and the triumph of legitimacy. The consequences were, of course, the restoration of this principle at home, first under the disguise of such sentimentalities as "Holy Alliance",[24] "eternal peace", "public weal", "confidence between prince and subject", etc., etc., afterwards undisguised by the bayonet and the dungeon. The impotency of the conquerors was sufficiently shown by this one fact, that, after all, the vanquished French people, with a hated dynasty forced upon them, and maintained by 150,000 foreign muskets, yet inspired such awe in the breasts of their victorious enemies, that they got a tolerably liberal constitution, while the other nations, with all their exertions, and all their boasting of liberty, got nothing but fine words first, and hard bullets afterwards. The putting down of the French Revolution was celebrated by the massacres of Republicans in the south of France; by the blaze of the inquisitorial pile and the restoration of

---

[a] Engels quotes "Rule, Britannia", a song by J. Thomson.— *Ed.*

native despotism in Spain and Italy, and by the gagging-bills and "Peterloo" in England.[25] We shall now see that in Germany things took a similar course.

The Kingdom of Prussia was the first of all German states to declare war against Napoleon. It was then governed by Frederick William III, nicknamed "The Just", one of the greatest blockheads that ever graced a throne. Born to be a corporal and to inspect the buttons of an army; dissolute, without passion, and a morality-monger at the same time, unable to speak otherwise but in the infinite tense, surpassed only by his son[a] as a writer of proclamations; he knew only two feelings—fear and corporal-like imperiousness. During the first half of his reign his predominating state of mind was the fear of Napoleon, who treated him with the generosity of contempt in giving him back half his kingdom, which he did not think worth the keeping. It was this fear which led him to allow a party of half-and-half reformers to govern in his stead, Hardenberg, Stein, Schön, Scharnhorst, etc., who introduced a more liberal organisation of municipalities, abolition of servitude, commutation of feudal services into rent, or a fixed sum of twenty-five years purchase, and above all, the military organisation, which gives the people a tremendous power, and which some time or other will be used against the Government. They also "prepared" a constitution which, however, has not yet made its appearance. We shall soon see what turn the affairs of Prussia took after the putting down of the French Revolution.

The "Corsican monster" being got into safe custody, there was immediately a great congress of great and petty despots held at Vienna, in order to divide the booty and the prize-money, and to see how far the ante-revolutionary state of things could be restored. Nations were bought and sold, divided and united, just as it best suited the interests and purposes of their rulers. There were only three states present who knew what they were about—England, intending to keep up and extend her commercial supremacy, to retain the lion's share out of the colonial plunder, and to weaken all the remainder—France, not to suffer too much, and weaken all others—Russia, to get increase of strength and territory, and to weaken all others; the remainder were directed by sentimentalities, petty egotism, and some of them even by a sort of ridiculous disinterestedness. The consequence was, that France spoiled the job for the great German states; that Russia got the best part of Poland; and England extended her maritime power more by the peace than

[a] Frederick William IV.—*Ed.*

by the war, and obtained the superiority in all continental markets—of no use for the English people, but means of enormous enrichment to the English middle classes. The German states, who thought of nothing but of their darling principle of legitimacy, were cheated once more, and lost by the peace everything they had won by the war. Germany remained split up into thirty-eight states, whose division hinders all internal progress, and makes France more than a match for her; and who, continuing [to be] the best market for English manufactures, served only to enrich the English middle classes. It is all well for this section of the English people to boast of the generosity which prompted them to send enormous sums of money to keep up the war against Napoleon; but, if we even suppose that it was them, and not the working people, who in reality had to pay these subsidies—they only intended, by their generosity, to re-open the continental markets, and in this they succeeded so well that the profits they have drawn since the peace, from Germany alone, would repay those sums at least six times over. It is really middle-class generosity which first makes you a present in the shape of subsidies, and afterwards makes you repay it six-fold in the shape of profits. Would they have been so eager to pay those subsidies, if at the end of the war, the reverse had been likely to be the case, and England been inundated with German manufactures, instead of Germany being kept in manufacturing bondage by a few English capitalists?

However, Germany was cheated on all hands, and mostly by her own so-called friends and allies. This I should not much care for myself, as I know very well that we are approaching to a reorganisation of European society, which will prevent such tricks on the one hand, and such imbecilities on the other; what I want to show is, first, that neither the English people, nor any other people profited by cheating the German despots, but that it all was for the benefit of other despots; or of one particular class, whose interest is opposed to the people; and second, that the very first act of the German restored despots showed their thorough incapacity. We now turn to the home affairs of Germany.

We have seen who were the parties that, with the aid of English money and Russian barbarism, put down the French Revolution. They were divided into two sections; first, the violent partisans of old "Christian-Germanic" society, the peasantry and the enthusiastic youth, who were impelled by the fanaticism of servitude, of nationality, of legitimacy and religion; and second, the more sober middle-class men, who wished "to be let alone", to make money and to spend it without being bothered with the impudent interference of great historical events. The latter party were satisfied as soon as they had obtained the peace, the right to buy in the cheapest market, to drink coffee without admixture of chicory, and to be excluded from all political affairs. The "Christian Germanics", however, now became the active supporters of the restored governments, and did everything in their power to screw history back to 1789. As to those who wished to see the people enjoy some of the fruits of their exertions, they had been strong enough to make their watchwords the battle-cry of 1813, but not the practice of 1815. They got some fine promises of constitutions, free press, etc., and that was all; in practice everything was carefully left as it had been previously. The Frenchified parts of Germany were purged, as far as possible, from the traces of "foreign despotism", and those provinces only which were situated on the left of the Rhine retained their French institutions. The Elector of Hesse[a] went so far as to restore even the *pig-tails of his soldiers,* which had been cut off by the impious hands of the French. In short, Germany, as well as every other country, offered the picture of a shameless reaction which was only distinguished by a character of timidity and weakness; it did not even elevate itself to that degree of energy with which revolutionary principles were combated in Italy, Spain, France and England.

The cheating system to which Germany had been subjected at the Congress of Vienna, now commenced to be practised between the different German states themselves. Prussia and Austria, in order to weaken the power of the different states, forced them to give some sort of mongrel constitutions, which weakened the governments, without imparting any power to the people, or even the middle classes. Germany being constituted a confederacy of states, whose embassies, sent by the governments alone, formed the diet, there was no risk that the people might become too strong, as every state was bound by the resolutions of the diet, which were law for all Germany, without being subject to the approval of any representative assembly. In this diet it was a matter of course that Prussia and Austria ruled absolutely; they only had to threaten the lesser princes to abandon them in their struggle with their representative assemblies, in order to frighten them into implicit obedience. By these means, by their overwhelming power, and by their being the true representatives of that principle from which every German prince derives his power, they have made themselves the absolute rulers of Germany. Whatever may be done in the small states is without any effect in practice. The struggles of the Liberal middle classes of Germany

---

[a] Ludwig I.— *Ed.*

remained fruitless as long as they were confined to the smaller southern states; they became important as soon as the middle classes of Prussia were aroused from their lethargy. And as the Austrian people can hardly be said to belong to the civilised world, and, in consequence, submit quietly to their paternal despotism, the state which may be taken as the centre of German modern history, as the barometer of the movements of public opinion, is Prussia.

After the downfall of Napoleon, the King of Prussia spent some of his happiest years. He was cheated, it is true, on every hand. England cheated him; France cheated him; his own dear friends, the Emperors of Austria and Russia,[a] cheated him over and over again; but he, in the fulness of his heart, did not even find it out; he could not think of the possibility of there being any such scoundrels in the world who could cheat Frederick William III, "The Just". He was happy. Napoleon was overthrown. He had *no fear.* He pressed Article 13 of the Fundamental Federative Act of Germany, which promised a constitution for every state. He pressed the other article about the liberty of the press.[26] Nay, on the 22nd of May, 1815, he issued a proclamation commencing with these words—words in which his benevolent happiness was beautifully blended with his corporal-like imperiousness—*"There shall be a representation of the people!"* He went on to order that a commission should be named to prepare a constitution for his people; and even in 1819, when there had been revolutionary symptoms in Prussia, when reaction was rifest all over Europe, and when the glorious fruit of the Congresses was in its full blossom, even then he declared that, in future, no public loan should be contracted without the assent of the future representative assemblies of the kingdom.

Alas! this happy time did not last. The fear of Napoleon was but too soon replaced in the king's mind by the *fear of the revolution.* But of that in my next.

I have only one word to add. Whenever in English democratic meetings the "patriots of all countries" are toasted, *Andreas Hofer* is sure to be amongst them. Now, after what I have said on the enemies of Napoleon in Germany, is Hofer's name worthy to be cheered by democrats? Hofer was a stupid, ignorant, bigoted, fanatical peasant, whose enthusiasm was that of La Vendée,[27] that of "Church and Emperor". He fought bravely—but so did the Vendéans against the Republicans. He fought for the paternal despotism of Vienna and Rome. Democrats of England, for the sake of the honour of the German people, leave that bigot out of the question in future.

---

[a] Ferdinand I and Alexander I.—*Ed.*

Germany has better patriots than him. Why not mention Thomas Münzer, the glorious chief of the peasant insurrection of 1525, who was a real democrat, as far as possible, at that time? Why not glorify George Forster, the German Thomas Paine, who supported the French Revolution in Paris up to the last, in opposition to all his countrymen, and died on the scaffold? Why not a host of others, who fought for realities, and not for delusions?

I am, dear Sir, yours respectfully,

Your German Correspondent

LETTER III

TO THE EDITOR OF *THE NORTHERN STAR*

[*The Northern Star* No. 438, April 4, 1846]

Dear Sir,—I really must beg of you and your readers to excuse my apparent negligence in not continuing sooner the series of letters on the above subject which I commenced writing for this paper. You may, however, rest assured that nothing but the necessity of devoting some weeks to the German movement exclusively could detain me from the pleasant task I have undertaken, of informing the English democracy of the state of things in my native country.

Your readers will, perhaps, have some recollection of the statements made in my first and second letters. I there related how the old, rotten state of Germany was rooted up by the French armies from 1792 to 1813; how Napoleon was overthrown by the union of the *feudalists,* or aristocrats, and the *bourgeois,* or trading middle classes of Europe; how, in the subsequent peace arrangements the German princes were cheated by their allies, and even by vanquished France; how the German Federative Act, and the present political state of Germany was brought about; and how Prussia and Austria, by inducing the lesser states to give constitutions, made themselves the exclusive masters of Germany. Leaving Austria, as a half-barbarian country, out of the question, we come to the result that Prussia is the battle-field on which the future fate of Germany is to be decided.

We said in our last, that Frederick William III, King of Prussia, after being delivered from the fear of Napoleon, and spending a few happy, because fearless years, acquired another bugbear to frighten him—"the revolution". The way in which "the revolution" was introduced into Germany we shall now see.

After the downfall of Napoleon, which I must repeat again, by the kings and aristocrats of the time, was totally identified with the putting down of the French Revolution, or, as they called it, *the* revolution, after 1815, in all countries, the anti-revolutionary party held the reins of government. The feudalist aristocrats ruled in all cabinets from London to Naples, from Lisbon to St. Petersburg. However, the middle classes, who had paid for the job and assisted in doing it, wanted to have their share of the power. It was by no means their interest which was placed in the ascendant by the restored governments. On the contrary, middle-class interests were neglected everywhere, and even openly set at nought. The passing of the English Corn Law of 1815[28] is the most striking example of a fact which was common to all Europe; and yet the middle classes were more powerful then than ever they had been. Commerce and manufactures had been extending everywhere, and had swelled the fortunes of the fat bourgeois; their increased well-being was manifested in their increased spirit of speculation, their growing demand for comforts and luxuries. It was impossible, then, that they should quietly submit to be governed by a class whose decay had been going on for centuries—whose interests were opposed to those of the middle classes—whose momentary return to power was the very work of the bourgeois. The struggle between the middle classes and the aristocracy was inevitable; it commenced almost immediately after the peace.

The middle classes being powerful by money only, cannot acquire political power but by making money the only qualification for the legislative capacity of an individual. They must merge all feudalistic privileges, all political monopolies of past ages, in the one great privilege and monopoly of *money*. The political dominion of the middle classes is, therefore, of an essentially *liberal* appearance. They destroy all the old differences of several estates co-existing in a country, all arbitrary privileges and exemptions; they are obliged to make the elective principle the foundation of government—to recognise equality in principle, to free the press from the shackles of monarchical censorship, to introduce the jury, in order to get rid of a separate class of judges, forming a state in the state. So far they appear thorough democrats. But they introduce all the improvements so far only, as thereby all former individual and hereditary privileges are replaced by the privilege of *money*. Thus the principle of election is, by property qualifications for the right of electing and being elected, retained for their own class. Equality is set aside again by restraining it to a mere "equality before the law", which means equality in spite of the inequality of rich and poor—equality within the limits of the chief inequality existing—which means, in short, nothing else but giving *inequality* the name of equality. Thus the liberty of the press is, of itself, a middle-class privilege, because printing requires *money*, and buyers for the printed productions, which buyers must have money again. Thus the jury is a middle-class privilege, as proper care is taken to bring none but "respectables" into the jury-box.

I have thought it necessary to make these few remarks upon the subject of middle-class government in order to explain two facts. The first is, that in all countries, during the time from 1815 to 1830, the essentially democratic movement of the working classes was more or less made subservient to the liberal movement of the bourgeois. The working people, though more advanced than the middle classes, could not yet see the total difference between liberalism and democracy—emancipation of the middle classes and emancipation of the working classes; they could not see the difference between liberty of *money* and liberty of *man*, until money had been made politically free, until the middle class had been made the exclusively ruling class. Therefore the democrats of Peterloo were going to petition, not only for Universal Suffrage, but for Corn Law repeal at the same time; therefore, the proletarians fought in 1830 in Paris, and threatened to fight in 1831 in England, for the political interest of the bourgeoisie. In all countries the middle classes were, from 1815 to 1830, the most powerful component, and, therefore, the leaders of the revolutionary party. The working classes are necessarily the instruments in the hands of the middle classes, as long as the middle classes are *themselves revolutionary* or progressive. The distinct movement of the working classes is, therefore, in this case always of a secondary importance. But from that very day when the middle classes obtain full political power—from the day on which all feudal and aristocratic interests are annihilated by the power of *money*—from the day on which the middle classes *cease* to be progressive and revolutionary, and become stationary themselves, from that very day the working-class movement takes the lead and becomes the *national movement. Let the Corn Laws be repealed today, and tomorrow the Charter is the leading question in England—tomorrow the Chartist movement will exhibit that strength, that energy, that enthusiasm and perseverance which ensures success.*

The second fact, for the explanation of which I ventured to make some few remarks on middle-class government, refers to Germany exclusively. The Germans being a nation of theorists, and little experienced in practice, took the common fallacies brought forward by the French and English middle classes to be sacred truths. The middle classes of Germany were glad to be left alone to their little private business, which was all in the "small way"; wherever they had obtained a constitution, they boasted of their liberty, but interfered little in the political business of the state; wherever they had none, they were glad to be saved the trouble of electing deputies and reading their speeches. The working people wanted that great lever which in France and England aroused them—extensive manufactures—and the consequence of it, middle-class rule. They, therefore, remained quiet. The peasantry in those parts of Germany where the modern French institutions had been again replaced by the old feudal regime, felt oppressed, but this discontent wanted another stimulus to break out in open rebellion. Thus, the revolutionary party in Germany, from 1815 to 1830, consisted of *theorists* only. Its recruits were drawn from the universities; it was made up of none but students.

It had been found impossible in Germany to re-introduce the old system of 1789. The altered circumstances of the time forced the governments to invent a new system, which has been peculiar to Germany. The aristocracy was willing to govern, but too weak; the middle classes were neither willing to govern nor strong enough—both, however, were strong enough to induce the government to some concessions. The form of government, therefore, was a sort of mongrel monarchy. A constitution, in some states, gave an appearance of guarantee to the aristocracy and middle classes; for the remainder there was everywhere a *bureaucratic* government—that is, a monarchy which pretends to take care of the interests of the middle class by a good administration, which administration is, however, directed by aristocrats, and whose proceedings are shut out as much as possible from the eyes of the public. The consequence is the formation of a separate class of administrative government officers, in whose hands the chief power is concentrated, and which stands in opposition against all other classes. It is the barbarian form of middle-class rule.

But this form of government satisfied neither the "Aristocrats", "Christian Germanics", "Romantics", "Reactionaries", nor the "Liberals". They, therefore, united against the governments, and formed the secret societies of the students. From the union of those two sects—for parties they cannot be called—arose that sect of mongrel Liberals, who in their secret societies dreamt of a German Emperor wearing crown, purple, sceptre, and all the remainder of that sort of apparatus, not to forget a long grey or red beard, surrounded by an assembly of estates in which clergy, nobility, burgesses, and peasants should be duly separated. It was the most ridiculous mixing up of feudal brutality with modern middle-class fallacies that could be imagined. But that was just the thing for the students, who wanted enthusiasm, no matter for what, nor at what price. Yet these ridiculous idiosyncrasies, together with the revolutions in Spain, Portugal and Italy, the movements of the Carbonari in France, and the Reformation in England,[29] frightened the monarchs almost out of their wits. Frederick William III got his bugbear, "the revolution"—under which name all these different and partly discordant movements were comprised.

A number of incarcerations and wholesale prosecutions quashed this "revolution" in Germany; the French bayonets in Spain, and the Austrian in Italy, secured for a while the ascendancy of legitimate kings and rights divine. Even the right divine of the Grand Turk to hang and quarter his Grecian subjects was for a while maintained by the Holy Alliance; but this case was too flagrant, and the Greeks were allowed to slip from under the Turkish yoke.[30]

At last, the three days of Paris[31] gave the signal for a general outbreak of middle-class, aristocratic, and popular discontent throughout Europe. The aristocratic Polish revolution was put down; the middle classes of France and Belgium succeeded in securing to themselves political power[32]; the English middle classes likewise obtained this end by the Reform Bill; the partly popular, partly middle-class, partly national insurrections of Italy, were suppressed; and in Germany numerous insurrections and movements betokened a new era of popular and middle-class agitation.

The new and violent character of liberal agitation in Germany, from 1830 to 1834, showed that the middle classes had now taken up the question for themselves. But Germany being divided into many states, almost each of which had a separate line of customs and separate rates of duty, there was no community of interest in these movements. The middle classes of Germany wanted to become politically free, not for the purpose of arranging public matters in accordance with their *interest*, but because they were ashamed of their servile position in comparison to Frenchmen and Englishmen. Their movement wanted the substantial basis which had ensured the success of Liberalism in France and England; their interest in the question was far more theoretical than practical; they were, upon an average, what is called disinterested. The French bourgeois of 1830 were not. Laffitte said, the day after the revolution: "Now we, the bankers, will govern"; and they do up to this hour. The English middle classes, too, knew very well what they were about when they fixed the ten-pound qualification [33]; but the German middle classes being, as aforesaid, men in a small way of business, were mere enthusiasts—admirers of "liberty of the press", "trial by jury", "constitutional guarantees for the people", "rights of the people", "popular representation", and such like, which they thought not means, but ends; they took the shadow for the substance, and therefore got nothing. However, this middle-class movement was sufficient to bring about several dozens of revolutions, of which two or three contrived somehow to succeed; a great number of popular meetings, a deal of talk and newspaper-boasting, and a very slight beginning of a democratic movement among students, working men, and peasants.

I shall not enter into the rather tedious details of this blustering and unsuccessful movement. Wherever somewhat important had been won, as liberty of the press in Baden, the German Diet stepped in and put a stop to it. The whole farce was concluded by a repetition of the wholesale imprisonments of 1819 and 1823, and, by a secret league of all German princes, concluded in 1834, at a Conference of delegates at Vienna, to resist all further progress of Liberalism.[34] The resolutions of this Conference were published some years ago.[a]

From 1834 to 1840, every public movement in Germany died out. The agitators of 1830 and 1834 were either imprisoned or scattered in foreign countries, where they had fled. Those who had kept much of their middle-class timidity during the times of agitation, continued to struggle against the growing rigour of the censor, and the growing neglect and indifference of the middle classes. The leaders of Parliamentary opposition went on speechifying in the Chambers, but the governments found means to secure the votes of the majorities. There appeared no further chance of bringing about any public movement whatsoever in Germany; the governments had it all their own way.

In all these movements the middle classes of *Prussia* took almost *no part.* The working people uttered their discontent throughout that country in numerous riots, having, however, no defined purpose, and therefore no result. The apathy of the Prussians was the principal strength of the German confederacy. It showed that the time for a general middle-class movement in Germany was not yet come.

---

[a] C. Th. Welcker, *Wichtige Urkunden für den Rechtszustand der deutschen Nation*, Mannheim, 1844.—*Ed.*

In my next,[a] I shall pass to the movement of the last six years, unless I can bring together the necessary materials for characterising the spirit of the German governments by some of their own doings, in comparison to which those of your precious Home Secretary[b] are pure and innocent.[35]

I am, in the meantime, dear Sir,

respectfully,

Your German Correspondent

Febr. 20th,[36] 1846

Written between October 15, 1845 and February 20, 1846

First published in *The Northern Star* Nos. 415, 417, 438, October 25, November 8, 1845 and April 4, 1846

Reprinted from the newspaper

---

[a] Engels' letter did not appear in the following numbers.—*Ed.*

[b] Sir James Robert George Graham.—*Ed.*

Karl Marx

STATEMENT

According to the *Rheinischer Beobachter* of January 18, issue No. 18, the *Trier'sche Zeitung* contains an announcement by the Editorial Board according to which, among a number of writers, Marx also is named as a contributor to this newspaper. In order to prevent any confusion I state that I have *never* written a *single* line for this paper, whose bourgeois philanthropic, by no means communist tendencies are entirely alien to me.

Brussels, January 18, 1846

Karl Marx

First published in *Trier'sche Zeitung* No. 26, January 26, 1846

Printed according to the newspaper

Published in English for the first time

Karl Marx and Frederick Engels

[CIRCULAR AGAINST KRIEGE][37]

At a meeting attended by the undermentioned Communists: *Engels, Gigot, Heilberg, Marx, Seiler, Weitling, von Westphalen* and *Wolff*, the following resolutions concerning the New York German-language journal

"*Der Volks-Tribun*" *edited by Hermann Kriege*

were passed unanimously—with the single exception of Weitling "who voted against". The appendix explains the motives behind the resolutions.

Resolutions:

1. The line taken by the editor of the *Volks-Tribun*, Hermann Kriege, is not communist.
2. Kriege's childish pomposity in support of this line is compromising in the highest degree to the Communist Party, both in Europe and America, inasmuch as he is held to be the literary representative of German communism in New York.
3. The fantastic emotionalism which Kriege is preaching in New York under the name of "communism" must have an extremely damaging effect on the workers' morale if it is adopted by them.
4. The present resolutions, together with the grounds for them, shall be communicated to the Communists in Germany, France and England.
5. One copy shall be sent to the editors of the *Volks-Tribun* with the request that these resolutions together with the grounds for them should be printed in the forthcoming issues of the *Volks-Tribun*.

Brussels, May 11, 1846

Engels, Phil. Gigot,
Louis Heilberg, K. Marx,
Seiler, von Westphalen, Wolff

3—1826

SECTION ONE

HOW COMMUNISM BECAME LOVE-SICK

No. 13 of the *Volks-Tribun* contains an article entitled: "An die Frauen".

1) "Women, priestesses of *love.*"

2) "It is *love* that has sent us."

3) "Apostles of *love.*"

a) Literary interlude: "The flaming eyes of humanity", "the sounds of truth".

b) Woman's hypocritical and ignorant *captatio benevolentiae*[a]: "Even in the attire of a queen you cannot deny your *femininity*... nor have you learned to speculate upon the tears of the unhappy; you are too soft-hearted to let a *mother's* poor child starve so that you may profit."

4) "The future of the *beloved* child."

5) "*Beloved* sisters."

6) "O give ear to us, you are betraying *love* if you do not do so."

8) "Of *love.*"

8) "Of *love.*"

9) "For the sake of *love.*"

10) "The most sacred labour of *love* which we entreat of you" (whimper).

c) Literary-biblical platitude: "Woman is destined to bear the son of man", whereby the fact is proclaimed that men do not bear children.

11) "The *holy spirit* of community must evolve from the *heart of* LOVE."

---

[a] Thirst for approval.—*Ed.*

1.

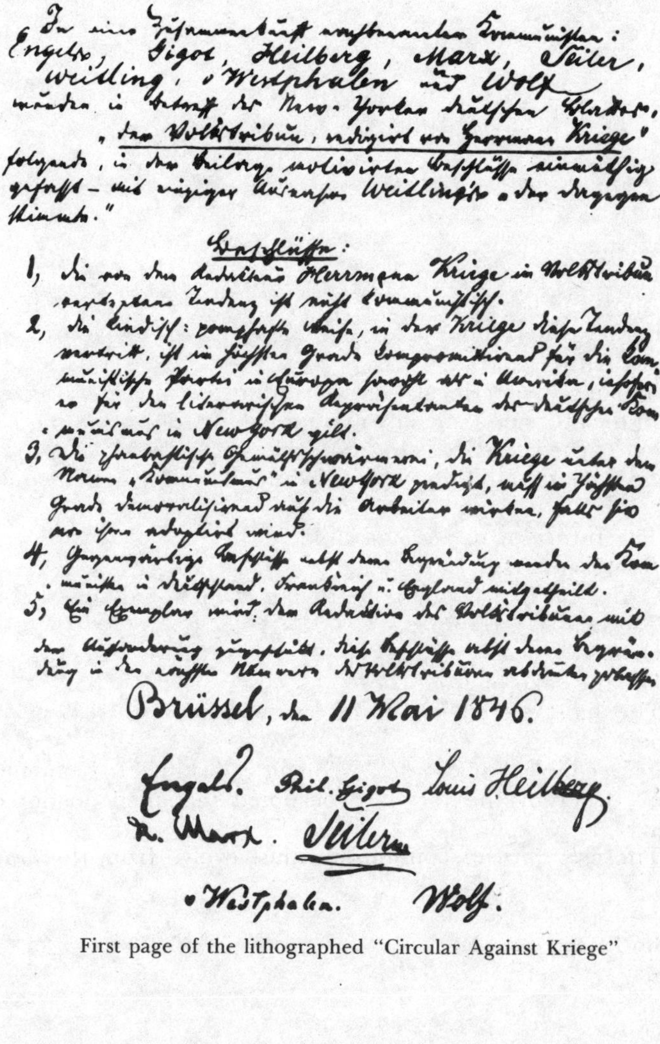

In einer Zusammenkunft nachbenannter Kommunisten: Engels, Gigot, Heilberg, Marx, Seiler, Weitling, v. Westphalen und Wolff wurden in Betreff des New-Yorker deutschen Blattes, „Der Volkstribun, redigirt von Hermann Kriege" folgende, in der Beilage motivirten Beschlüsse einmüthig gefaßt – mit einziger Ausnahme Weitlings, der dagegen stimmte."

Beschlüsse:

1, Die von dem Redakteur Hermann Kriege im Volkstribun vertretene Tendenz ist nicht kommunistisch.

2, Die kindisch-pompöse Weise, in der Kriege diese Tendenz vertritt, ist im höchsten Grade kompromittirend für die kommunistische Partei in Europa sowohl als in Amerika, insofern er für den literarischen Repräsentanten des deutschen Kommunismus in New-York gilt.

3, Die phantastische Gemüthsschwärmerei, die Kriege unter dem Namen „Kommunismus" in New-York predigt, muß im höchsten Grade demoralisirend auf die Arbeiter wirken, falls sie von ihnen adoptirt wird.

4, Gegenwärtige Beschlüsse nebst der Begründung werden den Kommunisten in Deutschland, Frankreich u. England mitgetheilt.

5, Ein Exemplar wird der Redaktion des Volkstribunen mit der Aufforderung zugeschickt, diese Beschlüsse nebst der Begründung in der nächsten Nummer des Volkstribunen abdrucken zu lassen.

Brüssel, den 11 Mai 1846.

Engels. Phil. Gigot. Louis Heilberg.
K. Marx. Seiler.
v. Westphalen. Wolff.

First page of the lithographed "Circular Against Kriege"

d) Interpolated Ave Maria: "*Blessed, thrice blessed* are you women, being chosen to pronounce the *first consecration* of the long-*promised* kingdom of bliss."

12) "*Beloved* sisters."

13) "Not *love* but hatred" (contrasting bourgeois and communist society).

14) "You *loved* ones."

15) "Raise *love* on to the throne."

16) "Active people in *loving* community."

17) "True priestesses of *love*."

e) Aesthetic parenthesis: "If your trembling soul has not yet forgotten the flight sublime"—(a feat whose feasibility has yet to be demonstrated).

18) "The world of *love*."

19) "The kingdom of hatred and the kingdom of *love*."

f) An attempt to hoodwink women: "And therefore you have a most mighty voice in politics too. You but need to use your influence, and all the old kingdom of hatred will fall in ruins to make way for the new kingdom of *love*."

g) Philosophical fanfare to drown reflection: "The ultimate goal of their activity is that all mankind should take an ever-joyful delight in itself."

20) "Your *love*." At this point women are required to be "unstinting" in their love so that it may "embrace all mankind with equal surrender". A demand that is as indecent as it is extravagant.

h) Fugue: "That thousands and yet more thousands of deserted orphans are abandoned to the fearful massacre of circumstances." What does this "fearfulness" consist in? In the "orphans" massacring the "circumstances" or the "circumstances" massacring the "orphans"?

i) Unveiling of the neo-communist policy: "We have no wish to lay hands on the private property of any man; what the usurer now has, let him keep; we merely wish to forestall the further pillaging of the people's assets and prevent capital from continuing to withhold from labour its rightful property." This purpose is to be achieved as follows: "Every poor man ... will instantly become a useful member of human society as soon as he is offered the opportunity of productive work." (According to this no one is more deserving in respect of "human society" than the capitalists, including those in New York against whom Kriege thunders so mightily.) "And this opportunity is assured him for ever, as soon as society gives him a piece of land on which he can produce food for himself and his family.... If this vast area of land" (the 1,400 million acres of the American state lands) "is *withdrawn from commerce and* ensured to labour *in limited quantities*, at *one* stroke all the poverty in America will have been eliminated; for each man will be given the opportunity to establish with his own hands an inviolable home for himself." That it does not lie in the legislators' power to decree either that the patriarchal system desired by Kriege shall not evolve into an industrial system or that the industrial and commercial states of the east coast of the United States shall revert to patriarchal barbarism—one had a right to expect that this would be realised. Meanwhile, for the day when the paradise just described will have arrived, Kriege prepares the following country-parson utterance: "And then we can teach men to *live together in peace*, to lighten for each other the burden and toil of their life and:

21) build the first dwelling-places on earth for celestial *love*" (each one 160 acres in area).

Kriege concludes his address to married women as follows: "Turn first to

22) the men of your *love*,

ask them ... to turn their backs on the politics of old,... show them their children, implore them in *their name*" (who are without reason) "to adopt reason." Secondly, to the "virgins":

23) "For your *lovers*

let *the liberation of the land be the touchstone of their human worth* and have no faith in

24) their *love*

until they have sworn fealty to mankind." (What is that supposed to mean?) If the virgins behave in this manner, he guarantees them that their children

25) "will become as *loving*

as they themselves" (that is, "the birds of heaven") and concludes this cant with another round of

26) "true priestesses of *love*", "great kingdom of community" and "consecration".

No. 13 of the *Volks-Trib[un]:—"Antwort an Sollta."*

27) "It" (the great spirit of community) "flashes from fraternal eyes as the fire of *love*."

28) "What is a woman without the man whom she can *love*, to whom she can surrender her *trembling soul*?"

29) "To join all mankind in *love*."

30) "Mother-*love*"....

31) "*Love* of mankind"....

32) "All the first sounds of *love*"....

33) "The radiance of *love*."

k) The purpose of communism is to "subject the whole life of mankind to its" (the sentient heart's) "beating".

34) "The sound of *love* flees before the rattle of money."

35) "Everything may be achieved by *love* and surrender."

In this *one* issue, then, we have love in approximately thirty-five shapes. It is in perfect accordance with this amorous slobbering that Kriege, in his "Antwort an Sollta" and elsewhere, presents communism as the love-imbued opposite of selfishness and reduces a revolutionary movement of world-historical importance to the few words: love—hate, communism—selfishness. Part and parcel of it is likewise the cowardice with which he here panders to the usurer by promising to let him keep what he already has and with which further on he assures that he does not want "to destroy the *cherished sentiments* of *family life*, of belonging to one's *native land* and *people*" but "only to fulfil them". This cowardly, hypocritical presentation of communism not as "destruction" but as "fulfilment" of existing evils and of the illusions which the bourgeoisie have about them, is found in every issue of the *Volks-Tribun*. This hypocrisy and cowardice are matched by the attitude which he adopts in discussions with politicians. He declares it (No.10[a]) a sin against communism to attack political visionaries like Lamennais and Börne who dabble in Catholicism, with the result that men like Proudhon, Cabet, Dézamy, in short all the French Communists, are just men "who call themselves Communists". The fact that the German Communists have left Börne as far behind as the French have Lamennais, is something Kriege could have discovered back in Germany, Brussels and London.

We leave Kriege to reflect for himself on the enervating effect this love-sickness cannot fail to have on both sexes and the mass hysteria and anaemia it must produce in the "virgins".

SECTION TWO

THE *VOLKS-TRIBUN*'S POLITICAL ECONOMY AND ITS *ATTITUDE TOWARDS YOUNG AMERICA*[38]

We fully recognise that the American national Reformers' movement is historically justified. We know that this movement has set its sights on a goal which, although for the moment it would

[a] Hermann Kriege an Harro Harring.—*Ed.*

further the industrialism of modern bourgeois society, nevertheless, as the product of a proletarian movement, as an attack on landed property in general and more particularly in the circumstances obtaining in America, will by its own inner logic inevitably press on to communism. Kriege, who has joined the Anti-Rent movement along with the German Communists in New York, pastes over this plain fact with his customary communist and extravagant phrases, without ever going into the positive substance of the movement, thereby proving that he is quite unclear in his own mind about the connection between Young America and circumstances prevailing in America. In addition to the individual passages which in passing we have already quoted, we would give another example of how his humanitarianising quite smothers the issue of land-distribution to the small farmer on an American scale.

In No. 10, "Was wir wollen", we read:

"They"—that is, the Americ[an] National Reformers—"call the soil the *communal* heritage of all mankind ... and want the legislative power of the people to take steps *to preserve as the inalienable communal property of all mankind* the 1,400 mill[ion] acres of land which have not yet fallen into the hands of rapacious speculators."

In order communally to "preserve for all mankind" this "*communal* heritage", this "inalienable *communal property*", he adopts the plan of the National Reformers: "to place 160 acres of American soil at the command of every farmer, from whatever country he may hail, so that he may feed himself", or, as it is put in No. 14, "Antwort" to Conze:

"Of this as yet untouched property of the people no one shall take more than 160 acres into his possession, and that only if he farms it himself."

So in order that the soil shall remain "inalienable *communal* property", for "all mankind" to boot, a start must be made without delay on *dividing it up*; Kriege here imagines he can use the law to *forbid* the necessary consequences of this division, that is, concentration, industrial progress, etc. He considers 160 acres of land as an ever-constant measure, as if the value of such an area did not vary according to its quality. The "farmers" will have to exchange, if not their land itself, then at least the produce of their land, with each other and with third parties, and when this juncture has been reached, it will soon become apparent that one "farmer", even though he has no capital, will, simply by his work and the greater initial productivity of his 160 acres, reduce his neighbour to the status of his *farm labourer*. And is it not then immaterial whether "the land" or the *produce* of the land "falls into the hands of rapacious speculators"?

Let us for the moment take Kriege's present to mankind seriously.

1,400 million acres are to be "preserved as the inalienable communal property of all mankind". Specifically, 160 acres are to be the portion of each "farmer". From this we can calculate the size of Kriege's "all mankind"—exactly 8¾ million "farmers", each of whom as head of family represents a family of five, a sum total therefore of 43¾ million people. We can likewise calculate how long "all eternity" will last, for the duration of which "the proletariat in its capacity as humanity" may "claim" "the whole earth"—at least in the United States. If the population of the United States continues to grow at the same rate as hitherto (i.e., if it doubles in 25 years), this "all eternity" will not last out 40 years; within this period the 1,400 mill[ion] acres will be settled, and there will be *nothing* left for future generations to "claim". But since the release of the land would greatly increase immigration, Kriege's "all eternity" might well be foreclosed even earlier. The more so when one considers that land for 44 million would not even suffice to channel off the now existing pauper-population of Europe, where every tenth man is a pauper and the British Isles alone supply 7 million. Similar economic naivety is to be found in No.13, "An die Frauen", in which Kriege says that if the city of New York were to release its 52,000 acres on Long Island, this would suffice to relieve New York "at one stroke" of all its pauperism, poverty and crime for all time.

If Kriege had seen the free-land movement as a first, in certain circumstances necessary, form of the proletarian movement, as a movement which because of the social position of the class from which it emanates must necessarily develop into a communist movement, if he had shown how communist tendencies in America could, to begin with, only emerge in this agrarian form which appears to be a contradiction of all communism, then no objection could have been raised. As things are, however, he declares what is after all a still subordinate form of movement of real specific people to be a matter for mankind *in general*, presents it, against his better knowledge, as the ultimate, supreme goal of all movement in general, and thereby transforms the specific aims of the movement into sheer, extravagant nonsense.

In the same essay (No.10) he however continues his paean unperturbed, as follows:

> "In this way, therefore, the old dreams of the Europeans at last came true, on this side of the ocean a plot was prepared for them which they needed only to settle and

make fruitful with the labour of their hands, and they would be able proudly to proclaim to all the tyrants of the world:

> This is *my* hut
> Which you did not build,
> This is *my* hearth
> Whose fire you envy me."[a]

He could have added: This is *my* midden, which I and my wife, child, farm labourer, maid-servant and cattle have produced. Who are these Europeans then, whose "dreams" here come true? Not the communist workers, but bankrupt shopkeepers and master-craftsmen or ruined cottagers striving for the bliss of becoming petty bourgeois and peasants once more in America. And what kind of "wish" is this which the 1,400 million acres are to make reality? None other than that *everybody* should be turned into a *private-property-owner*, a wish that is just as practicable and communist as that everybody should be turned into an emperor, king or pope. The following sentence shall serve as a final sample of Kriege's insight into communist revolutionary movements and economic conditions:

"*Every* man should at least learn enough of *every* trade *to be able to stand on his own feet for a while* if necessary, if misfortune should sever him from human society."[b]

It is of course much easier to "gush" "love" and "surrender" than to concern oneself with the development of real conditions and practical questions.

SECTION THREE

METAPHYSICAL TRUMPETINGS

No. 13 of the *Volks-Trib[un]*: "Antwort an Sollta".

1) Kriege here asserts he is "not accustomed to performing on a logical tight-rope in the barren desert of theory". That he is walking on a "tight-rope", not a logical one, it is true, but one spun from philosophical and love-besotted phrases, is clear from every issue of the *Volks-Tribun*.

2) The proposition that "each separate person lives individually" (which is itself nonsense) is expressed by Kriege as he walks the following illogical "tight-rope": "as long as the human species continues to find its representation in individuals at all",

3) "putting an end to the present state of things" is supposed to depend on the "pleasure" of the "creative spirit of mankind", which does not exist anywhere.

---

[a] A paraphrased stanza from Goethe's *Prometheus*.— *Ed.*

[b] H. Kriege, "Antwort an Cattanio".—*Ed.*

4) The following is the ideal of the communist man: "He bears the stamp of the species" (and who does not do so by the mere fact of his existence?), "determines his own goals according to the goals of the species" (as if the species were a person who could have goals) "and seeks to be completely his own, solely in order to dedicate himself to the species with everything that he is and is capable of becoming" (total self-sacrifice and self-abasement before a vaporous fantasy-concept).

5) The relationship of the individual to the species is also described in the following extravagant nonsense: "All of us and our particular activities are but symptoms of the great movement which is afoot in the inner depths of mankind." "In the inner depths of mankind"—where is that? According to this proposition, then, real people are only "symptoms", features of a "movement" that is afoot "in the depths" of a phantom conjured up by thinking.

6) This country parson transforms the struggle for a communist society into "the search for that great spirit of community". He pictures this "great spirit" "foaming full and fine from the *cup of communion*" and as "the *holy spirit* flashing from fraternal eyes".

Now that the revolutionary communist movement has thus been transformed into the "search" for the holy spirit and holy communion, Kriege can of course also assert that this spirit "needs *only* to be *recognised* for all men to be joined together in love".

7) This metaphysical conclusion is preceded by the following confusion of *communism* with *communion*: "The spirit that conquers the world, the spirit that commands the storm and the thunder and lightning (!!!!), the spirit that heals the blind and the lepers, the spirit that offers all men to drink of *one* wine" (we prefer a variety of kinds) "and to eat of *one* bread" (the French and English Communists are rather more demanding), "the spirit *that is eternal and omnipresent*, that is the spirit of community." If this "spirit" is "eternal and omnipresent", it is quite beyond comprehension how, according to Kriege, private property has managed to exist for so long. But, true enough, it has not been "recognised" and was thus "eternal and omnipresent" solely in his own imagination.

Kriege is therefore here preaching *in the name of communism* the old fantasy of religion and German philosophy which is the *direct antithesis of communism. Faith*, more specifically, faith in the "holy spirit of community" is the last thing required for the achievement of communism.

SECTION FOUR

FLIRTATIONS WITH RELIGION

It is self-evident that Kriege's amorous slobberings and his antithesis to selfishness are no more than the inflated utterances of a mind that has become utterly and completely absorbed in religion. We shall see how Kriege, who in Europe always claimed to be an atheist, here seeks to foist off all the infamies of Christianity under the signboard of communism and ends, perfectly consistently, with *man's self-desecration.*

In No.10, "Was wir wollen" and "H[ermann] Kriege an Harro Harring" define the purpose of the communist struggle in the following terms:

1) "To make a truth of the *religion of love* and a reality of the long yearned-for community of the blessed denizens of heaven." Kriege merely overlooks the fact that these obsessions of Christianity are only the fantastic expression of the existing world and that their "reality" therefore *already exists* in the evil conditions of this existing world.

2) "We demand in the name of that *religion of love* that the hungry should be given food, the thirsty be given drink and the naked clothed."—A demand which has been reiterated ad nauseam for 1,800 years already, without the slightest success.

3) "We teach the practice of *love*" in order to

4) "receive *love*".

5) "In their *realm of love* there is no room for devils."

6) "It is his" (man's) "*most sacred* need to *merge* his own person and whole individuality in the society of *loving beings,* towards whom he can retain nothing but

7) his *boundless love.*" One might think that with this boundlessness the theory of love had reached its highest peak, a peak so high that one can think of nothing higher; and yet the ascent continues.

8) "This hot outpouring of love, this surrender to all, this *divine urge* towards community—what else is this but the Communists' *innermost religion* which is only lacking in the appropriate external world to express itself in the fulness of human life." The present "external world" however seems to be quite sufficient for Kriege to lend the most lavish "expression" to his "innermost religion", his "divine urge", his "surrender to all" and his "hot outpouring" in the "fulness" of his own "human life".

9) "Do we not have the right to take the long pent-up desires of the religious heart seriously and march into battle in the name of the poor, the unhappy, and the rejected, for the final realisation of the sublime realm of brotherly love?" Kriege marches into battle, then, in order to take seriously the desires not of the real and the secular, but of the religious heart, not those of the heart made bitter by real need but those of the heart inflated by a fantasy of bliss. He forthwith offers proof of his "religious heart" by marching into battle as a priest, in the name of others, that is, in the name of the "poor", and in such a manner as to make it absolutely plain that he does not need communism for himself, he would have it that he is marching into battle in a spirit of pure, generous, dedicated, effusive self-sacrifice for the "poor, the unhappy and the rejected" who are in need of it—a feeling of elation which swells the heart of this worthy man in times of isolation and dejection, and outweighs all the troubles of this evil world.

10) Kriege concludes his pompous prating: "Any man who does not support such a party can with justice be treated as an enemy of mankind." This intolerant sentence appears to be in contradiction to "surrender to *all*", and the "religion of love" towards all. It is however a perfectly consistent conclusion of this new religion, which like every other mortally detests and persecutes all its enemies. The enemy of the party is quite consistently turned into a heretic, by transforming him from an enemy of the actually existing *party* who is *combated*, into a sinner against *humanity*—which only exists in the imagination—who must be *punished*.

11) In the letter to Harro Harring we read: "Our aim is to make all the poor of the world rebel against Mammon, under whose scourge they are condemned to work themselves to death, and when we have toppled the fearsome tyrant from his ancient throne, our aim will be to *unite* mankind by *love*, our aim will be to *teach* men to work communally and enjoy communally until the long-promised kingdom of joy finally comes about." In order to work up a fury against the present-day sovereignty of money, he first has to transform it into the idol Mammon. This idol is toppled—how, we do not discover; the revolutionary movement of the proletariat of all countries shrinks to no more than a rebellion—and when this toppling is complete, then the prophets—"we"—appear to "teach" the proletariat what is to be done next. These prophets "teach" their disciples, who here appear in remarkable ignorance of their own interests, how they are "to work and enjoy communally", not, indeed, for the sake of "working and enjoying communally" but rather just so that the scriptures shall be fulfilled and a

number of visionaries shall not have prophesied in vain 1,800 years ago.—This prophetical manner is found elsewhere as well, for example:

In No. 8, "Was ist das Proletariat?" and "Andreas Dietsch", with

a) "Proletarians,... the hour of your redemption has come."

b) "A thousand hearts beat joyfully in anticipation of the promised time"—in other words, "of that great realm of love ... for the long yearned-for realm of love."

c) In No. 12, "Antwort an Koch, den Antipfaffen",

"Already the gospel of the infinite redemption of the world goes quivering from eye to eye" and—even—"from hand to hand". This miracle of the "quivering gospel", this nonsense about the "infinite redemption of the world" is in perfect accordance with another miracle, namely that the long-abandoned prophecies of the old evangelists are unexpectedly fulfilled by Kriege.

12) Seen from this religious point of view, the answer to all *real questions* can only consist in a few *images* of extravagant religiosity which befog all sense, in a few high-sounding catchwords, such as "mankind", "humanity", "species", etc., and in turning every *real action* into a *fantastic phrase.* This is particularly evident in the essay "Was ist das Proletariat?" (No. 8). The answer given to this title-question is: "The proletariat is *mankind*",—a *deliberate* lie, according to which the Communists are aiming at the abolition of mankind. This answer, "mankind", is supposed to be the same as the one Sieyès gave to the question: What is the tiers-état?[39] Proof enough of how Kriege befuddles historical facts. He then forthwith provides more proof of this in his bigoted presentation of the American Anti-Rent movement: "And how would it be in the end if this proletariat, in its capacity as mankind" (a necessary character-mask for its appearance on the scene—a moment ago the proletariat was mankind, now mankind is only a capacity of the proletariat), "laid claim to the whole earth as its undisputed property for all eternity?" One observes how even an extremely simple, practical movement is transformed into empty phrases like "mankind", "undisputed property", "all eternity", etc., and for that reason rests content with a mere "claim".—Apart from the usual catchwords such as "outcast", etc., which is joined by the religious "accursed", all Kriege's statements about the proletariat amount to no more than the following mythological-biblical images:

"Prometheus bound",
"the Lamb of God which bears the sins of the world",
"the Wandering Jew",

and finally he brings up the following remarkable question: "Is mankind to wander for ever, then, a homeless vagabond, about the earth?" Meanwhile it is precisely the exclusive settlement of a part of "mankind" on the land which is his particular bugbear!

13) The real point about Kriege's religion is revealed in the following passage: "We have other things to do than worry about our *miserable selves*, we belong to mankind." With this shameful and nauseating grovelling before a "mankind" that is separate and distinct from the "self" and which is therefore a metaphysical and in his case even a religious fiction, with what is indeed the most utterly "miserable" slavish self-abasement, this religion ends up like any other. Such a doctrine, preaching the voluptuous pleasure of cringing and self-contempt, is entirely suited to valiant—*monks*, but never to men of action, least of all in a time of struggle. It only remains for these valiant monks to castrate their "miserable selves" and thereby provide sufficient proof of their confidence in the ability of "mankind" to reproduce itself!—If Kriege has nothing better to offer than these sentimentalities in pitiful style, it would indeed be wiser for him to translate his "Père Lamennais" again and again in each issue of the *Volks-Tribun*.

What the practical consequences are of Kriege's religion of infinite mercy and boundless surrender, is shown by the pleas for work which feature in almost every issue of the *Volks-Tribun*. We read, for instance, in No. 8:

"Arbeit! Arbeit! Arbeit!"

"Is there no one amongst all the wise[a] gentlemen who does not consider it a waste of effort to provide sustenance for deserving families and preserve helpless young people from poverty and despair? Firstly there is Johann Stern from Mecklenburg, still without work, and he is only asking to work himself to skin and bone for the benefit of some capitalist and at the same time earn enough bread as will suffice to sustain him for his work,—is that asking too much, then, in civilised society?—And then Karl Gescheidtle from Baden, a young man of the most excellent qualities and not without higher education—he looks so trustworthy and good, I guarantee he is honesty itself.... And an old man, too, and several other young people are begging for occupation for their hands, for their daily bread.—Let any person who can help delay no longer, or his conscience will one day rob him of his sleep when he most needs it. It is true you might say: There are thousands crying out in vain for work, and we certainly can't help all of them—you could, no doubt, but you are slaves of selfishness and have no heart to do anything. But for as long as you will not help all, at least show that you have left still a vestige of human feeling and help as many individuals as is in your power."

---

[a] In *Volks-Tribun* No. 8: rich.—*Ed.*

Of course, if they wished, they could help more than is in their power. That is how it is in practice, that is the real implementation of the self-abasement and degradation which this new religion teaches.

SECTION FIVE

KRIEGE'S PERSONAL STAND

The nature of Kriege's personal stand in his journal cannot fail to be evident from the above quotations; we will therefore only single out a small number of points.

Kriege appears as a *prophet* and therefore necessarily also as an emissary from a secret league of Essenes,[40] the "League of Justice". Hence, when he is not speaking in the name of the "oppressed", he is speaking in the name of "justice", which is not ordinary justice, however, but the justice of the "League of Justice". He not merely envelops *himself* in a fog of mystery, but *history* too. He envelops the real historical development of communism in the various countries of Europe, which he is not acquainted with, in a fog of mystery, by ascribing the origin and progress of communism to fabulous, novelettish and fictitious intrigues by this league of Essenes. There is evidence of this in every issue, especially in the reply to Harro Harring, which also contains the most absurd fantasies about the power of this league.

As a true *apostle of love* Kriege addresses himself firstly to women, whom he cannot believe to be so depraved as to resist a heart beating with love, secondly, to the newly discovered agitators "filially and conciliatorily",—as a "son"—as a "brother"—as "brother of the heart"—and finally as a *human being* to the rich. Hardly has he arrived in New York when he sends out circulars to all rich German merchants, presses the popgun of love to their chests, takes very good care not to say what he wants of them, signs variously as "A Human Being", "A Friend of Man" or "A Fool"—and, "would you believe it, my friends?", nobody responds to his high-falutin' tomfoolery. This can surprise no one but Kriege himself.—The familiar phrases of love we have already quoted are occasionally spiced with ejaculations like (No. 12, "Antwort an Koch"): "Hurrah! Long live community, long live equality, long live love!" Practical questions and doubts (cf. No. 14, "Antwort" to Conze) he can only explain to himself as deliberate malice and obtuseness. As a true prophet and exponent of love, he expresses all the hysterical irritation which a sensitive soul who has been snubbed feels towards the mockers, the unbelievers and those people in the old world whom the sweet warmth of his love fails to transmute into "the blessed denizens of heaven". It is in such a mood of sulky sentimentality that he cries out to them in No. 11, under the heading, "Frühling": "Therefore, you who mock us now, you shall soon have *faith*, for you shall know, spring is coming."

Written between April 20 and May 11, 1846

First published as a lithographic circular in May 1846

Signed: *Engels, K. Marx and others*

Printed according to the lithographic circular

Published in English for the first time

Frederick Engels

VIOLATION OF THE PRUSSIAN CONSTITUTION[41]

There exists a law in Prussia, dated 17th of January[a] 1820, forbidding the King to contract any State Debts without the sanction of the States-General, an assembly which it is very well known, does not yet exist in Prussia.[42] This law is the only guarantee the Prussians have for ever getting the constitution which, since 1815, has been promised to them. The fact of the existence of such a law not being generally known out of Prussia, the government succeeded in 1823 in borrowing *three millions of pounds* in England—first violation. After the French revolution of 1830, the Prussian government being obliged to make extensive preparations for a war which was then likely to break out, they not having any money, made the "interests for transatlantic trade",[43] a government concern, borrow twelve millions of dollars (£1,700,000), which, of course, were under the guarantee of the government, and spent by the government—second violation. Not to speak of the small violations, such as loans of a few hundred thousands of pounds by the same concern, the King of Prussia[b] has, at this moment, committed a third great violation. The credit of this concern being as it seems exhausted, the Bank of Prussia, being just in the same way, exclusively a government concern, has been empowered by the King to issue banknotes to the amount of ten millions of dollars (£1,350,000). This, deducting $3^1/_3$ millions as deposit and $^2/_3$ million for the increased expenses of the establishment, amounts in reality to an "indirect loan" of six millions of dollars or nearly one million of pounds, which the government will be responsible for, as up to this time no private capitalists are

[a] *The Northern Star* mistakenly gives 22nd of June.—*Ed.*

[b] Frederick William IV.—*Ed.*

partners to the Bank of Prussia. It is to be hoped that the Prussians, particularly the middle classes, who are most interested in the constitution, will not let this pass without an energetic protest.

Written in May 1846

First published in *The Northern Star* No. 446, May 30, 1846 with an editorial note: "From Our German Correspondent"

Reprinted from the newspaper

Karl Marx and Frederick Engels

LETTER
FROM THE BRUSSELS COMMUNIST CORRESPONDENCE COMMITTEE TO G. A. KÖTTGEN[44]

Brussels, June 15, 1846

TO G[USTAV] A[DOLF] KÖTTGEN FOR FURTHER CIRCULATION

We hasten to answer your call, communicated to us a few days ago, as follows:

We are in full agreement with your view that the German Communists must emerge from the isolation in which they have hitherto existed and establish durable mutual contacts with one another; similarly, that associations for the purpose of reading and discussion are necessary. For Communists must first of all clear things up among themselves, and this cannot be done satisfactorily without regular meetings to discuss questions concerning communism. We therefore also agree with you completely that cheap, easily understandable books and pamphlets with a communist content must be widely circulated. Both of these things, the former as well as the latter, should be taken up soon and energetically. You recognise the necessity of establishing regular money contributions; but your suggestion to support the authors by means of these contributions, to provide a comfortable life for them we must for our part reject. In our view the contributions should be used only for the printing of cheap communist leaflets and pamphlets and to cover the costs of correspondence, including that from here abroad. It will be necessary to fix a minimum sum for the monthly contributions, so that the amount of money that can be used for common purposes can be accurately determined at any moment. It is furthermore necessary that you should communicate to us the names of the members of your communist association — since we have to know, as you know of us, who it is we are dealing with. Finally, we await your statement of the size of the monthly contributions earmarked for common purposes, since the printing of several popular pamphlets ought to be proceeded with as soon as possible. That these pamphlets cannot be published in Germany is evident and needs no proof.

With regard to the Federal Diet, the King of Prussia, the assemblies of the estates, etc., you cherish really extensive illusions. A memorandum could only be effective if there already existed in Germany a strong and organised Communist Party, but neither is the case. A petition is only useful when at the same time it appears as a threat, behind which there stands a compact and organised mass. The only thing you could do, given suitable circumstances in your area, would be to produce a petition furnished with *numerous* and impressive workers' signatures.

We do not consider the time to be appropriate yet for a communist congress. Only when communist associations have been formed in the whole of Germany and means for action have been collected will delegates from the individual associations be able to gather for a congress with any prospect of success. And this will not be likely to occur before next year.

Until then the sole means of cooperation is the clarification of questions by letter and regular correspondence.

We have already, from time to time, been engaged in correspondence from here with the English and French Communists, as well as with the German Communists abroad. Whenever reports on the communist movement in England and France reach us, we shall communicate them to you, and we shall enclose anything else which comes to our notice in our current correspondence with you.

We request you to specify a *safe* address to us (and in future not to print the complete name, like G. A. Köttgen, on the seal, since this permits immediate identification of the sender as well as the recipient).

Write to us, however, at the following *completely safe* address:

Monsieur Ph[ilippe] Gigot, 8, rue de Bodenbroek, Bruxelles.

K. Marx, F. Engels, Ph. Gigot, F. Wolff[a]

Weerth sends his regards, is at the moment in Amiens.

If you should carry out your intention with the petition, it would lead to nothing but the C[ommunist] Party publicly proclaiming its weakness, and at the same time giving to the Government the names of the people it has specially to watch. If you cannot produce a working men's petition with at least 500 signatures, then petition rather, as the bourgeoisie in Trier wish to do, for a progressive

[a] Wilhelm (full name Friedrich Wilhelm) Wolff.— *Ed.*

property tax, and if, even then, the bourgeoisie of the area do not join in, eh bien,[a] join them for the time being in public demonstrations, proceed jesuitically, put aside teutonic probity, true-heartedness and decency, and sign and push forward the bourgeois petitions for freedom of the press, a constitution, and so on. When this has been achieved a new era will dawn for c[ommunist] propaganda. Our means will be increased, the antithesis between bourgeoisie and proletariat will be sharpened. In a party one must support everything which helps towards progress, and have no truck with any tedious moral scruples. For the rest, you must elect a standing committee for your correspondence, which will draft and discuss the letters to be written to us, and meet regularly. Otherwise matters will become disorganised. For drafting the letters you must elect the person you consider most capable. Personal considerations must be utterly disregarded, they ruin everything. The names of the committee members must naturally be communicated to us.

Salut.

Signatories, as overleaf

First published in Russian in the journal *Bolshevik* No. 3, February 1933

Printed according to the manuscript

Published in English for the first time

[a] Well and good.—*Ed.*

Frederick Engels

THE PRUSSIAN BANK QUESTION[45]

You will probably have already heard that the King of Prussia's plan of making money out of paper has been found impracticable. Two of the administrators of the State Debts refused to sign the new banknotes, as they considered them to be a new public debt, therefore subject to the guarantee of the States-General. Frederick William IV, to show that he can make as much money as he likes, has now hit upon a far better plan. Instead of making ten millions, he makes thirty—twenty millions of paper-money and ten of good, solid gold and silver coin. He proposes that ten millions of capital be raised by shares, "which shares it appears shall bring no dividends, but merely $3^1/_2$ per cent. interest and which shall not be transferable unless at the owner's death, in order to keep them out of the reach of speculation"!!! Now would you call such things *shares*? Why not? His Majesty of Prussia decrees that they *are* shares, and fosters the fond hope that he will find a lot of capitalists stupid enough to invest ten millions of dollars in such not transferable, leaden, three-and-a-half Bank Stock! And that at a time, too, when by speculating in railway shares they can make quite another percentage. When the King will have found the parcel of fools he is in want of, and thus borrowed ten millions in *coin*, he will issue *twenty* millions in banknotes, making "a sum total of thirty millions" increase of the national liabilities. Really this is raising the wind with a vengeance. Raising thirty millions, because one can't get ten.

Written at the end of June 1846

First published in *The Northern Star* No. 451, July 4, 1846 with an editorial note: "From Our German Correspondent"

Reprinted from the newspaper

Karl Marx and Frederick Engels

ADDRESS OF THE GERMAN DEMOCRATIC COMMUNISTS OF BRUSSELS TO MR. FEARGUS O'CONNOR[46]

Sir.— We embrace the occasion of your splendid success at the Nottingham election to congratulate you, and through you the English Chartists, on this signal victory. We consider the defeat of a Free-Trade minister[a] at the show of hands by an enormous Chartist majority, and at the very time, too, when Free-Trade principles are triumphant in the Legislature,[47] we consider this, Sir, as a sign that the working classes of England are very well aware of the position they have to take after the triumph of Free Trade. We conclude from this fact that they know very well that now, when the middle classes have carried their chief measure, when they have only to replace the present weak go-between cabinet by an energetical, really middle-class ministry, in order to be the acknowledged ruling class of your country, that now the great struggle of capital and labour, of *bourgeois* and *proletarian* must come to a decision. The ground is now cleared by the retreat of the landed aristocracy from the contest; middle class and working class are the only classes betwixt whom there can be a possible struggle. The contending parties have their respective battle-cries forced upon them by their interests and mutual position:— the middle class— "extension of commerce by any means whatsoever, and a ministry of Lancashire cotton-lords to carry this out";— the working class— "a democratic reconstruction of the Constitution upon the basis of the People's Charter",[48] by which the working class will become the ruling class of England. We

---

[a] John Cam Hobhouse.— *Ed.*

rejoice to see the English working men fully aware of this altered state of parties; of the new period Chartist agitation has entered into with the final defeat of the third party, the aristocracy; of the prominent position which Chartism henceforth will and must occupy, in spite of the "conspiracy of silence" of the middle-class press; and finally, of the new task, which by these new circumstances has devolved upon them. That they are quite aware of this task is proved by their intention *to go to the poll* at the next general election.

We have to congratulate you, Sir, in particular, upon your brilliant speech at the Nottingham election,[a] and the striking delineation given in it of the contrast between working-class democracy and middle-class liberalism.

We congratulate you besides on the unanimous vote of confidence in you, spontaneously passed by the whole Chartist body on the occasion of Thomas Cooper, the would-be *respectable*'s calumnies.[49] The Chartist party cannot but profit by the exclusion of such disguised bourgeois, who, while they show off with the name of Chartist for popularity's sake, strive to insinuate themselves into the favour of the middle classes by personal flattery of their literary representatives (such as the Countess of Blessington, Charles Dickens, D. Jerrold, and other "friends" of Cooper's), and by propounding such base and infamous old women's doctrines as that of "non-resistance".

Lastly, Sir, we have to thank you and your coadjutors for the noble and enlightened manner in which *The Northern Star* is conducted. We hesitate not a moment in declaring that the *Star* is the only English newspaper (save, perhaps, the *People's Journal*, which we know from the *Star* only), which knows the real state of parties in England; which is really and essentially democratic; which is free from national and religious prejudice; which sympathises with the democrats and working men (now-a-days the two are almost the same), all over the world; which in all these points speaks the mind of the English working class, and therefore is the only English paper really worth reading for the continental democrats. We hereby declare that we shall do everything in our power to extend the circulation of *The Northern Star* on the continent, and to have extracts from it translated in as many continental papers as possible.

We beg to express these sentiments, Sir, as the acknowledged

---

[a] O'Connor. [Speech at the Nottingham Nomination Meeting.]—*Ed.*

representatives of many of the German Communists in Germany, for all their relations with foreign democrats.

For the German Democratic Communists of Brussels.

The Committee,

Engels
Ph. Gigot
Marx

Brussels, July 17th, 1846

First published in *The Northern Star* No. 454, July 25, 1846

Reprinted from the newspaper

Frederick Engels

[GOVERNMENT AND OPPOSITION IN FRANCE]

The Chambers are now assembled. The Chamber of Peers have, as usual, nothing to do, now that they have disposed of the case of Joseph Henry, the new-fashioned regicide. The Chamber of Deputies are busily engaged in verifying the returns of members, and they profit by this opportunity to show the spirit which animates them. Never, since the revolution of 1830, has there been displayed such bare-faced impudence and contempt of public opinion. Three-fifths, at least, of the Deputies are thorough friends of the ministry; or, in other words, either great capitalists, stock-jobbers and railway speculators of the Paris Exchange, bankers, large manufacturers, etc., or their obedient servants. The present legislature is, more than any preceding one, the fulfilment of the words of Laffitte, the day after the revolution of July: Henceforth we, the bankers, shall govern France. It is the most striking proof that the government of France is in the hands of the great monied aristocracy, the *haute-bourgeoisie.* The fate of France is decided, not in the Cabinet of the Tuileries,[50] not in the Palace of Peers, not even in the Palace of Deputies, but on the Exchange of Paris. The actual ministers are not Messrs. Guizot and Duchâtel, but Messrs. Rothschild, Fould, and the rest of the large Paris bankers, whose tremendous fortunes make them the most eminent representatives of the rest of their class. They govern the ministry, and the ministry take care that in the elections none but men devoted to the present system, and to those who profit by this system, are carried. This time they have had a most signal success; government patronage and bribery of every description, united to the influence of the chief capitalists, upon a limited number of voters (less than 200,000), who all belong, more or less, to their own class, the terror spread among monied men by the timely attempt to shoot the king, and ultimately the certainty that Louis-Philippe will not survive the present Chambers (whose powers expire in 1851), all these things united were sufficient to quench all serious opposition in most of the elective assemblies. And now, this precious Chamber having met, they take proper care of themselves. The independent electors have sent in hundreds of petitions and protests against the returns of ministerial members, stating and proving, or offering to prove, that almost in every case the elections have been carried by the grossest illegalities committed by government officers; proving bribery, corruption, intimidation, patronage of every description to have been employed. But the majority never take the slightest notice of these facts. Every opposition deputy who raises his voice to protest against such abomination is hooted down by hisses, noise, or cries of "Division, division". Every illegality is covered by a sanctioning vote. The money lords rejoice in their strength, and guessing it will not last very long, they make the best of the present moment.

You may easily imagine that out of this narrow circle of capitalists there exists a general opposition against the present government, and those whose interests it serves. The centre of this opposition is Paris, where the money lords have so little influence upon constituencies, that of the fourteen deputies of the department of the Seine only two are ministerialists and twelve belong to the opposition. The majority of the middle class, voters of Paris, belong to the party of Thiers and O. Barrot; they want to do away with the exclusive rule of Rothschild and Co., to recover an honourable and independent position for France in her external relations, and perhaps a little bit of electoral reform. The majority of non-voting tradesmen, shopkeepers, etc., are of a more radical cast, and demand an electoral reform, which would give them the vote; a number of them are also partisans of the *National* or *Réforme*, and join themselves to the democratic party, which embraces the great bulk of the working classes, and is itself divided into different sections, the most numerous of which, at least in Paris, is formed by the Communists. The present system is attacked by all these different sections, and, of course, by each in a different manner. But there has been started, a short time ago, a new mode of attack which deserves to be mentioned. A working man has written a pamphlet against the head of the system, not against Louis-Philippe, but against "Rothschild I. King of the Jews".[a] The success of this pamphlet (it

[a] [G. M. Dairnvaell,] *Histoire édifiante et curieuse de Rothschild I-er, roi des juifs*.—*Ed.*

has now gone through some twenty editions) shows how much this was an attack in the right direction. King Rothschild has been obliged to publish two defences against these attacks of a man whom nobody knows, and the whole of whose property consists in the suit of clothes he wears. The public have taken up the controversy with the greatest interest. Some thirty pamphlets have been published pro and con. The hatred against Rothschild and the money lords is enormous, and a German paper says, Rothschild might take this as a warning that he had better take up his headquarters somewhere else than upon the ever-burning volcano of Paris.

Written about September 1, 1846

Reprinted from the newspaper

First published in *The Northern Star* No. 460, September 5, 1846 with an editorial note: "From Our Own Correspondent"

Frederick Engels

THE PRUSSIAN CONSTITUTION

At last this long-expected piece of workmanship has made its appearance![51] At last—if we believe the *Times, Globe,* some French and some German papers—Prussia has passed over to the ranks of constitutional countries. *The Northern Star,* however, has already sufficiently proved that this so-called Constitution is nothing but a trap offered to the Prussian people to cheat them of the rights promised by the late king,[a] at the time he wanted popular support. That this is the fact, that Frederick William tries by this so-called Constitution to obtain money without being obliged to make concessions to public opinion, is certain beyond all doubt. The democratic papers of all countries—in France, particularly the *National* and *Réforme,* nay, the ministerial *Journal des Débats,*—agree in this opinion. The fettered German press itself stammers words which allow no other conclusion, but that the movement party in Prussia is quite aware of the sly intentions of their "open-hearted, generous" king. The question then is this: will the king succeed in his plans? Will the Central Assembly of Estates be either stupid or cowardly enough to guarantee a new loan, without securing to the people extended liberties, and thus give the king the means to continue the present system for an indefinite length of time?

We answer: No; they will not, they cannot.

The hitherto followed plan of government in Prussia was the consequence of the relative position of the nobility and the middle classes in Prussia. The nobility had lost too much of its former strength, wealth and influence, to dominate the king as formerly it

---

[a] Frederick William III.—*Ed.*

had done. The middle classes were not yet strong enough to overcome the dead weight of the nobility, which cramped their commercial and industrial progress. Thus the king, representing the central power of the state, and supported by the numerous class of government officers, civil and military, besides having the army at his disposal, was enabled to keep down the middle classes by the nobility, and the nobility by the middle classes, by flattering now the interests of the one, and then those of the other; and balancing, as much as possible, the influence of both. This stage of absolute monarchy has been gone through by almost all the civilised countries of Europe, and in those most advanced it has now given place to the government of the middle classes.

Prussia, the most advanced of German countries, had hitherto wanted a middle class, wealthy, strong, united and energetic enough to shake off the domination of absolutism, and to crush the remains of feudal nobility. The two contending elements, nobility and middle classes, are, however, placed in such circumstances, that by the natural progress of industry and civilisation, the one (the middle classes) must increase in wealth and influence, while the other (the nobility) must decrease, impoverish and lose more and more its ascendancy. While, therefore, the Prussian nobility and large landed proprietors, found themselves every year in a worse position, first, by the ruinous wars with France in the beginning of this century; then by the English Corn Laws,[52] which shut them out from the market of that country; then by the competition of Australia, in one of their chief productions, wool, and by many other circumstances—the middle classes of Prussia increased enormously in wealth, productive powers, and influence in general. The wars with France, the shutting out of English manufactured goods from the Continental markets, created manufacturing industry in Prussia; and when peace was re-established, the upstart manufacturers were powerful enough to force government to grant them protective duties (1818). Soon afterwards, the Zollverein was founded, a union which almost exclusively advanced the interests of the middle classes.[53] And, above all, the violent competitive struggle arising between the different trading and manufacturing nations during these last 30 years of peace, forced the somewhat indolent Prussian middle classes, either to allow themselves to be entirely ruined by foreign competition, or to set to work in good earnest, as well as their neighbours.

The progress of the middle classes was very little visible up to the year 1840, when the ascension to the throne of a new king[a] appeared

---

[a] Frederick William IV.—*Ed.*

to them the proper moment to show that, since 1815, things were rather changed in Prussia. I need not recapitulate how the middle-class movement has progressed since that time; how all parts of the kingdom acceded to it, until at last all the middle classes, a great part of the peasantry, and not a few of the nobility, joined in it. A representative constitution, liberty of the press, open courts of law, immovability of the judges, trial by jury—such were the demands of the middle classes. The peasantry or small landed proprietors saw very well—in the more enlightened parts of the kingdom, at least—that such measures were for their interests, too, being the only ones by which they could hope to free themselves from the remnants of feudality, and to have that influence upon the making of laws which it was desirable for them to possess. The poorer part of the nobility thought that the constitutional system might, perhaps, give them such a position in the legislature as their interests demanded; and that, at all events, this system could not be more ruinous to them than that under which they lived. It was principally the nobility of Prussia Proper and Posen, who, being severely oppressed by want of markets for their produce, acceded to the Liberal movement from such considerations.

The middle classes themselves got more and more into an uncomfortable position. They had increased their manufacturing and mining concerns, as well as their shipping, to a considerable extent; they were the chief furnishers for the whole market of the Zollverein; their wealth and numbers had increased very much. But during the last ten or fifteen years the enormous progress of English manufactures and mining operations have threatened them with a deadly competition. Every glut in the English market threw large quantities of English goods into the Zollverein, where they were sold at prices more ruinous to the Germans than to the English, because these latter made, during the times of flourishing trade, large profits in the American and other markets, while the Prussians could never sell their produce anywhere but within the circle of their own line of customs. Their shipping was almost excluded from the ports of foreign nations, while ships of all flags entered the Prussian ports on equal conditions with the Prussians. Thus, although there is comparatively little capital in Prussia, there commenced a difficulty of investing this capital profitably. Trade appeared to be labouring under a continual pressure; factories, machinery, stock in trade, were slowly, but continually, depreciated; and this general uneasiness was for a moment only interrupted by the railway speculations, which, within the last eight years, were started in Prussia. These speculations, by raising the value of ready money, increased the

Ich und Mein Haus, Wir wollen dem HERRN dienen.

Cartoon by Engels of Frederick William IV making the royal speech at the opening of the United Diet in Berlin, April 11, 1847. Published as a special supplement to the *Deutsche-Brüsseler-Zeitung* May 6, 1847

depreciation of stock in trade, and were themselves, on an average, not very profitable, on account of the comparatively thin population and trade of the greater part of the country. They offered, however, a still better chance of profit than other industrial investments; and thus every one who could dispose of some capital engaged in them. Very soon these speculations assumed, as usual, a feverish character, and ended in a crisis which now for about a twelve-month has oppressed the Prussian money markets. Thus the middle classes found themselves in a very uncomfortable position in the beginning of the present year: the money markets under the pressure of an extraordinary want of coin; the manufacturing districts requiring more than ever those protective duties which the government refused to grant; the coast towns requiring navigation laws as the only means to relieve them; and, over and above all, a rise in the corn markets, which brought the country to a state approaching famine. All these causes of discontent operated at the same time, and more strongly so upon the people; the Silesian linen-weavers in the greatest distress; the cotton factories stopped; in the large manufacturing district of the Rhine almost all hands out of work, the potato crop mostly ruined, and bread at famine prices. The moment was evidently come for the middle classes to take the government out of the hands of an imbecile king, weak nobility, and self-conceited bureaucracy, and to secure it to themselves.

It is a curious fact, but which is repeated at every revolutionary epoch, that at the very moment when the leading class of a movement is most favourably placed for the accomplishment of that movement, the old worn-out government is reduced to beg the assistance of this same leading class. Thus in 1789, in France, when famine, bad trade, and divisions among the nobility pushed, so to say, the middle classes to a revolution—at that very moment the government found its money resources exhausted, and was reduced to begin the revolution by the convocation of the States-General.[54] Thus in 1847 in Prussia. At the very moment when the more indolent Prussian middle classes are almost forced by circumstances to change the governmental system, at that moment the king, by want of money, is forced to commence that change of system, and to convocate in his turn the Prussian States-General. It is indubitable that the States would offer him much less resistance than they will now, if the money market was easy, the factories at full work (which would be caused by a flourishing trade and ready sale, and consequent high prices for manufactured goods in England) and corn at a reasonably low price. But so it is: in times of approaching revolution, the progressive classes of society have always all chances on their side.

I have, during the course of 1845 and 1846, more than once shown to the readers of the *Star*, that the King of Prussia was in a very embarrassed financial situation[a]; I have at the same time called their attention to the several clever plans by which his ministers sought to extricate him; and predicted that the whole affair must end by a convocation of the States-General. The event, then, was neither unexpected, nor, as it now is represented, caused by the free grace of his squandering majesty; nothing but sheer necessity, poverty and distress could move him to such a step, and there is not a child in Prussia but knows this. The only question, then, is this:—Will the Prussian middle classes, by investing a new loan with their guarantee, allow the king to go on as he has done hitherto and to disregard for another seven years their petitions and their wants?

We have already answered this question. They cannot do this. We have proved it from the situation of the respective classes, and we shall now prove it from the composition of the States-General themselves.

Members of high and low nobility	311
Do. for towns and peasantry	306

As the king has declared his intention to increase the members of the high nobility (80 in all) by new creations of peers, we may add to the nobility, about 30 more; 341 members of nobility, or government party. Deduct from this number the liberal fractions of the lower nobility, namely, all the nobility of Prussia Proper, two-thirds of that of Posen, and some members of the Rhenish, Silesian, Brandenburg and Westphalian nobility, say 70 liberal members, voting with the towns and peasantry, and the position of parties is as follows:—

Nobility, or government party	271
Towns and peasantry, or liberal opposition	376

Thus, even allowing that thirty or forty town or peasantry members from the remote districts should vote for the government, there will always be a liberal majority of from twenty-five to fifty votes remaining, and with a little energy on the part of the Liberals, it will be easy to meet every demand for money with another demand for liberal institutions. There is besides, no doubt, that, under present circumstances, the people will support the middle classes, and by their pressure from without, which indeed is very much

[a] See F. Engels' articles "Violation of the Prussian Constitution" and "The Prussian Bank Question" (this volume, pp. 52-53 and p. 57).—*Ed.*

wanted, strengthen the courage and enliven the energies of those within.

Thus, the Prussian constitution, insignificant in itself, is, for all that, the beginning of a new epoch for that country, and for all Germany. It marks the downfall of absolutism and nobility, and the ascendancy of the middle classes; it marks the beginning of a movement which will very soon lead to a representative constitution for the middle classes, a free press, independent judges and trial by jury, and which will end God knows where. It marks the repetition of 1789 in Prussia. And if the revolutionary movement which now begins, will directly interest the middle classes only, it is yet not at all indifferent to the interests of the people. From the moment the power of the middle classes is constituted, from that moment begins the separate and distinct democratic movement. In the struggle against despotism and aristocracy, the people, the democratic party, cannot but play a secondary part; the first place belongs to the middle classes. From the moment, however, the middle classes establish their own government, identify themselves with a new despotism and aristocracy against the people, from that moment democracy takes its stand as the only, the exclusive movement party; from that moment the struggle is simplified, reduced to two parties, and changes, by that circumstance, into a "war to the knife". The history of the French and English democratic parties fully proves this.

There is another circumstance to be remarked. The conquest of public power by the middle classes of Prussia will change the political position of all European countries. The alliance of the North will be dissolved. Austria and Russia, the chief spoliators of Poland, will be entirely isolated from the rest of Europe, for Prussia carries along with her the smaller states of Germany, who all have constitutional governments. Thus the balance of power in Europe will be entirely changed by the consequences of this insignificant constitution; the desertion of three-fourths of Germany from the camp of stationary Eastern Europe into that of progressive Western Europe. In February 1846, broke out the last Polish insurrection.[55] In February 1847, Frederick William convocates his States-General. *The vengeance of Poland is drawing nigh!*

Written at the end of February 1847

First published in *The Northern Star* No. 489, March 6, 1847 with an editorial note: "From Our German Correspondent"

Signed: *E.*

Reprinted from the newspaper

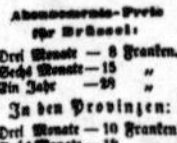

Deutsche-Brüsseler-Zeitung.

Redacteur: A. von Bornstedt.

N° 28. Brüssel, Donnerstag den 8. April 1847.

Karl Marx

[DECLARATION AGAINST KARL GRÜN]

Under the date-line *Berlin*, March 20, the *Trier'sche Zeitung* prints an article on my pamphlet now in printing, *Contradictions dans le système des contradictions économiques de M. Proudhon ou les misères de la philosophie.*[a] The Berlin correspondent[b] makes me out to be the author of a report printed in the *Rhein- u. Mosel-Zeitung* and elsewhere concerning this pamphlet, Proudhon's book[c] and the activities of its translator, Herr Grün.[56] He hails me time and again as "editor of the *former Rheinische Zeitung*" quite in the style of the Brussels or another correspondent. "Buttressed by a knowledge of the current state of the press in Germany", our friend peddles his insinuation. Not merely his insinuation, but his whole literary existence may, as far as I am concerned, be "*buttressed* by a knowledge of the current state of the press in Germany". I grant him the most practically proven "knowledge of the current state of the press in Germany". But this time it has not "*buttressed*" him.

The alleged Berlin correspondent need only read through my criticism of Proudhon in the *Critical Criticism*[d] in order to realise that the report which arouses his enmity might well originate in Brussels, but could not possibly originate with me, if only because it "*sets the same value*" on Proudhon and H[er]r Grün.

---

[a] The title of the work was changed later (see pp. 105-212 of this volume).—*Ed.*

[b] Obviously Eduard Meyen.—*Ed.*

[c] P. J. Proudhon, *Système des contradictions économiques, ou Philosophie de la misère*, T. I-II, Paris, 1846.—*Ed.*

[d] K. Marx and F. Engels, *The Holy Family or Critique of Critical Criticism* (see present edition, Vol. 4, pp. 23-54).—*Ed.*

My criticism of Proudhon is written *in French.* Proudhon himself will be able to reply. A letter he wrote to me before the publication of his book shows absolutely no inclination to leave it to Herr Grün and his associates to avenge him in the event of criticism on my part.[57]

"Concerning further the translator of P[roudhon]'s work on economics", our friend in Berlin need only add to the record that "*We here in Berlin* have *learnt much and of great diversity*" from Herr Grün's *Soziale Bewegung in Frankreich und Belgien* [Social Movement in France and Belgium] in order to place the value of this book above all doubt. And one must consider what it means when "We here in Berlin" "*learn*" anything at all, and in this case even "much and of great diversity", quantitatively and qualitatively at the same time! We here in Berlin!

Identifying me with the Brussels or another correspondent, the Berlin or alleged Berlin correspondent exclaims:

> Grün "has probably to make amends for the misfortune of having acquainted the German world with the results of foreign socialism *before* Herr Dr. Marx, 'editor of the *former Rheinische Zeitung*'".

Our friend undeniably betrays great ingenuity in forming his conjectures! I should like to confide to him, *sub rosa,*[a] that, admittedly in my own view, Herr Grün's *Soziale Bewegung in Frankreich und Belgien* and the French and the Belgian social movement—individual names and data excepted—have nothing in common with each other. At the same time, however, I must confide to him that I have experienced so little urge to acquaint "the German world" with the results of my studies of Herr Grün's *Soziale Bewegung in Frankreich und Belgien* that I have permitted a fairly comprehensive review of Grün's book, prepared a year ago, peacefully to sleep the sleep of the just in manuscript form, and only now that I have been challenged by our friend in Berlin shall I send it to the *Westphälisches Dampfboot* to be printed. The review forms an appendix to the book written jointly by *Fr. Engels* and me on "*the German ideology*" (critique of modern German philosophy as expounded by its representatives Feuerbach, B[runo] Bauer and Stirner, and of *German socialism* as expounded by its various prophets).[b] The circumstances which have hindered the printing of this manuscript and still hinder it will perhaps be set forth for the reader elsewhere as a contribution to the description of the "current state of the press in Germany". Nothing hindered the separate printing of my review of Grün's book, which in no way offends

---

[a] In secret.— *Ed.*

[b] See present edition, Vol. 5.— *Ed.*

against the censorship, except the slight obstacle that this book was not considered worthy of a special attack, and it was thought that only in a survey of the whole of the insipid and tasteless[a] literature of German socialism would some reference to Herr Grün be unavoidable. Now, however, after the article by our Berlin friend, the separate printing of this review has taken on the more or less humorous significance of showing the manner in which "the German world" "acquaints itself" with the "results of foreign socialism", and especially the desire and capacity "*We here in Berlin*" possess "to learn much and of great diversity". It will immediately be realised how strongly I was compelled to resort to petty attacks in petty little newspaper articles if I had otherwise been anxious to bring Herr Grün's "Social Movement in France and Belgium" to a standstill. Finally, even our Berlin friend will be unable to refrain from making public testimony that if I really harboured the intention of "acquainting the German world with the results of foreign socialism" in his sense, and truly feared a competitor in a predecessor, then I should be obliged daily to beseech fate, "Give me no predecessor, or even better, give me Herr Grün as a predecessor!"

A word more concerning "my conceit in imagining that I have scaled the topmost rung of human wisdom".

Who else could have inoculated me with this disease but Herr Grün who found in my expositions in the *Deutsch-Französische Jahrbücher*[b] the solution to the ultimate riddle (see, for example, the foreword to his *Bausteine*) in the same way as he finds it now in Proudhon's economics; who, as he now extols in Proudhon the true point of view, likewise assured his readers about me (see Grün's *Neue Anekdota*), that I had "negated the constitutional and radical point of view".[58] Herr Grün first poisons me, in order then to be able to blame me for the fact that his poison worked! Let our Berlin friend calm himself, however—I enjoy perfect health.

Brussels, April 3, 1847 *Karl Marx*

First published in the *Deutsche-Brüsseler-Zeitung* No. 28, April 8, 1847 and in the *Trier'sche Zeitung* No. 99, April 9, 1847

Printed according to the *Trier'sche Zeitung* text checked with the *Deutsche-Brüsseler-Zeitung*

Published in English for the first time

---

[a] The words "the insipid and tasteless" are missing in the *Trier'sche Zeitung*.— *Ed.*

[b] The reference is to K. Marx's articles "On the Jewish Question" and "Contribution to the Critique of Hegel's Philosophy of Law" (see present edition, Vol. 3).—*Ed.*

Frederick Engels

[THE CONSTITUTIONAL QUESTION IN GERMANY][59]

I

German socialist literature grows worse from month to month. It increasingly confines itself to the broad effusions of those *true socialists* whose whole wisdom amounts to an amalgam of German philosophy and German-philistine sentimentality with a few stunted communist slogans. It exhibits a peacefulness which enables it even under the censorship to state its most heartfelt opinions. Even the German police find little in it to take exception to—proof enough that it belongs not to the progressive, revolutionary elements but to the stale, reactionary elements in German literature.

To these *true socialists* belong not only those who term themselves socialists *par excellence*, but also the greater part of those writers in Germany who have accepted the party name of *Communists*. The latter indeed are, if possible, even worse.

Under these circumstances, it goes without saying that these *soi-disant* communist writers are in no way representative of the *Party* of the German Communists. They are neither recognised by the Party as its literary representatives nor do they represent its interests. On the contrary, they look after quite other interests, they defend quite other principles, which are opposed in every respect to those of the Communist Party.

The true socialists, to whom, as we have said, most German *soi-disant* communist writers belong, have learnt from the French Communists that the transition from the absolute monarchy to the modern representative state in no way abolishes the poverty of the great mass of the people, but only brings a new class, the bourgeoisie, to power. They have further learnt from the French Communists that it is precisely this bourgeoisie which, by means of its capital, presses most heavily upon the masses, and hence is the opponent *par excellence* of the Communists, or socialists respectively, as representatives of the mass of the people. They have not taken the trouble to compare Germany's level of social and political development with that of France, nor to study the conditions actually existing in Germany upon which all further development depends; hastily and without long reflection they have transferred their hastily acquired knowledge to Germany. Had they been Party men who aimed at a practical, tangible result, who represented particular interests common to an entire class, they would at least have paid attention to the way in which the opponents of the bourgeoisie in France, from the editors of *La Réforme* to the ultra-Communists, such as in particular the acknowledged representative of the great mass of the French proletariat, old Cabet, behave in their polemic against the bourgeoisie. It should really have struck them that these representatives of the Party not merely engage continually in politics of the day, but that even towards political measures such as proposals for electoral reforms, in which the proletariat has no *direct* interest, they nevertheless adopt an attitude far removed from sovereign disdain. But our true socialists are not Party men, they are German theoreticians. They are not concerned with practical interests and results, but with eternal truth. The interests which they strive to uphold are the interests of "man", the results they pursue are limited to philosophical "achievements". So they only needed to bring their new elucidations into harmony with their own philosophical conscience, in order then to noise abroad before the whole of Germany that political progress, like all politics, is evil, that constitutional freedom in particular elevates to the throne the bourgeoisie, the class most dangerous to the people, and that in general the bourgeoisie cannot be attacked enough.

In France, the rule of the bourgeoisie has for seventeen years been more complete than in any other country in the world. The attacks of the French proletarians, their Party chiefs and literary representatives on the bourgeoisie were therefore attacks on the ruling class, on the existing political system, they were *definitely revolutionary* attacks. How well the ruling bourgeoisie knows this is proven by the countless press trials and prosecutions of associations, the prohibition of meetings and banquets, the hundred police chicaneries with which it persecutes the Réformistes[60] and Communists. In Germany, things are completely different. In Germany the bourgeoisie is not only not in power, it is even the most dangerous enemy of the existing governments. For these the diversion mounted by the true socialists was very opportune. The struggle against the bourgeoisie, which only too often brought the French Communists imprisonment or exile, brought our true socialists nothing except the permission to print. The revolutionary heat in the polemics by the French proletariat dwindled in the cool breasts of the German theoreticians to a tepidness satisfying the censorship and in this emasculated state was a quite welcome ally for the German governments against the threatening bourgeoisie. True socialism managed to use the most revolutionary propositions that have ever been framed as a protective wall for the morass of the German status quo. True socialism is reactionary through and through.

The bourgeoisie long ago noticed this reactionary tendency of true socialism. But without further thought they took this trend for the literary representative also of German communism, and reproached the *Communists* publicly and privately with merely playing into the hands of the governments, the bureaucracy, and the nobility with their polemics against a representative system, trial by jury, freedom of the press, and their clamour against the bourgeoisie.

It is high time that the German Communists disowned the responsibility imputed to them for the reactionary deeds and desires of the true socialists. It is high time that the German Communists, who represent the German proletariat with its very clear, very tangible needs, broke in the most decisive manner with that literary clique—for it is nothing more—which does not know itself whom it represents, and so against its will tumbles into the arms of the German governments; which believes itself to be "realising man" and is realising nothing but the deification of the wretched German philistine. We Communists have in fact nothing in common with the theoretical phantasms and scruples of conscience of this crafty company. Our attacks on the bourgeoisie differ as much from those of the true socialists as from those of the reactionary nobles, e. g., the French legitimists or Young England.[61] The German status quo cannot exploit our attacks in any way, because they are directed still more against it than against the bourgeoisie. If the bourgeoisie, so to speak, our *natural* enemy, is the enemy whose overthrow will bring our party to power, the German status quo is still more our enemy, because it stands between the bourgeoisie and us, because it hinders us from coming to grips with the bourgeoisie. For that reason we do not exclude ourselves in any way from the great mass of opposition to the German status quo. We only form its most advanced section—a section which at the same time through its unconcealed *arrière pensée* against the bourgeoisie takes up a quite definite position.

With the meeting of the Prussian United Diet the struggle against the German status quo reaches a turning point. On the attitude of this Diet depends the continuation or the end of the status quo. The parties in Germany, which are still very vague, confused and fragmented through ideological subtleties, are thus faced with the necessity to clarify for themselves what interests they represent, what tactics they must follow, to demarcate themselves from other parties and to become practical. The youngest of these parties, the Communist Party, cannot evade this necessity. It must likewise clarify for itself its position, its plan of campaign, its means of action, and the first step to this is to disavow the reactionary socialists who try to insinuate themselves among the Communists. It can take this step all the sooner because it is strong enough to refuse assistance from all allies who would discredit it.

II

THE STATUS QUO AND THE BOURGEOISIE

The status quo in Germany is as follows.

While in France and England the bourgeoisie has become powerful enough to overthrow the nobility and to raise itself to be the ruling class in the state, the German bourgeoisie has not yet had such power. It has indeed a certain influence upon the governments, but in all cases where there is a collision of interests, this influence must give way to that of the landed nobility. While in France and England the *towns* dominate the *countryside,* in Germany the countryside dominates the towns, agriculture dominates trade and industry. This is the case not only in the absolute, but also in the constitutional, monarchies of Germany, not only in Austria and Prussia, but also in Saxony, Württemberg and Baden.

The cause of this is that in its stage of civilisation Germany lags behind the Western countries. In the latter it is predominantly trade and industry which provide the mass of the population with their livelihood, but with us it is agriculture. England exports no agricultural produce whatever, but is in constant need of supplies from abroad; France imports at least as much agricultural produce as it exports, and both countries base their wealth above all on their exports of industrial products. Germany, on the contrary, exports few industrial goods, but a great quantity of corn, wool, cattle, etc. When Germany's political system was established—in 1815, the overwhelming importance of agriculture was even greater than now and it was increased still more at that time by the fact that it was precisely the almost exclusively agricultural parts of Germany that had participated most zealously in the overthrow of the French Empire.

The political representative of agriculture is, in Germany as in most European countries, the *nobility*, the class of big landed proprietors. The political system corresponding to the exclusive dominance of the nobility is the feudal system. The feudal system has everywhere declined in the same degree in which agriculture has ceased to be the decisive branch of production in a country, in the same degree in which an industrial class has formed itself beside the agricultural, towns beside villages.

The class newly forming itself beside the nobility and the peasants more or less dependent on it is not the bourgeoisie, which today rules in the civilised countries and is striving for mastery in Germany; it is the class of the *petty bourgeoisie.*

The present political system of Germany is nothing more than a compromise between the nobility and the petty bourgeoisie, which amounts to resigning power into the hands of a third class: the bureaucracy. In the composition of this class the two high contracting parties participate according to their respective status; the nobility, which represents the more important branch of production, reserves to itself the higher positions, the petty bourgeoisie contents itself with the lower and only in exceptional circumstances puts forward candidates for the higher administration. Where the bureaucracy is subjected to direct control, as in the constitutional states of Germany, the nobility and petty bourgeoisie share in it in the same way; and that here also the nobility reserves to itself the lion's share is easily understood. The petty bourgeoisie can never overthrow the nobility, nor make itself equal to it; it can do no more than weaken it. To overthrow the nobility, another class is required, with wider interests, greater property and more determined courage: *the bourgeoisie.*

In all countries the bourgeoisie emerges from the petty bourgeoisie with the development of world trade and large-scale industry, with the accompanying free competition and centralisation of property. The petty bourgeoisie represents inland and coastal trade, handicrafts, manufacture based on handwork—branches of industry which operate within a limited area, require little capital, have a slow turnover and give rise to only local and sluggish competition. The bourgeoisie represents world trade, the direct exchange of products of all regions, trade in money, large factory industry based on the use of machinery—branches of production which demand the greatest possible area, the greatest possible capital and the quickest possible turnover, and give rise to universal and stormy competition. The petty bourgeois represents *local,* the bourgeois *general* interests. The petty bourgeois finds his position sufficiently safeguarded if, while exercising indirect influence on state legislation, he participates directly in provincial administration and is master of his local municipality. The bourgeois cannot protect his interests without direct, constant control of the central administration, foreign policy and legislation of his state. The classical creation of the petty bourgeoisie were the free cities of the German Reich, that of the bourgeoisie is the French representative state. The petty bourgeois is conservative as soon as the ruling class makes a few concessions to him; the bourgeois is revolutionary until he himself rules.

What then is the attitude of the German bourgeoisie to the two classes that share political rule?

While a rich and powerful bourgeoisie has been formed in England since the seventeenth and in France since the eighteenth century, one can speak of a German bourgeoisie only since the beginning of the nineteenth century. There were before then, it is true, a few rich shipowners in the Hanseatic towns, a few rich bankers in the interior, but no class of big capitalists, and least of all of big *industrial* capitalists. The creator of the German bourgeoisie was Napoleon. His continental system[62] and the freedom of trade made necessary by its pressure in Prussia gave the Germans a manufacturing industry and expanded their mining industry. After a few years these new or expanded branches of production were already so important, and the bourgeoisie created by them so influential, that by 1818 the Prussian government saw that it was necessary to allow them protective tariffs. The Prussian Customs Act of 1818 was the first official recognition of the bourgeoisie by the government. It was admitted, though reluctantly and with a heavy heart, that the bourgeoisie had become a class indispensable for the country. The next concession to the bourgeoisie was the Customs Union.[63] The admission of most of the German states into the Prussian customs system was no doubt originally occasioned simply by fiscal and political considerations, but no one benefited from it as much as did the German, more especially the Prussian, bourgeoisie. Although the Customs Union here and there brought a few small advantages to the nobility and petty bourgeoisie, on the whole it harmed both groups still more through the rise of the bourgeoisie, keener competition and the supplanting of the previous means of production. Since then the bourgeoisie, especially in Prussia, has developed rather quickly. Although its advance during the last thirty years has not been nearly as great as that of the English and French bourgeoisie, it has nevertheless established most branches of modern industry, in a few districts supplanted peasant or petty-bourgeois patriarchalism, concentrated capital to some extent, produced something of a proletariat, and built fairly long stretches of railroad. It has at least reached the point of having either to go further and make itself the ruling class or to renounce its previous conquests, the point where it is the only class that can at the moment bring about progress in Germany, can at the moment rule Germany. It is already in fact the leading class in Germany, and its whole existence depends upon its becoming legally so as well.

With the rise of the bourgeoisie and its growing influence coincides, indeed, the growing impotence of the hitherto official ruling classes. The nobility has become more and more impoverished and encumbered with debts since the time of Napoleon. The buying free from corvée raised the production costs of corn for the nobility and exposed it to competition from a new class of independent small peasants—disadvantages which in the long run were far from being compensated for by the peasants overreaching themselves when they bought themselves free. Russian and American competition limited the market for its corn, Australian and in some years South Russian that of its wool. And the more the production costs and competition increased, the more was exposed the incapacity of the nobility to work its estates profitably, and to apply the newest advances in agriculture. Like the French and English nobility of the last century, the German nobility employed the rising level of civilisation only to squander its fortune magnificently on pleasures in the big cities. Between the nobility and the bourgeoisie began that competition in social and intellectual education, in wealth and display, which everywhere precedes the political dominance of the bourgeoisie and ends, like every other form of competition, with the victory of the richer side. The provincial nobility turned into a Court nobility, only thereby to be ruined all the more quickly and surely. The three per cent revenues of the nobility went down before the fifteen per cent profit of the bourgeoisie, the three-per-centers resorted to mortgages, to credit banks for the nobility and so on, in order to be able to spend in accordance with their station, and only ruined themselves so much the quicker. The few landed gentry wise enough not to ruin themselves formed with the newly-emerging bourgeois landowners a new class of *industrial landowners.* This class carries on agriculture without feudal illusions and without the nobleman's nonchalance, as a business, an industry, with the bourgeois appliances of capital, expert knowledge and work. Such a class is so far from being incompatible with the rule of the bourgeoisie that in France it stands quite peacefully alongside it and participates according to its wealth in its rule. It constitutes the section of the bourgeoisie which exploits agriculture.

The nobility has therefore become so impotent, that a part of it has already gone over to the bourgeoisie.

The petty bourgeoisie was already in a weak position in relation to the nobility; still less can it hold out against the bourgeoisie. Next to the peasants, it is the most pathetic class that has ever meddled with history. With its petty local interests, it advanced no further even in its heyday (the later Middle Ages) than to local organisations, local struggles and local advances, to an existence *on sufferance* alongside the nobility, never to general, political, dominance. With the emergence of the bourgeoisie it loses even the *appearance* of historical initiative. Wedged in between nobility and bourgeoisie, under pressure alike from the political preponderance of the former and from the competition of the heavy capital of the latter, it split into two sections. The one, that of the richer and big-city petty bourgeoisie, joins the revolutionary bourgeoisie more or less timidly; the other, recruited from the poorer burghers, especially those of the small provincial towns, clings to the existing state of things and supports the nobility with the whole weight of its inertia. The more the bourgeoisie develops, the worse becomes the position of the petty bourgeoisie. Gradually this second section also realises that under existing conditions its ruin is certain, whereas under the rule of the bourgeoisie, alongside the *probability* of that ruin, it enjoys at least the *possibility* of advancing into the ranks of the bourgeoisie. The more certain its ruin, the more it ranges itself under the banner of the bourgeoisie. As soon as the bourgeoisie has come to power, the petty bourgeoisie splits again. It supplies recruits to every section of the bourgeoisie, and besides forms, between the bourgeoisie and the proletariat now emerging with its interests and demands, a chain of more or less radical political and socialist sects, which one can study more closely in the English or French Chamber of Deputies and the daily press. The more sharply the bourgeoisie penetrates into the undisciplined and poorly armed swarms of petty bourgeoisie with the heavy artillery of its capital, with the closed columns of its joint-stock companies, the more helpless the petty bourgeoisie becomes, the more disorderly its flight, until no other way of escape remains to it than either to muster behind the long files of the proletariat and to march under its banner—or to surrender to the bourgeoisie at its discretion. This diverting spectacle can be observed in England at every trade crisis, and in France at the present moment. In Germany we have only arrived at that phase when the petty bourgeoisie in a moment of despair and squeezed for money forms the heroic resolution to renounce the nobility and place its trust in the bourgeoisie.

The petty bourgeoisie is therefore just as little able as the nobility to raise itself to be the ruling class in Germany; on the contrary, it places itself every day more and more under the command of the bourgeoisie.

There remain the peasants and the propertyless classes.

The peasants, among whom we include here only the small peasant tenants or proprietors, with the exclusion of the day labourers and farm labourers—the peasants form a similarly helpless class as do the petty bourgeoisie, from whom, however, they differ to their advantage through their greater courage. But they are similarly incapable of all historical initiative. Even their emancipation from the fetters of serfdom comes about only under the protection of the bourgeoisie. Where the absence of nobility and bourgeoisie allows them to rule, as in the mountain cantons of Switzerland and in Norway, pre-feudal barbarisms, local narrow-mindedness, and dull, fanatical bigotry, loyalty and rectitude rule with them. Where, as in Germany, the nobility continues to exist beside them, they are squeezed, just like the petty bourgeoisie, between the nobility and the bourgeoisie. To protect the interests of agriculture against the growing power of trade and industry, they must join with the nobility. To safeguard themselves against the overwhelming competition of the nobility and especially the bourgeois landowners, they must join with the bourgeoisie. To which side they finally adhere depends upon the nature of their property. The big farmers of eastern Germany, who themselves exercise a certain feudal dominance over their farm labourers, are in all their interests too closely involved with the nobles to dissociate themselves from them in earnest. The small landowners in the west who have emerged from the breaking up of the estates of the nobility, and the small farmers in the east who are subject to patrimonial jurisdiction and still partly liable to corvée labour, are oppressed too directly by the nobles or stand too much in opposition to them not to adhere to the side of the bourgeoisie. That this is actually the case is proved by the Prussian provincial diets.

Rule by the peasants is also, therefore, fortunately unthinkable. The peasants themselves think of it so little that they have for the greatest part already placed themselves at the disposal of the bourgeoisie.

And the propertyless, in common parlance the working, classes? We shall soon speak of them at greater length[64]; for the moment it is sufficient to point to the division among them. This division into farm labourers, day labourers, handicraft journeymen, factory workers and lumpen proletariat, together with their dispersal over a great, thinly populated expanse of country with few and weak central points, already renders it impossible for them to realise that their interests are common, to reach understanding, to constitute themselves into *one* class. This division and dispersal makes nothing else possible for them but restriction to their immediate, everyday interests, to the wish for a good wage for good work. That is, it restricts the workers to seeing their interest in that of their employers, thus making every single section of the workers into an auxiliary army for the class employing them. The farm labourer and day labourer supports the interests of the noble or farmer on whose estate he works. The journeyman stands under the intellectual and political sway of his master. The factory worker lets himself be used by the factory owner in the agitation for protective tariffs. For a few talers the lumpen proletarian fights out with his fists the squabbles between bourgeoisie, nobility and police. And where two classes of employers have contradictory interests to assert, there exists the same struggle between the classes of workers they employ.

So little is the mass of the workers in Germany prepared to assume the leadership in public matters.

To summarise. The nobility is too much in decline, the petty bourgeoisie and peasants are, by their whole position in life, too weak, the workers are still far from sufficiently mature to be able to come forward as the ruling class in Germany. There remains only the bourgeoisie.

The poverty of the German status quo consists chiefly in this: no single class has hitherto been strong enough to establish its branch of production as the national branch of production *par excellence* and thus to set itself up as the representative of the interests of the whole nation. All the estates and classes that have emerged in history since the tenth century: nobles, serfs, peasants subject to corvée labour, free peasants, petty bourgeoisie, journeymen, manufactory workers, bourgeoisie and proletarians, all exist alongside one another. Those among these estates and classes who in consequence of their property represent a branch of production, namely the nobles, free peasants, petty bourgeoisie and bourgeoisie, have participated in political rule in proportion to their number, their wealth, and their share in the total production of the country. The result of this division is that, as we have said, the nobility has got the lion's share, the petty bourgeoisie the smaller share, and that *officially* the bourgeoisie count only as petty bourgeoisie and the peasants as *peasants* do not count at all, because they, with the slight influence they possess, divide themselves between the other classes. This regime represented by the bureaucracy is the political summing-up of the general impotence and contemptibility, of the dull boredom and the sordidness of German society. It is matched by the breaking up of Germany into thirty-eight local and provincial states together with the breaking up of Austria and Prussia into autonomous provinces from within and by the disgraceful helplessness against exploitation and kicks from without. The cause of this general poverty lies in the general lack of capital. In poverty-stricken Germany every single class has borne from the beginning the mark of civic mediocrity, and in comparison with the same classes in other countries has been poor and depressed. How petty bourgeois appears the high and low German nobility since the twelfth century beside the rich and carefree French and English nobility, so full of the joy of living and so purposeful in their whole behaviour! How tiny, how insignificant and parochial appear the burghers of the German free cities of the Reich and the Hanseatic towns beside the rebellious Parisian burghers of the fourteenth and fifteenth centuries, the London Puritans of the seventeenth century! How petty bourgeois still appear our principal magnates in industry, finance, shipping, beside the Stock Exchange princes of Paris, Lyons, London, Liverpool and Manchester! Even the working classes in Germany are thoroughly petty bourgeois. Thus the petty bourgeoisie have at least the consolation in their depressed social and political position of being the standard class of Germany; and of having imparted to all other classes their specific depression and their concern over their existence.

How is this poverty to be overcome? Only *one* way is possible: *one* class must become strong enough to make the rise of the whole nation dependent upon *its* rise, to make the advancement of the interests of all other classes dependent upon the advancement and development of *its* interests. The interest of this *one* class must become for the time being the national interest, and this class itself must become for the time being the representative of the nation. From that moment, this class and with it the majority of the nation, finds itself in contradiction with the political status quo. The political status quo corresponds to a state of affairs which has ceased to exist: to the conflict of interests of the different classes. The new interests find themselves restricted, and even a part of the classes in whose favour the status quo was established no longer sees its own interests represented in it. The abolition of the status quo, peacefully or by force, is the necessary consequence. In its place enters dominance by the class which for the moment represents the majority of the nation, and under whose rule a new development begins.

As the lack of capital is the basis of the status quo, of the general weakness, so possession of capital, its concentration in the hands of *one* class, can alone give this class the power to supplant the status quo.

Does this class, which can overthrow the status quo, exist now in Germany? It exists, although, compared with the corresponding class in England and France, in a perhaps very petty bourgeois way; but still it exists and, indeed, in the bourgeoisie.

The bourgeoisie is the class which in all countries overthrows the compromise established between nobility and petty bourgeoisie in the bureaucratic monarchy, and thus to begin with conquers power for itself.

The bourgeoisie is the only class in Germany which at least gives a great part of the industrial landowners, petty bourgeoisie, peasants, workers and even a minority among the nobles a share in its interests, and has united these under its banner.

The party of the bourgeoisie is the only one in Germany that definitely knows with what it must replace the status quo; the only one that does not limit itself to abstract principles and historical deductions, but wishes to carry into effect very definite, concrete and immediately practicable measures; the only one which is at least organised to some extent on a local and provincial basis and has a sort of plan of campaign, in short, it is the party which fights first and foremost against the status quo and is directly interested in its overthrow.

The party of the bourgeoisie is therefore the only one that at present has a chance of success.

The only question then is: Is the bourgeoisie compelled by necessity to conquer political rule for itself through the overthrow of the status quo, and is it strong enough, given its own power and the weakness of its opponents, to overthrow the status quo?

We shall see.

The decisive section of the German bourgeoisie are the factory owners. On the prosperity of industry depends the prosperity of the whole domestic trade, of the Hamburg and Bremen and, to some extent, Stettin sea trade, of banking; on it depend the revenues of the railways, and with that the most significant part of the Stock Exchange business. Independent of industry are only the corn and wool exporters of the Baltic towns and the insignificant class of importers of foreign industrial products. The needs of the factory owners thus represent the needs of the whole bourgeoisie and of the classes at present dependent upon it.

The factory owners are further divided into two sections: the one gives the initial processing to raw materials and sends them into trade half-finished, the other takes over the half-finished materials and brings them to market as finished commodities. To the first group belong the spinners, to the second the weavers. In Germany the first section also includes the iron producers.[a]

... to introduce newly invented techniques, to establish good communications, to obtain cheap machines and raw materials, to train skilled workers, requires an entire industrial system; it requires the interlocking of all branches of industry, sea-ports which are tributary to the industrial interior and carry on a flourishing trade. All this has long ago been proved by the economists. But such an industrial system requires also nowadays, when England is almost the only country that has no competition to fear, a complete protective system embracing all branches of industry threatened by foreign competition, and modifications to this system must always be made according to the position of industry. Such a system the existing Prussian Government *cannot* give, nor can all the governments of the Customs Union. It can only be set up and operated by the ruling bourgeoisie itself. And for this reason also the German bourgeoisie can no longer do without political power.

Such a protective system, moreover, is all the more necessary in Germany, since there manufacture lies in its death throes. Without systematic tariff protection the competition of English machinery will kill manufacture, and the bourgeoisie, petty bourgeoisie and workers hitherto maintained by it will be ruined. Reason enough for the German bourgeoisie to ruin what remains of manufacture rather with *German* machines.

Protective tariffs are therefore necessary for the German bourgeoisie and only by that bourgeoisie itself can they be introduced. If only for that reason, then, it must seize state power.

But it is not only by insufficient tariffs that the factory owners are hindered in the complete utilisation of their capital; they are also hindered by the *bureaucracy*. If in the matter of customs legislation they meet with indifference from the government, in their relations with the bureaucracy they meet with its most direct hostility.

The bureaucracy was set up to govern petty bourgeoisie and peasants. These classes, dispersed in small towns or villages, with interests which do not reach beyond the narrowest local boundaries, have necessarily the restricted horizons corresponding to their restricted mode of life. They cannot govern a large state, they can have neither the breadth of vision nor the knowledge to balance the different conflicting interests. And it was exactly at *that* stage of

[a] Here four pages of the manuscript are missing.—*Ed.*

civilisation when the petty bourgeoisie was most flourishing that the different interests were most complicatedly intertwined (one need only think of the guilds and their conflicts). The petty bourgeoisie and the peasants cannot, therefore, do without a powerful and numerous bureaucracy. They must let themselves be kept in leading strings so as to escape the greatest confusion, and not to ruin themselves with hundreds and thousands of lawsuits.

But the bureaucracy, which is a necessity for the petty bourgeoisie, very soon becomes an unbearable fetter for the bourgeoisie. Already at the stage of manufacture official supervision and interference become very burdensome; factory industry is scarcely possible under such control. The German factory owners have hitherto kept the bureaucracy off their backs as much as possible by bribery, for which they can certainly not be blamed. But this remedy frees them only from the lesser half of the burden; apart from the impossibility of bribing *all* the officials with whom a factory owner comes into contact, bribery does not free him from perquisites, honorariums to jurists, architects, mechanics, nor from other expenses caused by the system of supervision, nor from extra work and waste of time. And the more industry develops, the more "conscientious officials" appear—that is, officials who either from pure narrow-mindedness or from bureaucratic hatred of the bourgeoisie, pester the factory owners with the most infuriating chicaneries.

The bourgeoisie, therefore, is compelled to break the power of this indolent and pettifogging bureaucracy. From the moment the state administration and legislature fall under the control of the bourgeoisie, the independence of the bureaucracy ceases to exist; indeed from this moment, the tormentors of the bourgeoisie turn into their humble slaves. Previous regulations and decrees, which served only to lighten the work of the officials at the expense of the industrial bourgeoisie, give place to new regulations which lighten the work of the industrialists at the expense of the officials.

The bourgeoisie is all the more compelled to do this as soon as possible because, as we have seen, all its sections are directly concerned in the quickest possible increase of factory industry, and factory industry cannot possibly grow under a regime of bureaucratic harassment.

The subordination of the customs and the bureaucracy to the interest of the industrial bourgeoisie are the two measures with the implementation of which the bourgeoisie is most directly concerned. But that does not by any means exhaust its needs. The bourgeoisie is compelled to subject the whole system of legislation, administration and justice in almost all the German states to a thoroughgoing revision, for this whole system serves to maintain and uphold a social condition which the bourgeoisie is continually working to overthrow. The conditions under which nobility and petty bourgeoisie can exist side by side are absolutely different from the conditions of life of the bourgeoisie, and only the former are officially recognised in the German states. Let us take the Prussian status quo as an example. If the petty bourgeoisie could subject themselves to the judicial as well as to the administrative bureaucracy, if they could entrust their property and persons to the discretion and torpidity of an "independent", i. e., bureaucratically self-sufficient judicial class, which in return offered them protection against the encroachments of the feudal nobility and at times also against those of the administrative bureaucracy, the bourgeoisie cannot do so. For lawsuits concerning property the bourgeoisie requires at least the protection of publicity, and for criminal trials moreover that of the jury as well, the constant control of justice through a deputation of the bourgeoisie.—The petty bourgeois can put up with the exemption of nobles and officials from common legal procedure because his official humiliation in this way fully corresponds to his lower social status. The bourgeois, who must either be ruined or make his class the first in society and state, cannot do this.—The petty bourgeois can, without prejudice to the smooth course of his way of life, leave legislation on landed property to the nobility alone; in fact he must, since he has enough to do to protect his own urban interests from the influence and encroachment of the nobles. The bourgeois cannot in any way leave the regulation of property relationships in the countryside to the discretion of the nobility, for the complete development of his own interests requires the fullest possible industrial exploitation of agriculture too, the creation of a class of industrial farmers, free saleability and mobilisation of landed property. The need of the landowner to procure money on mortgage gives to the bourgeois here an opportunity and forces the nobility to allow the bourgeoisie, at least in relation to the mortgage laws, to influence legislation concerning landed property.—If the petty bourgeois, with his small scale of business, his slow turnover and his limited number of customers concentrated in a small area, has not found the miserable old Prussian legislation on trade too oppressive but has even been grateful for the bit of protection it provided, the bourgeois cannot bear it any longer. The petty bourgeois, whose highly simple transactions are seldom dealings between merchant and merchant, but almost always only sales from retailer or producer direct to consumer—the petty bourgeois seldom goes bankrupt and easily accommodates himself to the old Prussian bankruptcy laws. According to these laws, debts on bills are paid off from total assets before book debts, but customarily the whole assets are devoured by court costs. The laws are framed first of all in the interests of the judicial bureaucracy who administer the assets, and then in the interests of the non-bourgeois as opposed to the bourgeois. The noble in particular, who draws or receives bills on the purchaser or consignee of the corn he has dispatched, is thereby covered, and so are in general all those who have something to sell only once a year and draw the proceeds of that sale in a single transaction. Among those engaged in trade, the bankers and wholesalers are again protected, but the factory owner is rather neglected. The bourgeois, whose dealings are *only* from merchant to merchant, whose customers are scattered, who receives bills on the whole world, who must move in the midst of a highly complicated system of transactions, who is involved at every moment in a bankruptcy—the bourgeois can only be ruined by these absurd laws.—The petty bourgeois is interested in the general policy of his country only in so far as he wants to be left in peace; his narrow round of life makes him incapable of surveying the relations of state to state. The bourgeois, who has to deal or to compete with the most distant countries, cannot work his way up without the most direct influence on the foreign policy of his state.—The petty bourgeois could let the bureaucracy and nobility levy taxes on him, for the same reasons that he subjected himself to the bureaucracy; the bourgeois has a quite direct interest in having the public burdens so distributed that they affect *his* profit as little as possible.

In short, if the petty bourgeois can content himself with opposing to the nobility and the bureaucracy his inert weight, with securing for himself influence on the official power through his *vis inertiae*,[a] the bourgeois cannot do this. He must make his class dominant, his interests crucial, in legislation, administration, justice, taxation and foreign policy. The bourgeoisie must develop itself to the full, daily expand its capital, daily reduce the production costs of its commodities, daily expand its trade connections and markets, daily improve its communications, *in order not to be ruined.* The competition on the world market compels it to do so. And to be able to develop freely and to the full, what it requires is precisely political dominance, the subordination of all other interests to its own.

That in order not to be ruined the German bourgeoisie requires political dominance *now,* we have shown above in connection with the question of protective tariffs and with its attitude to the bureaucracy.

---

[a] Force of inertia.—*Ed.*

But the most striking proof of this is *the present state of the German money and commodity market.*

The prosperity of English industry in 1845 and the railway speculations to which it led had on this occasion a stronger effect on France and Germany than at any earlier lively period of business. The German factory owners did good business, which stimulated German business in general. The agricultural districts found a willing market for their corn in England. The general prosperity enlivened the money market, facilitated credit and attracted on to the market a large number of small amounts of capital, of which in Germany there were so many lying half idle. As in England and France, only somewhat later and in somewhat—[a]

Written in March-April 1847

First published in Russian in: Marx and Engels, *Works* (first Russian edition), Vol. V, Moscow, 1929 and in German in: Marx/Engels, *Gesamtausgabe*, Erste Abteilung, Bd. 6, Berlin, 1932

Printed according to the manuscript

Published in English for the first time

[a] Here the manuscript breaks off.— *Ed.*

Frederick Engels

PROTECTIVE TARIFFS OR FREE TRADE SYSTEM

From the instant that lack of money and credit forced the King of Prussia to issue the Letters Patent of February 3,[65] no reasonable person could doubt any longer that the absolute monarchy in Germany and the "Christian-Germanic" management as it has hitherto existed, also known under the name of "paternal government", had, in spite of all bristling resistance and sabre-rattling speeches from the throne, abdicated for ever. The day had now dawned from which the bourgeoisie in Germany can date its rule. The Letters Patent themselves are nothing but an acknowledgement, though still wrapped in a great deal of Potsdam mist and fog, of the power of the bourgeoisie. A good deal of this mist and fog has already been blown away by a little weak puffing from the United Diet, and very soon the whole Christian-Germanic misty phantom will be dissolved into its nothingness.

But as soon as the rule of the middle classes began, the first demand to be made was bound to be that the whole trade policy of Germany, or of the Customs Union,[66] should be wrested from the incompetent hands of German princes, their ministers, and arrogant, but in commercial and industrial matters utterly unimaginative and ignorant bureaucrats, and be made dependent upon and decided by those who possess both the necessary insight and the most immediate interest in the matter. In other words: the question of protective and differential tariffs or free trade must fall within the sole decision of the bourgeoisie.

The United Diet in Berlin has shown the Government that the bourgeoisie knows what it needs; in the recent tariff negotiations it was made clear to the Spandau System of Government,[67] in pretty plain and bitter words, that it is incapable of grasping, protecting and promoting the material interests concerned. The Cracow affair[68] alone would have been sufficient to brand the foreheads of Holy-Alliance William[a] and his ministers with the stamp of the crudest ignorance of, or the most culpable treachery against, the welfare of the nation. To the horror of his all-highest Majesty and his Excellencies a host of other things came up for discussion, in the course of which royal and ministerial capabilities and discernment—living as well as defunct—could feel anything but flattered.

In the bourgeoisie itself, indeed, two different views dominate with regard to industry and trade. Nonetheless there is no doubt that the party in favour of protective, or, rather, differential tariffs is by far the most powerful, numerous and predominant. The bourgeoisie cannot, in fact, even maintain itself, cannot consolidate its position, cannot attain unbounded power unless it shelters and fosters its industry and trade by artificial means. Without protection against foreign industry it would be crushed and trampled down within a decade. It is quite easily possible that not even protection will help it much or for long. It has waited too long, it has lain too peacefully in the swaddling clothes in which it has been trussed so many years by its precious princes. It has been outflanked and overtaken on every side, it has had its best positions taken from it, while at home it peacefully let its knuckles be rapped and did not even have enough energy to rid itself of its partly imbecile, partly extremely cunning paternal schoolmasters and disciplinarians.

Now a new page has been turned. The German princes can henceforth only be the servants of the bourgeoisie, only be the dot over the "i" of the bourgeoisie. In so far as there is still time and opportunity for the latter's rule, protection for German industry and German trade is the only foundation on which it may rest. And what the bourgeoisie wants and must want of the German princes, it will also be able to achieve.

There exists, however, alongside the bourgeoisie, a quite considerable number of people called proletarians—the working and propertyless class.

The question therefore arises: What does this class gain from the introduction of the protective system? Will it thereby receive more wages, be able to feed and clothe itself better, house itself more healthily, afford somewhat more time for recreation and education, and some means for the more sensible and careful upbringing of its children?

---

[a] Frederick William IV.—*Ed.*

The gentlemen of the bourgeoisie who advocate the protective system never fail to push the well-being of the working class into the foreground. To judge by their words, a truly paradisial life will commence for the workers with the protection of industry, Germany will then become a Canaan "flowing with milk and honey"[a] for the proletarians. But listen on the other hand to the free trade men speaking, and only under *their* system would the propertyless be able to live "like God in France", that is, in the greatest jollity and merriment.

Among both parties there are still plenty of limited minds who more or less believe in the truth of their own words. The intelligent among them know very well that this is all vain delusion, merely calculated, furthermore, to deceive and win the masses.

The intelligent bourgeois does not need to be told that whether the system in force is that of protective tariffs or free trade or a mixture of both, the worker will receive no bigger wage for his labour than will just suffice for his scantiest maintenance. From the one side as from the other, the worker gets precisely what he needs to keep going as a labour-machine.

It might thus appear to be a matter of indifference to the proletarian, to the propertyless, whether the protectionists or the free traders have the last word.

Since, however, as has been said above, the bourgeoisie in Germany requires protection against foreign countries in order to clear away the medieval remnants of a feudal aristocracy and the modern vermin by the Grace of God, and to develop purely and simply its own proper, innermost essence (!)—then the working class also has an interest in what helps the bourgeoisie to unimpeded rule.

Not until only *one* class—the bourgeoisie—is seen to exploit and oppress, until penury and misery can no longer be blamed now on this estate, now on that, or simply on the absolute monarchy and its bureaucrats—only then will the last decisive battle break out, the battle between the propertied and the propertyless, between the bourgeoisie and the proletariat.

Only then will the field of battle have been swept clean of all unnecessary barriers, of all that is misleading and accessory; the position of the two hostile armies will be clear and visible at a glance.

With the rule of the bourgeoisie, the workers, compelled by circumstances, will also make the infinitely important advance that they will no longer come forward as individuals, as at the most a couple of hundreds or thousands, in rebellion against the established

[a] Exodus 3:8.—*Ed.*

order, but all together, as *one* class, with its specific interests and principles, with a common plan and united strength, they will launch their attack on the last and the worst of their mortal enemies, the bourgeoisie.

There can be no doubt as to the outcome of this battle. The bourgeoisie will and must fall to the ground before the proletariat, just as the aristocracy and the absolute monarchy have received their coup de grâce from the middle class.

With the bourgeoisie, private property will at the same time be overthrown, and the victory of the working class will put an end to all class or caste rule for ever.

Written at the beginning of June 1847

First published in the *Deutsche-Brüsseler-Zeitung* No. 46, June 10, 1847

Printed according to the newspaper

Published in English for the first time

Frederick Engels

DRAFT OF A COMMUNIST CONFESSION OF FAITH[69]

Question 1: *Are you a Communist?*
Answer: Yes.
Question 2: *What is the aim of the Communists?*
Answer: To organise society in such a way that every member of it can develop and use all his capabilities and powers in complete freedom and without thereby infringing the basic conditions of this society.
Question 3: *How do you wish to achieve this aim?*
Answer: By the elimination of private property and its replacement by community of property.
Question 4: *On what do you base your community of property?*
Answer: Firstly, on the mass of productive forces and means of subsistence resulting from the development of industry, agriculture, trade and colonisation, and on the possibility inherent in machinery, chemical and other resources of their infinite extension.

Secondly, on the fact that in the consciousness or feeling of every individual there exist certain irrefutable basic principles which, being the result of the whole of historical development, require no proof.

Question 5: *What are such principles?*
Answer: For example, every individual strives to be happy. The happiness of the individual is inseparable from the happiness of all, etc.
Question 6: *How do you wish to prepare the way for your community of property?*
Answer: By enlightening and uniting the proletariat.

Entwurf des Kommunistischen Glaubensbekenntnisses.

Frage 1. – Bist Du Kommunist?
Antwort. – Ja.

— 2. Was ist der Zweck der Kommunisten? –
Die Gesellschaft so einzurichten, daß jedes Mitglied derselben seine sämmtlichen Anlagen u. Kräfte in vollständiger Freiheit und ohne dadurch die Grundbedingungen dieser Gesellschaft anzutasten, entwickeln und bethätigen kann.

— 3. Wie wollt Ihr diesen Zweck erreichen? –
Durch die Aufhebung des Privateigenthums, an dessen Stelle die Gütergemeinschaft tritt.

— 4. Worauf begründet Ihr Eure Gütergemeinschaft?
– Erstens auf die durch die Entwicklung der Industrie, des Ackerbaus, des Handels und der Colonisation erzeugte Masse von Produktionskräften und Lebensmitteln, und die in der Maschinerie, den Chemischen u. andern Hülfsmitteln liegende Möglichkeit ihrer Vermehrung ins Unendliche.
– Zweitens darauf, daß im Bewußtsein oder Gefühl eines jeden Menschen gewisse Sätze als unumstößliche Grundsätze existiren, Sätze welche als Resultat der ganzen geschichtlichen Entwicklung keines Beweises bedürfen.

— 5. Welches sind solche Sätze? –
– z. B. Jeder Mensch strebt danach, glücklich zu sein. Das Glück des Einzelnen ist unzertrennbar von dem Glücke Aller, u.s.w.

— 6. Auf welche Weise wollt Ihr Eure Gütergemeinschaft vorbereiten? –
– Durch Aufklärung und Vereinigung des Proletariats.

— 7. Was ist das Proletariat? –
– Das Proletariat ist diejenige Klasse der Gesellschaft, welche ausschließlich von ihrer Arbeit und nicht vom Profit irgend eines Kapitals lebt; diejenige Klasse, deren Wohl und Weh, deren Leben und Tod daher von dem Wechsel der guten und schlechten Geschäftszeiten, mit einem Wort von den Schwankungen der Konkurrenz abhängt.

Beginning of Engels' manuscript, "Draft of a Communist Confession of Faith"

Question 7: *What is the proletariat?*

Answer: The proletariat is that class of society which lives exclusively by its labour and not on the profit from any kind of capital; that class whose weal and woe, whose life and death, therefore, depend on the alternation of times of good and bad business; in a word, on the fluctuations of competition.

Question 8: *Then there have not always been proletarians?*

Answer: No. There have always been *poor* and *working classes*; and those who worked were almost always the poor. But there have not always been proletarians, just as competition has not always been free.

Question 9: *How did the proletariat arise?*

Answer: The proletariat came into being as a result of the introduction of the machines which have been invented since the middle of the last century and the most important of which are: the steam-engine, the spinning machine and the power loom. These machines, which were very expensive and could therefore only be purchased by rich people, supplanted the workers of the time, because by the use of machinery it was possible to produce commodities more quickly and cheaply than could the workers with their imperfect spinning wheels and hand-looms. The machines thus delivered industry entirely into the hands of the big capitalists and rendered the workers' scanty property which consisted mainly of their tools, looms, etc., quite worthless, so that the capitalist was left with everything, the worker with nothing. In this way the factory system was introduced. Once the capitalists saw how advantageous this was for them, they sought to extend it to more and more branches of labour. They divided work more and more between the workers so that workers who formerly had made a whole article now produced only a part of it. Labour simplified in this way produced goods more quickly and therefore more cheaply and only now was it found in almost every branch of labour that here also machines could be used. As soon as any branch of labour went over to factory production it ended up, just as in the case of spinning and weaving, in the hands of the big capitalists, and the workers were deprived of the last remnants of their independence. We have gradually arrived at the position where almost *all* branches of labour are run on a factory basis. This has increasingly brought about the ruin of the previously existing middle class, especially of the small master craftsmen, completely transformed the previous position of the workers, and two new classes which are gradually swallowing up all other classes have come into being, namely:

I. The class of the big capitalists, who in all advanced countries are in almost exclusive possession of the means of subsistence and those means (machines, factories, workshops, etc.) by which these means of subsistence are produced. This is the *bourgeois* class, or the *bourgeoisie*.

II. The class of the completely propertyless, who are compelled to sell their labour[70] to the first class, the bourgeois, simply to obtain from them in return their means of subsistence. Since the parties to this trading in labour are not *equal*, but the bourgeois have the advantage, the propertyless must submit to the bad conditions laid down by the bourgeois. This class, dependent on the bourgeois, is called the class of the *proletarians* or the *proletariat*.

Question 10: *In what way does the proletarian differ from the slave?*

Answer: The slave is sold once and for all, the proletarian has to sell himself by the day and by the hour. The slave is the property of one master and for that very reason has a guaranteed subsistence, however wretched it may be. The proletarian is, so to speak, the slave of the entire bourgeois *class*, not of one master, and therefore has no guaranteed subsistence, since nobody buys his labour if he does not need it. The slave is accounted a *thing* and not a member of civil society. The proletarian is recognised as a *person*, as a member of civil society. The slave *may*, therefore, have a better subsistence than the proletarian but the latter stands at a higher stage of development. The slave frees himself by *becoming a proletarian*, abolishing from the totality of property relationships *only* the relationship of *slavery*. The proletarian can free himself only by abolishing *property in general*.

Question 11: *In what way does the proletarian differ from the serf?*

Answer: The serf has the use of a piece of land, that is, of an instrument of production, in return for handing over a greater or lesser portion of the yield. The proletarian works with instruments of production which belong to someone else who, in return for his labour, hands over to him a portion, determined by competition, of the products. In the case of the serf, the share of the labourer is determined by his own labour, that is, by himself. In the case of the proletarian it is determined by competition, therefore in the first place by the bourgeois. The serf has guaranteed subsistence, the proletarian has not. The serf frees himself by driving out his feudal lord and becoming a property owner himself, thus entering into competition and joining for the time being the possessing class, the privileged class. The proletarian frees himself by doing away with property, competition, and all class differences.

Question 12: *In what way does the proletarian differ from the handicraftsman?*

Answer: As opposed to the proletarian, the so-called handicraftsman, who still existed nearly everywhere during the last century and still exists here and there, is at most a *temporary* proletarian. His aim is to acquire capital himself and so to exploit other workers. He can often achieve this aim where the craft guilds still exist or where freedom to follow a trade has not yet led to the organisation of handwork on a factory basis and to intense competition. But as soon as the factory system is introduced into handwork and competition is in full swing, this prospect is eliminated and the handicraftsman becomes more and more a proletarian. The handicraftsman therefore frees himself *either* by becoming a bourgeois or in general passing over into the middle class, *or*, by becoming a proletarian as a result of competition (as now happens in most cases) and joining the movement of the proletariat—i. e., the more or less conscious communist movement.

Question 13: *Then you do not believe that community of property has been possible at any time?*

Answer: No. Communism has only arisen since machinery and other inventions made it possible to hold out the prospect of an all-sided development, a happy existence, for all members of society. Communism is the theory of a liberation which was not possible for the slaves, the serfs, or the handicraftsmen, but only for the proletarians and hence it belongs of necessity to the 19th century and was not possible in any earlier period.

Question 14: *Let us go back to the sixth question. As you wish to prepare for community of property by the enlightening and uniting of the proletariat, then you reject revolution?*

Answer: We are convinced not only of the uselessness but even of the harmfulness of all conspiracies. We are also aware that revolutions are not made deliberately and arbitrarily but that everywhere and at all times they are the necessary consequence of circumstances which are not in any way whatever dependent either on the will or on the leadership of individual parties or of whole classes. But we also see that the development of the proletariat in almost all countries of the world is forcibly repressed by the possessing classes and that thus a revolution is being forcibly worked for by the opponents of communism. If, in the end, the oppressed proletariat is thus driven into a revolution, then we will defend the cause of the proletariat just as well by our deeds as now by our words.

Question 15: *Do you intend to replace the existing social order by community of property at one stroke?*

Answer: We have no such intention. The development of the masses cannot be ordered by decree. It is determined by the development of the conditions in which these masses live, and therefore proceeds gradually.

Question 16: *How do you think the transition from the present situation to community of property is to be effected?*

Answer: The first, fundamental condition for the introduction of community of property is the political liberation of the proletariat through a democratic constitution.

Question 17: *What will be your first measure once you have established democracy?*

Answer: Guaranteeing the subsistence of the proletariat.

Question 18: *How will you do this?*

Answer. I. By limiting private property in such a way that it gradually prepares the way for its transformation into social property, e. g., by progressive taxation, limitation of the right of inheritance in favour of the state, etc., etc.

II. By employing workers in national workshops and factories and on national estates.

III. By educating all children at the expense of the state.

Question 19: *How will you arrange this kind of education during the period of transition?*

Answer: All children will be educated in state establishments from the time when they can do without the first maternal care.

Question 20: *Will not the introduction of community of property be accompanied by the proclamation of the community of women?*

Answer: By no means. We will only interfere in the personal relationship between men and women or with the family in general to the extent that the maintenance of the existing institution would disturb the new social order. Besides, we are well aware that the family relationship has been modified in the course of history by the property relationships and by periods of development, and that consequently the ending of private property will also have a most important influence on it.

Question 21: *Will nationalities continue to exist under communism?*

Answer: The nationalities of the peoples who join together according to the principle of community will be just as much compelled by this union to merge with one another and thereby supersede themselves as the various differences between estates and classes disappear through the superseding of their basis—private property.

Question 22: *Do Communists reject the existing religions?*

Answer: All religions which have existed hitherto were expressions of historical stages of development of individual peoples or groups of peoples. But communism is that stage of historical development which makes all existing religions superfluous and supersedes them.[a]

In the name and on the mandate of the Congress.

Secretary: *Heide*[b]

President: *Karl Schill*[c]

London, June 9, 1847

Written by Engels

First published in the book *Gründungsdokumente des Bundes der Kommunisten (Juni bis September 1847)*, Hamburg, 1969

Printed according to the photocopy of the manuscript

[a] Here the text written in Engels' hand ends.—*Ed.*

[b] Alias of Wilhelm Wolff in the League of the Just.—*Ed.*

[c] Alias of Karl Schapper in the League of the Just.—*Ed.*

Karl Marx

THE POVERTY OF PHILOSOPHY

ANSWER TO THE *PHILOSOPHY OF POVERTY* BY M. PROUDHON[71]

Written in the first half of 1847

First published separately in Paris and Brussels in 1847

Printed according to the edition of 1847 with the author's changes and the changes in the German edition of 1885 and the French edition of 1896

Translated from the French

MISÈRE

DE

LA PHILOSOPHIE

RÉPONSE A

LA PHILOSOPHIE DE LA MISÈRE

DE M. PROUDHON.

Par Karl Marx.

PARIS.
A. FRANK,
69, rue Richelieu

BRUXELLES.
C. G. VOGLER,
2, petite rue de la Madeleine.

1847

Cover of the first edition of Marx's *The Poverty of Philosophy*

FOREWORD

M. Proudhon has the misfortune of being peculiarly misunderstood in Europe. In France, he has the right to be a bad economist, because he is reputed to be a good German philosopher. In Germany, he has the right to be a bad philosopher, because he is reputed to be one of the ablest of French economists. Being both a German and an economist at the same time, we desire to protest against this double error.

The reader will understand that in this thankless task we have often had to abandon our criticism of M. Proudhon in order to criticise German philosophy, and at the same time to give some observations on political economy.

Karl Marx

Brussels, June 15, 1847

M. Proudhon's work is not just a treatise on political economy, an ordinary book; it is a bible. "Mysteries", "Secrets Wrested from the Bosom of God", "Revelations"—it lacks nothing. But as prophets are discussed nowadays more conscientiously than profane writers, the reader must resign himself to going with us through the arid and gloomy erudition of "Genesis", in order to ascend later, with M. Proudhon, into the ethereal and fertile realm of *super-socialism.* (See Proudhon, *Philosophie de la misère,* Prologue, p. III, line 20.)

CHAPTER I

A SCIENTIFIC DISCOVERY

§1. THE OPPOSITION BETWEEN USE VALUE AND EXCHANGE VALUE

"The capacity of all products, whether natural or industrial, to contribute to man's subsistence is specifically termed *use value*; their capacity to be given in exchange for one another, *exchange value*.... How does use value become exchange value?... The genesis of the idea of" (exchange) "value has not been noted by economists with sufficient care. It is necessary, therefore, for us to dwell upon it. Since a very large number of the things I need occur in nature only in moderate quantities, or even not at all, I am forced to assist in the production of what I lack. And as I cannot set my hand to so many things, I shall *propose* to other men, my collaborators in various functions, to cede to me a part of their products in *exchange* for mine." (Proudhon, tome I, chap. II, [pp. 33-34].)

M. Proudhon undertakes to explain to us first of all the double nature of value, the "*distinction in value*" [I 34], the process by which use value is transformed into exchange value. It is necessary for us to dwell with M. Proudhon upon this act of transubstantiation. The following is how this act is accomplished, according to our author.

A very large number of products are not to be found in nature, they are products of industry. If man's needs go beyond nature's spontaneous production, he is forced to have recourse to industrial production. What is this industry in M. Proudhon's view? What is its origin? A single individual, feeling the need for a very great number of things, "cannot set his hand to so many things". So many needs to satisfy presuppose so many things to produce—there are no products without production. So many things to produce presuppose at once more than one man's hand helping to produce them. Now, the moment you postulate more than one hand helping in production, you at once presuppose a whole production based on the division of labour. Thus need, as M. Proudhon presupposes it, itself presupposes the whole division of labour. In presupposing the division of labour, you get exchange, and, consequently, exchange value. One might as well have presupposed exchange value from the very beginning.

But M. Proudhon prefers to go the roundabout way. Let us follow him in all his detours, which always bring us back to his starting point.

In order to emerge from the condition in which everyone produces in isolation and to arrive at exchange, "I turn to my collaborators in various functions," says Mr. Proudhon. I myself, then, have collaborators, all with different functions. And yet, for all that, I and all the others, always according to M. Proudhon's supposition, have got no farther than the solitary and hardly social position of the Robinsons. The collaborators and the various functions, the division of labour and the exchange it implies, are already to hand.

To sum up: I have certain needs which are founded on the division of labour and on exchange. In presupposing these needs, M. Proudhon has thus presupposed exchange, exchange value, the very thing of which he purposes to "note the genesis with more care than other economists".

M. Proudhon might just as well have inverted the order of things, without in any way affecting the accuracy of his conclusions. To explain exchange value, we must have exchange. To explain exchange, we must have the division of labour. To explain the division of labour, we must have needs which render necessary the division of labour. To explain these needs, we must "*presuppose*" them, which is not to deny them—contrary to the first axiom in M. Proudhon's prologue: "To presuppose God is to deny Him." (Prologue, p. I.)

How does M. Proudhon, who assumes the division of labour as the known, manage to explain exchange value, which for him is always the unknown?

"A man" sets out to "*propose* to other men, his collaborators in various functions", that they establish exchange, and make a distinction between use value and exchange value. In accepting this proposed distinction, the collaborators have left M. Proudhon no other "care" than that of recording the fact, of marking, of "noting" in his treatise on political economy "the genesis of the idea of value". But he has still to explain to us the "genesis" of this proposal, to tell us at last how this single individual, this Robinson, suddenly had the idea of making "to his collaborators" a proposal of the type *known* and how these collaborators accepted it without the slightest protest.

M. Proudhon does not enter into these genealogical details. He merely places a sort of historical stamp upon the fact of exchange, by presenting it in the form of a motion supposed to have been made by a third party, tending to establish exchange.

That is a sample of the "*historical and descriptive method*" [I 30] of M. Proudhon, who professes a superb disdain for the "historical and descriptive methods" of the Adam Smiths and Ricardos.

Exchange has a history of its own. It has passed through different phases.

There was a time, as in the Middle Ages, when only the superfluous, the excess of production over consumption, was exchanged.

There was again a time, when not only the superfluous, but all products, all industrial existence, had passed into commerce, when the whole of production depended on exchange. How are we to explain this second phase of exchange—marketable value at its second power?

M. Proudhon would have a reply ready-made: Assume that a man has "*proposed* to other men, his collaborators in various functions", to raise marketable value to its second power.

Finally, there came a time when everything that men had considered as inalienable became an object of exchange, of traffic and could be alienated. This is the time when the very things which till then had been communicated, but never exchanged; given, but never sold; acquired, but never bought—virtue, love, conviction, knowledge, conscience, etc.—when everything finally passed into commerce. It is the time of general corruption, of universal venality, or, to speak in terms of political economy, the time when everything, moral or physical, having become a marketable value, is brought to the market to be assessed at its truest value.

How, again, can we explain this new and last phase of exchange—marketable value at its third power?

M. Proudhon would have a reply ready-made: Assume that a person has "*proposed* to other persons, his collaborators in various functions", to make a marketable value out of virtue, love, etc., to raise exchange value to its third and last power.

We see that M. Proudhon's "historical and descriptive method" is applicable to everything, it answers everything, explains everything. If it is a question above all of explaining historically "the genesis of an economic idea", it postulates a man who proposes to other men, his collaborators in various functions, that they perform this act of genesis and that is the end of it.

We shall hereafter accept the "genesis" of exchange value as an accomplished act; it now remains only to expound the relation between exchange value and use value. Let us hear what M. Proudhon has to say:

"Economists have very well brought out the double character of value, but what they have not pointed out with the same precision is its *contradictory nature*; this is where our criticism begins.... It is a small thing to have drawn attention to this surprising contrast between use value and exchange value, in which economists have been wont to see only something very simple: we must show that this alleged simplicity conceals a profound mystery into which it is our duty to penetrate.... In technical terms, use value and exchange value stand in inverse ratio to each other." [I 36, 38]

If we have thoroughly grasped M. Proudhon's thought the following are the four points which he sets out to establish:

1. Use value and exchange value form a "surprising contrast", they are in opposition to each other.

2. Use value and exchange value are in inverse ratio, in contradiction, to each other.

3. Economists have neither observed nor recognised either the opposition or the contradiction.

4. M. Proudhon's criticism begins at the end.

We, too, shall begin at the end, and, in order to clear the economists from M. Proudhon's accusations, we shall let two sufficiently well-known economists speak for themselves.

Sismondi: "It is the opposition between use value and exchange value to which commerce has reduced everything, etc." (*Études*,[a] t. II, p. 162, Brussels edition.)

Lauderdale: "In proportion as the riches of individuals are increased by an augmentation of the exchange value, the national wealth" (use value) "is generally diminished; and in proportion as the mass of individual riches is diminished, by the diminution of the exchange value, its opulence is generally increased." (*Recherches sur la nature et l'origine de la richesse publique*; traduit par Lagentie de Lavaïsse, Paris, 1808 [p. 33; cf. Eng. ed., p. 50].)

Sismondi founded on the *opposition* between use value and exchange value his principal doctrine, according to which diminution in revenue is proportional to the increase in production.

Lauderdale founded his system on the inverse ratio of the two kinds of value, and his doctrine was indeed so popular in *Ricardo*'s time that the latter could speak of it as of something generally known.

"It is through confounding the ideas of exchange value and riches" (use value) "that it has been asserted, that by diminishing the quantity of commodities, that is to say, of the necessaries, conveniences, and enjoyments of human life, riches may be increased." (Ricardo, *Des principes de l'économie politique*, traduit par Constancio,

---

[a] Simonde de Sismondi, *Études sur l'économie politique*.—*Ed.*

annoté par J. B. Say, Paris, 1835; tome II, chap. "Sur la valeur et les richesses" [p. 65; cf. Eng. ed., p. 323].)

We have just seen that the economists before M. Proudhon had "drawn attention" to the profound mystery of opposition and contradiction. Let us now see how M. Proudhon in his turn explains this mystery after the economists.

The exchange value of a product falls as the supply increases, the demand remaining the same; in other words, the more abundant a product is *relatively to the demand*, the lower is its exchange value, or price. *Vice versa*: The weaker the supply relatively to the demand, the higher rises the exchange value or the price of the product supplied; in other words, the greater the scarcity in the products supplied, relatively to the demand, the higher the prices. The exchange value of a product depends upon its abundance or its scarcity, but always in relation to the demand. Take a product that is more than scarce, unique of its kind if you will: this unique product will be more than abundant, it will be superfluous, if there is no demand for it. On the other hand, take a product multiplied into millions, it will always be scarce if it does not satisfy the demand, that is, if there is too great a demand for it.

These are what we should almost call truisms, yet we have had to repeat them here in order to render M. Proudhon's mysteries comprehensible.

"So that, following up the principle to its ultimate consequences, one would come to the conclusion, the most logical in the world, that the things whose use is indispensable and whose quantity is unlimited should be had for nothing, and those whose utility is nil and whose scarcity is extreme should be of incalculable price. To cap the difficulty, these extremes are impossible in practice: on the one hand, no human product could ever be unlimited in magnitude; on the other, even the scarcest things must perforce be useful to a certain degree, otherwise they would be quite valueless. Use value and exchange value are thus inexorably bound up with each other, although by their nature they continually tend to be mutually exclusive." (Tome I, p. 39.)

What caps M. Proudhon's difficulty? That he has simply forgotten about *demand*, and that a thing can be scarce or abundant only insofar as it is in demand. The moment he leaves out demand, he identifies exchange value with *scarcity* and use value with *abundance*. In reality, in saying that things "whose *utility* is *nil* and *scarcity extreme* are of *incalculable price*", he is simply declaring that exchange value is merely scarcity. "Scarcity extreme and utility nil" means pure scarcity. "Incalculable price" is the maximum of exchange value, it is pure exchange value. He equates these two terms. Therefore exchange value and scarcity are equivalent terms. In arriving at these alleged "extreme consequences", M. Proudhon has in fact carried to the extreme, not the things, but the terms which express them, and, in so doing, he shows proficiency in rhetoric rather than in logic. He merely rediscovers his first hypotheses in all their nakedness when he thinks he has discovered new consequences. Thanks to the same procedure he succeeds in identifying use value with pure abundance.

After having equated exchange value and scarcity, use value and abundance, M. Proudhon is quite astonished not to find use value in scarcity and exchange value, nor exchange value in abundance and use value; and seeing that these extremes are impossible in practice, he can do nothing but believe in mystery. Incalculable price exists for him, because buyers do not exist, and he will never find any buyers, so long as he leaves out demand.

On the other hand, M. Proudhon's abundance seems to be something spontaneous. He completely forgets that there are people who produce it, and that it is to their interest never to lose sight of demand. Otherwise, how could M. Proudhon have said that things which are very useful must have a very low price, or even cost nothing? On the contrary, he should have concluded that abundance, the production of very useful things, should be restricted if their price, their exchange value, is to be raised.

The old vine-growers of France in petitioning for a law to forbid the planting of new vines; the Dutch in burning Asiatic spices, in uprooting clove trees in the Moluccas, were simply trying to reduce abundance in order to raise exchange value. During the whole of the Middle Ages this same principle was acted upon, in limiting by laws the number of journeymen a single master could employ and the number of implements he could use. (See Anderson, *History of Commerce.*[a])

After having represented abundance as use value and scarcity as exchange value—nothing indeed is easier than to prove that abundance and scarcity are in inverse ratio—M. Proudhon identifies use value with *supply* and exchange value with *demand.* To make the antithesis even more clear-cut, he substitutes a new term, putting "*estimation value*" for *exchange value.* [I 32] The battle has now shifted its ground, and we have on one side *utility* (use value, supply), on the other, *estimation* (exchange value, demand).

Who is to reconcile these two contradictory forces? What is to be done to bring them into harmony with each other? Is it possible to find in them even a single point of comparison?

---

[a] A. Anderson, *An Historical and Chronological Deduction of the Origin of Commerce from the Earliest Accounts to the Present Time* (Marx gives the title in French).— *Ed.*

Certainly, cries M. Proudhon, there is one—*free will.* The price resulting from this battle between supply and demand, between utility and estimation will not be the expression of eternal justice.

M. Proudhon goes on to develop this antithesis.

"In my capacity as a *free buyer,* I am judge of my needs, judge of the suitability of an object, judge of the price I am *willing* to pay for it. On the other hand, in your capacity as a *free producer,* you are master of the *means of execution,* and in consequence, you have the power to reduce your expenses." (Tome I, p. 41.)

And as demand, or exchange value, is identical with estimation, M. Proudhon is led to say:

"It is proved that it is man's *free will* that gives rise to the opposition between use value and exchange value. How can this opposition be removed, so long as free will exists? And how can the latter be sacrificed without sacrificing man?" (Tome I, p. 41.)

Thus there is no possible way out. There is a struggle between two as it were incommensurable powers, between utility and estimation, between the free buyer and the free producer.

Let us look at things a little more closely.

Supply does not represent exclusively utility, demand does not represent exclusively estimation. Does not the demander also supply a certain product or the token representing all products, viz., money; and as supplier, does he not represent, according to M. Proudhon, utility or use value?

Again, does not the supplier also demand a certain product or the token representing all products, viz., money? And does he not thus become the representative of estimation, of estimation value or of exchange value?

Demand is at the same time a supply, supply is at the same time a demand. Thus M. Proudhon's antithesis, in simply identifying supply and demand, the one with utility, the other with estimation, is based only on a futile abstraction.

What M. Proudhon calls use value is called estimation value by other economists, and with just as much right. We shall quote only Storch (*Cours d'économie politique,* Paris, 1823 [tome I], pp. 48 and 49).

According to him, *needs* are the things for which we feel the need; *values* are things to which we attribute value. Most things have value only because they satisfy needs engendered by estimation. The estimation of our needs may change; therefore the utility of things, which expresses only a relation of these things to our needs, may also change. Natural needs themselves are continually changing. Indeed, what could be more varied than the objects which form the staple food of different peoples!

The conflict does not take place between utility and estimation; it takes place between the marketable value demanded by the supplier and the marketable value supplied by the demander. The exchange value of the product is each time the resultant of these contradictory appreciations.

In final analysis, supply and demand bring together production and consumption, but production and consumption based on individual exchanges.

The product supplied is not useful in itself. It is the consumer who determines its utility. And even when its quality of being useful is admitted, it does not exclusively represent utility. In the course of production, it has been exchanged for all the costs of production, such as raw materials, wages of workers, etc., all of which are marketable values. The product, therefore, represents, in the eyes of the producer, a sum total of marketable values. What he supplies is not only a useful object, but also and above all a marketable value.

As to demand, it will only be effective on condition that it has means of exchange at its disposal. These means are themselves products, marketable values.

In supply and demand, then, we find, on the one hand, a product which has cost marketable values, and the need to sell; on the other, means which have cost marketable values, and the desire to buy.

M. Proudhon opposes the *free buyer* to the *free producer*. To the one and to the other he attributes purely metaphysical qualities. It is this that makes him say: "It is proved that it is man's *free will* that gives rise to the opposition between use value and exchange value." [I 41]

The producer, the moment he produces in a society founded on the division of labour and on exchange (and that is Mr. Proudhon's hypothesis), is forced to sell. M. Proudhon makes the producer master of the means of production; but he will agree with us that his means of production do not depend on *free will*. Moreover, many of these means of production are products which he gets from the outside, and in modern production he is not even free to produce the amount he wants. The actual degree of development of the productive forces compels him to produce on such or such a scale.

The consumer is no freer than the producer. His estimation depends on his means and his needs. Both of these are determined by his social position, which itself depends on the whole social organisation. True, the worker who buys potatoes and the kept woman who buys lace both follow their respective estimations. But the difference in their estimations is explained by the difference in the positions which they occupy in society, and which themselves are the product of social organisation.

Is the entire system of needs founded on estimation or on the whole organisation of production? Most often, needs arise directly from production or from a state of affairs based on production. World trade turns almost entirely round the needs, not of individual consumption, but of production. Thus, to choose another example, does not the need for lawyers suppose a given civil law which is but the expression of a certain development of property, that is to say, of production?

It is not enough for M. Proudhon to have eliminated the elements just mentioned from the relation of supply and demand. He carries abstraction to the extreme limits when he fuses all producers into *one single* producer, all consumers into *one single* consumer, and sets up a struggle between these two chimerical personages. But in the real world, things happen otherwise. The competition among the suppliers and the competition among the demanders form a necessary part of the struggle between buyers and sellers, of which marketable value is the result.

After having eliminated the cost of production and competition, M. Proudhon can as he likes reduce the formula of supply and demand to an absurdity.

> "Supply and demand," he says, "are merely two *ceremonial forms* that serve to bring use value and exchange value face to face, and to lead to their reconciliation. They are the two electric poles which, when connected, must produce the phenomenon of affinity called *exchange*." (Tome I, pp. 49 and 50.)

One might as well say that exchange is merely a "ceremonial form" for introducing the consumer to the object of consumption. One might as well say that all economic relations are "ceremonial forms" serving immediate consumption as go-betweens. Supply and demand are neither more nor less relations of a given production than are individual exchanges.

What, then, does all M. Proudhon's dialectic consist in? In the substitution for use value and exchange value, for supply and demand, of abstract and contradictory notions like scarcity and abundance, utility and estimation, *one* producer and *one* consumer, both of them *knights of free will*.

And what was he aiming at?

At arranging for himself a means of introducing later on one of the elements he had set aside, the *cost of production*, as the *synthesis* of use value and exchange value. And it is thus that in his eyes the cost of production constitutes *synthetic value* or *constituted value*.

§ 2. CONSTITUTED VALUE OR SYNTHETIC VALUE

"Value" (marketable value) "is the corner-stone of the economic structure." [I 32] "*Constituted*" value is the corner-stone of the system of economic contradictions.

What then is this "*constituted value*" which is all M. Proudhon has discovered in political economy?

Once utility is admitted, labour is the source of value. The measure of labour is time. The relative value of products is determined by the labour time required for their production. Price is the monetary expression of the relative value of a product. Finally, the *constituted* value of a product is purely and simply the value which is constituted by the labour time incorporated in it.

Just as Adam Smith discovered the *division of labour*, so he, M. Proudhon, claims to have discovered "*constituted value*". This is not exactly "something unheard of", but then it must be admitted that there is nothing unheard of in any discovery of economic science. M. Proudhon, who appreciates to the full the importance of his own invention, seeks nevertheless to tone down the merit thereof "in order to reassure the reader as to his claims to originality, and to win over minds whose timidity renders them little favourable to new ideas". [I 52] But in assessing the contribution made by each of his predecessors to the understanding of value, he is forced to confess openly that the largest portion, the lion's share, falls to himself.

> "The synthetic idea of value had been vaguely perceived by Adam Smith.... But with Adam Smith this idea of value was entirely intuitive. Now, society does not change its habits merely on the strength of intuitions: its decisions are made only on the authority of facts. The antinomy had to be stated more palpably and more clearly: J. B. Say was its chief interpreter." [I 66]

Here, in a nutshell, is the history of the discovery of synthetic value: Adam Smith—vague intuition; J. B. Say—antinomy; M. Proudhon—constituting and "constituted" truth. And let there be no mistake about it: all the other economists, from Say to Proudhon, have merely been trudging along in the rut of antinomy.

> "It is incredible that for the last forty years so many men of sense should have fumed and fretted at such a simple idea. But no, *values are compared without there being any point of comparison between them and with no unit of measurement*; this, rather than embrace the revolutionary theory of equality, is what the *economists of the nineteenth century* are resolved to uphold against all comers. *What will posterity say about it?*" (Tome I, p. 68.)

Posterity, so abruptly invoked, will begin by getting muddled over the chronology. It is bound to ask itself: are not Ricardo and his school economists of the nineteenth century? Ricardo's system, posing as a principle that "the relative value of commodities depends exclusively on the amount of labour required for their production", dates from 1817.[a] Ricardo is the head of a whole school dominant in England since the Restoration.[72] The Ricardian doctrine sums up severely, remorselessly, the whole of the English bourgeoisie, which is itself the type of the modern bourgeoisie. "What will posterity say about it?" It will not say that M. Proudhon did not know Ricardo, for he talks about him, he talks at length about him, he keeps coming back to him, and concludes by calling his system "trash". If ever posterity does interfere, it will say perhaps that M. Proudhon, afraid of offending his readers' Anglophobia, preferred to make himself the responsible editor of Ricardo's ideas. In any case, it will think it very naïve that M. Proudhon should give as a "revolutionary theory of the future" what Ricardo expounded scientifically as the theory of present-day society, of bourgeois society, and that he should thus take for the solution of the antinomy between utility and exchange value what Ricardo and his school presented long before him as the scientific formula of one single side of this antinomy, that of *exchange value*. But let us leave posterity aside once and for all, and confront M. Proudhon with his predecessor Ricardo. Here are some extracts from this author which summarise his doctrine on value:

"Utility then is not the measure of *exchangeable value*, although it is absolutely essential to it." (Tome I, p. 3 *of Principes de l'économie politique, etc.*, traduit de l'anglais par F. S. Constancio, Paris, 1835 [Eng. ed., p. 2].)

"Possessing utility, commodities derive their exchangeable value from two sources: from their scarcity, and from the quantity of labour[b] required to obtain them. There are some commodities, the value of which is determined by their scarcity alone. No labour can increase the quantity of such goods, and therefore their value cannot be lowered by an increased supply. Some rare statues and pictures, etc. are all of this description. Their value ... varies with the varying wealth and inclinations of those who are desirous to possess them." (Tome I, pp. 4 and 5, *l. c.* [Eng. ed., p. 2].) "These commodities, however, form a very small part of the mass of commodities daily exchanged in the market. By far the greatest part of those goods which are the objects of desire, are procured by labour; and they may be multiplied, not in one country alone, but in many, almost without any assignable limit, if we are disposed to bestow the labour necessary to obtain them." (Tome I, p. 5, *l. c.* [Eng. ed., p. 3].) "In speaking then of commodities, of their exchangeable value, and of the laws which regulate their relative prices, we mean always such commodities only as can be increased in quantity by the exertion of human industry, and on the production of which competition operates without restraint." (Tome I, p. 5 [Eng. ed., p. 3].)

---

[a] D. Ricardo, *On the Principles of Political Economy, and Taxation*, London, 1817.—*Ed.*

[b] The 1847 edition did not have the words "of labour", which were added in the copy with corrections in Marx's hand.—*Ed.*

Ricardo quotes Adam Smith, who, according to him, "*so accurately* defined the original source of exchangeable value" (Adam Smith, Book I, Chap. 5[a]), and he adds:

"That this" (i. e., labour time) "is really the foundation of the exchangeable value of all things, excepting those which cannot be increased by human industry, is a doctrine of the utmost importance in political economy; for from no source do so many errors, and so much difference of opinion in that science proceed, as from the vague ideas which are attached to the word *value*." (Tome I, p. 8 [Eng. ed., p. 4].) "If the quantity of labour realised in commodities regulate their exchangeable value, every increase of the quantity of labour must augment the value of that commodity on which it is exercised, as every diminution must lower it." (Tome I, p. 8 [Eng. ed., p. 4].)

Ricardo goes on to reproach Smith:

1. "With having himself erected another standart measure of value than labour, sometimes the value of corn, at other times the quantity of labour an object can command in the market," etc. (Tome I, pp. 9 and 10 [cf. Eng. ed., p. 5].)

2. "With having admitted the principle without qualification and at the same time restricted its application to that early and rude state of society, which precedes both the accumulation of stock and the appropriation of land." (Tome I, p. 21.[b])

Ricardo endeavours to prove that the ownership of land, that is, rent, cannot change the relative value of commodities and that the accumulation of capital has only a passing and fluctuating effect on the relative values determined by the comparative quantity of labour expended on their production. In support of this thesis, he gives his famous theory of rent, analyses capital, and ultimately finds nothing in it but accumulated labour. Then he develops a whole theory of wages and profits, and proves that wages and profits rise and fall in inverse ratio to each other, without affecting the relative value of the product. He does not neglect the influence that the accumulation of capital and its different aspects (fixed capital and circulating capital), as also the rate of wages, can have on the proportional value of products. In fact, these are the chief problems with which Ricardo is concerned.

"Economy in the use of labour never fails to reduce the relative value* of a commodity, whether the saving be in the labour necessary to the manufacture of the

* Ricardo, as is well known, determines the value of a commodity by "the quantity of labour necessary for its production". Owing, however, to the prevailing form of exchange in every mode of production based on production of commodities, including therefore the capitalist mode of production, this value is not expressed directly in quantities of labour but in quantities of some other commodity. The value of a commodity expressed in a quantity of some other commodity (whether money or not) is termed by Ricardo its relative value. *F. E.* [*Note to the German edition, 1885.* The copy with corrections in Marx's hand has here a marginal note: *nota* ("la valeur relative")]

[a] A. Smith, *An Inquiry into the Nature and Causes of the Wealth of Nations*.— *Ed.*

[b] In the third edition of Ricardo's book (London, 1821) this part of the text is omitted.—*Ed.*

commodity itself, or in that necessary to the formation of the capital, by the aid of which it is produced." (Tome I, p. 28 [Eng. ed., pp. 19-20]). "Consequently as long as a day's work continues to give one the same quantity of fish and the other the same quantity of game, the natural rate of the respective exchange prices will always be the same despite variations of wages and profit and despite all the effects of accumulation of capital." (Tome I, p. 32 [cf. Eng. ed., pp. 21-22].) "In making labour the foundation of the value of commodities and the comparative quantity of labour which is necessary to their production, the rule which determines the respective quantities of goods which shall be given in exchange for each other, we must not be supposed to deny the accidental and temporary deviations of the actual or market price of commodities from this, their primary and natural price." (Tome I, p. 105, *l. c.* [Eng. ed., p. 80].) "It is the cost of production which must ultimately regulate the price of commodities, and not, as has been often said, the proportion between supply and demand." (Tome II, p. 253 [Eng. ed., p. 460].)

Lord Lauderdale had developed the variations of exchange value according to the law of supply and demand, or of scarcity and abundance relatively to demand. In his opinion the value of a thing can increase when its quantity decreases or when the demand for it increases; it can decrease owing to an increase of its quantity or owing to the decrease in demand. Thus the value of a thing can change through eight different causes, namely, four causes that apply to the thing itself, and four causes that apply to money or to any other commodity which serves as a measure of its value. Here is Ricardo's refutation:

"Commodities which *are monopolised*, either by an individual, or by a company, vary according to the law which Lord Lauderdale has laid down: they fall in proportion as the sellers augment their quantity, and rise in proportion to the eagerness of the buyers to purchase them; their price has no necessary connexion with their natural value: but the prices of commodities, which are subject to competition, and whose quantity may be increased in any moderate degree, will ultimately depend, not on the state of demand and supply, but on the increased or diminished cost of their production." (Tome II, p. 259 [Eng. ed., p. 465].)

We shall leave it to the reader to make the comparison between this simple, clear, precise language of Ricardo's and M. Proudhon's rhetorical attempts to arrive at the determination of relative value by labour time.

Ricardo shows us the real movement of bourgeois production, which constitutes value. M. Proudhon, leaving this real movement out of account, "fumes and frets" in order to invent new processes and to achieve the reorganisation of the world on a would-be new formula, which formula is no more than the theoretical expression of the real movement which exists and which is so well described by Ricardo. Ricardo takes present-day society as his starting point to demonstrate to us how it constitutes value—M. Proudhon takes constituted value as his starting point to constitute a new social world with the aid of this value. For him, M. Proudhon, constituted value must complete a circle and become once more the constituting factor in a world already entirely constituted according to this mode of evaluation. The determination of value by labour time is, for Ricardo, the law of exchange value; for M. Proudhon, it is the synthesis of use value and exchange value. Ricardo's theory of values is the scientific interpretation of actual economic life; M. Proudhon's theory of values is the utopian interpretation of Ricardo's theory. Ricardo establishes the truth of his formula by deriving it from all economic relations, and by explaining in this way all phenomena, even those like rent, accumulation of capital and the relation of wages to profits, which at first sight seem to contradict it; it is precisely that which makes his doctrine a scientific system: M. Proudhon, who has rediscovered this formula of Ricardo's by means of quite arbitrary hypotheses, is forced thereafter to seek out isolated economic facts which he twists and falsifies to pass them off as examples, already existing applications, beginnings of realisation of his regenerating idea. (See our § 3. *Application of Constituted Value.*[a])

Now let us pass on to the conclusions M. Proudhon draws from value constituted (by labour time).

— A certain quantity of labour is equivalent to the product created by this same quantity of labour.

— Each day's labour is worth as much as another day's labour; that is to say, if the quantities are equal, one man's labour is worth as much as another man's labour: there is no qualitative difference. With the same quantity of labour, one man's product can be given in exchange for another man's product. All men are wage workers getting equal pay for an equal labour time. Perfect equality rules the exchanges.

Are these conclusions the strict, natural consequences of value "constituted" or determined by labour time?

If the relative value of a commodity is determined by the quantity of labour required to produce it, it follows naturally that the relative value of labour, or wages, is likewise determined by the quantity of labour needed to produce the wages. Wages, that is, the relative value or the price of labour, are thus determined by the labour time needed to produce all that is necessary for the maintenance of the worker.

"*Diminish the cost of production* of hats, and their price will ultimately fall to their new natural price, although the demand should be doubled, trebled, or quadrupled. *Diminish the cost of subsistence of men*, by diminishing the natural price of the food and

---

[a] See this volume, pp. 144-60.—*Ed.*

clothing by which life is sustained, and wages will ultimately fall, notwithstanding that the demand for labourers may very greatly increase." (Ricardo, tome II, p. 253 [Eng. ed., p. 460].)

Doubtless, Ricardo's language is as cynical as can be. To put the cost of manufacture of hats and the cost of maintenance of men on the same plane is to turn men into hats. But do not make an outcry at the cynicism of it. The cynicism is in the facts and not in the words which express the facts. French writers like MM. Droz, Blanqui, Rossi and others take an innocent satisfaction in proving their superiority over the English economists, by seeking to observe the etiquette of a "humanitarian" phraseology; if they reproach Ricardo and his school for their cynical language, it is because it annoys them to see economic relations exposed in all their crudity, to see the mysteries of the bourgeoisie unmasked.

To sum up: Labour, being itself a commodity, is measured as such by the labour time needed to produce the labour-commodity. And what is needed to produce this labour-commodity? Just enough labour time to produce the objects indispensable to the constant maintenance of labour, that is, to keep the worker alive and in a condition to propagate his race. The natural price of labour is no other than the minimum wage.* If the current rate of wages rises above the natural price, it is precisely because the law of value posed as a principle by M. Proudhon happens to be counterbalanced by the consequences of the varying relations of supply and demand. But the minimum wage is nonetheless the centre towards which the current rates of wages gravitate.

Thus relative value, measured by labour time, is inevitably the formula of the present enslavement of the worker, instead of being, as M. Proudhon would have it, the "revolutionary theory" of the emancipation of the proletariat.

Let us see now to what extent the application of labour time as a

* The thesis that the "natural", i.e., normal, price of labour power coincides with the minimum wage, i.e., with the equivalent in value of the means of subsistence absolutely indispensable for the life and procreation of the worker, was first put forward by me in *Outlines of a Critique of Political Economy (Deutsch-Französische Jahrbücher*, Paris, 1844) and in *The Condition of the Working Class in England.*[73] As seen here, Marx at that time accepted the thesis. Lassalle took it over from both of us. Although, however, in reality wages have a constant tendency to approach the minimum, the above thesis is nevertheless incorrect. The fact that labour power is regularly and on the average paid below its value cannot alter its value. In *Capital,* Marx has put the above thesis right (Section on the Buying and Selling of Labour Power) and also (Chapter 25: *The General Law of Capitalist Accumulation*) analysed the circumstances which permit capitalist production to depress the price of labour power more and more below its value. *F. E.* [*Note to the German edition, 1885.*]

measure of value is incompatible with the existing class antagonism and the unequal distribution of the product between the immediate worker and the owner of accumulated labour.

Let us take a particular product, for example, linen. This product, as such, contains a definite quantity of labour. This quantity of labour will always be the same, whatever the reciprocal position of those who have collaborated to create this product.

Let us take another product: broadcloth, which has required the same quantity of labour as the linen.

If there is an exchange of these two products, there is an exchange of equal quantities of labour. In exchanging these equal quantities of labour time, one does not change the reciprocal position of the producers, any more than one changes anything in the situation of the workers and manufacturers among themselves. To say that this exchange of products measured by labour time results in an equality of payment for all the producers is to suppose that equality of participation in the product existed before the exchange. When the exchange of broadcloth for linen has been accomplished, the producers of broadcloth will share in the linen in a proportion equal to that in which they previously shared in the broadcloth.

M. Proudhon's illusion is brought about by his taking for a consequence what could be at most but a gratuitous supposition.

Let us go further.

Does labour time, as the measure of value, suppose at least that the days are *equivalent*, and that one man's day is worth as much as another's? No.

Let us suppose for a moment that a jeweller's day is equivalent to three days of a weaver; the fact remains that any change in the value of jewels relative to that of woven materials, unless it be the transitory result of the fluctuations of demand and supply, must have as its cause a reduction or an increase in the labour time expended in the production of one or the other. If three working days of different workers be related to one another in the ratio of 1:2:3, then every change in the relative value of their products will be a change in this same proportion of 1:2:3. Thus values can be measured by labour time, in spite of the inequality of value of different working days; but to apply such a measure we must have a comparative scale of the different working days: it is competition that sets up this scale.

Is your hour's labour worth mine? That is a question which is decided by competition.

Competition, according to an American economist, determines how many days of simple labour are contained in one day's compound labour. Does not this reduction of days of compound labour to days of simple labour suppose that simple labour is itself taken as a measure of value? If the mere quantity of labour functions as a measure of value regardless of quality, it presupposes that simple labour has become the pivot of industry. It presupposes that labour has been equalised by the subordination of man to the machine or by the extreme division of labour; that men are effaced by their labour; that the pendulum of the clock has become as accurate a measure of the relative activity of two workers as it is of the speed of two locomotives. Therefore, we should not say that one man's hour is worth another man's hour, but rather that one man during an hour is worth just as much as another man during an hour. Time is everything, man is nothing; he is, at the most, time's carcase. Quality no longer matters. Quantity alone decides everything; hour for hour, day for day; but this equalising of labour is not by any means the work of M. Proudhon's eternal justice; it is purely and simply a fact of modern industry.

In the automatic workshop, one worker's labour is scarcely distinguishable in any way from another worker's labour: workers can only be distinguished one from another by the length of time they take for their work. Nevertheless, this quantitative difference becomes, from a certain point of view, qualitative, in that the time they take for their work depends partly on purely material causes, such as physical constitution, age and sex; partly on purely negative moral causes, such as patience, imperturbability, diligence. In short, if there is a difference of quality in the labour of different workers, it is at most a quality of the last kind, which is far from being a distinctive peculiarity. This is what the state of affairs in modern industry amounts to in the last analysis. It is upon this equality, already realised in automatic labour, that M. Proudhon wields his smoothing-plane of "equalisation", which he means to establish universally in "time to come"!

All the "equalitarian" consequences which M. Proudhon deduces from Ricardo's doctrine are based on a fundamental error. He confounds the value of commodities measured by the quantity of labour embodied in them with the value of commodities measured by "*the value of labour*". If these two ways of measuring the value of commodities merged into one, it could be said indifferently that the relative value of any commodity is measured by the quantity of labour embodied in it; or that it is measured by the quantity of labour it can buy; or again that it is measured by the quantity of labour which can acquire it. But this is far from being so. The value of labour [74] can no more serve as a measure of value than the value of any other commodity. A few examples will suffice to explain still better what we have just stated.

If a muid[a] of corn cost two days' labour instead of one, it would have twice its original value; but it would not set in operation double the quantity of labour, because it would contain no more nutritive matter than before. Thus the value of the corn, measured by the quantity of labour used to produce it, would have doubled; but measured either by the quantity of labour it can buy or by the quantity of labour with which it can be bought, it would be far from having doubled. On the other hand, if the same labour produced twice as many clothes as before, their relative value would fall by half; but, nevertheless, this double quantity of clothing would not thereby be reduced to disposing over only half the quantity of labour, nor could the same labour command double the quantity of clothing; for half the clothes would still go on rendering the worker the same service as before.

Thus it is going against economic facts to determine the relative value of commodities by the value of labour. It is moving in a vicious circle, it is to determine relative value by a relative value which itself needs to be determined.

It is beyond doubt that M. Proudhon confuses the two measures, measure by the labour time needed for the production of a commodity and measure by the value of the labour.

> "Any man's labour," he says, "can buy the value it represents." [I 81]

Thus, according to him, a certain quantity of labour embodied in a product is equivalent to the worker's payment, that is, to the value of labour. It is the same reasoning that makes him confuse cost of production with wages.

> "What are wages? They are the cost price of corn, etc., the integral price of all things. Let us go still further. Wages are the proportionality of the elements which compose wealth." [I 110]

What are wages? They are the value of labour.

Adam Smith takes as the measure of value, now the labour time needed for the production of a commodity, now the value of labour. Ricardo exposes this error by showing clearly the disparity of these two ways of measuring. M. Proudhon outdoes Adam Smith in error by identifying the two things which the latter had merely put in juxtaposition.

It is in order to find the proper proportion in which workers should share in the products, or, in other words, to determine the

---

[a] An old French measure equivalent to 18 hectolitres.— *Ed.*

relative value of labour, that M. Proudhon seeks a measure for the relative value of commodities. To find out the measure for the relative value of commodities he can think of nothing better than to give as the equivalent of a certain quantity of labour the sum total of the products it has created, which is as good as supposing that the whole of society consists merely of immediate workers who receive their own produce as wages. In the second place, he takes for granted the equivalence of the working days of different workers. In short, he seeks the measure of the relative value of commodities in order to arrive at equal payment for the workers, and he takes the equality of wages as an already established fact, in order to go off on the search for the relative value of commodities. What admirable dialectic!

"Say and the economists after him have observed that labour being itself subject to valuation, being a commodity like any other commodity, it is moving in a vicious circle to treat it as the principle and the determining cause of value.... In so doing, these economists, if they will allow me to say so, show a prodigious carelessness. Labour is said to have *value* not as a commodity itself, but in view of the values which it is supposed to contain potentially. The value of labour is a figurative expression, an anticipation of the cause for the effect. It is a fiction of the same stamp as the *productivity of capital*. Labour produces, capital has value.... By a sort of ellipsis one speaks of the value of labour.... Labour like liberty ... is a thing vague and indeterminate by nature, but defined qualitatively by its object, that is to say, it becomes a reality by the product." [I 61]

"But is there any need to dwell on this? The moment the economist" (read M. Proudhon) "changes the name of things, *vera rerum vocabula*, he is implicitly confessing his impotence and proclaiming himself not privy to the cause." (Proudhon, tome I, p. 188.)

We have seen that M. Proudhon makes the value of labour the "determining cause" of the value of products to such an extent that for him *wages*, the official name for the "value of labour", form the integral price of all things. That is why Say's objection troubles him. In labour-commodity, which is a grim reality, he sees nothing but a grammatical ellipsis. Thus the whole of existing society, founded on labour-commodity, is henceforth founded on a poetic licence, a figurative expression. If society wants to "eliminate all the drawbacks" that assail it, well, let it eliminate all the ill-sounding terms, change the language; and to this end it has only to apply to the Academy for a new edition of its dictionary. After all that we have just seen, it is easy for us to understand why M. Proudhon, in a work on political economy, has to enter upon long dissertations on etymology and other parts of grammar. Thus he is still learnedly discussing the antiquated derivation of *servus*[a] from *servare*[b]. These

[a] A slave, servant.— *Ed.*
[b] To preserve.— *Ed.*

philological dissertations have a deep meaning, an esoteric meaning—they form an essential part of M. Proudhon's argument.

Labour,[a] inasmuch as it is bought and sold, is a commodity like any other commodity, and has, in consequence, an exchange value. But the value of labour, or labour as a commodity, produces as little as the value of wheat, or wheat as a commodity, serves as food.

Labour has more or less "value," according to whether food commodities are more or less dear, whether the supply and demand of hands exist to such or such a degree, etc., etc.

Labour is not a "vague thing"; it is always some definite labour, it is never labour in general that is sold and bought. It is not only labour which is qualitatively defined by the object; but also the object which is determined by the specific quality of labour.

Labour, insofar as it is sold and bought, is itself a commodity. Why is it bought? "In view of the values it is supposed to contain potentially." But if a certain thing is said to be a commodity, there is no longer any question as to the reason why it is bought, that is, as to the utility to be derived from it, the application to be made of it. It is a commodity as an object of traffic. All M. Proudhon's arguments are limited to this: labour is not bought as an immediate object of consumption. No, it is bought as an instrument of production, as a machine would be bought. As a commodity, labour has value and does not produce. M. Proudhon might just as well have said that there is no such thing as a commodity, since every commodity is acquired merely for some utilitarian purpose, and never as a commodity in itself.

In measuring the value of commodities by labour, M. Proudhon vaguely glimpses the impossibility of excluding labour from this same measure, insofar as labour has a value, labour-commodity. He has a misgiving that it is turning the minimum wage into the natural and normal price of immediate labour, that it is accepting the existing state of society. So, to get away from this fatal consequence, he faces about and asserts that labour is not a commodity, that it cannot have value. He forgets that he himself has taken the value of labour as a measure, he forgets that his whole system rests on labour-commodity, on labour which is bartered, sold, bought, exchanged for produce, etc., on labour, in fact, which is an immediate source of income for the worker. He forgets everything.

---

[a] In the copy with corrections in Marx's hand and the one presented in 1876 to N. Utina after the word "travail" ("labour") is added "la force du travail" ("labour power"). The same addition is made in the 1896 French edition.—*Ed.*

To save his system, he consents to sacrifice its basis.

Et propter vitam vivendi perdere causas![a]

We now come to a new definition of "*constituted* value".

"Value is the *proportional relation* of the products which constitute wealth." [I 62]

Let us note in the first place that the simple phrase "relative or exchange value" implies the idea of some relation in which products are exchanged reciprocally. By giving the name "proportional relation" to this relation, no change is made in the relative value, except in the expression. Neither the depreciation nor the enhancement of the value of a product destroys its quality of being in some "proportional relation" with the other products which constitute wealth.

Why then this new term, which introduces no new idea?

"Proportional relation" suggests many other economic relations, such as proportionality in production, the correct proportion between supply and demand, etc., and M. Proudhon is thinking of all that when he formulates this didactic paraphrase of marketable value.

In the first place, the relative value of products being determined by the comparative amount of labour used in the production of each of them, proportional relations, applied to this special case, stand for the respective quota of products which can be manufactured in a given time, and which in consequence are given in exchange for one another.

Let us see what advantage M. Proudhon draws from this proportional relation.

Everyone knows that when supply and demand are evenly balanced, the relative value of any product is accurately determined by the quantity of labour embodied in it, that is to say, that this relative value expresses the proportional relation precisely in the sense we have just attached to it. M. Proudhon inverts the order of things. Begin, he says, by measuring the relative value of a product by the quantity of labour embodied in it, and supply and demand will infallibly balance one another. Production will correspond to consumption, the product will always be exchangeable. Its current price will express exactly its true value. Instead of saying like everyone else: when the weather is fine, a lot of people are to be seen going out for a walk, M. Proudhon makes his people go out for a walk in order to be able to ensure them fine weather.

[a] And for the sake of life to lose the reasons for living (Juvenal, *Satires*, VIII).—*Ed.*

What M. Proudhon gives as the consequence of marketable value determined *a priori* by labour time could be justified only by a law couched more or less in the following terms:

Products will in future be exchanged in the exact ratio of the labour time they have cost. Whatever may be the proportion of supply to demand, the exchange of commodities will always be made as if they had been produced proportionately to the demand. Let M. Proudhon take it upon himself to formulate and lay down such a law, and we shall relieve him of the necessity of giving proofs. If, on the other hand, he insists on justifying his theory, not as a legislator, but as an economist, he will have to prove that the *time* needed to create a commodity indicates exactly the degree of its *utility* and marks its proportional relation to the demand, and in consequence, to the total amount of wealth. In this case, if a product is sold at a price equal to its cost of production, supply and demand will always be evenly balanced; for the cost of production is supposed to express the true relation between supply and demand.

Actually, M. Proudhon sets out to prove that the labour time needed to create a product indicates its correct proportional relation to needs, so that the things whose production costs the least time are the most immediately useful, and so on, step by step. The mere production of a luxury object proves at once, according to this doctrine, that society has spare time which allows it to satisfy a need for luxury.

M. Proudhon finds the very proof of his thesis in the observation that the most useful things cost the least time to produce, that society always begins with the easiest industries and successively "starts on the production of objects which cost more labour time and which correspond to a higher order of needs". [I 57]

M. Proudhon borrows from M. Dunoyer the example of extractive industry—fruit-gathering, pasturage, hunting, fishing, etc. —which is the simplest, the least costly of industries, and the one by which man began "the first day of his second creation". [I 78] The first day of his first creation is recorded in Genesis, which shows us God as the world's first manufacturer.

Things happen in quite a different way from what M. Proudhon imagines. The very moment civilisation begins, production begins to be founded on the antagonism of orders, estates, classes, and finally on the antagonism of accumulated labour and immediate labour. No antagonism, no progress. This is the law that civilisation has followed up to our days. Till now the productive forces have been developed by virtue of this system of class antagonisms. To say now that, because all the needs of all the workers were satisfied, men could devote themselves to the creation of products of a higher order—to more complicated industries—would be to leave class antagonism out of account and turn all historical development upside down. It is like saying that because, under the Roman emperors, muraena were fattened in artificial fishponds, therefore there was enough to feed abundantly the whole Roman population. Actually, on the contrary, the Roman people had not enough to buy bread with, while the Roman aristocrats had slaves enough to throw as fodder to the muraena.

The price of food has almost continuously risen, while the price of manufactured and luxury goods has almost continuously fallen. Take the agricultural industry itself: the most indispensable objects, like corn, meat, etc., rise in price, while cotton, sugar, coffee, etc., continually fall in a surprising proportion. And even among comestibles proper, the luxury articles, like artichokes, asparagus, etc., are today relatively cheaper than foodstuffs of prime necessity. In our age, the superfluous is easier to produce than the necessary. Finally, at different historical epochs, the reciprocal price relations are not only different, but opposed to one another. In the whole of the Middle Ages, agricultural products were relatively cheaper than manufactured products; in modern times they are in inverse ratio. Does this mean that the utility of agricultural products has diminished since the Middle Ages?

The use of products is determined by the social conditions in which the consumers find themselves placed, and these conditions themselves are based on class antagonism.

Cotton, potatoes and spirits are objects of the most common use. Potatoes have engendered scrofula; cotton has to a great extent driven out flax and wool, although wool and flax are, in many cases, of greater utility, if only from the point of view of hygiene; finally, spirits have got the upper hand of beer and wine, although spirits used as an alimentary substance are everywhere recognised to be poison. For a whole century, governments struggled in vain against the European opium; economics prevailed, and dictated its orders to consumption.

Why are cotton, potatoes and spirits the pivots of bourgeois society? Because the least amount of labour is needed to produce them, and, consequently, they have the lowest price. Why does the minimum price determine the maximum consumption? Is it by any chance because of the absolute utility of these objects, their intrinsic utility, their utility insomuch as they correspond, in the most useful manner, to the needs of the worker as a man, and not of the man as a worker? No, it is because in a society founded on *poverty* the *poorest* products have the fatal prerogative of being used by the greatest number.

To say now that because the least costly things are in greater use, they must be of greater utility, is saying that the wide use of spirits, because of their low cost of production, is the most conclusive proof of their utility; it is telling the proletarian that potatoes are more wholesome for him than meat; it is accepting the present state of affairs; it is, in short, making an apology, with M. Proudhon, for a society without understanding it.

In a future society, in which class antagonism will have ceased, in which there will no longer be any classes, use will no longer be determined by the *minimum* time of production; but the time of production[a] devoted to an article[b] will be determined by the degree of its social[c] utility.

To return to M. Proudhon's thesis; since the labour time necessary for the production of an article is not the expression of its degree of utility, the exchange value of this same article, determined beforehand by the labour time embodied in it, can never regulate the correct relation of supply to demand, that is, the proportional relation in the sense M. Proudhon attributes to it at the moment.

It is not the sale of a given product at the price of its cost of production that constitutes the "proportional relation" of supply to demand, or the proportional quota of this product relatively to the sum total of production; it is the *variations in demand and supply* that show the producer what amount of a given commodity he must produce in order to receive at least the cost of production in exchange. And as these variations are continually occurring, there is also a continual movement of withdrawal and application of capital in the different branches of industry.

"It is only in consequence of such variations that capital is *apportioned* precisely, in the requisite abundance and no more, to the production of the different commodities which happen to be in demand. With the rise or fall of price, profits are elevated above, or depressed below their general level, and capital is either encouraged to enter into, or is warned to depart from, the particular employment in which the variation has taken place."—"When we look to the markets of a large town, and observe how regularly they are supplied both with home and foreign commodities, in the quantity

---

[a] The 1896 French edition has "production sociale".—*Ed.*

[b] In the copy with corrections in Marx's hand and the one presented to N. Utina the words "à un objet" are replaced by "aux différents objets". This change was also made in the 1896 French edition.—*Ed.*

[c] The word "sociale", which is not in the 1847 edition, was added in the copy with corrections in Marx's hand and the one which he presented to N. Utina and also in the 1896 French edition.—*Ed.*

in which they are required, under all the circumstances of varying demand, arising from the caprice of taste, or a change in the amount of population, without often producing either the effects of a glut from a too abundant supply, or an enormously high price from the supply being unequal to the demand, we must confess that the principle which apportions capital to each trade *in the precise amount that is required*, is more active than is generally supposed." (Ricardo, tome I, pp. 105[-106] and 108 [Eng. ed., pp. 80 and 82].)

If M. Proudhon admits that the value of products is determined by labour time, he should equally admit that it is the fluctuating movement alone that[a] makes labour time the measure of value. There is no ready constituted "proportional relation", but only a constituting movement.

We have just seen in what sense it is correct to speak of "proportion" as of a consequence of value determined by labour time. We shall see now how this measure by time, called by M. Proudhon the "law of proportion", becomes transformed into a law of *disproportion*.

Every new invention that enables the production in one hour of that which has hitherto been produced in two hours depreciates all similar products on the market. Competition forces the producer to sell the product of two hours as cheaply as the product of one hour. Competition implements the law according to which the relative value of a product is determined by the labour time needed to produce it. Labour time serving as the measure of marketable value becomes in this way the law of the continual *depreciation* of labour. We will say more. There will be depreciation not only of the commodities brought into the market, but also of the instruments of production and of whole plants. This fact was already pointed out by Ricardo when he said:

"By constantly increasing the facility of production, we constantly diminish the value of some of the commodities before produced." (Tome II, p. 59 [Eng. ed., p. 321].)

Sismondi goes further. He sees in this "value *constituted*" by labour time the source of all the contradictions of modern industry and commerce.

"Mercantile value," he says, "is always determined in the long run by the quantity of labour needed to obtain the thing evaluated: it is not what it has actually cost, but what it would cost in future with, perhaps, perfected means; and this quantity, although difficult to evaluate, is always faithfully established by competition... It is on

---

[a] In the copy with corrections in Marx's hand the words "in societies founded on individual exchanges" are added here and then struck out; in the copy presented to N. Utina this addition was made except for the word "individual".— *Ed.*

this basis that the demand of the seller as well as the supply of the buyer is reckoned. The former will perhaps declare that the thing has cost him ten days' labour; but if the latter realises that it can henceforth be produced with eight days' labour, in the event of competition proving this to the two contracting parties, the value will be reduced, and the market price fixed at eight days only. Of course, each of the parties believes that the thing is useful, that it is desired, that without desire there would be no sale; but the fixing of the price has nothing to do with utility." (*Études, etc.*, t. II, p. 267, Brussels edition.)

It is important to emphasise the point that what determines value is not the time taken to produce a thing, but the *minimum* time it could possibly be produced in, and this minimum is ascertained by competition. Suppose for a moment that there is no more competition and consequently no longer any means to ascertain the minimum of labour necessary for the production of a commodity; what will happen? It will suffice to spend six hours' work on the production of an object, in order to have the right, according to M. Proudhon, to demand in exchange six times as much as he who has taken only one hour to produce the same object.

Instead of a "proportional relation", we have a disproportional relation, at any rate if we insist on sticking to relations, good or bad.

The continual depreciation of labour is only one side, one consequence of the evaluation of commodities by labour time. The excessive raising of prices, overproduction and many other features of industrial anarchy have their explanation in this mode of evaluation.

But does labour time used as a measure of value give rise at least to the proportional variety of products that so fascinates M. Proudhon?

On the contrary, monopoly in all its monotony follows in its wake and invades the world of products, just as to everybody's knowledge monopoly invades the world of the instruments of production. It is only in a few branches of industry, like the cotton industry, that very rapid progress can be made. The natural consequence of this progress is that the products of cotton manufacture, for instance, fall rapidly in price: but as the price of cotton goes down, the price of flax must go up in comparison. What will be the outcome? Flax will be replaced by cotton. In this way, flax has been driven out of almost the whole of North America. And we have obtained, instead of the proportional variety of products, the dominance of cotton.

What is left of this "proportional relation"? Nothing but the pious wish of an honest man who would like commodities to be produced in proportions which would permit of their being sold at an honest price. In all ages good-natured bourgeois and philanthropic economists have taken pleasure in expressing this innocent wish.

Let us hear what old *Boisguillebert* says:

"The price of commodities," he says, "must always be *proportionate*; for it is such mutual understanding alone that can enable them to exist together *so as to give themselves to one another at any moment*" (here is M. Proudhon's continual exchangeability) "and reciprocally give birth to one another.... As wealth, then, is nothing but this continual intercourse between man and man, craft and craft, etc., it is a frightful blindness to go looking for the cause of misery elsewhere than in the cessation of such traffic brought about by a disturbance of proportion in prices." (*Dissertation sur la nature des richesses*, Daire ed. [pp. 405, 408].)

Let us listen also to a modern economist:

"The great law as necessary to be affixed to production, that is, the *law of proportion*,[a] which alone can preserve the continuity of value.... The equivalent must be guaranteed.... All nations have attempted, at various periods of their history, by instituting numerous commercial regulations and restrictions, to effect, in some degree, the object here explained.... But the natural and inherent selfishness of man ... has urged him to break down all such regulations.... Proportionate production[a] is the realisation of the entire truth of the Science of Social Economy." (W. Atkinson, *Principles of Political Economy*, London, 1840, pp. 170-95.)

Fuit Troja.[b] This correct proportion between supply and demand, which is beginning once more to be the object of so many wishes, ceased long ago to exist. It has passed into the stage of senility. It was possible only at a time when the means of production were limited, when exchange took place within very restricted bounds. With the birth of large-scale industry this correct proportion had to come to an end, and production is inevitably compelled to pass in continuous succession through vicissitudes of prosperity, depression, crisis, stagnation, renewed prosperity, and so on.

Those who, like Sismondi, wish to return to the correct proportion of production, while preserving the present basis of society, are reactionary, since, to be consistent, they must also wish to bring back all the other conditions of industry of former times.

What kept production in correct, or more or less correct, proportions? It was demand that dominated supply, that preceded it. Production followed close on the heels of consumption. Large-scale industry, forced by the very instruments at its disposal to produce on an ever-increasing scale, can no longer wait for demand. Production precedes consumption, supply compels demand.

In existing society, in industry based on individual exchange, anarchy of production, which is the source of so much misery, is at the same time the source of all progress.

Thus, one or the other:

---

[a] In the original the English term is given in parentheses after the French.— *Ed.*

[b] Troy is no more (Virgil, *Aeneid*, 2, 325).— *Ed.*

Either you want the correct proportions of past centuries with present-day means of production, in which case you are both reactionary and utopian.

Or you want progress without anarchy: in which case, in order to preserve the productive forces, you must abandon individual exchange.

Individual exchange is consistent only with the small-scale industry of past centuries and its corollary of "correct proportion", or else with large-scale industry and all its train of misery and anarchy.

After all,[a] the determination of value by labour time—the formula M. Proudhon gives us as the regenerating formula of the future—is therefore[b] merely the scientific expression of the economic relations of present-day society, as was clearly and precisely demonstrated by Ricardo long before M. Proudhon.

But does the "*equalitarian*" application of this formula at least belong to M. Proudhon? Was he the first to think of reforming society by transforming all men into immediate workers exchanging equal amounts of labour? Is it for him to reproach the Communists—these people devoid of all knowledge of political economy, these "obstinately foolish men", these "paradise dreamers"—with not having found, before him, this "solution of the problem of the proletariat"?

Anyone who is in any way familiar with the trend of political economy in England cannot fail to know that almost all the socialists in that country have, at different periods, proposed the equalitarian application of the Ricardian theory. We could quote for M. Proudhon: Hodgskin, *Political Economy*, 1827[75]; William Thompson, *An Inquiry into the Principles of the Distribution of Wealth Most Conducive to Human Happiness*, 1824; T. R. Edmonds, *Practical Moral and Political Economy*, 1828, etc., etc., and four pages more of *etc.* We shall content ourselves with listening to an English *Communist*, Mr. Bray. We shall give the decisive passages in his remarkable work, *Labour's Wrongs and Labour's Remedy*, Leeds, 1839, and we shall dwell some time upon it, firstly, because Mr. Bray is still little known in France, and, secondly, because we think that we have discovered in him the key to the past, present and future works of M. Proudhon.

---

[a] In the 1847 edition this sentence begins with the words: "D'après tout ce que nous venons de dire." In the copy with corrections in Marx's hand and the one presented to N. Utina "D'après" is changed to "Après" and the rest of the phrase is crossed out; this correction was reproduced in the 1896 French edition.—*Ed.*

[b] The word "therefore" ("donc") is not in the 1847 edition; it was added in the copy with corrections in Marx's hand and the one presented to N. Utina; this addition is reproduced in the 1896 French edition.—*Ed.*

"The only way to arrive at truth is to go at once to First Principles.... Let us ... go at once to the source from whence governments themselves have arisen.... By thus going to the origin of the thing, we shall find that every form of government, and every social and governmental wrong, owes its rise to the existing social system—to *the institution of property as it at present exists*[a]—and that, therefore, if we would end our wrongs and our miseries at once and for ever, *the present arrangements of society must be totally subverted*.... By thus fighting them upon their own ground, and with their own weapons, we shall avoid that senseless chatter respecting '*visionaries*' and '*theorists*', with which they are so ready to assail.... Before the conclusions arrived at by such a course of proceeding can be overthrown, the economists must unsay or disprove those established truths and principles on which their own arguments are founded." (Bray, pp. 17 and 41.) "It is *labour alone which bestows value*[b].... Every man has an undoubted right to all that his honest labour can procure him. When he thus appropriates the fruits of his labour, he commits no injustice upon any other human being; for he interferes with no other man's right of doing the same with the produce of his labour.... All these ideas of superior and inferior—of master and man—may be traced to the neglect of First Principles, and to the consequent rise of *inequality* of possessions[c], and such ideas will never be eradicated, nor the institutions founded upon them be subverted, so long as this inequality is maintained. Men have hitherto blindly hoped to remedy the present unnatural state of things ... by destroying *existing inequality*, and leaving untouched the *cause* of the inequality; but it will shortly be seen ... that government[d] is not a cause, but a consequence—that it is not the creator, but the created—that it is *the offspring of inequality of possessions*[e]; and that the inequality of possessions is inseparably connected with our present social system." (Bray, pp. 33, 36 and 37.)

"Not only are the greatest advantages, but strict justice also, on the side of a system of equality.... Every man is a link, and an indispensable link, in the chain of effects—the beginning of which is but an idea, and the end, perhaps, the production of a piece of cloth. Thus, although we may entertain different feelings towards the several parties, it does not follow that one should be better paid for his labour than another. The inventor will ever receive, in addition to his just pecuniary reward, that which genius only can obtain from us—the tribute of our admiration....

"From the very nature of labour and exchange, strict justice requires that all exchangers should be not only *mutually*, but that they should likewise be *equally*, benefited.[f] Men have only two things which they can exchange with each other, namely, labour, and the produce of labour.... If a just system of exchanges were acted upon, the value of all articles would be determined by *the entire cost of production*; and *equal values should always exchange for equal values*.[g] If, for instance, it takes a hatter one

---

[a] In the original the end of the phrase beginning with the words "the institution of property ..." is given in English in parentheses after the French.—*Ed.*

[b] In the original this phrase is given in English in parentheses after the French.—*Ed.*

[c] In the original the words "and to the consequent rise of inequality of possessions" are given in English in parentheses after the French.—*Ed.*

[d] Bray has here: "misgovernment".—*Ed.*

[e] In the original the words "the offspring of inequality of possessions" are given in English in parentheses after the French.—*Ed.*

[f] In the original the words "all exchangers should be" to the end of the sentence are given in English in parentheses after the French.—*Ed.*

[g] In the original this sentence is given in English in parentheses after the French.—*Ed.*

day to make a hat, and a shoemaker the same time to make a pair of shoes—supposing the material used by each to be of the same value—and they exchange these articles with each other, they are not only mutually but equally benefited: the advantage derived by either party cannot be a disadvantage to the other, as each has given the same amount of labour, and the materials made use of by each were of equal value. But if the hatter should obtain *two* pair of shoes for *one* hat—time and value of material being as before—the exchange would clearly be an unjust one. The hatter would defraud the shoemaker of one day's labour; and were the former to act thus in all his exchanges, he would receive, for the labour of *half a year*, the product of some other person's *whole year*.... We have heretofore acted upon no other than this most unjust system of exchanges—the *workmen have given* the capitalist the labour of a whole year, in exchange for the value of only half a year[a]—and from this, and not from the assumed inequality of bodily and mental powers in individuals, has arisen the inequality of wealth and power.... It is an inevitable condition of inequality of exchanges—of buying at one price and selling at another—that capitalists shall continue to be capitalists, and working men to be working men—the one a class of tyrants and the other a class of slaves—to eternity.... The whole transaction, therefore, plainly shews that the capitalists and proprietors do no more than give the working man, for his labour of one week, a part of the wealth which they obtained from him the week before!—which just amounts to giving him *nothing* for *something*[b].... The whole transaction ... between the producer and the capitalist is ... a mere farce: it is, in fact, in thousands of instances, no other than a barefaced though *legalised robbery*.[c]" (Bray, pp. 45, 48, 49 and 50.)

"... the gain of the employer will never cease to be the loss of the employed—until the exchanges between the parties are equal; and exchanges never can be equal while society is divided into capitalists and producers—the last living upon their labour and the first bloating upon the profit of that labour....

"It is plain," continues Mr. Bray, "that, establish whatever form of government we will ... we may talk of morality and brotherly love ... no reciprocity can exist where there are unequal exchanges.... Inequality of exchanges, as being the cause of inequality of possessions, is the secret enemy that devours us." [d] (Bray, pp. 51 and 52.)

"It has been deduced, also, from a consideration of the intention and end of society, not only that all men should labour, and thereby become exchangers, but that equal values should always exchange for equal values—and that, as the gain of one man ought never to be the loss of another, value should ever be determined by cost of production. But we have seen, that, under the present arrangements of society ... the gain of the capitalist and the rich man is always the loss of the workman—that this result will invariably take place, and the poor man be left entirely at the mercy of the rich man, under any and every form of government, so long as there is inequality of exchanges—and that equality of exchanges can be ensured only under social arrangements in which labour is universal.... If exchanges were equal, would the wealth of the present capitalists gradually go from them to the working classes." (Bray, pp. 53-55.)

---

[a] In the original the words from "the workmen" to "half a year" are given in English in parentheses after the French.—*Ed.*

[b] In the original the words "nothing for something" are given in English in parentheses after the French.—*Ed.*

[c] In the original this phrase is given in parentheses in English after the French.—*Ed.*

[d] In the original the words from "no reciprocity" to "devours us" are given in English in parentheses after the French.—*Ed.*

"So long as this system of unequal exchanges is tolerated, the producers will be almost as poor and as ignorant and as hardworked as they are at present, even if *every governmental burthen be swept away* and *all taxes be abolished* ... nothing but a total change of system — an equality of labour and exchanges — can alter this state of things and guarantee true equality of rights.... The producers have but to make an effort — and by them must every effort for their own redemption be made — and their chains will be snapped asunder for ever.... As an end, the political equality is there a failure ... as a means, also, it is there a failure.[a]

"Where equal exchanges are maintained, the gain of one man cannot be the loss of another; for every exchange is then simply a *transfer*, and not a sacrifice, of labour and wealth. Thus, although under a social system based on equal exchanges, a parsimonious man may become rich, his wealth will be no more than the accumulated produce of his own labour. He may exchange his wealth, or he may give it to others ... but a rich man cannot continue wealthy for any length of time after he has ceased to labour. Under equality of exchanges, wealth cannot have, as it now has, a procreative and apparently self-generating power, such as replenishes all waste from consumption; for, unless it be renewed by labour, wealth, when once consumed, is given up for ever. That which is now called *profit* and *interest* cannot exist as such in connection with equality of exchanges; for producer and distributor would be alike remunerated, and the sum total of their labour would determine the value of the article created and brought to the hands of the consumer.

"The principle of equal exchanges, therefore, must from its very nature ensure *universal labour.*" (Bray, pp. 67, 88, 89, 94, 109-10.)

After having refuted the objections of the economists to *communism*, Mr. Bray goes on to say:

"If, then, a changed character be essential to the success of the social system of community in its most perfect form — and if, likewise, the present system affords no circumstances and no facilities for effecting the requisite change of character and preparing man for the higher and better state desired — it is evident that these things must necessarily remain as they are, ... or else some preparatory step must be discovered and made use of — some movement partaking partly of the present and partly of the desired system" (the system of community), "some intermediate resting-place, to which society may go with all its faults and its follies, and from which it may move forward, imbued with those qualities and attributes without which the system of community and equality cannot as such have existence." (Bray, p. 134.)

"The whole movement would require only co-operation in its simplest form.... Cost of production would in every instance determine value; and equal values would always exchange for equal values. If one person worked a whole week, and another worked only half a week, the first would receive double the remuneration of the last; but this extra pay of the one would not be at the expense of the other, nor would the loss incurred by the last man fall in any way upon the first. Each person would exchange the wages he individually received for commodities of the same value as his respective wages; and in no case could the gain of one man or one trade be a loss to another man or another trade. The labour of every individual *would alone determine* his gains or his losses....

"...By means of general and local boards of trade[b] ... the quantities of the various

---

[a] In the original this sentence is given in English in parentheses after the French.— *Ed.*

[b] In the original the last three words are given in English in parentheses after the French.— *Ed.*

commodities required for consumption—the relative value of each in regard to each other—the number of hands required in various trades and descriptions of labour—and all other matters connected with production and distribution, could in a short time be as easily determined for a nation as for an individual company under the present arrangements.... Individuals would compose families, and families towns, as under the existing system.... The present distribution of people in towns and villages, bad as it is, would not be directly interfered with.... Under this joint-stock system, the same as under that now existing, every individual would be at liberty to accumulate as much as he pleased, and to enjoy such accumulations when and where he might think proper.... The great productive section of the community ... is divided into an indefinite number of smaller sections, all working, producing and exchanging their products on a footing of the most perfect equality.... And the joint-stock modification (which is nothing but a concession to present-day society in order to obtain communism), by being so constituted as to admit of *individual property* in productions in connection with a *common property* in productive powers—making every individual dependent on his own exertions, and at the same time allowing him an equal participation in every advantage afforded by nature and art—is fitted to take society as it is, and to prepare the way for other and better changes." (Bray, pp. 158, 160, 162, [163], 168, [170 and] 194.)

We only need to reply in a few words to Mr. Bray who without us and in spite of us has managed to supplant M. Proudhon, except that Mr. Bray, far from claiming the last word on behalf of humanity, proposes merely measures which he thinks good for a period of transition between existing society and a community regime.

One hour of Peter's labour exchanges for one hour of Paul's labour. That is Mr. Bray's fundamental axiom.

Let us suppose Peter has twelve hours' labour before him, and Paul only six. Peter will be able to make with Paul an exchange of only six for six. Peter will consequently have six hours' labour left over. What will he do with these six hours' labour?

Either he will do nothing—in which case he will have worked six hours for nothing; or else he will remain idle for another six hours to get even; or else, as a last resource, he will give these six hours' labour, which he has no use for, to Paul into the bargain.

What in the end will Peter have earned more than Paul? Some hours of labour? No! He will have gained only hours of leisure; he will be forced to play the loafer for six hours. And in order that this new right to loaf might be not only relished but sought after in the new society, this society would have to find in idleness its highest bliss, and to look upon labour as a heavy shackle from which it must break free at all costs. And again, to return to our example, if only these hours of leisure that Peter has gained in excess of Paul were really a gain! Not in the least. Paul, beginning by working only six hours, attains by steady and regular work a result that Peter secures only by beginning with an excess of work. Everyone will want to be

Paul, there will be a competition to occupy Paul's position, a competition in idleness.

Well, then! What has the exchange of equal quantities of labour brought us? Overproduction, depreciation, excess of labour followed by unemployment; in short, economic relations such as we see in present-day society, minus the competition of labour.

No! We are wrong! There is still an expedient which may save this new society, the society of Peters and Pauls. Peter will consume by himself the product of the six hours' labour which he has left. But since he has no longer to exchange in order to have produced, he has no need to produce in order to exchange; and the whole hypothesis of a society founded on the exchange and division of labour will fall to the ground. Equality of exchange will have been saved by the simple fact that exchange will have ceased to be: Paul and Peter will arrive at the position of Robinson.

Thus, if all the members of society are supposed to be immediate workers, the exchange of equal quantities of hours of labour is possible only on condition that the number of hours to be spent on material production is agreed on beforehand. But such an agreement negates individual exchange.

We still come to the same result, if we take as our starting point not the distribution of the products created but the act of production. In large-scale industry, Peter is not free to fix for himself the time of his labour, for Peter's labour is nothing without the co-operation of all the Peters and all the Pauls who make up the workshop. This explains very well the dogged resistance which the English factory owners put up to the *Ten Hours Bill*. They knew only too well that a two hours' reduction of labour granted to women and children[76] would carry with it an equal reduction of working hours for adult men. It is in the nature of large-scale industry that working hours should be equal for all. What is today the result of capital and the competition of workers among themselves will be tomorrow, if you sever the relation between labour and capital, an actual agreement based upon the relation between the sum of productive forces and the sum of existing needs.

But such an agreement is a condemnation of individual exchange, and we are back again at our first conclusion!

In principle, there is no exchange of products—but there is the exchange of the labour which co-operates in production. The mode of exchange of products depends upon the mode of exchange of the productive forces. In general, the form of exchange of products corresponds to the form of production. Change the latter, and the former will change in consequence. Thus in the history of society we see that the mode of exchanging products is regulated by the mode of producing them. Individual exchange corresponds also to a definite mode of production which itself corresponds to class antagonism. There is thus no individual exchange without the antagonism of classes.

But the honest conscience refuses to see this obvious fact. So long as one is a bourgeois, one cannot but see in this relation of antagonism a relation of harmony and eternal justice, which allows no one to gain at the expense of another. For the bourgeois, individual exchange can exist without any antagonism of classes. For him, these are two quite unconnected things. Individual exchange, as the bourgeois conceives it, is far from resembling individual exchange as it is practised.

Mr. Bray turns the *illusion* of the respectable bourgeois into an *ideal* he would like to attain. In a purified individual exchange, freed from all the elements of antagonism he finds in it, he sees an "*equalitarian*" relation which he would like society to adopt.

Mr. Bray does not see that this equalitarian relation, this *corrective ideal* that he would like to apply to the world, is itself nothing but the reflection of the actual world; and that therefore it is totally impossible to reconstitute society on the basis of what is merely an embellished shadow of it. In proportion as this shadow takes on substance again, we perceive that this substance, far from being the transfiguration dreamt of, is the actual body of existing society.*

§ 3. APPLICATION OF THE LAW OF THE PROPORTIONALITY OF VALUE

A) Money

"Gold and silver were the first commodities to have their value constituted." [I 69]

Thus gold and silver are the first applications of "value constituted" ... by M. Proudhon. And as M. Proudhon constitutes the

* Mr. Bray's theory, like all theories, has found supporters who have allowed themselves to be deluded by appearances. *Equitable-labour-exchange bazaars*[77] have been set up in London, Sheffield, Leeds and many other towns in England. These bazaars have all ended in scandalous failures after having absorbed considerable capital. The taste for them has gone for ever. You are warned, M. Proudhon! [*Note by Marx.* The copy with corrections in Marx's hand has "Nota!" in the margin opposite this note.]

It is known that Proudhon did not take this warning to heart. In 1849 he himself made an attempt with a new Exchange Bank in Paris. The bank, however, failed before it had got going properly: a court case against Proudhon had to serve to cover its collapse. *F. E.* [*Note to the German edition, 1885.*]

value of products determining it by the comparative amount of labour embodied in them, the only thing he had to do was to prove that *variations* in the value of gold and silver are always explained by variations in the labour time taken to produce them. M. Proudhon has no intention of doing so. He speaks of gold and silver not as commodities, but as money.

His only logic, if logic it be, consists in juggling with the capacity of gold and silver to be used as *money* for the benefit of all the commodities which have the property of being evaluated by labour time. Decidedly there is more naïveté than malice in this jugglery.

A useful product, being evaluated by the labour time needed to produce it, is always acceptable in exchange. Witness, cries M. Proudhon, gold and silver, which exist in my desired conditions of "exchangeability"! Gold and silver, then, are value which has reached a state of constitution: they are the incorporation of M. Proudhon's idea. He could not have been happier in his choice of an example. Gold and silver, apart from their capacity of being commodities, evaluated like other commodities in labour time, have also the capacity of being the universal agents of exchange, of being money. By now considering gold and silver as an application of "*value constituted*" by labour time, nothing is easier than to prove that all commodities whose value is constituted by labour time will always be exchangeable, will be money.

A very simple question occurs to M. Proudhon. Why have gold and silver the privilege of typifying "constituted value"?

> "The special function which usage has devolved upon the precious metals, that of serving as a medium for trade, is purely conventional, and any other commodity could, less conveniently perhaps, but just as authentically, fulfil this function. Economists recognise this, and cite more than one example. What then is the reason for this universal preference for metals as money? And what is the explanation of this specialisation of the functions of silver — which has no analogy in political economy?... Is it possible to *reconstruct the series* from which *money* seems to have broken away, and hence to trace it back to its true principle?" [I 68, 69]

By formulating the question in these terms, M. Proudhon has already presupposed the existence of *money*. The first question he should have asked himself was, why, in exchanges as they are actually constituted, it has been necessary to individualise exchangeable value, so to speak, by the creation of a special agent of exchange. Money is not a thing, it is a social relation. Why is the money relation a production relation like any other economic relation, such as the division of labour, etc.? If M. Proudhon had properly taken account of this relation, he would not have seen in money an exception, an element detached from a series unknown or needing reconstruction.

He would have realised, on the contrary, that this relation is a link, and, as such, closely connected with a whole chain of other economic relations; that this relation corresponds to a definite mode of production neither more nor less than does individual exchange. What does *he* do? He starts off by detaching money from the actual mode of production as a whole, and then makes it the first member of an imaginary series, of a series to be reconstructed.

Once the necessity for a specific agent of exchange, that is, for money, has been recognised, all that remains to be explained is why this particular function has devolved upon gold and silver rather than upon any other commodity. This is a secondary question, which is explained not by the chain of production relations, but by the specific qualities inherent in gold and silver as substances. If all this has made economists for once "go outside the domains of their own science, to dabble in physics, mechanics, history and so on" [I 69], as M. Proudhon reproaches them with doing, they have merely done what they were compelled to do. The question is no longer within the domain of political economy.

"What no economist," says M. Proudhon, "has either seen or understood is the *economic reason* which has determined, in favour of the precious metals, the favour they enjoy." [I 69]

This economic reason which nobody—with good ground indeed—has seen or understood, M. Proudhon has seen, understood and bequeathed to posterity.

"What nobody else has noticed is that, of all commodities, gold and silver were the first to have their value attain constitution. In the patriarchal period, gold and silver were still bartered and exchanged in ingots but even then they showed a visible tendency to become dominant and received a marked preference. *Little by little* the sovereigns took possession of them and affixed their seal to them: and of this sovereign consecration was born money, that is, the commodity *par excellence*, which, notwithstanding all the shocks of commerce, retains a definite proportional value and makes itself accepted for all payments.... The distinguishing characteristic of gold and silver is due, I repeat, to the fact that, thanks to their metallic properties, to the difficulties of their production, and above all to the intervention of state authority, they early won stability and authenticity as commodities." [I 69, 70]

To say that, of all commodities, gold and silver were the first to have their value constituted, is to say, after all that has gone before, that gold and silver were the first to attain the status of money. This is M. Proudhon's great revelation, this is the truth that none had discovered before him.

If, by these words, M. Proudhon means that of all commodities gold and silver are the ones whose time of production was known the earliest, this would be yet another of the suppositions with which he is so ready to regale his readers. If we wished to harp on this patriarchal erudition, we would inform M. Proudhon that it was the time needed to produce objects of prime necessity such as iron, etc., which was the first to be known. We shall spare him Adam Smith's classic bow.[78]

But, after all that, how can M. Proudhon go on talking about the constitution of a value, since a value is never constituted all alone? It is constituted, not by the time needed to produce it all alone, but in relation to the quota of each and every other product which can be created in the same time. Thus the constitution of the value of gold and silver presupposes an already completed constitution of a number of other products.

It is then not the commodity that has attained, in gold and silver, the status of "constituted value", it is M. Proudhon's "constituted value" that has attained, in gold and silver, the status of money.

Let us now make a closer examination of these *economic reasons* which, according to M. Proudhon, have bestowed upon gold and silver the advantage of being raised to the status of money sooner than other products, thanks to their having passed through the constitutive phase of value.

These economic reasons are: the "visible tendency to become dominant", the "marked preference" even in the "patriarchal period" [I 69], and other circumlocutions about the actual fact—which increase the difficulty, since they multiply the fact by multiplying the incidents which M. Proudhon brings in to explain the fact. M. Proudhon has not yet exhausted all the so-called economic reasons. Here is one of sovereign, irresistible force:

> "Money is born of sovereign consecration: the sovereigns took possession of gold and silver and affixed their seal to them." [I 69]

Thus the whim of sovereigns is for M. Proudhon the highest reason in political economy.

Truly, one must be destitute of all historical knowledge not to know that it is the sovereigns who in all ages have been subject to economic conditions, but they have never dictated laws to them. Legislation, whether political or civil, never does more than proclaim, express in words, the will of economic relations.

Was it the sovereign who took possession of gold and silver to make them the universal agents of exchange by affixing his seal to them? Or was it not, rather, these universal agents of exchange which took possession of the sovereign and forced him to affix his seal to them and thus give them a political consecration?

The impress which was and is still given to silver is not that of its value but of its weight. The stability and authenticity M. Proudhon speaks of apply only to the standard of the money; and this standard indicates how much metallic matter there is in a coined piece of silver.

"The sole intrinsic value of a silver mark," says Voltaire, with his habitual good sense, "is a mark of silver, half a pound weighing eight ounces. The weight and the standard alone form this intrinsic value." (Voltaire, *Système de Law.*[a])

But the question: how much is an ounce of gold or silver worth, remains nonetheless. If a cashmere from the *Grand Colbert* stores bore the trade mark *pure wool,* this trade mark would not tell you the value of the cashmere. There would still remain the question: how much is wool worth?

"Philip I, King of France," says M. Proudhon, "mixes with Charlemagne's Tours pound a third of alloy, imagining that, having the monopoly of the manufacture of money, he could do what is done by every tradesman who has the monopoly of a product. What was actually this debasement of the currency for which Philip and his successors have been so much blamed? It was perfectly sound reasoning from the point of view of commercial practice, but very unsound economic science, viz., to suppose that, as supply and demand regulate value, it is possible, either by producing an artificial scarcity or by monopolising manufacture, to increase the estimation and consequently the value of things; and that this is true of gold and silver as of corn, wine, oil or tobacco. But Philip's fraud was no sooner suspected than his money was reduced to its true value, and he himself lost what he had thought to gain from his subjects. The same thing has happened as a result of every similar attempt." [I 70-71]

It has been proved times without number that, if a prince takes into his head to debase the currency, it is he who loses. What he gains once at the first issue he loses every time the falsified coinage returns to him in the form of taxes, etc. But Philip and his successors were able to protect themselves more or less against this loss, for, once the debased coinage was put into circulation, they hastened to order a general re-minting of money on the old footing.

And besides, if Philip I had really reasoned like M. Proudhon, he would not have reasoned well "from the commercial point of view". Neither Philip I nor M. Proudhon displays any mercantile genius in imagining that it is possible to alter the value of gold as well as that of every other commodity merely because their value is determined by the relation between supply and demand.

If King Philip had decreed that one muid of wheat was in future to be called two muids of wheat, he would have been a swindler. He would have deceived all the rentiers, all the people who were entitled to receive a hundred muids of wheat. He would have been the cause

[a] Voltaire, *Histoire du parlement,* chapitre LX "Finances et système de Law pendant la régence."—*Ed.*

of all these people receiving only fifty instead of a hundred. Suppose the king owed a hundred muids of wheat; he would have had to pay only fifty. But in commerce a hundred such muids would never have been worth more than fifty. By changing the name we do not change the thing. The quantity of wheat, whether supplied or demanded, will be neither decreased nor increased by this mere change of name. Thus, the relation between supply and demand being just the same in spite of this change of name, the price of wheat will undergo no real change. When we speak of the supply and demand of things, we do not speak of the supply and demand of the name of things. Philip I was not a maker of gold or silver, as M. Proudhon says; he was a maker of names for coins. Pass off your French cashmeres as Asiatic cashmeres, and you may deceive a buyer or two; but once the fraud becomes known, your so-called Asiatic cashmeres will drop to the price of French cashmeres. When he put a false label on gold and silver, King Philip could deceive only so long as the fraud was not known. Like any other shopkeeper, he deceived his customers by a false description of his wares, which could not last for long. He was bound sooner or later to suffer the rigour of commercial laws. Is this what M. Proudhon wanted to prove? No. According to him it is from the sovereign and not from commerce that money gets its value. And what has he really proved? That commerce is more sovereign than the sovereign. Let the sovereign decree that one mark shall in future be two marks, commerce will keep on saying that these two marks are worth no more than one mark was formerly.

But, for all that, the question of value determined by the quantity of labour has not been advanced a step. It still remains to be decided whether the value of these two marks (which have become what one mark was once) is determined by the cost of production or by the law of supply and demand.

M. Proudhon continues:

> "It should even be borne in mind that if, instead of debasing the currency, it had been in the king's power to double its bulk, the exchange value of gold and silver would immediately have dropped by half, always for reasons of proportion and equilibrium." [I 71]

If this opinion, which M. Proudhon shares with the other economists, is valid, it argues in favour of the latter's doctrine of supply and demand, and in no way in favour of M. Proudhon's proportionality. For, whatever the quantity of labour embodied in the doubled bulk of gold and silver, its value would have dropped by half, the demand having remained the same and the supply having doubled. Or can it be, by any chance, that the "*law of proportionality*" would become confused this time with the so much disdained law of supply and demand? This correct proportion of M. Proudhon's is indeed so elastic, is capable of so many variations, combinations and permutations, that it might well coincide for once with the relation between supply and demand.

To make "every commodity acceptable in exchange, if not in fact then at least in law," on the basis of the role of gold and silver is, then, to misunderstand this role. Gold and silver are acceptable in law only because they are acceptable in fact; and they are acceptable in fact because the present organisation of production needs a universal agent of exchange. Law is only the official recognition of fact.

We have seen that the example of silver as an application of value which has attained constitution was chosen by M. Proudhon only to smuggle through his whole doctrine of exchangeability, that is to say, to prove that every commodity assessed by its cost of production must attain the status of money. All this would be very fine, were it not for the awkward fact that precisely gold and silver, as money, are of all commodities the only ones not determined by their cost of production; and this is so true that in circulation they can be replaced by paper. So long as there is a certain proportion observed between the requirements of circulation and the amount of money issued, be it paper, gold, platinum or copper money, there can be no question of a proportion to be observed between the intrinsic value (cost of production) and the nominal value of money. Doubtless, in international trade, money is determined, like any other commodity, by labour time. But it is also true that gold and silver in international trade are means of exchange as products and not as money. In other words, they lose this characteristic of "stability and authenticity", of "sovereign consecration", which, for M. Proudhon, forms their specific characteristic. Ricardo understood this truth so well that after basing his whole system on value determined by labour time, and after saying: "*Gold and silver,* like all other commodities, are valuable only in proportion to the quantity of labour necessary to produce them, and bring them to market", he adds, nevertheless, that the value of *money* is not determined by the labour time its substance embodies, but by the law of supply and demand only.

"Though it" (paper money) "has no intrinsic value, yet, by limiting its quantity, its value in exchange is as great as an equal denomination of coin, or of bullion in that coin. On the same principle, too, namely, by a limitation of its quantity, a debased coin would circulate at the value it should bear, if it were of the legal weight and fineness, and not at the value of the quantity of metal which it actually contained. In the history of the British coinage, we find, accordingly, that the currency was never depreciated in the same proportion that it was debased; the reason of which was, that it never was increased in quantity, in proportion to its diminished intrinsic value." (Ricardo, *loc. cit.* [II 206-07; Eng. ed., pp. 422-23].)

This is what J. B. Say observes on this passage of Ricardo's:

"This *example* should suffice, I think, to convince the author that the basis of all value is not the amount of labour needed to make a commodity, but the need felt for that commodity, balanced by its scarcity."[a]

Thus money, which for Ricardo is no longer a value determined by labour time, and which J. B. Say therefore takes as an example to convince Ricardo that the other values could not be determined by labour time either, this money, I say, taken by J. B. Say as an example of a value determined exclusively by supply and demand, becomes for M. Proudhon the example *par excellence* of the application of value constituted ... by labour time.

To conclude, if money is not a "value constituted" by labour time, it is all the less likely that it could have anything in common with M. Proudhon's correct "proportion". Gold and silver are always exchangeable, because they have the special function of serving as the universal agent of exchange, and in no wise because they exist in a quantity proportional to the sum total of wealth; or, to put it still better, they are always proportional because, alone of all commodities, they serve as money, the universal agent of exchange, whatever their quantity in relation to the sum total of wealth.

"A circulation can never be so abundant as to overflow; for by diminishing its value, in the same proportion you will increase its quantity, and by increasing its value, diminish its quantity." (Ricardo [II 205; Eng. ed., p. 422].)

"What an imbroglio political economy is!" cries M. Proudhon. [I 72]

"'Cursed gold!' cries a Communist flippantly" (through the mouth of M. Proudhon). "You might as well say: Cursed wheat, cursed vines, cursed sheep!—for just like gold and silver, *every commercial value* must attain its strict and exact determination." [I 73]

The idea of making sheep and vines attain the status of money is not new. In France, it belongs to the age of Louis XIV. At that period, money having begun to establish its omnipotence, the depreciation of all other commodities was being complained of, and the time when "every commercial value" might attain its strict and exact determination, the status of money, was being eagerly invoked. Even in the writings of Boisguillebert, one of the oldest of French economists, we find:

---

[a] Say's note to the French edition of Ricardo's book, tome II, p. 207.—*Ed.*

"Money then, by the arrival of innumerable competitors in the form of commodities themselves, re-established in their true values, will be thrust back again within its natural limits."[a] (*Économistes financiers du XVIIIe siècle*, Daire edition, p. 422.)

One sees that the first illusions of the bourgeoisie are also their last.

B) Surplus Left by Labour

"In works on political economy we read this absurd hypothesis: *If the price of everything were doubled....* As if the price of everything were not the proportion of things—and one could double a proportion, a relation, a law!" (Proudhon, tome I, p. 81.)

Economists have fallen into this error through not knowing how to apply the "law of proportionality" and "constituted value".

Unfortunately in the very same work by M. Proudhon, tome I, p. 110, we read the absurd hypothesis that, "if wages rose generally, the price of everything would rise". Furthermore, if we find the phrase in question in works on political economy, we also find an explanation of it.

"When one speaks of the price of all commodities going up or down, one always excludes some one commodity. The excluded commodity is, in general, money or labour." (*Encyclopaedia Metropolitana, or Universal Dictionary of Knowledge*, Vol. VI, Article *Political Economy*, by Senior, London, 1836. Regarding the phrase under discussion, see also J. St. Mill: *Essays on Some Unsettled Questions of Political Economy*, London, 1844, and Tooke: *A History of Prices, etc.*, London, 1838.)

Let us pass now to the *second application* of "constituted value", and of other proportions—whose only defect is their lack of proportion. And let us see whether M. Proudhon is happier here than in the *monetisation* of sheep.

"An axiom generally admitted by economists is that all labour must leave a surplus. In my opinion this proposition is universally and absolutely true: it is the corollary of the law of proportion, which may be regarded as the summary of the whole of economic science. But, if the economists will permit me to say so, the principle that *all labour must leave a surplus* is meaningless according to their theory, and is not susceptible of any *demonstration*." (Proudhon [I 73].)

To prove that all labour must leave a surplus, M. Proudhon personifies society; he turns it into a *person-society*—a society which is not by any means a society of persons, since it has its laws apart, which have nothing in common with the persons of which society is composed, and its "own intelligence", which is not the intelligence of

[a] P. Boisguillebert, *Dissertation sur la nature des richesses....*— *Ed.*

common men, but an intelligence devoid of common sense. M. Proudhon reproaches the economists with not having understood the personality of this collective being. We have pleasure in confronting him with the following passage from an American economist, who accuses the economists of just the opposite:

"The moral *entity*—the grammatical being[a] called a nation, has been clothed in attributes that have no real existence except in the imagination of those who metamorphose a word into a thing.... This has given rise to many difficulties and to some deplorable misunderstandings in political economy." (Th. Cooper, *Lectures on the Elements of Political Economy*, Columbia, 1826.[79])

"This principle of the surplus left by labour," continues M. Proudhon, "is true of individuals only because it emanates from society, which thus confers on them the benefit of its own laws." [I 75]

Does M. Proudhon thereby mean merely that the production of the social individual exceeds that of the isolated individual? Is M. Proudhon referring to this surplus of the production of associated individuals over that of non-associated individuals? If so, we could quote for him a hundred economists who have expressed this simple truth without any of the mysticism with which M. Proudhon surrounds himself. This, for example, is what Mr. Sadler says:

"Combined labour produces results which individual exertion could never accomplish. As mankind, therefore, multiply in number, the products of their united industry would greatly exceed the amount of any mere arithmetical addition calculated on such an increase.... In the mechanical arts, as well as in pursuits of science, a man may achieve more in a day ... than a solitary ... individual could perform in his whole life.... Geometry says ... that the whole is only equal to the sum of all its parts; as applied to the subject before us, this axiom would be false. Regarding labour, the great pillar of human existence[b], it may be said that the entire product of combined exertion almost infinitely exceeds all which individual and disconnected efforts could possibly accomplish." (T. Sadler, *The Law of Population*, London, 1830 [pp. 83, 84].)

To return to M. Proudhon. The surplus left by labour, he says, is explained by the person-society. The life of this person is guided by laws which are the opposite of those which govern the activities of man as an individual. He desires to prove this by "*facts*".

"The discovery of an economic process can never provide the inventor with a profit equal to that which he procures for society.... It has been remarked that railway enterprises are much less a source of wealth for the contractors than for the state.... The average cost of transporting commodities by road is 18 centimes per ton per kilometre, from the collection of the goods to their delivery. It has been calculated that

---

[a] In the original both terms are given in English in parentheses after the French.— *Ed.*

[b] In the original the words "the great pillar of human existence" are given in English in parentheses after the French.— *Ed.*

at this rate an ordinary railway enterprise would not obtain 10 per cent net profit, a result approximately equal to that of a road-transport enterprise. But let us suppose that the speed of rail transport compared with that of road transport is as 4 is to 1. Since in society time is value itself, the railway would, prices being equal, present an advantage of 400 per cent over road transport. Yet this enormous advantage, very real for society, is far from being realised in the same proportion for the carrier, who, while bestowing upon society an extra value of 400 per cent, does not for his own part draw 10 per cent. To bring the matter home still more pointedly, let us suppose, in fact, that the railway puts up its rate to 25 centimes, the cost of road transport remaining at 18: it would instantly lose all its consignments. Senders, receivers, everybody would return to the van, to the primitive waggon if necessary. The locomotive would be abandoned. A social advantage of 400 per cent would be sacrificed to a private loss of 35 per cent. The reason for this is easily grasped: the advantage resulting from the speed of the railway is entirely social, and each individual participates in it only in a minute proportion (it must be remembered that at the moment we are dealing only with the transport of goods), while the loss strikes the consumer directly and personally. A social profit equal to 400 represents for the individual, if society is composed only of a million men, four ten-thousandths; while a loss of 33 per cent for the consumer would suppose a social deficit of 33 million." (Proudhon [I 75, 76].)

We may even overlook the fact that M. Proudhon expresses a quadrupled speed as 400 per cent of the original speed; but that he should bring into relation the percentage of speed and the percentage of profit and establish a proportion between two relations which, although measured separately by percentages, are nevertheless incommensurable with each other, is to establish a proportion between the percentages without reference to denominations.

Percentages are always percentages, 10 per cent and 400 per cent are commensurable; they are to each other as 10 is to 400. Therefore, concludes M. Proudhon, a profit of 10 per cent is worth forty times less than a quadrupled speed. To save appearances, he says that, for society, time is money.[a] This error arises from his recollecting vaguely that there is a connection between value and labour time, and he hastens to identify labour time with transport time; that is, he identifies the few firemen, guards and conductors, whose labour time is actually transport time, with the whole of society. Thus at one blow, speed has become capital, and in this case he is entirely right in saying: "A profit of 400 per cent will be sacrificed to a loss of 35 per cent." After establishing this strange proposition as a mathematician, he gives us the explanation of it as an economist.

"A social profit equal to 400 represents for the individual, if society is composed only of a million men, four ten-thousandths."

---

[a] In the original the words "time is money" are given in English in parentheses after the French.— *Ed.*

Agreed; but we are dealing not with 400, but with 400 per cent, and a profit of 400 per cent represents for the individual 400 per cent, neither more nor less. Whatever be the capital, the dividends will always be in the ratio of 400 per cent. What does M. Proudhon do? He takes percentages for capital, and, as if he were afraid of his confusion not being manifest enough, "pointed" enough, he continues:

"A loss of 33 per cent for the consumer would suppose a social deficit of 33 million." A loss of 33 per cent for the consumer remains a loss of 33 per cent for a million consumers. How then can M. Proudhon say pertinently that the social deficit in the case of a 33 per cent loss amounts to 33 million, when he knows neither the social capital nor even the capital of a single one of the persons concerned? Thus it was not enough for M. Proudhon to have confused *capital* with *percentage*; he surpasses himself by identifying the *capital* sunk in an enterprise with the *number* of interested parties.

"To bring the matter home still more pointedly let us suppose in fact" a given capital. A social profit of 400 per cent divided among a million participants, each of them interested to the extent of one franc, would give 4 francs profit per head—and not 0.0004, as M. Proudhon alleges. Likewise a loss of 33 per cent for each of the participants represents a social deficit of 330,000 francs and not of 33 million (100:33=1,000,000:330,000).

M. Proudhon, preoccupied with his theory of the person-society, forgets to divide by 100 and gets a loss of 330,000 francs; but 4 francs profit per head makes 4 million francs profit for society. There remains for society a net profit of 3.670,000 francs. This accurate calculation proves precisely the contrary of that which M. Proudhon wanted to prove: namely, that the profits and losses of society are not in inverse ratio to the profits and losses of individuals.

Having rectified these simple errors of pure calculation let us take a look at the consequences which we would arrive at, if we admitted this relation between speed and capital in the case of railways, as M. Proudhon gives it—minus the mistakes in calculation. Let us suppose that a transport four times as rapid costs four times as much; this transport would not yield less profit than cartage, which is four times slower and costs a quarter of the amount. Thus, if cartage takes 18 centimes, rail transport could take 72 centimes. This would be, according to "the rigour of mathematics", the consequence of M. Proudhon's suppositions—always minus his mistakes in calculation. But here he is all of a sudden telling us that if, instead of 72 centimes, rail transport takes only 25, it would instantly lose all its consignments. Decidedly we should have to go back to the van, to the primitive waggon even. Only, if we have any advice to give M. Proudhon, it is not to forget, in his *Programme of the Progressive Association*, to divide by 100. But, alas! it is scarcely to be hoped that our advice will be listened to, for M. Proudhon is so delighted with his "progressive" calculation, corresponding to the "progressive association", that he cries most emphatically:

"I have already shown in Chapter II, by the solution of the antinomy of value, that the advantage of every useful discovery is incomparably less for the inventor, whatever he may do, than for society. I have carried the demonstration in regard to this point *to the rigour of mathematics*!" [I 241]

Let us return to the fiction of the person-society, a fiction which has no other aim than that of proving this simple truth—that a new invention which enables a given amount of labour to produce a greater number of commodities, lowers the marketable value of the product. Society, then, makes a profit, not by obtaining more exchange values, but by obtaining more commodities for the same value. As for the inventor, competition makes his profit fall successively to the general level of profits. Has M. Proudhon proved this proposition as he wanted to? No. This does not prevent him from reproaching the economists with failure to prove it. To prove to him on the contrary that they have proved it, we shall cite only Ricardo and Lauderdale—Ricardo, the head of the school which determines value by labour time, and Lauderdale, one of the most uncompromising defenders of the determination of value by supply and demand. Both have expounded the same proposition:

"By constantly increasing the facility of production, we constantly diminish the value of some of the commodities before produced, though by the same means we not only add to the national riches, but also to the power of future production.... As soon as by the aid of machinery, or by the knowledge of natural philosophy, you oblige natural agents to do the work which was before done by man, the exchangeable value of such work falls accordingly. If ten men turned a corn mill, and it be discovered that by the assistance of wind, or of water, the labour of these ten men may be spared, the flour which is the produce partly of the work performed by the mill, would immediately fall in value, in proportion to the quantity of labour saved; and the society would be richer by the commodities which the labour of the ten men could produce, the funds destined for their maintenance being in no degree impaired." (Ricardo [II 59, 82; Eng. ed., pp. 321-22, 336].)

Lauderdale, in his turn, says:

"In every instance where capital is so employed as to produce a profit, it uniformly arises, either—from its supplanting a portion of labour, which would otherwise be performed by the hand of man; or—from its performing a portion of labour, which is beyond the reach of the personal exertion of man to accomplish.... The small profit which the proprietors of machinery generally acquire, when compared with the wages of labour, which the machine supplants, may perhaps create a suspicion of the rectitude of this opinion. Some fire-engines, for instance, draw more water from a coalpit in one day than could be conveyed on the shoulders of three hundred men, even assisted by the machinery of buckets; and a fire-engine undoubtedly performs its labour at a much smaller expense than the amount of the wages of those whose labour it thus supplants. This is, in truth, the case with all machinery. All machines must execute the labour that was antecedently performed at a cheaper rate than it could be done by the hand of man.... If such a privilege is given for the invention of a machine, which performs, by the labour of one man, a quantity of work that used to take the labour of four; as the possession of the exclusive privilege prevents any competition in doing the work, but what proceeds from the labour of the workmen, their wages, as long as the patent continues, must obviously form the measure of the patentee's charge; that is to secure employment, he has only to charge a little less than the wages of the labour which the machine supplants. But when the patent expires, other machines of the same nature are brought into competition; and then his charge must be regulated on the same principle as every other, according to the abundance of machines.... The profit of capital employed..., though it arises from supplanting labour, comes to be regulated, not by the value of the labour it supplants, but, as in all other cases, by the competition among the proprietors of capital; and it will be great or small in proportion to the quantity of capital that presents itself for performing the duty, and the demand for it." [Pp. 119, 123, 124-25, 134; Eng. ed., pp. 161, 166-67, 168-69, 181-82.]

Finally, then, so long as the profit is greater than in other industries, capital will be thrown into the new industry until the rate of profit falls to the general level.

We have just seen that the example of the railway was scarcely suited to throw any light on the fiction of the person-society. Nevertheless, M. Proudhon boldly resumes his discourse:

"With these points cleared up, nothing is easier than to explain how labour must leave a surplus for each producer." [I 77]

What now follows belongs to classical antiquity. It is a poetical narrative intended to refresh the reader after the fatigue which the rigour of the preceding mathematical demonstrations must have caused him. M. Proudhon gives his person-society the name of *Prometheus*, whose high deeds he glorifies in these terms:

"First of all, Prometheus emerging from the bosom of nature awakes to life, in a delightful inertia," etc., etc. "Prometheus sets to work, and on this first day, the first day of the second creation, Prometheus' product, i.e., his wealth, his well-being, is equal to ten. On the second day, Prometheus divides his labour, and his product becomes equal to a hundred. On the third day and on each of the following days, Prometheus invents machines, discovers new utilities in bodies, new forces in nature.... With every step of his industrial activity, there is an increase in the number of his products, which marks an enhancement of happiness for him. And since, after all, to consume is for him to produce, it is clear that every day's consumption, using up only the product of the day before, leaves a surplus product for the next day." [I 77, 78]

This Prometheus of M. Proudhon's is a queer character, as weak in logic as in political economy. So long as Prometheus merely teaches us the division of labour, the application of machinery, the exploitation of natural forces and scientific power, multiplying the productive forces of men and giving a surplus compared with the produce of labour in isolation, this new Prometheus has the misfortune only of coming too late. But the moment Prometheus starts talking about production and consumption he becomes really ludicrous. To consume, for him, is to produce; he consumes the next day what he produced the day before, so that he is always one day in advance; this day in advance is his "surplus left by labour". But, if he consumes one day what he produced the day before, he must, on the first day, which had no day before, have done two days' work in order to be one day in advance later on. How did Prometheus earn this surplus on the first day, when there was neither division of labour, nor machinery, nor even any knowledge of physical forces other than fire? Thus the question, for all its being carried back "to the first day of the second creation", has not advanced a single step forward. This way of explaining things savours both of Greek and of Hebrew, it is at once mystical and allegorical. It gives M. Proudhon a perfect right to say:

> "I have proved by theory and by facts the principle that all labour must leave a surplus." [I 79]

The "facts" are the famous progressive calculation; the theory is the myth of Prometheus.

> "But," continues M. Proudhon, "this principle, while being as certain as an arithmetical proposition, is as yet far from being realised by everyone. Whereas, with the progress of collective industry, every day's individual labour produces a greater and greater product, and whereas therefore, by a necessary consequence, the worker with the same wage[a] ought to become richer every day, there actually exist estates in society which profit and others which decay." [I 79-80]

In 1770 the population of the United Kingdom of Great Britain was 15 million, and the productive population was 3 million. The scientific power of production equalled a population of about 12 million individuals more. Therefore there were, altogether, 15 million of productive forces. Thus the productive power was to the population as 1 is to 1; and the scientific power was to the manual power as 4 is to 1.

In 1840 the population did not exceed 30 million: the productive population was 6 million. But the scientific power amounted to 650 million; that is, it was to the whole population as 21 is to 1, and to manual power as 108 is to 1.

---

[a] In the copy with corrections in Marx's hand the words "with the same wage" are underscored and the word "Nota" is written in the margin.— *Ed.*

In English society the working day thus acquired in seventy years a surplus of 2,700 per cent productivity; that is, in 1840 it produced 27 times as much as in 1770. According to M. Proudhon, the following question should be raised: why was not the English worker of 1840 twenty-seven times as rich as the one of 1770? In raising such a question one would naturally be supposing that the English could have produced this wealth without the historical conditions in which it was produced, such as: private accumulation of capital, modern division of labour, automatic workshops, anarchical competition, the wage system—in short, everything that is based upon class antagonism. Now, these were precisely the necessary conditions of existence for the development of productive forces and of the surplus left by labour. Therefore, to obtain this development of productive forces and this surplus left by labour, there had to be classes which profited and classes which decayed.

What then, ultimately, is this Prometheus resuscitated by M. Proudhon? It is society, social relations based on class antagonism. These relations are not relations between individual and individual, but between worker and capitalist, between farmer and landlord, etc. Wipe out these relations and you annihilate all society, and your Prometheus is nothing but a ghost without arms or legs; that is, without automatic workshops, without division of labour—in a word, without everything that you gave him to start with in order to make him obtain this surplus left by labour.

If then, in theory, it sufficed to interpret, as M. Proudhon does, the formula of the surplus left by labour in the equalitarian sense, without taking into account the actual conditions of production, it should suffice, in practice, to share out equally among the workers all the wealth at present acquired, without changing in any way the present conditions of production. Such a distribution would certainly not assure a high degree of comfort to the individual participants.

But M. Proudhon is not so pessimistic as one might think. As proportionality is everything for him, he has to see in his fully equipped Prometheus, that is, in present-day society, the beginnings of a realisation of his favourite idea.

> "But everywhere, too, the progress of wealth, that is, the *proportion of values,* is the dominant law; and when economists hold up against the complaints of the social party the progressive growth of the public wealth, and the improved conditions of even the most unfortunate classes, they unwittingly proclaim a truth which is the condemnation of their theories." [I 80]

What is, actually, collective wealth, public fortune? It is the wealth of the bourgeoisie—not that of each bourgeois in particular. Well, the economists have done nothing but show how, in the existing relations of production, the wealth of the bourgeoisie has grown and must grow still further. As for the working classes, it still remains a very debatable question whether their condition has improved as a result of the increase in so-called public wealth. If the economists, in support of their optimism, cite the example of the English workers employed in the cotton industry, they see the condition of the latter only in the rare moments of trade prosperity. These moments of prosperity are to the periods of crisis and stagnation in the "correct proportion" of 3 to 10. But perhaps also, in speaking of improvement, the economists were thinking of the millions of workers who had to perish in the East Indies so as to procure for the million and a half workers employed in the same industry in England three years' prosperity out of ten.

As for the temporary participation in the increase of public wealth, that is a different matter. The fact of temporary participation is explained by the theory of the economists. It is the confirmation of this theory and not its "condemnation", as M. Proudhon calls it. If there were anything to be condemned, it would surely be the system of M. Proudhon, who would reduce the worker, as we have shown, to the minimum wage, in spite of the increase in wealth. It is only by reducing the worker to the minimum wage that he would be able to apply the correct proportion of values, of "value constituted" by labour time. It is because wages, as a result of competition, oscillate now above, now below, the price of food necessary for the sustenance of the worker, that he can participate to a certain extent in the development of collective wealth, and can also perish from want. This is the whole theory of the economists who have no illusions on the subject.

After his lengthy digressions on railways, on Prometheus, and on the new society to be reconstituted on "constituted value", M. Proudhon collects himself; emotion overpowers him and he cries in fatherly tones:

> "I *beseech* the economists to question themselves for one moment, in the silence of their hearts—far from the prejudices that trouble them and regardless of the employment they are engaged in or hope to obtain, of the interests they subserve, or the approbation to which they aspire, of the honours which nurse their vanity—let them say whether before this day the principle that all labour must leave a surplus appeared to them with this chain of premises and consequences that we have revealed." [I 80]

CHAPTER II

THE METAPHYSICS OF POLITICAL ECONOMY

§ 1. THE METHOD

Here we are, in the heart of Germany. We shall now have to talk metaphysics while talking political economy. And in this again we shall but follow M. Proudhon's "contradictions". Just now he forced us to speak English, to become pretty well English ourselves. Now the scene is changing. M. Proudhon is transporting us to our dear fatherland and is forcing us, whether we like it or not, to become German again.

If the Englishman transforms men into hats, the German transforms hats into ideas. The Englishman is Ricardo, a rich banker and distinguished economist; the German is Hegel, an ordinary professor of philosophy at the University of Berlin.

Louis XV, the last absolute monarch and representative of the decadence of French royalty, had attached to his person a physician who was himself France's first economist. This physician, this economist, represented the imminent and certain triumph of the French bourgeoisie. Doctor Quesnay made a science out of political economy; he summarised it in his famous *Tableau économique.* Besides the thousand and one commentaries on this table which have appeared, we possess one by the doctor himself. It is the "Analyse du *Tableau économique*", followed by "seven *observations importantes*".

M. Proudhon is another Dr. Quesnay. He is the Quesnay of the metaphysics of political economy.

Now metaphysics—indeed all philosophy—can be summed up, according to Hegel, in method. We must, therefore, try to elucidate the method of M. Proudhon, which is at least as obscure as *Tableau économique.* It is for this reason that we are making seven more or less important observations. If Dr. Proudhon is not pleased with our observations, well, then, he will have to become an Abbé Baudeau[a] and give the "explanation of the economico-metaphysical method" himself.

First Observation

"We are not giving a *history according to the order in time,* but *according to the sequence of ideas.* Economic *phases* or *categories* are in their *manifestation* sometimes contemporary, sometimes inverted.... Economic theories have nonetheless their *logical sequence* and their *serial relation in the understanding*: it is this order that we flatter ourselves to have discovered." (Proudhon, tome I, pp. 145 and 146.)

M. Proudhon most certainly wanted to frighten the French by flinging quasi-Hegelian phrases at them. So we have to deal with two men: first with M. Proudhon, and then with Hegel. How does M. Proudhon distinguish himself from other economists? And what part does Hegel play in M. Proudhon's political economy?

Economists express the relations of bourgeois production, the division of labour, credit, money, etc., as fixed, immutable, eternal categories. M. Proudhon, who has these ready-made categories before him, wants to explain to us the act of formation, the genesis of these categories, principles, laws, ideas, thoughts.

Economists explain how production takes place in the above-mentioned relations, but what they do not explain is how these relations themselves are produced, that is, the historical movement which gave them birth. M. Proudhon, taking these relations for principles, categories, abstract thoughts, has merely to put into *order* these thoughts, which are to be found alphabetically arranged at the end of every treatise on political economy. The economists' material is the active, energetic life of man; M. Proudhon's material is the dogmas of the economists. But the moment we cease to pursue the historical movement of production relations, of which the categories are but the theoretical expression, the moment we want to see in these categories no more than ideas, spontaneous thoughts, independent of real relations, we are forced to attribute the origin of these thoughts to the movement of pure reason. How does pure, eternal, impersonal reason give rise to these thoughts? How does it proceed in order to produce them?

If we had M. Proudhon's intrepidity in the matter of Hegelianism we should say: it is distinguished in itself from itself. What does this mean? Impersonal reason, having outside itself neither a base on which it can pose itself, nor an object to which it can oppose itself,

[a] An allusion to the book: N. Baudeau, *Explication du Tableau économique.*—*Ed.*

nor a subject with which it can compose itself, is forced to turn head over heels, in posing itself, opposing itself and composing itself—position, opposition, composition. Or, to speak Greek—we have thesis, antithesis and synthesis. For those who do not know the Hegelian language, we shall give the ritual formula: affirmation, negation and negation of the negation. That is what language means. It is certainly not Hebrew (with due apologies to M. Proudhon); but it is the language of this pure reason, separate from the individual. Instead of the ordinary individual with his ordinary manner of speaking and thinking we have nothing but this ordinary manner purely and simply—without the individual.

Is it surprising that everything, in the final abstraction—for we have here an abstraction, and not an analysis—presents itself as a logical category? Is it surprising that, if you let drop little by little all that constitutes the individuality of a house, leaving out first of all the materials of which it is composed, then the form that distinguishes it, you end up with nothing but a body; that, if you leave out of account the limits of this body, you soon have nothing but a space—that if, finally, you leave out of account the dimensions of this space, there is absolutely nothing left but pure quantity, the logical category? If we abstract thus from every subject all the alleged accidents, animate or inanimate, men or things, we are right in saying that in the final abstraction, the only substance left is the logical categories. Thus the metaphysicians who, in making these abstractions, think they are making analyses, and who, the more they detach themselves from things, imagine themselves to be getting all the nearer to the point of penetrating to their core—these metaphysicians in turn are right in saying that things here below are embroideries of which the logical categories constitute the canvas. This is what distinguishes the philosopher from the Christian. The Christian, in spite of logic, has only one incarnation of the *Logos*; with the philosopher there is no end to incarnations. If all that exists, all that lives on land and under water can be reduced by abstraction to a logical category—if the whole real world can be drowned thus in a world of abstractions, in the world of logical categories—who need be astonished at it?

All that exists, all that lives on land and under water, exists and lives only by some kind of movement. Thus the movement of history produces social relations; industrial movement gives us industrial products, etc.

Just as by dint of abstraction we have transformed everything into a logical category, so one has only to make an abstraction of every characteristic distinctive of different movements to attain movement in its abstract condition—purely formal movement, the purely logical formula of movement. If one finds in logical categories the substance of all things, one imagines one has found in the logical formula of movement the *absolute method*, which not only explains all things, but also implies the movement of things.

It is of this absolute method that Hegel speaks in these terms:

> "Method is the absolute, unique, supreme, infinite force, which no object can resist; it is the tendency of reason to find itself again, to recognise itself in every object."[80] (*Logic*,[a] Vol. III.)

All things being reduced to a logical category, and every movement, every act of production, to method, it follows naturally that every aggregate of products and production, of objects and of movement, can be reduced to applied metaphysics. What Hegel has done for religion, law, etc., M. Proudhon seeks to do for political economy.

So what is this absolute method? The abstraction of movement. What is the abstraction of movement? Movement in abstract condition. What is movement in abstract condition? The purely logical formula of movement or the movement of pure reason. Wherein does the movement of pure reason consist? In posing itself, opposing itself, composing itself; in formulation itself as thesis, antithesis, synthesis; or, yet again, in affirming itself, negating itself and negating its negation.

How does reason manage to affirm itself, to pose itself as a definite category? That is the business of reason itself and of its apologists.

But once it has managed to pose itself as a thesis, this thesis, this thought, opposed to itself, splits up into two contradictory thoughts—the positive and the negative, the yes and the no. The struggle between these two antagonistic elements comprised in the antithesis constitutes the dialectic movement. The yes becoming no, the no becoming yes, the yes becoming both yes and no, the no becoming both no and yes, the contraries balance, neutralise, paralyse each other. The fusion of these two contradictory thoughts constitutes a new thought, which is the synthesis of them. This thought splits up once again into two contradictory thoughts, which in turn fuse into a new synthesis. Of this travail is born a group of thoughts. This group of thoughts follows the same dialectic movement as the simple category, and has a contradictory group as antithesis. Of these two groups of thoughts is born a new group of thoughts, which is the synthesis of them.

---

[a] G. W. F. Hegel, *Wissenschaft der Logik.*— *Ed.*

Just as from the dialectic movement of the simple categories is born the group, so from the dialectic movement of the groups is born the series, and from the dialectic movement of the series is born the entire system.

Apply this method to the categories of political economy, and you have the logic and metaphysics of political economy, or, in other words, you have the economic categories that everybody knows translated into a little-known language which makes them look as if they had newly blossomed forth in an intellect of pure reason; so much do these categories seem to engender one another, to be linked up and intertwined with one another by the very working of the dialectic movement. The reader must not get alarmed at these metaphysics with all their scaffolding of categories, groups, series and systems. M. Proudhon, in spite of all the trouble he has taken to scale the heights of the *system of contradictions*, has never been able to raise himself above the first two rungs of simple thesis and antithesis; and even these he has mounted only twice, and on one of these two occasions he fell over backwards.

Up to now we have expounded only the dialectics of Hegel. We shall see later how M. Proudhon has succeeded in reducing it to the meanest proportions. Thus, for Hegel, all that has happened and is still-happening is only just what is happening in his own mind. Thus the philosophy of history is nothing but the history of philosophy, of his own philosophy. There is no longer a "history according to the order in time", there is only "the sequence of ideas in the understanding". He thinks he is constructing the world by the movement of thought, whereas he is merely reconstructing systematically and classifying by the absolute method the thoughts which are in the minds of all.

Second Observation

Economic categories are only the theoretical expressions, the abstractions of the social relations of production. M. Proudhon, holding things upside down like a true philosopher, sees in actual relations nothing but the incarnation of these principles, of these categories, which were slumbering—so M. Proudhon the philosopher tells us—in the bosom of the "impersonal reason of humanity".

M. Proudhon the economist understands very well that men make cloth, linen or silk materials in definite relations of production. But what he has not understood is that these definite social relations are just as much produced by men as linen, flax, etc. Social relations are closely bound up with productive forces. In acquiring new productive forces men change their mode of production; and in changing their mode of production, in changing the way of earning their living, they change all their social relations. The hand-mill gives you society with the feudal lord; the steam-mill, society with the industrial capitalist.

The same men who establish their social relations in conformity with their material productivity, produce also principles, ideas and categories, in conformity with their social relations.

Thus these ideas, these categories, are as little eternal as the relations they express. They are *historical and transitory products.*

There is a continual movement of growth in productive forces, of destruction in social relations, of formation in ideas; the only immutable thing is the abstraction of movement—*mors immortalis.*[a]

Third Observation

The production relations of every society form a whole. M. Proudhon considers economic relations as so many social phases, engendering one another, resulting one from the other like the antithesis from the thesis, and realising in their logical sequence the impersonal reason of humanity.

The only drawback to this method is that when he comes to examine a single one of these phases, M. Proudhon cannot explain it without having recourse to all the other relations of society; which relations, however, he has not yet made his dialectic movement engender. When, after that, M. Proudhon, by means of pure reason, proceeds to give birth to these other phases, he treats them as if they were newborn babes. He forgets that they are of the same age as the first.

Thus, to arrive at the constitution of value, which for him is the basis of all economic evolutions, he could not do without division of labour, competition, etc. Yet in the *series,* in the *understanding* of M. Proudhon, in the *logical sequence,* these relations did not yet exist.

In constructing the edifice of an ideological system by means of the categories of political economy, the limbs of the social system are

[a] These words are from Lucretius' poem *On the Nature of Things,* Book III, line 882 ("mortalem vitam mors immortalis ademit"— "mortal life has been usurped by death the immortal").— *Ed.*

dislocated. The different limbs of society are converted into so many separate societies, following one upon the other. How, indeed, could the single logical formula of movement, of sequence, of time, explain the structure of society, in which all relations coexist simultaneously and support one another?

Fourth Observation

Let us see now to what modifications M. Proudhon subjects Hegel's dialectics when he applies it to political economy.

For him, M. Proudhon, every economic category has two sides—one good, the other bad. He looks upon these categories as the petty bourgeois looks upon the great men of history: *Napoleon* was a great man; he did a lot of good; he also did a lot of harm.

The *good side* and the *bad side*, the *advantages* and the *drawbacks*, taken together form for M. Proudhon the *contradiction* in every economic category.

The problem to be solved: to keep the good side, while eliminating the bad.

Slavery is an economic category like any other. Thus it also has its two sides. Let us leave alone the bad side and talk about the good side of slavery. Needless to say we are dealing only with direct slavery, with Negro slavery in Surinam, in Brazil, in the Southern States of North America.

Direct slavery is just as much the pivot of bourgeois industry as machinery, credits, etc. Without slavery you have no cotton; without cotton you have no modern industry. It is slavery that gave the colonies their value; it is the colonies that created world trade, and it is world trade that is the precondition of large-scale industry. Thus slavery is an economic category of the greatest importance.

Without slavery North America, the most progressive of countries, would be transformed into a patriarchal country. Wipe North America off the map of the world, and you will have anarchy—the complete decay of modern commerce and civilisation. Cause slavery to disappear and you will have wiped America off the map of nations.*

* This was perfectly correct for the year 1847. At that time the world trade of the United States was limited mainly to import of immigrants and industrial products, and export of cotton and tobacco, i.e., of the products of southern slave labour. The Northern States produced mainly corn and meat for the slave States. It was only when the North produced corn and meat for export and also became an industrial country, and when the American cotton monopoly had to face powerful competition, in In-

Thus slavery, because it is an economic category, has always existed among the institutions of the peoples. Modern nations have been able only to disguise slavery in their own countries, but they have imposed it without disguise upon the New World.

What would M. Proudhon do to save slavery? He would formulate the *problem* thus: preserve the good side of this economic category, eliminate the bad.

Hegel has no problems to formulate. He has only dialectics. M. Proudhon has nothing of Hegel's dialectics but the language. For him the dialectic movement is the dogmatic distinction between good and bad.

Let us for a moment consider M. Proudhon himself as a category. Let us examine his good and his bad side, his advantages and his drawbacks.

If he has the advantage over Hegel of setting problems which he reserves the right of solving for the greater good of humanity, he has the drawback of being stricken with sterility when it is a question of engendering a new category by dialectical birth-throes. What constitutes dialectical movement is the coexistence of two contradictory sides, their conflict and their fusion into a new category. The very setting of the problem of eliminating the bad side cuts short the dialectical movement. It is not the category which is posed and opposed to itself, by its contradictory nature, it is M. Proudhon who gets excited, perplexed and frets and fumes between the two sides of the category.

Caught thus in a blind alley, from which it is difficult to escape by legal means, M. Proudhon takes a real flying leap which transports him at one bound into a new category. Then it is that to his astonished gaze is revealed the *serial relation in the understanding.*

He takes the first category that comes handy and attributes to it arbitrarily the quality of supplying a remedy for the drawbacks of the category to be purified. Thus, if we are to believe M. Proudhon, taxes remedy the drawbacks of monopoly; the balance of trade, the drawbacks of taxes; landed property, the drawbacks of credit.

By taking the economic categories thus successively, one by one, and making one the *antidote* to the other, M. Proudhon manages to make with this mixture of contradictions and antidotes to contradictions, two volumes of contradictions, which he rightly entitles: *Le Système des contradictions économiques.*

dia, Egypt, Brazil, etc., that the abolition of slavery became possible. And even then this led to the ruin of the South, which did not succeed in replacing the open Negro slavery by the disguised slavery of Indian and Chinese coolies, *F. E.* [*Note to the German edition, 1885.*]

Fifth Observation

"In the absolute reason all these ideas ... are equally simple, and general.... In fact, we attain knowledge only by a *sort of scaffolding* of our ideas. But truth in itself is independent of these dialectical symbols and free from the combinations of our minds." (Proudhon, tome II, p. 97.)

Here all of a sudden, by a kind of switch-over of which we now know the secret, the metaphysics of political economy has become an illusion. Never has M. Proudhon spoken more truly. Indeed, from the moment the process of the dialectic movement is reduced to the simple process of opposing good to bad, of posing problems tending to eliminate the bad, and of administering one category as an antidote to another, the categories are deprived of all spontaneity; the idea "no longer *functions*"; there is no life left in it. It is no longer posed or decomposed into categories. The sequence of categories has become a sort of *scaffolding*. Dialectics has ceased to be the movement of absolute reason. There is no longer any dialectics but only, at the most, absolutely pure morality.

When M. Proudhon spoke of the *serial relation in the understanding*, of the *logical sequence of categories*, he declared positively that he did not want to give *history according to the order in time*, that is, in M. Proudhon's view, the historical sequence in which the categories have *manifested* themselves. Thus for him everything happened in the *pure ether of reason*. Everything was to be derived from this ether by means of dialectics. Now that he has to put this dialectics into practice, his reason is in default. M. Proudhon's dialectics runs counter to Hegel's dialectics, and now we have M. Proudhon reduced to saying that the order in which he gives the economic categories is no longer the order in which they engender one another. Economic evolutions are no longer the evolutions of reason itself.

What then does M. Proudhon give us? Real history, which is, according to M. Proudhon's understanding, the sequence in which the categories have *manifested* themselves in order of time? No! History as it takes place in the idea itself? Still less! That is, neither the profane history of the categories, nor their sacred history! What history does he give us then? The history of his own contradictions. Let us see how they go, and how they drag M. Proudhon in their train.

Before entering upon this examination, which gives rise to the sixth important observation, we have yet another, less important observation to make.

Let us admit with M. Proudhon that real history, history according to the order in time, is the historical sequence in which ideas, categories and principles have manifested themselves.

Each principle has had its own century in which to manifest itself. The principle of authority, for example, had the eleventh century, just as the principle of individualism had the eighteenth century. In logical sequence, it was the century that belonged to the principle, and not the principle that belonged to the century. In other words it was the principle that made the history, and not the history that made the principle. When, consequently, in order to save principles as much as to save history, we ask ourselves why a particular principle was manifested in the eleventh or in the eighteenth century rather than in any other, we are necessarily forced to examine minutely what men were like in the eleventh century, what they were like in the eighteenth, what were their respective needs, their productive forces, their mode of production, the raw materials of their production—in short, what were the relations between man and man which resulted from all these conditions of existence. To get to the bottom of all these questions—what is this but to draw up the real, profane history of men in every century and to present these men as both the authors and the actors of their own drama? But the moment you present men as the actors and authors of their own history, you arrive—by a detour—at the real starting point, because you have abandoned those eternal principles of which you spoke at the outset.

M. Proudhon has not even gone far enough along the sideroad which an ideologist takes to reach the main road of history.

Sixth Observation

Let us take the sideroad with M. Proudhon.

We shall concede that economic relations, viewed as *immutable laws, eternal principles, ideal categories,* existed before active and energetic men did; we shall concede further that these laws, principles and categories had, since the beginning of time, slumbered "in the impersonal reason of humanity". We have already seen that, with all these changeless and motionless eternities, there is no history left; there is at most history in the idea, that is, history reflected in the dialectic movement of pure reason. M. Proudhon, by saying that, in the dialectic movement, ideas are no longer "*differentiated*", has done away with both the *shadow of movement* and the *movement of shadows,* by means of which one could still have created at least a semblance of history. Instead of that, he imputes to history his own impotence. He lays the blame on everything, even the French language.

"It is inexact then," says M. Proudhon the philosopher, "to say that something *appears*, that something *is produced*: in civilisation as in the universe, everything has existed, has acted, from eternity.... *This applies to the whole of social economy*." (Tome II. p. 102.)

So great is the productive force of the contradictions which *function* and which make M. Proudhon function, that, in trying to explain history, he is forced to deny it; in trying to explain the successive appearance of social relations, he denies that *anything* can *appear*: in trying to explain production, with all its phases, he questions whether *anything can be produced*!

Thus, for M. Proudhon, there is no longer any history: no longer any sequence of ideas. And yet his book still exists; and it is precisely that book which is, to use his own expression, "*history according to the sequence of ideas*". How shall we find a formula, for M. Proudhon is a man of formulas, to help him to clear all these contradictions *in one leap*?

To this end he has invented a new reason, which is neither the pure and virgin absolute reason, nor the common reason of men living and acting in different periods, but a reason quite apart—the reason of the person-society—of the subject, *humanity*—which under the pen of M. Proudhon figures at times also as "*social genius*", "*general reason*", or finally as "*human reason*". This reason, decked out under so many names, betrays itself nevertheless, at every moment, as the individual reason of M. Proudhon, with its good and its bad side, its antidotes and its problems.

"Human reason does not create truth", hidden in the depths of absolute, eternal reason. It can only unveil it. But such truths as it has unveiled up to now are incomplete, insufficient and consequently contradictory. Hence, economic categories, being themselves truths discovered, revealed by human reason, by social genius, are equally incomplete and contain within themselves the germ of contradiction. Before M. Proudhon, social genius saw only the *antagonistic elements*, and not the *synthetic formula*, both hidden simultaneously in *absolute reason*. Economic relations, which merely realise on earth these insufficient truths, these incomplete categories, these contradictory notions, are consequently contradictory in themselves, and present two sides, one good, the other bad.

To find complete truth, the notion, in all its fullness, the synthetic formula that is to annihilate the antinomy, this is the problem of social genius. This again is why, in M. Proudhon's illusion, this same social genius has been carried from one category to another without ever having been able, despite all its battery of categories, to snatch from God, from absolute reason, a synthetic formula.

"At first, society" (social genius) "poses a primary fact, puts forward a *hypothesis*... a veritable antinomy, whose antagonistic results develop in the social economy in the same way as its consequences could have been deduced in the mind; so that industrial movement, following in all things the deduction of ideas, splits up into two currents, one of useful effects, the other of subversive results.... To bring harmony into the constitution of this two-sided principle, and to solve this antinomy, society gives rise to a *second*, which will soon be followed by a third; and the *progress of social genius* will take place in this manner, until, having exhausted all its contradictions—I suppose, but it is not proved that there is a limit to human contradictions—it returns in one leap to all its former positions and in *a single formula* solves all its problems." (Tome I, p. 133.)

Just as the *antithesis* was before turned into an *antidote*, so now the *thesis* becomes a *hypothesis*. This change of terms, coming from M. Proudhon, has no longer anything surprising for us! Human reason, which is anything but pure, having only incomplete vision, encounters at every step new problems to be solved. Every new thesis which it discovers in absolute reason and which is the negation of the first thesis, becomes for it a synthesis, which it accepts rather naïvely as the solution of the problem in question. It is thus that this reason frets and fumes in ever renewing contradictions until, coming to the end of the contradictions, it perceives that all its theses and syntheses are merely contradictory hypotheses. In its perplexity, "human reason, social genius, returns in one leap to all its former positions and in a single formula solves all its problems". This unique formula, by the way, constitutes M. Proudhon's true discovery. It is *constituted value*.

Hypotheses are made only in view of some aim. The aim that social genius, speaking through the mouth of M. Proudhon, set itself in the first place, was to eliminate the bad in every economic category, in order to have nothing left but the good. For it, the good, the supreme good, the real practical aim, is *equality*. And why did the social genius aim at equality rather than inequality, fraternity, Catholicism, or any other principle? Because "humanity has successively realised so many separate hypotheses only in view of a superior hypothesis" [I 12], which precisely is equality. In other words: because equality is M. Proudhon's ideal. He imagines that the division of labour, credit, the workshop—all economic relations—were invented merely for the benefit of equality, and yet they always ended up by turning against it. Since history and the fiction of M. Proudhon contradict each other at every step, the latter concludes that there is a contradiction. If there is a contradiction, it exists only between his fixed idea and real movement.

Henceforth the good side of an economic relation is that which affirms equality; the bad side, that which negates it and affirms inequality. Every new category is a hypothesis of the social genius to eliminate the inequality engendered by the preceding hypothesis. In short, equality is the *primordial intention*, the *mystical tendency*, the *providential aim* that the social genius has constantly before its eyes as it whirls in the circle of economic contradictions. Thus *Providence* is the locomotive which makes the whole of M. Proudhon's economic baggage move better than his pure and volatilised reason. He has devoted to providence a whole chapter, which follows the one on taxes.[81]

Providence, providential aim, this is the great word used today to explain the march of history. In fact, this word explains nothing. It is at most a rhetorical form, one of the various ways of paraphrasing facts.

It is a fact that in Scotland landed property acquired a new value through the development of English industry. This industry opened up new outlets for wool. In order to produce wool on a large scale, arable land had to be transformed into pastures. To effect this transformation, the estates had to be concentrated. To concentrate the estates, small holdings had first to be abolished, thousands of tenants had to be driven from their native soil and a few shepherds in charge of millions of sheep to be installed in their place. Thus, by successive transformations, landed property in Scotland has resulted in men being driven out by sheep. Now say that the providential aim of the institution of landed property in Scotland was to have men driven out by sheep, and you will have made providential history.

Of course, the tendency towards equality belongs to our century. To say now that all former centuries, with entirely different needs, means of production, etc., worked providentially for the realisation of equality is, first of all, to substitute the means and the men of our century for the men and the means of earlier centuries and to misunderstand the historical movement by which the successive generations transformed the results acquired by the generations that preceded them. Economists know very well that the very thing that was for the one a finished product was for the other but the raw material for new production.

Suppose, as M. Proudhon does, that social genius produced, or rather improvised, the feudal lords with the providential aim of transforming the *settlers* into *responsible* and *equally-placed workers*: and you will have effected a substitution of aims and of persons worthy of the Providence that instituted landed property in Scotland, in order to give itself the malicious pleasure of having men driven out by sheep.

But since M. Proudhon takes such a tender interest in Providence, we refer him to the *Histoire de l'économie politique* of M. de Villeneuve-Bargemont, who likewise goes in pursuit of a providential aim. This aim, however, is not equality, but Catholicism.

Seventh and Last Observation

Economists have a singular method of procedure. There are only two kinds of institutions for them, artificial and natural. The institutions of feudalism are artificial institutions, those of the bourgeoisie are natural institutions. In this they resemble the theologians, who likewise establish two kinds of religion. Every religion which is not theirs is an invention of men, while their own is an emanation from God. When the economists say that present-day relations—the relations of bourgeois production—are natural, they imply that these are the relations in which wealth is created and productive forces developed in conformity with the laws of nature. These relations therefore are themselves natural laws independent of the influence of time. They are eternal laws which must always govern society. Thus there has been history, but there is no longer any. There has been history, since there were the institutions of feudalism, and in these institutions of feudalism we find quite different relations of production from those of bourgeois society, which the economists try to pass off as natural and as such, eternal.

Feudalism also had its proletariat—serfage, which contained all the germs of the bourgeoisie. Feudal production also had two antagonistic elements which are likewise designated by the name of the *good side* and the *bad side* of feudalism, irrespective of the fact that it is always the bad side that in the end triumphs over the good side. It is the bad side that produces the movement which makes history, by providing a struggle. If, during the epoch of the domination of feudalism, the economists, enthusiastic over the knightly virtues, the beautiful harmony between rights and duties, the patriarchal life of the towns, the prosperous condition of domestic industry in the countryside, the development of industry organised into corporations, guilds and fraternities, in short, everything that constitutes the good side of feudalism, had set themselves the problem of eliminating everything that cast a shadow on this picture—serfdom, privileges, anarchy—what would have happened? All the elements which called forth the struggle would have been destroyed, and the development of the bourgeoisie nipped in the bud. One would have set oneself the absurd problem of eliminating history.

After the triumph of the bourgeoisie there was no longer any question of the good or the bad side of feudalism. The bourgeoisie took possession of the productive forces it had developed under feudalism. All the old economic forms, the corresponding civil relations, the political system which was the official expression of the old civil society, were smashed.

Thus feudal production, to be judged properly, must be considered as a mode of production founded on antagonism. It must be shown how wealth was produced within this antagonism, how the productive forces were developed at the same time as class antagonisms, how one of the classes, the bad side, the drawback of society, went on growing until the material conditions for its emancipation had attained full maturity. Is not this as good as saying that the mode of production, the relations in which productive forces are developed, are anything but eternal laws, but that they correspond to a definite development of men and of their productive forces, and that a change in men's productive forces necessarily brings about a change in their[a] relations of production? As the main thing is not to be deprived of the fruits of civilisation, of the acquired productive forces, the traditional forms in which they were produced must be smashed. From this moment the revolutionary class becomes conservative.

The bourgeoisie begins with a proletariat which is itself a relic of the proletariat[b] of feudal times. In the course of its historical development, the bourgeoisie necessarily develops its antagonistic character, which at first is more or less disguised, existing only in a latent state. As the bourgeoisie develops, there develops in its bosom a new proletariat, a modern proletariat; there develops a struggle between the proletarian class and the bourgeois class, a struggle which, before being felt, perceived, appreciated, understood, avowed and proclaimed aloud by both sides, expresses itself, to start with, merely in partial and momentary conflicts, in subversive acts.

---

[a] In the 1847 edition the word "leurs" ("their") is not used; in the copy with corrections in Marx's hand and the one presented to N. Utina the word "leurs" is inserted instead of "les" ("the"). The correction was reproduced in the German edition of 1885 and the French edition of 1896.— *Ed.*

[b] In the copy with corrections in Marx's hand the words "du proletariat" ("of the proletariat") are underscored and the words "de la classe travailleuse" ("of the class of workers") are written in Engels' hand in the margin. These latter words are reproduced in the copy presented to N. Utina.— *Ed.*

On the other hand, if all the members of the modern bourgeoisie have the same interests inasmuch as they form a class as against another class, they have opposite, antagonistic interests inasmuch as they stand face to face with one another. This opposition of interests results from the economic conditions of their bourgeois life. From day to day it thus becomes clearer that the production relations in which the bourgeoisie moves have not a simple, uniform character, but a dual character; that in the selfsame relations in which wealth is produced, poverty is produced also; that in the selfsame relations in which there is a development of the productive forces, there is also a force producing repression; that these relations produce *bourgeois wealth*, i. e., the wealth of the bourgeois class, only by continually annihilating the wealth of the individual members of this class and by producing an ever-growing proletariat.

The more the antagonistic character comes to light, the more the economists, the scientific representatives of bourgeois production, find themselves in conflict with their own theory; and different schools arise.

We have the *fatalist* economists, who in their theory are as indifferent to what they call the drawbacks of bourgeois production as the bourgeois themselves are in practice to the sufferings of the proletarians who help them to acquire wealth. In this fatalist school there are Classics and Romantics. The Classics, like Adam Smith and Ricardo, represent a bourgeoisie which, while still struggling with the relics of feudal society, works only to purge economic relations of feudal taints, to increase the productive forces and to give a new upsurge to industry and commerce. The proletariat that takes part in this struggle and is absorbed in this feverish labour experiences only passing, accidental sufferings, and itself regards them as such. Economists like Adam Smith and Ricardo, who are the historians of this epoch, have no other mission than that of showing how wealth is acquired in bourgeois production relations, of formulating these relations into categories, into laws, and of showing how superior these laws, these categories, are for the production of wealth to the laws and categories of feudal society. Poverty is in their eyes merely the pang which accompanies every childbirth, in nature as in industry.

The Romantics belong to our own age, in which the bourgeoisie is in direct opposition to the proletariat; in which poverty is engendered in as great abundance as wealth. The economists now pose as blasé fatalists, who, from their elevated position, cast a proudly disdainful glance at the human machines who manufacture wealth. They copy all the developments given by their predecessors, and the indifference which in the latter was merely naïveté becomes in them coquetry.

Next comes the *humanitarian school*, which takes to heart the bad side of present-day production relations. It seeks, by way of easing its conscience, to palliate even if slightly the real contrasts; it sincerely deplores the distress of the proletariat, the unbridled competition of the bourgeois among themselves; it counsels the workers to be sober, to work hard and to have few children; it advises the bourgeois to put a judicious ardour into production. The whole theory of this school rests on interminable distinctions between theory and practice, between principles and results, between idea and application, between content and form, between essence and reality, between law and fact, between the good side and the bad side.

The *philanthropic* school is the humanitarian school carried to perfection. It denies the necessity of antagonism; it wants to turn all men into bourgeois; it wants to realise theory insofar as it is distinguished from practice and contains no antagonism. It goes without saying that, in theory, it is easy to make an abstraction of the contradictions that are met with at every moment in actual reality. This theory would therefore become idealised reality. The philanthropists, then, want to retain the categories which express bourgeois relations, without the antagonism which constitutes them and is inseparable from them. They think they are seriously fighting bourgeois practice, and they are more bourgeois than the others.

Just as the *economists* are the scientific representatives of the bourgeois class, so the *socialists* and the *Communists* are the theoreticians of the proletarian class. So long as the proletariat is not yet sufficiently developed to constitute itself as a class, and consequently so long as the very struggle of the proletariat with the bourgeoisie has not yet assumed a political character, and the productive forces are not yet sufficiently developed in the bosom of the bourgeoisie itself to enable us to catch a glimpse of the material conditions necessary for the emancipation of the proletariat and for the formation of a new society, these theoreticians are merely utopians who, to meet the wants of the oppressed classes, improvise systems and go in search of a regenerating science. But in the measure that history moves forward, and with it the struggle of the proletariat assumes clearer outlines, they no longer need to seek science in their minds; they have only to take note of what is happening before their eyes and to become its mouthpiece. So long as they look for science and merely make systems, so long as they are at the beginning of the struggle, they see in poverty nothing but poverty, without seeing in it the revolutionary, subversive side, which will overthrow the old society. From the moment they see this side, science, which is produced by the historical movement and associating itself consciously with it, has ceased to be doctrinaire and has become revolutionary.

Let us return to M. Proudhon.

Every economic relation has a good and a bad side; it is the one point on which M. Proudhon does not give himself the lie. He sees the good side expounded by the economists; the bad side he sees denounced by the socialists. He borrows from the economists the necessity of eternal relations; he borrows from the socialists the illusion of seeing in poverty nothing but poverty. He is in agreement with both in wanting to fall back upon the authority of science. Science for him reduces itself to the slender proportions of a scientific formula; he is the man in search of formulas. Thus it is that M. Proudhon flatters himself on having given a criticism of both political economy and communism: he is beneath them both. Beneath the economists, since, as a philosopher who has at his elbow a magic formula, he thought he could dispense with going into purely economic details; beneath the socialists, because he has neither courage enough nor insight enough to rise, be it even speculatively, above the bourgeois horizon.

He wants to be the synthesis—he is a composite error.

He wants to soar as the man of science above the bourgeois and the proletarians; he is merely the petty bourgeois, continually tossed back and forth between capital and labour, political economy and communism.

§ 2. DIVISION OF LABOUR AND MACHINERY

The division of labour, according to M. Proudhon, opens the series of *economic evolutions.*

Good side of the division of labour { "Considered in its essence, the division of labour is the manner in which *equality* of conditions and of intelligence is realised." (Tome I, p. 93.)

Bad side of the division of labour	"The division of labour has become for us an instrument of poverty." (Tome I, p. 94.) Variant "Labour, by *dividing itself according to the law* which is peculiar to it and which is the primary condition of its fruitfulness, ends in the negation of its aims and destroys itself." (Tome I, p. 94.)
Problem to be solved	To find the "recomposition which wipes out the drawbacks of the division, while retaining its useful effects." (Tome I, p. 97.)

The division of labour is, according to M. Proudhon, an eternal law, a simple, abstract category. Therefore the abstraction, the idea, the word must suffice for him to explain the division of labour at different historical epochs. Castes, corporations, manufacture, large-scale industry must be explained by the single word *divide.* First study carefully the meaning of "divide", and you will have no need to study the numerous influences which give the division of labour a definite character in each epoch.

Certainly, it would be oversimplifying things to reduce them to M. Proudhon's categories. History does not proceed so categorically. It took three whole centuries in Germany to establish the first big division of labour, the separation of the towns from the country. In proportion as this one relation of town and country was modified, the whole of society was modified. To take only this one aspect of the division of labour, you have the republics of antiquity and you have Christian feudalism; you have old England with its barons and you have modern England with its cotton lords.[a] In the fourteenth and fifteenth centuries, when there were as yet no colonies, when America did not yet exist for Europe, when Asia existed only through the intermediary of Constantinople, when the Mediterranean was the centre of commercial activity, the division of labour had a very different form, a very different aspect from that of the seventeenth century, when the Spanish, the Portuguese, the Dutch, the English, and the French had colonies established in all parts of

[a] In the original the words "cotton lords" are given in English in parentheses after the French.— *Ed.*

the world. The extent of the market, its physiognomy, give to the division of labour at different periods a physiognomy, a character, which it would be difficult to deduce from the single word *divide*, from the idea, from the category.

"All economists since Adam Smith," says M. Proudhon, "have pointed out the *advantages* and *drawbacks* of the law of division, but insist much more on the first than on the second, because that was more serviceable for their optimism, and none of them has ever wondered what could be the drawbacks to a law.... How does the same principle, pursued vigorously to its consequences, lead to diametrically opposite results? Not one economist before or since A. Smith has even perceived that here was a problem to elucidate. Say goes to the length of recognising that in the division of labour the same cause that produces the good engenders the bad." [I 95-96]

Adam Smith goes further than M. Proudhon thinks. He saw clearly that

"the difference of natural talents in different men is, in reality, much less than we are aware of; and the very different genius which appears to distinguish men of different professions, when grown up to maturity, is not so much the *cause* as the *effect* of the division of labour".[a]

In principle, a porter differs less from a philosopher than a mastiff from a greyhound. It is the division of labour which has set a gulf between them. All this does not prevent M. Proudhon from saying elsewhere that Adam Smith had not the slightest idea of the drawbacks produced by the division of labour. It is this again that makes him say that J. B. Say was the *first* to recognise "that in the division of labour the same cause that produces the good engenders the bad". [I 96]

But let us listen to Lemontey; *Suum cuique.*

"M. J. B. Say has done me the honour of adopting in his excellent treatise on political economy the principle *that I brought to light* in this fragment on the moral influence of the division of labour. The somewhat frivolous title of my book[b] doubtless prevented him from citing me. It is only to this motive that I can attribute the silence of a writer too rich in his own stock to disavow so modest a loan." (Lemontey [,"Influence morale de la division du travail"], *Œuvres complètes*, tome I, p. 245, Paris, 1840.)

Let us do him this justice: Lemontey wittily exposed the regrettable consequences of the division of labour as it is constituted today, and M. Proudhon found nothing to add to it. But now that, through the fault of M. Proudhon, we have been drawn into this question of priority, let us say again, in passing, that long before M.

---

[a] A. Smith, *Recherches sur la nature et les causes de la richesse des nations*, t. I, Paris, 1802, pp. 33-34; Eng. ed., pp. 56-57.—*Ed.*

[b] P. E. Lemontey, *Raison, folie, chacun son mot; petit cours de morale mis a la portée des vieux enfants.— Ed.*

Lemontey, and seventeen years before Adam Smith, who was a pupil of A. Ferguson, the last-named gave a clear exposition of the subject in a chapter which deals specifically with the division of labour.

> "It may even be doubted, whether the measure of national capacity increases with the advancement of arts. Many mechanical arts ... succeed best under a total suppression of sentiment and reason; and ignorance is the mother of industry as well as of superstition. Reflection and fancy are subject to err; but a habit of moving the hand, or the foot, is independent of either. Manufactures, accordingly, prosper most, where the mind is least consulted, and where the workshop may, without any great effort of imagination, be considered as an engine, the parts of which are men.... The general officer may be a great proficient in the knowledge of war, while the skill of the soldier is confined to a few motions of the hand and the foot. The former may have gained what the latter has lost.... And thinking itself, in this age of separations, may become a peculiar craft." (A. Ferguson, *Essai sur l'histoire de la société civile*, Paris, 1783 [II 108, 109, 110; Eng. ed., pp. 280, 281].)

To bring this literary survey to a close, we expressly deny that "*all* economists have insisted far more on the advantages than on the drawbacks of the division of labour". It suffices to mention Sismondi.

Thus, as far as the *advantages* of the division of labour are concerned, M. Proudhon had nothing further to do than to paraphrase more or less pompously the general propositions known to everybody.

Let us now see how he derives from the division of labour, taken as a general law, as a category, as a thought, the *drawbacks* which are attached to it. How is it that this category, this law implies an unequal distribution of labour to the detriment of M. Proudhon's equalitarian system?

> "At this solemn hour of the division of labour, the storm winds begin to blow over humanity. Progress does not take place for all in an equal and uniform manner.... It begins by taking possession of a small number of the privileged.... It is this preference for persons on the part of progress that has for so long kept up the belief in the natural and providential inequality of conditions, has given rise to castes, and hierarchically constituted all societies." (Proudhon, tome I, p. 94.)

The division of labour created castes. Now, castes are the drawbacks of the division of labour; thus it is the division of labour that has engendered the drawbacks. *Quod erat demonstrandum.* Will you go further and ask what made the division of labour create castes, hierarchical constitutions and privileged persons? M. Proudhon will tell you: Progress. And what made progress? Limitation. Limitation, for M. Proudhon, is discrimination of persons on the part of progress.

After philosophy comes history. It is no longer either descriptive history or dialectical history, it is comparative history. M. Proudhon establishes a parallel between the present-day printing worker and the printing worker of the Middle Ages; between the worker of Creusot[82] and the country blacksmith; between the man of letters of today and the man of letters of the Middle Ages, and he weighs down the balance on the side of those who belong more or less to the division of labour as the Middle Ages constituted or transmitted it. He opposes the division of labour of one historical epoch to the division of labour of another historical epoch. Was that what M. Proudhon had to prove? No. He should have shown us the drawbacks of the division of labour in general, of the division of labour as a category. Besides, why stress this part of M. Proudhon's work, since a little later we shall see him formally retract all these alleged arguments?

"The first effect of fractional labour," continues M. Proudhon, "after the *depravation of the soul,* is the lengthening of the shifts, which grow in inverse ratio to the sum total of intelligence expended.... But as the length of the shifts cannot exceed sixteen to eighteen hours per day, since the compensation cannot be taken out of the time, it will be taken out of the price, and the wages will diminish.... What is certain, and the only thing for us to note, is that the *universal conscience* does not assess at the same rate the work of a foreman and the labour of an unskilled worker. It is *therefore* necessary to reduce the price of the day's work; so that the worker, after having been afflicted in his soul by a degrading function, cannot escape being struck in his body by the meagreness of his remuneration." [I 97, 98]

We pass over the logical value of these syllogisms, which Kant would call paralogisms which lead astray.

This is the substance of it:

The division of labour reduces the worker to a degrading function; to this degrading function corresponds a depraved soul; to the depravation of the soul is befitting an ever-increasing wage reduction. And to prove that this reduction is befitting to a depraved soul, M. Proudhon says, to relieve his conscience, that the universal conscience wills it thus. Is M. Proudhon's soul to be reckoned as a part of the universal conscience?

Machinery is, for M. Proudhon, "the logical antithesis of the division of labour" [I 135], and in support of his dialectics, he begins by transforming the machinery into the *workshop.*

After presupposing the modern workshop, in order to make poverty the outcome of the division of labour, M. Proudhon presupposes poverty engendered by the division of labour, in order to come to the workshop and be able to represent it as the dialectical negation of that poverty. After striking the worker morally by a *degrading function,* physically by the meagreness of the wage; after putting the worker under the *dependence of the foreman,* and debasing his work to the *labour of an unskilled worker*, he lays the blame again on the workshop and the machinery for *degrading* the worker "by giving him a *master*", and he completes his abasement by making him "sink from the rank of artisan to that of *navvy*". [I 164] Excellent dialectics! And if he only stopped there! But no, he has to have a new history of the division of labour, not any longer to derive the contradictions from it, but to reconstruct the workshop after his own fashion. To attain this end he finds himself compelled to forget all he has just said about division.

Labour is organised, is divided differently according to the instruments it has at its disposal. The hand-mill presupposes a different division of labour from the steam-mill. Thus it is slapping history in the face to want to begin with the division of labour in general, in order to arrive subsequently at a specific instrument of production, machinery.

Machinery is no more an economic category than the bullock that drags the plough. Machinery is merely a productive force. The modern workshop, which is based on the application of machinery, is a social production relation, an economic category.

Let us see now how things happen in M. Proudhon's brilliant imagination.

"In society, the incessant appearance of machinery is the antithesis, the inverse formula of the division of labour: it is the *protest* of the industrial genius against *fractional and homicidal labour.* What, actually, is a machine? *A way of uniting different portions of labour* which had been separated by the division of labour. Every machine can be defined as a summary of several operations.... Thus through the machine there will be a *restoration of the worker*.... Machinery, which in political economy places itself in contradiction to the division of labour, represents synthesis, which in the human mind is opposed to analysis.... Division merely separated the different parts of labour, letting each one devote himself to the speciality which most suited him; the workshop groups the workers according to the relation of each part to the whole.... It introduces the principle of authority in labour.... But this is not all; the *machine* or the *workshop,* after degrading the worker by giving him a master, completes his abasement by making him sink from the rank of artisan to that of navvy.... The period we are going through at the moment, that of machinery, is distinguished by a special characteristic, the *wage system.* The wage system is *subsequent* to the division of labour and to exchange." [I 135, 136, 161, 164, 161]

Just a simple remark to M. Proudhon. The separation of the different parts of labour, leaving to each one the opportunity of devoting himself to the speciality best suited to him—a separation which M. Proudhon dates from the beginning of the world—exists only in modern industry under the rule of competition.

M. Proudhon goes on to give us a most "interesting genealogy", to show how the workshop arose from the division of labour and the wage system from the workshop.

1) He supposes a man who "noticed that by dividing up production into its different parts and having each one performed by a separate worker" the forces of production would be multiplied.

2) This man, "grasping the thread of this idea, tells himself that, by forming a permanent group of workers selected for the special purpose he *sets* himself, he will obtain a more sustained production, etc." [I 161]

3) This man makes a *proposal* to other men, to make them grasp his idea and the thread of his idea.

4) This man, at the beginning of industry, deals on *terms of equality* with *his companions* who later become *his workmen.*

5) "One realises, in fact, that this original equality had rapidly to disappear in view of the advantageous position of the master and the dependence of the wage worker." [I 163]

There we have another example of M. Proudhon's *historical and descriptive method.*

Let us now examine, from the historical and economic point of view, whether the workshop or the machine really introduced the *principle of authority* in society subsequently to the division of labour; whether it rehabilitated the worker on the one hand, while submitting him to authority on the other; whether the machine is the recomposition of divided labour, the *synthesis* of labour as opposed to its *analysis.*

Society as a whole has this in common with the interior of a workshop, that it too has its division of labour. If one took as a model the division of labour in a modern workshop, in order to apply it to a whole society, the society best organised for the production of wealth would undoubtedly be that which had a single chief employer, distributing tasks to the different members of the community according to a previously fixed rule. But this is by no means the case. While inside the modern workshop the division of labour is meticulously regulated by the authority of the employer, modern society has no other rule, no other authority for the distribution of labour than free competition.

Under the patriarchal system, under the caste system, under the feudal and guild system, there was division of labour in the whole of society according to fixed rules. Were these rules established by a legislator? No. Originally born of the conditions of material production, they were raised to the status of laws only much later. In this way these different forms of the division of labour became so many bases of social organisation. As for the division of labour in the workshop, it was very little developed in all these forms of society.

It can even be laid down as a general rule that the less authority presides over the division of labour inside society, the more the division of labour develops inside the workshop, and the more it is subjected there to the authority of a single person. Thus authority in the workshop and authority in society, in relation to the division of labour, are in *inverse ratio* to each other.

The question now is what kind of workshop it is in which the occupations are very much separated, where each worker's task is reduced to a very simple operation, and where the authority, capital, groups and directs the work. How was this workshop brought into existence? In order to answer this question we shall have to examine how manufacturing industry, properly so-called, has developed. I am speaking here of that industry which is not yet modern industry, with its machinery, but which is already no longer the industry of the artisans of the Middle Ages, nor domestic industry. We shall not go into great detail: we shall merely give a few main points to show that history cannot be made with formulas.

One of the most indispensable conditions for the formation of manufacturing industry was the accumulation of capital, facilitated by the discovery of America and the import of its precious metals.

It is sufficiently proved that the increase in the means of exchange resulted in the depreciation of wages and land rents, on the one hand, and the growth of industrial profits on the other. In other words: to the extent that the propertied class and the class of workers, the feudal lords and the people, sank, to that extent the capitalist class, the bourgeoisie, rose.

There were yet other circumstances which contributed simultaneously to the development of manufacturing industry: the increase of commodities put into circulation from the moment trade penetrated to the East Indies by way of the Cape of Good Hope; the colonial system; the development of maritime trade.

Another point which has not yet been sufficiently appreciated in the history of manufacturing industry is the disbanding of the numerous retinues of feudal lords, whose subordinate ranks became vagrants before entering the workshop. The creation of the workshop was preceded by an almost universal vagrancy in the fifteenth and sixteenth centuries. The workshop found, besides, a powerful support in the many peasants who, continually driven from the country owing to the transformation of the fields into pastures and to the progress in agriculture which necessitated fewer hands for the tillage of the soil, went on congregating in the towns during whole centuries.

The growth of the market, the accumulation of capital, the modification in the social position of the classes, a large number of persons being deprived of their sources of income, all these are historical preconditions for the formation of manufacture. It was not, as M. Proudhon says, friendly agreements between equals that brought men together into the workshop. It was not even in the bosom of the old guilds that manufacture was born. It was the merchant that became the head of the modern workshop, and not the old guildmaster. Almost everywhere there was a desperate struggle between manufacture and the crafts.

The accumulation and concentration of instruments and workers preceded the development of the division of labour inside the workshop. Manufacture consisted much more in the bringing together of many workers and many crafts in one place, in one room, under the command of one capital, than in the analysis of labour and the adaptation of a special worker to a very simple task.

The utility of a workshop consisted much less in the division of labour as such than in the circumstance that work was done on a much larger scale, that many unnecessary expenses were saved, etc. At the end of the sixteenth and at the beginning of the seventeenth century, Dutch manufacture scarcely knew any division of labour.

The development of the division of labour supposes the assemblage of workers in a workshop. There is not one single example, whether in the sixteenth or in the seventeenth century, of the different branches of one and the same craft being exploited separately to such an extent that it would have sufficed to assemble them all in one place so as to obtain a complete, ready-made workshop. But once the men and the instruments had been brought together, the division of labour, such as it had existed in the form of the guilds, was reproduced, necessarily reflected inside the workshop.

For M. Proudhon, who sees things upside down, if he sees them at all, the division of labour, in Adam Smith's sense, precedes the workshop, which is a condition of its existence.

Machinery, properly so-called, dates from the end of the eighteenth century. Nothing is more absurd than to see in machinery the *antithesis* of the division of labour, the *synthesis* restoring unity to divided labour.

The machine is a uniting of the instruments of labour, and by no means a combination of different operations for the worker himself.

"When," by the division of labour, "each particular operation has been simplified to the use of a simple instrument, the linking-up of all these instruments, set in motion by a single engine, constitutes a machine." (Babbage, *Traité sur l'Économie des machines, etc.*, Paris, 1833 [p. 230; cf. Eng. ed., p. 171].)

Simple tools; accumulation of tools; composite tools; setting in motion of a composite tool by a single hand engine, by man; setting in motion of these instruments by natural forces; machines; system of machines having one motor; system of machines having an automatic motor—this is the progress of machinery.

The concentration of the instruments of production and the division of labour are as inseparable one from the other as are, in the political sphere, the concentration of public powers and the division of private interests. England, with the concentration of the land, this instrument of agricultural labour, has at the same time division of agricultural labour and the application of machinery to the exploitation of the soil. France, which has the division of the instruments, the small holdings system, has, in general, neither division of agricultural labour nor application of machinery to the soil.

For M. Proudhon the concentration of the instruments of labour is the negation of the division of labour. In reality we find again the reverse. As the concentration of instruments develops, the division develops also, and *vice versa.* This is why every big mechanical invention is followed by a greater division of labour, and each increase in the division of labour gives rise in turn to new mechanical inventions.

We need not recall the fact that the great progress of the division of labour began in England after the invention of machinery. Thus the weavers and spinners were for the most part peasants like those one still meets in backward countries. The invention of machinery brought about the separation of manufacturing industry from agricultural industry. The weaver and the spinner, united but lately in a single family, were separated by the machine. Thanks to the machine, the spinner can live in England while the weaver resides in the East Indies. Before the invention of machinery, the industry of a country was carried on chiefly with raw materials that were the products of its own soil; in England—wool, in Germany—flax, in France—silks and flax, in the East Indies and the Levant—cotton, etc. Thanks to the application of machinery and of steam, the division of labour was able to assume such dimensions that large-scale industry, detached from the national soil, depends entirely on the world market, on international exchange, on an international division of labour. Finally—the machine has so great an influence on the division of labour, that when, in the manufacture of some object, a means has been found to produce parts of it mechanically, the manufacture splits up immediately into two branches independent of each other.

Need we speak of the *providential* and philanthropic *aim* that M. Proudhon discovers in the invention and first application of machinery?

When in England the market had become so far developed that manual labour was no longer adequate, the need for machinery was felt. Then came the idea of applying mechanical science, already quite developed in the eighteenth century.

The automatic workshop opened its career with acts which were anything but philanthropic. Children were kept at work by means of the whip; they were made an object of traffic and contracts were undertaken with the orphanages. All the laws on the apprenticeship of workers were repealed, because, to use M. Proudhon's phraseology, there was no further need of *synthetic* workers. Finally, from 1825 onwards,[83] almost all the new inventions were the result of collisions between the worker and the employer who sought at all costs to depreciate the worker's specialised ability. After each new strike of any importance, there appeared a new machine. So little indeed did the worker see in the application of machinery a sort of rehabilitation, *restoration*—as M. Proudhon would say—that in the eighteenth century he resisted for a very long time the incipient domination of automation.

"Wyatt," says Doctor Ure, "... invented the series of fluted rollers (the spinning fingers usually ascribed to Arkwright).... The main difficulty did not ... lie so much in the invention of a proper self-acting mechanism ... as ... in training human beings to renounce their desultory habits of work, and to identify themselves with the unvarying regularity of the complex automation. To devise and administer a successful code of factory discipline, suited to the necessities of factory diligence, was the Herculean enterprise, the noble achievement of Arkwright."[a]

In short, with the introduction of machinery the division of labour inside society has increased, the task of the worker inside the workshop has been simplified, capital has been concentrated, the human being has been further dismembered.

When M. Proudhon wants to be an economist, and to abandon for a moment the "evolution in serial relation in the understanding", then he goes and draws erudition from Adam Smith, from a time when the automatic workshop was only just coming into existence. Indeed, what a difference between the division of labour as it existed in Adam Smith's day and as we see it in the automatic workshop! In order to make this properly understood, we need only quote a few passages from Dr. Ure's *Philosophie des manufactures*.

---

[a] A. Ure, *Philosophie des manufactures*, t. I, Bruxelles, 1836, pp. 23, 21, 22, Eng. ed., pp. 16 and 15.—*Ed.*

"When Adam Smith wrote his immortal elements of economics, automatic machinery being hardly known, he was properly led to regard the division of labour as the grand principle of manufacturing improvement; and he showed, in the example of pin-making, how each handicraftsman, being thereby enabled to perfect himself by practice in one point, became a quicker and cheaper workman. In each branch of manufacture he saw that some parts were, on that principle, of easy execution, like the cutting of pin wires into uniform lengths, and some were comparatively difficult, like the formation and fixation of their heads; and therefore he concluded that to each a workman of appropriate value and cost was naturally assigned. This *appropriation* forms the very essence of the division of labour.... But what was in Dr. Smith's time a topic of useful illustration, cannot now be used without risk of misleading the public mind as to the right principle of manufacturing industry. In fact, the division, or rather adaptation of labour to the different talents of men, is little thought of in factory employment. On the contrary, wherever a process requires peculiar dexterity and steadiness of hand, it is withdrawn as soon as possible from the cunning workman, who is prone to irregularities of many kinds, and it is placed in charge of a peculiar mechanism, so self-regulating, that a child may superintend it....

"The principle of the factory system then is to substitute mechanical science for hand skill, and the partition of a process into its essential constituents, for the division or gradation of labour among artisans. On the handicraft plan, labour more or less skilled was usually the most expensive element of production ... but on the automatic plan, skilled labour gets progressively superseded, and will, eventually, be replaced by mere overlookers of machines.

"By the infirmity of human nature it happens, that the more skilful the workman, the more self-willed and intractable he is apt to become, and, of course, the less fit a component of a mechanical system, in which, by occasional irregularities, he may do great damage to the whole. The grand object therefore of the modern manufacturer is, through the union of capital and science, to reduce the task of his workpeople to the exercise of vigilance and dexterity—faculties, *when concentrated to one process,* speedily brought to perfection in the young....

"On the gradation system, a man must serve an apprenticeship of many years before his hand and eye become skilled enough for certain mechanical feats; but on the system of decomposing a process into its constituents, and embodying each part in an automatic machine, a person of common care and capacity may be entrusted with any of the said elementary parts after a short probation, and may be transferred from one to another, on any emergency, at the discretion of the master. Such translations are utterly at variance with the old practice of the division of labour, which fixed one man to shaping the head of a pin, and another to sharpening its point, with most irksome and spirit-wasting uniformity.... But on the *equalisation* plan of self-acting machines, the operative needs to call his faculties only into agreeable exercise.... As his business consists in tending the work of a well-regulated mechanism, he can learn it in a short period; and when he transfers his services from one machine to another, he varies his task, and enlarges his views, by thinking on those general combinations which result from his and his companions' labours. Thus, that cramping of the faculties, that narrowing of the mind, that stunting of the frame, which were ascribed, and not unjustly, ... to the division of labour, cannot, in common circumstances, occur under the *equable distribution of industry*....

"It is, in fact, the constant aim and tendency of every improvement in machinery to supersede human labour altogether, or to diminish its cost, by substituting the industry of women and children for that of men; or that of ordinary labourers for trained artisans.... This tendency to employ merely children with watchful eyes and nimble fingers, instead of journeymen of long experience, shows how the scholastic dogma of the division of labour into degrees of skill has been exploded by our enlightened manufacturers." (André Ure, *Philosophie des manufactures ou Économie industrielle*, t. I, chap. I [pp. 27-30, 32-35; Eng. ed., pp. 19-23].)

What characterises the division of labour inside modern society is that it engenders specialities, specialists, and with them craft-idiocy.

"We are struck with admiration," says Lemontey, "when we see among the ancients the same person distinguishing himself to a high degree as philosopher, poet, orator, historian, priest, administrator, general of an army. Our souls are appalled at the sight of so vast a domain. Each one of us plants his hedge and shuts himself up in his enclosure. I do not know whether by this parcellation the field is enlarged, but I do know that man is belittled." [Op. cit., p. 213.]

What characterises the division of labour in the automatic workshop is that labour has there completely lost its specialised character. But the moment every special development stops, the need for universality, the tendency towards an integral development of the individual begins to be felt. The automatic workshop wipes out specialists and craft-idiocy.

M. Proudhon, not having understood even this one revolutionary side of the automatic workshop, takes a step backward and proposes to the worker that he make not only the twelfth part of a pin, but successively all twelve parts of it. The worker would thus come to know and realise the pin. This is M. Proudhon's synthetic labour. Nobody will contest that to make a movement forward and another movement backward is also to make a synthetic movement.

To sum up, M. Proudhon has not gone further than the petty-bourgeois ideal. And to realise this ideal, he can think of nothing better than to take us back to the journeyman or, at most, to the master craftsman of the Middle Ages. It is enough, he says somewhere in his book, to have created a masterpiece once in one's life, to have felt oneself just once to be a man. Is not this, in form as in content, the masterpiece demanded by the craft guild of the Middle Ages?

§3. COMPETITION AND MONOPOLY

Good side of competition	"Competition is as essential to labour as division.... It is necessary ... for the *advent of equality*." [I 186, 188]
Bad side of competition	"The principle is the negation of itself. Its most certain result is to ruin those whom it drags in its train." [I 185]

General reflection	"The *drawbacks* which follow in its wake, just as the good it provides ... both flow logically from the principle." [I 185-86]
Problem to be solved	"To seek the principle of *accommodation*, which must be derived from a law superior to liberty itself." [I 185] Variant "There can, therefore, be no question here of destroying competition, a thing as impossible to destroy as liberty; we have only to find its equilibrium, I would be ready to say its *police*." [I 223]

M. Proudhon begins by defending the eternal necessity of competition against those who wish to replace it by *emulation*.*

There is no "purposeless emulation", and as "the object of every passion is necessarily analogous to the passion itself—a woman for the lover, power for the ambitious, gold for the miser, a garland for the poet—the object of industrial emulation is necessarily *profit*.... Emulation is nothing but competition itself." [I 187]

Competition is emulation with a view to profit. Is industrial emulation necessarily emulation with a view to profit, that is, competition? M. Proudhon proves it by affirming it. We have seen that, for him, to affirm is to prove, just as to suppose is to deny.

If the immediate *object* of the lover is the woman, the immediate object of industrial emulation is the product and not the profit.

Competition is not industrial emulation, it is commercial emulation. In our time industrial emulation exists only in view of commerce. There are even phases in the economic life of modern nations when everybody is seized with a sort of craze for making profit without producing. This speculation craze, which recurs periodically, lays bare the true character of competition, which seeks to escape the need for industrial emulation.

If you had told an artisan of the fourteenth century that the privileges and the whole feudal organisation of industry were going to be abrogated in favour of industrial emulation, called competition, he would have replied that the privileges of the various corporations, guilds and fraternities were organised competition. M. Proudhon

* The Fourierists. *F. E.* [*Note to the German edition, 1885.*]

does not improve upon this when he affirms that "emulation is nothing but competition itself".

> "Ordain that from the first of January 1847, labour and wages shall be guaranteed to everybody: immediately an immense relaxation will succeed the high tension of industry." [I 189]

Instead of a supposition, an affirmation and a negation, we have now an ordinance that M. Proudhon issues purposely to prove the necessity of competition, its eternity as a category, etc.

If we imagine that ordinances are all that is needed to get away from competition, we shall never get away from it. And if we go so far as to propose to abolish competition while retaining wages, we shall be proposing nonsense by royal decree. But nations do not proceed by royal decree. Before framing such ordinances, they must at least have changed from top to bottom the conditions of their industrial and political existence, and consequently their whole manner of being.

M. Proudhon will reply, with his imperturbable assurance, that it is the hypothesis of "a transformation of our nature without historical antecedents", and that he would be right in "*excluding* us from the discussion" [I 191], we know not in virtue of which ordinance.

M. Proudhon does not know that all history is nothing but a continuous transformation of human nature.

> "Let us stick to the facts.... The French Revolution was made for industrial liberty as much as for political liberty; and although France, in 1789, had not perceived—let us say it openly—all the consequences of the principle whose realisation it demanded, it was mistaken neither in its wishes nor in its expectations. Whoever attempts to deny this loses, in my view, the right to criticism. I will never dispute with an adversary who puts as principle the spontaneous error of twenty-five million men.... Why then, if competition had not been a *principle* of social economy, a *decree of fate, a necessity of the human soul,* why, instead of *abolishing* corporations, guilds and fraternities, did nobody think rather of *repairing* the whole?" [I 191, 192]

So, since the French of the eighteenth century abolished corporations, guilds and fraternities instead of modifying them, the French of the nineteenth century must modify competition instead of abolishing it. Since competition was established in France in the eighteenth century as a result of historical needs, this competition must not be destroyed in the nineteenth century because of other historical needs. M. Proudhon, not understanding that the establishment of competition was bound up with the actual development of the men of the eighteenth century, makes of competition a necessity of the *human soul, in partibus infidelium.*[84] What would he have made of the great Colbert for the seventeenth century?

After the revolution comes the present state of affairs. M. Proudhon equally draws facts from it to show the eternity of competition, by proving that all industries in which this category is not yet sufficiently developed, as in agriculture, are in a state of inferiority and decay.

To say that there are industries which have not yet reached the stage of competition, that others again are below the level of bourgeois production, is drivel which gives not the slightest proof of the eternity of competition.

All M. Proudhon's logic amounts to this: competition is a social relation in which we are now developing our productive forces. To this truth, he gives no logical development, but only forms, often very well developed, when he says that competition is industrial emulation, the present-day mode of freedom, responsibility in labour, constitution of value, a condition for the advent of equality, a principle of social economy, a decree of fate, a necessity of the human soul, an inspiration of eternal justice, liberty in division, division in liberty, an economic category.

> "*Competition* and *association* rely on each other.... Far from excluding each other they are not even *divergent*. Whoever says competition already supposes a *common aim*. Competition is therefore not *egoism*, and the most deplorable error committed by socialism is to have regarded it as the overthrow of society." [I 223]

Whoever says competition says common aim, and that proves, on the one hand, that competition is association; on the other, that competition is not egoism. And whoever says *egoism*, does he not say common aim? Every egoism operates in society and by the fact of society. Hence it presupposes society, that is to say, common aims, common needs, common means of production, etc., etc. Is it, then, by mere chance that the competition and association which the socialists talk about are not even divergent?

Socialists know well enough that present-day society is founded on competition. How could they accuse competition of overthrowing present-day society which they want to overthrow themselves? And how could they accuse competition of overthrowing the society to come, in which they see, on the contrary, the overthrow of competition?

M. Proudhon says, later on, that competition is the *opposite of monopoly*, and consequently cannot be the *opposite of association*.

Feudalism was, from its origin, opposed to patriarchal monarchy; it was thus not opposed to competition, which was not yet in existence. Does it follow that competition is not opposed to feudalism?

In actual fact, *society, association* are denominations which can be given to every society, to feudal society as well as to bourgeois society, which is association founded on competition. How then can there be socialists, who, by the single word *association*, think they can refute competition? And how can M. Proudhon himself wish to defend competition against socialism by describing competition by the single word *association*?

All we have just said makes up the beautiful side of competition as M. Proudhon sees it. Now let us pass on to the ugly side, that is the negative side, of competition, its drawbacks, its destructive subversive injurious qualities.

There is something dismal about the picture M. Proudhon draws of it.

Competition engenders misery, it foments civil war, it "changes natural zones", mixes up nationalities, causes trouble in families, corrupts the public conscience, "subverts the notion of equity, of justice", of morality, and what is worse, it destroys free, honest trade, and does not even give in exchange *synthetic value*, fixed, honest price. [I 203] It disillusions everyone, even economists. It pushes things so far as to destroy its very self.

After all the ill M. Proudhon says of it, can there be for the relations of bourgeois society, for its principles and its illusions, a more disintegrating, more destructive element than competition?

It must be noted that competition always becomes the more destructive for bourgeois *relations* in proportion as it urges on a feverish creation of new productive forces, that is, of the material conditions of a new society. In this respect at least, the bad side of competition would have its good points.

"Competition as an economic position or phase, considered in its origin, is the necessary result ... of the theory of the reduction of general expenses." [I 235]

For M. Proudhon, the circulation of the blood must be a consequence of Harvey's theory.

"*Monopoly* is the inevitable doom of competition, which engenders it by a continual negation of itself. This generation of monopoly is in itself a justification of it.... Monopoly is the natural opposite of competition ... but since competition is necessary, it implies the idea of monopoly, for monopoly is, as it were, the seat of each competing individuality." [I 236, 237]

We rejoice with M. Proudhon that he can for once at least properly apply his formula of thesis and antithesis. Everyone knows that modern monopoly is engendered by competition itself.

As for the content, M. Proudhon clings to poetic images. Competition made "of every subdivision of labour a sort of sovereignty in which each individual stood with his power and his independence." [I 186] Monopoly is "the *seat* of each competing individuality". The sovereignty is worth at least as much as the seat.

M. Proudhon speaks only of modern monopoly engendered by competition. But we all know that competition was engendered by feudal monopoly. Thus competition was originally the opposite of monopoly and not monopoly the opposite of competition. So that modern monopoly is not a simple antithesis, it is on the contrary the true synthesis.

Thesis: Feudal monopoly, before competition.

Antithesis: Competition.

Synthesis: Modern monopoly, which is the negation of feudal monopoly insofar as it implies the system of competition, and the negation of competition insofar as it is monopoly.

Thus modern monopoly, bourgeois monopoly, is synthetic monopoly, the negation of the negation, the unity of opposites. It is monopoly in the pure, normal, rational state. M. Proudhon is in contradiction with his own philosophy when he turns bourgeois monopoly into monopoly in the crude, *primitive*, contradictory, spasmodic state. M. Rossi, whom M. Proudhon quotes several times on the subject of monopoly, seems to have a better grasp of the synthetic character of bourgeois monopoly. In his *Cours d'économie politique*, he distinguishes between artificial monopolies and natural monopolies. Feudal monopolies, he says, are artificial, that is, arbitrary; bourgeois monopolies are natural, that is, rational.

Monopoly is a good thing, M. Proudhon reasons, since it is an economic category, an emanation "from the impersonal reason of humanity". Competition, again, is a good thing, since it also is an economic category. But what is not good is the reality of monopoly and the reality of competition. What is still worse is that competition and monopoly devour each other. What is to be done? Look for the synthesis of these two eternal thoughts, wrest it from the bosom of God, where it has been deposited from time immemorial.

In practical life we find not only competition, monopoly and the antagonism between them, but also the synthesis of the two, which is not a formula, but a movement. Monopoly produces competition, competition produces monopoly. Monopolists compete among themselves; competitors become monopolists. If the monopolists restrict their mutual competition by means of partial associations, competition increases among the workers; and the more the mass of the proletarians grows as against the monopolists of one nation, the more desperate competition becomes between the monopolists of different nations. The synthesis is such that monopoly can only maintain itself by continually entering into the struggle of competition.

To make the dialectical transition to the *taxes* which come after *monopoly*, M. Proudhon talks to us about the *social genius* which, after *zigzagging intrepidly onward*,

> "after striding with a jaunty step, *without repenting* and without halting, *reaches the corner of monopoly*, casts backward a *melancholy* glance, and, after profound reflection, assails all the objects of production with taxes, and creates a whole administrative organisation, in order that *all employments be given to the proletariat* and *paid by the men of monopoly*". [I 284, 285]

What can we say of this genius, which, while fasting, walks about in a zigzag? And what can we say of this walking which has no other object than to destroy the bourgeois by taxes, whereas taxes are the very means of giving the bourgeois the wherewithal to preserve themselves as the ruling class?

Merely to give a glimpse of the manner in which M. Proudhon treats economic details, it suffices to say that, according to him, the *tax on consumption* was established with a view to equality, and to relieve the proletariat.

The tax on consumption has assumed its true development only since the rise of the bourgeoisie. In the hands of industrial capital, that is, of sober and economical wealth, which maintains, reproduces and increases itself by the direct exploitation of labour, the tax on consumption was a means of exploiting the frivolous, gay, prodigal wealth of the fine lords who did nothing but consume. James Steuart clearly developed this original purpose of the tax on consumption in his *Recherche des principes de l'économie politique*, which he published ten years before Adam Smith.

> "Under the pure monarchy, the prince seems jealous, as it were, of growing wealth, and therefore imposes taxes upon people who are growing richer,—taxes on production, Under constitutional government they are calculated chiefly to affect those who are growing poorer,—taxes on consumption. Thus the monarch imposes a tax upon industry ... the poll-tax and *taille*, for example, are proportioned to the supposed opulence of everyone liable to them. Everyone is taxed in proportion to the gain he is supposed to make. In constitutional governments, impositions are more generally laid upon consumption. Everyone is taxed according to his expenditure." [II 190-91; cf. Eng. ed., pp. 353, 354][85]

As for the *logical sequence* of taxes, of the balance of trade, of credit—in the understanding of M. Proudhon—we would only remark that the English bourgeoisie, on attaining its political constitution under William of Orange, created all at once a new system of taxes, public credit and the system of protective duties, as soon as it was in a position freely to develop its conditions of existence.

This brief summary will suffice to give the reader a true idea of M. Proudhon's lucubrations on the police or on taxes, the balance of trade, credit, communism and population. We defy the most indulgent criticism to treat these chapters seriously.

§4. PROPERTY OR RENT

In each historical epoch, property has developed differently and under a set of entirely different social relations. Thus to define bourgeois property is nothing else than to give an exposition of all the social relations of bourgeois production.

To try to give a definition of property as of an independent relation, a category apart, an abstract and eternal idea, can be nothing but an illusion of metaphysics or jurisprudence.

M. Proudhon, while seeming to speak of property in general, deals only with *landed property,* with *rent.*

"The origin of rent, as of property, is, so to speak, extra-economic: it rests in psychological and moral considerations which are only very distantly connected with the production of wealth." (T. II, p. 269.)

So M. Proudhon declares himself incapable of understanding the economic origin of rent and of property. He admits that this incapacity obliges him to resort to psychological and moral considerations, which, indeed, while only distantly connected with the production of wealth, have yet a very close connection with the narrowness of his historical views. M. Proudhon affirms that there is something *mystical* and *mysterious* about the origin of property. Now, to see mystery in the origin of property—that is, to make a mystery of the relation between production itself and the distribution of the instruments of production—is not this, to use M. Proudhon's language, a renunciation of all claims to economic science?

M. Proudhon

"*confines* himself to recalling that at the seventh epoch of economic evolution" (*credit*) "when fiction had caused reality to vanish, and human activity threatened to lose itself in empty space, it had become necessary to *bind man more closely to nature.* Now rent was the price of this new contract." (T. II, p. 265.)

L'homme aux quarante écus foresaw a M. Proudhon of the future:

"Mr. Creator, by your leave; everyone is master in his own world; but you will never make me believe that the one we live in is made of glass."[a]

---

[a] Voltaire, "L'homme aux quarante écus", *Œuvres complètes de Voltaire,* t. 45, Gotha, 1787, p. 44.—*Ed.*

In your world, where credit was a means of *losing oneself in empty space*, it is very possible that property became necessary in order to *bind man to nature*. In the world of real production, where landed property always precedes credit, M. Proudhon's *horror vacui* could not exist.

The existence of rent once admitted, whatever its origin, it becomes a subject of a violent contention between the farmer and the landed proprietor. What is the ultimate result of this contention, in other words, what is the average amount of rent? This is what M. Proudhon says:

"Ricardo's theory answers this question. In the beginnings of society, when man, new to earth, had before him nothing but huge forests, when the earth was vast and when industry was beginning to come to life, rent must have been nil. Land, as yet unformed by labour, was an object of utility; it was not an exchange value, it was common, not social. Little by little, the multiplication of families and the progress of agriculture caused the price of land to make itself felt. Labour came to give the soil its worth: from this, rent came into being. The more fruit a field yielded with the same amount of labour, the higher it was valued; hence the tendency of proprietors was always to arrogate to themselves the whole amount of the fruits of the soil, less the wages of the farmer—that is, less the costs of production. Thus property followed on the heels of labour to take from it all the product that exceeded the actual expenses. As the proprietor fulfils a mystic duty and represents the community as against the *colonus*, the farmer is, by the dispensation of Providence, no more than a responsible labourer, who must account to society for all he reaps above his legitimate wage.... In essence and by destination, then, rent is an instrument of distributive justice, one of the thousand means that the genius of economy employs to attain to equality. It is an immense land valuation which is carried out contradictorily by the proprietors and the farmers, without any possible collusion,[a] in a higher interest, and whose ultimate result must be to equalise the possession of the land between the exploiters of the soil and the industrialists.... It needed no less than this magic of property to snatch from the *colonus* the surplus of his product which he cannot help regarding as his own and of which he considers himself to be exclusively the author. Rent, or rather property, has broken down agricultural egoism and created a solidarity that no power, no partition of the land could have brought into being.... The moral effect of property having been secured, at present what remains to be done is to distribute the rent." [II 270-72]

All this tumult of words may be reduced firstly to this: Ricardo says that the excess of the price of agricultural products over their cost of production, including the ordinary profit and interest on the capital, gives the measure of the rent. M. Proudhon does better. He makes the proprietor intervene, like a *deus ex machina*,[b] and snatch from the

[a] The original has a misprint: "collision" instead of "collusion".—*Ed.*

[b] Literally: god out of the machine. (In the theatre of antiquity actors playing the role of gods made their appearance by means of stage machinery.) Figuratively, a person who appears unexpectedly to save a situation.—*Ed.*

colonus all the surplus of his production over the cost of production. He makes use of the intervention of the proprietor to explain property, of the intervention of the rent-receiver to explain rent. He answers the problem by formulating the same problem and adding an extra syllable.[a]

Let us note also that in determining rent by the difference in fertility of the soil, M. Proudhon assigns a new origin to it, since land, before being assessed according to different degrees of fertility, "was not", in his view, "an exchange value, but was common". What, then, has happened to the fiction about rent having come into being *through the necessity* of bringing back *to the land* man who *was about to lose himself in the infinity of empty space*?

Now let us free Ricardo's doctrine from the providential, allegorical and mystical phrases in which M. Proudhon has been careful to wrap it.

Rent, in the Ricardian sense, is property in land in its bourgeois state, that is, feudal property which has become subject to the conditions of bourgeois production.

We have seen that, according to the Ricardian doctrine, the price of all objects is determined ultimately by the cost of production, including the industrial profit; in other words, by the labour time employed. In manufacturing industry, the price of the product obtained by the minimum of labour regulates the price of all other commodities of the same kind, seeing that the cheapest and most productive instruments of production can be multiplied to infinity and that free competition necessarily gives rise to a market price, that is, a common price for all products of the same kind.

In agricultural industry, on the contrary, it is the price of the product obtained by the greatest amount of labour which regulates the price of all products of the same kind. In the first place, one cannot, as in manufacturing industry, multiply at will the instruments of production possessing the same degree of productivity, that is, plots of land with the same degree of fertility. Then, as population increases, land of an inferior quality begins to be exploited, or new outlays of capital, proportionately less productive than before, are made upon the same plot of land. In both cases a greater amount of labour is expended to obtain a proportionately smaller product. The needs of the population having rendered necessary this increase of labour, the product of the land whose exploitation is the more costly

[a] *Propriété* (property) is explained by the intervention of the *propriétaire* (proprietor); *rente* (rent), by the intervention of the *rentier* (rent-receiver).—*Ed.*

has as certain a sale as has that of a piece of land whose exploitation is cheaper. As competition levels the market price, the product of the better soil will be paid for as dearly as that of the inferior. It is the excess of the price of the products of the better soil over the cost of their production that constitutes rent. If one could always have at one's disposal plots of land of the same degree of fertility; if one could, as in manufacturing industry, have recourse continually to cheaper and more productive machines, or if the subsequent outlays of capital produced as much as the first, then the price of agricultural products would be determined by the cost price of commodities produced by the best instruments of production, as we have seen with the price of manufactured products. But from this moment rent would have disappeared also.

For the Ricardian doctrine to be generally true, it is essential[a] that capital should be freely applicable to different branches of industry; that a strongly developed competition among capitalists should have brought profits to an equal level; that the farmer should be no more than an industrial capitalist claiming for the use of his capital on inferior land[b] a profit equal to that which he would draw from his capital if it were applied in any kind of manufacture[c]; that agricultural exploitation should be subjected to the regime of large-scale industry; and finally, that the landowner himself should aim at nothing beyond the money return.

It may happen, as in Ireland, that rent does not yet exist,[d] although the letting of land has reached an extreme development there. Rent being the excess not only over wages, but also over industrial profit,

---

[a] In the copy with corrections in Marx's hand and in the one presented to N. Utina, the beginning of the phrase was altered as follows: "Pour que la doctrine de Ricardo—les prémisses une fois accordées—soit généralement vraie, il faut encore" ("For the Ricardian doctrine, once the premises granted, to be generally true it is moreover essential..."). —*Ed.*

[b] In the copy with corrections in Marx's hand and in the one presented to N. Utina the words "à la terre" ("on the land") are substituted for "à des terrains-inférieurs" ("on inferior land"). The correction is reproduced in the French edition of 1896.—*Ed.*

[c] The edition of 1847 had "par exemple, à l'industrie cotonnière" ("for example, in cotton industry") instead of "dans une manufacture quelconque" ("in any kind of manufacture"). The change was made in the copy with corrections in Marx's hand and in the one presented to N. Utina, and reproduced in the German edition of 1885 and the French edition of 1896.—*Ed.*

[d] In the 1847 edition this sentence began as follows: "En Irlande, la rente n'existe pas encore" ("In Ireland rent does not yet exist"). The changes were made in the copy with corrections in Marx's hand and in the one presented to N. Utina, and reproduced in the German edition of 1885 and the French edition of 1896.— *Ed.*

it cannot exist where the landowner's income is nothing but a deduction from wages.[a]

Thus, far from converting the exploiter of the land, the farmer, into a *simple labourer*, and "snatching from the *colonus* the surplus of his product which he cannot help regarding as his own", rent confronts the landowner, not with the slave, the serf, the payer of tribute, the wage labourer, but with the industrial capitalist. Once constituted as rent, landed property has in its possession only the surplus over production costs, which are determined not only by wages but also by industrial profit. It is therefore from the landowner that rent snatched a part of his income.[b] Hence, there was a big lapse of time before the feudal farmer was replaced by the industrial capitalist. In Germany, for example, this transformation began only in the last third of the eighteenth century. It is in England alone that this relation between the industrial capitalist and the landed proprietor has been fully developed.

So long as there was only M. Proudhon's *colonus*, there was no rent. The moment rent exists, the *colonus* is no longer the farmer, but the worker, the farmer's *colonus*. The abasement of the labourer, reduced to the role of a simple worker, day labourer, wage-earner, working for the industrial capitalist; the intervention of the industrial capitalist, exploiting the land like any other factory; the transformation of the landed proprietor from a petty sovereign into a vulgar usurer: these are the different relations expressed by rent.

Rent, in the Ricardian sense, is patriarchal agriculture transformed into commercial industry, industrial capital applied to land, the town bourgeoisie transplanted into the country. Rent, instead of *binding man to nature*, has merely bound the exploitation of the land to competition. Once established as rent, landed property itself is the *result of competition*, since from that time onwards it depends on the market value of agricultural produce. As rent, landed property is

---

[a] In the 1847 edition the end of this sentence read: "elle ne saurait exister dans les pays où, comme en Irlande, le revenu du propriétaire n'est qu'un prélèvement sur le salaire" ("It cannot exist in those countries where, as in Ireland, the landowner's income is a deduction from wages"). The changes were made in the copy with corrections in Marx's hand and in the one presented to N. Utina, and reproduced in the German edition of 1885 and the French edition of 1896.—*Ed.*

[b] In the copy with corrections in Marx's hand and in the one presented to N. Utina this paragraph has many changes, some of which are illegible. In the German edition of 1885 the last two sentences were omitted and instead the following sentence was added after the words "the industrial capitalist": "who exploits the soil by means of his wage workers, and who pays to the landowner as rent only the surplus over the production costs, including profit on capital". In the French edition of 1896 the two sentences mentioned are also omitted.— *Ed.*

mobilised and becomes an article of commerce. Rent is possible only from the moment when the development of urban industry, and the social organisation resulting therefrom, force the landowner to aim solely at commercial profit, at the money his agricultural products fetch—in fact to look upon his landed property only as a machine for coining money. Rent has so completely divorced the landed proprietor from the soil, from nature, that he has no need even to know his estates, as is to be seen in England. As for the farmer, the industrial capitalist and the agricultural worker, they are no more bound to the land they exploit than are the employer and the worker in the factories to the cotton and wool they manufacture; they feel an attachment only for the price of their production, the monetary product. Hence the jeremiads of the reactionary parties, who offer up all their prayers for the return of feudalism, of the good old patriarchal life, of the simple manners and the fine virtues of our forefathers. The subjection of the soil to the laws which dominate all other industries is and always will be the subject of interested condolences. Thus it may be said that rent has become the motive power which has introduced idyll into the movement of history.

Ricardo, after postulating bourgeois production as necessary for determining rent, applies the conception of rent, nevertheless, to the landed property of all ages and all countries. This is an error common to all the economists, who represent the bourgeois relations of production as eternal categories.

From the providential aim of rent—which is, for M. Proudhon, the transformation of the *colonus* into a *responsible worker*, he passes to the equalised distribution of rent.

Rent, as we have just seen, is constituted by the *equal price* of the products of lands of *unequal fertility*, so that a hectolitre of corn which has cost ten francs is sold for twenty francs if the cost of production rises to twenty francs upon soil of inferior quality.

So long as necessity forces the purchase of all the agricultural products brought into the market, the market price is determined by the cost of the most expensive product. Thus it is this equalisation of price, resulting from competition and not from the different fertilities of the lands, that secures for the owner of the better soil a rent of ten francs for every hectolitre that his farmer sells.

Let us suppose for a moment that the price of corn is determined by the labour time needed to produce it, and at once the hectolitre of corn obtained from the better soil will sell at ten francs, while the hectolitre of corn obtained on the inferior soil will cost twenty francs. This being admitted, the average market price will be fifteen francs, whereas, according to the law of competition, it is twenty francs. If the average price were fifteen francs, there would be no occasion for any distribution, whether equalised or otherwise, for there would be no rent. Rent exists only when one can sell for twenty francs the hectolitre of corn which has cost the producer ten francs. M. Proudhon supposes equality of the market price, with unequal costs of production, in order to arrive at an equalised sharing out of the product of inequality.

We understand such economists as Mill, Cherbuliez, Hilditch and others demanding that rent should be handed over to the state to serve in place of taxes. That is a frank expression of the hatred the industrial capitalist bears towards the landed proprietor, who seems to him a useless thing, an excrescence upon the general body of bourgeois production.

But first to make the price of the hectolitre of corn twenty francs in order then to make a general distribution of the ten francs overcharge levied on the consumer, is indeed enough to make the *social genius* pursue *its zigzag course mournfully*—and knock its head against some *corner*.

Rent becomes, under M. Proudhon's pen,

> "an immense *land valuation* which is carried out contradictorily by the proprietors and the farmers ... in a higher interest, and whose ultimate result must be to equalise the possession of the land between the exploiters of the soil and the industrialists". [II 271]

For any land valuation based upon rent to be of practical value, the conditions of present society must not be departed from.

Now we have shown that the rent paid by the farmer to the landowner expresses the rent with any exactitude only in the countries most advanced in industry and commerce. Moreover, this rent often includes interest paid to the landowner on capital incorporated in the land. The location of the land, the nearness of towns, and many other circumstances influence the farm rent and modify the land rent. These peremptory reasons would be enough to prove the inaccuracy of a land valuation based on rent.

On the other hand, rent could not be the invariable index of the degree of fertility of the land, since every moment the modern application of chemistry is changing the nature of the soil, and geological knowledge is just now, in our days, beginning to revolutionise all the old estimates of relative fertility. It is only about twenty years since vast lands in the eastern counties of England were cleared; they had been left uncultivated due to the lack of proper comprehension of the relation between the humus and the composition of the sub-soil.

Thus history, far from supplying, in rent, a ready-made land valuation, does nothing but change and turn topsy-turyy the land valuations already made.

Finally, fertility is not so natural a quality as might be thought; it is closely bound up with the social relations of the time. A piece of land may be very fertile for corn growing, and yet the market price may induce the cultivator to turn it into an artificial pastureland and thus render it infertile.

M. Proudhon has improvised his land valuation, which has not even the value of an ordinary land valuation, only to give substance to the *providentially equalitarian aim* of rent.

> "Rent," continues M. Proudhon, "is the interest paid on a capital which never perishes, namely—land. And as the capital is capable of no increase in matter, but only of an indefinite improvement in its use, it comes about that while the interest or profit on a loan (*mutuum*) tends to diminish continually through abundance of capital, rent tends always to increase through the perfecting of industry, from which results the improvement in the use of the land.... Such, in its essence, is rent." (Tome II, p. 265.)

This time, M. Proudhon sees in rent all the characteristics of interest, save that it is derived from capital of a specific nature. This capital is land, an eternal capital, "which is capable of no increase in matter, but only of an indefinite improvement in its use". In the progressive advance of civilisation, interest has a continual tendency to fall, whilst rent continually tends to rise. Interest falls because of the abundance of capital; rent rises owing to the improvements brought about in industry, which result in an ever better utilisation of land.

Such, in its essence, is the opinion of M. Proudhon.

Let us first examine how far it is true to say that rent is interest on capital.

For the landed proprietor himself rent represents the interest on the capital that the land has cost him, or that he would draw from it if he sold it. But in buying or selling land he only buys or sells rent. The price he pays to make himself a receiver of rent is regulated by the rate of interest in general and has nothing to do with the actual nature of rent. The interest on capital invested in land is in general lower than the interest on capital invested in manufacture or commerce. Thus, for those who make no distinction between the interest that the land represents to the owner and the rent itself, the interest on land as capital diminishes still more than does the interest on other capital. But it is not a question of the purchase or sale price of rent, of the marketable value of rent, of capitalised rent, it is a question of rent itself.

Farm rent can imply again, apart from rent proper, the interest on the capital incorporated in the land. In this instance the landowner receives this part of the farm rent, not as a landowner but as a capitalist; but this is not the rent proper that we are to deal with.

Land, so long as it is not exploited as a means of production, is not capital. Land as capital can be increased just as much as all the other instruments of production. Nothing is added to its matter, to use M. Proudhon's language, but the lands which serve as instruments of production are multiplied. The very fact of applying further outlays of capital to land already transformed into means of production increases land as capital without adding anything to land as matter, that is, to the extent of the land. M. Proudhon's land as matter is the earth in its limitation. As for the eternity he attributes to land, we grant readily it has this virtue as matter. Land as capital is no more eternal than any other capital.

Gold and silver, which yield interest, are just as lasting and eternal as land. If the price of gold and silver falls, while that of land keeps rising, this is certainly not because of its more or less eternal nature.

Land as capital is fixed capital; but fixed capital gets used up just as much as circulating capital. Improvements to the land need reproduction and upkeep; they last only for a time; and this they have in common with all other improvements used to transform matter into means of production. If land as capital were eternal, some lands would present a very different appearance from what they do today, and we should see the Roman Campagna, Sicily, Palestine, in all the splendour of their former prosperity.

There are even instances when land as capital might disappear, even though the improvements remain incorporated in the land.

In the first place, this occurs every time rent proper is wiped out by the competition of new and more fertile soils; secondly, the improvements which might have been valuable at one time cease to be of value the moment they become universal owing to the development of agronomy.

The representative of land as capital is not the landowner, but the farmer. The proceeds yielded by land as capital are interest and industrial profit, not rent. There are lands which yield such interest and profit but still yield no rent.

Briefly, land insofar as it yields interest is land capital, and as land capital it yields no rent, it is not landed property. Rent results from the social relations in which the exploitation of the land takes place. It cannot be a result of the more or less solid, more or less durable nature of the soil. Rent is a product of society and not of the soil.

According to M. Proudhon, "improvement in the use of the land"—a consequence "of the perfecting of industry"—causes the continual rise in rent. On the contrary, this improvement causes its periodical fall.

Wherein consists, in general, any improvement, whether in agriculture or in manufacture? In producing more with the same labour; in producing as much, or even more, with less labour. Thanks to these improvements, the farmer is spared from using a greater amount of labour for a relatively smaller product. He has no need, therefore, to resort to inferior soils, and instalments of capital applied successively to the same soil remain equally productive. Thus, these improvements, far from continually raising rent, as M. Proudhon says, become on the contrary so many temporary obstacles preventing its rise.

The English landowners of the seventeenth century were so well aware of this truth, that they opposed the progress of agriculture for fear of seeing their incomes diminish. (See Petty, an English economist of the time of Charles II.[a])

§ 5. STRIKES AND COMBINATIONS OF WORKERS

"Every upward movement in wages can have no other effect than a rise in the price of corn, wine, etc., that is, the effect of a dearth. For what are wages? They are the cost price of corn, etc.; they are the integrant price of everything. We may go even further: wages are the proportion of the elements composing wealth and consumed reproductively every day by the mass of the workers. Now, to double wages ... is to attribute to each one of the producers a greater share than his product, which is contradictory, and if the rise extends only to a small number of industries, it brings about a general disturbance in exchange; in a word, a *dearth*.... It is impossible, I declare, for strikes followed by an increase in wages not to culminate in a *general rise in prices*: this is as certain as that two and two make four." (Proudhon, tome I, pp. 110 and 111.)

We deny all these assertions, except that two and two make four.

In the first place, there is no *general rise in prices*. If the price of everything doubles at the same time as wages, there is no change in price, the only change is in terms.

Then again, a general rise in wages can never produce a more or less general rise in the price of goods. Actually, if every industry employed the same number of workers in relation to fixed capital or to the instruments used, a general rise in wages would produce a general fall in profits and the current price of goods would undergo no alteration.

---

[a] W. Petty, *Political Arithmetick* (1676).—*Ed.*

But as the relation of manual labour to fixed capital is not the same in different industries, all the industries which employ a relatively greater mass of fixed capital and fewer workers, will be forced sooner or later to lower the price of their goods. In the opposite case, in which the price of their goods is not lowered, their profit will rise above the general rate of profits. Machines are not wage-earners. Therefore, the general rise in wages will affect less those industries, which, compared with the others, employ more machines than workers. But as competition always tends to level the rate of profits, those profits which rise above the general rate cannot but be transitory. Thus, apart from a few fluctuations, a general rise in wages will lead, not as M. Proudhon says, to a general increase in prices, but to a partial fall, that is a fall in the current price of the goods that are made chiefly with the help of machines.

The rise and fall of profits and wages express merely the proportion in which capitalists and workers share in the product of a day's work, without influencing in most instances the price of the product. But that "strikes followed by an increase in wages culminate in a general rise in prices, in a dearth even"—these are notions which can blossom only in the brain of a poet who has not been understood.

In England, strikes have regularly given rise to the invention and application of new machines. Machines were, it may be said, the weapon employed by the capitalists to quell the revolt of specialised labour. The *self-acting mule*,[a] the greatest invention of modern industry, put out of action the spinners who were in revolt. If combinations and strikes had no other effect than that of making the efforts of mechanical genius react against them, they would still exercise an immense influence on the development of industry.

"I find," continues M. Proudhon, "in an article published by M. Léon Faucher ... September 1845,[b] that for some time the English workers have got out of the habit of *combination*, which is assuredly a progress for which one cannot but congratulate them: but this improvement in the morale of the workers comes chiefly from their economic education. 'It is not on the manufacturers,' cried a spinning-mill worker at a Bolton meeting, 'that wages depend. In periods of depression the masters are, so to speak, merely the whip with which necessity arms itself, and whether they want to or not, they have to deal blows. The regulative principle is the relation of supply to demand; and the masters have not this power'.... Well done," cries M. Proudhon, "these are well-trained workers, model workers," etc., etc. "Such poverty did not exist in England; it will not cross the Channel." (Proudhon, tome I, pp. 261 and 262.)

Of all the towns in England, Bolton is the one in which radicalism is the most developed. The Bolton workers are known to be the most

---

[a] This term is given in English in the original.— *Ed.*

[b] L. Faucher, "Les coalitions condamnées par les ouvriers anglais."—*Ed.*

revolutionary of all. At the time of the great agitation in England for the abolition of the Corn Laws,[86] the English manufacturers thought that they could cope with the landowners only by thrusting the workers to the fore. But as the interests of the workers were no less opposed to those of the manufacturers than the interests of the manufacturers were to those of the landowners, it was natural that the manufacturers should fare badly in the workers' meetings. What did the manufacturers do? To save appearances they organised meetings composed, to a large extent, of foremen, of the small number of workers who were devoted to them, and of the real *friends of trade.* When later on the genuine workers tried, as in Bolton and Manchester, to take part in these sham demonstrations, in order to protest against them, they were forbidden admittance on the ground that it was a *ticket meeting*[a]—a meeting to which only persons with entrance cards were admitted. Yet the posters placarded on the walls had announced public meetings. Every time one of these meetings was held, the manufacturers' newspapers gave a pompous and detailed account of the speeches made. It goes without saying that it was the foremen who made these speeches. The London papers reproduced them word for word. M. Proudhon has the misfortune to take foremen for ordinary workers, and enjoins them not to cross the Channel.

If in 1844 and 1845 strikes drew less attention than before, it was because 1844 and 1845 were the first two years of prosperity that English industry had had since 1837.[87] Nevertheless none of the *trades unions* had been dissolved.

Now let us listen to the foremen of Bolton. According to them manufacturers have no command over wages because they have no command over the price of products, and they have no command over the price of products because they have no command over the world market. For this reason they wish it to be understood that combinations should not be formed to extort an increase in wages from the masters. M. Proudhon, on the contrary, forbids combinations for fear they should be followed by a rise in wages which would bring with it a general dearth. We have no need to say that on one point there is an *entente cordiale* between the foremen and M. Proudhon: that a rise in wages is equivalent to a rise in the price of products.

But is the fear of a dearth the true cause of M. Proudhon's rancour? No. Quite simply he is annoyed with the Bolton foremen

---

[a] These two words are given in English in the original.—*Ed.*

because they determine value by *supply and demand* and hardly take any account of *constituted value,* of value which has passed into the state of constitution, of the constitution of value, including *permanent exchangeability* and all the other *proportionalities of relations* and *relations of proportionality,* with Providence at their side.

"A workers' strike is *illegal,* and it is not only the Penal Code that says so, it is the economic system, the necessity of the established order.... That each worker individually should dispose freely over his person and his hands, this can be tolerated, but that workers should undertake by combination to do violence to monopoly, is something society cannot permit." (Tome I, pp. 334 and 335.)

M. Proudhon wants to pass off an article of the Penal Code as a necessary and general result of bourgeois relations of production.

In England combination is authorised by an Act of Parliament, and it is the economic system which has forced Parliament to grant this legal authorisation. In 1825, when, under the Minister Huskisson, Parliament had to modify the law in order to bring it more and more into line with the conditions resulting from free competition, it had of necessity to abolish all laws forbidding combinations of workers.[88] The more modern industry and competition develop, the more elements there are which call forth and strengthen combination, and as soon as combination becomes an economic fact, daily gaining in solidity, it is bound before long to become a legal fact.

Thus the article of the Penal Code proves at the most that modern industry and competition were not yet well developed under the Constituent Assembly and under the Empire.[89]

Economists and socialists* are in agreement on one point: the condemnation of *combinations.* Only they have different motives for their act of condemnation.

The economists say to the workers: Do not combine. By combination you hinder the regular progress of industry, you prevent manufacturers from carrying out their orders, you disturb trade and you precipitate the invasion of machines which, by rendering your labour in part useless, force you to accept a still lower wage. Besides, whatever you do, your wages will always be determined by the relation of hands demanded to hands supplied, and it is an effort as ridiculous as it is dangerous for you to revolt against the eternal laws of political economy.

The socialists say to the workers: Do not combine, because what will you gain by it anyway? A rise in wages? The economists will

* That is, the socialists of that time: the Fourierists in France, the Owenites in England. *F. E.* [*Note to the German edition, 1885.*]

prove to you quite clearly that the few ha'pence you may gain by it for a few moments if you succeed, will be followed by a permanent fall. Skilled calculators will prove to you that it would take you years merely to recover, through the increase in your wages, the expenses incurred for the organisation and upkeep of the combinations. And we, as socialists, tell you that, apart from the money question, you will continue nonetheless to be workers, and the masters will still continue to be the masters, just as before. So no combination! No politics! For is not entering into combination engaging in politics?

The economists want the workers to remain in society as it is constituted and as it has been signed and sealed by them in their manuals.

The socialists want the workers to leave the old society alone, the better to be able to enter the new society which they have prepared for them with so much foresight.

In spite of both of them, in spite of manuals and utopias, combination has not ceased for an instant to go forward and grow with the development and growth of modern industry. It has now reached such a stage, that the degree to which combination has developed in any country clearly marks the rank it occupies in the hierarchy of the world market. England, whose industry has attained the highest degree of development, has the biggest and best organised combinations.

In England they have not stopped at partial combinations which have no other objective than a passing strike, and which disappear with it. Permanent combinations have been formed, *trades unions*, which serve as bulwarks for the workers in their struggles with the employers. And at the present time all these local *trades unions* find a rallying point in the *National Association of United Trades,*[90] the central committee of which is in London, and which already numbers 80,000 members. The organisation of these strikes, combinations, and *trades unions* went on simultaneously with the political struggles of the workers, who now constitute a large political party, under the name of *Chartists.*

The first attempts of workers to *associate* among themselves always take place in the form of combinations.

Large-scale industry concentrates in one place a crowd of people unknown to one another. Competition divides their interests. But the maintenance of wages, this common interest which they have against their boss, unites them in a common thought of resistance—*combination.* Thus combination always has a double aim, that of stopping competition among the workers, so that they can carry on general competition with the capitalist. If the first aim of resistance was merely the maintenance of wages, combinations, at first isolated, constitute themselves into groups as the capitalists in their turn unite for the purpose of repression, and in face of always united capital, the maintenance of the association becomes more necessary to them than that of wages. This is so true that English economists are amazed to see the workers sacrifice a good part of their wages in favour of associations, which, in the eyes of these economists, are established solely in favour of wages. In this struggle—a veritable civil war—all the elements necessary for a coming battle unite and develop. Once it has reached this point, association takes on a political character.

Economic conditions had first transformed the mass of the people of the country into workers. The domination of capital has created for this mass a common situation, common interests. This mass is thus already a class as against capital, but not yet for itself. In the struggle, of which we have pointed out only a few phases, this mass becomes united, and constitutes itself as a class for itself. The interests it defends become class interests. But the struggle of class against class is a political struggle.

In the bourgeoisie we have two phases to distinguish: that in which it constituted itself as a class under the regime of feudalism and absolute monarchy, and that in which, already constituted as a class, it overthrew feudalism and monarchy to make society into a bourgeois society. The first of these phases was the longer and necessitated the greater efforts. This too began by partial combinations against the feudal lords.

Much research has been carried out to trace the different historical phases that the bourgeoisie has passed through, from the commune up to its constitution as a class.

But when it is a question of making a precise study of strikes, combinations and other forms in which the proletarians carry out before our eyes their organisation as a class, some are seized with real fear and others display a *transcendental* disdain.

An oppressed class is the vital condition for every society founded on the antagonism of classes. The emancipation of the oppressed class thus implies necessarily the creation of a new society. For the oppressed class to be able to emancipate itself it is necessary that the productive powers already acquired and the existing social relations should no longer be capable of existing side by side. Of all the instruments of production, the greatest productive power[91] is the revolutionary class itself. The organisation of revolutionary elements as a class supposes the existence of all the productive forces which could be engendered in the bosom of the old society.

Does this mean that after the fall of the old society there will be a new class domination culminating in a new political power? No.

The condition for the emancipation of the working class is the abolition of all classes, just as the condition for the emancipation of the third estate, of the bourgeois order, was the abolition of all estates* and all orders.

The working class, in the course of its development, will substitute for the old civil society an association which will exclude classes and their antagonism, and there will be no more political power properly so-called, since political power is precisely the official expression of antagonism in civil society.

Meanwhile the antagonism between the proletariat and the bourgeoisie is a struggle of class against class, a struggle which carried to its highest expression is a total revolution. Indeed, is it at all surprising that a society founded on the *opposition* of classes should culminate in brutal *contradiction*, the shock of body against body, as its final denouement?

Do not say that social movement excludes political movement. There is never a political movement which is not at the same time social.

It is only in an order of things in which there are no more classes and class antagonisms that *social evolutions* will cease to be *political revolutions*. Till then, on the eve of every general reshuffling of society, the last word of social science will always be:

"Le combat ou la mort; la lutte sanguinaire ou le néant. C'est ainsi que la question est invinciblement posée."

George Sand.[a]

* Estates here in the historical sense of the estates of feudalism, estates with definite and limited privileges. The revolution of the bourgeoisie abolished the estates and their privileges. Bourgeois society knows only *classes*. It was, therefore, absolutely in contradiction with history to describe the proletariat as the "fourth estate".[92] *F. E.* [*Note to the German edition, 1885.*]

[a] "Combat or death, bloody struggle or extinction. Thus the question is inexorably put." (George Sand, *Jean Ziska. Épisode de la guerre des hussites.* Introduction.)—*Ed.*

Frederick Engels

THE DECLINE AND APPROACHING FALL OF GUIZOT.— POSITION OF THE FRENCH BOURGEOISIE

The English stage had better give over playing *The School for Scandal*,[a] for, indeed, the greatest school of this sort has been set up in Paris, in the Chamber of Deputies. The amount of scandalous matter collected and brought forward there during the last four or five weeks, is really unprecedented in the annals of parliamentary discussion. You recollect the inscription Mr. Duncombe once proposed for your own glorious House of Commons, "*The most degrading and infamous proceedings take place within these walls*". Well, here is a match for your own set of middle-class legislators; here are proceedings which will put British rascality to the blush. The honour of Old England is saved; Mr. Roebuck is outdone by M. de Girardin; Sir James Graham is beaten by M. Duchâtel.

I shall not undertake to give you the whole list of scandalous affairs brought to the light within the last few weeks; I shall not say a word about the several dozen of bribery cases brought before the juries; not a word about M. Gudin, the ordnance officer of the King, who, not without some degree of cleverness, made an attempt to introduce the habits of the swell mob into the palace of the Tuileries[93]; I shall not give you a lengthy report of the dirty affair of Gen. Cubières, peer of France, formerly Minister of War, who, under pretext of bribing the ministry into granting the concession of allowing the formation of a mining company, cheated the said company out of forty shares, which he coolly put into his own pocket, and on account of which he is now under trial before the Chamber of

[a] R. Sheridan, *The School for Scandal.* A comedy in five acts.— *Ed.*

Peers. No; I shall give you only a few choice bits—a few samples taken from two or three sittings of the Deputies, which will enable you to judge of the rest.

M. Emile de Girardin, deputy and editor of the daily paper *La Presse*, supporting in both characters the new party of *Progressive Conservatives*, and for a considerable time past one of the most violent opponents of the Ministry, whom until lately he had supported, is a man of great talent and activity, but without any principles. From the beginning of his public career he unhesitatingly employed any means to make himself an important public character. It was he who forced Armand Carrel, the celebrated editor of the *National*, to a duel, and shot him, thus delivering himself from a dangerous competitor. The support of such a man, proprietor of an influential paper, and member of the Chamber of Deputies, was of course very important to the government; but M. de Girardin sold his support (for he always *sold* it) at a very high price. There was a deal of business transacted between M. de Girardin and the Ministry, but not always to the complete satisfaction of both parties. In the meantime, M. de Girardin prepared himself for any turn which affairs might take. Foreseeing the probability of a rupture with the Guizot Ministry, he collected accounts of scandalous transactions, bribings, and traffickings, which he was in the best position to learn, and which were brought to him by his friends and agents in high places. The turn which party discussions took this session showed to him that the fall of Guizot and Duchâtel was approaching. He was one of the principal actors in the formation of the new "Progressive Conservative" party, and repeatedly threatened the government with the full weight of his wrath, if they persisted in their course. M. Guizot refused, in pretty scornful terms, any compromise with the new party. These detached themselves from the majority, and annoyed the government by their opposition. The financial and other discussions of the Chamber unveiled so much scandal, that MM. Guizot and Duchâtel were obliged to throw several of their colleagues overboard in order to save themselves. The vacant places, however, were filled by such insignificant men, that no party was satisfied, and the Ministry were rather weakened than fortified. Then came Cubières' affair, which elicited some doubts, even in the majority, as to the possibility to keep M. Guizot in office. Now, at last, when he saw the Ministry totally disorganised and weakened, now M. de Girardin thought the moment had arrived when he might bring forth his Pandora's box of scandal, and achieve the ruin of a tottering government, by revelations fit to shake the faith even of the "*belly*" of the Chamber.[94]

He commenced by accusing the Ministry of having sold a peerage for 80,000 francs, but of not having kept their promise, after pocketing the money! The House of Peers found themselves insulted by this assertion made in *La Presse*, and asked leave from the Deputies to bring M. de Girardin before their bar. This demand occasioned a discussion in the Deputies, in the course of which M. de Girardin fully maintained his assertion, declaring he was in possession of the proofs, but refusing to give any names, as he would not play the part of a *delator*. He said, however, that three times he had mentioned the matter privately to M. Guizot, who never denied the fact, and that once he spoke about it to M. Duchâtel, who replied—"It was done during my absence, and I afterwards disapproved of it; it was M. Guizot who did it." The whole of this was flatly denied by M. Duchâtel. "Then," said M. de Girardin, "I will give you the proof that the Ministry is quite in the habit of proposing such transactions"; and he read a letter from General Alexander de Girardin (the father, I believe, of M. Emile de Girardin; the latter is an illegitimate child) to the King. This letter expressed General de G.'s gratitude for the offer of a peerage made to him, but said at the same time, that M. Guizot having afterwards made it a condition of the grant that he (General de G.) should use his influence with M. Emile de G. to prevent him opposing the government, General de G. would be no party to such a transaction, and, therefore, declined the peerage. "O!" said M. Duchâtel, "if this is all, we will just mention that M. Emile de Girardin himself offered to us to cease his opposition if we would make him a peer, but we declined that offer." *Hinc illae lacrimae!*[a] But Duchâtel replied not a word to the allegation contained in the letter. The Chamber then voted that M. Emile de G. should be delivered up to the peers for trial. He was tried, sustained the allegation, but declared, the sold peerages not having been made out, he could not have attacked the Chamber of Peers, but only the government. The peers then *acquitted* him. Girardin then brought forward another scandalous affair. There was got up last year a large paper, called the *Epoque*, which was to support the government, to beat all opposition papers out of the market, and to supersede the costly support of M. de Girardin's *Presse*. The experiment signally failed; partly, too, through the intrigues of M. de Girardin himself, who has his finger in every pie of that sort. Now, M. Duchâtel had answered, when charged with bribing the press, that the government had never paid any subsidies to any paper. M. de Girardin, against this assertion, maintained the notorious fact, that M. Duchâtel, after

[a] Hence these tears. (Terence, *Andria*, Act I, Scene 1.)—*Ed.*

a deal of begging on the part of the editors of the *Epoque,* had told them: "Well, gold and silver I have none; but what I have that will I give unto you"; and had given them the privilege for a third opera-house for Paris, which privilege the "gents" of the *Epoque* sold for 100,000 f., of which sum 60,000 f. were spent in support of the paper, and the remaining 40,000 f. went nobody knows where to. This, too, was flatly denied by M. Duchâtel; but the fact is notorious.

There were, besides, some similar transactions brought forward by M. de Girardin, but these samples will be quite sufficient.

Yesterday, in the Chamber of Deputies, M. de Girardin again got up and read some letters, from which it appeared that M. Duchâtel has caused the discussion in the above peerage affair to be printed at the public expense, and sent it to all town councils in the country; but that in this ministerial report neither M. de Girardin's nor M. Duchâtel's speeches were correctly reported; but, on the contrary, both of them were arranged so as to make M. de Girardin appear as a ridiculous calumniator, and M. Duchâtel in the light of the purest and most virtuous of men. As to the matter itself, he repeated all his assertions, and defied the government either to have them disproved by a parliamentary committee, or to bring him before a jury as a slanderer. In both cases, he said, he should be bound to give the names of the parties and all particulars, and thus be enabled to prove his accusations without placing himself in the position of a common informer. This excited a general storm in the Chamber. M. Duchâtel denied; M. de Girardin re-asserted; M. Duchâtel re-denied; M. de Girardin re-reasserted, and so on, the whole accompanied by the shouts and counter-shouts of the "choruses" of the Chamber. Other opposition members again defied the Ministry to have the matter looked into either by parliamentary inquiry, or by a trial. At last M. Duchâtel said,—

> "A Parliamentary inquiry, gentlemen, would presuppose a doubt in the integrity of the government on the part of the majority; and, therefore, the day this inquiry should be granted our places would be occupied by others than us; if you have any doubt tell us so plainly, and we shall resign immediately."
>
> "Then," said M. de Girardin, "there remains nothing but a trial. I am ready to undergo it; place me before a jury, if you dare."
>
> "No," said M. Hébert, Minister of Justice, "we shall not, because the majority of the Chamber will judge."
>
> "But," said M. Odilon Barrot, "this is not a political question; it is a *legal* one, and such a question is not within our competence, but of that of the public courts of law. If M. de Girardin has calumniated the government in his paper, why do you not have him tried for it?"
>
> "We won't!"
>
> "Well, but there is a plain allegation against other parties, too, of trafficking in peerages; why not bring them up? And this affair with the *Epoque* and the opera

privilege—if you are no parties to that, as you say, why do you not bring up those who *are* parties to such villainous traffic? Here are plain incriminations, and even partial proofs of crimes said to have been committed; why do not the lawyers of the Crown prosecute the alleged perpetrators of these crimes, as is their duty?"

"We do not get up a prosecution," replied M. Hébert, "because the character of the allegations, and the character of those who bring them forward, is not such as to make the truth of these allegations anything like probable to the legal advisers of the Crown!"

All this was every moment interrupted by groaning, shouting, knocking and all sorts of noises in general. This incomparable sitting, which has shaken the Guizot Ministry to its very foundation, was concluded by a vote, which proves, that if the faith of the majority may be shaken, their system of voting is not!

"The Chamber, after having heard the explanations of the Ministry, and found them *satisfactory*, passes to the order of the day!"

What do you think of that? Which do you prefer, the ministry or the majority, the Deputies of France or your own Commons? M. Duchâtel or Sir James Graham? I dare say you will find the choice a difficult one. There is, however, one difference betwixt them. The English middle classes have, up to this day, to struggle against an aristocracy, which, although in a state of dissolution and decomposition, is not yet removed. The aristocracy of England always found some support in one fraction or the other of the middle classes themselves, and it was this division of the middle classes that saved the aristocracy from total ruin. At this moment the aristocracy is supported by the fund-holders, bankers, and owners of fixed incomes, and by a large part of the shipping trade against the manufacturers. The whole agitation for the repeal of the Corn Laws proves this.[95] The advanced fraction of the English middle classes, therefore (I mean the manufacturers) will yet be able to carry out some progressive political measures which will more and more decompose the aristocracy. They will even be *obliged* to do so; they must extend their markets, which they cannot do without reducing their prices, which reduction must be preceded by a reduced cost of production, which reduced cost of production is mainly obtained by reduced wages, for reducing which there is no safer means than reduced price of the necessaries of life; and, to obtain this, they have no other means but reducing the taxes. This is the logical chain which ties the manufacturers of England to the necessity of destroying the Established Church, and reducing, or "equitably adjusting", the National Debt. Both these measures, and others in the same spirit, they will be forced to carry out as soon as they find, which they must, the market of the world insufficient to continually and regularly buy up their produce. Thus the English middle classes are, as yet, in a progressive direction; they have an aristocracy and a privileged clergy to overthrow; there are certain progressive measures which they will be forced to carry, and which they are the fit and proper persons to carry. But the French middle classes are in a different position. There is no aristocracy of birth, nor a landed aristocracy, in that country. The revolution has swept it entirely away. Neither is there a privileged or Established Church; but on the contrary, both Catholic and Protestant clergy receive their salaries from the government, and are upon a footing of perfect equality. There is no important struggle possible in France between the fund-holders, bankers, shippers, and manufacturers, because, of all fractions of the middle classes the fund-holders and bankers (who, at the same time, are the principal shareholders in the railway, mining, and other companies) are decidedly the strongest fraction, and have, with a few interruptions only, ever since 1830, held the reins of government. The manufacturers, kept down by foreign competition in the foreign market, and threatened in their own, have no chance of growing to such a degree of power, that they successfully might struggle against the bankers and fund-holders. On the contrary, their chance decreases every year; their party in the Deputies, formerly one-half, is now not more than a third part of the Chamber. It results from all this that neither a single fraction, nor the whole of the ruling middle classes, are in a position to carry out anything like "progress"; that the government of the *bourgeoisie* is so fully established in France since the revolution of 1830, that the ruling class could do nothing but *wear themselves out.* This they have done. Instead of progressing, they were obliged to go backwards, to restrain the liberty of the press; to take away the right of free association and meeting; to make all sorts of exceptional laws in order to keep down the working people. And the scandalous affairs brought forward within the last few weeks are the evident proof that the ruling *bourgeoisie* of France are entirely worn out, totally "used up".

Indeed, the high *bourgeoisie* are in an awkward position. They had found, at last, in Guizot and Duchâtel, the men to govern them. They kept them in office seven years, and sent them at every election larger and larger majorities. And now, when all opposing fractions had been reduced to the utmost impotency in the Chamber,—now when Guizot and Duchâtel's days of glory seemed to have arrived, at that very moment a mass of scandal is discovered in the doings of the Ministry, that makes it impossible for them to remain in office, even if supported unanimously by the Chambers. There can be no doubt that Guizot and Duchâtel will, with their colleagues, resign very shortly; they may drag on their ministerial existence a few weeks longer, but their end is drawing nigh—very nigh. And who is to govern after them? God knows! They may say, as Louis XV, "after me the deluge, ruin, and confusion". Thiers is unable to bring together a majority. Molé is an old, worn-out, and insignificant man, who will meet all sorts of difficulties, and who, in order to secure the support of the majority, must commit similar scandalous actions, and therefore, end in the same way as Guizot. This is the principal difficulty. The present electors will always elect a majority like that now sitting; the present majority will always require a ministry like that of Guizot and Duchâtel, committing all sorts of scandal; any ministry doing so will be overthrown by the mere weight of public opinion. This is the vicious circle in which the present system moves. But to go on as heretofore is impossible. What, then, is to be done? There is no other course but to leave this circle, to pass a measure of Electoral Reform; and Electoral Reform means admission of the smaller tradesmen to the Suffrage, and this means, in France, "the beginning of the end". Rothschild and Louis Philippe know very well, both of them, that admission of the smaller "bourgeoisie" to the Suffrage means nothing but "LA RÉPUBLIQUE!"

Paris, June 26th, 1847

First published in *The Northern Star* No. 506, July 3, 1847 with an editorial note: "From our own correspondent in the French capital"

Reprinted from the newspaper

Karl Marx

THE COMMUNISM OF THE *RHEINISCHER BEOBACHTER*[96]

Brussels, September 5.—In issue No. 70 of this newspaper an article from the *Rh[einischer] Beobachter* is introduced with the words:

> "In issue No. 206 the *Rh[einischer] B[eobachter]* preaches communism as follows."

Whether or not this comment is intended ironically, Communists must protest against the idea that the *Rheinischer Beobachter* could preach "communism", and especially against the idea that the article communicated in issue No. 70 of the *D[eutsche]-B[rüsseler]-Z[eitung]* is communist.

If a certain section of German socialists has continually blustered against the liberal bourgeoisie, and has done so, in a manner which has benefited nobody but the German governments, and if at present government newspapers like the *Rh[einischer] Beobachter*, basing themselves on the empty phrases of these people, claim that it is not the liberal bourgeoisie but the government which represents the interests of the proletariat, then the Communists have nothing in common with either the former or the latter.

Certain people have admittedly wished to lay the responsibility for this on the German Communists, they have accused them of being in alliance with the government.

This accusation is ludicrous. The government cannot unite with the Communists, nor the Communists with the government, for the simple reason that of all the revolutionary parties in Germany the Communists are by far the most revolutionary, and that the government knows this better than anyone else.

Can Communists unite with a government which has pronounced them guilty of high treason and treats them as such?

Can the government propagate in its press principles, which, in France, are considered to be anarchistic, incendiary and destructive of all social relations, and to which this same government continually ascribes the very same characteristics?

It is inconceivable. Let us examine the so-called communism of the *Rheinischer Beobachter*, and we snall find that it is very innocent.

The article begins:

> "If we examine *our* (!) social condition, then the greatest distress and the most pressing want reveal themselves everywhere (!), and we have to admit that much has been neglected. This is, indeed, a fact, and the *only* (!) question which arises, is what causes it. We are convinced that our constitution does not bear the responsibility for this, for (!) as far as social conditions are concerned matters are (!) still worse in France and England. Nevertheless (!) liberalism seeks the remedy in representation alone; if the people were represented, it would help itself. This is quite illusory to be sure, but nonetheless (!) extremely (!!) plausible."

In this paragraph we see the *Beobachter* [observer] before us, in the flesh—the way he chews his pen, at a loss for an introduction, speculates, writes, crosses out, writes again, and then finally, after some considerable time, produces the above magnificent passage. In order to arrive at liberalism, his own inherited hobby-horse, he begins with "our social condition", that is, strictly speaking, the social condition of the *Beobachter*, which may very well have its unpleasantnesses. By means of the extremely trivial observation that our social condition is miserable and that much has been neglected, he arrives, by way of some very thorny sentences, at a point where the *only* question which arises for him, is what causes it. This question arises for him, however, *only* to disappear again at once. The *Beobachter* does not, in fact, tell us what causes it, neither does he tell us what does *not* cause it, he tells us merely what he is *convinced* does not cause it, and that is, of course, the Prussian constitution. From the Prussian constitution, by means of a bold "for", he arrives at France and England, and from here to Prussian liberalism is for him of course only a trifling leap, which, supported by the least motivated "nevertheless" conceivable, he accomplishes with ease. And thus at last he has reached his favourite terrain, where he can exclaim, "This is quite illusory to be sure, but nonetheless extremely plausible." *But nonetheless extremely!!!*

Is it possible that the Communists have sunk so low that the paternity of such utterances, such classical transitions, such questions, arising and disappearing with ease, such remarkable *Only*'s, *For*'s and *Nevertheless*'s, and above all the phrase "but nonetheless extremely", should be ascribed to them?

Besides the "Old General", Arnold Ruge, there are only a few men in Germany who can write in this way, and these few are all Consistorial Counsellors in Herr Eichhorn's ministry.

We cannot be required to go into the contents of this introductory passage. It has no content other than the awkwardness of its form, it is merely the portal through which we step into the hall where our observing Consistorial Counsellor is preaching a crusade against liberalism.

Let us listen:

"Liberalism has above all the advantage that its approach to the people takes easier and more pleasant forms than does that of the bureaucracy." (Indeed, not even Herr Dahlmann or Gervinus writes such clumsy and angular prose.) "It speaks of the welfare and the rights of the people. In reality, however, it only pushes the people forward in order thereby to intimidate the government; it considers the people only as cannon fodder in the great onslaught against the power of the government. To seize the power of the state—this is the true tendency of liberalism, the welfare of the people is only of secondary importance to it."

Does the Herr Consistorial Counsellor believe he has told the people anything new with this? The people, and in particular the communist section of the people, knows very well that the liberal bourgeoisie is only pursuing its own interests and that little reliance should be placed on its sympathy for the people. If, however, the Consistorial Counsellor concludes from this that the liberal bourgeoisie exploits the people for its own ends in so far as the people participates in the political movement, then we must answer him: "That is quite plausible for a Consistorial Counsellor, to be sure, but nonetheless extremely illusory."

The people, or, to replace this broad and vague expression by a definite one, the proletariat, has quite another way of reasoning than the gentlemen of the ecclesiastical ministry permit themselves to imagine. The proletariat does not ask whether the welfare of the people is a matter of secondary or of primary importance to the bourgeoisie, or whether the bourgeoisie *wishes* to use proletarians as cannon fodder or not. The proletariat does not ask what the bourgeoisie merely *wishes* to do, but what it *must* do. It asks whether the present political system, the rule of the bureaucracy, or the one the liberals are striving for, the rule of the bourgeoisie, will offer it the means to achieve its own purposes. To this end it only has to compare the political position of the proletariat in England, France and America with that in Germany to see that the rule of the bourgeoisie does not only place quite new weapons in the hands of the proletariat for the struggle *against* the bourgeoisie, but that it also secures for it a quite different status, the status of a recognised party.

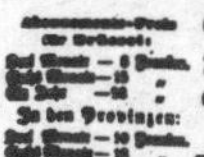

Deutsche-Brüsseler-Zeitung.

Redakteur: A. von Bornstedt.

Nº 73. Brüssel, Sonntag den 12. September 1847.

Einzelne Exemplare der „Deutschen-Brüsseler-Zeitung" zu 50 Cent., und einzelne Exemplare der König Ludwig-Lola-Montez-Lithographie, so wie von der allegorischen Darstellung des Königs von Preussen, auch der Eröffnung der Stände in Berlin, sind zu haben zu 50 Cent. im Bureau der Zeitung, 23, rue Botanique, vor dem Kölnischen- und Scharbecker-Thore, hinter dem botanischen Garten und an den Eisenbahn-Stationen zu Brüssel, Lüttich, Verviers, Mecheln u. s. w.

Zur Nachricht.

Die Erklärungen der drei Karrikaturen.

Der Kommunismus des Rheinischen Beobachters.

Deutscher Sozialismus in Versen und Prosa. 1) Karl Beck: „Lieder vom armen Mann, oder die Poesie des wahren Sozialismus."

An das Haus Rothschild.

A page of the *Deutsche-Brüsseler-Zeitung* with Marx's "Communism of the *Rheinischer Beobachter*" and the beginning of Engels' essays "German Socialism in Verse and Prose"

Does the Herr Consistorial Counsellor then believe that the proletariat, which is more and more adhering to the Communist Party, that the proletariat will be incapable of utilising the freedom of the press and the freedom of association? Let him just read the English and French working men's newspapers, let him just attend some time a single Chartist meeting!

But in the ecclesiastical ministry, where the *Rh[einischer] Beobachter* is edited, they have queer ideas about the proletariat. They think they are dealing with Pomeranian peasants or with Berlin loafers. They think they have reached the greatest depths of profundity when they promise the people no longer *panem et circenses*,[a] but *panem et religionem*[b] instead. They delude themselves that the proletariat wishes to be helped, they do not conceive that it expects help from nobody but itself. They do not suspect that the proletariat sees through all these empty consistorial phrases about the "welfare of the people" and bad social conditions just as well as through the similar phrases of the liberal bourgeoisie.

And why is the welfare of the people only of secondary importance to the bourgeoisie? The *Rh[einischer] Beobachter* replies:

> "The United Diet[97] has proved it, the perfidy of liberalism is exposed. The Income Tax was the acid test of liberalism, and it failed the test."

These well-meaning Consistorial Counsellors, imagining in their economic innocence that they can use the Income Tax to throw dust in the eyes of the proletariat!

The Slaughter and Milling Tax directly affects wages, the Income Tax affects the profit of capital. Extremely plausible, Herr Consistorial Counsellor, isn't it? But the capitalists will not and cannot allow their profits to be taxed with impunity. This follows from competition itself. So within a few months after the introduction of the Income Tax, wages will therefore have been reduced to precisely the extent by which they were actually raised by the abolition of the Slaughter and Milling Tax and by the reduced food prices resulting from this.

The level of wages expressed, not in terms of money, but in terms of the means of subsistence necessary to the working man, that is the level of *real*, not of *nominal* wages, depends on the relationship between demand and supply. An alteration in the mode of taxation may cause a momentary disturbance, but will not change anything in the long run.

---

[a] Bread and games.— *Ed.*

[b] Bread and religion.— *Ed.*

The only economic advantage of the Income Tax is that it is cheaper to levy, and this the Consistorial Counsellor does not mention. Incidentally the proletariat gains nothing from this circumstance either.

What, then, does all this talk about the Income Tax amount to?

In the first place, the proletariat is not at all, or only momentarily, interested in the whole matter.

In the second place, the government, which in levying the Slaughter and Milling Tax comes daily into direct contact with the proletariat and confronts it in a hateful fashion, the government remains in the background where the Income Tax is concerned, and forces the bourgeoisie to assume in full the odious business of pressing down wages.

The Income Tax would thus be of benefit to the government alone, hence the anger of the Consistorial Counsellors at its rejection.

But let us concede even for a moment that the proletariat has an interest in the matter; should this Diet have granted it?

By no means. It ought not to have granted moneys at all, it should have left the financial system exactly as it was so long as the government had not fulfilled all its demands. The refusal of moneys is, in all parliamentary assemblies, the means by which the government is forced to yield to the majority. This consistent refusal of moneys was the only thing in which the Diet behaved energetically, and that is why the disappointed Consistorial Counsellors have to try and render it suspicious in the eyes of the people.

"And yet," the *Rh[einischer] Beob[achter]* continues, "the organs of the liberal press quite appropriately raised the matter of the Income Tax."

Quite correct, and it is indeed a purely bourgeois measure. For this very reason, though, the bourgeoisie is able to reject it when it is proposed to it at the wrong time by ministers whom it cannot trust an inch.

We shall, incidentally, add this confession concerning the paternity of the Income Tax to the record; we shall find it useful later on.

After some exceptionally vacuous and confused twaddle the Consistorial Counsellor suddenly stumbles over the proletariat in the following manner:

"What *is* the proletariat?" (This is yet another of those questions which arise *only* to remain unanswered.) "It is no exaggeration when we" (that is, the Consistorial Counsellors of the *Rh[einischer] B[eobachter]*, not, however, the other profane newspapers) "state that one-third of the people has no basis for its existence, and another third is on the decline. The problem of the proletariat is the problem of the great majority of the people, it is the cardinal question."

How rapidly, indeed, these bureaucrats are brought to see reason by a single United Diet with a little opposition! How long is it since the government was prohibiting newspapers from maintaining such exaggerations as that we might have a proletariat in Prussia? Ever since the *Trier'sche Zeitung* among others—that innocent organ!—was threatened with closure because it maliciously wished to present the evil circumstances of the proletariat in England and France as existing also in Prussia? Be that as the government wishes. We shall similarly add to the record that the great majority of the people are proletarians.

"The Diet," it is further declared, "considered the question of principle to be the cardinal question, that is, the question of whether or not this exalted assembly should receive state power. And what was the people to receive? No railway, no annuity banks, no tax relief! Thrice happy people!"

Observe how our sleek-pated Consistorial Counsellor is gradually beginning to show his fox's ears. "The Diet considered the question of principle to be the main question." The blessed simplicity of this amiable blind-worm! The question as to whether a loan of 30 millions, an Income Tax providing a revenue not to be determined in advance, an annuity bank by means of which 400 to 500 millions can be raised on the domains—as to whether all this should be put at the disposal of the present dissolute and reactionary government, thus rendering it independent for an eternity, or whether it should be kept short, be rendered submissive to public opinion by the withdrawal of moneys, this our pussy-footing Consistorial Counsellor calls the question of principle!

"And what will the people receive?" asks the sympathetic Consistorial Counsellor. *"No railway"*—thus it will also avoid paying any taxes to cover the interest on the loan and the inevitable big losses in the running of this railway.

"No annuity banks!" Our Consistorial Counsellor acts just as if the government wished to give annuities to the proletarians, doesn't he? But, on the contrary, it wanted to give annuities to the *nobility*, for which the people would have had to pay. In this way it was to be made easier for the peasants to buy themselves free from compulsory labour service. If the peasants wait a few years more they will probably no longer need to *buy* themselves free. When the lords of the manor come under the pitchforks of the peasants, and this could easily happen before very long, then corvée system will cease of its own accord.

"No Income Tax." But so long as the Income Tax brings no income to the people, this is a matter of utter indifference to it.

"Thrice happy people," continues the Consistorial Counsellor, "you have at least won the question of principle! And if you do not understand what this is, then let your representatives explain it to you; perhaps you will forget your hunger in the course of their lengthy speeches!"

Who still dares to claim that the German press is not free? The *Rh[einischer] Beob[achter]* employs here with complete impunity a turn of phrase which many a French provincial jury would without more ado declare to be an incitement of the various classes of society against one another and cause to be punished.

The Consistorial Counsellor behaves, incidentally, in a terribly awkward manner. He wishes to flatter the people, and does not even credit it with knowing what a question of principle might be. Because he has to feign sympathy for the people's *hunger,* he takes his revenge by declaring it to be stupid and politically incompetent. The proletariat knows so well what the question of principle is that it does not reproach the Diet for having won it, but for *not* having won it. The proletariat reproaches the Diet for having stayed on the defensive, for not having attacked, for not having gone ten times further. It reproaches it with not having behaved decisively enough to make possible the participation of the proletariat in the movement. The proletariat was certainly incapable of showing any interest in the *Privileges of the Estates.* But a Diet demanding trial by jury, equality before the law, the abolition of the corvée system, freedom of the press, freedom of association and true representation, a Diet having once and for all broken with the past and formulating its demands according to the needs of the present instead of according to the old laws—such a Diet could count on the strongest support from the proletariat.

The *Beobachter* continues:

"And may God grant that this Diet should not absorb the power of the government, otherwise an insuperable brake will be put upon all social improvements."

The Herr Consistorial Counsellor may calm himself. A Diet that could not even get the better of the Prussian government will be given short shrift by the proletariat when the need arises.

"It has been said," the Consistorial Counsellor observes further, "that the Income Tax leads to revolution, to communism. To revolution, to be sure, that is to say, to a *transformation* of social relations, to the removal of *limitless poverty.*"

Either the Consistorial Counsellor wishes to mock his readers and merely say that the Income Tax removes *limitless* poverty in order to replace it with limited poverty, and more of a similar kind of bad Berlin jokes—or he is the greatest and most shameless ignoramus in economic matters alive. He does not know that in England the Income Tax has been in existence for seven years and has not transformed a single social relation, has not removed the least hair's breadth of limitless poverty. He does not know that it is precisely where the *most limitless* poverty exists in Prussia, in the weaving villages of Silesia and Ravensberg, among the small peasants of Silesia, Posen, the Mosel and the Vistula, that the Class Tax, that is, the Income Tax, is *in force.*

But who can reply seriously to such absurdities? It is further stated:

"Also to *communism,* as it happens to be understood.... Where all relations have been so intertwined with one another and brought into flux by trade and industry that the individual loses his footing in the currents of competition, by the nature of the circumstances he is *thrown upon the mercy* of society which *must* compensate in respect of the *particular* for the consequences of the *general* fluctuations. Hence society has a *duty of solidarity* in respect of the existence of its members."

And there we are supposed to have the communism of the *Rh*[*einischer*] *Beobachter*! Thus—in a society such as ours, where nobody is *secure* in his existence, in his position in life, society is duty bound to secure everybody's existence. First the Consistorial Counsellor admits that the existing society *cannot* do this, and then he demands of it that it should nevertheless perform this impossible feat.

But it should compensate in respect of the particular for that for which it can show no consideration in its general fluctuations, this is what the Consistorial Counsellor means.

"One-third of the people has no basis for its existence, and another third is on the decline."

Ten million individuals, therefore, are to be individually *compensated for.* Does the Consistorial Counsellor believe in all seriousness that the *pauvre*[a] Prussian government will be able to achieve this?

To be sure, and what is more by means of the Income Tax, which leads to communism, as it *happens to be understood* by the *Rh*[*einischer*] *Beobachter.*

Magnificent. After bemusing us with confused balderdash about alleged communism, after declaring that society has a duty of solidarity in respect of the existence of its members, that it *has to* care for them, although it cannot do so, after all these aberrations, contradictions and impossible demands, we are urged to accept the Income Tax as the measure which will resolve all contradictions,

---

[a] Poor.—*Ed.*

make all impossibilities possible and restore the solidarity of all members of society.

We refer to Herr von Duesberg's memorandum on the Income Tax, which was presented to the Diet.[a] In this memorandum employment had already been found for the last penny of the revenue from the Income Tax. The hard-pressed government had not a farthing to spare for the compensation in respect of the particular for general fluctuations, for the fulfilment of society's duties of solidarity. And if, instead of ten million, only ten individuals had been through the nature of circumstances thrown upon Herr von Duesberg's mercy, Herr von Duesberg would have rejected all ten of them.

But no, we are mistaken; besides the Income Tax the Herr Consistorial Counsellor has yet another means for introducing communism, as he happens to understand it:

> "What is the Alpha and Omega of the Christian faith? The dogma of original sin and redemption. And therein lies the association in solidarity of humanity in its highest potential: One for all and all for one."

Thrice happy people! The *cardinal question* is solved for all eternity! Under the double wings of the Prussian eagle and the Holy Ghost, the proletariat will find two inexhaustible springs of life: first, the surplus from the Income Tax above the ordinary and extraordinary needs of the state, which surplus equals zero, and second, the revenues from the heavenly domains of original sin and redemption, which likewise equal zero. These two zeroes provide a splendid basis for the one-third of the people which has no basis for its existence, a powerful support for the other third which is on the decline. Imaginary surpluses, original sin and redemption will undoubtedly satisfy the people's hunger in quite another way than the long speeches of liberal deputies! It is further stated:

> "We also pray, in the Lord's prayer: 'Lead us not into temptation.' And what we supplicate for ourselves we ought to practise with regard to our fellow human beings. Our social conditions undoubtedly tempt man, and the excess of poverty incites to crime."

And *we*, gentlemen, we bureaucrats, judges and Consistorial Counsellors of the Prussian state, practise this consideration by having people broken on the wheel, beheaded, locked up and flogged to our heart's content, thereby "leading" the proletariat "into the temptation" to have us later similarly broken on the wheel, beheaded, locked up and flogged. Which will not fail to occur.

---

[a] Duesberg, von. *Denkschrift, betreffend die Aufhebung der Mahl- und Schlachtsteuer, die Beschränkung der Klassensteuer und die Erhebung einer Einkommensteuer.*—*Ed.*

"Such conditions," declares the Consistorial Counsellor, "*must not* be tolerated by a Christian state, it must remedy them."

Indeed, with absurd blusterings about society's duties of solidarity, with imaginary surpluses and unacceptable bills of exchange on God the Father, Son and Company.

"We can also save ourselves all this tedious talk of communism," opines our observing Consistorial Counsellor. "If only those who have the vocation for it develop the social principles of Christianity, then the Communists will soon fall silent."

The social principles of Christianity have now had eighteen hundred years to be developed, and need no further development by Prussian Consistorial Counsellors.

The social principles of Christianity justified the slavery of antiquity, glorified the serfdom of the Middle Ages and are capable, in case of need, of defending the oppression of the proletariat, even if with somewhat doleful grimaces.

The social principles of Christianity preach the necessity of a ruling and an oppressed class, and for the latter all they have to offer is the pious wish that the former may be charitable.

The social principles of Christianity place the Consistorial Counsellor's compensation for all infamies in heaven, and thereby justify the continuation of these infamies on earth.

The social principles of Christianity declare all the vile acts of the oppressors against the oppressed to be either a just punishment for original sin and other sins, or trials which the Lord, in his infinite wisdom, ordains for the redeemed.

The social principles of Christianity preach cowardice, self-contempt, abasement, submissiveness and humbleness, in short, all the qualities of the rabble, and the proletariat, which will not permit itself to be treated as rabble, needs its courage, its self-confidence, its pride and its sense of independence even more than its bread.

The social principles of Christianity are sneaking and hypocritical, and the proletariat is revolutionary.

So much for the social principles of Christianity.

Further:

"We have acknowledged social reform to be the most distinguished vocation of the monarchy."

Have we? There has not been a single word of this hitherto. However, let it stand. And what does the social reform of the monarchy consist in? In promulgating an Income Tax stolen from the liberal press, which is to provide surpluses the Minister of Finance knows nothing about, in the abortive Land Annuity Banks, in the Prussian Eastern Railway, and in particular in the profits from a vast capital of original sin and redemption!

"The interests of the monarchy itself makes this advisable"—how low, then, the monarchy must have sunk!

"The distress in society demands this"—for the moment it demands protective tariffs far more than dogmas.

"The gospel recommends this"—this is recommended by everything in general, only not by the terrifyingly barren condition of the Prussian State treasury, this abyss, which, within three years, will irrevocably have swallowed up the 15 Russian millions. The gospel recommends a great deal besides, among other things also castration as the beginning of social reform with oneself (Matth[ew] 19:12).

"The monarchy," declares our Consistorial Counsellor, "is one with the people."

This pronouncement is only another form of the old "*l'état c'est moi*",[a] and precisely the same form, in fact, as was used by Louis XVI against his rebellious estates on June 23, 1789: "If you do not obey, then I shall send you back home"—"*et seul je ferai le bonheur de mon peuple*".[b]

The monarchy must indeed be very hard-pressed if it decides to make use of this formula, and our learned Consistorial Counsellor certainly knows how the French people thanked Louis XVI for its use on that occasion.

"The throne," the Herr Consistorial Counsellor assures us further, "must rest on the broad foundation of the people, there it stands best."

So long, that is, as those broad shoulders do not, with one powerful heave, throw this burdensome superstructure into the gutter.

"The *aristocracy*," thus concludes the Herr Consistorial Counsellor, "leaves the monarchy its dignity and gives it a poetical adornment, but removes real power from it. The *bourgeoisie* robs it of both its power and its dignity, and only gives it a civil list. The *people* preserves to the monarchy its power, its dignity and its poetry."

In this passage the Herr Consistorial Counsellor has unfortunately taken the boastful appeal *To His People*, made by Frederick William in his Speech from the Throne,[98] too seriously. Its last word is—overthrow of the aristocracy, overthrow of the bourgeoisie, creation of a monarchy drawing its support from the people.

If these demands were not pure fantasies they would contain in themselves a complete revolution.

We have not the slightest wish to argue in detail that the

---

[a] "*I am* the state" (expression attributed to Louis XIV).—*Ed.*

[b] "And alone I shall create the happiness of my people."—*Ed.*

aristocracy cannot be overthrown in any other manner than by the bourgeoisie and the people together, that rule of the people in a country where the aristocracy and the bourgeoisie still exist side by side is a piece of sheer nonsense. One cannot reply to such yarn-spinnings from one of Eichhorn's Consistorial Counsellors with any serious development of ideas.

We merely wish to make some well-intentioned comments to those gentlemen who would like to rescue the apprehensive Prussian monarchy by means of a somersault into the people.

Of all political elements the people is by far the most dangerous for a king. Not the people of which Frederick William speaks, which offers thanks with moist eyes for a kick and a silver penny; this people is completely harmless, for it only exists in the king's imagination. But the real people, the proletarians, the small peasants and the plebs—this is, as Hobbes says, *puer robustus, sed malitiosus*,[a] a robust, but ill-natured youth, which permits no kings, be they lean or fat, to get the better of him.

This people would above all else extort from His Majesty a constitution, together with a universal franchise, freedom of association, freedom of the press and other unpleasant things.

And if it had all this, it would use it to pronounce as rapidly as possible on the *power*, the *dignity* and the *poetry* of the monarchy.

The current worthy occupant of this monarchy could count himself fortunate if the people employed him as a public barker of the Berlin Artisans' Association with a civil list of 250 talers and a cool pale ale daily.

If the Consistorial gentlemen now directing the destiny of the Prussian monarchy and the *Rhein[ischer] Beobachter* should doubt this, then let them merely cast a glance at history. History provides a quite different horoscopes for kings who appealed to their people.

Charles I of England also appealed *to His People* against his estates. He called his people to arms against parliament. The people, however, declared itself to be against the king, threw all the members who did not represent the people out of parliament and finally caused parliament, which had thus become the real representative of the people, to behead the king. Thus ended the appeal of Charles I to his people. This occurred on January 30, 1649, and has its bicentenary in the year 1849.

Louis XVI of France likewise appealed *to His People*. Three years long he appealed from one section of the people to another, he sought *His* people, the true people, the people filled with enthusiasm

[a] Th. Hobbes, *Elementa philosophica de cive*.— *Ed.*

for him, and found it nowhere. Finally he found it in the encampment of Koblenz, behind the ranks of the Prussian and Austrian army. This, however, was too much of a good thing for his people in France. On August 10, 1792 it locked up the appellant in the Temple and summoned the National Convention, which represented it in every respect.

This Convention declared itself competent to judge the *appeal* of the ex-king, and after some consultation the appellant was taken to the Place de la Révolution, where he was guillotined on January 21, 1793.

That is what happens when kings *appeal to Their People.* Just what happens, however, when Consistorial Counsellors wish to found a democratic monarchy, we shall have to wait and see.

Written on September 5, 1847

First published in the *Deutsche-Brüsseler-Zeitung* No. 73, September 12, 1847

Printed according to the newspaper

Published in full in English for the first time

Frederick Engels

GERMAN SOCIALISM IN VERSE AND PROSE[99]

1

KARL BECK, *LIEDER VOM ARMEN MANN*, OR THE POETRY OF TRUE SOCIALISM

[*Deutsche-Brüsseler-Zeitung* No. 73, September 12, 1847]

Songs about the Poor Man begins with a song to a wealthy house.

TO THE HOUSE OF ROTHSCHILD

To prevent misunderstandings, the poet addresses God as "LORD" and the house of Rothschild as *Lord.*

Right at the beginning he records his petty-bourgeois illusion that the "rule of gold" obeys Rothschild's "whims"; an illusion which gives rise to a whole series of fancies about the power of the house of Rothschild.

It is not the destruction of Rothschild's real power, of the social conditions on which it is based, which the poet threatens; he merely desires it to be humanely applied. He laments that bankers are not socialist philanthropists, not enthusiasts for an ideal, not benefactors of mankind, but just—bankers. Beck sings of the cowardly petty-bourgeois wretchedness, of the "poor man", the *pauvre honteux* with his poor, pious and contradictory wishes of the "little man" in all his manifestations, and not of the proud, threatening, and revolutionary proletarian. The threats and reproaches which Beck showers on the house of Rothschild, sound, for all his good intentions, even more farcical to the reader than a Capuchin's sermon. They are founded on the most infantile illusion about the power of the Rothschilds, on total ignorance of the connection between this power and existing conditions, and on a complete misapprehension about the means which the Rothschilds had to use to acquire power and to retain power. Pusillanimity and lack of understanding, womanish sentimentality and the wretched, prosaically sober attitudes of the petty bourgeoisie, these are the muses of this lyre, and in vain they do violence to themselves in an attempt to appear terrible. They only appear ridiculous. Their forced bass is constantly breaking into a comic falsetto, their dramatic rendering of the titanic struggle of an

Enceladus only succeeds in producing the farcical, disjointed jerks of a puppet.

> The rule of gold obeys your whims
> . . . .
> Oh, would your works could be as splendid
> And your heart as great as is your power! (p. 4).

It is a pity that Rothschild has the *power* and our poet the *heart.* "Were but the two of them one, it had been too much for the earth." (Herr Ludwig of Bavaria.)[a]

The first figure with whom Rothschild is confronted is of course the minstrel himself, to be precise, the *German* minstrel who dwells in "lofty, heavenly garrets".

> Singing of justice, light and freedom,
> The one true GOD in trinity,
> The lute of the bards is with melody inspired:
> Now men with listening ears will follow
> The spirits (p. 5).

This "GOD", borrowed from the *Leipziger Allgemeine Zeitung*'s motto,[100] precisely because of his existence as a trinity, has no effect on the Jew Rothschild but produces quite magical effects on German youth.

> Restored to health, youth speaks a warning
> . . . .
> And the fertile seed of inspiration
> Sprouts up in myriad splendid names (p.[p. 5-]6).

Rothschild's verdict on the German poets is different:

> The song the spirits had us sing,
> You call it hunger for fame and food [p. 6].

Although youth is speaking a warning and its myriad splendid names are sprouting up, their splendour consisting in the very fact that they never get further than mere inspiration, although "the bugles bravely sound for battle" and "the heart beats so loud at night",

> The foolish heart, it feels the stress
> Of a celestial impregnation (p. 7).

That foolish heart, that Virgin Mary!—although

> Youth like a sombre *Saul* (by Karl Beck,[b] published
> by Engelmann, Leipzig, 1840),
> At odds with GOD and with itself [p. 8.],

for all that and all that, Rothschild maintains the armed peace which, as Beck believes, depends on him alone.

---

[a] Free rendering of two lines from Ludwig I of Bavaria's, "Florenz".—*Ed.*

[b] An allusion to Karl Beck's tragedy *Saul.*—*Ed.*

The newspaper report that the Holy See has sent Rothschild the Order of the Redeemer provides our poet with the chance to demonstrate that Rothschild is no redeemer; similarly it could just as well have been the occasion for the equally interesting proof that Christ, Redeemer though he was, was nevertheless not a knight of the Order of the Redeemer.

> You, a redeemer? (p. 11).

And he then proves to him that unlike Christ he never *wrestled* in bitter night, he never sacrificed proud earthly power

> For a merciful gladdening mission
> To you entrusted by the great SPIRIT (p. 11).

It must be said of the great SPIRIT that it does not exhibit much spiritual sagacity in its choice of missionaries and has approached the wrong man for acts of *mercy*. The only *great thing* about it is its block capitals.

Rothschild's paucity of talent as a redeemer is amply demonstrated to him by means of three examples: how he reacted towards the July Revolution, the Poles and the Jews.

> Up rose the dauntless scion of the Franks (p. 12),

in a word, the July Revolution broke out.

> Were you prepared? Did your gold resound
> Happy as the twittering of larks in welcome
> To the springtime stirring in the world?
> Which made young again those yearning hopes
> Sleeping deeply buried in our breasts,
> And brought them back into the living world? (p. 12).

The springtime that was stirring was the springtime of the bourgeoisie, to whom gold, Rothschild's gold as much as any other, does indeed resound happy as the twittering of larks. To be sure, the hopes which at the time of the Restoration were sleeping deeply buried not only in the breast but also in the Carbonari Ventes[101] were at that time made young again and brought back into the living world, and Beck's *poor man* was left to pick up the crumbs. But as soon as Rothschild had convinced himself that the new government had firm foundations, he was happy enough to set his larks twittering—at the usual interest rates, of course.

Just how completely Beck is entangled in petty-bourgeois illusions is shown by the saintly status Laffitte is accorded in comparison with Rothschild:

> Close-nestling beside your much-coveted halls
> Is a burgher's dwelling of holy repute (p. 13),

in other words, Laffitte's dwelling. The inspired petty bourgeois is proud of the bourgeois character of his house compared with the much-coveted halls of the Hotel Rothschild. His ideal, the Laffitte of his imagination, must naturally also live in true bourgeois simplicity; the Hotel Laffitte shrinks into a German burgher's dwelling. Laffitte himself is depicted as a virtuous householder, a man pure in heart, he is compared with Mucius Scaevola and is said to have sacrificed his fortune in order to put *mankind* and the century (is Beck perhaps thinking of the Paris *Siècle*[a]?) back on their feet again. He is called a youthful dreamer and finally a beggar. His funeral is touchingly described:

> Accompanying the funeral cortège
> Marched with muffled tread the Marseillaise (p. 14).

Alongside the Marseillaise went the carriages of the royal family, and right behind them M. Sauzet, M. Duchâtel and all the *ventrus*[102] and *loups-cerviers*[b] of the Chamber of Deputies.

How the Marseillaise really must have *muffled* her tread, though, when Laffitte led his *compère*,[c] the Duke of Orléans, in triumph to the *Hôtel de Ville* after the July revolution and made the striking statement that *from now on the bankers would rule*?

In the case of the *Poles*, criticism goes no further than that Rothschild did not show enough charity to the emigrés. The attack on Rothschild is here reduced to the level of a small-town anecdote and quite loses the appearance of an attack on the power of money in general which is represented by Rothschild. We all know how the bourgeoisie has welcomed the Poles with open arms and even with enthusiasm wherever it is in power.

An example of this compunction: enter a Pole, begging and praying. Rothschild gives him a silver coin, the Pole

> Trembling with joy accepts the silver coin
> And speaks his blessing on you and your line [p. 16],

a predicament from which the Polish Committee in Paris has so far on the whole saved the Poles. The whole episode with the Pole only serves to permit our poet to strike an attitude:

> But I hurl back that beggar's happiness
> Contemptuously into your money-bag,
> Avenging thus mankind offended! (p. 16),

---

[a] Century.—*Ed.*

[b] Pot-bellies and profiteers.—*Ed.*

[c] The French word has a double meaning: firstly, kinsman; secondly, accomplice.—*Ed.*

such a bull's-eye at the money-bag requiring much practice and skill in throwing. Finally Beck insures himself against proceedings for assault and battery by acting not in his own name but in that of mankind.

As early as p. 9 Rothschild is taken to task for accepting a patent of citizenship from Austria's fat imperial city,

Where your much-harassed fellow-Jews
Pay for their daylight and their air.

Beck really believes that with this Viennese patent of citizenship Rothschild has obtained the blessings of freedom.

Now, on p. 19, he is asked:

Have you set your own people free
That ever hopes and meekly suffers?

Rothschild ought then to have become the redeemer of the Jews. And how ought Rothschild to have set about this? The Jews had chosen him as *king* because his gold weighed the heaviest. He should have taught them how to despise gold, "how to suffer deprivation for the world's sake" (p. 21).

He ought to have wiped their memories clean of selfishness, cunning and the practice of usury, in short, he ought to have appeared in sackcloth and ashes as a preacher of morality and atonement. Our poet's daring demand is the equivalent of requiring Louis-Philippe to teach the bourgeoisie of the July revolution to abolish property. If either were so insane, they would lose their power forthwith, but the Jews would not wipe their memories clean of haggling, nor the bourgeoisie theirs of property.

On p. 24 Rothschild is criticised for bleeding the bourgeoisie white, as though it were not desirable that the bourgeoisie should be bled white.

On p. 25 he is said to have led the princes astray. *Ought* they not to be *led astray*?

We have already evidence enough of the fabulous power Beck attributes to Rothschild. But he goes on in a crescendo. Having indulged on p. 26 in fantasies as to all the things he (Beck) would do if he were *propriétaire* of the *sun*, that is, not even the hundredth part of what the sun is doing without him—it suddenly occurs to him that Rothschild is not the only *sinner*, but that other wealthy men exist besides him. However:

You occupied in eloquence the teacher's chair,
Attentively the rich sat as your pupils;
Your task: to lead them out into the world,
Your role: to be their *conscience.*
They have gone wild—and you looked on,
They are corrupted—and yours is the blame (p. 27).

So Lord Rothschild could have prevented the development of trade and industry, competition, the concentration of property, the national debt and *agiotage*, in short, the whole development of modern bourgeois society, if only he had had somewhat more *conscience*. It really requires *toute la désolante naïveté de la poésie allemande*[a] for one to dare to publish such nursery tales. Rothschild is turned into a regular Aladdin.

Still not satisfied, Beck confers on Rothschild

> The dizzy grandeur of the mission
> . . . .
> *The whole world's sufferings* to assuage [p. 28],

a mission which all the capitalists in the whole world are not remotely capable of fulfilling. Does our poet not realise then that the more sublime and awe-inspiring he attempts to appear, the more ridiculous he becomes? that all his criticisms of Rothschild are transmuted into the most slavish flattery? that he is extolling Rothschild's power as the most cunning panegyrist could not have extolled it? Rothschild must congratulate himself when he sees what a monstrous form his puny personality assumes as reflected in the mind of a German poet.

After our poet has so far versified the romantic and ignorant fantasies of a German petty bourgeois concerning what is within the power of a big capitalist if only he were a man of good will, after he has puffed up the fantasy of this power as far as it will go in the puffed-up dizzy grandeur of his mission, he gives vent to the moral indignation of a petty bourgeois at the discrepancy between ideal and reality, in an emotional paroxysm which would give rise to fits of laughter even in a Pennsylvanian Quaker:

> Alas, alack, when in long night (December 21)
> I pondered with a fevered brow
> . . . .
> Then did my locks *rear* up on end,
> Methought I was at GOD's own heartstrings tugging,
> A bellman at the fire-bell (p. 28),

which must surely have been the last nail in the old man's coffin. He thinks the "spirits of history" have thus entrusted him with ideas, which he is not *permitted* either to whisper or proclaim aloud. In fact he comes to the desperate decision to dance the cancan in his grave:

> But when in mouldering shroud I lie,
> My corse shall shake with joyful tremors,
> When down to me (the corse) the tiding comes
> That victims on the altars smoke (p. 29).

[a] All the utterly depressing naïvety of German poetry.—*Ed.*

I begin to find young Karl disturbing.[a]

Thus ends the song about the House of Rothschild. There now follows, as is customary with *modern* lyric poets, a rhymed reflection on this canto and the role the poet has played in it.

> I know your mighty arm
> Can chastise me till the blood does flow (p. 30),

in other words, he can give him fifty of the best. The Austrian never forgets the birch. In the face of this danger, a feeling of exaltation gives him strength:

> At GOD's *command* and without fear
> I sang full freely what I knew [p. 30].

The German poet always sings to command. Of course, the master is responsible and not the servant, and so Rothschild has to face up to GOD and not to Beck, his servant. It is indeed the general practice of *modern* lyric poets:

1. To boast of the danger they think they are exposing themselves to in their harmless songs;
2. to take a thrashing and then commend themselves to God.

The song "To the House of Rothschild" closes with a few stirring sentiments about the aforementioned song, which is here slanderously described in the following terms:

> Free it is and proud, it may command you,
> Tell you the things by which in faith it swears (p. 32),

that is, by its own excellence, as instanced in this conclusion. We fear that Rothschild may take Beck to court, not on account of the song, but on account of this piece of perjury.

[*Deutsche-Brüsseler-Zeitung* No. 74, September 16, 1847]

O, SCATTER THE GOLDEN BLESSING!

The rich are called upon to give support to *those in need,*

> Until your industry for wife and child
> Security ensured [p. 35].

---

[a] Quoted ironically from Schiller's tragedy *Don Carlos,* Act I, Scene 6.— *Ed.*

And all this is to happen

> That you may keep your *virtue*
> As a *burgher* and a *man* [p. 35],

summa summarum, a good *philistine*.[a] Beck is thereby reduced to his ideal.

SERVINGMAN AND MAID

The poet takes as his theme two souls most pleasing to God and describes in an exceptionally dull fashion how they only come to share a chaste marriage-bed only after many years of cheese-paring and moral living.

> To kiss? Shame would o'ercome them! To dally? O so discreetly!
> Flowers there were indeed—the flowers on the frosted pane;
> A dance on crutches, O God!, a poor butterfly in winter,
> Half in the bloom of childhood, half in withered age [p. 50].

Instead of concluding with this, the one good verse in the whole poem, he then sets them crowing and quivering, and all for joy over their few chattels, that "at their *own* hearth their *own* settles stand", a cliché uttered not ironically but with heartfelt tears of pathos. Nor will he have done at that:

> God alone is their Lord, who bids the stars shine in the darkness
> And observes with a kindly eye the slave who breaks his chains [p. 50].

And with this any point in the ending is happily blunted. Beck's indecision and lack of self-confidence constantly reveal themselves in the fact that he spins out every poem for as long as he can, and can never complete it until some piece of sentimentality has betrayed his petty-bourgeois outlook. The Kleistian hexameters appear to be deliberately chosen so as to subject the reader to the same boredom as the two lovers bring upon themselves by their craven morality during their long period of trial.

THE JEWISH SECOND-HAND DEALER

There are some naive, appealing bits in the description of the Jewish second-hand dealer, e.g.:

> The week flies by, five days only
> The week allows you for your work.
> Bestir yourself, don't pause for breath,

---

[a] In German there is a pun on the words: *Bürger*—burgher, *Mann*—man, *Bürgersmann*—philistine.—*Ed.*

Earn, earn your daily bread.
Saturdays the *Father* does forbid you,
Sundays are forbidden by the *Son* [p. 55].

But later Beck succumbs completely to that kind of blathering about the Jews which is typical of the liberal Young Germans.[103] The poetry dries up so entirely that one might think one was listening to a scrofulous speech in the scrofulous Saxon Assembly of Estates: You cannot become a craftsman, nor an "alderman of the mercers' guild", nor tiller of the soil, nor professor, but a career in medicine is open to you. This finds poetical expression as follows:

A working trade they would deny you,
Deny you too a field to till.
You may not from the teacher's chair
Offer discourse to the young;
. . . .
You may heal the country's sick [p. 57].

Could one not in the same way versify the Collected Statutes of Prussia and set Herr Ludwig of Bavaria's verse to music?

Having declaimed to his son:

You must labour and be grasping,
Always covetous of property and gold [p. 57],

the Jew consoles him with:

Your *honesty* endures for ever [pp. 57-58].

LORELEI

This Lorelei is none other than Gold.

Then did turpitude flood in
Upon all purity of spirit,
Drowning all things sound [p. 64].

This Deluge of the spirit and drowning of all things sound is a most depressing mixture of the banal and the bombastic. There follow petty tirades against the evil and immorality of money.

Its (love's) quest is money and precious stones
And never hearts nor parity of souls,
No simple hut for dwelling [p. 67].

If money had done no more than discredit this German quest for hearts and parity of souls and Schiller's *meanest hut* with its space for a happy loving pair,[a] its revolutionary effects would deserve recognition.

---

[a] An allusion to Schiller's poem "Der Jüngling am Bache".— *Ed.*

DRUM-SONG

In this poem our socialist poet once more shows how through being trapped in the German petty-bourgeois misery, he is constantly obliged to spoil what little effect he achieves.

A regiment marches off with its band playing. The people call upon the soldiers to make common cause with them. The reader is glad that the poet is at last summoning up courage. But oh dear! We finally discover that the occasion is merely the Emperor's name-day and the people's words are only the improvised and unspoken reverie of a youth watching the parade. Probably a gymnasium boy:

> Thus dreams a youth with burning heart [p. 76].

Whilst in the hands of Heine the same material, with the same point, would contain the most bitter satire on the German people, in Beck's case all that emerges is a satire on the poet himself, who identifies himself with the powerlessly rapturous youth. In Heine's case, the raptures of the bourgeoisie are deliberately high-pitched, so that they may equally deliberately then be brought down to earth with a bump; in Beck's case it is the poet himself who is associated with these fantasies and who naturally also suffers the consequences when he comes crashing down to earth. In the case of the one the bourgeoisie feels indignation at the poet's impertinence, in the case of the other reassurance at the attitudes of mind they have in common. The Prague uprising[104] in any case presented him with an opportunity to work up material of a quite different character from this farce.

THE EMIGRANT

> I broke a bough from off a tree,
> The keeper made complaint,
> The master bound me to a post
> And dealt me this grave injury [p. 86].

The only thing missing here is the *complaint* delivered in similarly versified form.

THE WOODEN LEG

Here the poet tries his hand at narrative and fails in a really pathetic fashion. This complete inability to tell a story and create a situation, which is evident throughout the book, is characteristic of the poetry of true socialism. True socialism, in its vagueness, provides no opportunity to relate the individual facts of the narrative to general conditions and thus bring out what is striking or significant about them. That is why the true socialists shy away from history in their prose as well. Where they cannot avoid it, they content themselves either with philosophical constructions or with producing an arid and boring catalogue of isolated instances of misfortune and *social cases.* Furthermore, they all lack the necessary talent for narrative, both in prose and poetry, and this is connected with the vagueness of their whole outlook.

THE POTATO

Tune: *Morgenrot, Morgenrot!*

Sacred bread!

You that came in our distress,
You that came *at heaven's bidding*
Into the world, that men might eat—
Farewell, for now you are dead! [p. 105].

In the second verse he calls the potato

...that little relic
Left to us from Eden,

and describes potato-blight:

Among angels the plague rampages.

In the third verse Beck advises *the poor* to put mourning on:

You, the poor!
Go and put mourning on.
You now have need of nought,
Alas, all you own is gone,
Weep, who still have tears to shed!

Dead in the sand
Lies your *God,* o melancholy land.
Yet let these words speak comfort to you:
Never did redeemer perish
Who did not later rise again! [p. 106].

Weep, who still have tears to shed, with the poet! Were he not as bereft of energy as his *poor man* is of wholesome potatoes, he would have rejoiced at the substance acquired last autumn by that bourgeois god, the potato, one of the pivots of the existing bourgeois society. The landowners and burghers of Germany would have done themselves no harm by having this poem sung in the churches.

For this effort Beck deserves a garland of potato-blossom.

THE OLD MAID

We shall not look more closely at this poem since it drags on interminably, extending over full ninety pages with unspeakable boredom. The old maid, who in civilised countries is mostly only a nominal occurrence, is in Germany admittedly a significant "social case".

The most common kind of socialist self-complacent reflection is to say that all would be well if only it were not for the poor on the other side. This argument may be developed with any conceivable subject-matter. At the heart of this argument lies the philanthropic petty-bourgeois hypocrisy which is perfectly happy with the *positive* aspects of existing society and laments only that the *negative* aspect of poverty exists alongside them, inseparably bound up with present society, and only wishes that this society may continue to exist *without the conditions of its existence.*

Beck develops this argument in this poem often in the most trivial possible way, for example, in connection with Christmas:

O day that gently edifies men's hearts,
You would be gentler still and doubly dear—
Did there not lodge in *poor* children's hearts
Whose orphan gaze surveys the festive
Rooms of their rich playmates,
Envy and the seeds of sin,
Along with rabid blasphemy!
Yes . . . .
... more sweetly would the children's merry cheer
Sound to my ears in the Christmas candlelight,
If only in damp caverns destitution
Were not shivering on putrid straw [p. 149].

There are, by the way, occasional fine passages in this amorphous and interminable poem, for example the description of the lumpen proletariat:

Who day by day unwearyingly
Hunt garbage in the fetid gutters;
Who flit like sparrows after food,
Mending pans and grinding knives,
Starching linen with stiff fingers,
Pushing breathless at the heavy cart,
Laden with but scarcely ripened fruits,
Crying piteously: Who'll buy, who'll buy?
Who fight over a copper in the dirt;
Who at the corner-stones each day
Sing praise to the God in whom they believe,
But scarcely dare hold out their hands,
Begging being against the law;
Who with deaf ears, beset by hunger,

Pluck the harp and blow upon the flute,
Year in, year out, the same old tune—
Beneath each window, at each gate—
Setting the nursemaid's feet adance
But hearing not the melody themselves;
Who after dusk illuminate the city
But have no light for their own home;
Who shoulder burdens and split firewood,
Who have no master, and who have too many;
Who dash to pray, procure and steal
And drown with drink the vestige of a soul [pp. 158-160].

Beck here rises for the first time above the usual morality of the German bourgeoisie by putting these lines in the mouth of an old beggar whose daughter is asking for his permission to go to a rendezvous with an officer. In the above lines he gives her an embittered picture of the classes to which her child would then belong, he derives his objections from her immediate social position and does not preach morality to her, and for this he deserves credit.

THOU SHALT NOT STEAL

The virtuous servant of a Russian, whom the servant himself characterises as a worthy master, robs his apparently sleeping master during the night in order to maintain his old father. The Russian follows him surreptitiously and looks over his shoulder just as he is penning the following note to the same old man:

Take this money! I have stolen!
Father, pray to our Redeemer
That he may one day from his throne
Allow forgiveness to his servant!
I will labour and earn money,
And from my palliasse chase fatigue,
Till I can pay my worthy master
Back the money I have stolen [p. 241].

The virtuous servant's worthy master is so moved by these awful revelations that he cannot speak, but places his hand on the servant's head in blessing.

But the latter's life had left him—
And *his heart had broken with terror* [p. 242].

Can anything more comical be committed to paper? Beck here descends lower than Kotzebue and Iffland, the servant's tragedy surpasses even the middle-class tragedy.

NEW GODS AND OLD SORROWS

In this poem, Ronge, the Friends of Light,[105] the New Jews, the barber, the washerwoman and the Leipzig citizen with his modicum of liberty are often effectively lampooned. At the end, the poet defends himself against the philistines who will criticise him for it, although he too

> The song of light
> Sang out into the storm and night [p. 298].

He then himself propounds a doctrine of brotherly love and practical religion, modified by socialism and founded on a kind of nature-deism, and thus enlists one aspect of his opponents against the other. So Beck can never let matters rest until he has spoilt his own case, because he is himself too much entangled in German misery and gives too much thought to himself, to the poet, in his verse. With the *modern* lyrical poets in general, the bard has reverted to a fabulously trimmed, heroically posturing figure. He is not an active person situated in real society, who writes poetry, but "*the* poet", hovering in the clouds, these clouds being none other than the nebulous fantasies of the German bourgeoisie.—Beck constantly drops from the most heroical bombast into the soberest of bourgeois prose styles, and from a petty warlike wit against present conditions into a sentimental acceptance of them. It is constantly occurring to him that it is he himself *de quo fabula narratur.*[a] That is why his songs are not revolutionary in effect, but resemble

> Three doses of salts
> To calm the blood (p. 293).

The conclusion to the whole volume is therefore most appropriately provided by the following weak wail of resignation:

> *When will life upon this earth*
> *Be bearable, O God?*
> In *longing* I am doubly strong
> And hence in patience doubly wearied [p. 324].

Beck has incontestably more talent and at the outset more energy too than most of the German scribbling fraternity. His great lament is the German misery, amongst whose theoretical manifestations also belong Beck's pompously sentimental socialism and Young German reminiscences. Until social conflicts in Germany are given a more acute form by a more distinct differentiation between classes and a momentary acquisition of political power by [the] bourgeoisie, there

---

[a] About whom the story is being told.— *Ed.*

can be little hope for a German poet in Germany itself. On the one hand, it is impossible for him to adopt a revolutionary stance in German society because the revolutionary elements themselves are not yet sufficiently developed, and on the other, the chronic misery surrounding him on all sides has too debilitating an effect for him to be able to rise above it, to be free of it and to laugh at it, without succumbing to it again himself. For the present the only advice we can give to all German poets who still have a little talent is to emigrate to civilised countries.

2

KARL GRÜN, *ÜBER GÖTHE VOM MENSCHLICHEN STANDPUNKTE*, DARMSTADT, 1846

[Deutsche-Brüsseler-Zeitung No. 93, November 21, 1847]

Herr Grün relaxes after the exertions of his "Soziale *Bewegung* in Frankreich und Belgien" by glancing at the *lack of* social *movement*[a] in his native land. For the sake of variety, he decides to take a look at "the human aspect" of the elderly Goethe. He has exchanged his seven-league boots for carpet-slippers, donned his dressing-gown and stretches himself, full of self-satisfaction, in his arm-chair:

"We are not writing a commentary, we are only picking out what is there for all to see" (p. 244).

He has made things really snug for himself:

"I had put some roses and camellias in my room, and mignonette and violets by the open window" (p. III). "And above all, no commentaries! ...But here, the complete works on the table and a faint scent of roses and mignonette in the room! Let us just see where we get to.... Only a rogue offers more than he has!" (pp. IV, V).

For all his nonchalance, Herr Grün nevertheless performs deeds of the stoutest heroism in this book. But this will not surprise us when we have heard him himself say that he is the man who "was on the point of despairing at the *triviality* of public and private affairs" (p. III), who "felt Goethe's restraining hand whenever he was in danger of being submerged by extravagance and lack of form" (ibid.), whose heart is "full with the sense of human destiny", "who has listened to the soul of man—though it should mean descending into hell!" (p. IV). Nothing will surprise us any more after learning that previously he had "once addressed a question to Feuerbachian

[a] In German there is a pun on the words *Bewegung*—movement and *Stillstand*—lack of movement.—*Ed.*

man" which was indeed "easy to answer" but which nevertheless appears to have been too difficult for the man in question (p. 277); and when we see how Herr Grün on p. 198 "leads self-awareness out of a cul de sac", on p. 102 even plans to visit "the court of the Russian Emperor" and on p. 305 cries out to the world with a voice of thunder: "*Anathema upon any man* who would proclaim new and permanent social relations by law!" We are prepared for anything when Herr Grün undertakes on p. 187 "to take a closer look at idealism" and "show it up for the guttersnipe it is", when he speculates on "becoming a man of property",

> a "rich, rich man of property, to be able to pay the property tax, to obtain a seat in the Chamber of Representatives of mankind, to be included in the list of jurymen who judge between what is human and what is not".

How could he fail to achieve this, standing as he does, "on the nameless ground of the universally human"? (p. 182). He does not even tremble before "the night and its *horrors*" (p. 312), such as murder, adultery, robbery, whoring, licentiousness and puffed-up pride. It is true that on p. 99 he confesses he has also "known the infinite pang of man as he discovers himself at the very point of his own insignificance", it is true he "discovers" himself before the public eye at this "point" on the occasion of the lines:

> You compare but with the spirit in your mind,
> Not me[a]

to be precise, as follows:

> "These words are as when thunder and lightning occur together, with the earth opening up at the same time. These words are like the veil of the temple being rent in twain and the graves being opened ... the twilight of the Gods is upon us and the chaos of old is come again ... the stars collide, in an instant a single comet tail incinerates our little earth, and all that exists is henceforth but billowing smoke and vapour. And if one imagines the most atrocious destruction, ... it is all *but as nothing* against the annihilation contained in these eleven words!" (pp. 235, 236).

It is true, "at the furthermost frontier of theory", namely on p. 295, Herr Grün has a sensation "of icy water running down his back, real terror quivers through his limbs"—but he overcomes all this with ease, for after all he is a member of the "great order of freemasons of mankind"! (p. 317).

Take it all in all,[b] with such qualities Herr Grün will perform valiantly on any field of battle. Before we proceed to his productive

---

[a] J. W. Goethe, *Faust*, Part I, Scene 1 ("Night").— *Ed.*

[b] Engels gives this phrase in English. (Shakespeare, *Hamlet*, Act I, Scene 2 [paraphrased]).—*Ed.*

examination of Goethe, let us accompany him to some of the secondary areas of his activity.

Firstly to the field of the natural sciences, for according to p. 247 "the understanding of nature" is "the sole positive science" and at the same time "nonetheless the fulfilment of humanistic" (*vulgo*: human) "man". Let us carefully collate the positive pronouncements Herr Grün makes concerning this sole positive science. He does not actually go into the subject at all extensively, he merely lets fall a few remarks while pacing his room, so to speak, in the interval between daylight and darkness, but the miracles he performs are "nonetheless" the "most positive" for that.

In connection with the *Système de la Nature*[106] ascribed to Holbach, he reveals:

> "We cannot here expound how the System of Nature breaks off half-way, how it breaks off at the point *where freedom and self-determination had to break out from the necessity of the cerebral system*" (p. 70).

Herr Grün could indicate the precise point at which this or that "breaks out" "from the necessity of the cerebral system" and man would thus be slapped on the inside of his skull as well. Herr Grün could give the most certain and most detailed information on a point which has hitherto escaped all observation, in other words the productive processes of consciousness in the brain. But alas! In a book on the human aspect of Goethe we "cannot expound this in detail".

Dumas, Playfair, Faraday and Liebig have hitherto innocently subscribed to the view that oxygen is a gas which has neither taste nor smell. Herr Grün, however, who of course knows that the prefix "oxy-" means *sharp* to the *taste*, declares on p. 75 that "oxygen" is "sharp-tasting". In the same way, on p. 229 he contributes new facts to acoustics and optics; by postulating a "purifying uproar and brightness", he places the purificatory power of sound and light beyond all doubt.

Not content with such dazzling contributions to the "sole positive science", not content with the theory of inward slaps, on p. 94 Herr Grün discovers a new bone:

> "Werther is the man who has no vertebra, who has not yet developed as subject."

Until now it had been mistakenly thought that man had some two dozen vertebrae. Herr Grün reduces these numerous bones not just to the normal singular form but goes on to discover that this one and only vertebra has the remarkable property of making man "subject". The "subject" Herr Grün deserves an extra vertebra for this discovery.

Finally our casual naturalist summarises his "sole positive science" of nature as follows:

> "Is not the core of nature
> Mankind at heart?[a]

"The core of nature is mankind at heart. At the heart of mankind is the core of nature. Nature has its core at mankind's heart" (p. 250).

To which we would add, with Herr Grün's permission: Mankind at heart is the core of nature. At heart the core of nature is mankind. At the heart of mankind nature has its core.

With this eminently "positive" piece of enlightenment we leave the field of natural science, and turn to *economics*, which unfortunately, according to the above, is *not* a "positive science". Regardless of this, Herr Grün, hoping for the best, proceeds extremely "positively" here too.

"Individual set himself against individual, *and thus* universal competition arose" (p. 211).

In other words, that obscure and mysterious conception German socialists have of "universal competition" came into being, "and thus competition arose". No reasons are indicated, no doubt, because economics is not a positive science.

"In the Middle Ages base metal was still bound by fealty, courtly love and piety; the sixteenth century burst this fetter, and money was set free" (p. 241).

MacCulloch and Blanqui, who have hitherto been under the misapprehension that money was "bound in the Middle Ages" by deficient communications with America and the granite masses that covered the veins of "base metal" in the Andes,[b] MacCulloch and Blanqui will be addressing a vote of thanks to Herr Grün for this revelation.

Herr Grün seeks to give a positive character to *History*, which is likewise not a "positive science", by juxtaposing the traditional facts and a series of facts of his imagination.

On p. 91, "Addison's Cato stabbed himself on the English stage a century before Werther", thereby testifying to a remarkable weariness of life. For by this account, he "stabbed" himself when his author, who was born in 1672, was still a babe in arms.[107]

On p. 175 Herr Grün corrects Goethe's *Tag- und Jahreshefte* to the effect that the freedom of the press was by no means "declared" by the German governments in 1815 but only "promised". So the

---

[a] J. W. Goethe, "Ultimatum" (Zyklus "Gott und Welt").—*Ed.*

[b] The reference is to the books: J. R. MacCulloch, *The Principles of Political Economy* and A. Blanqui, *Histoire de l'économie politique en Europe*.—*Ed.*

horrors retailed to us by the philistines of the Sauerland and elsewhere concerning the four years of press freedom from 1815 to 1819, are all just a dream: how at that time the press exposed all their dirty linen and petty scandals to the light of day and how finally the Federal Decrees of 1819[108] put an end to this reign of terror by public opinion.

Herr Grün goes on to tell us that the Free Imperial City of Frankfurt was not a state at all but "no more than a piece of civil society" (p. 19). Germany, he says, has no states of any kind, and people are at last beginning "to realise increasingly the peculiar advantages of this stateless condition of Germany" (p. 257), which advantages consist especially in the cheapness of flogging. The German autocrats will thus be obliged to say: "*la société civile, c'est moi*"[a]—although they fare badly in this, for according to p. 101, civil society is only "an abstraction".

If, however, the Germans have no state, they have instead "a massive bill-of-exchange on truth, and this bill-of-exchange must be realised, paid up and changed for jingling coin" (p. 5). This bill-of-exchange is no doubt payable at the same office where Herr Grün pays his "property tax", "to obtain a seat in the Chamber of Representatives of mankind".

[*Deutsche-Brüsseler-Zeitung* No. 94, November 25, 1847]

The most important "positive" things he enlightens us about concern the French Revolution, on whose "significance" he delivers a special "digression". He begins with the oracular utterance that the contradiction between historical law and rational law is indeed important, for both are of historical origin. Without wishing in any way to belittle Herr Grün's discovery, which is as new as it is important, that rational law too arose in the course of history, we would diffidently venture the observation that a quiet encounter in the quiet of his chamber with the first volumes of *Buchez*'s *Histoire parlementaire* should show him what part this contradiction played in the Revolution.

Herr Grün, however, prefers to give us an extensive proof of the evil nature of the Revolution which eventually boils down to the one, ponderously massive complaint against it: that it "did not examine the concept of man" [p. 195]. Indeed such a grievous sin of omission is unforgivable. If only the Revolution had examined the concept of man, there would have been no question of a ninth Thermidor or an eighteenth Brumaire[109]; Napoleon would have contented himself

[a] *I* am civil society.—*Ed.*

with his general's commission and maybe in his old age written drilling regulations "from the human aspect".—We further learn, in the course of our enlightenment, "about the significance of the Revolution", that basically there is no difference between deism and materialism, and why not. From this we see with some pleasure that Herr Grün has not yet quite forgotten his Hegel. Cf. for example Hegel's *Geschichte der Philosophie,* III, pp. 458, 459 and 463, second edition.—Then, likewise to enlighten us "about the significance of the Revolution", a number of points about competition are made, of which we anticipated the most important above; further, long excerpts from the writings of Holbach are given, in order to prove that he explained crime as having its origin in the state; "the significance of the Revolution" is similarly elucidated by a generous anthology from Thomas More's *Utopia,* which *Utopia* is in turn elucidated to the effect that in the year of 1516 it prophetically portrayed no less than—"*present-day* England" (p. 225), down to the most minute details. And at last, after all these *vues* and *considérants,* on which he digresses at length over 36 pages, the final verdict follows on p. 226: "The Revolution is the realisation of Machiavellianism." An example which is a warning to all those who have not yet examined the concept of "man"!

By way of consolation for the unfortunate French, who have achieved nothing but the realisation of Machiavellianism, on p. 73 Herr Grün dispenses one little drop of balm:

> "In the eighteenth century the French people was like a Prometheus among the nations, who asserted *human rights* as against those of the gods."

Let us not dwell on the fact that it must presumably have "examined the concept of man" after all, nor on the fact that it "asserted" human rights not "as against those of the gods" but those of the king, the aristocracy and the clergy, let us pass over these trifles and veil our heads in silent grief: for something "human" has happened to Herr Grün himself here.

Herr Grün, you see, has forgotten that in previous publications (cf. for instance the article in Volume I of the *Rheinische Jahrbücher,*[a] "Die soziale Bewegung" etc.) he had not merely expatiated upon and "popularised" a certain argument concerning human rights that is to be found in the *Deutsch-Französische Jahrbücher,*[b] but with the truest plagiaristic zeal had even carried it to nonsensical extremes. He has forgotten that there he had pilloried human rights as the rights of

---

[a] K. Grün, "Politik und Socialismus".— *Ed.*

[b] See Marx's "On the Jewish Question" (present edition, Vol. 3, pp. 160-68).—*Ed.*

the *épicier*,[a] the philistine, etc.; here he suddenly transforms them into "*human* rights", the rights of "man". The same thing happens to Herr Grün on pp. 251 and 252, where "the right with which we were born and which, alas, is universally ignored", from *Faust*, is turned into "your natural right, your human right, the right to translate one's ideas into practice and enjoy the fruits of one's labours"; although Goethe opposes it directly to "law and rights", which "are *passed on from generation to generation* like an everlasting disease",[b] in other words the traditional law of the *ancien régime*, with which only the "*innate*, ageless and inalienable human rights" of the Revolution, but by no means the rights of "*man*" conflict. This time, it is true, Herr Grün had to forget his previous point, so that Goethe should not forfeit his human aspect.

Herr Grün has however not yet completely forgotten what he learned from the *Deutsch-Französische Jahrbücher* and other publications of the same tendency. On p. 210 he defines the freedom in France at that time, for example, as "the freedom of unfree (!), common (!!) beings (!!!)". This non-being has arisen from the *common being* on pp. 204 and 205 of the *Deutsch-Französische Jahrbücher*[c] and from the translations of these pages into the current language of German socialism of that time. Arguments which make abstract of philosophy and contain expressions from law, economics, etc., are incomprehensible to the true socialists, who therefore have the general habit of condensing them in the twinkling of an eye into a single brief catchphrase, studded with philosophical expressions and then committing this nonsense to memory for use on any conceivable occasion. In this way, the legal "common being" in the *Deutsch-Französische Jahrbücher* has been transformed into the above philosophico-nonsensical "general being"; political liberation, democracy, has acquired its philosophical short formula in "liberation from the unfree general being", and this the true socialist can put in his pocket without having to fear that his erudition will prove too heavy for him.

On p. XXVI Herr Grün exploits what is said in the *Holy Family* about sensationism and materialism[d] in a manner similar to that which he uses in respect of the above-mentioned quotations from Holbach and their socialist interpretation, the hint contained in that publication that links with the socialist movement of the present day

[a] Grocer, shopkeeper.—*Ed.*

[b] J. W. Goethe, *Faust*, Act I, Scene 4 ("Faust's Study").—*Ed.*

[c] K. Marx, "On the Jewish Question" (see present edition, Vol. 3, pp. 165-66).—*Ed.*

[d] See present edition, Vol. 4, pp. 124-34.—*Ed.*

are to be found in the materialists of the eighteenth century, including Holbach.

Let us pass on to *philosophy*. For which Herr Grün has a thorough-going contempt. As early as p. VII he informs us that he "has no further use for religion, philosophy and politics", that these three "have existed and will never rise again from their dissolution" and that from all of them and from philosophy in particular he "will retain nothing more than man himself *and* the social being capable of social activity". The social being capable of social activity and the above-mentioned human man are, it is true, sufficient to console us for the irreversible downfall of religion, philosophy and politics. But Herr Grün is far too modest. He has not only "retained" "humanistic man" and various "beings" from philosophy, but he is also the proud possessor of a considerable, if confused, mass of Hegelian tradition. How could it be otherwise, when several years ago he knelt in reverence on a number of occasions before the bust of Hegel? We shall be asked not to introduce such scurrilous and scandalous personal details; but Herr Grün himself confided this secret to the man from the press. We shall not at this juncture say where. We have already quoted Herr Grün's sources with chapter and verse so frequently that we may for once request a like service of Herr Grün. To give him at once further proof of our kind intentions towards him, we will confide to him the fact that he took his final verdict in the free-will controversy, which he gives on p. 8, from Fourier's *Traité de l'Association*, section "*du libre arbitre*". Only the idea that the theory of free will is an "aberration of the *German* mind" is a peculiar "aberration" on the part of Herr Grün himself.

We are at last getting closer to Goethe. On p. 15 Herr Grün allows Goethe the right to exist. For Goethe and Schiller are the resolution of the contradiction between "pleasure without activity", i. e., Wieland, and "activity without pleasure", i. e., Klopstock. "Lessing first based man on himself." (One wonders whether Herr Grün can emulate him in this acrobatic feat.)—In this philosophic construction, we have all of Herr Grün's sources together. The form of the construction, the basis of the whole thing is Hegel's world-famous stratagem for the reconciliation of contradictions. "Man based on himself" is Hegelian terminology applied to Feuerbach. "Pleasure without activity" and "activity without pleasure", this contradiction on which Herr Grün sets Wieland and Klopstock to play the above variations, is borrowed from the Complete Works of M[oses] Hess. The only source which we miss is literary history itself, which has not the remotest inkling of the above hotch-potch and is therefore rightly ignored by Herr Grün.

Whilst we are on the subject of Schiller, the following observation of Herr Grün's should be apposite: "Schiller was everything one can be, insofar as one is not Goethe" (p. 311). Beg pardon, one can also be Herr Grün.—Incidentally, our author is here ploughing the same furrow as Ludwig of Bavaria:

> Rome, thou art lacking in Naples' gifts, she in those
> that thou layst claim to;
> Were but the two of you one, it had been too much for the earth.[a]

This historical construction prepares the way for Goethe's entry into German literature. "Man based on himself" by Lessing can continue his evolution only in Goethe's hands. For to Herr Grün belongs the credit of having discovered "man" in Goethe, not natural man, begotten by man and woman in the pleasures of the flesh, but man in the higher sense, dialectical man, the *caput mortuum*[b] in the crucible, in which God the Father, Son and Holy Ghost have been calcined, the *cousin germain* of Homunculus in *Faust*—in short, not man as Goethe speaks of him, but man *as such*, as Herr Grün speaks of him. Who is "man as such", then, of whom Herr Grün speaks?

"There is nothing in Goethe that is not *human* content" (p. XVI).—On p. XXI we hear "that Goethe so portrayed and conceived of *man as such as we wish to realise him today*".—On p. XXII: "Goethe today, and that means his works, is a *true compendium of humanity*."—Goethe "is *humanity fulfilled*" (page XXV).—"Goethe's literary works are (!) *the ideal of human society*" (p. 12).—"Goethe could not become a national poet because he was destined to be the *poet of all that is human*" (p. 25).—Yet, according to p. 14, "*our nation*"—that is, the Germans—is nevertheless supposed to "discern its own essence transfigured" in Goethe.

This is the first revelation about "the essence of man", and we may trust Herr Grün all the more in this matter because he has no doubt "examined the concept of man" with the utmost thoroughness. Goethe portrays "man" as Herr Grün wishes to realise him, and at the same time he portrays the German nation transfigured—"man" is thus none other than "the German transfigured". We have confirmation of this throughout. Just as Goethe is not "a national poet" but "the poet of all that is human", so too the German nation is not a "national" nation, but the nation "of all that is human". For this reason we read on p. XVI again: "Goethe's literary works, emanating from life, ... neither had nor have anything to do with reality." Just like "man", just like "the Germans". And on p. 4: "At this very time *French* socialism aims to bring happiness to *France*,

[a] Ludwig I of Bavaria, "Florenz" (paraphrased).— *Ed.*

[b] Distillation product, distillate.— *Ed.*

German writers have their eyes on *the human race*." (While "the human race" is for the most part accustomed to "having" them not before "their eyes" but before a somewhat opposite part of the anatomy.) On innumerable occasions Herr Grün therefore expresses his pleasure at the fact that Goethe wanted "to liberate man *from within*" (e. g., p. 225), which truly Germanic form of liberation has so far refused to emerge from "*within*"!

Let us duly note this first revelation then: "Man" is the *German* "*transfigured*".

[*Deutsche-Brüsseler-Zeitung* No. 95, November 28, 1847]

Let us now observe how Herr Grün pays homage to "the poet of all that is human", the "human content in Goethe". We shall thereby best discover who "man" is, of whom Herr Grün is speaking. We shall find that Herr Grün here reveals the most secret thoughts of true socialism, which is typical of the way his general craving to outshout all his cronies leads him rashly to trumpet out to the world matters which the rest of the band prefer to keep to themselves. His transformation of Goethe into "the poet of all that is human" was incidentally facilitated for him by the fact that Goethe himself had a habit of using the words "man" and "human" with a special kind of emphasis. Goethe, it is true, used them only in the sense in which they were applied in his own day and later also by Hegel, for instance the attribute "human" was bestowed on the Greeks in particular as opposed to heathen and Christian barbarians, long before these expressions acquired their mystically philosophical meaning through Feuerbach. With Goethe especially they usually have a most unphilosophical and flesh-and-blood meaning. To Herr Grün belongs the credit of being the first to have turned Goethe into a disciple of Feuerbach and a true socialist.

We cannot of course speak of Goethe himself in any detail here. We would just draw attention to one point. In his works Goethe's attitude to contemporary German society is a dual one. Sometimes he is hostile towards it; he attempts to escape from what he finds repulsive in it, as in *Iphigenie* and above all throughout the Italian journey; he rebels against it as Götz, Prometheus and Faust, he lashes it with his bitterest satire as Mephistopheles. But then sometimes he is on friendly terms with it, "accommodates" himself to it, as in the majority of the *Zahme Xenien* and many prose writings; he celebrates it, as in the *Maskenzüge*, even defends it against the oncoming movement of history, as particularly in all the writings in which he comes to speak of the French Revolution. It is not just some aspects of German life which Goethe accepts in contrast to others which are repugnant to him. More frequently it is a question of the different moods he is in; there is a continuing battle within him between the poet of genius who feels revulsion at the wretchedness of his environment, and the cautious offspring of the Frankfurt patrician or the Weimar privy-councillor who finds himself compelled to come to terms with and accustom himself to it. Goethe is thus at one moment a towering figure, at the next petty; at one moment an obstinate, mocking genius full of contempt for the world, at the next a circumspect, unexacting, narrow philistine. Not even Goethe was able to conquer the wretchedness of Germany; on the contrary, it conquered him, and this victory of wretchedness over the greatest of Germans is the most conclusive proof that it cannot be surmounted at all "from within". Goethe was too universal, too active a nature, too much a man of flesh and blood to seek refuge from this wretchedness in a Schillerian flight to the Kantian ideal; he was too keen-sighted not to see how ultimately such a flight amounted to no more than the exchange of a prosaic form of wretchedness for a grandiloquent one. His temperament, his energies, his whole mental attitude disposed him to the practical life, and the practical life he found around him was wretched. This dilemma of having to exist in an environment which he could only despise, and yet being bound to this environment as the only one in which he could be active, this dilemma always faced Goethe, and the older he became, the more the mighty poet withdrew *de guerre lasse*[a] behind the insignificant Weimar minister. Unlike Börne and Menzel, we do not criticise Goethe for not being liberal[b] but for being capable of occasional philistinism as well, not for being unsusceptible to any enthusiasm for German freedom but for sacrificing his spasmodically erupting and truer aesthetic instinct to a petty-bourgeois fear of all major contemporary historical movements, not for being a man of the court but for being capable of attending with such solemn gravity to the pettiest affairs and *menus plaisirs*[c] of one of the pettiest of the little German courts, at the time when a Napoleon was flushing out the great Augean stable that was Germany. We criticise him not from a moral or from a party point of view, but at the very most from the aesthetic and historical point of view; we measure Goethe neither by moral nor by political nor by "human" standards. We cannot here involve ourselves in a description of Goethe's relationship to his

[a] Tired of the struggle.—*Ed.*
[b] L. Börne, *Pariser Briefe*; W. Menzel, *Die deutsche Literatur.*—*Ed.*
[c] Little entertainments (involving supplementary expenditure).—*Ed.*

whole age, his literary precursors and contemporaries, his process of development and his station in life. We therefore restrict ourselves simply to noting the facts.

We shall see in respect of which of these aspects Goethe's works are a "true compendium of humanity", "humanity fulfilled" and the "ideal of human society".

Let us first of all take Goethe's critique of the existing society and then move on to the positive description of the "ideal of human society". In view of the wealthy content of Grün's book, it goes without saying that in either area we are only highlighting a few points of characteristic brilliance.

As a critic of society Goethe does indeed perform miracles. He "condemns civilisation" (pp. 34-36) by giving voice to a few romantic complaints that it blurs everything that is characteristic and distinctive about man. He "prophesies the world of the bourgeoisie" (p. 78) by depicting in *Prometheus tout bonnement*[a] the origin of private property. On p. 229 he is "judge over the world..., the Minos of civilisation". But all these things are mere trifles.

On p. 253 Herr Grün quotes *Catechisation*:

> Reflect, my child! From whom have you these talents?
> You cannot have them from yourself, you know.—
> Why, father gave me everything.—
> And who gave them to him?—My grandfather.—
> No, no! From whom could he, your grandfather, receive them?—
> Well, he just *took* them.

Hurrah! trumpets Herr Grün at the top of his voice, *la propriété, c'est le vol*[b]—Proudhon in person![c]

Leverrier can go back home with his planet and surrender his medal to Herr Grün—for this is something greater than Leverrier, this is something greater even than Jackson and his sulphuric ether fumes. For the man who condensed Proudhon's theft thesis, which is indeed disquieting for many peaceful members of the bourgeoisie, to the innocuous dimensions of the above epigram by Goethe—the only reward for him is the *grand cordon* of the Legion of Honour.

The *Bürgergeneral* presents more difficulties. Herr Grün gazes at it for a while from every side, makes a few doubtful grimaces, which is unusual for him, and begins to cogitate: "true enough ... somewhat wishy-washy ... this does not amount to a condemnation of the Revolution" (p. 150).... Wait! now he has it! What is the object at

[a] Quite simply.—*Ed.*

[b] Property is theft.—*Ed.*

[c] An allusion to P. J. Proudhon, *Qu'est-ce que la propriété?*—*Ed.*

issue? *A jug of milk*[110] and so: "Let us not ... forget that here once again ... it is the *property question* that is being brought to the fore" (p. 151).

If two old women are quarrelling beneath Herr Grün's window over the head of a salted herring, may Herr Grün never find it too much trouble to descend from his room with its fragrance of "roses" and mignonette to inform them that for them too "it is the property question that is being brought to the fore". The gratitude of all right-thinking people will be the best reward for him.

[*Deutsche-Brüsseler-Zeitung* No. 96, December 2, 1847]

Goethe performed one of the greatest feats of criticism when he wrote *Werther. Werther* is not by any means merely a sentimental love-story, as those who have hitherto read Goethe "from the human aspect" believed.

In *Werther* "the human content has found so fitting a form that nothing can be found in any of the literatures of the world which might even remotely deserve to be set beside it" (p. 96). "Werther's love for Lotte is a mere instrument, a vehicle for the tragedy of the radical pantheism of emotion.... Werther is the man who has no vertebra, who has not yet become a subject" (p. 93 [p. 94]). Werther shoots himself not from infatuation but "because he, that unhappy pantheistic spirit, could not come to terms with the world" (p. 94). "*Werther* depicts the whole rotten condition of society with artistic mastery, it seizes the wrongs of society by their deepest roots, by their philosophico-religious basis" (which "basis" everybody knows to be of more recent origin than the "wrongs"), "by the vague and nebulous understanding.... Pure, well-ventilated conceptions of true human nature" (and above all vertebra, Herr Grün, vertebra!) "would be the death of that state of wretchedness, those worm-eaten, crumbling conditions which we call bourgeois life!" [p. 95].

An example of how "*Werther* depicts the rotten condition of society with artistic mastery". Werther writes:

"Adventures? Why do I use this silly word ... our false bourgeois relationships, they are the real adventures, they are the real monstrosities!"[a]

This cry of lamentation from a lachrymose emotionalist at the discrepancy between bourgeois reality and his no less bourgeois illusions about this reality, this faint-hearted sigh which derives solely from a lack of the most ordinary experience, is given out by Herr Grün on p. 84 as incisive social criticism. Herr Grün even asserts that the "despairing agony of life" which the above words express, "this

[a] J. W. Goethe, "Briefe aus der Schweiz" (written in the form of excerpts from letters supposedly found among the papers of the main character of *Die Leiden des jungen Werthers*).— *Ed.*

unhealthy urge to turn things on their heads so that they should at least acquire a different appearance" (!) "ultimately dug for itself the burrow of the French Revolution". The Revolution, previously the realisation of Machiavellianism, here becomes merely the realisation of the sufferings of young Werther. The guillotine of the Place de la Révolution is only a pale imitation of Werther's pistol.

By the same token it is self-evident, according to p. 108, that in *Stella* too Goethe is dealing with "social material", although here only "the most disreputable circumstances" (p. 107) are depicted. True socialism is much more broad-minded than our Lord Jesus. For where two or three are forgathered—they need not even do so in its name—then it is in the midst of them and there is "social material". Like its disciple Herr Grün, it generally bears a striking resemblance to "that kind of dull-witted, self-satisfied nosey-parker who makes everything his business but gets to the bottom of nothing" (p. 47).

Our readers will perhaps remember a letter Wilhelm Meister writes to his brother-in-law[a] in the last volume of the *Lehrjahre*, in which, after a few rather trite comments on the advantages of growing up in well-to-do circumstances, the superiority of the aristocracy over the narrow-minded bourgeoisie is acknowledged and the subordinate position of the latter as well as of all other non-aristocratic classes is sanctioned on the grounds that it is not possible to change it for the present. It is said that only the individual is able in certain circumstances to attain a level of equality with the aristocracy.[b] Herr Grün remarks apropos of this:

> "What Goethe says of the pre-eminence of the upper classes of society is *absolutely true* if one takes upper class as identical with educated class, and in Goethe's case this is so" (p[p]. 264[-65]).

And there let the matter rest.

Let us come to the much-discussed central point: Goethe's attitude to politics and to the French Revolution. Here Herr Grün's book provides an object lesson in what it means to endure through thick and thin; here Herr Grün's devotion gives a good account of itself.

So that Goethe's attitude towards the Revolution may appear justified, Goethe must of course be *above* the Revolution and have transcended it even before it took place. As early as p. XXI we therefore learn:

> "Goethe had so far outstripped the *practical* development of his age that he felt he could only adopt towards it an attitude of rejection, a defensive attitude."

---

[a] Werner.—*Ed.*

[b] J. W. Goethe, *Wilhelm Meisters Lehrjahre*, Buch 5, Kap. 3.—*Ed.*

And on p. 84, apropos of *Werther*, who, as we saw already, embodies the whole Revolution *in nuce*[a]: "History shows 1789, Goethe shows 1889." Similarly on pp. 28 and 29 Goethe is obliged in a few brief words "radically to dispose of all the shouting about liberty" since back in the seventies he had an article[b] printed in the *Frankfurter Gelehrte Anzeigen* which does not at all discuss the liberty which the "shouters" are demanding, but only engages in a few general and fairly sober reflections on liberty as such, the concept of liberty. Furthermore: because in his doctoral dissertation[c] Goethe propounded the thesis that it was actually the duty of every legislator to introduce a certain form of worship—a thesis which Goethe himself treats merely as an amusing paradox, inspired by all manner of small-town clerical bickering in Frankfurt (which Herr Grün *himself* quotes)—because of this "the student Goethe discarded the whole dualism of the Revolution and the present French state like an old pair of shoes" (pp. 26 and 27). It would appear as if Herr Grün has inherited "the student Goethe's worn-out shoes" and used them to sole the seven-league boots of his "social movement" with.

This of course now sheds a new light for us on Goethe's statements about the Revolution. It is now clear that being high above it, having "disposed of it" as long as fifteen years previously, having "discarded it like an old pair of shoes" and being a hundred years in advance of it, he could have no sympathy with it and could take no interest in a nation of "shouters for liberty", with whom he had settled his accounts way back in the year seventy-three. Herr Grün now has an easy time of it. Goethe may turn as much trite inherited wisdom into elegant distiches, he may philosophise upon it with as much philistine narrow-mindedness, he may shrink with as much petty-bourgeois horror from the great ice-floes which threaten his peaceable poet's niche, he may behave with as much pettiness, cowardice and servility as he will, but he cannot carry things too far for his patient gloss-writer. Herr Grün lifts him up on his tireless shoulders and carries him through the mire; indeed he transfers the whole mire to the account of true socialism, just to ensure that Goethe's boots stay clean. From the *Campagne in Frankreich* to the *Natürliche Tochter*, Herr Grün takes on responsibility (pp. 133-170) for everything, everything without exception, he shows a devotion

---

[a] In the germ.— *Ed.*

[b] J. W. Goethe, "Alexander von Joch über Belohnung und Strafen nach türkischen Gesetzen".— *Ed.*

[c] J. W. Goethe, "De Legislatoribus".— *Ed.*

which might move a Buchez to tears. And if all this does not help, if the mire is just too deep, then a higher social exegesis is harnessed to the task, then Herr Grün [p. 137] paraphrases as follows:

> The sad destiny of France, let the mighty think on it,
> But verily the lowly should ponder it more.
> The mighty perished; but who defends the multitude
> From the multitude? The multitude was tyrant to itself.[a]

"Who defends", shouts Herr Grün for all he is worth, with italics, question marks and all the "vehicles of the tragedy of the radical pantheism of emotion" [p. 93], "who, in particular, defends the unpropertied multitude, the so-called rabble, against the propertied multitude, the legislating rabble?" (p. 137). "Who in particular defends" Goethe against Herr Grün?

In this way Herr Grün explains the whole series of worldly-wise bourgeois precepts contained in the Venetian *Epigramme*:

> they "are like a slap in the face delivered by the hand of *Hercules* which only now" (after the danger is past for the philistine) "appear to us to smack home really tolerably now that we have a great and *bitter* experience" (bitter indeed for the philistine) "behind us" (p. 136).

From the *Belagerung von Mainz* Herr Grün

> "would not wish to pass over the following passage for anything in the world: "On Tuesday ... I hastened ... to *pay homage* to his *Highness*, and had the *great good fortune* to *wait upon* the Prince ... *my ever gracious Lord*", etc. [p. 147].

The passage in which Goethe lays his humble devotion at the feet of Herr Rietz, the King of Prussia's[b] Gentleman, Cuckold and Pimp of the Bedchamber, Herr Grün does not think fit to quote.

[*Deutsche-Brüsseler-Zeitung* No. 97, December 5, 1847]

Apropos of the *Bürgergeneral* and the *Ausgewanderte* we read:

> "Goethe's whole antipathy towards the Revolution, whenever it was expressed in literary form, was concerned with the eternal lament at seeing people driven out from circumstances of *well-deserved* and *well-accustomed* property, which intriguers and envious men, etc., then usurped ... this same *injustice of robbery*. ...His *peaceful, domesticated* nature became indignant at this violation of the right of property, which, being *arbitrarily* inflicted, made destitute refugees of whole masses of people" (p. 151).

Let us without more ado put this passage to the account of "man" whose "peaceful, domesticated nature" feels so much at ease in

[a] J. W. Goethe, "Venezianische Epigramme".—*Ed.*
[b] Frederick William II.—*Ed.*

"well-deserved and well-accustomed", to put it bluntly, well-earned "circumstances of property" that it declares the tempest of the Revolution which sweeps away these circumstances *sans façon* to be "arbitrary" and the work of "intriguers and envious men", etc.

In the light of this it does not surprise us that Herr Grün "finds the purest pleasure" (p. 165) in the bourgeois idyll *Hermann und Dorothea*, its timid, worldly-wise small-townsfolk and lamenting peasants who take to their heels in superstitious fear before the sans-culotte army and the horrors of war. Herr Grün

"even accepts with relief the pusillanimous role which is assigned at the end ... to the German people:

> It befits not a German to be at the head of a movement
> Fleeing in terror, nor to waver first this way, then that."[a]

Herr Grün is right to shed tears of sympathy for the victims of cruel times and to raise his eyes to heaven in patriotic despair at such strokes of fate. There are enough ruined and degenerate people anyway, who have no "human" heart in their bosoms, who prefer to join in singing the *Marseillaise* in the Republican camp and perhaps even make lewd jokes in Dorothea's deserted bedchamber. Herr Grün is a decent fellow who waxes indignant at the lack of feeling with which for instance a Hegel looks down on the "little, dumb flowers" which have been crushed underfoot by the onrush of history and mocks at the "litany of private virtues of modesty, humility, love of one's fellow-men and charity" which is held out "against the deeds of world history and those who perform them".[b] Herr Grün is right to do this. He will no doubt receive his reward in heaven.

Let us conclude these "human" remarks on the Revolution with the following: "A real humorist might well take the liberty of finding the *Convention itself infinitely ridiculous*", and until this "real humorist" is found, Herr Grün meanwhile provides the necessary instructions (pp. 151, 152).

Herr Grün similarly sheds some surprising light upon Goethe's attitude towards politics after the Revolution. Just one example. We already know of the profound resentment "man" feels in his heart towards the liberals. The "poet of all that is human" must of course not be allowed to go to his rest without having specifically had it out with them, without having pinned an explicit memorandum on Messrs Welcker, Itzstein and their cronies. This memorandum our

---

[a] J. W. Goethe, *Hermann und Dorothea*, 9. Gesang ("Urania").— *Ed.*

[b] G. W. F. Hegel, *Vorlesungen über die Philosophie der Geschichte*, Einleitung.— *Ed.*

"self-satisfied nosey-parker" unearths in the following of the *Zahme Xenien* (p. 319):

All that is just the same old tripe,
Do acquire some savvy!
Don't be forever just marking time,
But make some progress!

Goethe's verdict: "Nothing is more repulsive than the *majority*, for it consists of a few strong leaders, of rogues who accommodate themselves, of weaklings who adapt themselves, and the mass jogging along behind without having the faintest idea what it wants"[a]—this verdict so typical of the philistine, whose ignorance and short-sightedness are only possible within the narrow bounds of a petty German principality, appears to Herr Grün as "the critique of the later" (i.e. modern) "constitutional state".[b] How important it is one may discover "for instance in any Chamber of Deputies you care to choose" (p. 268). According to this, it is only out of ignorance that the "belly" of the French Chamber looks after itself and its like in such an excellent manner. A few pages later, on p. 271, Herr Grün finds "the *July Revolution*" "misbegotten", and as early as p. 34 the *Customs Union*[111] is sharply criticised because it "makes yet *more expensive* the rags the unclothed and the shivering need to cover their nakedness, in order to make the pillars of the throne (!!), the liberal-minded money-masters" (whom everyone knows to be opposed to "the throne" throughout the Customs Union) "somewhat more resistant to decay". Everyone knows how in Germany the philistines always bring out the "unclothed" and "shivering" whenever it is a question of combating protective tariffs or any other progressive bourgeois measure, and "man" joins their number.

What light does Goethe's critique of society and the state, as seen through Herr Grün's eyes, now shed on "the essence of man"?

Firstly, "man", according to p. 264, exhibits a most marked respect for "the educated estates" in general and a seemly deference towards a high aristocracy in particular. And then he is distinguished by a mighty terror of any great mass movement and any determined social action, at the approach of which he either scuttles timidly back into his fireside corner or takes to his heels with all his goods and chattels. As long as it lasts, such a movement is "a bitter experience" for him; scarcely is it over than he takes up a dominant position at the front of the stage and with the hand of Hercules delivers slaps in

---

[a] J. W. Goethe, *Über Naturwissenschaft im Allgemeinen, einzelne Betrachtungen und Aphorismen.*— *Ed.*

[b] The German original has: "Gesetzesstaat".—*Ed.*

the face which only now appear to him to smack home really tolerably, and finds the whole business "infinitely ridiculous". And throughout he remains wholeheartedly attached to "circumstances of well-deserved and well-accustomed property"; apart from that he has a very "peaceful and domesticated nature", is undemanding and modest and does not wish to be disturbed in his quiet little pleasures by any storms. "Man is happy within a restricted sphere" (p. 191, as the *first sentence* of Part Two has it); he envies no one and gives thanks to his maker if he is left in peace. In short, "man", who, as we have already seen, is *German* by birth, is gradually beginning to turn into the spit image of a *German petty bourgeois.*

What actually does Goethe's critique of society as conveyed by Herr Grün amount to? What does "man" find in society to take exception to? Firstly that it does not correspond to his illusions. But these illusions are precisely the illusions of an ideologising philistine, especially a young one, and if philistine reality does not correspond to these illusions, this is only because they are illusions. For that very reason they correspond all the more fully to philistine reality. They differ from it only as the ideologising expression of a condition in general differs from that condition, and there can therefore be no further question of them being realised. A striking example of this is provided by Herr Grün's commentary on *Werther.*

Secondly "man's" polemic is directed against everything that threatens Germany's philistine régime. His whole polemic against the Revolution is that of a philistine. His hatred of the liberals, the July Revolution and protective tariffs is the absolutely unmistakable expression of the hatred an oppressed, inflexible petty bourgeois feels for the independent, progressive bourgeois. Let us give two further examples of this.

Every one knows that the guild system marked the period of efflorescence of the petty bourgeoisie. On p. 40 Herr Grün says, speaking on behalf of Goethe, in other words, of "man": "In the Middle Ages the corporation brought together *one strong man* in defensive alliance with other *strong men.*" The guildsmen of those days are "strong men" in the eyes of "man".

But in Goethe's day the guild system was already in decay, competition was bursting in from all sides. As a true philistine, Goethe gives voice to a heart-rending wail at one point in his memoirs[a] which Herr Grün quotes on p. 88, about the rot setting among the petty bourgeoisie, the ruination of well-to-do families, the decay of family life associated with this, the loosening of domestic

[a] J. W. Goethe, "Aus meinem Leben", Teil 2, Buch 7.—*Ed.*

bonds and other petty-bourgeois lamentations which in civilised countries are treated with well-deserved contempt. Herr Grün, who scents a capital criticism of modern society in this passage, can so little moderate his delight that he has its whole "human content" printed in italics.

Let us now turn to the positive "human content" in Goethe. We can proceed more quickly now that we are on the track of "man".

Before all else let us report the glad tidings that "Wilhelm Meister deserts his parental home" and that in *Egmont* "the citizens of Brussels are demanding privileges and liberties" for no other reason than to "become men" (p. XVII).

Herr Grün has detected affinities with Proudhon in the elderly Goethe once before. On p. 320 he has this pleasure once again:

"What he wanted, what we all want, to save our personalities, *anarchy* in the true sense of the word, on this topic Goethe has the following to say:

Now why should anarchy have for me
Such attraction in modern times?
Each lives according to his lights
And that is profit for me as well",[a] etc.

Herr Grün is beside himself with joy at finding in Goethe that truly "human" social anarchy which was first proclaimed by Proudhon and adopted by acclamation by the German true socialists. This time he is mistaken however. Goethe is speaking of the already existing "anarchy in modern times", which already "is" profit for him and by which each lives according to his lights, in other words of the independence in sociable intercourse which has been brought about by the dissolution of the feudal system and the guilds, by the rise of the bourgeoisie, and the exclusion of patriarchalism from the social life of the educated classes. Simply for *grammatical* reasons there can therefore be no question of the Herr Grün's beloved *future* anarchy in the higher sense. Goethe is here not talking at all about "what he wanted" but about what he found around him.

But such a little slip should not disturb us. For we do have the poem: *Eigentum.*

I know that nothing is mine own
Save the idea that peacefully
Secretes itself from my spirit,
And every instant of happiness
Which destiny beneficent
Gives me to savour fully.

---

[a] J. W. Goethe, *Zahme Xenien,* IV.—*Ed.*

If it is not clear that in this poem "property as it has existed up to now vanishes into smoke" (p. 320), Herr Grün's comprehension has come to a standstill.

[*Deutsche-Brüsseler-Zeitung* No. 98, December 9, 1847]

But let us leave these entertaining little exegetical diversions of Herr Grün's to their fate. They are in any case legion and each invariably leads on to others still more surprising. Let us rather resume our search for "man".

"Man is happy within a restricted sphere," as we have read. So is the philistine.

"Goethe's early works were of *purely social*" (i.e. human) "character.... Goethe clung to what was *most immediate, smallest, most domesticated*" (p. 88).

The first positive thing we discover about "man" is his delight in the "smallest, domesticated" still-life of the petty bourgeoisie.

"If we can find a place in the world," says Goethe, as summarised by Herr Grün, "where to rest with our possessions, a field to provide us with food, a house to shelter us—is that not a Fatherland for us?"

And, exclaims Herr Grün,

"How these words express our deepest thoughts today!" (p. 32).

Essentially "man" is dressed in a *redingote à la propriétaire* and by that too reveals himself as a thoroughbred *épicier*.[a]

The German bourgeois, as everyone knows, is a fanatic for freedom at most for a brief moment, in his youth. That is characteristic of "man" too. Herr Grün mentions with approval how in his later years Goethe "damns" the "urge for freedom" which still haunts *Götz*, that "product of a free and ill-bred boy", and even quotes this cowardly recantation in extenso on p. 43. What Herr Grün understands by freedom can be deduced from the fact that in the same passage he identifies the freedom of the French Revolution with that of the free Switzers at the time of Goethe's Swiss journey, in other words, modern, constitutional and democratic freedom with the dominance of patricians and guilds in medieval Imperial Cities and especially with the early Germanic barbarism of cattle-rearing Alpine tribes. The montagnards of the Bernese Oberland even have the same name as the Montagnards of the National Convention![b]

---

[a] Grocer.— *Ed.*

[b] Play on words: "*montagnards*"—literally "mountain-dwellers"; this was also the name taken by the Jacobins, the representatives of the Mountain Party in the Convention during the French Revolution.— *Ed.*

The respectable bourgeois is a sworn enemy of all frivolity and mockery of religion: "man" likewise. If Goethe on various occasions expressed himself in a truly bourgeois manner on this topic, Herr Grün takes this as another aspect of the "human content in Goethe". And to make the point quite credible, Herr Grün assembles not merely these grains of gold, but on p. 62 even adds a number of meritorious sentiments of his own, to the effect that "those who mock religion ... are empty vessels and simpletons", etc. Which does much credit to his feelings as "man" and bourgeois.

The bourgeois cannot live without a "king he loves", a father to his country whom he holds dear. Nor can "man". That is why on p. 129 Karl August is for Goethe a "most excellent Prince". Stout old Herr Grün, still enthusing for "most excellent Princes" in the year 1846!

An event is of interest to the bourgeois insofar as it impinges directly on his private circumstances.

> "To Goethe even the events of the day become alien objects which either add to or detract from his *bourgeois comforts* and which may arouse in him an aesthetic or *human* but never a political interest" (p. 20).

Herr Grün "thus finds a human interest in a thing" if he notices that it "either adds to or detracts from his bourgeois comforts". Herr Grün here confesses as openly as possible that bourgeois comforts are the chief thing for "man".

Faust and *Wilhelm Meister* provide Herr Grün with an occasion for special chapters. Let us take *Faust* first.

On p. 116 we are told:

> "Only the fact that Goethe came upon a clue to the mystery of the organisation of plants" enabled him "to complete his delineation of humanistic man" (for there is no way of escaping "human" man) "Faust. *For* Faust is brought to the peak of his own nature (!) just as much as by natural science."

We have already had examples of how that "humanistic man", Herr Grün, "is brought to the peak of his own nature by natural science". We observe that this is inherent in the race.

Then on p. 231 we hear that the "bones of brute and human skeletons" in the first scene signifies "the abstraction of our whole life"—and Herr Grün treats *Faust* in general exactly as though he had the Revelation of St. John the Theologian before him. The macrocosm signifies "Hegelian philosophy", which at the time when Goethe was writing this scene (1806) happened to exist only in Hegel's mind or at most in the manuscript of the *Phänomenologie* which Hegel was then working on. What has chronology to do with "human content"?

The depiction of the moribund Holy Roman Empire in the Second Part of *Faust* Herr Grün (p. 240) imagines without more ado to be a depiction of the monarchy of Louis XIV, "in which," he adds, "we *automatically* have the Constitution and the Republic!" "Man" naturally "of himself has" everything that other people first have to provide for themselves by dint of toil and exertion.

On p. 246 Herr Grün confides to us that the Second Part of *Faust* has become, with regard to its scientific aspect, "the canon of modern times, just as Dante's *Divine Comedy* was the canon of the Middle Ages". We would commend this to natural scientists who have hitherto sought very little in the Second Part of *Faust*, and to historians, who have sought something quite other than a "canon of the Middle Ages" in the Florentine's pro-Ghibelline poem![112] It seems as though Herr Grün is looking at history with the same eyes as Goethe, according to p. 49, looked at his own past: "In Italy Goethe surveyed his past *with the eyes* of the Belvedere Apollo", eyes which *pour comble de malheur*[a] do not even have eyeballs.

Wilhelm Meister is "a Communist", i.e. "in theory, on the basis of aesthetic outlook" (!!) (p. 254).

> On nothing does he set great store,
> And yet the whole wide world is his[b] (p. 257).

Of course, he has enough money, and the world belongs to him, as it belongs to every bourgeois, without his needing to go to the trouble of becoming "a communist on the basis of aesthetic outlook".—Under the auspices of this "nothing" on which Wilhelm Meister sets great store and which, as we see from p. 256, is indeed an extensive and most substantial "nothing", even hangovers are eliminated. Herr Grün "drains every cup to the lees, without ill effect, without a headache". So much the better for "man" who may now quietly worship Bacchus with impunity. For the day when all these things shall come to pass, Herr Grün has meanwhile already discovered the drinking song for "true man" in *On nothing do I set great store*—"this song will be sung when mankind has arranged its affairs in a manner worthy of itself"; but Herr Grün has reduced it to three verses and expunged those parts unsuitable for youth and "man".

In *W[ilhelm] M[eister]* Goethe sets up

> "the ideal of human society". "Man is not a teaching but a living, acting and creating being." "Wilhelm Meister is this man." "The essence of man is activity" (an essence he shares with any flea) pp. 257, 258, 261.

Finally the *Wahlverwandtschaften.* This novel, moral enough in itself, is moralised even more by Herr Grün, so that it almost seems as

[a] As the final misfortune.—*Ed.*
[b] J. W. Goethe, "Vanitas! Vanitatum vanitas!" (paraphrased).—*Ed.*

though he were concerned to recommend the *Wahlverwandtschaften* as a suitable text-book for schools for young ladies. Herr Grün explains that Goethe

> "distinguished between love and marriage, so that for him love was a *search of marriage* and marriage was love *found* and fulfilled" (p. 286).

By this token, then, love is the *search* of "love that has been found". This is further elucidated to the effect that after "the freedom of youthful love", marriage must come about as "the final relationship of love" (p. 287). Exactly as in civilised countries a wise father first allows his son to sow his wild oats for a few years and then finds him a suitable wife as a "final relationship". However, whilst people in civilised countries have long passed the stage of regarding this "final relationship" as something morally binding, whilst on the contrary in those countries the husband keeps mistresses and his wife retaliates by cuckolding him, the philistine once again rescues Herr Grün:

> "If man has had a really free choice, ... if two people base their union on their mutual rational wishes" (there is no mention here of passion, flesh and blood) "it would require the outlook of a *libertine* to regard the upsetting of this relationship as a trifle, as not so fraught with suffering and unhappiness as Goethe did. But there can be no question of *libertinism* with Goethe" (p. 288).

This passage qualifies the timid polemic against morality which Herr Grün permits himself from time to time. The philistine has arrived at the realisation that there is all the more reason for having to turn a blind eye to the behaviour of the young since it is precisely the most dissolute young men who afterwards make the best husbands. But if they should misbehave themselves again after the wedding—then no mercy, no pity on them; for that "would require the outlook of a libertine".

"The outlook of a libertine!" "Libertinism!" One can just picture "man" as large as life before one, as he places his hand on his heart, and overflowing with pride exclaims: No! I am pure of all frivolity, of "fornication and licentiousness", I have never deliberately ruined the happiness of a contented marriage, I have always practised fidelity and honesty and have never lusted after my neighbour's wife—I am no "libertine"!

"Man" is right. He is not made for amorous affairs with beautiful women, he has never turned his mind to seduction and adultery, he is no "libertine", but a man of conscience, an honourable, virtuous, German philistine. He is

> ...l'épicier pacifique,
> Fumant sa pipe au fond de sa boutique;
> Il craint sa femme et son ton arrogant;

De la maison il lui laisse l'empire,
Au moindre signe obéit sans mot dire
Et vit ainsi cocu, battu, content.[a]

(Parny, *Goddam*, chant III.)

There remains just one observation for us to make. If above we have only considered one aspect of Goethe, that is the fault of Herr Grün alone. He does not present Goethe's towering stature at all. He either skims hurriedly over all works in which Goethe was really great and a genius, such as the *Römische Elegieen* of Goethe the "libertine", or he inundates them with a great torrent of trivialities, which only proves that he can make nothing of them. On the other hand, with what is for him uncommon industry he seeks out every instance of philistinism, petty priggery and narrow-mindedness, collates them, exaggerates them in the manner of a true literary hack, and rejoices every time he is able to find support for his own narrow-minded opinions on the authority of Goethe, whom he furthermore frequently distorts.

History's revenge on Goethe for ignoring her every time she confronted him face to face was not the yapping of Menzel nor the narrow polemic of Börne. No,

Just as Titania in the land of fairy magic
Found Nick Bottom in her arms,[b]

so one morning Goethe found Herr Grün in his arms. Herr Grün's apologia, the warm thanks he stammers out to Goethe for every philistine word, that is the bitterest revenge which offended history could pronounce upon the greatest German poet.

Herr Grün, however, "can close his eyes in the awareness that he has not disgraced his destiny of being a man" (p. 248).

Written in 1846 and early 1847

First published in the *Deutsche-Brüsseler-Zeitung* Nos. 73, 74, 93, 94, 95, 96, 97 and 98; September 12 and 16, November 21, 25 and 28, December 2, 5 and 9, 1847

Printed according to the newspaper

Published in English for the first time

---

[a] ... the peaceful tradesman,
Smoking his pipe at the back of his shop;
He fears his wife and her domineering tone;
He leaves to her the government of the house,
Without a word he obeys her slightest signal;
Thus he lives, cuckolded, beaten and content.— *Ed.*

[b] J. W. Goethe, *Warnung* (Zyklus "Epigrammatisch").—*Ed.*

Frederick Engels

THE ECONOMIC CONGRESS[113]

It is well known that here there are several lawyers, officials, doctors, rentiers, merchants, etc., who, under pretence of an Association pour le libre échange (à l'instar de Paris),[a] give one another instruction in the elements of political economy. For the last three days of the past week these gentlemen were swimming in bliss. They held their great congress of the greatest economists of all countries, they enjoyed the ineffable delights of hearing the truths of economics expounded, no longer from the mouths of a M[onsieur] Jules Bartels, a Le Hardy de Beaulieu, a Faider or Fader[b] or other unknown celebrities, no, but from the mouths of the leading masters of the science. They were enraptured, enchanted, divinely happy, transported to the seventh heaven.

Less enraptured, however, were the masters of the science themselves. They had come prepared for an easy battle, and the battle was very hard for them; they believed that they had only to come, see and conquer, and they conquered only in the voting, whereas they were decisively defeated in the discussion on the second day, and only by means of intrigues did they avoid a new and still more decisive defeat on the third day. Even if their divinely happy public noticed nothing of all this, they themselves could not but feel it painfully.

We attended the congress. From the very beginning we had no particular respect for these masters of science, whose principal

---

[a] Association for Free Trade (after the example of Paris).— *Ed.*

[b] Pun— *Fader*, from "fade" (dull, insipid), *Faider*, name of a participant in the economic congress.— *Ed.*

learning consists in continually contradicting one another and themselves with the greatest equanimity. But we confess that this congress robbed us of the last tiny vestige of respect we might have had for those with whose writings and speeches we were less well acquainted. We confess that we were astounded to have to hear such platitudes and insipidities, such universally familiar trivialities. We confess that we had not expected these men of science to be incapable of telling us anything more valuable than the first elements of economics, which might well be new for children of seven or eight, but which must be presumed to be common knowledge for adults, and in particular for members of Associations pour le libre échange. However, the gentlemen knew their public better than we.

The Englishmen comported themselves best at the congress. They had the greatest interest in the matter; they have the opening up of the continental markets at heart; for them the question of free trade is a matter of life and death. They showed this clearly enough, too; they, who nowhere speak anything but their English, condescended, in the interest of their beloved free trade,[a] to speak French. One could clearly see how powerfully the matter affected their purses. The Frenchmen performed in the manner of pure ideologists and scientific dreamers. They did not even distinguish themselves by any French *esprit* or originality of conception. But at least they spoke good French, and that is something one seldom hears in Brussels.—The Dutchmen were tedious and professorial. The Dane, Herr David, was quite incomprehensible. The Belgians for the most part played the role of passive listeners, or at any rate never transcended the limits of their national industry—*contrefaçon*.[b] And finally the Germans, with the exception of Weerth, who, however, spoke more as an Englishman than a German, formed the *partie honteuse* of the whole congress. The palm would have fittingly been theirs, if a Belgian had not after all conquered it for his nation.

First day. General discussion. Belgium opened it with M. Faider, who, in his entire behaviour, in his deportment and language, brought before us the whole of that strutting foppishness which gives itself such repulsive airs in the streets and promenades of Brussels. M. Faider peddled nothing but empty phrases, and hardly raised himself to the most elementary economic truths. Let us not detain

[a] English in the original.—*Ed.*

[b] Imitation.—*Ed.*

ourselves with him for as long as he detained us with his outpourings of dishwater soup.

M. Wolowski, Professor etc. in Paris, mounted the rostrum. A smug, rhetorical, superficial, Frenchified Polish Jew, who has managed to combine in himself the bad qualities of all three nations with none of the good. M. Wolowski whipped up huge enthusiasm by means of a previously arranged, sophistically surprising speech. Unfortunately, however, this speech was not M. Wolowski's property, it was patched together from the *Sophismes économiques* of M. Frédéric Bastiat. This was naturally something the Brussels *claqueurs* could not know.—M. Wolowski regretted that a *German* protectionist would be opposing him and that the French protectionists had allowed the initiative to be taken from them in this way. For this he was punished. When concluding his speech M. Wolowski became comical in the highest degree. He came to speak of the working classes, to whom he promised golden mountains from free trade, and in whose name he made a hypocritically furious attack on the protectionists. Yes! He exclaimed, working himself up into a rhetorical falsetto, yes, these protectionists, "*ces gens qui n'ont rien là qui batte pour les classes laborieuses*"[a]—here he pounded himself on his round little belly—these protectionists are the people who prevent us from fulfilling our most heartfelt wishes and help the workers out of their poverty! Unfortunately, his whole fury was too artificial to make any impression on the few workers who were present in the gallery.

Herr Rittinghausen from Cologne, the representative of the German fatherland, read out an infinitely tedious essay in defence of the protective system. He spoke as a true German. With the most pitiful grimaces in the world he lamented Germany's sorry condition and its industrial impotence, and he downright beseeched the Englishmen that they might, after all, allow Germany to protect itself against their superior competition. Why, he said, gentlemen, you wish to give us freedom of trade, you wish us to compete freely with all nations, when we still have guilds almost everywhere, when we may not even compete freely *among ourselves*?

M. Blanqui, Professor, Deputy, and Progressive Conservative from Paris, author of a wretched economic history[b] and other inferior books, principal pillar of the so-called École française of economics, answered Herr Rittinghausen. A well-fed, stand-offish man with a face in which hypocritical severity, unctuousness and philanthropy

[a] "These people with nothing here which beats for the toiling classes."—*Ed.*

[b] A. Blanqui, *Histoire de l'économie politique en Europe*.—*Ed.*

are repulsively blended. Knight of the Legion of Honour, *cela va sans dire.*[a] M. Blanqui spoke with the greatest possible volubility and the least possible wit, and this, naturally, was just the thing to impress the Brussels Free Traders. What he said is moreover ten times less significant than what he has previously written. Let us not detain ourselves with these empty phrases.

Then came Dr. Bowring, radical Member of Parliament and heir to the wisdom of Bentham, whose skeleton he owns.[114] He is himself a kind of Bentham skeleton. It was noticeable that the elections were over; Mr. Bowring no longer found it necessary to make concessions to the people, but spoke instead in the manner of a genuine bourgeois. He spoke fluent and correct French, with a strong English accent, and emphasised the effect of his words with the most vehement and droll gesticulations that we recall ever having seen. Mr. Bowring, the representative of the highly interested English bourgeoisie, declared that at last the time had come for all egoism to be cast aside and for each to establish his own prosperity on that of the others. Naturally the old economic "truth" cropped up that one can do more business with a millionaire and therefore make more out of him than out of the possessor of a mere thousand talers.—Finally, there was yet another inspired hymn to *cet envoyé du ciel,*[b] the smuggler.

After him spoke M. Duchateau, President of the Valenciennes Association pour la protection du travail national,[c] defending, as a result of M. Wolowski's provocation, the French protective system. He repeated, with great calm and lucidity, the well-known principles of the protectionists, in the quite correct opinion that these were sufficient to make the whole congress bitter for the free-trade gentlemen. He was undoubtedly the best speaker of the day.

Mr. Ewart, Member of Parliament, answered him, in almost incomprehensible French, with the stalest and most platitudinous shibboleths of the Anti-Corn-Law League, long since known by heart to almost every street urchin in England.

We mention M. Campan, a delegate from the Free Trade Society of Bordeaux, merely for the sake of the record. What he said was so insignificant that we can no longer recall a single word of it.

Colonel Thompson, Member of Parliament, reduces the question to a simple story—in a certain town there exist cab-drivers who make a journey for $1^1/_2$ francs. Now an omnibus is introduced, which

---

[a] That goes without saying.—*Ed.*

[b] This ambassador from heaven.—*Ed.*

[c] Association for the protection of national labour.—*Ed.*

makes the same trip for 1 franc. Thus the cab-driver would say that $^1/_2$ franc per trip is withdrawn from trade. But is that true? Where does the $^1/_2$ franc go to? Aha! the passenger will buy something else for it, perhaps pies, cakes or the like. Thus the half franc enters trade after all, and the consumer gets more satisfaction from it. Here we have the case of the protectionists, who defend the cab-driver, and that of the Free Traders, who wish to introduce the omnibus. The only thing that the good Colonel Thompson forgets is that competition soon eliminates this advantage of the consumer, and takes from him for one thing exactly what he gains on another.

The final speaker was M. Dunoyer, a Counsellor of State in Paris, author of several books, among others *De la liberté du travail*, in which he accuses the workers of producing far too many children. He spoke with the vehemence proper to a Counsellor of State, and moreover very insignificantly. M. Dunoyer is a well-nourished *ventru*[a] with a bald skull and the red, forward-thrusting face of a dog, he is evidently accustomed to brook no contradictions, but is by no means as terrifying as he would like to be. M. Blanqui said of his cheap invective against the proletariat: "*M. Dunoyer dit aux peuples les mêmes vérités austères qu'au dernier siècle les Voltaire et Rousseau disaient aux princes.*"[b]

With this the general discussion was closed. We shall report on the discussion of the individual questions on the second and third days in the next issue.[115]

Written between September 19 and 22, 1847

First published in the *Deutsche-Brüsseler-Zeitung* No. 76, September 23, 1847

Printed according to the newspaper

Published in English for the first time

---

[a] Belly, paunch.—*Ed.*

[b] "M. Dunoyer tells the same hard truths to the people as did the Voltaires and Rousseaus to the princes in the last century."—*Ed.*

Karl Marx

THE PROTECTIONISTS, THE FREE TRADERS AND THE WORKING CLASS[116]

The protectionists have never protected small industry, handicraft proper. Have Dr. List and his school in Germany by any chance demanded protective tariffs for the small linen industry, for hand loom-weaving, for handicraft production? No, when they demanded protective tariffs they did so only in order to oust handicraft production with machines and patriarchal industry with modern industry. In a word, they wish to extend the dominion of the bourgeoisie, and in particular of the big industrial capitalists. They went so far as to proclaim aloud the decline and fall of small industry and the petty bourgeoisie, of small farming and the small peasants, as a sad but inevitable and, as far as the industrial development of Germany is concerned, necessary occurrence.

Besides the school of Dr. List there exists in Germany, the land of schools, yet another school, which demands not merely a system of protective tariffs, but a system of import prohibition proper. The leader of this school, Herr v. Gülich, has written a very scholarly history of industry and trade,[a] which has also been translated into French. Herr v. Gülich is a sincere philanthropist; he is in earnest with regard to protecting handicraft production and national labour. Well now! What did he do? He began by refuting Dr. List, proved that in List's system the welfare of the working class is only a sham and a pretence, a ringing piece of hollow rhetoric, and then, for his part, he made the following proposals:

1. To prohibit the importation of foreign manufactured products;

---

[a] G. Gülich, *Geschichtliche Darstellung des Handels, der Gewerbe und des Ackerbaus der bedeutendsten handeltreibenden Staaten unserer Zeit.*—*Ed.*

2. to place very heavy import duties on raw materials originating abroad, like cotton, silk etc., etc., in order to protect wool and nationally produced linen;
3. likewise on colonial products, in order to replace sugar, coffee, indigo, cochineal, valuable timbers etc., etc., with national products;
4. to place high taxes on nationally produced machines, in order to protect handicraft production against the machine.

It is evident that Herr v. Gülich is a man who accepts the system with all its consequences. And what does this lead to? Not merely preventing the entry of foreign industrial products, but also hindering the progress of national industry.

Herr List and Herr v. Gülich form the limits between which the system moves. If it wishes to protect industrial progress, then it at once sacrifices handicraft production, labour; if it wishes to protect labour, then industrial progress is sacrificed.

Let us return to the protectionists proper, who do not share the illusions of Herr v. Gülich.

If they speak consciously and openly to the working class, then they summarise their philanthropy in the following words: It is better to be exploited by one's fellow-countrymen than by foreigners.

I do not think the working class will be for ever satisfied with this solution, which, it must be confessed, is indeed very patriotic, but nonetheless a little too ascetic and spiritual for people whose only occupation consists in the production of riches, of material wealth.

But the protectionists will say: "So when all is said and done we at least preserve the present state of society. Good or bad, we guarantee the labourer work for his hands, and prevent his being thrown on to the street by foreign competition." I shall not dispute this statement, I accept it. The preservation, the conservation of the present state of affairs is accordingly the best result the protectionists can achieve in the most favourable circumstances. Good, but the problem for the working class is not to preserve the present state of affairs, but to transform it into its opposite.

The protectionists have one last refuge. They say that their system makes no claim to be a means of social reform, but that it is nonetheless necessary to begin with social reforms in one's own country, before one embarks on economic reforms internationally. After the protective system has been at first reactionary, then conservative, it finally becomes conservative-progressive. It will suffice to point out the contradiction lurking in this theory, which at first sight appears to have something seductive, practical and rational to it. A strange contradiction! The system of protective tariffs places in the hands of the capital of one country the weapons which enable it to defy the capital of other countries; it increases the strength of this capital in opposition to foreign capital, and at the same time it deludes itself that the very same means will make that same capital small and weak in opposition to the working class. In the last analysis that would mean appealing to the philanthropy of capital, as though capital as such could be a philanthropist. In general, social reforms can never be brought about by the weakness of the strong; they must and will be called to life by the strength of the weak.

Incidentally, we have no need to detain ourselves with this matter. From the moment the protectionists concede that social reforms have no place in their system and are not a result of it, and that they form a special question—from this moment on they have already abandoned the social question. I shall accordingly leave the protectionists aside and speak of Free Trade in its relationship to the condition of the working class.

Written in the second half of September 1847

First published in *Zwei Reden über die Freihandels- und Schutzzollfrage von Karl Marx*, Hamm, 1848

Printed according to the 1848 edition

Published in English for the first time

Frederick Engels

THE FREE TRADE CONGRESS AT BRUSSELS

On the 16th, 17th, and 18th of September, there was held here (Brussels) a congress of political economists, manufacturers, tradesmen, etc., to discuss the question of Free Trade. There were present about 150 members of all nations. There assisted, on the part of the English Free Traders, Dr. Bowring, M. P., Col. Thompson, M. P., Mr. Ewart, M. P., Mr. Brown, M. P., James Wilson, Esq., editor of the *Economist*, etc.; from France had arrived M. Wolowski, professor of jurisprudence; M. Blanqui, deputy, professor of political economy, author of a history of that science,[a] and other works; M. Horace Say, son of the celebrated economist[b]; M. Ch. Dunoyer, member of the Privy Council, author of several works upon politics and economy, and others. From Germany there was no Free Trader present, but Holland, Denmark, Italy, etc., had sent representatives. Señor Ramon de la Sagra, of Madrid, intended to come, but came too late. The assistance of a whole host of Belgian Free Traders need hardly be mentioned, it being a matter of course.

Thus the celebrities of the science had met to discuss the important question—whether Free Trade would benefit the world? You will think the discussions of such a splendid assembly—discussions carried on by economical stars of the first magnitude—must have been interesting in the highest degree. You will say that men like Dr. Bowring, Colonel Thompson, Blanqui and Dunoyer, must have pronounced speeches the most striking, must have produced arguments the most convincing, must have represented all questions under a light the most novel and surprising imaginable. Alas! Sir, if you had been present, you would have been piteously undeceived.

---

[a] A. Blanqui, *Histoire de l'économie politique en Europe*.—*Ed.*

[b] Jean Baptiste Say.—*Ed.*

Your glorious expectations, your fond illusions would have vanished within less than an hour. I have assisted at innumerable public meetings and discussions. I heard the League pour forth their Anti-Corn-Law[117] arguments more than a hundred times, while I was in England, but never, I can assure you, never did I hear such dull, tedious, trivial stuff, brought forward with such a degree of self-complacency. I was never before so disappointed. What was carried on did not merit the name of a discussion—it was mere pot-house talk. The great scientific luminaries never ventured themselves upon the field of political economy, in the strict sense of the word. I shall not repeat to you all the worn-out stuff which was brought forward on the first two days. Read two or three numbers of the *League* or the *Manchester Guardian,* and you will find all that was said, except, perhaps, a few specious sentences brought forward by M. Wolowski, which he, however, had stolen from M. Bastiat's (chief of the French Free Traders) pamphlet of *Sophismes économiques.* Free Traders did not expect to meet with any other opposition, but that of M. Rittinghausen, a German Protectionist, and generally an insipid fellow. But up got M. Duchateau, a French manufacturer and Protectionist—a man who spoke for his purse, just as Mr. Ewart or Mr. Brown spoke for theirs, and gave them such a terrible opposition, that on the second day of the discussion, a great number, even of Free Traders, avowed that they had been beaten in argument. They took, however, their revenge at the vote—the resolutions passed, of course, almost unanimously.

On the third day, a question was discussed which interests your readers. It was this: "Will the carrying out of universal Free Trade benefit the working classes?" The affirmative was supported by Mr. Brown, the South Lancashire Free Trader, in a lengthy speech, in English; he and Mr. Wilson were the only ones who spoke that language, the remainder all spoke French—Dr. Bowring, very well—Colonel Thompson, tolerably—Mr. Ewart, dreadfully. He repeated a part of the old League documents, in a whining tone, very much like a Church-of-England parson.

After him got up Mr. *Weerth,* of Rhenish Prussia. You know, I believe, this gentleman—a young tradesman whose poetry is well known and very much liked throughout Germany, and who, during several years' stay in Yorkshire, was an eye-witness of the condition of the working people. He has a great many friends amongst them there, who will be glad to see that he has not forgotten them. As his speech will be to your readers the most interesting feature of the whole Congress, I shall report it at some length. He spoke as follows[118]:

"Gentlemen—You are discussing the influence of Free Trade upon the condition of the working classes. You profess the greatest possible sympathy for those classes. I am very glad of it, but yet I am astonished not to see a representative of the working classes amongst you! The monied classes of France are represented by a peer—those of England by several M.P.s.—those of Belgium by an ex-minister—and even those of Germany by a gentleman who gave us a faithful description of the state of that country. But where, I ask you, are the representatives of the working men? I see them nowhere; and, therefore, gentlemen, allow me to take up the defence of their interests. I beg to speak to you on behalf of the working people, and principally on behalf of those five millions of English working men, amongst whom I spent several of the most pleasant years of my life, whom I know and whom I cherish. (Cheers.) Indeed, gentlemen, the working people stand in need of some generosity. Hitherto they have not been treated like men, but like beasts of burden, nay—like merchandise, like machines; the English manufacturers know this so well, that they never say, we employ so many workmen, but so many hands. The monied classes, acting upon this principle, have never hesitated a moment to profit by their services as long as they require them, and then turn them out upon the streets, as soon as there is no longer any profit to be squeezed out of them. Thus the condition of these outcasts of modern society has become such, that it cannot be made worse. Look wherever you like; to the banks of the Rhone; into the dirty and pestilential lanes of Manchester, Leeds, and Birmingham; on the hills of Saxony and Silesia, or the plains of Westphalia; everywhere you will meet with the same pale starvation, the same gloomy despair, in the eyes of men who in vain claim their rights and their position in civilised society." (Great sensation.)

Mr. Weerth then declared his opinion to be, that the protective system in reality did not protect the working people, but that Free Trade—and he told it them plainly and distinctly, although he himself was a Free Trader—that Free Trade would never change their miserable condition. He did not at all join in the delusions of the Free Traders, as to the beneficial effects of the carrying out of their system upon the working classes. On the contrary, Free Trade, the full realisation of free competition, would force the working people as much into a keener competition amongst themselves as it would make capitalists compete more selfishly against each other. The perfect freedom of competition would inevitably give an enormous impulse to the invention of new machinery, and thus supersede more workmen than even now were daily superseded. It would stimulate production in every way, but for this very reason it would stimulate overproduction, overstocking of markets, and commercial revulsions, just in the same measure. The Free Traders pretended that those terrible revulsions would cease under a system of commercial freedom; why, just the contrary would be the case, they would increase and multiply more than ever. Possible, nay certain it was, that at first the greater cheapness of provisions would benefit the workpeople,—that a lessened cost of production would increase consumption and the demand for labour, but that advantage very soon would be turned into misery, the competition of the working people amongst themselves would soon reduce them to the former level of misery and starvation. After these and other arguments (which appeared to be quite novel to the meeting, for they were listened to with the greatest attention, although *The Times* reporter deigns to rid himself of them with the impudent but significant sneer—"Chartist commonplace"[a]), Mr. *Weerth* concluded as follows:

"And do not think, gentlemen, that these are but my individual opinions; they are the opinions, too, of the English working men, a class whom I cherish and respect, because they are intelligent and energetic men, indeed, (cheers, "by courtesy") I shall prove that by a few facts. During full six years, the gentlemen of the League, whom we see here, courted the support of the working people, but in vain. The working men never forgot that the capitalists were their natural enemies; they recollected the League riots of 1842,[119] and the masters' opposition against the Ten Hours Bill. It was only towards the end of 1845, that the Chartists, the élite of the working classes, associated for a moment with the League, in order to crush their common enemy, the landed aristocracy. But it was for a moment only, and never were they deceived by the delusive promises of Cobden, Bright and Co., nor did they hope the fulfilment of cheap bread, high wages, and plenty to do. No, not for a moment did they cease to trust in their own exertions only; to form a distinct party, led on by distinct chiefs, by the indefatigable Duncombe, and by Feargus O'Connor, who, in spite of all calumnies,—(here Mr. Weerth looked at Dr. Bowring, who made a quick, convulsive movement)—who, in spite of all calumnies, within a few weeks will sit upon the same bench with you in the House of Commons.[120] In the name, then, of those millions who do not believe that Free Trade will do wonders for them, I call upon you to seek for some other means to effectively better their condition. Gentlemen, I call upon you for your own interests. You have no longer to fear the Emperor of all the Russias; you dread not an invasion of Cossacks, but if you do not take care you will have to fear the irruption of your own workmen, and they will be more terrible to you than all the Cossacks in the world. Gentlemen, the workpeople want no more words from you, they want deeds. And you have no reason to be astonished at that. They recollect very well, that in 1830 and 31, when they conquered the Reform Bill for you in London, when they fought for you in the streets of Paris and Brussels,[121] that then they were courted, shaken hands with, and highly praised; but that when a few years after they demanded bread, then they were received with grape shot and the bayonet. ("Oh! no, no! yes, yes! Buzançais, Lyons.")[122] I repeat, therefore, to you, carry your Free Trade, it will be well; but think, at the same time, about other measures for the working classes, or you will repent it." (Loud cheers.)

Immediately after Mr. Weerth, up got Dr. *Bowring* to reply.

"Gentlemen," said he, "I can tell you that the hon. member who has just sat down has not been elected by the English working people to represent them in this Congress. On the contrary, the English people generally have given us their suffrages for this purpose, and, therefore, we claim our places as their true representatives."

He then went on to show the beneficial effects of Free Trade, as proved by the increased importation of articles of food into England

---

[a] "Free Trade Congress in Brussels" in *The Times*, September 20, 1847.—*Ed.*

since the introduction of last year's tariff.[a] So many eggs, so many cwt. of butter, cheese, ham, bacon, so many heads of cattle, etc., etc.; who could have eaten all that if not the working people of England? He quite forgot, however, telling us what quantities of the same articles have been produced less in England since foreign competition has been admitted. He took it for granted that increased importation was a decisive proof of increased consumption. He never mentioned wherefrom the working people of Manchester, Bradford, and Leeds, who now walk the streets and cannot get work, wherefrom these men got the money to pay for this supposed increase of consumption and Free Trade comforts, for we never heard of the masters making them presents of eggs, butter, cheese, ham, and meat, for not working at all. He never said a word about the present depressed state of the trade, which in every public paper is represented as really unexampled. He seemed not to know that all the predictions of the Free Traders since the carrying of the measures have proved just the reverse of reality. He had not a word of sympathy for the sufferings of the working classes, but, on the contrary, represented their present gloomy condition as the brightest, happiest, and most comfortable they could reasonably desire.

The English working people, now, may choose betwixt their two representatives. A host of others followed, who spoke about every imaginable subject upon earth, except upon the one under discussion. Mr. M'Adam, M. P. for Belfast (?), spun an eternally long yarn upon flax-spinning in Ireland, and almost killed the meeting with statistics. Mr. Ackersdijk, a Dutch professor, spoke about Old Holland and Young Holland, the university of Liège, Walpole, and De Witt. M. Van de Casteele spoke about France, Belgium, and the ministry. M. Asher, of Berlin, about German patriotism and some new article he called spiritual manufacture. M. Den Tex, a Dutchman, about God knows what. At last, the whole meeting being half asleep, was awakened by M. Wolowski, who returned to the question and replied to Mr. Weerth. His speech, like all speeches delivered by Frenchmen, proved how much the French capitalists dread the fulfilment of Mr. Weerth's prophecies; they speak with such pretended sympathy, such canting and whining of the sufferings of the working classes, that one might take it all for good earnest, were it not too flagrantly contradicted by the roundness of their bellies, by the stamp of hypocrisy deeply imprinted on their faces, by the pitiful remedies they propose and by the unmistakeably striking contrast between their words and their deeds. Nor have they

[a] i.e., the lifting of heavy duties on imported corn in 1846.—*Ed.*

ever succeeded in deceiving one single working man. Then, up got the Duc d'Harcourt, peer of France, and claimed, too, for the French capitalists, deputies, etc., present the right of representing the French working people. They do so in the same way as Dr. Bowring represents the English Chartists. Then spoke Mr. James Wilson, repeating most brazen-facedly the most worn-out League arguments, in the drowsy tone of a Philadelphia quaker.

You see from this, what a nice discussion it was. Dr. Marx, of Brussels, whom you know as by far the most talented representative of German Democracy, had also claimed his turn to speak. He had prepared a speech, which, if it had been delivered, would have made it impossible for the congressional "gents" to vote upon the question. But Mr. Weerth's opposition had made them shy. They resolved to let none speak, of whose orthodoxy they were not quite sure. Thus, Messrs Wolowski, Wilson, and the whole precious lot spoke against time, and when it was four o'clock, there were still six or seven gentlemen who wanted to speak, but the chairman[a] closed the discussion abruptly, and the whole set of fools, ignorants, and knaves called a congress of political economists, voted all votes against one (the poor German fool of a Protectionist aforesaid)—the Democrats did not vote at all—that Free Trade is extremely beneficial to the working people, and will free them from all misery and distress.

As Mr. Marx's speech, although not delivered, contains the very best and most striking refutation of this barefaced lie, which can be imagined, and as its contents, in spite of so many hundred pages having been written *pro* and *con* upon the subject, will yet read quite novel in England, I enclose you some extracts from it.

SPEECH OF DR. MARX ON PROTECTION, FREE TRADE, AND THE WORKING CLASSES

There are two sects of protectionists. The first sect, represented in Germany by Dr. List, who never intended to protect manual labour, on the contrary, they demanded protective duties in order to crush manual labour by machinery, to supersede patriarchal manufacture by modern manufacture. They always intended to prepare the reign of the monied classes (the *bourgeoisie*), and more particularly that of the large manufacturing capitalists. They openly proclaimed the ruin of petty manufacturers, of small tradesmen, and small farmers, as an event to be regretted, indeed, but quite inevitable, at the same time. The second school of protectionists, required not only

[a] Charles de Brouckère.—*Ed.*

protection, but absolute prohibition. They proposed to protect manual labour against the invasion of machinery, as well as against foreign competition. They proposed to protect by high duties, not only home manufactures, but also home agriculture, and the production of raw materials at home. And where did this school arrive at? At the prohibition, not only of the importation of foreign manufactured produce, but of the progress of the home manufacture itself. Thus the whole protective system inevitably got upon the horns of this dilemma. Either it protected the progress of home manufactures, and then it sacrificed manual labour, or it protected manual labour, and then it sacrificed home manufactures. Protectionists of the first sect, those who conceived the progress of machinery, of division of labour, and of competition, to be irresistible, told the working classes, "At any rate if you are to be squeezed out, you had better be squeezed by your own countrymen, than by foreigners." Will the working classes for ever bear with this? I think not. Those who produce all the wealth and comforts of the rich, will not be satisfied with that poor consolation. They will require more substantial comforts in exchange for substantial produce. But the protectionists say, "After all, we keep up the state of society as it is at present. We ensure to the working man, somehow or other, the employment he wants. We take care that he shall not be turned out of work in consequence of foreign competition." So be it. Thus, in the best case, the protectionists avow that they are unable to arrive at anything better than the continuation of the status quo. Now the working classes want not the continuation of their actual condition, but a change for the better. A last refuge yet stands open to the protectionist. He will say that he is not at all adverse to social reform in the interior of a country, but that the first thing to ensure their success will be to shut out any derangement which might be caused by foreign competition. "My system," he says, "is no system of social reform, but if we are to reform society, had we not better do so within our own country, before we talk about reforms in our relations with other countries?" Very specious, indeed, but under this plausible appearance, there is hid a very strange contradiction. The protectionist system, while it gives arms to the capital of a country against the capital of foreign countries, while it strengthens capital against foreigners, believes that this capital, thus armed, thus strengthened, will be weak, impotent, and feeble, when opposed to labour. Why, that would be appealing to the mercy of capital, as if capital, considered as such, could ever be merciful. Why, social reforms are never carried by the weakness of the strong, but always by the strength of the weak. But it is not at all necessary to insist on this point. From the moment the protectionists agree that social reforms do not necessarily follow from, and that they are not part and parcel of their system, but form quite a distinct question, from that moment they abandon the question, which we discuss. We may, therefore, leave them in order to review the effects of Free Trade upon the condition of the working classes. The problem: What will be the influence of the perfect unfettering of trade upon the situation of the working classes, is very easy to be resolved. It is not even a problem. If there is anything clearly exposed in political economy, it is the fate attending the working classes under the reign of Free Trade. All those laws developed in the classical works on political economy, are strictly true under the supposition only, that trade be delivered from all fetters, that competition be perfectly free, not only within a single country, but upon the whole face of the earth. These laws, which A. Smith, Say, and Ricardo have developed, the laws under which wealth is produced and distributed—these laws grow more true, more exact, then cease to be mere abstractions, in the same measure in which Free Trade is carried out. And the master of the science, when treating of any economical subject, tells us every moment that all their reasonings are founded upon the supposition that all fetters, yet existing, are to be removed from trade. They are quite right in following this method. For they make no arbitrary abstractions, they only remove from their reasoning a series of accidental circumstances. Thus it can justly be said, that the economists—Ricardo and others—know more about society as it will be, than about society as it is. They know more about the future than about the present. If you wish to read in the book of the future, open Smith, Say, Ricardo. There you will find described, as clearly as possible, the condition which awaits the working man under the reign of perfect Free Trade. Take, for instance, the authority of Ricardo, authority than which there is no better. What is the natural normal price of the labour of, economically speaking, a working man? Ricardo replies, "Wages reduced to their minimum—their lowest level." Labour is a commodity as well as any other commodity.[123] Now the price of a commodity is determined by the time necessary to produce it. What then is necessary to produce the commodity of labour? Exactly that which is necessary to produce the sum of commodities indispensable to the sustenance and the repairing of the wear and tear of the labourer, to enable him to live and to propagate, somehow or other, his race. We are, however, not to believe that the working man will never be elevated above this lowest level, nor that he never will be depressed below it. No, according to this law, the working classes will be for a time more happy, they will have for a time more than the minimum, but this surplus will be the supplement only for what they will have less than the minimum at another time, the time of industrial stagnation. That is to say, that during a certain space of time, which is always periodical, in which trade passes through the circle of prosperity, overproduction, stagnation, crisis—that, taking the average of what the labourer received more, and what he received less, than the minimum, we shall find that on the whole he will have received neither more or less than the minimum; or, in other words, that the working class, as a class, will have conserved itself, after many miseries, many sufferings, and many corpses left upon the industrial battle field. But what matters that? The class exists, and not only it exists, but it will have increased. This law, that the lowest level of wages is the natural price of the commodity of labour, will realise itself in the same measure with Ricardo's supposition that Free Trade will become a reality. We accept every thing that has been said of the advantages of Free Trade. The powers of production will increase, the tax imposed upon the country by protective duties will disappear, all commodities will be sold at a cheaper price. And what, again, says Ricardo? "That labour being equally a commodity, will equally sell at a cheaper price"—that you will have it for very little money indeed, just as you will have pepper and salt. And then, in the same way as all other laws of political economy will receive an increased force, a surplus of truth, by the realisation of Free Trade—in the same way the law of population, as exposed by Malthus, will under the reign of Free Trade develop itself in as fine dimensions as can possibly be desired. Thus you have to choose: Either you must disavow the whole of political economy as it exists at present, or you must allow that under the freedom of trade the whole severity of the laws of political economy will be applied to the working classes. Is that to say that we are against Free Trade? No, we are for Free Trade, because by Free Trade all economical laws, with their most astounding contradictions, will act upon a larger scale, upon a greater extent of territory, upon the territory of the whole earth; and because from the uniting of all these contradictions into a single group, where they stand face to face, will result the struggle which will itself eventuate in the emancipation of the proletarians.

Written at the end of September 1847

First published in *The Northern Star* No. 520, October 9, 1847 with an editorial note: "From Our German Correspondent"

Reprinted from the newspaper

Frederick Engels

THE COMMUNISTS AND KARL HEINZEN[124]

FIRST ARTICLE

[*Deutsche-Brüsseler-Zeitung* No. 79, October 3, 1847]

Brussels, September 26. Today's number of the *D[eutsche]-Br[üsseler]-Z[ei]t[un]g* contains an article by Heinzen[a] in which under the pretext of defending himself against a trivial accusation by the editors, he embarks on a long polemic against the Communists.

The editors advise both sides to drop the polemic. In that case however they ought only to reproduce that part of Heinzen's article in which Heinzen really defends himself against the accusation of having attacked the Communists first. Even if "Heinzen has no paper at his disposal", that is no reason for placing one at his disposal for the publication of attacks which the editors of the paper themselves consider stupid.

Incidentally, no greater service could have been rendered to the Communists than has been rendered through the publication of this article. Sillier and more narrow-minded criticisms than those Heinzen here makes of the Communists have never been made of any party. The article is the most dazzling vindication of the Communists. It proves that if they had not already attacked Heinzen, they would be obliged to do so at once.

At the very outset Herr Heinzen presents himself as the representative of all the non-communist German radicals; his intention is to debate with the Communists as one party with another. He "is entitled to demand", he announces with the greatest assurance what "must be expected of" the Communists, what "must be demanded of them", what the "duty of real Communists is". He

[a] Published as a statement in the Polemik column with a note by the editors entitled "Karl Heinzen und die Kommunisten".—*Ed.*

identifies *his* differences with the Communists in all respects with those "the German republicans and democrats" have with them and speaks of "*we*" in the name of these republicans.

Who is Herr Heinzen, then, and what does he represent?

Herr Heinzen is a former liberal, lower-ranking civil servant who in 1844 was still enthusiastic about legitimate progress and the wretched German Constitution, and who at best confessed in a confidential whisper that a republic might be desirable and possible, of course in the far distant future. Herr Heinzen was wrong however about the possibility of legal resistance in Prussia. The bad book he wrote on the bureaucracy[a] (even Jacob Venedey wrote a far better book about Prussia years ago[b]) compelled him to flee the country. Now the truth dawned on him. He declared legal resistance to be impossible, became a revolutionary and naturally a republican as well. In Switzerland he made the acquaintance of that *savant sérieux*[c] Ruge, who taught him the little philosophy he has, consisting of a confused hotch-potch of Feuerbachian atheism and humanism, reminiscences of Hegel and rhetorical phrases from Stirner. Thus equipped, Herr Heinzen considered himself mature and inaugurated his revolutionary propaganda, leaning on Ruge to the right and Freiligrath to the left.

We are most certainly not criticising Herr Heinzen for his transition from liberalism to bloodthirsty radicalism. But we do maintain that he has made this transition as a result of merely personal circumstances. As long as Herr Heinzen was able to put up legal resistance, he attacked all those who admitted the necessity of a revolution. Scarcely was legal resistance rendered impossible for *him* when he declared it to be impossible absolutely, without taking into account that for the present this resistance is still perfectly possible for the German bourgeoisie, which is constantly putting up a highly legal resistance. Scarcely had the way back been cut off for *him* when he declared the necessity of an immediate revolution. Instead of studying conditions in Germany, taking overall stock of them and deducing from this what progress, what development and what steps were necessary and possible, instead of obtaining for himself a clear picture of the complex situation of the individual classes in Germany with regard to each other and to the government and concluding from this what policy was to be followed, instead, in a word, of accommodating himself to the development of Germany, Herr

[a] K. Heinzen, *Die Preussische Bureaukratie.—Ed.*

[b] J. Venedey, *Preussen und Preussenthum.— Ed.*

[c] Serious scholar.— *Ed.*

Heinzen quite unceremoniously demands that the development of Germany should accommodate itself to him.

Herr Heinzen was a violent opponent of philosophy as long as it remained *progressive*. Scarcely had it become reactionary, scarcely had it become the refuge of all waverers, weaklings and literary hacks, when Herr Heinzen did himself the disservice of joining it. And worse still, fate would have it that Herr Ruge, who himself has been a mere proselyte all his life, has found his only proselyte in Herr Heinzen. Herr Heinzen is thus condemned to provide Herr Ruge with the consolation that at least one person believed he had penetrated his verbal edifices.

For what end is Herr Heinzen actually working then? For the instant establishment of a German republic combining American and 1793 traditions with a few measures borrowed from the Communists, and looking very black, red and gold.[125] As a result of its industrial lethargy, Germany occupies such a wretched position in Europe that it can never seize an initiative, never be the first to proclaim a great revolution, never establish a republic on its own account without France and England. Any German republic that is supposed to be created independently of the development of the civilised countries, any German revolution that is supposed to be carried out on its own and, as happens in Herr Heinzen's case, leaves the real development of classes in Germany totally out of consideration, any such republic or revolution is nothing but black, red and gold day-dreaming. And in order to make this glorious German republic even more glorious, Herr Heinzen garnishes it with Feuerbachian, Rugified humanism, and proclaims it as the kingdom "of man" which is almost at hand. And the Germans are supposed to make something of all this topsy-turvy day-dreaming?

But how does the great "agitator" Herr Heinzen conduct his propaganda? He declares the princes to be the chief authors of all poverty and distress. This assertion is not only ridiculous but exceedingly damaging. Herr Heinzen could not flatter the German princes, those impotent and feeble-minded puppets, more than by attributing to them fantastic, preternatural, daemonic omnipotence. If Herr Heinzen asserts that the princes can do so much evil, he is thereby also conceding them the power to perform as many good works. The conclusion this leads to is not the necessity of a revolution but the pious desire for a virtuous prince, for a good Emperor Joseph. In any case, the people know far better than Herr Heinzen who their oppressors are. Herr Heinzen will never transfer to the princes the hatred which the serf feels for the feudal lord and the worker for his employer. But of course Herr Heinzen is working in the interests of the landowners and capitalists when he puts the blame for the exploitation of the people by these two classes not on them but on the princes; and the exploitation by the landowners and capitalists is after all surely responsible for nineteen-twentieths of all the misery in Germany!

Herr Heinzen calls for an immediate insurrection. He has leaflets printed[a] to this effect and attempts to distribute them in Germany. We would ask whether blindly lashing out with such senseless propaganda is not injurious in the highest degree to the interests of German democracy. We would ask whether experience has not proved how useless it is. Whether, at a time of far greater unrest, in the thirties, hundreds of thousands of such leaflets, pamphlets, etc., were not distributed in Germany and whether a single one of them had any success whatever. We would ask whether any person who is in his right mind at all can imagine that the people will pay any attention whatever to political sermonising and exhortations of this kind. We would ask whether Herr Heinzen has ever done anything else in his leaflets except exhort and sermonise. We would ask whether it is not positively ridiculous to trumpet calls for revolution out into the world in this way, without sense or understanding, without knowledge or consideration of circumstances.

What is the task of a party press? To debate, first and foremost, to explain, to expound, to defend the party's demands, to rebut and refute the claims and assertions of the opposing party. What is the task of the German democratic press? To demonstrate the necessity for democracy by the worthlessness of the present government, which by and large represents the nobility, by the inadequacy of the constitutional system that brings the bourgeoisie to the helm, by the impossibility of the people helping itself so long as it does not have political power. Its task is to reveal the oppression of the proletarians, small peasants and urban petty bourgeoisie, for in Germany these constitute the "people", by the bureaucracy, the nobility and the bourgeoisie; how not only political but above all social oppression has come about, and by what means it can be eliminated; its task is to show that the conquest of political power by the proletarians, small peasants and urban petty bourgeoisie is the first condition for the application of these means. Its task is further to examine the extent to which a rapid realisation of democracy may be expected, what resources the party can command and what other parties it must ally itself with as long as it is too weak to act alone.—Well, and has Herr Heinzen done even one of these things?

[a] K. Heinzen, "Teutsche Revolution. Gesammelte Flugschriften".—*Ed.*

No. He has not put himself to so much trouble. He has revealed absolutely nothing to the people, in other words to the proletarians, small peasants and urban petty bourgeoisie. He has never examined the position of the classes and parties. He has done nothing but play variations on the *one* theme: Fight'em, fight'em, fight'em!

And to whom does Herr Heinzen address his revolutionary sermonising? First and foremost to the small peasants, to that class which in our day and age is least of all capable of seizing a revolutionary initiative. For 600 years, all progressive movements have issued so exclusively from the towns that the independent democratic movements of country people (Wat Tyler, Jack Cade, the Jacquerie, the Peasants' War[126]) were firstly always reactionary manifestations and were secondly always crushed. The industrial proletariat of the towns has become the vanguard of all modern democracy; the urban petty bourgeoisie and still more the peasants depend on its initiative completely. The French Revolution of 1789 and the most recent history of England, France and the eastern states of America prove this. And Herr Heinzen hopes the peasants will fight now, in the nineteenth century?

But Herr Heinzen also promises social reforms. Of course, the indifference of the people towards his appeals has gradually forced him to. And what kind of reforms are these? They are such as the *Communists* themselves suggest in preparation for the abolition of private property. The only point Herr Heinzen makes that deserves recognition he has borrowed from the Communists, the Communists whom he attacks so violently, and even that is reduced in his hands to utter nonsense and mere day-dreaming. All measures to restrict competition and the accumulation of capital in the hands of individuals, all restriction or suppression of the law of inheritance, all organisation of labour by the state, etc., all these measures are not only possible as revolutionary measures, but actually necessary. They are possible because the whole insurgent proletariat is behind them and maintains them by force of arms. They are possible, despite all the difficulties and disadvantages which are alleged against them by economists, because these very difficulties and disadvantages will compel the proletariat to go further and further until private property has been completely abolished, in order not to lose again what it has already won. They are possible as preparatory steps, temporary transitional stages towards the abolition of private property, but not in any other way.

Herr Heinzen however wants all these measures as permanent, final measures. They are not to be a preparation for anything, they are to be definitive. They are for him not a means but an end. They are not designed for a revolutionary but for a peaceful, bourgeois condition. But this makes them impossible and at the same time reactionary. The economists of the bourgeoisie are quite right in respect of Herr Heinzen when they present these measures as reactionary compared with free competition. Free competition is the ultimate, highest and most developed form of existence of private property. All measures, therefore, which start from the basis of private property and which are nevertheless directed against free competition, are reactionary and tend to restore more primitive stages in the development of property, and for that reason they must finally be defeated once more by competition and result in the restoration of the present situation. These objections the bourgeoisie raises, which lose all their force as soon as one regards the above social reforms as pure *mesures de salut public,* as revolutionary and transitory measures, these objections are devastating as far as Herr Heinzen's peasant-socialist black, red and gold republic is concerned.

Herr Heinzen of course imagines that property relations, the law of inheritance, etc., can at will be altered and trimmed to shape. Herr Heinzen—one of the most ignorant men of this century—may, of course, not know that the property relations of any given era are the necessary result of the mode of production and exchange of that era. Herr Heinzen may not know that one cannot transform large-scale landownership into small-scale without the whole pattern of agriculture being transformed, and that otherwise large-scale landownership will very rapidly re-assert itself. Herr Heinzen may not know what a close relationship exists between today's large-scale industry, the concentration of capital and the creation of the proletariat. Herr Heinzen may not know that a country as industrially dependent and subservient as Germany can never presume to undertake on its own account a transformation of its property relations other than one that is in the interests of the bourgeoisie and of free competition.

In short: with the Communists these measures have sense and reason because they are not conceived as arbitrary measures but as consequences which will necessarily and of themselves ensue from the development of industry, agriculture, trade and communications, from the development of the class struggle between bourgeoisie and proletariat which is dependent on these; which will ensue not as definitive measures but as transitory ones, *mesures de salut public* arising from the transitory struggle between the classes itself.

With Herr Heinzen, they have neither sense nor reason, because they take the form of quite arbitrarily conceived, obtusely bourgeois visions of putting the world to rights; because there is no mention of a connection between these measures and historical development; because Herr Heinzen is not in the least concerned about the material feasibility of his proposals; because it is not his aim to formulate industrial necessities but on the contrary to overturn them by decree.

The same Herr Heinzen who is only able to adopt the demands of the Communists after he has so cruelly confused them and transformed them into pure fantasies, that same Herr Heinzen criticises the Communists for "confusing the minds of the uneducated", for "chasing fantasies" and for "failing to keep their feet on the ground (!) of reality"!

There we have Herr Heinzen in all his activity as an agitator, and we make no bones about our opinion that it brings nothing but harm and discredit upon the whole German radical party. A party writer requires quite different qualities from those possessed by Herr Heinzen, who, as we said, is one of the most ignorant men of our century. Herr Heinzen may have the best will in the world, he may be the most steadfast man in his convictions in the whole of Europe. We also know that he is personally a man of honour and has courage and endurance. But all that does not make him a party writer. To be that, one requires more than convictions, good will and a stentorian voice, to be that, one requires a little more intelligence, a little more lucidity, a better style and more knowledge than Herr Heinzen possesses and, as long experience has proved, than he is capable of acquiring.

Herr Heinzen's flight has faced him with the necessity of becoming a party writer nevertheless. He was compelled to try to form a party of his own among the radicals. Thus he got into a situation he was not equal to, in which through his unsuccessful efforts to meet the demands of this situation he only makes himself ridiculous. He would make the German radicals look equally ridiculous if they left him the pretence that he was representing them, that he was making himself ridiculous in their name.

But Herr Heinzen does not represent the German radicals. They have quite other representatives, e.g., Jacoby and others. Herr Heinzen represents no one and is recognised by no one as their representative, apart perhaps from some few German bourgeois who sent him money for the purposes of agitation. But we are mistaken: one class in Germany recognises him as its representative, adores him and roars its head off for him, outshouts whole tables of drinkers in the taverns for him (just as, according to Herr Heinzen, the Communists "outshouted the whole literary opposition"). This class is the numerous, enlightened, noble-minded and influential class of *commis-voyageurs*.[a]

And this Herr Heinzen demands that the Communists should recognise him as representative of the radical bourgeoisie and debate with him in that capacity?

For the moment, these are reasons enough to justify the polemic the Communists are conducting against Herr Heinzen. In the next issue we shall investigate the criticisms which Herr Heinzen makes of the Communists in No. 77 of the paper.

If we were not completely convinced that Herr Heinzen is utterly incompetent as a party writer, we would advise him to subject Marx's *Misère de la Philosophie* to close study. But as things are, in response to his advice to us to read Fröbel's *Neue Politik*,[b] we can only give him the alternative advice to maintain absolute silence and wait quietly until "the fighting starts". We are convinced that Herr Heinzen will prove as good a batallion commander as he is a bad writer.

So that Herr Heinzen cannot complain about anonymous attacks, we are signing this article.

F. Engels

SECOND ARTICLE

[*Deutsche-Brüsseler-Zeitung* No. 80, October 7, 1847]

The Communists—this we established in the first article—are attacking Heinzen not because he is no Communist, but because he is a bad democratic party writer. They are attacking him not in their capacity as *Communists* but in their capacity as *democrats*. It is purely coincidental that it is precisely the Communists who have opened the polemic against him; even if there were no Communists at all in the world, the democrats would still have to take the field against Heinzen. In this whole controversy it is only a question of: 1. whether Herr Heinzen as a party writer and agitator is capable of serving German democracy, which we deny; 2. whether Herr Heinzen's manner of agitation is a correct one, whether it is merely tolerable, which we likewise deny. It is therefore a question neither of communism nor of democracy, but just of Herr Heinzen's person and his personal eccentricities.

---

[a] Commercial travellers.—*Ed.*

[b] J. Fröbel, "System der socialen Politik", zweite Auflage der *Neuen Politik*, Th. I-II (the first edition entitled *Neue Politik* appeared under the pen-name "Junius").—*Ed.*

Far from starting futile quarrels with the democrats, in the present circumstances, the Communists for the time being rather take the field as democrats themselves in all practical party matters. In all civilised countries, democracy has as its necessary consequence the political rule of the proletariat, and the political rule of the proletariat is the first condition for all communist measures. As long as democracy has not been achieved, thus long do Communists and democrats fight side by side, thus long are the interests of the democrats at the same time those of the Communists. Until that time, the differences between the two parties are of a purely theoretical nature and can perfectly well be debated on a theoretical level without common action being thereby in any way prejudiced. Indeed, understandings will be possible concerning many measures which are to be carried out in the interests of the previously oppressed classes immediately after democracy has been achieved, e.g. the running of large-scale industry and the railways by the state, the education of all children at state expense, etc.

Now to Herr Heinzen.

Herr Heinzen declares the Communists had begun a quarrel with him, not he with them. The well-known argument of the street-porter, then, which we will readily concede to him. He calls his conflict with the Communists "the absurd split which the Communists have provoked in the camp of the German radicals". He says that as long as three years ago he had been concerned to prevent the approaching split as far as his powers and circumstances might permit. These fruitless exertions were followed, he says, by attacks on him by the Communists.

Herr Heinzen, as everyone perfectly well knows, was not yet in the *radical camp* three years ago. At that time Herr Heinzen was progressive-within-the-law and liberal. A split with him was therefore by no means a split in the camp of the *radicals*.

Herr Heinzen met some Communists here in Brussels at the beginning of 1845. Far from attacking Herr Heinzen for his ostensible political radicalism, they rather took the greatest trouble to bring the then liberal Herr Heinzen over to just this radicalism. But in vain. Herr Heinzen only became a democrat in Switzerland.

"I later became more and more convinced (!) of the need for a vigorous struggle against the Communists"—in other words, of the need for an absurd split in the radical camp! We ask the German democrats whether someone who contradicts himself so absurdly is fitted to be a party writer?

But who are the Communists by whom Herr Heinzen claims he was attacked? The above innuendoes and particularly the ensuing reproaches against the Communists show who it was clearly. The Communists, we read,

> "were outshouting the whole camp of the literary opposition, confusing the minds of the uneducated, decrying even the most radical men in the most uninhibited manner, ... they were intent on paralysing the political struggle as far as possible, ... indeed, they were finally positively allying themselves ... even with reaction. Furthermore they often descended, obviously as a result of their doctrine, to *base and false intrigues* in practical life...."

Out of the fog and vagueness of these criticisms looms an easily recognisable figure: that of the literary hack, Herr Karl Grün. Three years ago Herr Grün had some personal dealings with Herr Heinzen, whereupon Herr Grün attacked Herr Heinzen in the *Trier'sche Zeitung*, Herr Grün attempted to outshout the whole camp of the literary opposition, Herr Grün strove to paralyse the political struggle as far as possible, etc.

But since when has Herr Grün been a representative of communism? If he thrust himself on the Communists three years ago, he has never been recognised as a Communist, he has never openly declared himself to be a Communist, and more than a year ago he thought it proper to inveigh against the Communists.

Moreover, even at that time, for Herr Heinzen's benefit, Marx repudiated Herr Grün, just as he later publicly showed him up in his true colours at the first opportunity.[a]

Concerning Herr Heinzen's final "base and false" insinuation about the Communists, one incident which occurred between Herr Grün and Herr Heinzen, and nothing more, lies behind this. This incident concerns the two gentlemen in question and not the Communists at all. We are not even so exactly acquainted with this incident as to be able to pass judgment on it. But let us assume Herr Heinzen is in the right. If he then, after Marx and other Communists have repudiated his adversary, after it has been shown beyond all doubt that his adversary was never a Communist, if Herr Heinzen then still presents the incident as a necessary consequence of communist doctrine, it is monstrously perfidious of him.

And furthermore, if in his above reproaches Herr Heinzen has in mind persons other than Herr Grün, he can only mean those true socialists whose admittedly reactionary theories have long ago been repudiated by the Communists. All members of this now completely

---

[a] The reference is apparently to the "Declaration Against Karl Grün" (see this volume, pp. 72-74) and Chapter IV of Volume II of *The German Ideology* published in August-September 1847 in the journal *Das Westphälische Dampfboot* as an article under the title "Karl Grün: *Die Soziale Bewegung in Frankreich und Belgien* (Darmstadt, 1845) or the Historiography of True Socialism".—*Ed.*

dissolved movement who are capable of learning anything have come over to the Communists and are now themselves attacking true socialism wherever it still shows itself. Herr Heinzen is thus again speaking with his customary crass ignorance when he once more disinters these superannuated visions in order to lay them at the Communists' door. Whilst Herr Heinzen here reproaches the true socialists, whom he confuses with the Communists, he subsequently makes the same nonsensical criticisms of the Communists as the true socialists did. He thus has not even the right to attack the true socialists, he belongs, in one respect, to them himself. And whilst the Communists were writing sharp attacks on these socialists, the same Herr Heinzen was sitting in Zurich being initiated by Herr Ruge into those fragments of true socialism which had found a niche for themselves in the latter's confused brain. Herr Ruge had indeed found a pupil worthy of him!

But what of the real Communists then? Herr Heinzen speaks of honourable exceptions and talented men, of whom he foresees that they will reject communist solidarity (!). The Communists *have* already rejected solidarity with the writings and actions of the true socialists. Of all the above reproaches, not a single one applies to the Communists, unless it be the conclusion of the whole passage, which reads as follows:

> "The Communists ... in the arrogance of their imagined superiority laughed to scorn everything which is indispensable for forming the basis of an association of *honourable people.*"

Herr Heinzen appears to be alluding here to the fact that Communists have made fun of his sternly moral demeanour and mocked all those sacred and sublime ideas, virtue, justice, morality, etc., which Herr Heinzen imagines form the basis of all society. We accept this reproach. The Communists will not allow the moral indignation of that *honourable* man Herr Heinzen to prevent them from mocking these *eternal verities.* The Communists, moreover, maintain that these eternal verities are by no means the basis, but on the contrary the product, of the society in which they feature.

If, incidentally, Herr Heinzen foresaw that the Communists would reject solidarity with those people he takes it into his head to associate with them—what is the point of all his absurd reproaches and lying insinuations? If Herr Heinzen only knows the Communists from hearsay, as almost appears to be the case, if he knows so little who they are that he demands they should designate themselves more closely, and so to speak *introduce themselves* to him, what brazenness is this he exhibits in polemicising against them?

"A designation of those ... who ... actually represent communism or manifest it in its pure form would ... probably have to exclude completely the vast majority of those who base themselves upon communism and are *used for it*, and it would hardly be the people from the *Trier'sche Zeitung* alone who would protest against the assertion of such a claim."

And a few lines later:

"Those who are really Communists now *must be allowed* the consistency and *honesty*" (what a decent philistine speaks here!) "of coming forward and openly professing their doctrine and declaring their dissociation from those who are not Communists.... *They are under the moral obligation*" (how typical of the philistine these expressions are) "not to maintain *unscrupulously* (!) the *confusion* which is created in the minds of a thousand *suffering, uneducated minds* by the impossibility (!!), dreamt of or falsely advertised as a possibility, of finding a way, based on real conditions, to implement that doctrine (!). It is the *duty*" (the philistine again) "of the real Communists either completely to clarify things for all their unenlightened adherents and to lead them to a definite goal, or else to *detach themselves* from them and *not to use them.*"

If Herr Ruge had produced these last three periods, he could have been well pleased. Entirely matching the philistine demands is the philistine confusion of thought, which is concerned only with the matter and not with the form and for that very reason says the exact opposite of what it wants to say. Herr Heinzen demands that the real Communists should detach themselves from the merely seeming ones. They should put an end to the confusion which (that is what he *wants* to say) arises from the mixing up of two different trends. But as soon as the two words "Communists" and "confusion" collide in his mind, confusion arises there too. Herr Heinzen loses the thread; his constantly reiterated formula, that the Communists *in general* are confusing the minds of the uneducated, trips him up, he forgets the real Communists and the unreal Communists, he stumbles with farcical clumsiness over a host of impossibilities dreamt of or falsely advertised as possibilities, and finally falls flat on his face on the solid ground of real conditions, where he regains his faculty of reflection. Now he is reminded that he meant to talk about something quite different, that it was not a question of whether this or that was possible. He returns to his theme, but is still so dazed that he does not even cross out that magnificent sentence in which he executed the somersault just described.

So much for the style. Regarding the matter, we repeat that, honest German that he is, Herr Heinzen comes too late with his demands, and that the Communists repudiated those true socialists long ago. But then we see here once again that the application of sly insinuations is by no means irreconcilable with the character of a decent philistine. For Herr Heinzen gives it clearly enough to be understood that the communist writers are only using the communist workers. He says in almost as many words that if these writers were to come forward openly with their intentions, the vast majority of those who are being used for communism would be excluded completely. He regards the communist writers as prophets, priests or preachers who possess a secret wisdom of their own but deny it to the uneducated in order to keep them on leading-strings. All his decent philistine demands that things *be clarified* for the *unenlightened* and that these persons must not be *used*, obviously proceed from the assumption that the literary representatives of communism have an interest in keeping the workers in the dark, as though they were merely using them, just as the *Illuminati*[127] wished to use the common people in the last century. This insipid idea also causes Herr Heinzen to burst forth with always inopportune talk about confusion in the minds of the uneducated, and compels him, as a penalty for not speaking his mind plainly, to perform stylistic somersaults.

We merely take note of these insinuations, we do not take issue with them. We leave it to the communist workers to pass judgment on them themselves.

At last, after all these preliminaries, diversions, appeals, insinuations and somersaults by Herr Heinzen, we come to his theoretical attacks on and reflections about the Communists.

Herr Heinzen

> "discerns the core of the communist doctrine simply in ... the abolition of private property (including that earned through labour) and in the principle of the communal utilisation of the earth's riches which follows inescapably from that abolition."

Herr Heinzen imagines communism is a certain *doctrine* which proceeds from a definite theoretical principle as its *core* and draws further conclusions from that. Herr Heinzen is very much mistaken. Communism is not a doctrine but a *movement*; it proceeds not from principles but from *facts*. The Communists do not base themselves on this or that philosophy as their point of departure but on the whole course of previous history and specifically its actual results in the civilised countries at the present time. Communism has followed from large-scale industry and its consequences, from the establishment of the world market, of the concomitant uninhibited competition, from the ever more violent and more universal trade crises, which have already become full-fledged crises of the world market, from the creation of the proletariat and the concentration of capital, from the ensuing class struggle between proletariat and bourgeoisie. Communism, insofar as it is a theory, is the theoretical expression of the position of the proletariat in this struggle and the theoretical summation of the conditions for the liberation of the proletariat.

Herr Heinzen will now no doubt realise that in assessing communism he has to do rather more than discern its core simply in the abolition of private property; that he would do better to undertake certain studies in political economy than to gabble wildly about the abolition of private property; that he cannot know the first thing about the *consequences* of the abolition of private property if he does not also know its conditions.

However, in this respect, Herr Heinzen labours under such gross ignorance that he even says "the communal utilisation of the earth's riches" (another fine expression) is the *consequence* of the abolition of private property. Precisely the contrary is the case. Because large-scale industry, the development of machinery, communications and world trade are assuming such gigantic proportions that their exploitation by individual capitalists is becoming daily more impossible; because the mounting crises of the world market are the most striking proof of this; because the productive *forces* and the *means* of exchange which characterise the present *mode* of production and exchange are daily becoming increasingly more than individual exchange and private property can manage; because, in a word, the moment is approaching when communal management of industry, of agriculture and of exchange will become a material necessity for industry, agriculture and exchange themselves—for this reason private property will be abolished.

So when Herr Heinzen forcibly separates the abolition of private property, which is of course the condition for the liberation of the proletariat, from the conditions that attach to it, when he considers it quite out of all connection with the real world simply as an ivory-tower fantasy, it becomes a pure cliché about which he can only talk platitudinous nonsense. This he does as follows:

"By its above-mentioned casting-off of all private property..., communism necessarily also abolishes *individual existence.*" (So Herr Heinzen is reproaching us for wanting to turn people into Siamese twins.) "The consequence of this is once more ... the incorporation of each individual into a perhaps (!!) communally organised barracks ... economy." (Would the reader kindly note that this is avowedly only the consequence of Herr Heinzen's own absurd remarks about individual existence.) "By these means communism destroys ... individuality ... independence ... freedom." (The same old twaddle as we had from the true socialists and the bourgeoisie. As though there was any individuality to be destroyed in the individuals whom the division of labour has today turned against their will into cobblers, factory workers, bourgeois, lawyers, peasants, in other words, into slaves of a particular form of labour and of the mores, way of life, prejudices and blinkered attitudes, etc., that go with that form of labour!) "It sacrifices the individual person with its necessary attribute or basis" (that "*or*" is marvellous) "of *earned* private property to the 'phantom of the community or society'" (is Stirner here as well?), "whereas the community cannot and should not" (should not!!) "be the aim but only the means for each individual person."

Herr Heinzen attaches particular importance to *earned* private property and in so doing once again proves his crass unfamiliarity with the matter on which he is speaking. Herr Heinzen's philistine justice, which allows to each man what he has earned, is unfortunately frustrated by large-scale industry. As long as large-scale industry is not so far advanced that it frees itself completely from the fetters of private property, thus long does it permit no other distribution of its products than that at present occurring, thus long will the capitalist pocket his profit and the worker increasingly know by practice just what a minimum wage is. M. Proudhon attempted to develop a system for *earned* property which would relate it to existing conditions, and, we all know, he failed spectacularly. Herr Heinzen, it is true, will never risk a similar experiment, for in order to do so he would need to study, and he will not do that. But let the example of M. Proudhon teach him to expose his earned property less to public scrutiny.

And if Herr Heinzen reproaches the Communists for chasing fantasies and failing to keep their feet on the ground of reality—to whom does this reproach properly apply?

Herr Heinzen goes on to say a number of other things which we need not enter into. We merely observe that his sentences get worse and worse the further he proceeds. The clumsiness of his language, which can never find the right word, would of itself suffice to discredit any party which acknowledged him as its literary representative. The solidity of his conviction constantly makes him say something quite different from what he intends to say. Thus each of his sentences contains a twofold nonsense: firstly the nonsense he intends to say, and secondly the one he doesn't intend to say but nevertheless says. We gave an example of it above. It only remains for us to observe that Herr Heinzen repeats his old superstition about the power of the princes when he says that the *power* which must be overthrown and which is none other than the power of the State, is and always has been the progenitor and preserver of all injustice, and that his aim is to establish a *State really based on justice* (!) and within this fantasy structure

"to undertake all those social reforms which have emerged in the course of events in general (!), as correct (!) in theory and possible (!) in practice"!!!

His intentions are as good as his style is bad, and that is the fate of the well-meaning in this bad world.

From seduction by the *Zeitgeist*,
Nature-nurtured sansculotte,
Dancing badly, but yet bearing
Good intentions in a bosom rough;
. . . .
Void of talent, yet a character.[a]

Our articles will fill Herr Heinzen with all the righteous indignation of an outraged honest philistine, but for all that he is not going to give up either his style of writing or his discreditable and ineffectual manner of agitation. We found his threat to string us up on the nearest lamp-post when the day for action and decision comes most entertaining.

In short: the Communists must co-operate with the German radicals and desire to do so. But they reserve the right to attack any writer who discredits the entire party. This, and no other, was our intention in attacking Heinzen.

Brussels, October 3, 1847

F. Engels

N. B. We have just received a pamphlet written by a worker[b]: *Der Heinzen'sche Staat, eine Kritik von Stephan*, Bern, Rätzer. If Herr Heinzen wrote half so well as this worker, he might be well satisfied. From this pamphlet Herr Heinzen can see clearly enough, amongst other things, why the workers want nothing to do with his peasant republic. We also observe that this pamphlet is the first written by a worker which does not adopt a moral attitude but attempts to trace the political struggles of the present back to the struggle of the various classes of society with one another.

Written on September 26 and October 3, 1847

First published in the *Deutsche-Brüsseler-Zeitung* Nos. 79 and 80, October 3 and 7, 1847
Signed: *F. Engels*

Printed according to the newspaper

Published in English for the first time

---

[a] H. Heine, *Atta Troll*, ch. 24.—*Ed.*
[b] Stephan Born.—*Ed.*

Mardi 26 Octobre 1847.

PRIX DE L'ABONNEMENT:

	Paris.	Départ.	Etrang
Pour 1 an.	45 fr.	50 fr.	66 fr.
— 6 mois.	23	26	35
— 3 mois.	12	13	18
— 1 mois.	4	5	

BUREAUX A PARIS:
Rue J.-J.-Rousseau, n° 3.
HÔTEL DE BULLION.

LA REFORME

PRIX DES INSERTIONS:
Librairie, en petit texte: 75 cent. la ligne.
Industrie, en nompareille: 85 cent. —
RÉCLAMES { Libr. 1 fr. 50 / Ind. 1 fr. 80 cent. —

AFFRANCHIR tout ce qui concerne
Rédaction et l'Administration.

Frederick Engels

[THE COMMERCIAL CRISIS IN ENGLAND.— THE CHARTIST MOVEMENT.—IRELAND][128]

The commercial crisis to which England finds itself exposed at the moment is, indeed, more severe than any of the preceding crises. Neither in 1837 nor in 1842 was the depression as universal as at the present time. All the branches of England's vast industry have been paralysed at the peak of its development; everywhere there is stagnation, everywhere one sees nothing but workers thrown out on the streets. It goes without saying that such a state of affairs gives rise to extreme unrest among the workers who, exploited by the industrialists during the period of commercial prosperity, now find themselves dismissed *en masse* and abandoned to their fate. Consequently meetings of discontented workers are rapidly increasing. *The Northern Star*, the organ of the Chartist workers, uses more than seven of its large columns to report on meetings held in the past week[a]; the list of meetings announced for the present week fills another three columns. The same newspaper mentions a brochure published by a worker, Mr. John Noakes,[b] in which the author makes an open and direct attack on the right of the aristocracy to own its lands.

"English soil," he says, "is the property of the people, from whom our aristocrats seized it either by force or by trickery. The people must see that their inalienable right to property prevails; the proceeds of the land should be public property and used in the interest of the public. Perhaps I shall be told that these are revolutionary remarks.

---

[a] Reports on the Chartist meetings in *The Northern Star* No. 521, October 16, 1847.—*Ed.*

[b] John Noakes, *The Right of the Aristocracy to the Soil, considered.* The report on its publication appeared in *The Northern Star* No. 522, October 23, 1847.—*Ed.*

Revolutionary or not, it is of no concern; if the people cannot obtain that which they need in a law, they must get it without law."

It will not seem surprising that in these circumstances the Chartists should have recourse to most unusual measures; their leader, the famous Feargus O'Connor, has just announced that he is shortly to leave for Scotland, where he will call meetings in all the towns and collect signatures for the national petition for the People's Charter, which will be sent to the next Parliament. At the same time, he announced that before the opening of Parliament, the Chartist press is to be increased by the addition of a daily newspaper, the *Democrat.*[129]

It will be recalled that at the last elections Mr. Harney, editor-in-chief of *The Northern Star,* was put forward as the Chartist candidate for Tiverton, a borough which is represented in Parliament by Lord Palmerston, the Foreign Secretary. Mr. Harney, who won on the show of hands, decided to retire when Lord Palmerston demanded a poll.[130] Now something has happened which shows how the feelings of the inhabitants of Tiverton differ from those of the small number of parliamentary electors. There was a vacancy to fill on the borough council; the municipal electors, a far more numerous class than that of the parliamentary electors, gave the vacant seat to Mr. Rowcliffe, the person who had proposed Mr. Harney at the elections. Moreover, the Chartists are preparing all over England for the municipal elections which will take place throughout the country at the beginning of November.

But let us turn now to England's greatest manufacturing district, Lancashire, a part of the country which has suffered under the burden of industrial stagnation more than any other. The situation in Lancashire is alarming in the highest degree. Most of the factories have already stopped work entirely, and those which are still operating employ their workers for only two or at the most three days a week. But this is still not all: the industrialists of Ashton, a very important town for the cotton industry, have announced to their workers that in a week's time they are going to reduce wages by 10 per cent. This news, which is causing alarm among the workers, is spreading across the country. A few days later a meeting of workers' delegates from all over the county was held in Manchester; this meeting resolved to send a deputation to the owners to induce them not to carry out the threatened reduction and, if this deputation achieved no results, to announce a strike of all workers employed in the Lancashire cotton industry. This strike, together with the strike of the Birmingham iron-workers and miners which has already started, would not fail to assume the same alarming dimensions which signalled the last general strike, that of 1842.[131] It could quite well become even more menacing for the government.

In the meantime starving Ireland is writhing in the most terrible convulsions. The workhouses are overflowing with beggars, the ruined property owners are refusing to pay the Poor Tax, and the hungry people gather in their thousands to ransack the barns and cattle-sheds of the farmers and even of the Catholic priests, who were still sacred to them a short time ago.

It looks as though the Irish will not die of hunger as calmly next winter as they did last winter. Irish immigration to England is getting more alarming each day. It is estimated that an average of 50,000 Irish arrive each year; the number so far this year is already over 220,000. In September, 345 were arriving daily and in October this figure increased to 511. This means that the competition between the workers will become stronger, and it would not be at all surprising if the present crisis caused such an uproar that it compelled the government to grant reforms of a most important nature.

Written on October 23, 1847

First published in *La Réforme*, October 26, 1847

Printed according to the newspaper

Translated from the French

Frederick Engels

THE MASTERS AND THE WORKERS IN ENGLAND[132]

TO THE WORKER EDITORS OF *L'ATELIER*

Gentlemen,

I have just read in your October issue an article entitled: *Les maîtres et les ouvriers en Angleterre*; this article mentions a meeting reported by *la Presse* of so-called delegates of workers employed in the Lancashire cotton industry, a meeting which took place on August 29 last in Manchester. The resolutions passed at this meeting were such as to prove to *la Presse* that there is perfect harmony between capital and labour in England.

You did quite well, gentlemen, to reserve your judgment on the authenticity of a report which a newspaper of the French bourgeoisie has published, based on newspapers of the English bourgeoisie. The report is accurate, it is true; the resolutions were adopted just as *la Presse* gives them; there is only one small statement lacking in accuracy, but it is precisely this small inaccuracy that is the crux of the matter: the meeting which *la Presse* describes was not a meeting of *workers*, but a meeting of *foremen*.

Gentlemen, I spent two years in the heart of Lancashire itself, and these two years were spent among the workers; I saw them both at their public meetings and in their small committees, I knew their leaders and their speakers, and I think I can assure you that in no other country in the world will you find men more sincerely devoted to democratic principles or more firmly resolved to cast off the yoke of the capitalist exploiters, under which they find themselves suffering at present, than these Lancashire cotton factory workers. How, gentlemen, could these same workers whom I have seen with my own eyes throw several dozen factory owners off a meeting hall platform, whom I have seen, their eyes glinting and fists raised, cast terror into the ranks of the bourgeois gathered on this platform, how, I repeat, could these same workers today pass a vote of thanks to their masters because the latter were kind enough to prefer a reduction in working hours to a reduction in wages?

But let us take a slightly closer look at the matter. Does not the reduction in work mean precisely the same thing for the worker as a reduction in wages? Evidently it does; in both cases the worker's position deteriorates to an equal extent. There was therefore no possible reason for the workers to thank their masters for having preferred the first method of reducing the worker's income to the second. However, gentlemen, if you study the English newspapers for late August, you will see that the cotton manufacturers had good reason to prefer a reduction in working hours to one in wages. At that time the price of raw cotton was rising; the same issue of the London *Globe* which reports the meeting in question[a] also says that *the Liverpool speculators were going to take over the cotton market* to produce an artificial rise in price. What do the Manchester manufacturers do in such cases? They send their foremen to meetings and make them pass resolutions like those which *la Presse* communicated to you. This is a tried and tested device which is used each time the speculators try to raise the price of cotton. It is a warning to the speculators to be careful not to attempt to raise the price too high; for in that case the manufacturers would reduce consumption and in so doing, inevitably produce a drop in price. So the meeting which gives *la Presse* grounds for so much rejoicing and acclamation is nothing but one of those foremen's assemblies which do not fool anyone in England.

In order to give you further proof of the extent to which this meeting was the exclusive work of the capitalists, it should suffice to tell you that the only newspaper to which the resolutions were sent, the newspaper from which all the other newspapers borrowed them, was the *Manchester Guardian*, the organ of the manufacturers. The democratic workers' paper, *The Northern Star*, also gives them; but adds that it has taken them from this capitalist newspaper, a damning observation in the eyes of the workers.[b]

Yours, etc.

Written about October 25, 1847

First published in the journal *l'Atelier* No. 2, November 1847

Printed according to the journal

Translated from the French

[a] "General Suspension of Labour in Cotton Factories", in *The Globe*, September 2, 1847.—*Ed.*

[b] *The Northern Star* No. 515, September 4, 1847.—*Ed.*

Karl Marx

MORALISING CRITICISM AND CRITICAL MORALITY[133]

A CONTRIBUTION TO GERMAN CULTURAL HISTORY CONTRA KARL HEINZEN

[*Deutsche-Brüsseler-Zeitung* No. 86, October 28, 1847]

Shortly before and during the period of the Reformation there developed amongst the Germans a type of literature whose very name is striking—*grobian* literature. In our own day we are approaching an era of revolution analogous to that of the sixteenth century. Small wonder that among the Germans grobian literature is emerging once more. Interest in historical development easily overcomes the aesthetic revulsion which this kind of writing provokes even in a person of quite unrefined taste and which it provoked back in the fifteenth and sixteenth centuries.

Flat, bombastic, bragging, thrasonical, putting on a great show of rude vigour in attack, yet hysterically sensitive to the same quality in others; brandishing the sword with enormous waste of energy, lifting it high in the air only to let it fall down flat; constantly preaching morality and constantly offending against it; sentiment and turpitude most absurdly conjoined; concerned only with the point at issue, yet always missing the point; using with equal arrogance petty-bourgeois scholarly semi-erudition against popular wisdom, and so-called "sound common sense" against science; discharging itself in ungovernable breadth with a certain complacent levity; clothing a philistine message in a plebeian form; wrestling with the literary language to give it, so to speak, a purely corporeal character; willingly pointing at the writer's body in the background, which is itching in every fibre to give a few exhibitions of its strength, to display its broad shoulders and publicly to stretch its limbs; proclaiming a healthy mind in a healthy body; unconsciously infected by the sixteenth century's most abstruse controversies and by its fever of the body; in thrall to dogmatic, narrow thinking and at the same time appealing to petty practice in the face of all real thought; raging against reaction, reacting against progress; incapable of making the opponent seem ridiculous, but ridiculously abusing him through the whole gamut of tones; Solomon and Marcolph, Don Quixote and Sancho Panza, a visionary and a philistine in one person; a loutish form of indignation, a form of indignant loutishness; and suspended like an enveloping cloud over it all, the self-satisfied philistine's consciousness *of his own virtue*—such was the *grobian literature* of the sixteenth century. If our memory does not deceive us, the German folk anecdote has set up a lyrical monument to it in the song of *Heineke, der starke Knecht*. To Herr Heinzen belongs the credit of being one of the re-creators of grobian literature and in this field one of the German swallows healding the coming springtime of the nations.

Heinzen's manifesto against the Communists in No. 84 of the *Deutsche-Brüsseler-Zeitung* has been our most immediate instigation in studying that degenerate variety of literature whose historically interesting aspect for Germany we have indicated. We shall describe the literary species represented by Herr Heinzen on the basis of his manifesto, exactly as literary historians characterise the writers of the sixteenth century from the surviving writings of the sixteenth century, for instance the "goose-preacher".[a]

[*Deutsche-Brüsseler-Zeitung* No. 87, October 31, 1847]*

Biron. Hide thy head, Achilles: here comes Hector in arms.

. . . .

King. Hector was but a Troyan in respect of this.
Boyet. But is this Hector?
Dumain. I think Hector was not so clean-timbered.

. . . .

Biron. This cannot be Hector.
Dumain. He's a god or a painter; for he makes faces.**

But that Herr Heinzen is Hector, of that there is no doubt.

"I have long been visited," he confesses to us, "by a premonition that I would fall by the hand of a communist Achilles. Now that I have been attacked by a Thersites, the danger thus averted makes me bold once more," etc.

Only a Hector can have a premonition that he will fall by the hand of an Achilles.

* My reason for answering Herr Heinzen is not to rebut the attack on Engels. Herr Heinzen's article does not need a rebuttal. I am answering because Heinzen's manifesto furnishes entertaining material for analysis. *K. M.*[134]

** Shakespeare, *Love's Labour Lost* [Act V, Scene 1].[135]

a Thomas Murner.—*Ed.*

Or did Herr Heinzen derive his picture of Achilles and Thersites not from Homer but from Schlegel's translation of Shakespeare?

If that is so, he assigns to himself the part of Ajax.

Let us look at Shakespeare's Ajax.

Ajax. I will beat thee into handsomeness.

Thersites. I shall sooner rail thee into wit; but thy horse will sooner con an oration than thou learn a prayer without book. Thou canst strike, canst thou? a red murrain o' thy jade's tricks!

Ajax. Toadstool, learn me the proclamation.

. . . .

Thersites. Thou art proclaimed a fool, I think.

. . . .

Ajax. You whoreson cur.

Thersites. Do, do.

Ajax. Thou stool for a witch!

Thersites. Ay, do, do;... thou scurvy-valiant ass! thou art here but to thrash Trojans; and thou art bought and sold among those of any wit, like a barbarian slave ... a great deal of your wit too lies in your sinews, or else there be liars.

. . . .

Thersites. A wonder!

Achilles. What?

Thersites. Ajax goes up and down the field, asking for himself.

Achilles. How so?

Thersites. He must fight singly tomorrow, and is so prophetically proud of an heroical cudgelling that he raves in saying nothing.

Achilles. How can that be?

Thersites. Why, he stalks up and down like a peacock, a stride and a stand; ruminates like a hostess that hath no arithmetic but her brain to set down her reckoning; bites his lip with a politic regard, as who would say "There were wit in this head, an 'twould out"... I had rather be a tick in a sheep than such a *valiant ignorance*.*

Whichever character-mask Herr Heinzen now appears wearing—Hector or Ajax—scarcely has he entered the arena when he proclaims to the spectators in a mighty voice that his adversary has not dealt him the "coup de grâce". With all the composure and epic breadth of an ancient Homeric hero, he expounds the reasons for his escape. "I owe my escape," he tells us, "to an error on *nature's* part." "Nature" has not "fitted" me for my adversary's level. He towers over him, the taller by two heads, and that is why the two "swinging blows" of his "little executioner" could not reach his "literary neck". Herr Engels, it is stressed most emphatically and repeatedly, Herr Engels is "little", a "little executioner", a "little person". He then says, with one of those turns of phrase such as we only come across in the old heroic lays, or in the puppet play of the giant Goliath and the small David: "If you were hanging that high"—from a lamp-

---

* Shakespeare, *Troilus and Cressida* [Act II, Scene 1 and Act III, Scene 3].

post—"nobody would ever find you again". That is the giant's humour, at once whimsical and spine-chilling.

It is not just his "neck", but his whole "nature", his whole body for which Herr Heinzen thus finds "literary" application. He has put his "little" adversary beside him in order to set off his own physical perfection in fitting contrast. The deformed "dwarf" carries an *executioner's axe* under his tiny arm, perhaps one of those little guillotines which were given to children as toys in 1794. He, the terrible warrior on the other hand, wields no other weapon in his furious-playful arrogance than the—"birch-rod", of which, he informs us, he has long made use to "chastise" the "naughtiness" of those bad "boys", the Communists. The giant is content to confront his "insect-sized foe" as a *pedagogue,* instead of crushing the *rash* little fellow underfoot. He is content to speak to him as *the children's friend,* to teach him a lesson in morality and reprimand him with the utmost severity for vicious wickedness, especially "lying", "silly, puerile lying", "insolence", his "boyish tone", lack of respect and other shortcomings of youth. And if in the process the schoolmasterly warrior's rod sometimes swishes cruelly about the pupil's ears, if from time to time over-vigorous language interrupts his moral sentences and even partially destroys their effect, one should not for a moment forget that a warrior cannot impart moral instruction in the same way as ordinary schoolmasters, for example a *Quintus Fixlein,* and that *nature* comes in again by the window if one chases her out of the door. One should furthermore reflect that what would repel us as obscenity from the mouth of an elf like Engels, has for ear and heart the splendid resonance of nature herself when it comes from the mouth of a colossus like Heinzen. And are we to measure the language of heroes by the restricted linguistic standards of the common citizen? No more so than we should think Homer descends to the level of, for instance, grobian literature, when he calls one of his favourite heroes, *Ajax,* "as stiff-necked as an ass".

The giant's intentions were honest when he showed the Communists his birch-rod in No. 77 of the *Deutsche-Brüsseler-Zeitung*.[a] And the "little" wretch for whose opinion he did not even ask—several times he expresses his warrior-like astonishment at the incomprehensible audacity of the pigmy—repaid him so unkindly. "It was not intended as a piece of advice," he complains. "Herr Engels wants to kill me, he wants to murder me, the *wicked* man."

And what of his own part? As when he faced the Prussian government, here too he had "enthusiastically begun a battle, in

---

[a] An article by Heinzen published as a statement in the Polemik column.—*Ed.*

which he bore peace proposals, a *heart of humane reconciliation* between the opposing forces of the age, beneath his warlike coat".* But: "*Enthusiasm* was dowsed with the acid-sharp water of malice."**

Isegrim showing his rage and fury, stretched out his paws and
Came at him with wide-gaping jaws and with powerful leaping.
Reineke, lighter than he, escaped his raging opponent,
And then hastily wetted his coarse-haired tail-brush with his
Acid-sharp water and trailed it through dust to load it with sand-grains.
Isegrim thought, now he had him at bay! But sly Reineke struck him
Over the eyes with his tail, preventing him seeing and hearing.
He had used such a strategem often, many a creature
Had to his cost felt the *noxious force of his acid-sharp water.****

[*Deutsche-Brüsseler-Zeitung* No. 90, November 11, 1847]

"I have *been a republican,* Herr Engels, as long as I have concerned myself with politics, and my *convictions* have not been turning about, they have been without *wavering* and *fickleness* unlike what has gone on in the heads of so many Communists.****

"It is true I have only just *become a revolutionary.* It is part of the Communists' tactics that, aware of their own *incorrigibility,* they criticise their adversaries as soon as they *correct themselves.*"*****

Herr Heinzen never *became* a republican, he has *been* one since his political birth. On his side, therefore, immutability, the immobility of a final state, consistency. On the side of his adversaries, wavering, fickleness, turning about. Herr Heinzen has not always *been* a revolutionary, he has *become* one. Now, of course, the *turning about* is on Herr Heinzen's side, but then the *immoral* character of turning about has been turned about too; it is now known as "correcting themselves". On the Communists' side, on the other hand, *immutability* has lost its character of *high morality.* What has become of it? "Incorrigibility."

Remaining constant or *turning about,* both are moral, both are immoral; moral on the side of the philistine, immoral on the side of his adversary. For the art of the philistine as critic consists in calling out *rouge et noir*[a] at the right time, the right word at the right time.

* Karl Heinzen, [*Ein*] *Steckbrief.*

** Ibid.

*** Goethe, *Reineke Fuchs* [Canto Twelve].

**** Heinzen's Manifesto, *Deutsche-Brüsseler-Zeitung* No. 84.

***** Ibid.

[a] Red and black (as at the gaming table) was given in the errata in the November 18 issue instead of the original "wohl und weh"—good and bad.—*Ed.*

Ignorance is generally considered a fault. We are accustomed to regard it as a *negative* quantity. Let us observe how the magic wand of the philistine as critic converts a minus quantity of intelligence into a plus quantity of morality.

Herr Heinzen reports amongst other things that he is still just as *ignorant* of *philosophy* as in 1844. Hegel's "language" he has "continued to find *indigestible*".

So much for the facts of the matter. Now for the moral processing of them.

Because Herr Heinzen has always found Hegel's language "indigestible", he has not, like "Engels and others", succumbed to the immoral arrogance of ever priding himself on that same Hegelian language, any more than, by all accounts so far, Westphalian peasants "pride themselves" on the Sanskrit language. However, true moral behaviour consists in avoiding the *motivation* for immoral behaviour, and how can one better secure oneself against immoral "priding oneself" on a language than by taking good care not to understand that language!

Herr Heinzen, who knows nothing of philosophy, has for that reason, as he thinks, not attended the philosophers' "school" either. His school was "sound common sense" and the "fulness of life".

"At the same time," he exclaims with the modest pride of the just, "this has preserved me from the danger of *denying* my school."

There is no more proven remedy for the moral danger of *denying* one's school than not going to school!

Any development, whatever its substance may be, can be represented as a series of different stages of development that are connected in such a way that one forms the *negation* of the other. If, for example, a people develops from absolute monarchy to constitutional monarchy, it *negates* its former political being. In no sphere can one undergo a development without negating one's previous mode of existence. *Negating* translated into the language of morality means: *denying*.

Denying! With this catchword the philistine as critic can condemn any development without understanding it; he can solemnly set up his undevelopable undevelopment beside it as moral immaculateness. Thus the religious phantasy of the nations has by and large stigmatised *history*, by transposing the age of innocence, the golden age, into *pre-history*, into the time when no historical development at all took place, and hence no negating and no denying. Thus in noisy eras of revolution, in times of strong, passionate negation and denial, as in the 18th century, there emerge honest, well-meaning men, well-bred, respectable satyrs like *Gessner*, who oppose the undevelopable state of the *idylls* to the corruption of history. It should nevertheless be observed to the credit of these idyll-poets, who were also critical moralists and moralising critics of a kind, that they conscientiously waver as to who should be accorded the palm of morality, the shepherd or the sheep.

But let us leave our worthy philistine undisturbed to pasture on his own diligence! Let us follow him to where he *fancies* he attacks the "heart of the matter". Throughout we shall find the same method.

"I cannot help it if Herr Engels and other Communists are too *blind* to realise that *power* also controls *property* and that injustice in *property relations* is only maintained by power.—I call any man a *fool* and a *coward* who bears the bourgeois malice on account of his *acquisition of money* and lets a king be on account of his *acquisition of power*." *

"Power also controls property!"

Property, at all events, is also a kind of power. Economists call capital, for instance, "power over the labour of others".

We are therefore faced with two kinds of power, on the one hand the power of property, in other words, of the property-owners, on the other hand political power, the power of the state. "Power also controls property" means: property does not control the political power but rather it is harassed by it, for example by arbitrary taxes, by confiscations, by privileges, by the disruptive interference of the bureaucracy in industry and trade and the like.

In other words: the bourgeoisie has not yet taken political shape as a class. The power of the state is not yet its own power. In countries where the bourgeoisie has already conquered political power and political rule is none other than the rule, not of the individual bourgeois over his workers, but of the bourgeois class over the whole of society, Herr Heinzen's dictum has lost its meaning. The propertyless of course remain untouched by political rule insofar as it directly affects property.

Whilst, therefore, Herr Heinzen fancied he was expressing a truth as eternal as it was original, he has only expressed the fact that the German bourgeoisie must conquer political power, in other words, he says what Engels says, but unconsciously, honestly thinking he is saying the opposite. He is only expressing, with some emotion, a transient relationship between the German bourgeoisie and the German state power, as an eternal truth, and thereby showing how to make a "solid core" out of a "movement".

* Heinzen's Manifesto, No. 84 of the *D[eutsche]-B[rüsseler]-Z[eitung]*.

"Injustice in property relations," continues Herr Heinzen, "is only maintained by power."

Either Herr Heinzen here understands "injustice in property relations" as the above-mentioned pressure to which the absolute monarchy still subjects the bourgeoisie even in its "most sacred" interests, in which case he is only repeating what has just been said—or he understands "injustice in property relations" as the economic conditions of the workers, in which case his pronouncement has the following meaning:

The present *bourgeois* property relations are "maintained" by the state power which the bourgeoisie has organised for the protection of its property relations. The proletariat must therefore overthrow the political power where it is already in the hands of the bourgeoisie. It must itself become a power, in the first place a revolutionary power.

Again, Herr Heinzen is unconsciously saying the same thing as Engels is saying, but again in the steadfast conviction that he is saying the opposite. What he says he does not mean, and what he means he does not say.

Incidentally, if the bourgeoisie is politically, that is, by its state power, "maintaining injustice in property relations", it is not *creating* it. The "injustice in property relations" which is determined by the modern division of labour, the modern form of exchange, competition, concentration, etc., by no means arises from the political rule of the bourgeois class, but vice versa, the political rule of the bourgeois class arises from these modern relations of production which bourgeois economists proclaim to be necessary and eternal laws. If therefore the proletariat overthrows the political rule of the bourgeoisie, its victory will only be temporary, only an element in the service of the *bourgeois revolution* itself, as in the year 1794, as long as in the course of history, in its "movement", the material conditions have not yet been created which make necessary the abolition of the bourgeois mode of production and therefore also the definitive overthrow of the political rule of the bourgeoisie. The terror in France could thus by its mighty hammer-blows only serve to spirit away, as it were, the ruins of feudalism from French soil. The timidly considerate bourgeoisie would not have accomplished this task in decades. The bloody action of the people thus only prepared the way for it. In the same way, the overthrow of the absolute monarchy would be merely temporary if the economic conditions for the rule of the bourgeois class had not yet become ripe. Men build a new world for themselves, not from the "treasures of this earth", as grobian superstition imagines, but from the historical achievements of their declining world. In the course of their development they first have to *produce* the *material conditions* of a new[a] society itself, and no exertion of mind or will can free them from this fate.

It is characteristic of the whole *grobianism* of "sound common sense", which feeds upon the "fulness of life" and does not stunt its *natural* faculties with any philosophical or other studies, that where it succeeds in seeing *differences*, it does not see *unity*, and that where it sees *unity*, it does not see *differences*. If it propounds *differentiated determinants*, they at once become fossilised in its hands, and it can see only the most reprehensible sophistry when these wooden concepts are knocked together so that they take fire.

When Herr Heinzen, for instance, says that *money* and *power*, *property* and *rule*, the *acquisition of money* and the *acquisition of power* are not *the same*, he is committing a *tautology* inherent in the mere words themselves, and this merely verbal differentiation he considers an heroic deed which with all the faculties of a *clairvoyant* he brings into play against the Communists, who are so "blind" as not to stop in their tracks at this childlike first perception.

How "acquisition of money" turns into "acquisition of power", how "property" turns into "political rule", in other words, how instead of the rigid difference to which Herr Heinzen gives the force of *dogma*, there are rather effective relations between the two forces up to the point where they merge, of this he may swiftly convince himself by observing how the serfs *bought* their freedom, how the communes[136] *bought* their municipal rights, how the townspeople on the one hand, by trade and industry, attracted the money out of the pockets of the feudal lords and vaporised their landed property into bills of exchange, and on the other hand helped the absolute monarchy to its victory over the thus undermined feudal magnates, and *bought* privileges from it; how they later themselves exploited the financial crises of the absolute monarchy itself, etc., etc.; how the most absolute monarchies become dependent on the stock-exchange barons through the system of state debts—a product of modern industry and modern trade; how in international relations between peoples, industrial monopoly turns directly into political rule, as for instance, the Princes of the Holy Alliance in the "German war of liberation" were merely the hired mercenaries of England,[137] etc., etc.

This self-important *grobianism* of "sound common sense", however, by fixing such distinctions as between *acquisition of money*

---

[a] The word "new" was given in the errata in the November 18 issue instead of the original "more developed".—*Ed.*

and *acquisition of power* in the form of eternal truths whose nature is "acknowledged by all" to be "such and such", in the form of unshakeable *dogmas,* creates for itself the desired position for pouring out its moral indignation about the "blindness", "foolishness" or "wickedness" of the opponents of such articles of faith—an act of self-indulgence which in its blustering expectorations inevitably yields up a mess of rhetoric in which float a few meagre, bony truths.

Herr Heinzen will live to see the power of property even in Prussia achieve a *mariage forcé*[a] with political power. Let us hear what he says next:

"You are trying to make *social questions* the central concern of our age, and you fail to see that there is *no more important social question* than that of *monarchy* or *republic.*"*

A moment ago, Herr Heinzen saw only the *distinction* between the power of money and political power; now he sees only the *unity* of the *political* question and the *social* question. Of course he continues to see the "ridiculous blindness" and "cowardly ignominy" of his antagonists.

The *political* relationships of men are of course also *social, societal* relationships, like all relations between men and men. All questions that concern the relations of men with each other are therefore also social questions.

With this view, which belongs in a catechism for eight-year-old children, this grobian naivety believes it has not only said something but has affected the balance in the conflicts of modern times.

It so happens that the "social questions" which have been "dealt with in *our own* day" increase in importance in proportion as we leave behind us the realm of absolute monarchy. Socialism and communism did not emanate from Germany but from England, France and North America.

The first manifestation of a truly active communist party is contained within the bourgeois revolution, at the moment when the constitutional monarchy is eliminated. The most consistent *republicans,* in England the *Levellers,*[138] in France *Babeuf, Buonarroti,* etc., were the first to proclaim these "social questions". *The Babeuf Conspiracy,* by Babeuf's friend and party-comrade Buonarroti,[b] shows how these republicans derived from the "movement" of

* Heinzen's Manifesto, No. 84 [of the *Deutsche-Brüsseler-Zeitung*].

[a] Forced marriage.—*Ed.*

[b] Ph. Buonarroti, *Conspiration pour l'égalité dite de Babeuf.—Ed.*

history the realisation that the disposal of the social question of *rule by princes* and *republic* did not mean that even a single "social question" has been solved in the interests of the proletariat.

The *question of property* as it has been raised in "*our own* day" is quite unrecognisable even formulated as a question in the form Heinzen gives it: "whether it is *just* that one man should *possess* everything and another man nothing..., whether the individual *should be permitted* to possess anything at all" and similar simplistic questions of conscience and clichés about justice.

The question of property assumes different forms according to the different levels of development of industry in general and according to its particular level of development in the different countries.

For the *Galician* peasant, for instance, the question of property is reduced to the transformation of feudal landed property into small bourgeois landownership. For him it has the same meaning as it had for the *French* peasant before 1789, the *English* agricultural day labourer on the other hand has no relationship with the landowner at all. He merely has a relationship with the tenant farmer, in other words, with the industrial capitalist who is practising agriculture in factory fashion. This industrial capitalist in turn, who pays the landowner a rent, has on the other hand a direct relationship with the landowner. The abolition of landed property is thus the most important question of property as it exists for the English industrial bourgeoisie, and their struggle against the Corn Laws[139] had no other significance. The abolition of capital on the other hand is the question of property as it affects the English agricultural day labourer just as much as the English factory worker.

In the English as well as the French revolution, the question of property presented itself in such a way that it was a matter of asserting free competition and of abolishing all feudal property relations, such as landed estates, guilds, monopolies, etc., which had been transformed into fetters for the industry which had developed from the 16th to the 18th century.

In "*our own* day", finally, the significance of the question of property consists in it being a matter of eliminating the conflicts which have arisen from large-scale industry, the development of the world market and free competition.

The question of property, depending on the different levels of development of industry, has always been the vital question for a particular class. In the 17th and 18th centuries, when the point at issue was the abolition of *feudal* property relations, the question of property was the vital question for the *bourgeois* class. In the

19th century, when it is a matter of abolishing *bourgeois* property relations, the question of property is a vital question for the *working class*.

The question of property, which in "*our own* day" is a question of world-historical significance, has thus a meaning only in *modern bourgeois society*. The more advanced this society is, in other words, the further the bourgeoisie has developed economically in a country and therefore the more state power has assumed a bourgeois character, the more glaringly does the *social* question obtrude itself, in France more glaringly than in Germany, in England more glaringly than in France, in a constitutional monarchy more glaringly than in an absolute monarchy, in a republic more glaringly than in a constitutional monarchy. Thus, for example, the conflicts of the credit system, speculation, etc., are nowhere more acute than in North America. Nowhere, either, does *social* inequality obtrude itself more harshly than in the eastern states of North America, because nowhere is it less disguised by political inequality. If pauperism has not yet developed there as much as in England, this is explained by economic circumstances which it is not our task to elucidate further here. Meanwhile, pauperism is making the most gratifying progress.

"In this country, where there are no privileged orders, where all *classes* of society have *equal rights*" (the difficulty however lies in the existence of *classes*) "and where our population is far from ... pressing on the means of subsistence, it is indeed alarming to find the increase of pauperism progressing with such rapidity." (Report by Mr. Meredith to the Pennsylvania Congress.[140])

"It is proved that pauperism in Massachusetts has increased by three-fifths within 25 years." (From Niles' *Register*, Niles being an American.[a])

One of the most famous North American political economists, *Thomas Cooper*, who is also a radical, proposes:

1. To prohibit those without property from marrying.
2. To *abolish universal suffrage*,

for, he exclaims:

"Society was instituted for the protection of property.... What reasonable claim can they have, who by eternal economic laws will eternally be without property of their own, to legislate on the property of others? What common motive and common interest is there between these two *classes* of inhabitants?

"Either the working class is not revolutionary, in which case it represents the interests of the employers, on whom their livelihood depends. At the last election in New England, the master-manufacturers, to ensure votes for themselves, had the candidates' names printed on calico, and each of their workers wore such a piece of calico on their trouser-fronts.

---

[a] *Niles' Weekly Register.— Ed.*

"Or the working class becomes revolutionary, as a consequence of communal living together, etc., and then the *political power of the country* will sooner or later fall into its hands, and no property will be safe any more under this system."*

Just as in *England* the workers form a political party under the name of the *Chartists*, so do the workers in *North America* under the name of the *National Reformers*[142] and their battle-cry is not at all *rule of the princes* or the *republic*, but *rule of the working class* or the *rule of the bourgeois class*.

Since therefore it is precisely in modern bourgeois society with its corresponding forms of state, the constitutional or republican representative state, that the "question of property" has become the most important "social question", it is very much the narrow need of the *German* bourgeois that interjects: the question of the *monarchy* is the most important "*social* question of the time". It is in a very similar way that Dr. *List*, in the foreword to his *Nationalökonomie*,[a] expresses his so naïve irritation that *pauperism* and not protective tariffs should have been "misconstrued" as the most important social question of our time.

[*Deutsche-Brüsseler-Zeitung* No. 92, November 18, 1847]

The *distinction* between *money* and *power* was at the same time a *personal* distinction between the two combatants.

The "little" one appears as a kind of *cut-purse* who only takes on enemies who have "money". The daring muscle-man by contrast fights with the "mighty" of this earth.

Indosso la corazza, e l'elmo in testa.**

And, he mutters,

"and incidentally, you are better off than I".***

But best off of all are the "mighty" of the earth who visibly heave a sigh of relief whilst Herr Heinzen lashes out at his pupil:

"Like all Communists, you have now lost the capacity *to recognise the connection between politics and social conditions.*"****

We have just been present at a moral lesson, in which the great man revealed with surprising *simplicity* the *connection* between

* Thomas Cooper, *Lectures on [the Elements of] Political Economy*, Columbia, pp. 361 & 365.[141]

** Ariost[o, *L'*]*Orlando Furioso* [Canto I, 11]: Harness on his back and helmet on his head.

*** Heinzen's Manifesto, *Deutsche-Brüsseler-Zeitung* No. 84.

**** Ibid.

[a] F. List, *Das nationale System der politischen Oekonomie*.— *Ed.*

politics and *social conditions* in general. In the *rule of the princes* he now provides his pupil with a *tangible* application.

The princes, or the rule of the princes, he tells us, are the "chief authors of all poverty and distress". Where the rule of the princes is eliminated, this kind of explanation is of course eliminated too, and the *slave-economy*, which caused the downfall of the republics of antiquity, the slave-economy, which will provoke the most fearful conflicts in the southern states of republican North America,* the slave-economy can exclaim, like John Falstaff, "if reasons were as plenty as blackberries!"[a]

And in the first place, who or what has created the *princes* or the *rule of the princes*?

Once upon a time, the people had to place the most eminent personalities at their head to conduct general affairs. Later, this position became hereditary within families, etc. And eventually the stupidity and depravity of men tolerated this abuse for centuries.

If one were to summon a congress of all the most primitive would-be politicians in Europe, they would be able to give no other answer. And if one were to open all Herr Heinzen's works, they would provide no other answer.

Doughty "sound common sense" believes it explains the *rule of princes* by declaring itself *opposed* to it. The difficulty, from the standpoint of this norm of common sense, would, however, seem to consist in explaining how the opponent of sound common sense and of the moral dignity of man was born and how he dragged out his remarkably tenacious life for centuries. Nothing is simpler. The centuries did without sound common sense and the moral dignity of man. In other words, the sense and morality of centuries were in accordance with the rule of the princes instead of contradicting it. And it is precisely this sense and morality of past centuries which today's "sound common sense" does not understand. It does not understand it, but *despises* it. It takes refuge from history in morality, and now it can allow free rein to the whole armoury of its moral indignation.

In the same way as political "sound common sense" here explains the origin and continued existence of the rule of the princes as the work of unreason, in the same way does religious "sound common sense" explain heresy and unbelief as works of the devil. In the same

* Cf. on this topic the memoirs of Jefferson, who was one of the group of founders of the American Republic and was twice president.

[a] Shakespeare, *Henry IV*, Part One, Act II, Scene 4.—*Ed.*

way, irreligious "sound common sense" explains religion as the work of the devils, the priests.

However, once Herr Heinzen has by means of moral platitudes proved the *origin* of the rule of the princes, the "connection between the rule of the princes and social conditions" follows quite *naturally* from this. Listen:

"An individual man takes possession of the state for himself, sacrifices a whole nation, more or less, not just materially, but morally too, to his own person and its entourage; institutes within it a scale of humiliation by degrees, classifies it variously into *estates* like so many fat and lean cattle, and basically just for the benefit of his own, individual person *makes* each member of the state society *officially the enemy of the other.*"*

Herr Heinzen sees the princes at the peak of the social structure in Germany. He does not for a moment doubt that they have created its social foundation and are re-*creating* it each day. What *simpler* explanation could there be for the connection between the monarchy and social conditions, whose *official* political expression it is, than by having the princes *create* this connection! What is the connection between the representative assemblies and modern bourgeois society which they represent? They *created* it. The political deity with its apparatus and gradations has thus *created* the secular world, whose most sacred object it is. In the same way the *religious* deity will have created earthly conditions, which are fantastically and in deified form reflected in it.

The grobianism which retails such homespun wisdom with appropriate sentiment cannot of course fail to be equally astonished and morally outraged at the opponent who toils to demonstrate to it that the apple did not create the apple-tree.

Modern histories have demonstrated that *absolute monarchy* appears in those transitional periods when the old feudal estates are in decline and the medieval estate of burghers is evolving into the modern bourgeois class, without one of the contending parties having as yet finally disposed of the other. The elements on which absolute monarchy is based are thus by no means its own product; they rather form its social prerequisite, whose historical origins are too well known to be repeated here. The fact that absolute monarchy took shape later in Germany and is persisting longer, is explained solely by the stunted pattern of development of the German bourgeois class. The answers to the puzzles presented by this pattern of development are to be found in the history of trade and industry.

The decline of the philistine German free cities, the destruction of the knightly estate, the defeat of the peasants[143]—the resulting

* Heinzen's Manifesto, loc. cit.

territorial sovereignty of the princes—the decay of German industry and German trade, which were founded entirely on medieval conditions, at the very moment when the modern world market is opening up and large-scale manufacturing is arising—the depopulation and the barbaric conditions which the Thirty Years War[144] had left behind—the character of the national branches of industry which are now rising again—as of the small linen industry—to which patriarchal conditions and relations correspond, the nature of exported goods which for the most part derived from agriculture, and which therefore went almost exclusively to increase the material sources of wealth of the rural aristocracy and therefore its relative power *vis-à-vis* the townspeople—Germany's lowly position in the world market in general, as a result of which the subsidies paid by foreigners to the princes became a chief source of the national income, the dependence of the townspeople upon the court consequent upon this—etc., etc., all these relationships, within which the structure of German society and a political organisation in keeping with it were taking shape become, in the eyes of sound-common-sensical grobianism, just a few pithy utterances, whose pith however consists in the statement that the "rule of the princes in Germany" has created "German society" and is "re-creating" it each day.

The optical illusion, which enables sound common sense to "discern" the springhead of German society in the rule of the princes instead of the springhead of the rule of the princes in German society, is easily explained.

It perceives at first glance—and it always considers its first glance to be particularly perceptive—that the German princes are preserving and maintaining control over the old social conditions in Germany with which their political existence stands and falls, and that they *react* violently against the elements of decomposition. Equally, it sees on the other hand the elements of decomposition fighting against the power of the princes. The five sound senses thus unanimously testify that the rule of the princes is the *basis* of the old society, of its gradations, its prejudices and its contradictions.

When looked at more closely, these appearances however only refute the crude opinion of which they are the innocent occasion.

The violently reactionary role played by the rule of the princes only proves that in the pores of the old society a new society has taken shape, which furthermore cannot but feel the political shell—the natural covering of the old society—as an unnatural fetter and blow it sky-high. The more primitive these new elements of social decomposition, the more conservative will even the most vigorous reaction by the old political power appear. The more advanced these new elements of social decomposition, the more reactionary will even the most harmless attempt at conservation by the old political power appear. The reaction of the rule of the princes, instead of proving that it creates the old society, proves rather that its day is over as soon as the material conditions of the old society have become obsolete. Its reaction is at the same time the reaction of the old society which is still the *official* society and therefore also still in *official possession* of power or in possession of *official power.*

Once society's material conditions of existence have developed so far that the transformation of its official political form has become a vital necessity for it, the whole physiognomy of the old political power is transformed. Thus absolute monarchy now attempts, not to *centralise,* which was its actual progressive function, but to *decentralise.* Born from the defeat of the feudal estates and having the most active share in their destruction itself, it now seeks to retain at least the *semblance* of feudal distinctions. Formerly encouraging trade and industry and thereby at the same time the rise of the bourgeois class, as necessary conditions both for national strength and for its own glory, absolute monarchy now everywhere hampers trade and industry, which have become increasingly dangerous weapons in the hands of an already powerful bourgeoisie. From the *town,* the birth-place of its rise to power, it turns its alarmed and by now dull glance to the *countryside* which is fertile with the corpses of its old powerful opponents.

But by "the connection between politics and social conditions" Herr Heinzen actually understands only the connection between the rule of the princes in Germany and the distress and misery in Germany.

The monarchy, like every other form of state, is a direct burden on the working class on the material side only in the form of *taxes.* Taxes are the existence of the state expressed in economic terms. Civil servants and priests, soldiers and ballet-dancers, schoolmasters and police constables, Greek museums and Gothic steeples, civil list and services list—the common seed within which all these fabulous beings slumber in embryo is *taxation.*

And what reasoning citizen would not have referred the starving people to taxes, to the ill-gotten gains of the princes, as the source of its misery?

The German princes and Germany's distress! In other words, taxes on which the princes gorge themselves and which the people pay with their sweat and blood!

What inexhaustible material for speechifying saviours of mankind!

The monarchy is the cause of great expenditure. No doubt. Just consider the North American national budget and compare what our 38 petty fatherlands have to pay in order to be governed and disciplined! It is not the Communists who answer the thunderous outbursts of such self-important demagogy, no, it is the *bourgeois* economists such as Ricardo, Senior, etc., in just two words.

The economic existence of the state is *taxes.*

The economic existence of the worker is *wages.*

To be ascertained: the *relationship* between taxes and wages.

Competition necessarily reduces the average wage to the minimum, that is to say, to a wage which permits the workers penuriously to eke out their lives and the lives of their race. Taxes form a part of this minimum, for the political calling of the workers consists precisely in paying taxes. If all taxes which bear on the working class were abolished root and branch, the necessary consequence would be the reduction of wages by the whole amount of taxes which today goes into them. Either the employers' *profit* would rise as a direct consequence by the same quantity, or else no more than an alteration in the *form* of tax-collecting would have taken place. Instead of the present system, whereby the capitalist also advances, as part of the wage, the taxes which the worker has to pay, he [the capitalist] would no longer pay them in this roundabout way, but directly to the state.

If in North America wages are higher than in Europe, this is by no means the consequence of lower taxes there. It is the consequence of the territorial, commercial and industrial situation there. The demand for workers in relation to the supply of workers is significantly greater than in Europe. And any novice knows the truth of this already from Adam Smith.

For the bourgeoisie on the other hand both the way in which taxes are distributed and levied, and the use to which they are put, are a vital question, both on account of its influence on trade and industry and because taxes are the golden cord with which to strangle the absolute monarchy.

Having provided such profound insights into "the connection between politics and social conditions" and between "class relations" and the power of the state, Herr Heinzen cries out in triumph:

"The 'narrow-minded communist view' which only treats people in terms of 'classes' and *incites* them against one another according to their 'craft', is something I must confess I have been innocent of in my revolutionary propaganda, because I make allowance for the 'possibility' that 'humanity' is not always determined by 'class' or the 'size of one's purse'."

"Grobianist" common sense transforms the distinction between classes into the "distinction between the size of purses" and class contradictions into "craft-bickering". The size of one's purse is a purely quantitative distinction whereby any two individuals of the *same* class may be *incited* against one another at will. That the medieval *guilds* opposed each other "according to their *craft*" is common knowledge. But it is equally common knowledge that modern class distinctions are by no means based upon "craft" but rather that the division of labour brings about very *different* modes of work within the *same* class.

And this, his own "narrow-minded view", derived entirely from his very own "fulness of life" and his very own "sound common sense" is what Herr Heinzen humorously calls a "narrow-minded communist view".

But let us for a moment assume that Herr Heinzen knows what he is talking about, that he is therefore not talking about "the distinction between the size" of purses and "craft-bickering".

It is perfectly "possible" that what individual persons do is not "always" determined by the class to which they belong, although this is no more crucial to the class struggle than an aristocrat going over to the *tiers-état* was crucial to the French Revolution. And then these aristocrats at least joined *a specific* class, the revolutionary class, the bourgeoisie. But for Herr Heinzen all classes melt away before the solemn concept of "humanity".

However, if Herr Heinzen believes that *whole classes* which are based on *economic* conditions independent of their own will and are forced into the most virulent contradiction by these conditions, can by means of the quality of "humanity", which attaches to all men, shed their real relationships, how easy must it be for *one particular* prince to rise by the power of "humanity" above his "princely condition", above his "princely craft"? Why then does he resent it when Engels discerns a "good Emperor Joseph" behind his revolutionary phrases?

But if on the one hand Herr Heinzen obliterates *all* differences, by addressing himself vaguely to the "humanity" of the Germans, which would oblige him to include the princes in his exhortations too, on the other hand he nevertheless finds himself compelled to acknowledge the existence of *one difference* amidst German *humanity*, for without a difference there can be no contradiction and without a contradiction there can be no material for political sermonising.

So Herr Heinzen *divides* German humanity into *princes* and *subjects*. The perception and expression of this contradiction is on his part an exhibition of moral strength, a proof of personal daring, political understanding, outraged human feeling, serious-minded perspicacity and laudable bravery. And it would be a sign of intellectual blindness, of a policeman's mentality, to point out that there are privileged and unprivileged subjects; that the former by no means see humiliating gradations in the political hierarchy, but an elevating, upward line; that finally amongst the subjects whose subjection is considered a fetter, it is however considered a fetter in very different ways.

Along come the "narrow-minded" Communists now and see not only the political *difference* between *prince* and *subject* but also the social difference between *classes*.

Whereas Herr Heinzen's moral greatness a moment before consisted in perceiving and expressing the difference, his greatness now consists rather in overlooking it, averting his eyes from it and hushing it up. Expression of the *contradiction* ceases to be the language of revolution and becomes the language of reaction and the malicious "incitement" of brothers, united in their *humanity*, against one another.

It is common knowledge that shortly after the July revolution, the victorious bourgeoisie, in the *September Laws*, made the "incitement of the various classes of the nation against each other" a serious political offence, probably for reasons of "humanity" too, with penalties of imprisonment, fines, etc.[145] It is also common knowledge that the English bourgeois journals know no better way of denouncing the Chartist leaders and Chartist writers than by accusing them of inciting the various classes of the nation against each other. It is even common knowledge that German writers are lying in deep dungeons for this incitement of the various classes of the nation against each other.

Is not Herr Heinzen now speaking the language of the French September Laws, of the English bourgeois papers and the Prussian criminal code?

Not a bit of it. The well-meaning Herr Heinzen fears only that the Communists "were *seeking* to *ensure* the princes a revolutionary fontanel".[146]

Thus the *Belgian* liberals assure us that the *radicals* have a secret understanding with the Catholics; the *French* liberals assure us that the *democrats* have an understanding with the legitimists; the English free traders assure us that the *Chartists* have an understanding with the Tories. And the liberal Herr Heinzen assures us that the *Communists* have an understanding with the princes.

Germany, as I already made clear in the *Deutsch-Französische*

Jahrbücher,[a] has its own Christian-Germanic brand of bad luck. Its bourgeoisie has got so very far behind the times that it is beginning its struggle against absolute monarchy and seeking to create the foundation for its own political power at the moment when in all advanced countries the bourgeoisie is already engaged in the most violent struggle with the working class and when its political illusions are already antiquated in the European mind. In this country, where the political wretchedness of the absolute monarchy still persists with its whole appendage of run-down, semi-feudal estates and relationships, there also already partially exist, on the other hand, as a consequence of industrial development and Germany's dependence on the world market, the modern contradictions between bourgeoisie and working class and the struggle that results from them—examples are the workers' uprisings in Silesia and Bohemia.[147] The German bourgeoisie therefore already finds itself in conflict with the proletariat even before being politically constituted as a class. The struggle between the "subjects" has broken out even before princes and aristocracy have been chased out of the country, all the songs sung at Hambach[148] notwithstanding.

Herr Heinzen can think of no other explanation for these contradictory circumstances, which of course are also reflected in German literature, except by laying them on his opponents' *consciences* and interpreting them as a consequence of the counter-revolutionary activity of the Communists.

The German workers meanwhile know very well that the *absolute monarchy* does not waver for a moment, nor can it do so, in greeting them, in the *service of the bourgeoisie,* with cannon-balls and whip-lashes. Why, then, should they prefer the brutal harassment of the absolute government with its semi-feudal retinue to *direct bourgeois rule*? The workers know very well that it is not just politically that the bourgeoisie will have to make broader concessions to them than the absolute monarchy, but that in serving the interests of its trade and industry it will create, willy-nilly, the conditions for the uniting of the working class, and the uniting of the workers is the first requirement for their victory. The workers know that the abolition of *bourgeois* property relations is not brought about by preserving those of *feudalism*. They know that the revolutionary movement of the bourgeoisie against the feudal estates and the absolute monarchy can only accelerate their own revolutionary movement. They know that their own struggle against the bourgeoi-

[a] See K. Marx, "Contribution to the Critique of Hegel's Philosophy of Law". Introduction (present edition, Vol. 3, pp. 175-87).—*Ed.*

sie can only dawn with the day when the bourgeoisie is victorious. Despite all this they do not share Herr Heinzen's bourgeois illusions. They can and must accept the *bourgeois revolution* as a precondition for the *workers' revolution*. However, they cannot for a moment regard it as their *ultimate goal.*

That the workers really react in this way has been magnificently exemplified by the *English* Chartists in the most recent Anti-Corn Law League movement. Not for a moment did they believe the lies and inventions of the bourgeois radicals, not for a moment did they abandon the struggle against them, but quite consciously helped their enemies to victory over the Tories, and on the day after the abolition of the Corn Laws they were facing each other at the hustings, no longer Tories and free traders, but free traders and Chartists. And they won seats in parliament, in opposition to these bourgeois radicals.[149]

No more than Herr Heinzen understands the workers does he understand the *bourgeois liberals,* for all that he is unconsciously working in their service. He thinks it is necessary to repeat, where they are concerned, the old warnings against the "easy-going ways and submissiveness of the Germans". He, the philistine, takes in absolute earnest the obsequious expressions that were served up by a Camphausen or a Hansemann. The bourgeois gentlemen would smile at such naïvety. They know better where the shoe pinches. They are aware that in revolutions the *rabble* gets insolent and lays hands on things. The bourgeois gentlemen therefore seek as far as possible to make the change from *absolute* to *bourgeois* monarchy without a revolution, in an amicable fashion.

But the absolute monarchy in Prussia, as earlier in England and France, will not let itself be amicably changed into a bourgeois monarchy. It will not abdicate amicably. The princes' hands are tied both by their personal prejudices and by a whole bureaucracy of officials, soldiers and clerics—integral parts of absolute monarchy who are far from willing to exchange their ruling position for a subservient one in respect of the bourgeoisie. Then the feudal estates also hold back; for them it is a question of life or death, in other words, of property or expropriation. It is clear that the absolute monarch, for all the servile homage of the bourgeoisie, sees his true interest on the side of these estates.

The siren-songs of a Camphausen or a Hansemann will no more convince Frederick William IV, therefore, than the honeyed language of a Lally-Tollendal, a Mounier, a Malouet or a Mirabeau could talk a Louis XVI into casting in his lot with the bourgeoisie rather than with the feudal lords and remnants of the absolute monarchy.

But Herr Heinzen is concerned neither with the bourgeoisie nor with the proletariat in Germany. His party is the "party of men", in other words, of worthy and generous-minded dreamers who advocate "bourgeois" interests in the guise of "human" ends, without however clearly understanding the connection between the idealistic phrase and its real substance.

[*Deutsche-Brüsseler-Zeitung* No. 94, November 25, 1847]

To this party, the party of *men*, or to *humanity* resident in Germany, the founder of states Karl Heinzen offers the "best republic", the best republic he himself has hatched, the "federal republic with social institutions". *Rousseau* once designed a "best" political world for the Poles[a] as did *Mably* for the Corsicans.[150] The great citizen of Geneva has found an even greater successor.

> "I am contented"—what modesty!—"to claim that just as I can assemble a flower only from petals, so also I can assemble a republic only from republican elements."*

A man who knows how to *assemble* a flower from *petals*, even though it were only a *daisy*, cannot fail in the construction of the "best republic", let the wicked world think of it what it will.

Despite all slanderous tongues, the valiant founder of states takes as a model the charters of republican North America. Whatever seems offensive to him, he paints out with his grobian brush. Thus he brings about an amended edition—*in usum delphini*,[b] in other words for the use and edification of "German man". And having thus "outlined the features of the republic, that is, of a specific republic", he hoists his "little" disrespectful pupil up into the air "by his communist ears" and dashes him down with the question whether he too could "create" a world, and indeed a "best world"? And he does not desist from hoisting the "little one" up "into the air" by his "communist ears" until he has "banged" his "nose" against the gigantic picture of the "new" world, the best republic. For with his very own hands he has hung a colossal picture of the world, devised by himself, on the highest peak of the Swiss Alps.

* Heinzen's Manifesto, *Deutsche-Brüsseler-Zeitung* No. 84.

[a] J. J. Rousseau, *Considérations sur le gouvernement de Pologne, et sur sa réformation projettée.— Ed.*

[b] For the use of the Dauphin. (These words were used in the second half of the seventeenth century to mark the edition of Latin works intended for the heir to the French throne, from which "offensive" material had been removed.)— *Ed.*

"*Cacatum non est pictum,*"[a] hisses the voice of the impenitent "little" snake.

And horrified, the republican Ajax drops the communist Thersites to the ground and out of his shaggy bosom heaves the—terrible words:

"You are carrying absurdity to extremes, Herr Engels!"

And really, Herr Engels! Do you not believe "that the American federal system" is the "best political form" "which the art of politics has yet devised"? You shake your little head? What? You deny absolutely that the "American federal system" has been *devised* by "the art of politics"? And that "best political forms of society" exist *in abstracto*? That's going a bit too far!

You are at the same time so "devoid of shame and conscience" as to suggest to us that the honest German who wishes his faithful fatherland to enjoy the benefits of the North American Constitution—embellished and improved at that, that he resembles that idiotic merchant who copied his rich competitor's accounts and then imagined that having possession of this copy, he had also taken possession of the coveted wealth!

And you threaten us with the "executioner's axe" under your *little arm*, with the miniature guillotine which you were given as a toy in 1794? Barbaroux, you mumble, and other persons of impressive height and girth, were shortened by a full head in those days when we used to play guillotine because they happened to proclaim "the American federal system" to be "the best political form".[151] And such will be the fate of all other Goliaths, to whom it occurs in any democratic revolution in Europe and especially in Germany, which is still quite feudally fragmented, to wish to put the "American federal system" in place of the *one* indivisible republic and its levelling centralisation.

But good God! The men of the Comité de salut public[152] and those bloodhounds of Jacobins behind them were monsters, and Heinzen's "best republic" has been "devised" by the "statecraft of heretofore" as the "best political form" for "men", for good men, for human humans!

Really! "You are carrying absurdity to the extreme, Herr Engels!"

And what is more, this Herculean founder of states does not copy the North American "federal republic" in every detail. He adorns it with "social institutions", he will "regulate property relations according to rational principles", and the seven great "measures" with which he disposed of the "evils" of the old bourgeois society are

[a] "To shit is not to paint."—*Ed.*

by no means wretched, insubstantial garbage begged at the doors of—abominable modern socialist and communist soup-kitchens. It is to the "Incas" and "Campe's Books for Children"[153] that the great Karl Heinzen owes his recipes for the "humanisation of society", just as he owes the latter profound slogan not to the Pomeranian philosopher Ruge but rather to some "Peruvian" grown old in wisdom. And Herr Engels describes all this as arbitrarily concocted philistine dreams of world improvement!

We live of course in an age when "the better people are increasingly passing away" and the "best" are not even understood at all.

Take, for instance, any well-meaning citizen and ask his honest opinion as to what is wrong with present "property relations"? And the decent fellow will put his index finger to the tip of his nose, twice draw deep and pensive breath and then express his "humble" view that it is a shame that many people have "nothing", not even the barest necessities, and that others, to the detriment not only of propertyless wretches but also of honest citizens, are with aristocratic brazenness accumulating millions! *Aurea mediocritas!* Golden mediocrity! the honest member of the middle class will exclaim! It is just a matter of avoiding extremes! What rational political constitution would be compatible with these extremes, these oh so abominable extremes!

And now take a look at Heinzen's "federal republic" with "social institutions" and its seven measures for the "humanisation of society". We find that each citizen is assured a "minimum" of wealth below which he cannot fall, and a maximum of wealth is prescribed which he may not exceed.

Has not Herr Heinzen solved all the difficulties, then, by reiterating in the form of state decrees the pious desire of all good citizens that no person should have too little and none, indeed, too much, and simply by so doing made it reality?

And in the same manner, which is as simple as it is splendid, Herr Heinzen has resolved all economic conflicts. He has *regulated* property according to the *rational principles* corresponding to an honest bourgeois equity. And please do not object that the "rational rules" of property are precisely the "economic laws" on whose cold-blooded inevitability all well-meaning "measures" will necessarily founder, though they be recommended by Incas and Campe's Books for Children and cherished by the stoutest patriots!

How unfair to bring *economic* considerations into play against a man who, unlike some people, does not "boast of studies in political economy", but has from modesty managed so far in all his works rather to preserve the virginal appearance of still having before him his first study of political economy! It must be accounted very much to the credit of the man's primitive level of education that with solemn countenance he serves up to his little communist foe all the considerations which already in 1842 had penetrated to the German fulness of life through the channels of the Augsburg *Allgemeine Zeitung*,[154] such as those concerning "acquired" property, "personal freedom and individuality" and the like. It really does show how low the communist writers have fallen that they seek out opponents who are schooled in economics and philosophy, but on the other hand provide no answer to the "unpresuming" fancies of grobianist sound common sense, to which they would first have to teach the elements of the economic relations in existing bourgeois society, in order to be able subsequently to enter into debate with it.

Since *private property*, for instance, is not a simple relation or even an abstract concept, a principle, but consists in the totality of the *bourgeois* relations of production—for it is not a question of subordinate or extinct but of existing bourgeois private property—since all these bourgeois relations of production are class relations, an insight which any novice must have acquired from his Adam Smith or Ricardo—, a change in, or even the abolition of, these relations can only follow from a change in these classes and their relationships with each other, and a change in the relationship of classes is a historical change, a product of social activity as a whole, in a word, the product of a specific "historical movement". The writer may very well serve a movement of history as its mouthpiece, but he cannot of course create it.

For example, in order to explain the elimination of feudal property relations, modern historians have had to describe how the bourgeoisie evolved to the point where it had developed its conditions of life sufficiently to be able to eliminate all the feudal estates and its own feudal mode of existence and hence also feudal production relations, which were the economic foundation of these feudal estates. The elimination of feudal property relations and the foundation of modern bourgeois society were thus by no means the product of a particular doctrine based upon and elaborated from a specific principle as its *core*. It was much more the case that the principles and theories put forward by the writers of the bourgeoisie during its struggle against feudalism were nothing but the theoretical expression of a series of real events; indeed one can see that the extent to which this expression was more or less utopian, dogmatic or doctrinaire corresponded exactly to the degree of advancement of the phase of real historical development.

And in this respect Engels was rash enough to talk to his terrible opponent, the Herculean founder of states, about communism, insofar as it is theory, as the theoretical expression of a "movement".

But, expostulates the mighty man in honest indignation: "My purpose was to urge the practical consequences, to get the 'representatives' of communism to acknowledge those consequences", that is, those absurd consequences which, for a man who has only fantastic conceptions of bourgeois private property, are necessarily linked with its abolition. He thus wanted to compel Engels "to defend the whole absurdity" which according to Herr Heinzen's worthy scheme "he would have dug up". And Reineke Engels has so bitterly disappointed the honest Isegrim that he no longer finds in communism itself even a "core" to "bite on" and thus asks himself in wonderment "how this phenomenon is to be served up, so that it can be eaten"!

And in vain the honest fellow seeks to calm himself with ingenious turns of phrase, for example, by asking whether a historical movement is a "movement of the emotions", etc., and even conjures up the spirit of the great "Ruge" to interpret this riddle of nature for him!

"After what has happened," the disappointed man exclaims, "my heart is beating in a *Siberian fashion*, after what has happened I *smell only treachery* and *dream of malice.*"*

And really he explains the affair to himself finally by saying that Engels "denies his school", "beats a retreat that is as cowardly as it is ridiculous", "compromises the whole human race just so as to save his own person from being compromised", "denies the party or deserts it at the crucial moment", and a host of similar moralising outbursts of fury. Likewise Engels' distinctions between "true socialism" and "communism", between the utopian communist systems and critical communism—are all nothing but "treachery and malice". Indeed nothing but Jesuitical "after-thought" distinctions, because they appear not to have been put at least so far to Herr Heinzen, nor to have been blown his way by the tempest of the fulness of life!

And how ingeniously Herr Heinzen manages to interpret these contradictions to himself, insofar as they have found literary expression!

"Then there is Weitling, who is cleverer than you, and yet can certainly be considered a Communist."

* Karl Heinzen, *Steckbrief*.

Or else:

> "What if Herr Grün *claimed* to be a Communist and were to expel Herr Engels?"

Arrived at this point, it goes without saying, the honest fellow, who could not "emancipate himself to the extent of considering *loyalty* and *faith*, outmoded though they might be, to be superfluous amongst rational beings"—serves up the most absurd *lies*, for example, that Engels also intended to write about a "social movement in Belgium and France". But K[arl] Grün had "forestalled him". And then he had been "unable to find a publisher for his boring repetition" and other such fabrications Herr Heinzen has derived as "conclusions" from a "certain principle".

That moralising criticism has turned out to be so wretched is due to its "nature" and is by no means to be regarded as a personal shortcoming of the Telamonian Ajax. For all his stupidities and baseness, this St. Grobian has the moral satisfaction of being stupid and base with conviction and thus being a fellow with some stuffing in him.

Whatever the "facts" may do, which even the great Karl Heinzen allows to "run their course" unimpeded:

> "I," he proclaims, thrice beating his honest bosom, "I, meanwhile, bear my principle unflinchingly about with me and do not ditch it when a person asks me about it."

Heinrich LXXII of Reuss-Schleitz-Ebersdorf has also been parading his "principle" some 20 years now.

N.B. We would recommend Stephan's[a] critique, *Der Heinzen'sche Staat*, to the readers of the *Deutsche-Brüsseler-Zeitung*. The author has of course only used Herr Heinzen as a peg, he could just as well have seized upon any other literary nonentity in Germany to confront the reasoning and grumbling petty bourgeois with the viewpoint of the really revolutionary worker. Herr Heinzen knows of no other way of answering Stephan than by first of all *asserting* that what he has written is rubbish; so much for *objective* criticism. As he does not know Stephan personally, he resorts simply to calling him names like *gamin* and *commis-voyageur*.[b] But he has not yet blackened his opponent enough, he finally turns him into a policeman. One can see incidentally how just this last accusation is, since the French police,

---

[a] Stephan Born.— *Ed.*

[b] Guttersnipe and commercial traveller.— *Ed.*

presumably in league with Herr Heinzen, have confiscated 100 copies of Stephan's pamphlet.

Having given the worker Stephan a practical moral lesson as described above, he apostrophises him in the following ingenuous terms:

"For my own part, gladly though I would have engaged in discussions with a worker, I fail to see in insolence a fit substitute for competence."[a]

The German workers will feel elated at the prospect of the *democrat* Karl Heinzen engaging in discussions with them as soon as they approach the great man with due modesty. Herr Heinzen is seeking to conceal his incompetence concerning Herr Stephan by the insolence of his outburst.

K. M.

Written at the end of October 1847

First published in the *Deutsche-Brüsseler-Zeitung* Nos. 86, 87, 90, 92 and 94; October 28 and 31; November 11, 18 and 25, 1847

Printed according to the newspaper

Published in full in English for the first time

---

[a] K. Heinzen, "Ein 'Representant' der Kommunisten".—*Ed.*

Frederick Engels

PRINCIPLES OF COMMUNISM[155]

Question 1: What is communism?

Answer: Communism is the doctrine of the conditions for the emancipation of the proletariat.

Question 2: What is the proletariat?

Answer: The proletariat is that class of society which procures its means of livelihood entirely and solely from the sale of its labour[156] and not from the profit derived from any capital; whose weal and woe, whose life and death, whose whole existence depend on the demand for labour, hence, on the alternation of times of good and bad business, on the fluctuations resulting from unbridled competition. The proletariat, or class of proletarians, is, in a word, the working class of the nineteenth century.

Question 3: Then there have not always been proletarians?

Answer: No. Poor folk and working classes have always existed,[157] and the working classes have for the most part been poor. But such poor, such workers who live under the conditions just stated, that is, proletarians, have not always existed, any more than competition has always been free and unbridled.

Question 4: How did the proletariat arise?

Answer: The proletariat arose as a result of the industrial revolution which took place in England in the latter half of the last century and which has repeated itself since then in all the civilised countries of the world. This industrial revolution was brought about by the invention of the steam-engine, of various spinning machines, of the power-loom, and of a great number of other mechanical devices. These machines which were very expensive and, consequently, could only be purchased by big capitalists, changed the entire hitherto existing mode of production and supplanted the former workers because machines produced cheaper and better commodities than could the workers with their imperfect spinning-wheels and hand-looms. Thus, these machines delivered industry entirely into the hands of the big capitalists and rendered the workers' scanty property (tools, looms, etc.) quite worthless, so that the capitalists soon had their hands on everything and the workers were left with nothing. In this way the factory system was introduced into the manufacture of clothing materials.—Once the impetus had been given to the introduction of machinery and the factory system, this system was soon applied to all the other branches of industry, notably the calico and book-printing trades, pottery, and hardware industry. There was more and more division of labour among the individual workers, so that the worker who formerly had made a whole article now produced only a part of it. This division of labour made it possible to supply products more speedily and therefore more cheaply. It reduced the activity of each worker to a very simple, constantly repeated mechanical operation, which could be performed not only just as well but even much better by a machine. In this way, all these branches of industry came one after another under the domination of steam-power, machinery, and the factory system, just like spinning and weaving. But they thus fell at the same time completely into the hands of the big capitalists, and here too the workers were deprived of the last shred of independence. Gradually, in addition to actual manufacture, the handicrafts likewise fell increasingly under the domination of the factory system, for here also the big capitalists more and more supplanted the small craftsmen by the establishment of large workshops, in which many savings on costs can be made and there can be a very high division of labour. Thus we have now reached the point when in the civilised countries almost all branches of labour are carried on under the factory system, and in almost all branches handicraft and manufacture have been ousted by large-scale industry.—As a result, the former middle classes, especially the smaller master handicraftsmen, have been increasingly ruined, the former position of the workers has been completely changed, and two new classes which are gradually swallowing up all other classes have come into being, namely:

I. The class of big capitalists who already now in all civilised countries almost exclusively own all the means of subsistence and the raw materials and instruments (machinery, factories, etc.), needed for the production of these means of subsistence. This class is the bourgeois class or the bourgeoisie.

II. The class of the completely propertyless, who are compelled therefore to sell their labour to the bourgeois in order to obtain the necessary means of subsistence in exchange. This class is called the class of the proletarians or the proletariat.

Question 5: Under what conditions does this sale of the labour of the proletarians to the bourgeois take place?

Answer: Labour is a commodity like any other and its price is determined by the same laws as that of any other commodity. The price of a commodity under the domination of large-scale industry or of free competition, which, as we shall see, comes to the same thing, is on the average always equal to the cost of production of that commodity. The price of labour is, therefore, likewise equal to the cost of production of labour. The cost of production of labour consists precisely of the amount of the means of subsistence required for the worker to maintain himself in a condition in which he is capable of working and to prevent the working class from dying out. Therefore, the worker will not receive for his labour any more than is necessary for that purpose; the price of labour, or wages, will be the lowest, the minimum required for subsistence. Since business is now worse, now better, the worker will receive now more, now less, just as the factory owner receives now more, now less for his commodity. But just as on the average between good times and bad the factory owner receives for his commodity neither more nor less than the cost of its production, so also the worker will on the average receive neither more nor less than this minimum. This economic law of wages will come to be more stringently applied the more all branches of labour are taken over by large-scale industry.

Question 6: What working classes existed before the industrial revolution?

Answer: Depending on the different stages of the development of society, the working classes lived in different conditions and stood in different relations to the possessing and ruling classes. In ancient times the working people were the *slaves* of their owners, just as they still are in many backward countries and even in the southern part of the United States. In the Middle Ages they were the *serfs* of the landowning nobility, just as they still are in Hungary, Poland, and Russia. In the Middle Ages and up to the industrial revolution there were in the towns also journeymen in the service of petty-bourgeois craftsmen, and with the development of manufacture there gradually emerged manufactory workers, who were already employed by the bigger capitalists.

Question 7: In what way does the proletarian differ from the slave?

Answer: The slave is sold once and for all, the proletarian has to sell himself by the day and by the hour. Being the property of *one* master, the individual slave has, since it is in the interest of this master, a guaranteed subsistence, however wretched it may be; the individual proletarian, the property, so to speak, of the whole bourgeois *class*, whose labour is only bought from him when somebody needs it, has no guaranteed subsistence. This subsistence is guaranteed only to the proletarian *class* as a whole. The slave stands outside competition, the proletarian stands within it and feels all its fluctuations. The slave is accounted a thing, not a member of civil society; the proletarian is recognised as a person, as a member of civil society. Thus, the slave may have a better subsistence than the proletarian, but the proletarian belongs to a higher stage of development of society and himself stands at a higher stage than the slave. The slave frees himself by abolishing, among all the private property relationships, only the relationship of slavery and thereby only then himself becomes a proletarian; the proletarian can free himself only by abolishing private property in general.

Question 8: In what way does the proletarian differ from the serf?

Answer: The serf has the possession and use of an instrument of production, a piece of land, in return for handing over a portion of the yield or for the performance of work. The proletarian works with instruments of production belonging to another person for the benefit of this other person in return for receiving a portion of the yield. The serf gives, to the proletarian is given. The serf has a guaranteed subsistence, the proletarian has not. The serf stands outside competition, the proletarian stands within it. The serf frees himself either by running away to the town and there becoming a handicraftsman or by giving his landlord money instead of labour and products and becoming a free tenant; or by driving out his feudal lord and himself becoming a proprietor, in short, by entering in one way or another into the possessing class and competition. The proletarian frees himself by doing away with competition, private property and all class distinctions.

Question 9: In what way does the proletarian differ from the handicraftsman?[a]

Question 10: In what way does the proletarian differ from the manufactory worker?

Answer: The manufactory worker of the sixteenth to the eighteenth centuries almost everywhere still owned an instrument of production, his loom, the family spinning-wheels, and a little plot of

---

[a] Half a page is left blank by Engels in the manuscript. The answer is in the "Draft of a Communist Confession of Faith" (see this volume, p. 101).—*Ed.*

land which he cultivated in his leisure hours. The proletarian has none of these things. The manufactory worker lives almost always in the country and in more or less patriarchal relations with his landlord or his employer; the proletarian lives mostly in large towns, and stands to his employer in a purely money relationship. The manufactory worker is torn up from his patriarchal relations by large-scale industry, loses the property he still has and thereby only then himself becomes a proletarian.

Question 11: What were the immediate results of the industrial revolution and the division of society into bourgeois and proletarians?

Answer: Firstly, owing to the continual cheapening of the price of industrial products as a result of machine labour, the old system of manufacture or industry founded upon manual labour was completely destroyed in all countries of the world. All semi-barbarian countries, which until now had been more or less outside historical development and whose industry had until now been based on manufacture, were thus forcibly torn out of their isolation. They bought the cheaper commodities of the English and let their own manufactory workers go to ruin. Thus countries that for thousands of years had made no progress, for example India, were revolutionised through and through, and even China is now marching towards a revolution. It has reached the point that a new machine invented today in England, throws millions of workers in China out of work within a year. Large-scale industry has thus brought all the peoples of the earth into relationship with one another, thrown all the small local markets into the world market, prepared the way everywhere for civilisation and progress, and brought it about that everything that happens in the civilised countries must have its repercussions on all other countries. So if now in England or France the workers liberate themselves, this must lead to revolutions in all other countries, which sooner or later will also bring about the liberation of the workers in those countries.

Secondly, wherever large-scale industry replaced manufacture, the industrial revolution developed the bourgeoisie, its wealth and its power, to the highest degree and made it the first class in the land. The result was that wherever this happened, the bourgeoisie obtained political power and ousted the hitherto ruling classes—the aristocracy, the guild-burghers and the absolute monarchy representing both. The bourgeoisie annihilated the power of the aristocracy, the nobility, by abolishing entails or the ban on the sale of landed property, and all privileges of the nobility. It destroyed the power of the guild-burghers by abolishing all guilds and craft privileges. In place of both it put free competition, that is, a state of society in which everyone has the right to engage in any branch of industry he likes, and where nothing can hinder him in carrying it on except lack of the necessary capital. The introduction of free competition is therefore the public declaration that henceforward the members of society are only unequal in so far as their capital is unequal, that capital has become the decisive power and therefore the capitalists, the bourgeois, have become the first class in society. But free competition is necessary for the beginning of large-scale industry since it is the only state of society in which large-scale industry can grow. The bourgeoisie having thus annihilated the social power of the nobility and the guild-burghers, annihilated their political power as well. Having become the first class in society, the bourgeoisie proclaimed itself also the first class in the political sphere. It did this by establishing the representative system, which rests upon bourgeois equality before the law and the legal recognition of free competition, and which in European countries was introduced in the form of constitutional monarchy. Under these constitutional monarchies those only are electors who possess a certain amount of capital, that is to say, the bourgeois; these bourgeois electors elect the deputies, and these bourgeois deputies, by means of the right to refuse taxes, elect a bourgeois government.

Thirdly, the industrial revolution built up the proletariat in the same measure in which it built up the bourgeoisie. In the same proportion in which the bourgeois became wealthier, the proletarians became more numerous. For since proletarians can only be employed by capital and since capital only increases when it employs labour, the growth of the proletariat keeps exact pace with the growth of capital. At the same time it concentrates the bourgeois as well as the proletarians in large cities, in which industry can most profitably be carried on, and through this throwing together of great masses in *one* place it makes the proletarians conscious of their power. Further, the more it develops, the more machines are invented which displace manual labour, the more large-scale industry, as we already said, depresses wages to their minimum, and thereby makes the condition of the proletariat more and more unbearable. Thus, through the growing discontent of the proletariat, on the one hand, and through its growing power, on the other, the industrial revolution prepares a social revolution by the proletariat.

Question 12: What were the further results of the industrial revolution?

Answer: In the steam-engine and the other machines large-scale industry created the means of increasing industrial production in a short time and at slight expense to an unlimited extent. With this facility of production the free competition necessarily resulting from large-scale industry very soon assumed an extremely intense character; numbers of capitalists launched into industry, and very soon more was being produced than could be used. The result was that the goods manufactured could not be sold, and a so-called trade crisis ensued. Factories had to stand idle, factory owners went bankrupt, and the workers lost their bread. Everywhere there was the greatest misery. After a while the surplus products were sold, the factories started working again, wages went up, and gradually business was more brisk than ever. But before long too many commodities were again produced, another crisis ensued, and ran the same course as the previous one. Thus since the beginning of this century the state of industry has continually fluctuated between periods of prosperity and periods of crisis, and almost regularly every five to seven years a similar crisis has occurred,[158] and every time it has entailed the greatest misery for the workers, general revolutionary ferment, and the greatest danger to the entire existing system.

Question 13: What conclusions can be drawn from these regularly recurring trade crises?

Answer: Firstly, that although in the initial stages of its development large-scale industry itself created free competition, it has now nevertheless outgrown free competition; that competition and in general the carrying on of industrial production by individuals have become a fetter upon large-scale industry which it must and will break; that large-scale industry, so long as it is conducted on its present basis, can only survive through a general confusion repeating itself every seven years which each time threatens all civilisation, not merely plunging the proletarians into misery but also ruining a great number of bourgeois; therefore that either large-scale industry itself must be given up, which is utterly impossible, or that it absolutely necessitates a completely new organisation of society, in which industrial production is no longer directed by individual factory owners, competing one against the other, but by the whole of society according to a fixed plan and according to the needs of all.

Secondly, that large-scale industry and the unlimited expansion of production which it makes possible can bring into being a social order in which so much of all the necessities of life will be produced that every member of society will thereby be enabled to develop and exercise all his powers and abilities in perfect freedom. Thus, precisely that quality of large-scale industry which in present society produces all misery and all trade crises is the very quality which under a different social organisation will destroy that same misery and these disastrous fluctuations.

Thus it is most clearly proved:

1. that from now on all these ills are to be attributed only to the social order which no longer corresponds to the existing conditions;

2. that the means are available to abolish these ills completely through a new social order.

Question 14: What kind of new social order will this have to be?

Answer: Above all, it will have to take the running of industry and all branches of production in general out of the hands of separate individuals competing with each other and instead will have to ensure that all these branches of production are run by society as a whole, i.e., for the social good, according to a social plan and with the participation of all members of society. It will therefore do away with competition and replace it by association. Since the running of industry by individuals had private ownership as its necessary consequence and since competition is nothing but the manner in which industry is run by individual private owners, private ownership cannot be separated from the individual running of industry and competition. Hence, private ownership will also have to be abolished, and in its stead there will be common use of all the instruments of production and the distribution of all products by common agreement, or the so-called community of property. The abolition of private ownership is indeed the most succinct and characteristic summary of the transformation of the entire social system necessarily following from the development of industry, and it is therefore rightly put forward by the Communists as their main demand.

Question 15: The abolition of private property was therefore not possible earlier?

Answer: No. Every change in the social order, every revolution in property relations, has been the necessary result of the creation of new productive forces which would no longer conform to the old property relations. Private property itself arose in this way. For private property has not always existed, but when towards the end of the Middle Ages a new mode of production appeared in the form of manufacture which could not be subordinated to the then existing feudal and guild property, manufacture, having outgrown the old property relations, created a new form of ownership—private ownership. For manufacture and the first stage of development of large-scale industry, no other form of ownership was possible than private ownership and no other order of society than that founded upon private ownership. So long as it is not possible to produce so much that not only is there enough for all, but also a surplus for the increase of social capital and for the further development of the productive forces, so long must there always be a ruling class disposing of the productive forces of society, and a poor, oppressed class. How these classes are composed will depend upon the stage of development of production. In the Middle Ages, which were dependent upon agriculture, we find the lord and the serf; the towns of the later Middle Ages show us the master guildsman and the journeyman and day labourer; the seventeenth century has the manufacturer and the manufactory worker; the nineteenth century the big factory owner and the proletarian. It is obvious that hitherto the productive forces had not yet been so far developed that enough could be produced for all or to make private property a fetter, a barrier, to these productive forces. Now, however, when the development of large-scale industry has, *firstly*, created capital and productive forces on a scale hitherto unheard of and the means are available to increase these productive forces in a short time to an infinite extent; when, *secondly*, these productive forces are concentrated in the hands of a few bourgeois whilst the great mass of the people are more and more becoming proletarians, and their condition more wretched and unendurable in the same measure in which the riches of the bourgeois increase; when, *thirdly*, these powerful productive forces that can easily be increased have so enormously outgrown private property and the bourgeois that at every moment they provoke the most violent disturbances in the social order—only now has the abolition of private property become not only possible but even absolutely necessary.

Question 16: Will it be possible to bring about the abolition of private property by peaceful methods?

Answer: It is to be desired that this could happen, and Communists certainly would be the last to resist it. The Communists know only too well that all conspiracies are not only futile but even harmful. They know only too well that revolutions are not made deliberately and arbitrarily, but that everywhere and at all times they have been the necessary outcome of circumstances entirely independent of the will and the leadership of particular parties and entire classes. But they also see that the development of the proletariat is in nearly every civilised country forcibly suppressed, and that thus the opponents of the Communists are working with all their might towards a revolution. Should the oppressed proletariat in the end be goaded into a revolution, we Communists will then defend the cause of the proletarians by deed just as well as we do now by word.

Question 17: Will it be possible to abolish private property at one stroke?

Answer: No, such a thing would be just as impossible as at *one* stroke to increase the existing productive forces to the degree necessary for instituting community of property. Hence, the proletarian revolution, which in all probability is impending, will transform existing society only gradually, and be able to abolish private property only when the necessary quantity of the means of production has been created.

Question 18: What will be the course of this revolution?

Answer: In the first place it will inaugurate a *democratic constitution* and thereby, directly or indirectly, the political rule of the proletariat. Directly in England, where the proletariat already constitutes the majority of the people. Indirectly in France and in Germany, where the majority of the people consists not only of proletarians but also of small peasants and urban petty bourgeois, who are only now being proletarianised and in all their political interests are becoming more and more dependent on the proletariat and therefore soon will have to conform to the demands of the proletariat. This will perhaps involve a second fight, but one that can end only in the victory of the proletariat.

Democracy would be quite useless to the proletariat if it were not immediately used as a means of carrying through further measures directly attacking private ownership and securing the means of subsistence of the proletariat. Chief among these measures, already made necessary by the existing conditions, are the following:

1. Limitation of private ownership by means of progressive taxation, high inheritance taxes, abolition of inheritance by collateral lines (brothers, nephews, etc.), compulsory loans and so forth.

2. Gradual expropriation of landed proprietors, factory owners, railway and shipping magnates, partly through competition on the part of state industry and partly directly through compensation in assignations.

3. Confiscation of the property of all emigrants and rebels against the majority of the people.

4. Organisation of the labour or employment of the proletarians on national estates, in national factories and workshops, thereby putting an end to competition among the workers themselves and compelling the factory owners, as long as they still exist, to pay the same increased wages as the State.

5. Equal liability to work for all members of society until complete abolition of private ownership. Formation of industrial armies, especially for agriculture.

6. Centralisation of the credit and banking systems in the hands of the State by means of a national bank with state capital and the suppression of all private banks and bankers.

7. Increase of national factories, workshops, railways, and ships, cultivation of all uncultivated land and improvement of land already cultivated in the same proportion in which the capital and workers at the disposal of the nation increase.

8. Education of all children, as soon as they are old enough to do without the first maternal care, in national institutions and at the expense of the nation. Education combined with production.

9. The erection of large palaces on national estates as common dwellings for communities of citizens engaged in industry as well as agriculture, and combining the advantages of both urban and rural life without the one-sidedness and disadvantages of either.

10. The demolition of all insanitary and badly built dwellings and town districts.

11. Equal right of inheritance to be enjoyed by illegitimate and legitimate children.

12. Concentration of all means of transport in the hands of the nation.

Of course, all these measures cannot be carried out at once. But one will always lead on to the other. Once the first radical onslaught upon private ownership has been made, the proletariat will see itself compelled to go always further, to concentrate all capital, all agriculture, all industry, all transport, and all exchange more and more in the hands of the State. All these measures work towards such results; and they will become realisable and will develop their centralising consequences in the same proportion in which the productive forces of the country will be multiplied by the labour of the proletariat. Finally, when all capital, all production, and all exchange are concentrated in the hands of the nation, private ownership will automatically have ceased to exist, money will have become superfluous, and production will have so increased and men will be so much changed that the last forms of the old social relations will also be able to fall away.

Question 19: Will it be possible for this revolution to take place in one country alone?

Answer: No. Large-scale industry, already by creating the world market, has so linked up all the peoples of the earth, and especially the civilised peoples, that each people is dependent on what happens to another. Further, in all civilised countries large-scale industry has so levelled social development that in all these countries the bourgeoisie and the proletariat have become the two decisive classes of society and the struggle between them the main struggle of the day. The communist revolution will therefore be no merely national one; it will be a revolution taking place simultaneously in all civilised countries, that is, at least in England, America, France and Germany.[159] In each of these countries it will develop more quickly or more slowly according to whether the country has a more developed industry, more wealth, and a more considerable mass of productive forces. It will therefore be slowest and most difficult to carry out in Germany, quickest and easiest in England. It will also have an important effect upon the other countries of the world, and will completely change and greatly accelerate their previous manner of development. It is a worldwide revolution and will therefore be worldwide in scope.

Question 20: What will be the consequences of the final abolition of private ownership?

Answer: Above all, through society's taking out of the hands of the private capitalists the use of all the productive forces and means of communication as well as the exchange and distribution of products and managing them according to a plan corresponding to the means available and the needs of the whole of society, all the evil consequences of the present running of large-scale industry will be done away with. There will be an end of crises; the extended production, which under the present system of society means overproduction and is such a great cause of misery, will then not even be adequate and will have to be expanded much further. Instead of creating misery, overproduction beyond the immediate needs of society will mean the satisfaction of the needs of all, create new needs and at the same time the means to satisfy them. It will be the condition and the cause of new advances, and it will achieve these advances without thereby, as always hitherto, bringing the order of society into confusion. Once liberated from the pressure of private ownership, large-scale industry will develop on a scale that will make its present level of development seem as paltry as seems the manufacturing system compared with the large-scale industry of our time. This development of industry will provide society with a sufficient quantity of products to satisfy the needs of all. Similarly agriculture, which is also hindered by the pressure of private ownership and the parcelling of land from introducing the improvements already available and scientific advancements, will be given a quite new impulse, and place at society's disposal an ample quantity of products. Thus society will produce enough products to be able so to arrange distribution that the needs of all its members will be satisfied. The division of society into various antagonistic classes will thereby become superfluous. Not only will it become superfluous, it is even incompatible with the new social order. Classes came into existence through the division of labour and the division of labour in its hitherto existing form will entirely disappear. For in order to bring industrial and agricultural production to the level described, mechanical and chemical aids alone are not enough; the abilities of the people who set these aids in motion must also be developed to a corresponding degree. Just as in the last century the peasants and the manufactory workers changed their entire way of life, and themselves became quite different people when they were drawn into large-scale industry, so also will the common management of production by the whole of society and the resulting new development of production require and also produce quite different people. The common management of production cannot be effected by people as they are today, each one being assigned to a single branch of production, shackled to it, exploited by it, each having developed only *one* of his abilities at the cost of all the others and knowing only *one* branch, or only a branch of a branch of the total production. Even present-day industry finds less and less use for such people. Industry carried on in common and according to plan by the whole of society presupposes moreover people of all-round development, capable of surveying the entire system of production. Thus the division of labour making one man a peasant, another a shoemaker, a third a factory worker, a fourth a stockjobber, which has already been undermined by machines, will completely disappear. Education will enable young people quickly to go through the whole system of production, it will enable them to pass from one branch of industry to another according to the needs of society or their own inclinations. It will therefore free them from that one-sidedness which the present division of labour stamps on each one of them. Thus the communist organisation of society will give its members the chance of an all-round exercise of abilities that have received all-round development. With this, the various classes will necessarily disappear. Thus the communist organisation of society is, on the one hand, incompatible with the existence of classes and, on the other, the very establishment of this society furnishes the means to do away with these class differences.

It follows from this that the antagonism between town and country will likewise disappear. The carrying on of agriculture and industrial production by the same people, instead of by two different classes, is already for purely material reasons an essential condition of communist association. The scattering of the agricultural population over the countryside, along with the crowding of the industrial population into the big towns, is a state which corresponds only to an undeveloped stage of agriculture and industry, an obstacle to all further development which is already now making itself very keenly felt.

The general association of all members of society for the common and planned exploitation of the productive forces, the expansion of production to a degree where it will satisfy the needs of all, the termination of the condition where the needs of some are satisfied at the expense of others, the complete annihilation of classes and their antagonisms, the all-round development of the abilities of all the members of society through doing away with the hitherto existing division of labour, through industrial education, through change of activity, through the participation of all in the enjoyments provided by all, through the merging of town and country—such are the main results of the abolition of private property.

Question 21: What influence will the communist order of society have upon the family?

Answer: It will make the relation between the sexes a purely private relation which concerns only the persons involved, and in which society has no call to interfere. It is able to do this because it abolishes private property and educates children communally, thus destroying the twin foundation of hitherto existing marriage—the dependence through private property of the wife upon the husband and of the children upon the parents. Here also is the answer to the outcry of moralising philistines against the communist community of women. Community of women is a relationship that belongs altogether to bourgeois society and is completely realised today in prostitution. But prostitution is rooted in private property and falls with it. Thus instead of introducing the community of women, communist organisation puts an end to it.

Question 22: What will be the attitude of the communist organisation towards existing nationalities?

—remains[a]

Question 23: What will be its attitude towards existing religions?

—remains[b]

---

[a] Apparently this means that the answer remains the same as to Question 21 of the "Draft of a Communist Confession of Faith". See this volume, p. 103.—*Ed.*

[b] See answer to Question 22 of the "Draft of a Communist Confession of Faith", this volume, p. 103.—*Ed.*

Question 24: In what way do Communists differ from socialists?

Answer: The so-called socialists fall into three groups.

The first group consists of adherents of feudal and patriarchal society which has been or is still being daily destroyed by large-scale industry, world trade and the bourgeois society they have both brought into existence. From the ills of present-day society this group draws the conclusion that feudal and patriarchal society should be restored because it was free from these ills. Directly or deviously, all its proposals make for this goal. Despite all its professions of sympathy and its bewailing the misery of the proletariat, this group of *reactionary* socialists will be strongly opposed by the Communists, because

1. it is striving after something utterly impossible;
2. it seeks to establish the rule of the aristocracy, the guild-masters and the manufacturers, with their retinue of absolute or feudal monarchs, officials, soldiers and priests, a society which was indeed free from the vices of present society, but brought at least as many other evils in its train and did not even hold out the prospect of the emancipation of the oppressed workers through a communist organisation;
3. it always gives away its real intentions every time the proletariat becomes revolutionary and communist, when it immediately allies itself with the bourgeoisie against the proletarians.

The second group consists of adherents of present society in whom the evils inseparable from it have awakened fears for its survival. They therefore endeavour to preserve present society but to remove the evils bound up with it. With this end in view, some of them propose measures of mere charity, and others grandiose systems of reform which, under the pretext of reorganising society, would retain the foundations of present society, and thus present society itself. These *bourgeois socialists* will also have to be continuously fought by the Communists, since they work for the enemies of the Communists and defend the society which it is the Communists' aim to destroy.

Finally, the third group consists of democratic socialists, who in the same way as the Communists desire part of the measures listed in Question ...[a] not, however, as a means of transition to communism but as measures sufficient to abolish the misery of present society and to cause its evils to disappear. These *democratic socialists* are either proletarians who are not yet sufficiently enlightened regarding the conditions of the emancipation of their class, or they are

[a] The manuscript has a blank space here. See answer to Question 18.—*Ed.*

members of the petty bourgeoisie, a class which, until the winning of democracy and the realisation of the socialist measures following upon it, has in many respects the same interest as the proletariat. At moments of action the Communists will, therefore, have to reach an understanding with these democratic socialists, and in general for the time being pursue as much as possible a common policy with them, insofar as these democratic socialists do not enter the service of the ruling bourgeoisie and attack the Communists. It is obvious that this common action does not exclude the discussion of differences with them.

Question 25: What is the attitude of the Communists towards the other political parties of our day?

Answer: This attitude differs from country to country.—In England, France, and Belgium, where the bourgeoisie rules, the Communists still have for the time being a common interest with the various democratic parties, which is all the greater the more in the socialist measures they are now everywhere advocating the democrats approach the aims of the Communists, that is, the more clearly and definitely they uphold the interests of the proletariat and the more they rely on the proletariat. In *England*, for instance, the Chartists, who are all workers, are incalculably nearer to the Communists than are the democratic petty bourgeois or so-called radicals.

In *America*, where a democratic constitution has been introduced, the Communists must make common cause with the party that will turn this constitution against the bourgeoisie and use it in the interest of the proletariat, that is, with the national agrarian reformers.[160]

In *Switzerland* the radicals, although still a very mixed party, are yet the only people with whom the Communists can have anything to do, and, further, among these radicals those in the cantons of Vaud and of Geneva are the most advanced.

Finally, in *Germany* the decisive struggle between the bourgeoisie and the absolute monarchy is still to come. Since, however, the Communists cannot count on the decisive struggle between themselves and the bourgeoisie until the bourgeoisie rules, it is in the interests of the Communists to help bring the bourgeoisie to power as soon as possible in order as soon as possible to overthrow them again. The Communists must therefore always take the side of the liberal bourgeois against the governments but they must ever be on their guard against sharing the self-deceptions of the bourgeois or believing their false assurances about the benefits which the victory of the bourgeoisie will bring to the proletariat. The only advantages which the victory of the bourgeoisie will provide for the Communists will be: 1. various concessions which make easier for the Communists the defence, discussion and spreading of their principles and thus the unification of the proletariat into a closely knit, militant and organised class, and 2. the certainty that from the day when the absolute governments fall, comes the turn for the fight between bourgeois and proletarians. From that day onwards the party policy of the Communists will be the same as in the countries where the bourgeoisie already rules.

Written at the end of October 1847

First published separately in 1914

Printed according to the manuscript

Frederick Engels

[THE AGRARIAN PROGRAMME OF THE CHARTISTS][161]

About two years ago the Chartist workers founded an association with the object of buying land and dividing it among its members into small holdings.[162] It was hoped in this way to diminish the excessive competition between factory workers themselves, by keeping from the labour market some of these workers to form a quite new and essentially democratic class of small peasants. This project, whose author is none other than Feargus O'Connor himself, has had such success that the *Chartist Land Company* already numbers from two to three hundred thousand members,[a] that it disposes of social funds of £60,000 (a million and a half francs), and that its receipts, announced in *The Northern Star*, exceed £2,500 per week. In fact, the Company, of which I propose to give you later a more detailed account, has grown to such a size that it is already disquieting the landed aristocracy; for it is evident that this movement, if it continues to grow at the same rate as up to now, will end by becoming transformed into a national agitation for taking possession of the nation's land by the people. The bourgeoisie does not find this Company to its taste either; it sees it as a lever in the hands of the people which will allow the latter to free themselves without needing the help of the middle class. It is particularly the small bourgeoisie, more or less liberal, which looks askance at the Land Company because it already finds the Chartists much more independent of its support than before the founding of the association. Moreover, these same radicals, unable to explain the

[a] *The Northern Star* No. 524, November 6, 1847 has "consists of a vast number of members" instead of "already numbers from two to three hundred thousand members".—*Ed.*

indifference which the people show them and which is the inevitable consequence of their own lukewarm attitude, insist on attacking Mr. O'Connor continually as the sole obstacle to a reunion of the Chartist and radical parties. It was therefore enough that the Land Company should be the work of O'Connor to draw upon it all the hatred of the more or less radical bourgeois. At first they ignored it; when the conspiracy of silence could no longer be maintained they tried to prove that the Company was so organised as to end inevitably in the most scandalous bankruptcy; finally, when these means did not prevent the Company from prospering, they returned to the tactic that for ten years they had constantly used always without the least success against Mr. O'Connor. They sought to cast suspicions upon his character, to throw doubts on his disinterestedness, to destroy the right he claimed to call himself the incorruptible and unpaid administrator for the workers. When, therefore, some time ago, Mr. O'Connor published his annual report,[a] six more or less radical papers, which appear to have had a clandestine meeting, joined in attacking him. These papers were the *Weekly Dispatch*, the *Globe*, the *Nonconformist*, the *Manchester Examiner*, *Lloyd's Weekly Newspaper* and the *Nottingham Mercury*. They accused Mr. O'Connor of the most shameless thefts and misappropriations, which they sought to prove or to make probable by the figures of the report itself. Far from being satisfied with that, they pried into the private life of the celebrated agitator: a mountain of accusations, each graver than the other, was heaped on him, and his adversaries could well believe that he would be overwhelmed by it. But O'Connor, who for ten years has not ceased to fight the so-called radical press, did not flinch under these calumnies. He published in *The Northern Star* of the 23rd of this month a reply to the six papers.[b] This reply, a polemical masterpiece which recalls the best pamphlets of *William Cobbett*, refutes one accusation after another and, in its turn taking the offensive, launches against the six editors very severe attacks, full of superb disdain. This was enough completely to justify O'Connor in the people's eyes. *The Northern Star* of the 30th of this month contains the votes of complete confidence in O'Connor passed at public meetings of Chartists in more than fifty localities. But O'Connor wanted to give his adversaries the opportunity to attack him in front of the people. He invited them to maintain their charges at public

---

[a] F. O'Connor, "To the Members of the National Land Company" and "O'Connor, F., Esq. (Treasurer) in Account with the National Land Company".—*Ed.*

[b] F. O'Connor, "To the Editors of the *Nottingham Mercury*, the *Nonconformist*, the *Dispatch*, the *Globe*, the *Manchester Examiner* and *Lloyds' Trash*".—*Ed.*

meetings at Manchester and Nottingham. Not one of them turned up. At Manchester, O'Connor spoke for four hours before more than ten thousand men, who applauded him thunderously and unanimously confirmed their confidence in him. The crowd was so great that, besides the great meeting where O'Connor defended himself personally, it was necessary to hold another meeting in the public square, where ten to fifteen thousand other people, who were not able to enter the indoor meeting, were harangued by several other speakers.

When the meetings had ended, O'Connor declared that he would receive the contributions and subscriptions of the members of the Land Company, and the sum paid to him that evening exceeded £1,000 (25,000 francs).

At Nottingham, where O'Connor on the next day drew one of the greatest meetings which had ever taken place there, the same popular enthusiasm was caused by his speech.

This was at least the hundredth time that Mr. O'Connor has triumphed in this brilliant way over the calumnies of the bourgeois press. Imperturbable amidst all these attacks, the indefatigable patriot continues his work, and the unanimous confidence of the English people is the best proof of his courage, his energy, his incorruptibility.

Written on October 30, 1847

First published in *La Réforme*, November 1, 1847 and *The Northern Star* No. 524, November 6, 1847

Printed according to the text in *La Réforme*

Translated from the French

Frederick Engels

[THE CHARTIST BANQUET IN CONNECTION WITH THE ELECTIONS OF 1847][163]

In a letter of the day before yesterday I was concerned to defend the Chartists and their leader Feargus O'Connor against the attacks of the radical bourgeois press.[a] Today, to my great satisfaction, I can tell you something which confirms what I suggested about the spirit of the two parties. You will judge for yourselves to whom French democracy ought to give its sympathy: to the Chartists, sincere democrats without ulterior motives, or to the radical bourgeois who so carefully avoid using the words *people's charter, universal suffrage*, and limit themselves to proclaiming that they are partisans of *complete suffrage*![164]

Last month a banquet took place in London to celebrate the triumph of democratic opinion at the last elections. Eighteen radical members of Parliament were invited, but since the Chartists had initiated the banquet all these gentlemen defaulted, with the exception of O'Connor. The radicals, as we see, are behaving in a way which makes it quite predictable how they will honour their pledges made at the last elections.

One dispensed with their presence the more readily as they had sent one of their worthy representatives—Doctor Epps, a timid man and a petty reformer, conciliatory towards everybody except the active and energetic men of our opinions; a philanthropic bourgeois who burns, he says, to free the people, but who does not want the people to free themselves without him; in fact, a worthy partisan of bourgeois radicalism.

Doctor Epps proposed a first toast to the *sovereignty of the people*,

---

[a] See previous article.—*Ed.*

but so generally lukewarm apart from a few slightly livelier passages that several times it aroused murmurs among the assembly.

"I do not think," he said, "that the sovereignty of the people can be obtained through a revolution. The French fought three days[165]; they have been cheated out of national sovereignty. Nor do I think that it can be obtained by long speeches. Those who speak least do most. I do not like men who make a lot of noise; big words do not make big deeds."

These indirect sallies against the Chartists were received with numerous marks of disapproval. It could not be otherwise, above all when Doctor Epps added:

"The bourgeoisie has been slandered among the workers; as if the bourgeoisie was not the very class which alone can obtain political rights for the workers. ("No! No!") No? Is it not the bourgeois who are the electors? And is it not only the electors who can give the vote to those who do not have it? Is there anyone among you who would not become a bourgeois if he could? Ah! If the workers would give up their pots and their pipes, they would have money to support their political agitation, they could do much to contribute towards their freedom," etc., etc.

Such is the language of the men who reject O'Connor and the Chartists!

The speakers who succeeded Dr. Epps energetically rebutted the strange doctrines of the radical doctor, amid much applause by the assembly.

Mr. MacGrath, member of the executive committee of the Chartist Association,[166] recalled that the people ought not to have confidence in the bourgeoisie, that they had to win their own rights by themselves; it was not proper to the dignity of the people to beg for what really belonged to them.

Mr. Jones reminded the assembly that the bourgeoisie had always forgotten the people; and now that the bourgeoisie sees the growth of democracy, he said, it wants to use it to overthrow the landed aristocracy, and crush the democrats as soon as it has attained its objective.

Mr. O'Connor, replying still more directly to Dr. Epps, asked him who had crushed the country with an enormous debt, if it were not the bourgeoisie? Who had deprived the workers of their political and social rights if not the bourgeoisie? Who had, that very evening, refused to respond to the people's invitation, if it were not the seventeen honourable bourgeois to whom the democrats had so unfortunately given their votes? No, no, capital never represents labour! The lion and the lamb would lie down together before capitalists and workers were united by interests and feelings!

Mr. Harney, editor of *The Northern Star,* gave the last toast: "*Our democratic brethren throughout the world! May their present struggle for liberty and equality be crowned with success!*" Kings, aristocrats, priests and capitalists of all countries, he said, are allied together. May democrats of all lands follow the same example! Everywhere democracy marches forward. In France, banquet follows banquet in favour of electoral reform; and the movement is developing on such a scale that it must lead to a happy result. Let us hope that the masses, this time, will profit from this agitation, that the reform won by the French will be worth more than what we won in 1831.[167]

There can be no true reform as long as sovereignty does not wholly belong to the nation; there is no national sovereignty as long as the principles of the constitution of 1793[168] are not a reality.

Mr. Harney then gave a picture of the progress of democracy in Germany, Italy and Switzerland, and ended by disavowing, for his part, in the most energetic terms, the strange doctrines of Dr. Epps about the rights of the bourgeoisie.

Written on November 1, 1847

First published in *La Réforme*, November 6, 1847

Printed according to the newspaper

Translated from the French

Published in English for the first time

Frederick Engels

THE MANIFESTO OF M. DE LAMARTINE

You recently published this curious piece of workmanship.[169] It consists of two very distinct parts: *political* measures and *social* measures. Now the *political* measures are, one and all, taken from the Constitution of 1791,[170] with almost no alteration; that is, they are the return to the demands of the middle classes in the beginning of the revolution. At that time the whole of the middle classes, including even the smaller tradesmen, were invested with political power, while at present the participation in it is restrained to the large capitalists. What, then, is the meaning of the political measures proposed by M. de Lamartine? To give the government into the hands of the inferior *bourgeoisie,* but under the semblance of giving it to the whole people (this, and nothing else, is the meaning of his universal suffrage, with his double system of elections). And his *social* measures? Why, they are either things which presuppose that a successful revolution has already given the political power to the people—such as gratuitous education for all; or measures of pure charity, that is, measures to soften down the revolutionary energies of the proletarians; or mere high-sounding words without any practical meaning, such as extinction of mendicity by order in council, abolition of public distress by law, a ministry of the people's life, etc. They are, therefore, either totally useless to the people, or calculated to benefit them in such a degree only as will assure some sort of public tranquillity, or they are mere empty promises, which no man can keep—and in these two last cases they are worse than useless. In short, M. de Lamartine proves himself, both under a social and a political point of view, the faithful representative of the small tradesman, the inferior *bourgeoisie,* and [one] who shares in the illusion particular to this class: that he represents the working people. And, in the end he is foolish enough to address himself to the government with the demand of their support for his measures. Why, the present government of the great capitalists will do anything but that. The *Réforme*, therefore, is perfectly right in attacking, though with a deal of good will, and recognising his good intentions, the practicability both of his measures, and his mode of setting about having them carried.[a]

"Certainly," says the *Réforme*, "these are high words, revealing a mighty heart, a spirit sympathising with the cause of right. The fraternal feeling is panting visibly under the cloak of words, and our poets and philosophers will be excited by them into enthusiasm similar to that produced upon Periclean Greece by the sentence of Plato. But we have not now anything to do with Pericles, we live under the reign of Messrs Rothschild, Fulchiron and Duchâtel, that is under the triple incarnation of Money, blockheaded Fear, and Police; we have for a government, profits, privilege, and the municipal guard. Now, hopes M. de Lamartine that the league of consolidated interests, that the Sonderbund[b] of dollars, place and monopoly, will surrender and lay down arms at his appeal to national sovereignty and social fraternity? Why, for good as for evil, all things in this world are connected—one keeps up the other, nothing is isolated—and that is the reason why the most generous programme of the deputy for Mâcon[c] will pass like perfumed zephyrs of summer, will die like empty trumpet sounds, as long as they shall bear the motherstain of all monopoly—feudal violation of Right and of Equality. And this league of the privileged classes is particularly closely united at this very moment, when the governmental system is the prey of convulsive fear.

"As to the institutions he proposes, the official country and its leaders call such things the sweet meats of philosophy: Messrs Duchâtel and Guizot will laugh at them, and if the deputy for Mâcon does not look out elsewhere for arms and soldiers to defend his ideas, he will pass all his life at making fine words and no progress! And if he addresses himself to the million instead of the government, we tell him that he follows a false route, and never will win over to his system of graduated election, poor rate, and philanthropic charity, neither the Revolution, nor thinking men, nor the people. The principles, indeed, of social and political regeneration have been found fifty years ago. Universal suffrage, direct election, paid representation—these are the essential conditions of political sovereignty. Equality, liberty, fraternity—these are the principles which ought to rule all social institutions. Now, the poor rate is far from being based upon fraternity, whilst at the same time it is an insolent and very impotent denial of equality. What we want is not English middle-class expediency, but quite a new system of social economy, to realise the right and satisfy the wants of all."

A few days after appeared the second manifesto of M. de Lamartine upon the foreign policy of France. In this he maintains that the peace system followed by the French government after 1830, was the only convenient mode of action. He covers by pompous

---

[a] There follows a free translation of extracts from an article by Louis Blanc analysing Lamartine's "Déclaration de principes".—*Ed.*

[b] The allusion is to the Swiss Sonderbund, a separatist union of seven Catholic cantons.—*Ed.*

[c] Lamartine.—*Ed.*

sentences the infamous manner in which the French government first excited Italy and other countries to rebellion, and afterwards abandoned them to their fate. Here is the forcible reply of the *Réforme*[a] to this buttermilk manifesto:

"M. de Lamartine sacrifices the legitimate and only instrument of freeing us—the holy war of principle—to a theory of peace which will be a mere weakness, a lie, and even an act of treason, as long as the relations from people to people are based upon the policy of diplomatists, and the egotism of governments. No doubt, peace is the ultimate necessity of civilisation; but what is peace with Nicholas of Russia? The disemboweller of whole nations, the hangman who nails infants to the gallows, who carries on a deadly war against even hope and recollection, who drowns in her tears and her blood a great, a glorious country! For mankind, for civilisation, for France herself, peace with this madman of a Jack Ketch is cowardice; for justice, for right, for the revolution, it is a crime! What is peace with Metternich, who hires hosts of assassins, who confiscates for the benefit of crowned epilepsy,[b] the liberties of nations? What is peace with all those little Caesars of Europe, ruined debauchees, or villainous bigots who reign, to-day for the Jesuits, to-morrow for the courtezan? What is peace with the aristocratic and money-mongering English government, which tyrannises the seas, which kills liberty in Portugal, which squeezes money even out of the rags of its people? Peace with these Jews, these poison-mongers, we repeat it, is, for a country in revolution, cowardice, shame, crime, moral desertion, bankruptcy not only of interest, but of right and honour."

The other Paris papers have equally expressed their dissent from M. de Lamartine's programme in different respects.[171] He continues, however, illustrating its principles in his paper, the *Bien Public* of Mâcon. We shall in a few months be enabled to judge what effect his *new move* will make upon the Chamber of Deputies.

Written at the beginning of November 1847

First published in *The Northern Star* No. 525, November 13, 1847 with an editorial note: "From Our Paris Correspondent"

Reprinted from the newspaper

---

[a] "Programme de M. Lamartine".—*Ed.*

[b] Ferdinand I.—*Ed.*

Frederick Engels

THE CIVIL WAR IN SWITZERLAND[172]

At last the ceaseless bombast about the "cradle of freedom", about the "grandsons of William Tell and Winkelried", about the heroic victors of Sempach and Murten[173] is being brought to an end. At last it has been revealed that the cradle of freedom is nothing but the centre of barbarism and the nursery of Jesuits, that the grandsons of Tell and Winkelried can only be brought to reason by cannon-balls, and that the heroism at Sempach and Murten was nothing but the desperation of brutal and bigoted mountain tribes, obstinately resisting civilisation and progress.

It is really very fortunate that European democracy is finally getting rid of this *Ur*-Swiss, puritan and reactionary ballast. As long as the democrats concentrated on the virtue, the happiness and the patriarchal simplicity of these Alpine shepherds, they themselves still appeared in a reactionary light. Now that they are supporting the struggle of civilised, industrial, modern-democratic Switzerland against the crude, Christian-Germanic democracy of the primitive, cattle-breeding cantons, they represent progress everywhere, now the last reactionary glimmer disappears, now they show that they are learning to understand the meaning of democracy in the 19th century.

There are two regions in Europe where old Christian-Germanic barbarism has retained its most primitive form, almost down to acorn-eating—Norway and the High Alps, especially *Ur*-Switzerland.[174] Both Norway and *Ur*-Switzerland still provide us with genuine examples of that breed of men who once beat the Romans to death in good Westphalian style with clubs and flails in the Teutoburg Forest.[175] Both Norway and *Ur*-Switzerland are democratically organised. But there are many varieties of democracy and it is very necessary that the democrats of the civilised countries should at last decline responsibility for the Norwegian and *Ur*-Swiss forms of democracy.

The democratic movement in all civilised countries is, in the last analysis, striving for the political domination of the proletariat. It therefore presupposes that a proletariat exists, that a ruling bourgeoisie exists, that an industry exists which gives birth to the proletariat and which has brought the bourgeoisie to power.

There is nothing of all this either in Norway or in *Ur*-Switzerland. In Norway, we have the very famous peasant regiment (*bonde-regimente*); in *Ur*-Switzerland a number of rough shepherds who, despite their democratic constitution, are ruled by a few big landowners, Abyberg, etc., in patriarchal fashion. A bourgeoisie only exists in exceptional cases in Norway, and not at all in *Ur*-Switzerland. The proletariat is practically non-existent.

The democracy prevailing in civilised countries, *modern* democracy, has thus nothing whatever in common with Norwegian or *Ur*-Swiss democracy. It does not wish to bring about the Norwegian and *Ur*-Swiss state of affairs but something absolutely different. Let us nevertheless look a little closer at this primitive-Germanic democracy and deal first with *Ur*-Switzerland, which is what above all concerns us here.

Is there a German philistine who does not rave about William Tell, the liberator of his Fatherland; a schoolmaster who does not celebrate Morgarten, Sempach and Murten along with Marathon, Plataea and Salamis[176]; a hysterical old maid who does not go into raptures over the strong leg calves and sturdy thighs of the chaste Alpine youths? The glory of *Ur*-Swiss valour, freedom, skill and strength has been endlessly praised in verse and prose from Aegidius Tschudi to Johannes von Müller, from Florian to Schiller. The carbines and cannons of the twelve cantons now provide a commentary on these enthusiastic panegyrics.

The *Ur*-Swiss have drawn attention to themselves twice during the course of history. The first time, when they freed themselves gloriously from Austrian tyranny; the second at the present time, when they march off to fight in God's name for the Jesuits and the Fatherland.

On closer examination, the glorious liberation from the talons of the Austrian eagle does not look at all good. The House of Austria was progressive just once in the whole of its career; this was at the beginning of its existence when it allied itself with the urban petty bourgeoisie against the nobility, and sought to found a German monarchy. It was progressive in the most philistine of ways but it was progressive nonetheless. And who opposed it most resolutely? The *Ur*-Swiss. The struggle of the *Ur*-Swiss against Austria, the glorious oath on the Grütli,[177] Tell's heroic shot, the eternally memorable victory at Morgarten, all this was the struggle of stubborn shepherds against the onward march of historical development, the struggle of obstinate, rooted local interests against the interests of the whole nation, the struggle of crude ignorance against enlightenment, of barbarism against civilisation. They won their victory over the civilisation of the time, and as a punishment they were excluded from all further civilisation.

As if this were not enough, these simple, stiff-necked shepherds were soon punished in a quite different way. They escaped the domination of the Austrian nobility only to come under the yoke of the petty bourgeois of Zurich, Lucerne, Berne and Basel. These had already noted that the *Ur*-Swiss were just as strong and as stupid as their oxen. They agreed to join the Swiss Confederation and stayed peacefully at home behind their counters while the thick-headed Alpine shepherds fought out all their battles with the nobility and the princes for them. This is what happened at Sempach, Granson, Murten and Nancy.[178] In return, these people were allowed to arrange their internal affairs as they wished and so they remained in blissful ignorance of how they were being exploited by their dear fellow-Confederationists.

Since then nothing much has been heard of them. They busied themselves in all piety and propriety with milking the cows, with cheese-making, chastity and yodelling. From time to time they had folk assemblies at which they divided into horn-men, claw-men and other animal-like groups, and these gatherings never ended without a hearty, Christian-Germanic fight. They were poor but pure in heart, stupid but pious and well-pleasing to the Lord, brutal but broad-shouldered and had little brain but plenty of brawn. From time to time there were too many of them and then the young men went off on their "travels", i.e., enlisted in foreign armies where they displayed the most steadfast loyalty to the flag no matter what happened. One can only say of the Swiss that they let themselves be killed most conscientiously for their pay.

The greatest boast of these burly *Ur*-Swiss was that from time immemorial they had never deviated by a hair's breadth from the customs of their forefathers, that they had retained the simple, chaste, upright and virtuous customs of their fathers unsullied throughout the centuries. And this is true. Every attempt at civilisation was defeated by the granite walls of their mountains and of their heads. From the days when Winkelried's first ancestor led his cow, with the inevitable little pastoral bell round its neck, on to the virgin pastures of the Vierwaldstätter Lake, up to the present day, when the latest descendant of Winkelried has his gun blessed by the priest, all houses have been built in the same way, all cows milked in the same way, all pigtails plaited in the same way, all cheeses prepared according to the same recipe, all children made in the same way. Here, in the mountains, is Paradise, here the Fall of Man has not yet come to pass. And should some innocent Alpine lad happen to find his way to the great outside world and allow himself to be tempted for a moment by the seductions of the big cities, by the artificial charms of a decadent civilisation, by the vices of sinful countries, which have no mountains and where corn thrives—his innocence is so deep-rooted that he can never quite succumb. A sound strikes his ear, just two of those notes of the Alpine cowherd's call that sound like a dog's howling, and he falls on his knees, weeping and overwhelmed with remorse, and at once tears himself from the arms of seduction and will not rest until he lies at the feet of his old father! "Father, I have sinned against my ancient mountains and in thy sight, and am no more worthy to be called thy son."[a]

In recent times two invasions against these artless customs and primitive power have been attempted. The first was by the French in 1798. But these French, who spread a little civilisation everywhere else, failed with these *Ur*-Swiss. No trace of their presence has remained, they were unable to eliminate one single jot of the old customs and virtues. The second invasion took place about twenty years later and did at least bear a little fruit. This was the invasion of English travellers, of London lords and squires[b] and the hordes of chandlers, soap-manufacturers, grocers and bone merchants who followed them. This invasion at least ended the old hospitality and transformed the honest inhabitants of the Alpine huts, who previously hardly knew what money was, into the most mean and rascally swindlers anywhere to be found. But this advance made no impact at all on the old simple customs. This not so very virtuous chicanery fitted in perfectly with the patriarchal virtues of chastity, skill, probity and loyalty. Even their piety suffered no injury; the priests were delighted to give them absolution for all the deceptions practised on British heretics.

But it now looks as if all this moral purity is about to be thoroughly stirred up. It is to be hoped that the punitive detachments will do

[a] Luke 15:21 (paraphrased).—*Ed.*

[b] In the original the words "lords" and "squires" are in English.—*Ed.*

their best to finish off all the probity, primitive power and simplicity. Then moan, you philistines! For there will be no more poor but contented shepherds whose carefree peace of mind you might wish for yourselves on Sundays after you have made your cut out of selling coffee made of chicory and tea made of sloe leaves during the other six days of the week. Then weep, you schoolmasters, for there will be an end to your hopes for a new Sempach-Marathon and other classical feats. Then mourn, you hysterical virgins over thirty, for those six-inch leg calves, the thought of which solaced your solitary dreams, will soon be gone—gone the Antinous-like beauty of the powerful "Swiss peasant lads", gone the firm thighs and tight trousers which attract you so irresistibly to the Alps. Then sigh, tender and anaemic boarding-school misses, who when reading Schiller's works delighted in the chaste but oh so powerful love of the agile chamois hunters, for all your fond illusions are lost and now there is nothing left for you but to read the works of Henrik Steffens and fall for the frigid Norwegians.

But no more of that. The *Ur*-Swiss must be fought with weapons quite different from mere ridicule. Democracy has to settle accounts with them about matters quite different from their patriarchal virtues.

Who defended the Bastille on July 14, 1789 against the people who were storming it? Who shot down the workers of the Faubourg St. Antoine with grape-shot and rifle bullets from behind safe walls?—*Ur*-Swiss from the Sonderbund, grandsons of Tell, Stauffacher and Winkelried.

Who defended the traitor Louis XVI on August 10, 1792 from the just wrath of the people, in the Louvre and the Tuileries?—*Ur*-Swiss from the Sonderbund.

Who suppressed the Neapolitan revolution of 1798 with the help of Nelson?—*Ur*-Swiss from the Sonderbund.

Who re-established the absolute monarchy in Naples—with the help of Austrians—in 1823?—*Ur*-Swiss from the Sonderbund.

Who fought to the last on July 29, 1830, again for a treacherous king[a] and again shot Paris workers down from the windows and colonnades of the Louvre?—*Ur*-Swiss from the Sonderbund.

Who suppressed the insurrections in Romagna in 1830 and 1831, again along with the Austrians, with a brutality which achieved world notoriety?—*Ur*-Swiss from the Sonderbund.

In short, who holds the Italians down, to this day, forcing them to bow to the oppressive domination of their aristocrats, princes and

[a] Charles X.—*Ed.*

priests; who was Austria's right hand in Italy, who enables the bloodhound Ferdinand of Naples to keep a tight rein on his anguish-stricken people to this very moment, who has been acting as his executioners to this day carrying out the mass shootings he orders? Always, again and again, *Ur*-Swiss from the Sonderbund, again and again, the grandsons of Tell, Stauffacher and Winkelried!

In one word, wherever and whenever a revolutionary movement broke out in France either directly or indirectly advantageous to democracy, it was always *Ur*-Swiss mercenaries who fought it to the last, with the utmost resolution. And especially in Italy these Swiss mercenaries were always the most devoted servants and handy men of Austria. A just punishment for the glorious liberation of Switzerland from the talons of the two-headed eagle!

One should not think that these mercenaries were the refuse of their country, or that they were disavowed by their fellow-countrymen. Have not the people of Lucerne had a statue hewn out of the rock at their city gates by the pious Icelander Thorvaldsen, depicting a huge lion, bleeding from an arrow wound, covering the Bourbon fleur-de-lis with his paw, faithful unto death, in memory of the Swiss who died at the Louvre on August 10, 1792? This is the way Sonderbund honours the venal loyalty of its sons. It lives by the trade in human beings and glorifies it.

Can the English, French and German democrats have had anything in common with this kind of democracy?

Through its industry, its commerce and its political institutions, the bourgeoisie is already working everywhere to drag the small, self-contained localities which only live for themselves out of their isolation, to bring them into contact with one another, to merge their interests, to expand their local horizons, to destroy their local habits, strivings and ways of thinking, and to build up a great nation with common interests, customs and ideas out of the many hitherto mutually independent localities and provinces. The bourgeoisie is already carrying out considerable centralisation. The proletariat, far from suffering any disadvantage from this, will as a result rather be in a position to unite, to feel itself a class, to acquire a proper political point of view within the democracy, and finally to conquer the bourgeoisie. The democratic proletariat not only needs the kind of centralisation begun by the bourgeoisie but will have to extend it very much further. During the short time when the proletariat was at the helm of state in the French Revolution, during the rule of the Mountain party, it used all means—including grape-shot and the guillotine—to effect centralisation. When the democratic proletariat again comes to power, it will not only have to centralise every country separately but will have to centralise all civilised countries together as soon as possible.

Ur-Switzerland, on the other hand, has never done anything but obstruct centralisation; with really brutish obstinacy it has insisted on its isolation from the whole outside world, on its local customs, habits, prejudices, narrow-mindedness and seclusion. It has stood still in the centre of Europe at the level of its original barbarism, while all other nations, even the other Swiss, have gone forward. It stands pat on cantonal sovereignty with all the obduracy of the crude primitive Germans, that is, on the right to be eternally stupid, bigoted, brutal, narrow-minded, recalcitrant and venal if it so wishes, whether its neighbours like it or not. If their own brutish situation comes under discussion, they no longer recognise such things as majorities, agreements or obligations. But in the 19th century it is no longer possible for two parts of one and the same country to exist side by side without any mutual intercourse and influence. The radical cantons affect the Sonderbund, the Sonderbund affects the radical cantons, where, too, very crude elements still exist here and there. The radical cantons are, therefore, interested in getting the Sonderbund to abandon its bigotry, narrow-mindedness and obduracy, and if it won't, then its self-will must be broken by force; and this is what is happening at this moment.

The civil war which has now broken out can only help the cause of democracy. Even though there is still a great deal of primitive Germanic crudity to be found in the radical cantons, even though a peasant, or a bourgeois regiment, or a mixture of both is concealed behind their democracy, even though the most civilised cantons still lag behind the development of European civilisation and really modern elements only rise to the top slowly here and there, this is no great help to the Sonderbund. It is necessary, urgently necessary, that this last bastion of brutal, primitive Germanism, of barbarism, bigotry, patriarchal simplicity and moral purity, of immobility, of loyalty unto death to the highest bidder, should at last be destroyed. The more energetically the Swiss Diet sets to work and the more violently it shakes up this old nest of priests, the more claim it will have on the support of all really resolute democrats and the more it will prove that it understands its position. But of course the five great powers are there and the radicals themselves are afraid.

As far as the Sonderbund is concerned, it is significant that the true sons of William Tell have to beg the House of Austria, Switzerland's hereditary foe, for help just when Austria is baser, viler, meaner and more hateful than ever. This is yet another part of the punishment for the glorious liberation of Switzerland from the talons of the two-headed eagle and the much boasting that went with it. And for the cup of punishment to be filled to the brim Austria itself has to be in such a pass that it could not give William Tell's sons any help whatever.

Written about November 10, 1847

First published in the *Deutsche-Brüsseler-Zeitung* No. 91, November 14, 1847

Printed according to the newspaper

Published in English for the first time

Frederick Engels

THE REFORM MOVEMENT IN FRANCE

When, during the last session of the Legislative Chambers, M. E. de Girardin had brought to light those numerous and scandalous facts of corruption which he thought would overthrow the government; when, after all, the government had maintained themselves against the storm; when the celebrated Two Hundred and Twenty-Five[a] declared themselves "satisfied" as to the innocence of the ministry, all seemed to be over, and the Parliamentary Opposition, towards the close of the session, fell back into the same impotency and lethargy which they had manifested at the beginning. But all was not over. Though Messrs Rothschild, Fould, Foulchiron, and Co. were satisfied, the people were not, nor was a large portion of the middle classes. The majority of the French bourgeoisie, especially those of the second and third rank, could not but see that the present class of electors became more and more the obedient servants of a small number of bankers, stock-jobbers, railway-speculators, large manufacturers, landed and mining proprietors, whose interest was the only interest cared for by the government. They saw that there was no hope for them ever to regain the position in the Chambers which, since 1830, they had been losing more and more every day, unless they extended the suffrage. They knew that electoral and parliamentary Reform was a dangerous experiment for them to try; but what could they do? Seeing that the *haute finance*, the lords of Paris Exchange, bought up the government and both the Chambers; seeing their own interests openly trampled upon; they were obliged either to submit patiently, and await humbly and

[a] The majority in the Chamber of Deputies supporting the Guizot government.—*Ed.*

quietly the day when the encroachments of the ruling money lords would make them bankrupts, or to risk parliamentary Reform. They preferred the latter.

The Opposition, of all shades, therefore, united, some four months ago, in getting up a demonstration in favour of Electoral Reform. A public dinner was arranged and took place in July, at the Château-Rouge ball-rooms, at Paris. All fractions of Reformers were represented, and the assembly was rather mixed; but the Democrats, having been the most active, evidently predominated. They had made it a condition of their assistance, that the king's[a] health should not be drunk, but be replaced by a toast in favour of the sovereignty of the people; the committee knowing well that in the most democratic town of France they could not get up a decent demonstration without the Democrats, were obliged to comply. If I recollect rightly, you gave, at the time, a full account of the banquet,[179] which was in every respect more like a demonstration of the strength, both in number and intellect, of democracy at Paris, than anything else.

The *Journal des Débats* failed not to raise a terrible outcry about this banquet.

> "What! no toast to the king? and this toast not omitted by negligence, by want of a sense of propriety—no, this omission put as a condition for their support by part of the getters-up! Why, what pretty company this calm and peaceful M. Duvergier de Hauranne—this moral-force, monarchical M. Odilon Barrot have got into! Why, this is not mere republicanism—this is revolutionism, physical-forcism, socialism, utopianism, anarchism and communism! Ah, but, gentlemen, we know you—we have had samples of your bloody deeds, we have proofs of what you are contending for! Fifty years ago, gentlemen, you called yourselves the *club of the Jacobins*!"[180]

Next day's *National* replied to the fierce and furious vituperation of the *furiously moderate* paper by a host of quotations from Louis Philippe's private journal, written in 1790 and 1791, where every day's note of the then "Citizen Égalité[b] junior" commenced with the words:

> "To-day I was at the Jacobins"—"To-day I took the liberty of saying a few words at the Jacobins which were warmly applauded"—"To-day I was called to the office of door-keeper at the Jacobins", etc.[c]

The central committee of the Opposition had invited their friends in the country to imitate the example given by the metropolis, in

[a] Louis Philippe.—*Ed.*

[b] The name which Duke of Orleans, Louis Philippe's father, took during the French Revolution.—*Ed.*

[c] "Journal du duc de Chartre" in *Le National*, August 12, 1847.—*Ed.*

getting up everywhere similar banquets in favour of Reform. This was done accordingly, and a great number of Reform dinners were held in almost all parts of France. But not everywhere the same union of all fractions of Reformers could be made to prevail. In a great number of the smaller towns the middle-class Liberals were strong enough to carry the king's health being drunk, by which the Democrats were excluded. In other localities they tried to make it pass in the shape of a toast:—"The constitutional king, and the sovereignty of the people." This being not yet sufficient to the Democrats, they went on shuffling, and replaced the "constitutional king" by the "constitutional institutions", among which royalty, of course, was tacitly comprised. The great question now agitated among the provincial Liberals is, whether they are to give up even this, and to resign all attempts at carrying the king's health in whatever shape or disguise it be, or whether they are to separate openly from the Democrats, who, in that case, would get up separate and competing banquets. For the democratic party insist upon the original agreement, that the king be not mixed up at all with the affair, and if in one case the *National* has been wavering a little, the party of the *Réforme* stand firmly on the side of republicanism. In all the large towns the Liberals have been forced to give way, and if in the localities of lesser importance they have carried the king's health, it is because such banquets cost a great deal of money, and, therefore, the people are naturally excluded from them. On the occasion of the banquet of Bar-le-Duc, the *Réforme* says:

"Whoever would take such demonstration as a sample of the state of public opinion in France, would be very much mistaken indeed; they are got up by the middle classes only, and the people are entirely shut out from them. This agitation, if it be confined to the limits of the Bar-le-Duc banquet, will vanish like all *bourgeois* movements; like the Free Trade movement, which after a few hollow speeches died away very soon."[a]

The first large banquet, after that of Paris, was held at Strasburg, in the beginning of September. It was rather a democratic one, and a working man, at the close of it, proposed a toast to the organisation of labour, which term, in France, expresses that which in England the National Association of United Trades[181] are trying to carry out; viz. the freeing of labour from the oppression of capital by carrying on manufacturing, agricultural, and other purposes, for the account, either of the associated working men themselves, or of the people at large, under a democratic government.

Then came the banquets of Bar-le-Duc, a *bourgeois* demonstration, finished by the Mayor proposing the health of the Constitutional

[a] "Banquet de Bar-le-Duc".—*Ed.*

King (very constitutional, indeed); of Colmar, Rheims, and Meaux, all of them entirely dominated by the *bourgeoisie*, who, in those secondary towns, always have it all their own way.

But the banquet of Saint-Quentin, again, was more or less democratic; and that of Orleans, in the last days of September, was, from beginning to end, a thoroughly democratic meeting. Judge of it by the toast to the working classes, responded to by M. Marie, one of the most celebrated barristers of Paris, and a democrat. He commenced his speech in the following terms:

"To the working men—to those men, always neglected and forgotten, but always faithful to the interests of their country, always ready to die for its cause, be it in defending their native land against foreign aggression, be it in guarding our institutions, when menaced by inward foes! To those, from whom we demanded the days of July,[182] and who gave them to us; terrible in their actions, generous in their triumph, resplendent with courage, probity, and disinterestedness!"[a]

and concluded the toast in these words: "Liberty, equality, fraternity!" It is characteristic that the Orleans banquet was the only one at which we find it stated that covers were reserved for the representatives of the working people.

The banquets of Culommiers, Melun, and Cosne, again, were mere *bourgeoisie* gatherings. The "*Left Centre*", the middle-class Liberals of the *Constitutionnel* and *Siècle*, amused themselves in listening to the speeches of MM. Barrot, Beaumont, Drouyn de Lhuys, and such like retailers of Reform. At Cosne, the democrats openly declared against the demonstration, because the king's health was insisted upon. The same narrow spirit prevailed at the banquet of La Charité, on the Loire.

In return, the Reform dinner of Chartres was thoroughly democratic. No toast to the king—toasts for Electoral and Parliamentary Reform upon the largest base, for Poland and Italy, for the organisation of labour.

This week banquets will take place at Lille, Valenciennes, Avesnes, and throughout the Department of the North generally. Those of Lille and Valenciennes, at least, will probably take a decidedly democratic turn. In the South of France, at Lyons, and in the West, other demonstrations are preparing. The Reform Movement is far from being near to its close.

You see from this account that, from its very beginning, the Reform Movement of 1847 has been marked by a struggle betwixt the Liberals and the Democrats; that while the Liberals carried their ends in all the smaller localities, the Democrats were the stronger in

[a] Quoted from the article "Banquet réformiste du département du Loiret".—*Ed.*

all large towns: in Paris, Strasburg, Orleans, Chartres, and even in one smaller town, in Saint-Quentin; that the Liberals were very anxious of having the support of the Democrats; that they shuffled and made concessions, while the Democrats never retracted an iota of the condition under which they were ready to give their support, and that wherever the Democrats assisted, they had it all their own way. Thus, after all, the whole movement has been turned to the profit of democracy, for all those banquets which excited public attention in some degree, were, one and all, democratic.

The Reform movement was seconded by the Departmental Councils, who met in September, and who are entirely composed by *bourgeois*. The Councils of the Departments of the Côté-d'Or, of Finisterre, of the Aisne, the Moselle, the Haut-Rhin, the Oise, the Vosges, the North, and others, demanded, more or less, extensive reforms, all of them, of course, confined to the limits of *bourgeois* Liberalism.

But what, will you ask, are the reforms demanded? There are as many different systems of reform, as there are shades of Liberals and Radicals. The least thing asked for, is the extension of the Suffrage, to what is called the *capacities*, or what you, in England, would call the learned professions, even if they do not pay the 200 francs of direct taxes, which make, at present, a man a voter. Then the Liberals have some other propositions, more or less in common with the Radicals. These are:—

1st. The extension of the *incompatibilities*, or the declaring of certain government offices to be incompatible with the functions of a representative. The government have, at present, more than 150 of their subordinate employees in the Deputies, all of which may, at any moment, be cashiered, and are, therefore, entirely dependent upon the Ministry.

2nd. The enlargement of some electoral districts, some of which are composed of less than 150 voters, who are, therefore, entirely ruled through the influence of the government upon their local and personal interests.

3rd. The electing of all deputies of a Department in a full meeting of all the electors, assembled at its principal town, by which means local interests are intended to be more or less submerged in the common interests of the whole Department, and thus render nugatory the corruption and influence of the government.

Then, there are proposals for lowering the amount of the voting qualification in different degrees. The most radical of these propositions is that of the *National*, the paper of the Republican small tradesmen, for extending the suffrage to all men belonging to the National Guard. This would give the vote to the entire class of small tradesmen and shopkeepers, and extend the suffrage in the same degree as the Reform Bill has done in England; but the consequences of such a measure would, in France, be much more important. The small *bourgeoisie* in this country are so much oppressed and squeezed by the large capitalists, that they would be obliged to have recourse to direct aggressive measures against the moneylords, as soon as they get the suffrage. As I said in an article I sent you some months ago, they would be carried further and further, even against their own consent; they would be forced either to give up the positions already won, or to form an open alliance with the working classes, and that would, sooner or later, lead to the Republic.[a] They know this in some measure. Most of them support Universal Suffrage, and so does the *National*, which goes for the above measure only, as far as it is considered as a preliminary step in the road of reform. Of all Parisian daily papers, there is, however, but one which will not be satisfied with anything less than Universal Suffrage, and which, by the term "Republic", understands not merely Political Reforms, which will, after all, leave the working classes as miserable as before—but Social Reforms, and very definite ones too. This paper is the *Réforme*.

The Reform movement is, however, not to be considered as the totality of the agitation now going on in France. Far from it! At all these banquets be they Liberal or Democratic, the middle classes were predominating; that of Orleans was the only one in which working men took part. The movement of the working people is going on, side by side, with these banquets, silently, underground, almost invisible, for every one who does not take the trouble of looking after it. But it is going on more lively than ever. The government know this very well. They have given their permission to all these middle-class banquets; but when the typographic working men of Paris, in September, asked for the permission to hold their annual banquet, which, up to the present time, they had held every year, and which was in no manner of a political character, it was refused to them. The government are so afraid of the working people, that they do not allow them the slightest liberty. They are afraid, because the people have entirely given up all attempts at insurrection and rioting. The government desire a riot, they provoke it by every means. The police throw out small bombshells filled with incendiary papers; which, by the explosion of the shell, are spread all over the streets. A trades' affair in the Rue S. Honoré was profited by

[a] See this volume, p. 219.—*Ed.*

to make the most brutal attacks upon the people, in order to provoke them to riot and violence.[183] Tens of thousands assembled every evening during a fortnight; they were treated in the most infamous manner; they were on the very brink of repelling force by force; but they held out and no pretext for more gagging laws are to be forced from them. And think, what a tacit understanding, what a common feeling of what was to be done, at the moment, must have prevailed; what an effort it must have cost to the people of Paris, to submit to such infamous treatment rather than try a hopeless insurrection. What an enormous progress this forebearance proves in those very same working men of Paris, who seldom went into the streets, without battering to pieces every thing before them; who are accustomed to insurrection, and who go into a revolution just as gaily as they go to the wineshop! But if you would draw from this the conclusion that the revolutionary ardour of the people is decreasing, you would be quite mistaken. On the contrary, the necessity of a revolution, and a revolution more thoroughgoing, more radical by far than the first one, is deeper than ever felt by the working people here. But they know from the experience of 1830, that mere fighting will not do; that the enemy once beaten, they must establish measures that will guarantee the stability of their conquest; that will destroy not only the political, but the social power of capital, that will guarantee their social welfare, along with their political strength. And, therefore, they very quietly await their opportunity, but, in the meantime, earnestly apply themselves to the study of those questions of social economy, the solution of which will show what measures alone can establish, upon a firm basis, the welfare of all. Within a month or two, six thousand copies of M. Louis Blanc's work on "The Organisation of Labour",[a] have been sold in the workshops of Paris, and you must consider, that five editions of this book had been published before. They read likewise a number of other works upon these questions; they meet in small numbers of from ten to twenty, and discuss the different plans propounded therein. They talk not much of revolution, this being a thing admitting of no doubt, a subject upon which they one and all agree; and when the moment will have arrived, at which a collision between the people and the government will be inevitable, down they will be in the streets and squares at a moment's notice, tearing up the pavement, laying omnibuses, carts and coaches, across the streets, barricading every alley, making every narrow lane a fortress, and advancing, in spite of all resistance, from the Bastille to the Tuileries.[184] And then, I fear,

---

[a] Louis Blanc, *Organisation du travail*.—*Ed.*

most of the reform banquet gentry will hide themselves in the darkest corner of their houses, or be scattered like dead leaves before the popular thunderstorm. Then it will be all over with Messrs Odilon Barrot, de Beaumont and other Liberal thunderers, and then the people will judge them quite as severely as they now judge the Conservative Governments.

Written in early November 1847

First published in *The Northern Star* No. 526, November 20, 1847 with an editorial note: "From Our Paris Correspondent"

Reprinted from the newspaper

Frederick Engels

[THE CHARTIST MOVEMENT][185]

The opening of the recently elected Parliament that counts among its members distinguished representatives of the People's Party[186] could not but produce extraordinary excitement in the ranks of democracy. Everywhere the local Chartist associations are being reorganised. The number of meetings increases and the most diverse ways and means of taking action are being proposed and discussed. The Executive of the National Charter Association[187] has just assumed leadership of this movement, outlining in an address to the British democrats the plan of campaign which the party will follow during the present session.

"In a few days," we are told, "a meeting will be held which in the face of the people dares to call itself the assembly of the commons of England. In a few days this assembly, elected by only one class of society, will begin its iniquitous and odious work of strengthening the interests of this class, to the detriment of the people.

"The people must protest *en masse* at the very beginning against the exercise of the legislative functions usurped by this assembly. You, Chartists of the United Kingdom, you have the means to do so; it is your duty to use them to advantage. We therefore submit to you a new national petition with the demands of the People's Charter. Cover it with millions of your signatures. Make it possible for us to present it as the expression of the will of the nation, as the solemn protest of the people against every law passed without the consent of the people, as a Bill, finally, for the restoration of the sovereignty out of which the nation has been tricked for so many centuries.

"But the petition by itself will not suffice to meet the needs of the moment. True, we have won a seat in the legislative chamber by electing Mr. O'Connor. The democratic members will find him to be a vigilant and energetic leader. But O'Connor must be supported by *pressure from without*, and it is you who should create this pressure from without, this strong and imposing public opinion. Let the sections of our Association be reorganised everywhere; let all our former members rejoin our ranks; let meetings be called everywhere; let everywhere the Charter be made the issue of the day; let each locality contribute its share to increase our funds. Be active, give proof of the old energy of the English and the campaign we are opening will be the most glorious ever undertaken for the victory of democracy."[a]

The *Fraternal Democrats*,[188] a society consisting of democrats from almost every nation in Europe, has also just joined, openly and unreservedly, in the agitation of the Chartists. They adopted a resolution of the following tenor:

"Whereas the English people will be unable effectively to support democracy's struggle in other countries until it has won democratic government for itself; and

"whereas our society, established to succour the militant democracy of every country, is duty-bound to come to the aid of the English democrats in their effort to obtain an electoral reform on the basis of the Charter;

"therefore the Fraternal Democrats undertake to support with all their strength the agitation for the People's Charter."[b]

This fraternal society, which counts among its members the most distinguished democrats, both English and foreigners residing in London, is daily gaining in importance. It has grown to such proportions that the London liberals have considered it advisable to set up in opposition to it a bourgeois *International League*[189] headed by Free-Trade parliamentary celebrities. The sole object of this new association, whose leadership includes Dr. Bowring, Col. Thompson and other champions of Free Trade, is to carry on Free-Trade propaganda abroad under cover of philanthropic and liberal phrases. But it seems that the association will not make much headway. During the six months of its existence it has done almost nothing, whereas the Fraternal Democrats have openly come out against any act of oppression, no matter who may attempt to commit it. Hence the democrats, both English and foreign, in so far as the latter are represented in London, have attached themselves to the Fraternal Democrats, declaring at the same time that they will not allow themselves to be exploited for the benefit of England's Free-Trade manufacturers.

Written on November 21, 1847

First published in *La Réforme*, November 22, 1847

Printed according to the newspaper

Translated from the French

[a] "The Executive Committee to the Chartists of the United Kingdom", November 18, 1847.—*Ed.*

[b] Resolution of the Fraternal Democrats, November 15, 1847.—*Ed.*

Frederick Engels

SPLIT IN THE CAMP.— THE *RÉFORME* AND THE *NATIONAL*.— MARCH OF DEMOCRACY[190]

Since my last[a] the banquets of Lille, Avesnes, and Valenciennes, have been held. Avesnes was merely constitutional; Valenciennes half-and-half; Lille a decided triumph of democracy over middle-class intrigue. Here are, shortly, the facts concerning this most important meeting:—

Besides the liberals and the party of the *National* the democrats of the *Réforme* had been invited, and Messrs Ledru-Rollin and Flocon, editor of the last-named paper, had accepted the invitation. M. Odilon Barrot, the virtuous middle-class thunderer, was also invited. Every thing was ready, the toasts were prepared, when all of a sudden M. Odilon Barrot declared he could not assist, nor speak to his toast, "Parliamentary Reform", unless that reform was qualified by adding:—"as a means to insure the purity and sincerity of the institutions conquered in July 1830." This addition excluded, of course, the republicans. Great consternation of the committee ensued. M. Barrot was inflexible. At last it was resolved to submit the decision to the whole meeting. But the meeting very plainly declared they would have no alterations in the programme; they would not violate the understanding upon which the democrats had come to Lille. M. Odilon Barrot, along with his tail of liberal deputies and editors, scornfully retired; Messrs Flocon and Ledru-Rollin were sent for, the banquet took place in spite of the liberals, and M. Ledru's speech was rapturously applauded.

Thus the treacherous plot of the middle-class reformers resulted in a glorious triumph of democracy. M. Odilon Barrot had to decamp shamefully and will never dare to show his face again in the democratic city of Lille. His only excuse was, he had understood the

---

[a] See this volume, pp. 375-82.—*Ed.*

gentlemen of the *Réforme* intended to profit by the Lille banquet to get up a revolution—in the very depth of tranquillity!

A few days after, M. Barrot got some consolation in the Avesnes banquet, a mere family meeting of some middle-class liberals. Here he had the pleasure of toasting the King.[a] But at Valenciennes he was again obliged to pocket his favourite sentiment, dropped so sadly at Lille; no King's health was to be drunk, although the formidable getters-up of revolutions, at the shortest notice, were not at hand. The discomfited thunderer will have to devour his virtuous indignation until another hole-and-corner banquet will allow him to denounce "anarchism", "physical forcism", and "communism", to the astounded grocers and tallow-chandlers of some petty provincial town.

The Lille banquet produced extraordinary discussions in the press. The Conservative papers shouted triumph at the division in the ranks of the reformers. M. Thiers' old and drowsy *Constitutionnel*, and the *Siècle*, M. Barrot's "own", all of a sudden were seized with the most dreadful convulsions.

> "No," shouted the indignant *Siècle* to its shopkeeping public, "no, we are none of these anarchists, we have nothing in common with these restorers of the reign of terror, with these followers of Marat and Robespierre: we would prefer to their reign of blood the present system, were it even a hundred times worse than it is!"

And quite rightly; for such peaceful grocers and tallow-chandlers the white nightcap is a hundred times more fit than the red cap of the Jacobin. At the same time, however, that these papers heaped their vilest and most virulent abuse upon the *Réforme*, they treated the *National* with the utmost esteem. The *National*, indeed, has behaved, on this occasion, in a more than doubtful manner. Already at the banquet of Cosne, this paper blamed the conduct of several democrats who would not assist on account of the King's health being proposed. Now, again, it spoke very coolly of the Lille banquet, and deplored the accident which for a moment troubled the demonstration, while several provincial allies of the *National* openly attacked the conduct of Messrs Ledru and Flocon. The *Réforme* now asked of that paper a more explicit declaration. The *National* declared his article to be quite explicit enough. Then, asked the *Réforme*, what was the deplorable accident at Lille? What is it you deplore? Is it M. Barrot's or M. Ledru-Rollin's conduct you deplore? Is it M. Barrot's impudence or his bad luck you deplore? Is it M. Ledru's speech in favour of Universal Suffrage? Is it the discomfiture of monarchism, the triumph of democracy, you deplore? Do you avow, or not, what your provincial allies say on this occasion? Do you accept the praise

[a] Louis Philippe.—*Ed.*

of the *Siècle*, or do you take our part of the abuse it heaps upon us? Would you have advised M. Marie, your friend, to submit, if, at Orleans, M. Odilon Barrot had made similar pretensions? The *National* replied, from party motives they would have no controversy with the *Réforme*: they were not responsible for articles sent to provincial papers by a "*friend*" of theirs; as to the other questions, the past of the *National* allowed them to pass them unnoticed, and not to trouble themselves with a reply. The *Réforme* gave the whole of this reply, with this remark only:—"Our questions remain."[a] Democrats now have the documents under their eyes—they may judge for themselves. This they have done; a whole host of radical, and even liberal, papers of France have declared in the most decided terms for the *Réforme*.

The conduct of the *National*, indeed, deserves the strongest blame. This paper is getting more and more into the hands of the middle classes. It has of late always deserted the cause of democracy at the decisive moment; it has always preached union with the middle classes, and has on more than one occasion served none but Thiers and Odilon Barrot. If the *National* does not very soon change its conduct, it will cease to be counted as a democratic paper. And in this Lille affair, the *National*, out of mere personal antipathy against men more radical than itself, has not hesitated to sacrifice the very principles upon which [it] itself had contracted an alliance with the liberals in order to get up banquets. After what has passed, the *National* will never again be able to oppose seriously toasting the King at future banquets. The "past" of the *National* is not so very bright as to allow of its answering by silence only the questions of its contemporary. Think only of its defence of the Parisian Bastilles![191]

P.S.—The Reform Banquet of Dijon has come off this week. Thirteen hundred sat down at dinner. The whole affair was thoroughly democratic. No toast to the King, of course. All the speakers belonged to the party of the *Réforme*. MM. Louis Blanc, Flocon, E. Arago, and Ledru-Rollin, were the chief speakers. M. Flocon, editor of the *Réforme*, spoke to the toast of the foreign democrats, and mentioned the English Chartists in a very honourable manner. Next week I shall give you his speech at full length, as well as a full report of the whole proceedings of this most important meeting.[b]

Written at the end of November 1847

First published in *The Northern Star* No. 528, December 4, 1847

Reprinted from the newspaper

---

[a] *La Réforme*, November 16, 1847.—*Ed.*

[b] See this volume, pp. 397-401 and 409-11.—*Ed.*

Karl Marx and Frederick Engels

[ON POLAND]

SPEECHES AT THE INTERNATIONAL MEETING HELD IN LONDON ON NOVEMBER 29, 1847 TO MARK THE 17TH ANNIVERSARY OF THE POLISH UPRISING OF 1830 [192]

MARX'S SPEECH

The unification and brotherhood of nations is a phrase on the lips of all parties today, especially those of bourgeois free traders. A certain kind of brotherhood does of course exist among the bourgeois classes of all nations. It is the brotherhood of the oppressors against the oppressed, of the exploiters against the exploited. Just as, despite the competition and conflicts existing between the members of the bourgeoisie, the bourgeois class of one country is united by brotherly ties against the proletariat of that country, so the bourgeois of all countries, despite their mutual conflicts and competition on the world market, are united by brotherly ties against the proletariat of all countries. For the peoples to be able truly to unite, they must have common interests. And in order that their interests may become common, the existing property relations must be done away with, for these property relations involve the exploitation of some nations by others: the abolition of existing property relations is the concern only of the working class. It alone has also the means for doing this. The victory of the proletariat over the bourgeoisie is, at the same time, victory over the national and industrial conflicts which today range the peoples of the various countries against one another in hostility and enmity. And so the victory of the proletariat over the bourgeoisie is at the same time the signal of liberation for all oppressed nations.

The old Poland is lost in any case and we would be the last to wish for its restoration. But it is not only the old Poland that is lost. The old Germany, the old France, the old England, the whole of the old society is lost. But the loss of the old society is no loss for those who have nothing to lose in the old society, and this is the case of the great majority in all countries at the present time. They have rather everything to gain by the downfall of the old society, which is the condition for the establishment of a new society, one no longer based on class antagonisms.

Of all countries, England is the one where the contradiction between the proletariat and the bourgeoisie is most highly developed. The victory of the English proletarians over the English bourgeoisie is, therefore, decisive for the victory of all the oppressed over their oppressors. Hence Poland must be liberated not in Poland but in England. So you Chartists must not simply express pious wishes for the liberation of nations. Defeat your own internal enemies and you will then be able to pride yourselves on having defeated the entire old society.

ENGELS' SPEECH

Allow me, dear friends, to speak here today as an exception in my capacity as a German. For we German democrats have a special interest in the liberation of Poland. It was German princes who derived great advantages from the division of Poland and it is German soldiers who are still holding down Galicia and Posen. The responsibility for removing this disgrace from our nation rests on us Germans, on us German democrats above all. A nation cannot become free and at the same time continue to oppress other nations. The liberation of Germany cannot therefore take place without the liberation of Poland from German oppression. And because of this, Poland and Germany have a common interest, and because of this, Polish and German democrats can work together for the liberation of both nations.—I also believe that the first decisive blow which will lead to the victory of democracy, to the liberation of all European nations, will be struck by the English Chartists. I have lived in England for a number of years now and openly aligned myself with the Chartist movement during this period. The English Chartists will be the first to rise because it is precisely in England that the struggle between the bourgeoisie and the proletariat is the most intense. And why is it the most intense? Because in England, as a result of modern industry, of the introduction of machinery, all oppressed classes are being merged together into a single great class with common interests, the class of the proletariat; because as a consequence, on the opposite side all classes of oppressors have likewise been united into a single class, the bourgeoisie. The struggle has thus been simplified and so it will be possible to decide it by one single heavy blow. Isn't this so? The aristocracy no longer has any power in

England; the bourgeoisie alone rules and it has taken the aristocracy in tow. But the whole great mass of the people stands opposed to the bourgeoisie, united in a formidable phalanx, whose victory over the ruling capitalists draws nearer and nearer. And you have to thank machinery for this elimination of opposed interests which previously divided the different sections of workers, for this levelling of the living standards of all workers. Without machinery no Chartism, and although machinery may temporarily worsen your position it is nevertheless machinery that makes our victory possible. But not only in England; in all other countries it has had the same effect on the workers. In Belgium, in America, in France, in Germany it has evened out the position of all workers and daily continues to do so more and more; in all these countries the workers now have the same interest, which is the overthrow of the class that oppresses them—the bourgeoisie. This levelling of living standards, this identification of the party interests of the workers of all nations is the result of machinery, and so machinery is an enormous historical advance. What follows from this for us? Because the condition of the workers of all countries is the same, because their interests are the same, their enemies the same, they must also fight together, they must oppose the brotherhood of the bourgeoisie of all nations with a brotherhood of the workers of all nations.

First published in the *Deutsche-Brüsseler-Zeitung* No. 98, December 9, 1847

Printed according to the newspaper

Published in English for the first time

Frederick Engels

[THE ANNIVERSARY OF THE POLISH REVOLUTION OF 1830][193]

Dear Citizen!

I arrived yesterday evening just in time to attend the public meeting called to celebrate the anniversary of the Polish revolution of 1830.

I have been present at many similar celebrations but I have never seen such general enthusiasm, such perfect and cordial agreement between men of all nations.

The chairmanship was given to Mr. Arnott, an English workman.

The first speech was by Mr. Ernest Jones, editor of *The Northern Star*, who, while speaking against the behaviour of the Polish aristocracy during the insurrection of 1830, gave much praise to the efforts made by Poland to escape from the yoke of her oppressors. His brilliant and powerful speech was loudly applauded.

After him, M. Michelot gave a speech in French.

Mr. Schapper from Germany followed him. He told the meeting that the Brussels Democratic Association had delegated to London Mr. Marx, German democrat and one of its vice-presidents, to establish relations of correspondence between the Brussels society and the London society of Fraternal Democrats,[194] and also to prepare for a democratic congress of the different European nations.

Mr. Marx was received with prolonged applause, when he came forward to address the assembly.

In a speech in German, translated by Mr. Schapper, Mr. Marx declared that England would give the signal for the deliverance of Poland. Poland, he said, would be free only when the civilised nations of Western Europe had won democracy. Now, of all the democracies of Europe, the strongest and most numerous was that of England, organised throughout the whole country. It was in England that the antagonism between the proletariat and the bourgeoisie was most developed, that the decisive struggle between these two classes became more and more inevitable. It was therefore in England that in all probability the fight would begin which would end with the universal triumph of democracy and which would also break the Polish yoke. The success of other European democrats depended on the victory of the English Chartists; therefore Poland would be saved by England.

Mr. Harney, chief editor of *The Northern Star,* followed by thanking the democrats of Brussels for having immediately approached the democrats of London, taking no account of the advances made to them by the bourgeoisie of the London International League,[195] a society founded by the free traders in order to exploit foreign democrats in the interests of free trade and to compete with the society of Fraternal Democrats which was almost exclusively composed of workers.

Mr. Engels, from Paris, a German democrat, then declared that Germany had a special interest in the freedom of Poland because the German governments exercised their despotism over a part of Poland. German democracy ought to have at heart the ending of this tyranny which shamed Germany.

Mr. Tedesco, from Liège, in a vigorous speech, thanked the Polish fighters of 1830 for having loudly proclaimed the principle of insurrection. His speech, translated by Mr. Schapper, was warmly applauded.

After some remarks by Mr. Charles Keen, Colonel Oborski replied for Poland.

Mr. Wilson, an English workman who by his vigorous opposition recently almost brought about the break-up of a meeting of the International League, was the last to address the assembly.

On the proposal of Messrs Harney and Engels, three cheers were given for the three great European democratic newspapers: the *Réforme, The Northern Star,* and the *Deutsche-Brüsseler-Zeitung*; on the proposal of Mr. Schapper, three groans were given for the three anti-democratic papers: the *Journal des Débats, The Times* and the *Augsburg Zeitung*.[a]

The meeting ended with the singing of the *Marseillaise,* in which everybody joined, standing and with hats off.

Written on November 30, 1847

First published in *La Réforme,* December 5, 1847

Printed according to the newspaper

Translated from the French

Published in English for the first time

[a] Augsburg *Allgemeine Zeitung*.—*Ed.*

Frederick Engels

REFORM BANQUET AT LILLE.— SPEECH OF M. LEDRU-ROLLIN

In response to the toast:—"To the labourers,—to their imprescriptible rights,—to their sacred interests, hitherto unknown."[a]

"Citizens,—Yes, to the labourers! to their imprescriptible rights,—to their sacred interests, hitherto unknown. To the unalienable rights of man, proclaimed in principle, by two glorious revolutions[b]; but artfully eluded in their application, and successfully re-wrested from the people, and which are now only a glorious, yet bitter remembrance! Political rights to the people, it is said, is madness. How entrust them with them, in their state of incapacity, of ignorance, of moral depravity? To give the people political freedom is a blind and dangerous power; it is revolution—blood —anarchy—chaos! Gentlemen, you know the people; you in this industrial city, at once so wealthy and so poor, believe you this picture to be true! Oh! doubtless, if we cast our eyes over the pages of certain romance writers, to whom the grand side of things has appeared trivial, vulgar—who have sought for effect in the humorous, the fantastic, the exceptional, the people—is it thus! Taking the normal life of our towns, from one point, where criminals escaped from justice, find a refuge, the way of life, the dregs of society, they have said, 'Such are the people!' Doubtless such would still be the people, did we put faith in those mercenary writers, who, to terrify the wealthy, cry out against the invasion of the barbarians! *Barbarians!* they have cast that epithet upon the people, as the most outrageous of insults. Ah! if barbarians always signify men full of simplicity, of strength, of social and youthful energy, those barbarians can alone save our worn-out official world, fast hastening to decay in powerlessness and corruption. No; a thousand times no, it is not the people. It is not upon the theatre of crime and debauchery, that it must be sought for. To be acquainted with it, we must transport ourselves into those manufacturing towns, where the merchant, struggling against unrestricted competition which crushes him, between the tyrannical pressure

---

[a] Ledru-Rollin's speech at the banquet at Lille on November 7, 1847 was translated by Engels according to the report in *La Réforme*, November 10, 1847.—*Ed.*

[b] The reference is evidently to the revolutions of 1789-94 and 1830.—*Ed.*

of capital and opposition to wages, which eat him up, he is compelled to reduce those wages, in order to avoid bankruptcy and dishonour. Ah! believe not that the people, in their spirit of justice, always accuse the masters as the cause of that cruel necessity. Know they not that our industry fails for want of outlet; that we have seen the greatest number of the markets of the world closed against us; and that our commerce has perished, where our flag has been trampled under foot? Well; in the midst of those vicissitudes, of those fluctuations, of this crisis of wages, what befalls the workman? The labour of the father, no longer sufficing to procure bread for the family, the daughter prostitutes herself for food; the child must go to aid the formidable machine, and exhaust his unevolved strength; and by the side of those beauteous fabrics, the product of our industry, the eye wanders over rickety boys, faded girls, worn-out men, bent under the pressure of premature labour. And, nevertheless, of that physically decayed population—those who have escaped enervation, sickness—who have attained their proper height, will go forth to do battle for their country—nobly to encounter death beneath her banner. Such are the people of the towns, sociable, good, patient in the midst of those daily evils,—doing more, deriving from within themselves the light of knowledge, dealt out to them with such a niggardly hand, reading, sometimes composing verses upon their sufferings or their prospects, publishing journals, which enlighten and prepare those formidable problems, respecting the future fate of mankind! It is those people of the towns whom some writers, who only judge by their own flimsy minds, call barbarians!... In this slight and rapid sketch, we have only seen the people in their habitual life—their daily struggles; but were one of those unforeseen scourges, in which a fearful inundation sweeps off everything in its destructive course, a terrible fire, or a severe cholera suddenly to arise, who would be foremost in the cause of humanity? who would forget their families and their wives, upon their lowly couches? their children, who might die on the morrow? who would peril life, without counting the cost; and fly when the service was performed, without even leaving their names?—the people! Intelligence or devotedness, head or heart, the people are, therefore, worthy to exercise the rights to which they lay claim. And who are better aware of it than the citizens, who by the superhuman efforts of the people, have conquered the twofold tyranny of the nobility and the priesthood. It was to that clergy, to that nobility, as to the States of 1614, that a member of the *bourgeoisie* once said— 'You, our elder brothers, you, our younger brothers—for we are all brothers—forming but one and the same nation.' And the clergy and the nobles attempted to make that courageous member of the *third* retract and their minions to scourge him, regarding a plebeian as of a conquered and inferior race.... Not only are the people worthy to represent themselves, but if justice is to be rendered, they can only be efficiently represented *by themselves*. Who, then, in a legislative chamber knows sufficiently, at this present moment, their interests, their wants to dare to defend them? There are many men, gentlemen, who would unite in our principle of Reform; for it is now made evident—but they still dread the advance of democracy; yet never has a solemn and decisive movement, in the onward march of humanity, been preceded by more significant auguries! Let us pass rapidly in review those transcendent men of our own age. Towering above all, is one, whose prophetic speech is engraven on every heart. 'Before fifty years,' said Napoleon, 'Europe will be Cossack or Republican.'... It shall not be Cossack—and in this patriotic city exists the right so to say. If doubt could ever have prevailed, it would assuredly not have been in the midst of those whose love of national independence and of the revolution of 1792, transformed each citizen into a hero! Republican—but I pause, gentlemen—the laws of September[196] are in force, and in order to be strong, when armed in a good cause, we must know how to keep within the law. I shall, therefore, only permit myself to choose, as interpreters of my thoughts, a few men, whose very names shed a glory over their country. He, for example, who has sung the high hymn of legitimacy, and who has achieved renown, in essaying to restore the ancient ruins of the past. Chateaubriand, in his sincerity, has been unable to avoid regarding the approaching future of the world, as tending towards democracy.... Beranger, whose patriotic hymns will be eternally repeated by the world—hymns, which we, his contemporaries, ought to teach to our children as a prayer, whilst a Waterloo remains to be avenged!! Beranger believes in the approaching sovereignty of the people. And Lamartine, sparkling with poetry, with eloquence, has passed by legitimacy—he has traversed the marshes of the plain, in order to approach nearer to us. Though an ardent admirer of the Girondists, yet the noble candour of his mind leads him to draw conclusions favourable to the Radicals. There is a something, however, which still divides him from pure democracy; as for myself, I only behold the steps of giants, each day rapidly striding towards us. So much for men of letters, gentlemen, and that unanimous testimony rendered by such illustrations in favour of our party, might suffice for its hopes. But cast your eyes into the domain of science; behold a man who is at the summit of all—of whom the two worlds would deprive us—Arago! But for an imperious duty he would have been here in the midst of you. He would, much better than I am able, have spoken to you of the rights of the people; he who was the first to advocate their cause in another assembly, where to do so required no small amount of moral courage. Is not, then, Arago entirely for democracy? And in the arts, who with his powerful chisel draws forth, from marble, those men who have best served the people? Who confides to the eternity of bronze those grand revolutionary figures, to bequeath them to the admiration of future ages? David of Angers! Is he not, also, for the cause of the people? Well, when so many illustrious men declare in favour of democracy, or struggle for its attainment, how conclude otherwise than that right and Providence combat with us, and for us? Those are the teachings of talented men; but have not the teachings of the people also their manifestations? Look at Poland—heroic Poland—the last pulsations of whose heart still throb for liberty—no longer possessing an army; each day some martyr consecrates himself to her cause. Italy; she too longs for unity. She emerges from her ruins, which constituted her glory, in order to acquire fresh renown. May she on awakening distrust herself; let her remember Masaniello. Switzerland;— I feel that I ought well to weigh my words at this solemn moment. We can do one thing, gentlemen, we can unite ourselves for an instant, by recollection, by thought, with those whom we look upon as brothers, in order to pray that victory may be with them, as have hitherto been right and reason! The cause of Switzerland is ours, gentlemen; the Radicals there wage war against two things, which are the plague-spots of our era—aristocrats and worthless priests. Respect our creeds, but war against those who, under the mask of religion, are the abettors of despotism, and of tyranny. Short-sighted beings! who see not in this double association of genius and of the people, the near advent of a Messiah of equality! Thus then, O people, to whom I would sacrifice all that I possess of devotedness and strength, *hope,* and *believe.* Between this period, in which thy ancient faith is extinguished, and in which the new light has not yet been showered upon you, each evening in thy desolate dwelling piously repeat the immortal symbol—LIBERTY, EQUALITY, FRATERNITY! Yes, liberty for all; liberty of conscience; liberty of thought, liberty of association; for man cannot become moral without communing with man, and it is in order the better to subjugate him that he is isolated by a system of corruption. They know that a bundle of sticks cannot be broken. Equality likewise for all—equality in presence of civil law, equality in political matters, equality in education, in order that man may have no superior, except in morals or in virtue! Fraternity—inexhaustible source, from whence will spring noble and celebrated institutions; of association, of strength. Then labour will no longer be a right, it will be a duty. Let there be no more revenues, except from labour and for labour. Yes, salvation. O great and immortal symbol, thy advent draws nigh! People, may the plaudits bestowed on thy humble interpreter be wafted to thee, and prove at once a consolation and a hope!"

Compiled and translated into English in the first half of December 1847

Reprinted from the newspaper

First published in *The Northern Star* No. 530, December 18, 1847 with editorial note: "From Our Paris Correspondent"

Frederick Engels

REFORM MOVEMENT IN FRANCE.— BANQUET OF DIJON[197]

This meeting of the Democracy of the Department of the Côte d'Or, was incontestably the most splendid one of the whole series of Reform Banquets. 1,300 sat down to dinner. There were present deputations from almost all the neighbouring towns, and even a Swiss deputation, composed of citizens from Neufchâtel, Geneva and Lucerne. The character of the meeting is very clearly marked out by the names of the principal speakers—MM. Louis Blanc, Flocon, Ledru-Rollin, Etienne Arago—all of them belonging to the Ultra-Democratic party, represented by the *Réforme.* We need not say that Louis Philippe was not toasted at this dinner.

M. Signard, of Gray, a neighbouring town, spoke to the toast—"The Democrats of Lille who, at the late banquet of their town sternly refused to compromise with the sham-Liberals; and by their energy, union, and intelligence, saved the honour of Democracy."[a]

M. Etienne Arago, a well-known literary character of Paris, and who but recently brought upon the stage an exceedingly successful comedy, entitled *The Aristocracies,* then spoke to the sentiment—"The development of literature, science, and the fine arts"; exposing, in a brilliant speech, the rapid advance literature and science were sure to make under a free and democratic system.

At the toast—"The future progress of France", the chairman called upon M. Louis Blanc, who was very enthusiastically received by the meeting. He delivered a splendid speech, containing many

---

[a] Here and below speeches are quoted according to the reports on the banquet of Dijon printed in *La Réforme,* November 24 and 25, 1847.—*Ed.*

just and striking observations on the past development of France; on the conclusions to draw from it with regard to the future; on the particular character impressed indelibly upon the French Democratic Movement by the revolution. He was repeatedly and deservedly interrupted by applause. It was a speech quite worthy of the first historical writer France now possesses. There is, however, one point upon which we would make a few observations, which we hope will be taken in the same friendly spirit in which we write them.

M. Blanc says—

> "We want union in Democracy. And no one may deceive himself, we do not think and labour for France only, but for the whole world, because the future of France contains in it the future of mankind. In fact, we are placed in this admirable position, that, without ever ceasing to be national, we are necessarily cosmopolite, and are even more cosmopolite than national. Whoever would call himself a Democrat, and be at the same time an Englishman, would give the lie to the history of his own country, for the part which England has always played, has been a struggle of egotism against fraternity. In the same manner, he who is a Frenchman, and would not be a cosmopolite, would give the lie to his country's past; for France never could make predominant any idea, except it was for the benefit of the whole world. Gentlemen, at the time of the Crusades, when Europe went to conquer the grave of Christ, it was France who took the movement under her wing. Afterwards, when the priests would impose upon us the yoke of Papist supremacy, the Gallican bishops defended the rights of conscience. And in the last days of the ancient monarchy, who supported young, republican America?[198] France, always France! And what was true of monarchical France, how should it not be true of Republican France? Where, in the book of history, do we find anything resembling that admirable, self-sacrificing disinterestedness of the Republic, when, exhausted by the blood she had shed on our frontiers and on the scaffold, she found yet more blood to shed for her Batavian brethren?[199] When beaten or victorious, she enlightens her very enemies by the sparks of her genius! Let Europe send us sixteen armies, and we shall send her liberty in return."

Now, without intending to deprecate in any manner the heroic efforts of the French Revolution, and the immense gratitude the world owes to the great men of the Republic, we think that the relative position of France and England, with regard to cosmopolitism, is not at all justly delineated in the above sketch. We entirely deny the cosmopolitic[200] character ascribed to France before the revolution, and the times of Louis XI and Richelieu may serve as proofs. But what is it M. Blanc ascribes to France? That she never could make predominant any idea, except it was to benefit the whole world. Well, we should think M. Louis Blanc could not show us any country in the world which could do otherwise than France is said to have done. Take England, for instance, which M. Blanc places in direct opposition to France. England invented the steam-engine; England erected the railway; two things which, we believe, are worth a good many ideas. Well, did England invent them for herself, or for the world? The French glory in spreading civilisation everywhere, principally in Algiers. Well, who has spread civilisation in America, Asia, Africa, and Australia, but England?[201] Who founded the very Republic, in the freeing of which France took some part? England—always England. If France assisted in freeing the American Republic from English tyranny, England freed the Dutch Republic, just two hundred years sooner, from Spanish oppression.[202] If France gave, at the end of the last century, a glorious example to the whole world, we cannot silently pass by the fact that England, a hundred and fifty years sooner, gave that example,[203] and found at that time, not even France prepared to follow. And, as far as ideas are concerned, those very ideas, which the French philosophers of the 18th century—which Voltaire, Rousseau, Diderot, D'Alembert, and others, did so much to popularise—where had these ideas first been originated, but in England? Let us never forget Milton, the first defender of regicide, Algernon Sydney, Bolingbroke, and Shaftesbury, over their French more brilliant followers.

If an Englishman "would call himself a democrat he would give the lie to the history of his own country", says M. Blanc. Well, we consider it as the veriest proof of sterling democracy, that it *must* give the lie to its country, that it *must* repudiate all responsibility for a past filled up with misery, tyranny, class oppression, and superstition. Let the French not make an exception to the other democrats; let them not take the responsibility for the doings of their Kings and Aristocrats of former times. Therefore, what M. Blanc thinks a disadvantage to English democrats, we think to be a great advantage, that they *must* repudiate the past, and only look to the future.

A Frenchman is necessarily a cosmopolite. Yes, in a world ruled over by French influence, French manners, fashions, ideas, politics. In a world in which every nation has adopted the characteristics of French nationality. But that is exactly what the democrats of other nations will not like. Quite ready to give up the harshness of their own nationality, they expect the same from the French. They will not be satisfied in the assertion, on the part of the French, that they *are* cosmopolites; assertion which amounts to the demand urged upon all others to become Frenchmen.

Compare Germany. Germany is the fatherland of an immense number of inventions—of the printing press, for instance. Germany has produced—and this is recognised upon all hands—a far greater number of generous and cosmopolitic ideas than France and England put together. And Germany, in practice, has always been humiliated, always been deceived in all her hopes. She can tell best what French cosmopolitism has been. In the same measure as France has to complain—and quite justly—of the treachery of English policy, Germany has experienced a policy quite as treacherous on the part of France, from Louis XI down to Louis Philippe. If we were to apply the measure of M. Louis Blanc, the Germans would be the true cosmopolites, and yet they do not pretend to this.

So much upon this point. We wish to establish a discussion upon it, as this will only lead to a mutual understanding; to a firm union of French and English Democracy.

After M. Blanc, M. Flocon spoke to the toast: "The Democrats of Europe."

M. Flocon said:

"Look around you, listen to the voices which arise from foreign countries; complaints or menace; sighs or hopes; what tell they? They invoke the principle of the French Revolution; they proclaim in the face of all despotisms, its immortal motto: *Liberté, Egalité, Fraternité*. Yes, those very nations, which in the delusions of slavery and ignorance, made an impious war on the revolution; they now come by thousands to take up its standard, and promise to be most ardent defenders of the glorious principles they did not understand in times past. This striking fact is before the eyes of all the world, and I know nothing more terrible to our enemies, nothing which could more effectually recall to our minds our duty. In England, at the side of the old factions, in the face of the richest and most tyrannical aristocracy of the world, the people are organising. An immense association, conducted by experienced leaders, enrols daily thousands of working men, who will undertake to avenge the wrongs of humanity. And the rights of man are not a new watchword in England. At the time of the old civil wars, in the midst of religious fanaticism and political passions, several parties clearly saw the great social truth:

When Adam delved and Eve span
Where was then the gentleman?[204]

That was proclaimed by the Covenanters[205] almost three hundred years ago. The same question is again put; and the cotton lords disdain as much to listen to the complaint of the children of toil, as did the landlords in by-gone times. Therefore, asking what is right will not suffice, the people must be strong enough to take it, and the English people know this. In Belgium, at this very moment, a society is organising, uniting Democrats of all nations, a Democratic Congress[206] is being prepared. In Germany, while the princes play the game of granting gracious constitutions, the people prepare themselves for working out their own salvation."

The speaker then reviewed briefly the Polish, Italian, and Swiss movements, and closed his speech as follows:

"Yes, the seed of the revolution is germinating, the soil is fertile, the splendid flower of hope adorns the fields of the future. But the winter has been long, and we ought soon to take to the sickle, to make our harvest. Let us then take up again the work of the revolution, where our fathers left it. Let us make haste, else we shall have to take it up where they commenced." (*Loud applause.*)

The next toast: "The Sovereignty of the people", was spoken to by M. Ledru-Rollin, deputy.

Letters of apology were read from MM. François Arago, Lamennais, Dupont de L'Eure, and the meeting separated.

This demonstration proves that the provincial Democrats are more and more leaving the party of the *National*, in order to rally around the party of the *Réforme.*

Written in the first half of December 1847

First published in *The Northern Star* No. 530, December 18, 1847 with an editorial note: "From Our Paris Correspondent"

Reprinted from the newspaper

Karl Marx

REMARKS ON THE ARTICLE BY M. ADOLPHE BARTELS[207]

M. *Adolphe Bartels* claims that public life is finished for him. Indeed, he has withdrawn into private life and does not mean to leave it; he limits himself, each time some public event occurs, to hurling protests and proclaiming loudly that he believes he is his own master, that the movement has been made without him, M. Bartels, and in spite of him, M. Bartels, and that he has the right to refuse it his supreme sanction. It will be agreed that this is just as much a way of participating in public life as any other, and that by all these declarations, proclamations and protestations the public man hides behind the humble appearance of the private individual. This is the way in which the unappreciated and misunderstood genius reveals himself.

M. A. Bartels knows very well that the democrats of the different nations, in forming a body under the name of a democratic association, have had no other object but to exchange ideas and come to an understanding about the principles which will serve to bring about the union and fraternity of peoples. It goes without saying that, in a society which proposes such a goal for itself, it is the duty of all foreigners to state their opinions frankly, and it is truly ridiculous to call them *schoolmasters* every time they take the floor to fulfil this duty in the association to which they belong. If M. A. Bartels accuses foreigners of wanting to teach lessons it is because they refuse to take lessons from him.

M. A. Bartels will recall, no doubt, that in the provisional committee in which he took part he even proposed to make the Society of German Workers[208] the *nucleus* of the new society to be founded. I had to reject this proposal, in the name of the German workers. Might it perhaps be that M. A. Bartels meant to lay a trap for us, to contrive the means for a false denunciation?

M. Bartels is free to decry our doctrines as "filthy and barbarous". He does not criticise, he does not prove, he condemns; and he gives proof of his orthodoxy by condemning in advance what he does not understand.

We are more tolerant than M. A. Bartels. We overlook his "blue devils",[a] which are quite innocent devils.

M. A. Bartels being more theocratic than democratic, it is quite natural that he finds an accomplice in the *Journal de Bruxelles.* This paper accuses us of wanting to "*improve the human race*".[209] Let it calm down! Fortunately, we Germans are not unaware that since 1640 the *Congregatio de propaganda fide*[210] has had the monopoly in improving the human race. We are too modest and too few to want to compete with the reverend fathers in that humanitarian industry. Let them take the trouble to compare the report in the *Deutsche-Brüsseler-Zeitung*[b] with that of *The Northern Star,* and they will be able to assure themselves that it is only by a mistake that *The Northern Star* makes me say "Chartists—you will be hailed as the *saviours of the human race.*"[211]

The *Journal de Bruxelles* is moved by a more charitable spirit when it reminds us of the example of *Anacharsis Cloots* mounting the scaffold for having wanted to be more patriotic than the patriots of 1793 and 1794. In this respect the reverend fathers are free from all reproach. They have never been more patriotic than the patriots. On the contrary, they have always and everywhere been accused of wanting to be more reactionary than the reactionaries and, what is still worse, of wanting to be more governmental than the national government. When we think of the said experiences which they have just undergone in Switzerland, we are all ready to recognise that the admonitions they address to us so that we should avoid the opposite extreme and similar dangers, are of a generosity worthy of the early Christians. We thank them for this

Written about December 17, 1847

First published in French in the *Deutsche-Brüsseler-Zeitung* No. 101, December 19, 1847

Signed: *Karl Marx*

Printed according to the newspaper

Translated from the French

Published in English for the first time

[a] Blue devils—*delirium tremens.*—*Ed.*

[b] See this volume, pp. 388-90.—*Ed.*

Karl Marx

LAMARTINE AND COMMUNISM

Brussels, December 24. Once again the French papers carry a letter from M. de Lamartine. This time it is communism on which this poetic socialist at last gives his candid opinion having been challenged to do so by Cabet.[212] At the same time Lamartine promises to set forth his views *in detail* on this "important subject" in the near future. For the present he contents himself with a few brief, oracular utterances:

"My opinion of communism," he says, "may be summarised in a *feeling* (!), namely the following: were God to entrust me with a society of savages to civilise them and make into well-mannered people, the first institution I should give them would be that of property."

"The fact," continues M. Lamartine, "that man appropriates the elements to himself is a law of nature and a precondition of life. Man appropriates the air by breathing, space by striding through it, the land by cultivating it, and even time, by perpetuating himself through his children; property is the organisation of the life principle in the universe; communism would be the death of labour and of the whole of humanity."

"Your dream," M. Lamartine finally consoles M. Cabet, "is too beautiful for this earth."

M. Lamartine is thus an opponent of communism, and what is more not merely of a communist system; in fact, he enters the lists on behalf of the "perpetuity of private property". For his "feeling" tells him three things: 1. that property civilises people, 2. that it is the organisation of the life principle in the world, and 3. that its opposite, communism, is too beautiful a dream for this bad world.

No doubt M. Lamartine "feels" a better world, in which the "life principle" is differently "organised". In this bad world, however, it just so happens that "appropriation" is a precondition of life.

It is not necessary to analyse M. Lamartine's confused feeling in order to resolve it into its contradictions. We wish only to make one single observation. M. Lamartine believes he has proved the perpetuity of bourgeois property by pointing out that property in general forms the transition from the state of savagery to that of civilisation, and by giving us to understand that the process of breathing and the making of children presuppose the right of property just as much as does social private property.

M. Lamartine sees no distinction between the epoch of transition from savagery to civilisation and our own epoch, any more than between the "appropriation" of air and the "appropriation" of the products of society; for both of these are "appropriations", forsooth, just as both epochs are "epochs of transition"!

In his "detailed" polemic against communism M. Lamartine will no doubt find an opportunity to deduce "logically" from these general platitudes arising from his "feeling" a whole series of other, still more general platitudes.—Perhaps then we shall likewise find the opportunity to shed light upon his platitudes "in greater detail". —For the present we shall content ourselves with passing on to our readers the "feelings" which a monarchist-Catholic newspaper opposes to those of M. Lamartine. The *Union monarchique* namely, in yesterday's issue, speaks out against Lamartine's feelings as follows:

> "Here we see how these enlighteners of humanity leave it leaderless. The wretches! ... They have robbed the poor man of the God who comforted him;... they have taken Heaven from him;... they have left man alone with his want and his wretchedness. And then they come and say: 'You wish to possess the earth—it is not yours. You wish to enjoy the good things of life—they belong to others. You wish to share in wealth—that is out of the question. Stay poor, stay naked, stay abandoned—die!'"

The *Union monarchique* comforts the proletarians with God. The *Bien Public*, M. Lamartine's paper, comforts them with the "life principle".

Written on December 24, 1847

First published in the *Deutsche-Brüsseler-Zeitung* No. 103, December 26, 1847

Printed according to the newspaper

Published in English for the first time

Frederick Engels

THE *RÉFORME* AND THE *NATIONAL*[213]

Following the Lille banquet a controversy developed between the *Réforme* and the *National*, which has now led to a decisive split between the two papers.

The facts are as follows:

From the inception of the reform banquets the *National* has attached itself even more openly than before to the dynastic opposition.[214] At the Lille banquet M. Degeorge of the *National* withdrew together with Odilon Barrot. The *National* expressed its opinion of the Lille banquet in terms that were more than equivocal. Challenged by the *Réforme* to explain itself in more detail, it refused, with the excuse that it did not wish to start polemics with this newspaper. This was no reason at all for failing to comment on facts. To be brief, the *Réforme* did not let the matter drop and eventually attacked M. Garnier-Pagès of the *National* for a speech in which he denied the existence of classes and deleted the bourgeoisie and the proletariat in the general phrase of *citoyens français*. Now, at last, the *National* declared that it would defend its friends against a newspaper which cast suspicion on all worthy patriots, such as Carnot, Garnier-Pagès, etc.

The *National*, very soon defeated on every point, could finally hit upon no other expedient than to accuse the *Réforme* of communism.

"You speak of indefinite strivings, of theories and systems which arise among the people, you censure us for openly attacking these—to put it bluntly—communistic strivings. Very well then, declare yourselves directly, either for or against communism. We declare for all to hear that we have nothing in common with the Communists, with these people who deny property, family and country. When the day of battle comes we shall fight not with, but against these abominable strivings. We have no peace, no tolerance for these odious fantasies, for this absurd and barbarous (sauvage) system which bestialises man and reduces him to the level of a brute (le réduit à l'état de brute). And you believe the people would be with you? The people would surrender what little property they have earned in the sweat of their brow, their family, their country? You believe that the people would ever allow themselves to be persuaded that it is a matter of indifference whether or not Austria brings us under the yoke of her despotism, whether or not the Powers dismember France?"[a]

To such grounds against communism the *National* adds its plans for improving the condition of the workers—postal reform, financial reform, luxury taxes, state subsidies, the abolition of the *octrois*,[215] and free competition.

Correcting the ridiculous ideas of communism held by the *National* is not worth the effort. It is ludicrous, however, that the *National* is still parading the terrifying fantasy of a constantly threatening invasion by the "Great Powers", and that it still believes that beyond the Rhine and across the Channel there are millions of bayonets pointed against France, and hundreds of thousands of cannons aimed at Paris. The *Réforme* has quite correctly replied to this that in the event of an invasion by the Kings it will not be the fortifications which will serve as a rampart, but the peoples themselves.

With reference to the article from the *National* quoted above the *Réforme* declares:

"We are not communistic, and our reason is that communism disregards the laws of production, that it is not concerned with ensuring that enough is produced for the whole of society. But the economic proposals of the Communists stand closer to us than those of the *National*, which accepts the existing bourgeois economics without further ado. We shall defend the Communists against the police and the *National* also in the future, because we acknowledge at least their right of discussion, and because the doctrines that originate from the workers themselves always deserve consideration."

We thank the *Réforme* for the energetic way in which it has stood for true democracy as against the *National*. We thank the *Réforme* for defending communism against it. We willingly acknowledge that the *Réforme* has always defended the Communists whenever they have been persecuted by the government. *Alone* of all the Paris newspapers, the *Réforme* defended the materialistic Communists when they were dragged to court by M. Delangle[216]; on this same occasion M. Cabet almost conceded that the government was right as against the materialists. We are glad that the *Réforme*, even in the more or less undeveloped forms in which communism has so far appeared, has discovered a kernel of truth to which it stands closer

[a] Quoted from the leading article in *La Réforme*, December 21, 1847; the reply of this newspaper given below is from the same source.—*Ed.*

than it does to the representatives of bourgeois economics. On the other hand, we hope to be able to prove to the *Réforme* before long that communism as *we* defend it is still more closely related to the principles of the *Réforme* than to communism itself as it has hitherto been presented in France, and as it now is being spread, in part, abroad.

In its repudiation of the *National*, furthermore, the *Réforme* is only pronouncing the same judgment that the democratic movement in Germany, England and Belgium, indeed everywhere except in France, has long since passed on it.

Written at the end of December 1847

First published in the *Deutsche-Brüsseler-Zeitung* No. 104, December 30, 1847

Printed according to the newspaper

Published in English for the first time

Frederick Engels

LOUIS BLANC'S SPEECH AT THE DIJON BANQUET[217]

The Northern Star in its report of the Dijon banquet criticises the speech of Louis Blanc in remarks with which we completely concur. The union of the democrats of different nations does not exclude mutual criticism. It is impossible without such criticism. Without criticism there is no understanding and consequently no union. We reproduce the remarks of *The Northern Star* in order that we too, for our part, may protest against preconceptions and illusions which are in direct and hostile opposition to the trends of modern democracy and which should be abandoned if the union of democrats of different nations is to remain more than an empty phrase.

At the Dijon banquet, M. Blanc said:

"We want union in Democracy. And no one may deceive himself about this, we do not think and labour for France only, but for the whole world, because the future of France contains in it the future of mankind. In fact, we are placed in this admirable position, that, without ever ceasing to be national, we are necessarily cosmopolite, and are even more cosmopolite than national. Whoever would call himself a *Democrat,* and be at the same time an *Englishman, would give the lie* to the history of his own country, for the part which England has always played in history has been the struggle for egotism against 'fraternité'. In the same manner, he who is a Frenchman, and would not be a cosmopolite, would give the lie to his country's past; for France never could make predominant any idea, except it was for the benefit of the whole world. Gentlemen, at the time of the Crusades, when Europe went to conquer the grave of Christ, it was France who took the movement under her wing. Afterwards, when the priests would impose upon us the yoke of Papist supremacy, the Gallican bishops defended the rights of conscience. And in the last days of the ancient monarchy, who supported young, republican America? France, always France! And what was true of monarchical France, how should it not be true of republican France? Where, in the book of history, do we find anything resembling that admirable, self-sacrificing disinterestedness of the French Republic, when, exhausted by the blood she had shed on our frontiers and on the scaffold, she found yet more blood to shed for her

Batavian brethren? When beaten or victorious, she enlightened her very enemies by the sparks of her genius! Let Europe send us sixteen armies, and we shall send her liberty in return."

The Northern Star says with regard to this:

"Now, without intending to deprecate in any manner the heroic efforts of the French Revolution, and the immense gratitude the world owes to the great men of the Republic, we think that the relative position of France and England, with regard to cosmopolitism, is not at all justly delineated in the above sketch. We entirely deny the cosmopolitic character ascribed to France before the revolution, and the times of Louis XI and Richelieu may serve as proofs. But what is it M. Blanc ascribes to France? That she never could make predominant any idea, except it was to benefit the whole world. Well, we should think M. Louis Blanc could not show us any country in the world which could do otherwise than France is said to have done. Take England, for instance, which M. Blanc places in direct opposition to France. England invented the steam-engine; England erected the railway; two things which, we believe, are worth a good many ideas. Well, did England invent them for herself, or for the world? The French glory in spreading civilisation everywhere, principally in Algiers. Well, who has spread civilisation in America, Asia, Africa, and Australia, but England? Who founded the very Republic, in the freeing of which France took some part? England—always England. If France assisted in freeing the American Republic from English tyranny, England freed the Dutch Republic, just two hundred years sooner, from Spanish oppression. If France gave, at the end of the last century, a glorious example to the whole world, we cannot silently pass by the fact that England, a hundred and fifty years sooner, gave that example, and found at that time, not even France prepared to follow. And, as far as *ideas* are concerned, those very ideas, which the French philosophers of the 18th century—which Voltaire, Rousseau, Diderot, D'Alembert, and others, did so much to popularise—where had these ideas first been originated, but in England? Let us never forget Milton, the first defender of regicide, Algernon Sydney, Bolingbroke, and Shaftesbury, over their French more brilliant followers.

"'If an Englishman would call himself a democrat he would give the lie to the history of his own country,' says M. Blanc.

"Well, we consider it as the veriest proof of sterling democracy, that it *must* give the lie to its country, that it *must* repudiate all responsibility for a past filled up with misery, tyranny, class oppression, and superstition. Let the French not make an exception to the other democrats; let them not take the responsibility for the doings of their kings and aristocrats of former times. What M. Blanc thinks a disadvantage to English democrats, we think to be a great advantage, that they *must* repudiate the past, and only look to the future.

"'A Frenchman is necessarily a cosmopolite,' says M. Blanc. Yes, in a world ruled over only by French influence, French manners, fashions, ideas, politics. In a world in which every nation has adopted the characteristics of French nationality. But that is exactly what the democrats of other nations will not accept. Quite ready to give up the harshness of their own nationality, they expect the same from the French. They will not be satisfied in the assertion, on the part of the French, that they *are* cosmopolites by the mere fact that they are French, an assertion which amounts to the demand urged upon all others to *become* Frenchmen.

"Compare Germany. Germany is the fatherland of an immense number of inventions—of the printing press, for instance. Germany has produced—and this is recognised upon all hands—a far greater number of generous and cosmopolitic ideas than France and England put together. And Germany, in practice, has always been humiliated, always been deceived in all her hopes. She can tell best what French cosmopolitism has been. Just as France had to complain of the treachery of English policy, Germany experienced an equally treacherous policy on the part of France, from Louis XI down to Louis Philippe. If we were to apply the measure of M. Louis Blanc, the Germans would be the true cosmopolites. *However the German democrats are far from having any such pretensions.*"

Written in December 1847

First published in the *Deutsche-Brüsseler-Zeitung* No. 104, December 30, 1847

Printed according to the newspaper

Published in English for the first time

Frederick Engels

CHARTIST AGITATION

Since the opening of Parliament Chartist agitation has developed enormously. Petitions are being prepared, meetings held and Chartist agents are travelling everywhere. Besides the great National Petition for the People's Charter which this time, it is hoped, will collect four million signatures, two other petitions for the Chartist Land Company have just been submitted to the people; the first, edited by O'Connor and published in *The Northern Star* this week, can be summarised as follows:

"To the Honourable, the Commons of Great Britain and Ireland in Parliament assembled, Gentlemen:

"We, the undersigned, members of the Chartist Land Company and all workmen, considering that excessive speculation in the products of our work, the unlimited competition and the continual increase in the mechanical means of production have everywhere closed outlets for our work;

"that as the mechanical means of production increase, manual labour decreases and workers are sacked;

"that your recent decision about the temporary suspension of work on the railways will throw thousands of workers out of work, which will flood the labour market and will make the employers again reduce the wages already reduced so many times;

"that, nevertheless, we shall ask no more than to live from the products of our work;

"that we reject all poor rates as an insult, serving only to give the capitalists a reserve to throw at any moment on the labour market in order to reduce wages by means of competition between the workers themselves;

"that while manufacturing industry no longer knows how to employ the masses of proletarians which it has produced, agricultural industry still offers a vast field for our work, for it is sure that by the use of labour the yield of the land of our country can be at least quadrupled;

"that therefore we have formed a company for purchasing land whereby each may be enabled to earn a livelihood for himself and family without being at the expense of the parish or of individual charity, and without reducing the wages of other workers by competition.

"In this way we therefore pray you, gentlemen, to pass such a law which releases and affranchises the *Land Company* from paying the Stamp duties, as well as the duty on bricks, timber and other building materials and to pass the *Bill* which will be placed before you to this end."

The Bill has also been drafted by Feargus O'Connor, who is soon going to present it to Parliament.

The second petition demands the return to the people of the uncultivated land that is the property of the parishes. This land, which for thirty years has been sold in blocks to great landowners, ought, as the petition requests, to be divided into small fields to be leased or sold on easy terms of payment to the labourers of this land. This petition was adopted in London at a great meeting where Messrs Harney and Jones, editors of *The Northern Star*, supported it in the absence of O'Connor, who was kept in Parliament. It was also adopted at a large meeting in Norwich where Mr. Jones, who is one of the best speakers in England, again gave it his brilliant and irresistible support.

The National Petition has finally[a] been adopted by a large meeting in London. The principal speakers here were Messrs Keen, Schapper (German) and Harney. The address by the latter, above all, was marked by its democratic strength.

"What is our entire political and social system," he said, "but a gigantic fraud, erected and maintained for the benefit of idlers and impostors.

"Behold the Church! The bishops and archbishops appropriate to themselves enormous salaries while leaving the hard-working clergy only a few pounds a year. Millions of pounds, in the shape of tithes, are taken annually from the people; these tithes were originally destined mainly for the upkeep of the churches and the support of the poor; now there are separate rates for that, and the Church 'sacks' all the tithes. I ask, is not such a Church an organised imposture? (Cheers.)

"Behold our House of Commons, representing not the common people, but the aristocracy and the middle class, and dooming six-sevenths of the adult males of this country to political slavery by denying them the right to vote. Is not this house a legalised imposture? (Loud cheers.)

"Behold those venerable peers who, whilst the wail of distress is heard through the land, can sit, evening after evening, waiting for the Coercion Bill coming up from the Commons. Will any one be good enough to show me the utility of the Hospital of Incurables—will any one attempt to defend this hereditary imposture? (Cheers.)

"Of course, the respect I entertain for that blessed specimen of the 'wisdom of our ancestors'—the monarchy—forbids me to speak in other than the most loyal terms of so interesting a sovereign as Queen Victoria, who regularly, once a year, is delivered of a royal speech and a royal baby. (Laughter.) We have just had the speech, and I see an announcement that in March next we are to have the baby. Her most gracious Majesty expresses great concern for her people's sufferings, admires their patience, and

[a] December 20, 1847.—*Ed.*

promises them another baby—and when it comes to babies, she has never yet promised in vain. (Bursts of laughter.) Then, there is Prince Albert, a celebrated hatmaker, a capital breeder of pigs, and a distinguished Field Marshal and who, for all his services, is paid thirty thousand pounds a year. No, citizens, the monarchy is no imposture." (Laughter and applause.)

The speaker, having contrasted with this picture of official society the picture of the people's sufferings, concluded by demanding the adoption of the National Petition for the Charter. The petition was adopted unanimously. Mr. Duncombe will place it on the table in the House of Commons, when it has toured the country. I shall send you the translation of it as soon as I have obtained a copy.[218]

Written at the end of December 1847

First published in *La Réforme*, December 30, 1847

Printed according to the newspaper

Translated from the French

Published in English for the first time

Karl Marx

WAGES[219]

[A]

Explained already:

1. Wages=price of the commodity.

Hence, generally speaking, wages are determined in the same way as prices.

Human activity=commodity.

Manifestation of life, life activity, appears as mere means; existence divorced from this activity as purpose.

2. As commodity wages depend on competition, demand and supply.

3. The supply itself depends on the cost of production, i.e., on the labour time required for the production of a commodity.

4. Inverse proportion of profits and wages. Opposition of the two classes whose economic existence are profits and wages.[220]

5. Fight for increase or reduction of wages. Workers' associations.

6. Average or normal price of labour; the minimum is valid only for the class of workers, not for the individual. Combinations of workers to maintain wages.

7. Influence on wages of the removal of taxes, protective tariffs, reduction of armies, etc. The minimum is given on average as=the price of the necessary means of subsistence.

[B]

ADDITIONS

I. ATKINSON[a]

1. *Hand-loom weavers*[b] (working 15 hours per day). (Half a million of them.)[221]

---

[a] W. Atkinson, *Principles of Political Economy.— Ed.*

[b] Marx uses the English word.— *Ed.*

"Their distress[a] ... an inevitable condition of a species of labour easily learned, and constantly intruded on and superseded by cheaper means of production. A very short cessation of demand, where the competition for work is so great..., produces a crisis. ...improvements, which, by superseding manual labour more and more, infallibly bring with them in the transition much of *temporary suffering*. Example of the hand-loom cotton weavers of the Dacca district of India; either starved or were thrown back into agricultural labour by the competition of English machinery." (Excerpt from the speech of Dr. Bowring in the House of Commons, July 1835.)[b]

(This example on the passing from one trade to another to be used in respect of the debate on free trade.[222])

2. Something to be said on *population theory*.

3. Influence of changed and expanded division of labour on the fixing of wages.

II. CARLYLE[c]

1. Not only the quantity of wages[a] is to be considered. They vary in quality, depending on the play of circumstances.

2. The advantage of wages: that from now on necessity, interest, haggling, alone link the worker to the employer. No longer anything patriarchal, as in the Middle Ages.

Poor laws, extirpation of vermin, chargeable labourers.[223]

3. The greater part of labour is not skilled labour.[a]

4. The entire theory of Malthus and the economists amounts to saying that it lies with the workers to reduce the demand by not making any children.

III. M'CULLOCH[d]

"The wages earned by the labourer are only the common and ordinary rate of profit to the proprietors of the machine called *man*, thereto [*dazu*][e] a sum to replace the wear and tear of the machines, or, which is the same thing, to supply the place of the old and decayed labourers with new ones" [p. 319].[f]

---

[a] Marx uses the English word.— *Ed.*

[b] Bowring's speech is quoted in W. Atkinson, *Principles of Political Economy*, pp. 36-38.— *Ed.*

[c] Th. Carlyle, *Chartism*.— *Ed.*

[d] J. R. M'Culloch, *The Principles of Political Economy*.— *Ed.*

[e] M'Culloch has here: "exclusive of".— *Ed.*

[f] The words "to replace ... of the machines" and "new ones" are in English in the original.— *Ed.*

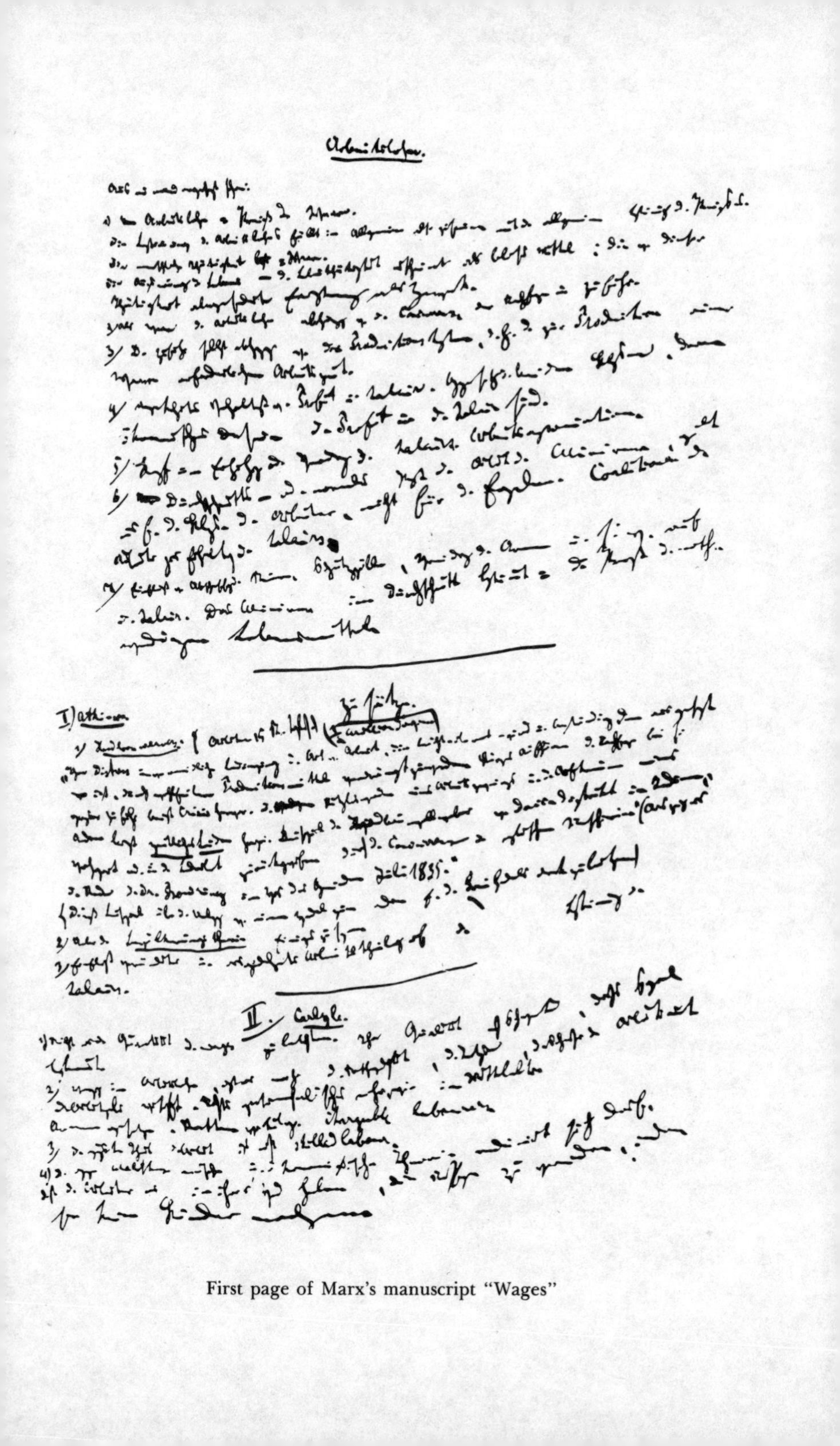

First page of Marx's manuscript "Wages"

IV. JOHN WADE[a]

1. "If the object sought be to render an operative a machine, whereby the greatest quantity of work in a given occupation may be extracted from him, no way so effective as division of labour" [p. 125].

2. A reduction of wages drives the workers either to reduce their spending or to increase their productivity, in factories operated by machines, for instance (and in general), by working longer hours; or, with handicraftsmen, hand-loom weavers, etc., by working harder in the same hour. But since their wages have been reduced precisely because the demand has slackened, they thereby increase the supply at the unfavourable moment. The consequence is that their wages drop still lower, and then the bourgeois come along and say "If the people would only work".

3. Altogether, the general law is that there cannot be *two market prices*, and that the *lower* market price prevails (given equal quality).

Take 1,000 workers of equal skill; 50 are without work; the price is then determined not by the 950 who are employed but by the 50 who are unemployed.

But this law of the *market price* weighs more heavily on the commodity labour than on other commodities, because the worker cannot lay up his commodity in store but must sell his life activity or, deprived of the means of subsistence, must die.

The saleable commodity labour differs from other commodities in particular by its *evanescent nature*, by the impossibility of *accumulating* it, and by the fact that the *supply* cannot be increased or reduced with the same facility as with other products.

4. The humanity of the capitalists consists in buying as much labour as possible at the cheapest price. Agricultural labourers earn more in summer than in winter, although in winter they need more food, fuel and warmer clothing.

5. The abolition of *Sunday*, for example, would be a sheer loss to the workers. The masters seek to reduce wages by leaving them nominally the same but making the workers work a quarter of an hour more, for example, shortening meal times, etc.

6. Wages affected by fashions, the changing seasons, and commercial fluctuations.[224]

7. If the worker, supplanted by the machine, goes into another industry, that is as a rule a *worse* one. He never gets back into his former position.

---

[a] J. Wade, *History of the Middle and Working Classes.—Ed.*

The machine and the division of labour replace dear by cheap labour.

One has suggested to the workers:

1) savings banks;

2) to learn all possible trades (so that when there is a surplus of workers in one industry the same occurs at once in all industries).

8. In times of stagnation:

a) cessation of work;

b) reduction of wages;

c) the same wage, but employment for fewer days in the week.[225]

9. Concerning the combinations of trade,[a] it is to be remarked:

1. The expenses of the workers (the costs). Invention of machines in consequence of the combinations. Other division of labour. Depression of wages. Deplacement[b] of factories to other localities.

2. If they were all to succeed in keeping wages so high that profits were significantly reduced below the average profits of other countries, or so that capital would grow more slowly, the industry of a country would be ruined, and the workers together with the masters even more so.

Although a reduction in taxes does not benefit the workers, a rise in taxation, on the other hand, harms them. The good thing in the rise in taxation in countries with a developed bourgeoisie is that the estate of small farmers and proprietors (craftsmen, etc.) is thereby ruined and thrown into the working class.

Influence of the Irish in England, the Germans in Alsace, on wages.

V. BABBAGE[c]

Truck system.[226]

VI. ANDREW URE[d]

General principle of modern industry: to replace adults by children, skilled workers by unskilled, men by women.

Equalisation of wages: Main feature of modern industry [see pp. 34, 35].

---

[a] The words "combinations of trade" are in English in the original.—*Ed.*

[b] The word "deplacement" is in English in the original.—*Ed.*

[c] Ch. Babbage, *Traité sur l'économie des machines et des manufactures.*—*Ed.*

[d] A. Ure, *Philosophie des manufactures, ou Économie industrielle.*—*Ed.*

VII. ROSSI[a]

Mr. *Rossi* thinks:

The manufacturer only advances to the worker his share in the product because the latter cannot wait for its sale. This is a speculation which has no direct bearing on the production process. If the worker can maintain himself until the product is sold he will, as an *associé*, claim his share in it afterwards.

Hence, wages are not a constituent element of the product as are capital and the land. They are a mere accident, a form of our social condition. Wages do not belong to capital.

Wages are not a factor indispensable to production. In a different organisation of labour they may disappear [see pp. 369, 370].

[VIII.] CHERBULIEZ[b]

1. "...The increase of the productive capital does not necessarily entail an increase of the *approvisionnement* for the workers. Raw materials and machinery can be increased while *approvisionnement* is reduced.

"The price of labour depends on a) the absolute quantity of the productive capital; b) on the proportions of the various elements of capital, two social facts on which the will of the workers cannot exert any influence.

2. "It is not so much the *absolute* consumption of the worker as his *relative* consumption which makes his position either happy or unhappy. Beyond the necessary consumption ... the *value* of what we enjoy is *essentially relative*" [pp. 103-04, 105, 109].

When one speaks of the fall or rise of wages one must never lose sight of the whole world market or of the position of the workers in the various countries.

Egalitarian and other attempts to fix wages justly.

The minimum wage itself changes and constantly falls. Example of spirits.

[IX.] BRAY[c]

SAVINGS BANKS

Triple machine in the hands of despotism and capital.

1. The money flows back into the national bank, which makes profits by lending it back to the capitalists.

---

[a] P. Rossi, *Cours d'économie politique.—Ed.*

[b] A. Cherbuliez, *Riche ou pauvre.—Ed.*

[c] J. F. Bray, *Labour's Wrong and Labour's Remedy.—Ed.*

2. The golden chain by which the government holds a large part of the working class.

3. By this means a new weapon is given into the hands of the capitalists as such [pp. 152, 153].

Once wages have fallen, they never rise to their previous height; absolute and relative wages.

[C]

I. HOW DOES THE GROWTH OF THE PRODUCTIVE FORCES AFFECT WAGES?[227]

[Cf. VI, 3][a]

Machinery: Division of labour.

Labour is simplified. Its cost of production is reduced. It becomes cheaper. The competition among the workers increases.

Passing from one industry to another. On this see Dr. Bowring himself in relation to the hand-loom cotton weavers in the region of Dacca in India, in Parliament 1835.

The new work into which the worker is flung, is worse than the former, more subordinate. Adult labour replaced by children's, men's by women's, more skilled by less skilled.

Either working hours increased or wages reduced.

Competition among workers not only in that one sells himself more cheaply than another, but also in that one does the work of two.

In general, the growth of the productive forces has the following consequences:

a) The position of the worker relative to that of the capitalist worsens, and the value of the things enjoyed is relative. The enjoyments themselves are indeed nothing but social enjoyments, relations, connections.

b) The worker becomes an increasingly one-sided productive force which produces as much as possible in as little time as possible. Skilled labour increasingly transformed into simple labour.

c) Wages become more and more dependent on the world market and the position of the worker increasingly subject to chance.

d) In productive capital the share of machinery and raw materials grows much faster than that of *approvisionnement*. The increase of productive capital is therefore not accompanied by a similar increase of the demand for labour.

---

[a] See this volume, pp. 428-34.—*Ed.*

Wages depend:

α) on the mass of productive capital as a whole;

β) on the proportion of its constituents.

The worker has no influence on either.

(Were it not for the fluctuations of wages, the worker would take no interest at all in the development of civilisation; he would remain stationary.)

In the competition of the workers with the machine it is to be noted that handworkers (e.g., hand-loom cotton weavers) suffer even more than machine workers directly employed in the factory.

Every development of new productive forces is at the same time a weapon against the workers. All improvements in the means of communication, for example, facilitate the competition of workers in different localities and turn local competition into national, etc.

The cheapening of all commodities, which however does not occur in the case of the most immediate means of subsistence, has as a result that the worker wears a collection of rags and his misery displays the colours of civilisation.

II. COMPETITION BETWEEN WORKERS AND EMPLOYERS

α) To determine relative wages it should be noted that one taler for one worker and One taler for One employer do not have the same value. The worker must buy everything worse and dearer. His taler commands neither so many nor such good commodities as that of the employer. The worker must be a *spendthrift* and buy and sell against all economic principles. We must remark in general that we have in mind here only one aspect, *wages* themselves. But the exploitation of the worker begins anew as soon as he exchanges the price for his labour back into other commodities.—*Épicier*,[a] pawnbroker, landlord, *tout le monde l'exploite encore une fois*.[b]

β) The employer, by commanding the means of employment, commands the means of subsistence of the worker, i.e., the latter's life depends on him; just as the worker himself degrades his life activity to a mere means of existence.

γ) The commodity labour has great disadvantages against other commodities. For the capitalist, competition with the workers is a mere question of profit, for the workers it is a question of their existence.

Labour is of a *more evanescent* nature than other commodities. It

[a] Grocer.—*Ed.*

[b] Everybody exploits him over again.—*Ed.*

cannot be accumulated. The *supply* cannot be increased or reduced with the same facility as with other commodities.

δ) Factory regime. Housing legislation. Truck system,[a] where the employer cheats the worker by raising the price of goods while leaving the nominal wage the same.

III. COMPETITION AMONG THE WORKERS THEMSELVES

a) By a general economic law there cannot be *two market prices.* The wages of 1,000 workers of the same skill are determined not by the 950 in employment but by the 50 unemployed. Influence of the *Irish* on the position of the *English workers* and of the Germans on the position of the Alsatian workers.

b) The workers compete with each other not merely by one offering himself more cheaply than another, but by one doing the work of two.

Advantages of the unmarried over the married worker, etc. Competition between workers from villages and towns.

IV. FLUCTUATIONS OF WAGES

They are occasioned by:

1) Changes in fashions.

2) The changing seasons.

3) Fluctuations in trade.

In case of a crisis

α) the workers will limit their spending, or, to increase their productivity, they will either work longer hours or produce more in the same hour. But since their wages have been reduced because the demand for their product has slackened, they increase the unfavourable proportion of the supply to the demand, and then the bourgeois says: if the people would only work. Their wages drop still lower through their overexertion.

β) In times of crisis:

Complete unemployment. Reduction in wages. No change in wages and reduction of the working days.[228]

γ) In all crises the following circular movement relates to the workers:

The employer cannot employ the workers because he cannot sell his product. He cannot sell his product because he has no buyers. He has no buyers because the workers have nothing to offer in exchange

---

[a] Marx uses the English term.—*Ed.*

but their labour, and precisely for that reason they cannot exchange their labour.

δ) When it is a question of a rise in wages, it is to be noted that one must always have in mind the world market and the fact that the rise in wages is ineffectual since workers in other countries are put out of work.

V. MINIMUM WAGE

1. The daily wage the worker takes home is the profit which his machine, his body, yields to its owner. Included in it is the sum necessary to replace the wear and tear[a] of the machine, or, what is the same thing, to replace old, worn-out workers by new ones.

2. It is inherent in the minimum wage that the abolition of Sunday, for example, would be a sheer loss to the worker. He would have to earn his wages in harder conditions. This is the purpose of the brave philanthropists who zealously argue against the observance of Sabbath.

3. Although the minimum wage is determined on average by the price of the most indispensable provisions, it is nevertheless to be remarked:

Firstly: that the minimum is different in different countries, the potato in Ireland, for example.[229]

Secondly: not only that. The minimum itself has a historical movement and sinks always further towards the absolutely lowest level. Example of brandy. Distilled first from draff, then from grain, finally from spirits.

Towards bringing about the really lowest level of the minimum contribute not only

1) the general development of the working machines, the division of labour, the increase in competition among the workers themselves and its liberation from local fetters, but also

2) the growth of taxation and the greater costliness of the state budget, for, although, as we have seen, the abolition of a tax does not benefit the worker, he is harmed by the introduction of any new tax so long as the minimum has not yet fallen to its lowest possible expression, and this is the case with all perturbations and difficulties of civil relations. The growth of taxation, incidentally, brings about the ruin of the small farmers, bourgeois and craftsmen.

Example—after the war of liberation.[230] The progress of industry, which brings with it cheaper products and substitutes.

---

[a] Marx uses the English term.—*Ed.*

3. This minimum tends to become the same in different countries.

4. When wages have once fallen and later rise again, they never rise, however, to their previous level.

In the course of development, there is a double fall in wages:

Firstly: relative, in proportion to the development of general wealth.

Secondly: absolute, since the quantity of commodities which the worker receives in exchange becomes less and less.

5. With the development of large-scale industry time becomes increasingly the measure of the value of commodities, hence also the measure of wages. Simultaneously the production of the commodity labour becomes cheaper and cheaper and costs less and less working time as civilisation progresses.

The peasant still has free time and can earn something on the side. But big industry (not manufacture) does away with this patriarchal situation. Every moment of the worker's life, of his very existence, thus becomes more and more a matter of haggling.

(Here add the following sections:

1. Suggestions for the improvement of the workers' position. Malthus; Rossi etc.; Proudhon; Weitling.

2. Workers' associations.

3. Positive significance of wage labour.)

VI. SUGGESTIONS FOR REMEDIES

1. One of the most popular suggestions is the system of *savings banks*.

We will say nothing at all of the impossibility for most of the workers to save.

The purpose, at least the strictly economic meaning of savings banks, is supposed to be: that by their own foresight and wisdom the workers can equalise the good working times with the bad, i.e., distribute their wages in the cycle through which the industrial movement runs in such a way that they actually never spend more than the minimum wage, that which is indispensable to sustain life.

But we have seen that the fluctuations of wages not only revolutionise the worker, but that without the temporary rise of wages above the minimum he would remain excluded from all advances of production, from public wealth, from civilisation, hence from all possibility of emancipation.

He must therefore turn himself into a bourgeois calculating machine, make thrift into a system, and give misery a stationary, conservative character.

In addition, the savings bank system is a triple machine of despotism:

α) The savings bank is the golden chain by which the government holds a large part of the working class. By it they not only acquire an interest in the preservation of the existing conditions. Not only does it lead to a split between that portion of the working class which takes part in the savings banks and the portion which does not. The workers themselves thus give into the hands of their enemies the weapons to preserve the existing organisation of society which subjugates them.

β) The money flows back into the national bank, this lends it again to the capitalists and both share in the profits and thus, with the money borrowed from the people at a miserable rate of interest—which only by this centralisation becomes a mighty industrial lever—increase their capital, their direct ruling power over the people.

2. Another suggestion, very popular with the bourgeoisie, is *education*, especially comprehensive *industrial education*.

α) We shall not draw attention to the trite contradiction which lies in the fact that modern industry replaces compound labour more and more with simple labour which requires no education; we shall not draw attention to the fact that it throws more and more children from the age of seven upwards behind the machine and turns them into a source of income not only for the bourgeois class but for their own proletarian parents; the factory system frustrates the school laws, example Prussia; nor shall we draw attention to the fact that the education of the mind, if the worker had such an education, has no direct effect at all on his wages, that education is altogether dependent on the conditions of life, and that by moral education the bourgeois understands indoctrination with bourgeois principles, and that, finally, the bourgeois class neither has the means, nor if it had them would it use them, to offer the people a real education.

We confine ourselves to stressing a purely economic viewpoint.

β) The true purpose which education has with the philanthropic economists is this: every worker should be trained in as many industries as possible, so that if by the introduction of new machines or by a change in the division of labour he is thrown out of one industry, he can as easily as possible find employment in another.

Assuming this to be possible:

The consequence would be that if there were a surplus of hands in one industry, this surplus would at once spread to all other industries, and even more than before the reduction of wages in one business would lead directly to a general reduction in wages.

Even as it is, since modern industry simplifies work everywhere and makes it easy to learn, the rise of wages in one industry at once causes an influx of workers into this industry and the reduction of wages will more or less directly assume a general character.

We cannot here, of course, consider all the many minor palliatives which are suggested from the bourgeois side.[a]

3. We must, however, turn to a third suggestion, which has had, and continues to have, very significant practical consequences—the *Malthusian theory*.

This entire theory, in so far as we have to consider it here, amounts to the following:

α) The level of wages depends on the proportion of the hands which offer themselves to the hands which are required.

Wages can rise in two ways.

Either when the capital which sets the labour in motion increases so rapidly that the demand for workers increases more rapidly, in quicker progression, than their supply.

Or, secondly, when the population is growing so slowly that competition among the workers remains weak although productive capital does not grow rapidly.

On one side of this proportion, namely the growth of productive capital, you workers can exert no influence.

But you can on the other side.

You can reduce the supply of workers, i.e., the competition among them, by making as few children as possible.

To reveal the utter stupidity, baseness and hypocrisy of this doctrine, the following is sufficient:

β) (This is to be included in I: How does the growth of the productive forces affect wages?)

Wages rise when the demand for labour grows. This demand grows when the capital grows which sets the labour in motion, i.e., when the productive capital grows.

Here there are two main points to be made:

Firstly: A main condition for the rise of wages is the growth of the productive capital, and its most rapid possible growth. The main condition for the worker to be in a passable position is, therefore, to depress his position in relation to the bourgeois class more and more, to increase as much as possible the power of his opponent, capital. That is, he can only be in a passable position provided he creates and reinforces the power which is hostile to him, his own opposite. On this condition of creating this hostile power, the means of

---

[a] Marx later added: "Pauperism".—*Ed.*

employment flow to him from that power and turn him anew into part of the productive capital and into the lever which increases the latter and hurls it into an accelerated movement of growth.

Incidentally, when one has grasped this relationship of capital and labour, all Fourierist and other attempts at mediation appear in their true absurdity.

Secondly: Having thus explained this crazy relationship, we must add a second, even more important element.

Namely, what does it mean: Growth of productive capital, and in what conditions does it take place?

Growth of capital=accumulation and concentration of capital. In the same measure in which capital is accumulated and concentrated, it leads:

to work on a larger scale and hence to a new division of labour which simplifies the work still more;

then to the introduction of machinery on a larger scale and to the introduction of new machinery.

That means, therefore, that in the measure in which productive capital grows, there grows

the competition among the workers because the division of labour is simplified and every branch of labour is open to everybody.

Competition also grows among them because in the same measure they have to compete with the machines and are thrown out of work by them. By constantly increasing the scale of operations and because the rate of interest tends to fall more and more through the competition among the capitals offered, the concentration and accumulation of productive capital brings about the following:

Small industrial enterprises are ruined and cannot stand up to competition with the big ones. Entire sections of the bourgeois class are thrown down into the working class. The competition among the workers is therefore increased by the ruin of the small industrialists which is fatally linked with the growth of productive capital.

And at the same time as the rate of interest falls, small capitalists formerly not participating in industry directly are forced to become industrial, i.e., to supply big industry with further victims. From this side, too, the working class is enlarged and competition among the workers increased.

While the growth of the productive forces leads to work on a larger scale, momentary overproduction becomes more and more necessary, the world market more and more extensive, and competition more universal. The crises, therefore, become more and more violent. So the workers are given a sudden encouragement to marry and multiply, they are agglomerated and concentrated in large masses, and their wages fluctuate more and more. Every new crisis, therefore, creates directly much bigger competition among the workers.

Speaking generally, the growth of the productive forces, with their more rapid means of communication, accelerated circulation and feverish turnover of capital consists in the fact that in the same time more can be produced, and hence, under the law of competition, more must be produced. That is, production takes place in more and more difficult conditions, and so that competition can be put up with in these conditions, production must take place on an ever growing scale and capital must be concentrated in fewer and fewer hands. And so that this producing on a larger scale may be fruitful, the division of labour and machinery must be constantly and disproportionately extended.

This producing in more and more difficult conditions also extends to the worker as part of capital. He must produce more, in more and more difficult conditions, i.e., for less and less wages and more work, at constantly decreasing production costs. So the minimum itself is constantly being reduced to greater exertions with minimum enjoyment.

The disproportion rises geometrically, not arithmetically.[a]

The growth of the productive forces therefore leads to increased power of big capital, to the machine called the worker becoming more and more simple, to an increase in direct competition among the workers through greater division of labour and use of machinery, through a positive premium being placed on the production of people, through the competition of the ruined sections of the bourgeois class, etc.

We can formulate the matter still more simply:

Productive capital consists of three constituent parts:

1) the raw material which is worked up;

2) the machines and materials such as coal, etc., which are necessary to drive the machines; buildings, etc.;

3) the part of capital intended for the maintenance of the workers.

Given the growth of productive capital, in what proportion do these three constituents stand to each other?

The growth of productive capital is linked with its concentration, and with that the fact that it can only be profitable if it is exploited on an ever larger scale.

A large part of capital will therefore be transformed directly into instruments of labour and will operate as such, and the more the

[a] This sentence was written by Marx in the margin.—*Ed.*

productive forces grow, the larger will be this part of capital which is directly transformed into machinery.

The growth of machinery and of the division of labour has the consequence that in a shorter time far more can be produced. Hence the store of raw materials must grow in the same proportion. In the course of the growth of the productive capital the part of capital transformed into raw materials necessarily increases.

There is still the third part of capital, that which is intended for the maintenance of the workers, i.e., transformed into wages.

In what proportion does the growth of this part of productive capital stand to the two others?

The greater division of labour causes a worker to produce as much as three, four, or five did formerly. Machinery has as a consequence the same proportion on a much larger scale.

It further stands to reason that the growth of the parts of productive capital transformed into machinery and raw materials is not accompanied by a similar growth of the part of productive capital intended for wages. In that case the purpose of the use of machinery and the increased division of labour would, of course, be thwarted. It stands to reason that the part of productive capital intended for wages does not grow in the same measure as the part intended for machinery and raw materials. Moreover, in the same measure in which productive capital grows, i.e., the power of capital as such, in the same measure there increases the disproportion between the capital invested in raw materials and machinery and that spent on wages. That means, therefore, that the part of productive capital intended for wages becomes smaller and smaller in relation to that which acts as machinery and raw material.

After the capitalist has put a larger capital into machinery, he is compelled to spend a larger capital on the purchase of raw materials and the fuels required to drive the machines. But if formerly he employed 100 workers, now he will need perhaps only 50. Otherwise he would have perhaps to double the other parts of his capital again, i.e., make the disproportion still greater. He will therefore dismiss 50, or else the 100 must work for the same price as formerly the 50 did. There are, therefore, redundant workers on the market.

With improved division of labour only the capital for raw material will have to be increased. The place of three workers will perhaps be taken by one.

But take the most favourable case. Let the capitalist expand his enterprise so that he can not only retain the previous number of his workers—and, of course, he does not care a fig about waiting until he can do so—but even increase it; in this case production must have been enormously expanded for it to be possible to retain the same number of workers or even increase it, and the proportion of workers to the productive forces has relatively become infinitely more a disproportion. Overproduction is thereby accelerated, and in the next crisis more workers than ever are unemployed.

It is, therefore, a general law which necessarily arises from the nature of the relation between capital and labour that in the course of the growth of the productive forces the part of productive capital which is transformed into machinery and raw material, i. e., capital as such, increases in disproportion to the part which is intended for wages; i. e., in other words, the workers must share among themselves an ever smaller part of the productive capital in relation to its total mass. Their competition, therefore, becomes more and more violent. In other words: the more productive capital grows, the more, in proportion, the means of employment and the means of subsistence for the workers are reduced, and the more rapidly, in other words, the working population grows in proportion to its means of employment. And this increases in the same measure in which the productive capital as a whole grows.

To compensate the above disproportion it must be enlarged in geometrical proportion, and in order afterwards, in a time of crisis, to readjust it, it is enlarged still more.

This law, which arises simply from the relation of the worker to capital, and which turns even the condition most favourable for him, the rapid growth of productive capital, into an unfavourable one, the bourgeois have changed from a social law into a law of nature by saying that by a law of nature the population grows more rapidly than the means of employment or the means of subsistence.

They fail to understand that the growth of this contradiction is inherent in the growth of productive capital.

We shall return to this later.

Productive force, in particular the social force of the workers themselves, not paid for, is even directed against them.

γ) First absurdity:

We have seen that when productive capital grows—the most favourable case presupposed by the economists—when, therefore, the demand for labour increases relatively, it is in the nature of modern industry and in the nature of capital that the means for the employment of workers do not grow in the same proportion, that the same circumstances which make productive capital grow, make the disproportion between the supply of labour and the demand for it grow still more rapidly, in a word, that the growth of the productive forces makes grow at the same time the disproportion between the number of workers and the means for their employment. This depends neither on the increase of means of subsistence nor on the increase of the population regarded by itself. It follows necessarily from the nature of large-scale industry and the relationship of labour and capital.

If the growth of productive capital progresses only slowly, however, if it remains stationary or even decreases, the number of workers is always too large in proportion to the demand for labour.

In both cases, the most favourable and the most unfavourable, it follows from the relationship of labour to capital, from the nature of capital itself, that the supply of labour will always be too great for the demand for labour.

δ) Leaving aside the nonsense that the entire working class cannot possibly take the decision not to make any children, their condition, on the contrary, makes the sexual instinct their chief pleasure and develops it one-sidedly.

After the bourgeoisie has depressed the existence of the workers to a minimum, it wants in addition to limit their acts of reproduction to a minimum.

ε) That the bourgeoisie, incidentally, does not and cannot mean these phrases and counsels seriously, is clear from the following:

Firstly: By replacing adults with children, modern industry places a veritable premium on the making of children.

Secondly: Big industry constantly requires a reserve army of unemployed workers for times of overproduction. The main purpose of the bourgeois in relation to the worker is, of course, to have the commodity labour as cheaply as possible, which is only possible when the supply of this commodity is as large as possible in relation to the demand for it, i.e., when the overpopulation is the greatest.

Overpopulation is therefore in the interest of the bourgeoisie, and it gives the workers good advice which it knows to be impossible to carry out.

ι) Since capital only increases when it employs workers, the increase of capital involves an increase of the proletariat, and, as we have seen, according to the nature of the relation of capital and labour, the increase of the proletariat must proceed relatively even faster.

κ) The above theory, however, which is also expressed as a law of nature, that population grows faster than the means of subsistence, is the more welcome to the bourgeois as it silences his conscience, makes hard-heartedness into a moral duty and the consequences of society into the consequences of nature, and finally gives him the opportunity to watch the destruction of the proletariat by starvation as calmly as other natural event without bestirring himself, and, on the other hand, to regard the misery of the proletariat as its own fault and to punish it. To be sure, the proletarian can restrain his natural instinct by reason, and so, by moral supervision, halt the law of nature in its injurious course of development.

λ) The poor laws may be regarded as an application of this theory. Extirpation of vermin. Arsenic. Workhouses.[a] Pauperism in general. The treadmill again within civilisation. Barbarism reappears, but created in the lap of civilisation itself and belonging to it; hence leprous barbarism, barbarism as leprosy of civilisation. Workhouses[a] the Bastilles of the workers. Separation of man and wife.

4. We will now briefly speak of those who want to improve the condition of the workers by a different way of fixing wages.

Proudhon.

5. Finally, among the remarks which philanthropic economists have made on wages, yet another view must be mentioned.

α) Among other economists *Rossi*, in particular, has expounded the following:

The manufacturer only advances to the worker his share in the product because the worker cannot wait for its sale. If the worker could maintain himself until the product was sold he would, as an *associé*, afterwards claim his share, as is the case between the actual and the industrial capitalist. That the worker's share has the particular form of wages is an accident, the result of a speculation, of a specific act which takes place alongside the production process and does not form any necessary constituent element of it. Wages are merely an accidental form of our social conditions. They do not necessarily belong to capital. They are not an indispensable factor of production. They can disappear under another organisation of society.

β) This whole trick amounts to the following: If the workers possessed enough accumulated labour, i.e., enough capital, not to have to live directly on the sale of their labour, the wage form would end. That is, if all workers were at the same time capitalists; which is to presuppose and preserve capital without the contrast of wage labour without which it cannot exist.

γ) Nevertheless, the following admission is to be observed: Wages are no accidental form of bourgeois production, but the whole of

---

[a] Marx uses the English word.—*Ed.*

bourgeois production is a passing historical form of production. All its relationships, capital as well as wages, rent, etc., are transitory and can be abolished at a certain point of development.

VII. WORKERS' ASSOCIATIONS

An element in the population theory was that it is supposed to lessen the competition among workers. The associations, by contrast, have the purpose of *removing* it and replacing it by *union* of workers.

The economists are right when they remark against the associations:

1. The costs which they cause the workers are mostly greater than the rise in the gains they want to get. In the long run they cannot withstand the laws of competition. These combinations bring about new machines, a new division of labour, removal from one place of production to another. In consequence of all this a reduction of wages.

2. If the combinations were to succeed in keeping the price of labour so high in one country that profits fell significantly in relation to the average profit in other countries, or so that capital was held up in its growth, stagnation and recession of industry would be the consequence, and the workers would be ruined together with their masters. For that, as we have seen, is the condition of the worker. His condition deteriorates by leaps and bounds when productive capital grows, and he is ruined from the start when it declines or remains stationary.

3. All these objections of the bourgeois economists are, as we have said, correct, but only correct from their point of view.[231] If in the associations it really were a matter only of what it appears to be, namely the fixing of wages, if the relationship between labour and capital were eternal, these combinations would be wrecked on the necessity of things. But they are the means of uniting the working class, of preparing for the overthrow of the entire old society with its class contradictions. And from this standpoint the workers are right to laugh at the clever bourgeois schoolmasters who reckon up to them what this civil war is costing them in fallen, injured, and financial sacrifices. He who wants to beat his adversary will not discuss with him the costs of the war. And how far the workers are from such mean-spiritedness is proved to the economists by the very fact that the best-paid workers form the most combinations and that the workers spend all they can scrape from their wages on forming

political and industrial associations and meeting [the costs] of this movement. And if in their moments of philanthropy Messrs the bourgeois and their economists are so gracious as to allow in the minimum wage, that is, in the minimum life, a little tea, or rum, or sugar and meat, it must by contrast appear to them as shameful as incomprehensible that the workers reckon in this minimum a little of the costs of war against the bourgeoisie and that out of their revolutionary activity they even make the maximum of their enjoyment of life.

VIII. POSITIVE ASPECT OF WAGE LABOUR

Before we conclude, let us draw attention to the positive aspect of wage labour.

α) If one says "positive aspect of wage labour" one says "positive aspect of capital", of large-scale industry, of free competition, of the world market, and I do not need to explain to you in detail how without these production relations neither the means of production—the material means for the emancipation of the proletariat and the foundation of a new society—would have been created, nor would the proletariat itself have taken to the unification and development through which it is really capable of revolutionising the old society and itself. *Equalisation* of wages.

β) Let us take wages themselves in the essence of their evil, that my activity becomes a commodity, that I become utterly and absolutely for sale.

Firstly: thereby everything patriarchal falls away, since haggling, purchase and sale remain the only connection, and the money relationship the sole relationship between employer and workers.

Secondly: the halo of sanctity is entirely gone from all relationships of the old society, since they have dissolved into pure money relationships.

Likewise, all so-called higher kinds of labour, intellectual, artistic, etc., have been turned into articles of commerce and have thereby lost their old sanctity. What a great advance it was that the entire regiment of clerics, doctors, lawyers, etc., hence religion, law, etc., ceased to be judged by anything but their commercial value.[a]

(*Thirdly*: since labour has become a commodity and as such subject to free competition, one seeks to produce it as cheaply as possible, i.e., at the lowest possible production cost. All physical labour has

[a] Here the manuscript has an insertion: "National, class, property relations."—*Ed.*

thereby become infinitely easy and simple for the future organisation of society.— To be put in general form.)

Thirdly: as the workers realised through the general saleability that everything was separable, dissoluble from itself, they first became free of their subjection to a given relationship. The advantage both over payment in kind and over the way of life prescribed purely by the (feudal) estate is that the worker can do what he likes with his money.

Written at the end of December 1847

First published in Russian in the journal *Sotsialisticheskoye khozyaistvo*, 1924 and in German in the journal *Unter dem Banner des Marxismus*, 1925

Printed according to the manuscript

Published in English for the first time

Frederick Engels

THE "SATISFIED" MAJORITY.—GUIZOT'S SCHEME OF "REFORM".—QUEER NOTIONS OF M. GARNIER-PAGÈS.—DEMOCRATIC BANQUET AT CHÂLON.—SPEECH OF M. LEDRU-ROLLIN.—A DEMOCRATIC CONGRESS.—SPEECH OF M. FLOCON.—THE *RÉFORME* AND THE *NATIONAL*

The French Chambers are now open, and we shall very soon have the pleasure of seeing what effect the Reform agitation has had upon the 225 "satisfied" members of the majority.[a] We shall see whether they will be satisfied, too, with the manner in which Guizot has exposed France in the Swiss question to the ridicule of all Europe. Why, this fat, corrupting and corrupted stock-jobbing, swindling, blood-sucking, and cowardly majority, are the very men to swallow down even that—to say "amen" to the trick which Palmerston, in return for the Spanish marriages, played on his worthy colleague Guizot[232]—to declare that never was France so great, so glorious, so respected, so "satisfied"—as at this very moment.

And it is at this very moment that all the papers of Paris, from the *Débats*[b] to the *Réforme*, discuss, as openly as can be done under the circumstances, the eventuality consequent upon the death of Louis Philippe. The *Débats* afraid of seeing the majority split itself up, warns them every day that this inevitable event, whenever it takes place, will be the signal for the general rendezvous of all political parties; that "republicanism", "communism", "anarchism", "terrorism", and so forth, will then break from their subterraneous caverns, to spread desolation, horror and destruction; that France will be lost—liberty, safety, property will be lost, unless the friends of order (M. Guizot and Co., of course) keep them down with a strong hand; that this perilous moment may occur any day; and that if M. Guizot is not supported in office, all will be lost. The other papers, the *Presse*,

[a] See this volume, pp. 216-17.—*Ed.*

[b] *Journal des Débats politiques et littéraires.—Ed.*

the *Constitutionnel*, the *Siècle*, on the contrary, say that quite the reverse will take place, that all the horrors of a bloody revolution will overrun the country, unless the abominable corruptor, Guizot, shall, at the moment of the king's death, have been replaced by their respective political heroes, by M. de Girardin, M. Thiers, or M. O. Barrot. The Radical papers discuss the question from another point of view, as we shall see by and by.

Thus, even the *Débats* agrees indirectly that "satisfied" France only awaits the proper moment for proving her dissatisfaction, in a manner which the frightened *bourgeois* imagination of the *Débats* depicts most ludicrously to its terrified reason. This, however, does not matter to the "satisfied" two hundred and twenty-five. They have a logic of their own. If the people are satisfied, then there is no reason for a change of system. If they are dissatisfied, why, then, their very dissatisfaction is a reason to stick more to the system; for if only one inch was abandoned, there would be a sudden eruption of all the horrors of revolution. Do whatever you like, these *bourgeois* will always draw the conclusion from it that they are the best rulers of the country.

Nevertheless, Guizot will give a small bit of reform. He will add to the electoral list the "capacities", that is, all persons possessing a university degree, lawyers, doctors, and other such humbugs. A glorious reform, indeed. But this will suffice to disarm the "Progressive Conservatives", or, as they call themselves now—for, in want of something else to do, they change names every quarter—the Conservative opposition. And it will be a ready stroke for M. Thiers, who, while sending his second, M. Duvergier de Hauranne, on a Reform banquetting errand, slily prepared his reform-plan, with which he was to surprise the Chambers, and which was equally the same as the one now to be proposed by his rival, Guizot.

There will be a deal of crying, shouting, and noise-making generally in the Chambers; but I hardly think M. Guizot has anything serious to apprehend from his faithful two hundred and twenty-five.

So much for the official world. In the meantime the Reform banquets and the polemic between the *National* and the *Réforme* have continued. The allied oppositions, that is, the left centre (M. Thiers' party), the left (M. Odilon Barrot's party) and the "sensible Radicals" (the *National*), had the banquets of Castres, Montpellier, Neubourg, and others; the ultra-Democrats (the *Réforme*), had the banquet of Châlon. The chief speaker of the banquets of Montpellier and Neubourg was M. Garnier-Pagès, brother of the well-known democrat of that name,[a] deceased a few years ago. But M. Garnier-Pagès, the younger, is far from being like his brother; he totally lacks that energy, that courage and never-compromising spirit which secured so prominent a position to the deceased leader of French Democracy. At Neubourg, M. Garnier-Pagès, the younger, came out with assertions proving him to be entirely ignorant of the actual state of society, and consequently of the means of improving it. While all modern democracy is based upon the great fact, that modern society is irreparably divided into two classes—the *bourgeoisie*, or possessors of all means of production and all produce, and the proletarians, or possessors of nothing but their labour to live upon; that the latter class is socially and politically oppressed by the former; while the acknowledged tendency of modern Democrats in all countries is to make political power pass from the middle classes to the working classes, these latter constituting the immense majority of the people—in the face of all these facts, M. Garnier boldly asserts that the division of the people into middle classes and working classes does in reality not exist, that it is a mischievous invention of M. Guizot's got up to divide the people; that in spite of Guizot he recognises that all Frenchmen *are* equal—that they all participate in the same life, and that he recognises in France none but *French citizens*! According to M. Garnier-Pagès, then, the monopolising of all instruments of production in the hands of the *bourgeoisie*, which abandons the proletarians to the tender mercies of the economical law of wages, reducing the share of the working men to the lowest level of food, is an invention of M. Guizot's too! According to him, the whole of that desperate struggle now going on in all civilised countries of the world, between Labour and Capital, a struggle the different phases of which are marked by coalitions, trades' unions, murders, riots, and bloody insurrections—a struggle whose reality is testified by the death of the proletarians shot at Lyons, at Preston, at Langenbielau, at Prague,[233] this struggle has been carried on upon no better grounds than a lying assertion of a French professor! What else do the words of M. Garnier-Pagès mean but this? "Let the capitalists continue to monopolise all powers of production—let the working man continue to live upon the merest pittance, but give him, as a compensation for his suffering, the *title* of citizen!" Ay, M. Pagès would under certain circumstances, and with certain restrictions, perhaps, consent to give the people the suffrage; but let them never think of profiting by the gift by passing measures which

[a] Etienne Joseph Louis Garnier-Pagès.—*Ed.*

would essentially alter the actual mode of production and distribution of wealth—which would, in course of time, give to the entire people the command of the productive powers of the country, and do away with all individual "employers"! The *Réforme* was perfectly right in styling this honourable gentleman a *bourgeois radical.*[a]

The Ultra-Democrats had, as I said before, only one banquet, but it was a bumper, and worth a dozen of the coalition party. More than two thousand citizens sat down to dinner at Châlon-sur-Saône. The *National* had been invited, but very significantly had not come. The men of the *Réforme*, accordingly, had it all their own way. M. Ledru-Rollin, who had been designated by the *National* as the chief of the ultra-democratic party, here, accepted this position. He explained his position and the position of his party, by relating in a brilliant abstract, the different phases of French democracy since 1789. He then justified himself against the attacks of the *National*, attacked that paper in turn, and proposed a jury of Democrats to be nominated from all parts of France—one-half by either party—to decide between the *Réforme* and the *National*.

> And now (he said), after having settled this home affair, would it not be a good thing if the French democracy entered into relation with the other democracies? There is at this moment a great movement going on in Europe amongst all the disinherited, who suffer by heart or by hunger. This is the moment to console them, to strengthen them, and to enter into communion with them.... Let us, then, hold a congress of Democrats of all nations, now, when the congress of kings has failed!... There is one republic in Europe, which just now has secured in its own territory the ascendancy of democracy—there is Switzerland, a country worthy of seeing the Democrats of all nations upon its free soil!... And thus, citizens, let me conclude, by coupling to my toast: "To the Unity of the French Revolution", that other one, "The Union of all Democracies".

This speech excited loud applause, and it merited it. We heartily rejoice in M. Ledru-Rollin's oratorial success at Châlon, but at the same time, must protest against an unguarded expression, which, we are sure, has been said without intention to hurt. M. Ledru-Rollin says, that the moment has arrived for French Democrats to console and to strengthen the suffering working men of other nations. The Democrats of *no country*, we are sure, want consolation from whomsoever it be. They admire the revolutionary pride of French Democrats, but they take for themselves the right to be quite as proud and independent. The four millions of English Chartists certainly are strong enough to do their own work for themselves. Glad as we are to see the French democracy take up with enthusiasm

---

[a] The reference is to the leading article in *La Réforme*, December 17, 1847.—*Ed.*

the idea of a Democratic Congress, and an alliance of all democracies, we expect, before all things, a perfect reciprocity and equality. Any alliance, which should not recognise this equality as its foundation, would itself be anti-democratic. We know, however, too well the profoundly democratic sentiments of the men of the *Réforme* to doubt of their perfectly agreeing with us; we only wish them to drop for the interest of our common cause, certain expressions, which far from expressing their real sentiments, are an inheritance from the time when the *National* alone represented the French Democracy.

At the same banquet, M. Flocon spoke to the toast:—"The Rights of Man and of the Citizen". He read the declaration of rights of the National Convention,[234] which he declared to be, up to this day, the faithful abstract of true Democratic principles. To this, what he called the true French principle, he opposed the present system of moneyocracy, which places man upon a lower level than even cattle, because man is overabundant, and costs more than he gives in nature when his labour is not required. This system, from the country in which it first arose, he called the English system.

> But lo, he said, while the English principle is introduced into the fatherland of the revolution, the English people themselves strive to throw its yoke off their shoulders, and write upon their banners the glorious motto:—"Liberty, Equality, Fraternity!" Thus, by one of those painful turns, of which history offers more than one example, the very nation which first gave truth to the world, fallen back into darkness and ignorance, would soon be obliged to ask from its neighbours the revolutionary traditions which itself could not conserve. Shall it ever come thus far with us? No, never, as long as there are Democrats like you, and meetings like this! No, we never will prop up the worm-eaten frame of those English institutions, which the English themselves will no longer support! (No, no!) Well then, to your tents, O Israel! Every one of you rally round his standard! Every one for his faith! Here, on our side, Democracy with her twenty-five millions of proletarians to free, whom she greets with the names of citizens, brothers, equal and free men; there the bastard-opposition, with her monopolies and aristocracy of capital! They speak of reducing the qualification by one-half; we, we proclaim the rights of man and of the citizen! (Loud and long-continued applause, which ended by the whole meeting singing the *Chant du départ.*[235])

We regret not to have room for giving more of the speeches delivered at this splendid and thoroughly Democratic banquet.

At last, the *Réforme* has forced the *National* to enter into a *polemic.* The former journal, in declaring its adhesion to the principles announced by M. Garnier-Pagès, at the Montpellier banquet, in a speech on the French revolution, at the same time disputed the right of men, like M. Garnier, who had sacrificed the interests of Democracy to M. Odilon Barrot and the middle-class opposition, to act as the representatives of the principles of the Revolution.[a] This, at last, brought out a reply from the *National*, in which Ledru-Rollin in his turn was attacked. The principal points of accusation against the *National* were: 1st. Its support of the bastilles around Paris, by which the inheritance of the revolution was placed under the control of twelve hundred pieces of cannon.[236] 2nd. Its silence last year, upon a pamphlet of M. Carnot,[b] in which he engaged the Democrats to join the Left Centre and the Left, to get them into office as soon as possible, to drop for the moment the Republican principle, and to agitate for an extension of the Suffrage within the limits of the Charter.[237] M. Garnier-Pagès, the younger, had about the same time announced similar principles; the pamphlet declared itself to be the expression of the opinion not of an individual, but of a party in the Chamber. The *Réforme* attacked both M. Garnier's speech and M. Carnot's (son of the celebrated member of the Convention and Republican minister of war[c]) pamphlet, and tried to provoke the *National* to a declaration.[d] But the *National* remained silent. The *Réforme* rightly declared that the policy proposed by both deputies would tend to nothing but to place the Democratic party wholly under the control of MM. Thiers and Barrot, and break it up entirely as a distinct party. 3rd. The *National* following up in practice during the Reform banquet agitation the policy proposed by M. Carnot. 4th. Its virulent and calumniating attacks upon the Communists, while proposing at the same time no practicable or effective remedy for the misery of the working people.

The dispute has been going on for a week at least. At last the *National* retired from the contest, after having conducted it in a very improper manner. It has been regularly beaten; but, in order to mask its defeat, it finally accepted M. Ledru's proposal of a Democratic jury.

We can only declare our full adhesion to the part the *Réforme* has taken in this affair. It has saved the honour, independence, and the strength of French Democracy as a distinct party. It has maintained the principles of the Revolution, which were endangered by the course pursued by the *National*. It has asserted the rights of the working classes in opposition to middle-class encroachments. It has unmasked these *bourgeois* radicals—who would make the people

[a] The reference is to the leading articles in *La Réforme*, December 15, 17 and 19, 1847.—*Ed.*

[b] L. H. Carnot, *Les radicaux et la charte*.—*Ed.*

[c] Lazare Nicolas Carnot.—*Ed.*

[d] The reference is to the leading article in *La Réforme*, December 20, 1847.—*Ed.*

believe that no class oppression exists—who will not see the frightful civil war of class against class in modern society,—and who have nothing but vain words for the working people. The *Réforme*, by keeping up this contest, until it has succeeded in forcing its haughty rival to break silence, to wave, to retract, to explain, and at last to withdraw,—the *Réforme*, we say, has well merited of Democracy.

Written at the beginning of January 1848

Reprinted from the newspaper

First published in *The Northern Star* No. 533, January 8, 1848 with an editorial note: "From Our Paris Correspondent"

Frederick Engels

[THE COERCION BILL FOR IRELAND AND THE CHARTISTS][238]

The Irish Coercion Bill came into force last Wednesday.[a] The Lord Lieutenant[b] was not slow in taking advantage of the despotic powers with which this new law invests him; the act has been applied all over the counties of Limerick and Tipperary and to several baronies in the counties of Clare, Waterford, Cork, Roscommon, Leitrim, Cavan, Longford and *King's County*.[239]

It remains to be seen what the effect of this odious measure will be. In this connection we already have the opinion of the class in whose interests the measure was taken, namely, the Irish landowners. They announce to the world in their organs that the measure will have no effect whatsoever. And in order to achieve this a whole country is being placed in a state of siege! To achieve this nine-tenths of the Irish representatives have deserted their country!

This is a fact. The desertion has been a general one. During the discussion of the Bill the O'Connell family itself became divided: John and Maurice, two of the deceased "Liberator's"[c] sons, remained faithful to their homeland, whereas their cousin,[d] Morgan O'Connell, not only voted for the Bill, but also spoke in its support on several occasions. There were only eighteen members who voted for the outright rejection of the Bill, and only twenty supported the amendment put forward by Mr. Wakley, the Chartist member for a borough on the outskirts of London, who demanded that the

[a] December 29, 1847.—*Ed.*

[b] Earl of Clarendon.—*Ed.*

[c] Daniel O'Connell.—*Ed.*

[d] Read "brother", a mistake in *La Réforme*.—Ed.

Coercion Bill should also be accompanied by measures aimed at reducing the causes of the crimes which it was proposed to repress. And among these eighteen and twenty voters there were also four or five English Radicals and two Irishmen representing English boroughs, meaning that out of the hundred members which Ireland has in Parliament there were only a dozen who put up serious opposition to the Bill.

This was the first discussion on an important question affecting Ireland which had been held since the death of O'Connell. It was to decide who would take the place of the great agitator in leading Ireland. Up to the opening of Parliament Mr. John O'Connell had been tacitly acknowledged in Ireland as his father's successor. But it soon became evident after the debate had begun that he was not capable of leading the party and, what is more, that he had found a formidable rival in Feargus O'Connor. This democratic leader about whom Daniel O'Connell said, "We are happy to make the English Chartists a present of Mr. F. O'Connor", put himself at the head of the Irish party in a single bound. It was he who proposed the outright rejection of the Coercion Bill; it was he who succeeded in rallying all the opposition behind him; it was he who opposed each clause, who held up the voting whenever possible; it was he who in his speeches summed up all the arguments of the opposition against the Bill; and finally it was he who for the first time since 1835 reintroduced the motion for *Repeal of the Union*,[240] a motion which none of the Irish members would have put forward.

The Irish members accepted this leader with a bad grace. As simple Whigs in their heart of hearts they fundamentally detest the democratic energy of Mr. O'Connor. He will not allow them to go on using the campaign for repeal as a means for overthrowing the Tories in favour of the Whigs and to forget the very word "repeal" when the latter come to power. But the Irish members who support repeal cannot possibly do without a leader like O'Connor and, although they are trying to undermine his growing popularity in Ireland, they are obliged to submit to his leadership in Parliament.

When the parliamentary session is over O'Connor will probably go on a tour of Ireland to revive the agitation for repeal and to found an Irish Chartist party. There can be no doubt that if O'Connor is successful in doing this he will be the leader of the Irish people in less than six months. By uniting the democratic leadership of the three kingdoms[a] in his hands, he will occupy a position which no agitator, not even O'Connell, has held before him.

---

[a] England, Scotland and Ireland.—*Ed.*

We will leave it to our readers to judge the importance of this future alliance between the peoples of the two islands. British democracy will advance much more quickly when its ranks are swelled by two million brave and ardent Irish, and poverty-stricken Ireland will at last have taken an important step towards her liberation.

Written on January 4, 1848

First published in *La Réforme*, January 8, 1848

Printed according to the newspaper

Translated from the French

Frederick Engels

FEARGUS O'CONNOR AND THE IRISH PEOPLE[241]

The first issue of *The Northern Star* for 1848 contains an address to the Irish people by *Feargus O'Connor*, the well-known leader of the English Chartists and their representative in Parliament. This address deserves to be read from beginning to end and carefully considered by every democrat, but our restricted space prevents us from reproducing it in full.

We would, however, be remiss in our duty if we were to pass it over in silence. The consequences of this forceful appeal to the Irish people will very soon be strongly felt and seen. Feargus O'Connor, himself of Irish descent, a Protestant and for over ten years a leader and main pillar of the great labour movement in England, must henceforth be regarded as the virtual chief of the Irish Repealers[242] and advocates of reform. His speeches in the House of Commons against the recently published disgraceful Irish Coercion Bill[243] have given him the first claim to this status, and the subsequently continued agitation for the Irish cause shows that Feargus O'Connor is just the man Ireland needs.

O'Connor is indeed seriously concerned about the well-being of the millions in Ireland. Repeal[a]—the abolition of the Union, that is, the achievement of an independent Irish Parliament—is not an empty word, not a pretext for obtaining posts for himself and his friends and for making profitable private business transactions.

In his address he shows the Irish people that Daniel O'Connell, that political juggler, led them by the nose and deceived them for thirteen years by means of the word "Repeal".

He shows in its true light the conduct of John O'Connell, who has taken up his father's political heritage and who like his father is prepared to sacrifice millions of credulous Irishmen for the sake of

[a] Here and below Engels uses the English term.—*Ed.*

his personal ventures and interests. All O'Connell's speeches at the Dublin Conciliation Hall[244] and all his hypocritical protestations and beautiful phrases will not obliterate the disrepute he has brought upon himself earlier and in particular now in the House of Commons during the debates on the Irish Coercion Bill.

The Irish people must and will see how things stand, and then it will kick out the entire gang of so-called Repealers, who under cover of this cloak laugh up their sleeves and in their purses and John O'Connell, the fanatical papist and political rogue, will be kicked out first of all.

If this were all the address contained, we should not have especially mentioned it.

But it is of much wider importance. For Feargus O'Connor speaks in it not only as an Irishman but also, and primarily, as an English democrat, as a Chartist.

With a lucidity which cannot escape even the most obtuse mind, O'Connor shows that the Irish people must fight with all their might and in close association with the English working classes and the Chartists in order to win the six points of the People's Charter—annual parliaments, universal suffrage, vote by ballot, abolition of the property qualification for members of Parliament, payment of M.P.s and the establishment of equal electoral districts. Only after these six points are won will the achievement of the Repeal have any advantages for Ireland.

Furthermore O'Connor points out that justice for Ireland has already been demanded earlier by the English workers in a petition which received $3^1/_2$ million signatures,[245] and that now the English Chartists have again protested against the Irish Coercion Bill in numerous petitions and that the oppressed classes in England and Ireland must at last fight together and conquer together or continue to languish under the same oppression and live in the same misery and dependence on the privileged and ruling capitalist class.

There can be no doubt that henceforth the mass of the Irish people will unite ever more closely with the English Chartists and will act with them according to a common plan. As a result the victory of the English democrats, and hence the liberation of Ireland, will be hastened by many years. That is the significance of O'Connor's address to the Irish people.

Written at the beginning of January 1848

First published in *Deutsche-Brüsseler-Zeitung* No. 3, January 9, 1848

Printed according to the newspaper

Karl Marx

SPEECH ON THE QUESTION OF FREE TRADE

DELIVERED TO THE DEMOCRATIC ASSOCIATION OF BRUSSELS AT ITS PUBLIC MEETING OF JANUARY 9, 1848[246]

Gentlemen,—The Repeal of the Corn Laws[247] in England is the greatest triumph of Free Trade in the nineteenth century. In every country where manufacturers discuss Free Trade, they have in mind chiefly Free Trade in corn or raw material generally. To burden foreign corn with protective duties is infamous, it is to speculate on the hunger of the people.

Cheap food, high wages,[a] for this alone the English Free Traders[b] have spent millions, and their enthusiasm has already infected their Continental brethren. And, generally speaking, all those who advocate Free Trade do so in the interests of the working class.[c]

But, strange to say, the people for whom cheap food is to be procured at all costs are very ungrateful. Cheap food is as ill reputed in England as is cheap government in France. The people see in these self-sacrificing gentlemen, in Bowring, Bright & Co., their worst enemies and the most shameless hypocrites.

Everyone knows that in England the struggle between Liberals and Democrats takes the name of the struggle between Free Traders and Chartists. Let us see how the English Free Traders have proved to the people the good intentions that animate them.

---

[a] In the 1848 French edition these words are repeated in English after the French.—*Ed.*

[b] In the 1848 French edition, here and below, as a rule, the English is used, though the French "libre-échangiste" also occurs sometimes.— *Ed.*

[c] In the 1848 French edition the end of this phrase reads: "to ease the condition of the working class".—*Ed.*

DISCOURS

SUR LA QUESTION

DU LIBRE ÉCHANGE,

PRONONCÉ A

L'ASSOCIATION DÉMOCRATIQUE

DE BRUXELLES,

Dans la Séance Publique du 9 Janvier 1848.

PAR CHARLES MARX.

Imprimé aux frais de l'Association Démocratique.

Messieurs,

L'abolition des lois céréales en Angleterre est le plus grand triomphe que le libre échange ait remporté au 19me siécle. Dans tous les pays où les fabricants parlent de libre échange ils ont principalement en vue le libre échange des grains et des matières premières en général. Frapper de droits protecteurs les grains étrangers, c'est infâme, c'est spéculer sur la famine des peuples.

First page of a separate edition of Marx's "Speech on the Question of Free Trade"
(Brussels, February 1848)

This is what they said to the factory hands,—

"The duty on corn is a tax upon wages; this tax you pay to the landlords, those medieval aristocrats; if your position is a wretched one, it is so only on account of the high price of the most indispensable articles of food."

The workers in turn asked of the manufacturers,—

"How is it that in the course of the last thirty years, while our commerce and manufacture[a] has immensely increased, our wages have fallen far more rapidly, in proportion, than the price of corn has gone up?

"The tax which you say we pay the landlords is about three pence a week per worker. And yet the wages of the hand-loom weaver fell, between 1815 and 1843, from 28s. per week to 5s., and the wages of the power-loom weaver, between 1823 and 1843, from 20s. per week to 8s.

"And during the whole of the time that portion of the tax which you say we pay the landlord has never exceeded three pence. And, then, in the year 1834, when bread was very cheap and business lively, what did you tell us? You said, 'If you are poor, it is only because you have too many children, and your marriages are more productive than your labor!'

"These are the very words you spoke to us, and you set about making new Poor Laws, and building workhouses, those bastilles of the proletariat."

To this the manufacturers replied,—

"You are right, worthy laborers: it is not the price of corn alone, but competition of the hands among themselves as well, which determines wages.

"But just bear in mind the circumstance that our soil consists of rocks and sandbanks only. You surely do not imagine that corn can be grown in flower-pots! If, instead of wasting our labor and capital upon a thoroughly sterile soil, we were to give up agriculture, and devote ourselves exclusively to commerce and manufacture, all Europe would abandon its factories, and England would form one huge factory town, with the whole of the rest of Europe for its agricultural districts."

While thus haranguing his own workingmen, the manufacturer is interrogated by the small tradesmen, who exclaim,—

"If we repeal the Corn Laws, we shall indeed ruin agriculture; but, for all that, we shall not compel other nations to give up their own

[a] The 1848 French edition has here and below "industry" instead of "commerce and manufacture".—*Ed.*

factories, and buy our goods. What will the consequences be? I lose my customers in the country, and the home market is destroyed."

The manufacturer turns his back upon the workingmen and replies to the shopkeeper,—

"As to that, you leave it to us! Once rid of the duty on corn, we shall import cheaper corn from abroad. Then we shall reduce wages at the very time when they are rising in the countries where we get our corn. Thus in addition to the advantages which we already enjoy we shall have lower wages, and, with all these advantages, we shall easily force the Continent to buy of us."

But now the farmers and agricultural laborers join in the discussion.

"And what, pray, is to become of us? Are we to help in passing a sentence of death upon agriculture, when we get our living by it? Are we to let the soil be torn from beneath our feet?"

For all answer the Anti-Corn Law League[248] contented itself with offering prizes for the three best essays upon the wholesome influence of the Repeal of the Corn Laws on English agriculture.

These prizes were carried off by Messrs Hope, Morse, and Greg, whose essays[a] were distributed broadcast throughout the agricultural districts.[b] One of the prize essayists devotes himself to proving that neither the tenant farmer nor the agricultural laborer would lose by the repeal of the Corn Laws, and that the landlord alone would lose.

"The English tenant farmer," he exclaims, "need not fear repeal, because no other country can produce such good corn so cheaply as England. Thus, even if the price of corn fell, it would not hurt you, because this fall would only affect rent, which would go down, while the profit of capital and the wages of labor remain stationary."

The second prize essayist, Mr. Morse, maintains, on the contrary, that the price of corn will rise in consequence of repeal. He is at infinite pains to prove that protective duties have never been able to secure a remunerative price for corn.

In support of his assertion he quotes the fact that, whenever foreign corn has been imported, the price of corn in England has gone up considerably, and that when little corn has been imported the price has fallen extremely. This prize-winner forgets that the importation was not the cause of the high price, but that the high price was the cause of the importation. In direct contradiction of his

---

[a] *The Three Prize Essays on Agriculture and the Corn Law.* Published by the National Anti-Corn Law League.—*Ed.*

[b] The 1848 French edition has: "whose books were circulated in the rural districts in thousands of copies."—*Ed.*

colleague he asserts that every rise in the price of corn is profitable to both the tenant farmer and laborer, but does not benefit the landlord.

The third prize essayist, Mr. Greg, who is a large manufacturer and whose work is addressed to the large tenant farmers, could not afford to echo such silly stuff. His language is more scientific.

He admits that the Corn Laws can increase rent only by increasing the price of corn, and that they can raise the price of corn only by inducing the investment of capital upon land of inferior quality, and this is explained quite simply.

In proportion as population increases, it inevitably follows, if foreign corn cannot be imported, that less fruitful soil must be placed under cultivation. This involves more expense and the product of this soil is consequently dearer. There being a demand for all the corn thus produced,[a] it will all be sold. The price for all of it will of necessity be determined by the price of the product of the inferior soil.[b] The difference between this price and the cost of production upon soil of better quality constitutes the rent paid for the use of the better soil.[c]

If, therefore, in consequence of the repeal of the Corn Laws, the price of corn falls, and if, as a matter of course, rent falls along with it, it is because inferior soil will no longer be cultivated. Thus the reduction of rent must inevitably ruin a part of the tenant farmers.

These remarks were necessary in order to make Mr. Greg's language comprehensible.

"The small farmers," he says, "who cannot support themselves by agriculture must take refuge in manufacture. As to the large tenant farmers, they cannot fail to profit by the arrangement: either the landlord will be obliged to sell them their land very cheap, or leases will be made out for long periods. This will enable tenant farmers to invest more capital in their farms, to use agricultural machinery on a larger scale, and to save manual labor, which will, moreover, be cheaper, on account of the general fall in wages, the immediate consequence of the repeal of the Corn Laws."

Dr. Bowring conferred upon all these arguments the consecration of religion, by exclaiming at a public meeting, "Jesus Christ is Free Trade, and Free Trade is Jesus Christ."

---

[a] The 1848 French edition does not have the words "thus produced".—*Ed.*

[b] The 1848 French edition has here "requiring greater expenses".—*Ed.*

[c] The 1848 French edition does not have the words "paid for the use of the better soil".—*Ed.*

It will be evident that all this cant was not calculated to make cheap bread tasteful to workingmen.

Besides, how should the workingmen understand the sudden philanthropy of the manufacturers, the very men still busy fighting against the Ten-Hours Bill, which was to reduce the working day of the mill hands from twelve hours to ten?[249]

To give you an idea of the philanthropy of these manufacturers I would remind you of the factory regulations in force in all their mills.

Every manufacturer has for his own private use a regular penal code by means of which fines are inflicted for every voluntary or involuntary offence. For instance, the hand pays so much when he has the misfortune to sit down on a chair, or whisper, or speak, or laugh; if he is a few moments late; if any part of a machine breaks, or if he turns out work of an inferior quality, etc. The fines are always greater than the damage really done by the workman. And to give the workingman every opportunity for incurring fines the factory clock is set forward, and he is given bad material to make into good stuff. An overseer unskilful in multiplying infractions of rules is soon discharged.

You see, gentlemen, this private legislation is enacted for the especial purpose of[a] creating such infractions, and infractions are manufactured for the purpose of making money. Thus the manufacturer uses every means of reducing the nominal wage, and even profiting by accidents over which the workers have no control.

And these manufacturers are the same philanthropists who have tried to persuade the workers that they were capable of going to immense expense for the sole and express purpose of improving the condition of these same workingmen! On the one hand they nibble at the workers' wages in the pettiest way, by means of factory legislation, and, on the other, they are prepared to make the greatest sacrifices to raise those wages by means of the Anti-Corn Law League.

They build great palaces, at immense expense, in which the League takes up[b] its official residence. They send an army of missionaries to all corners of England to preach the gospel of Free Trade; they print and distribute gratis thousands of pamphlets to enlighten the workingman upon his own interests. They spend enormous sums to buy over the press to their side. They organize a vast administrative system for the conduct of the Free Trade movement, and bestow all

---

[a] The 1848 French edition does not have the words "the especial purpose of".—*Ed.*

[b] The 1848 French edition has here "as it were".—*Ed.*

the wealth of their eloquence upon public meetings. It was at one of these meetings that a workingman cried out,—

"If the landlords were to sell our bones, you manufacturers would be the first to buy them, and to put them through the mill and make flour of them."

The English workingmen have appreciated to the fullest extent the significance of the struggle between the lords of the land and of capital. They know very well that the price of bread was to be reduced in order to reduce wages, and that the profit of capital would rise by as much as rent fell.

Ricardo, the apostle of the English Free Traders, the leading economist of our century, entirely agrees with the workers upon this point.

In his celebrated work upon Political Economy[a] he says:

> "If instead of growing our own corn ... we discover a new market from which we can supply ourselves ... at a cheaper price, wages will fall and profits rise. The fall in the price of agricultural produce reduces the wages, not only of the laborer employed in cultivating the soil, but also of all those employed in commerce or manufacture" [t. I, pp. 178-79; Eng. ed., p. 137].

And do not believe, gentlemen, that it is a matter of indifference to the workingman whether he receives only four francs on account of corn being cheaper, when he had been receiving five francs before.

Have not his wages always fallen in comparison with profit? And is it not clear that his social position has grown worse as compared with that of the capitalist? Beside which he loses actually. So long as the price of corn was higher and wages were also higher, a small saving in the consumption of bread sufficed to procure him other enjoyments. But as soon as bread is cheap, and wages are therefore low, he can save almost nothing on bread, for the purchase of other articles.

The English workingmen have shown the English[b] Free Traders that they are not the dupes of their illusions or of their lies; and if, in spite of this, the workers have made common cause with the manufacturers against the landlords, it is for the purpose of destroying the last remnant of feudalism, that henceforth they may have only one enemy to deal with. The workers have not miscalculated, for the landlords, in order to revenge themselves upon the manufacturers, have made common cause with the workers to carry the Ten-Hours Bill, which the latter had been vainly

---

[a] D. Ricardo, *Des principes de l'économie politique et de l'impôt.—Ed.*

[b] The 1848 French edition does not have the word "English".—*Ed.*

demanding for thirty years, and which was passed immediately after the repeal of the Corn Laws.

When Dr. Bowring, at the Congress of Economists,[a] drew from his pocket a long list to show how many head of cattle, how much ham, bacon, poultry, etc., is imported into England, to be consumed—as he asserted— by the workers, he forgot to state that at the same time the workers of Manchester and other factory towns were thrown out of work by the beginning of the crisis.

As a matter of principle in Political Economy, the figures of a single year must never be taken as the basis for formulating general laws. We must always take the average of from six to seven years, a period during which modern industry passes through the successive phases of prosperity, overproduction, crisis,[b] thus completing the inevitable cycle.

Doubtless, if the price of all commodities falls,—and this is the necessary consequence of Free Trade—I can buy far more for a franc than before. And the workingman's franc is as good as any other man's. Therefore, Free Trade must be advantageous to the workingman. There is only one little difficulty in this, namely that the workman, before he exchanges his franc for other commodities, has first exchanged his labor for the money of the capitalist.[c] If in this exchange he always received the said franc[d] while the price of all other commodities fell, he would always be the gainer by such a bargain. The difficulty does not lie in proving that, the price of all commodities falling, more commodities can be bought for the same sum of money.

Economists always take the price of labor at the moment of its exchange with other commodities, and altogether ignore the moment at which labor accomplishes its own exchange with capital. When it costs less to set in motion the machinery which produces commodities, then the things necessary for the maintenance of this machine, called workman, will also cost less. If all commodities are cheaper, labor, which is a commodity too, will also fall in price, and we shall see later that this commodity, labor, will fall far lower in proportion than all other commodities. If the workingman still pins his faith to the arguments of the economists, he will find, one fine

---

[a] See this volume, pp. 274-78 and pp. 282-90.—*Ed.*

[b] The 1848 French edition has "prosperity, overproduction, stagnation, crisis".—*Ed.*

[c] The 1848 French edition has "for capital" instead of "for the money of capitalist".—*Ed.*

[d] The 1848 French edition has "the said franc for the same work".—*Ed.*

morning,[a] that the franc has dwindled in his pocket, and that he has only five sous left.

Thereupon the economists will tell you,—

"We admit that competition among the workers will certainly not be lessened under Free Trade, and will very soon bring wages into harmony with the low price of commodities. But, on the other hand, the low price of commodities will increase consumption, the larger consumption will increase production, which will in turn necessitate a larger demand for labor and this larger demand will be followed by a rise in wages."

The whole line of argument amounts to this: Free Trade increases productive forces. When manufactures keep advancing, when wealth, when the productive forces, when, in a word, productive capital increases, the demand for the labor, the price of labor, and consequently the rate of wages, rises also.

The most favorable condition for the workingman is the growth of capital. This must be admitted: when capital remains stationary, commerce and manufacture are not merely stationary but decline, and in this case the workman is the first victim. He goes to the wall before the capitalist. And in the case of the growth of capital, under the circumstances, which, as we have said, are the best for the workingman, what will be his lot? He will go to the wall just the same. The growth of capital implies the accumulation and the concentration of capital. This centralization involves a greater division of labor and a greater use of machinery. The greater division of labor destroys the especial skill of the laborer; and by putting in the place of this skilled work labor which any one can perform it increases competition among the workers.

This competition becomes more fierce as the division of labor enables a single man to do the work of three. Machinery accomplishes the same result on a much larger scale. The accumulation of productive capital forces the industrial capitalist to work with constantly increasing means of production, ruins the small manufacturer, and drives him into the proletariat. Then, the rate of interest falling in proportion as capital accumulates, the little *rentiers* and retired tradespeople,[b] who can no longer live upon their small incomes, will be forced to look out for some business again and ultimately to swell the number of proletarians. Finally, the more productive capital grows, the more it is compelled to produce for a

[a] The 1848 French edition does not have the words "one fine morning".—*Ed.*

[b] The 1848 French edition does not have the words "and retired tradespeople".—*Ed.*

market whose requirements it does not know,—the more supply tries to force demand,[a] and consequently crises increase in frequency and in intensity. But every crisis in turn hastens the concentration of capital, adds to the proletariat. Thus, as productive capital grows, competition among the workers grows too, and grows in a far greater proportion. The reward of labor is less for all, and the burden of labor is increased for some at least.

In 1829 there were, in Manchester, 1,088 cotton spinners employed in 36 factories. In 1841 there were but 448, and they tended 53,353 more spindles than the 1,088 spinners did in 1829. If manual labor had increased in the same proportion as productive force, the number of spinners ought to have risen to 1,848; improved machinery had, therefore, deprived 1,400 workers of employment.

We know beforehand the reply of the economists—the people thus thrown out of work will find other kinds of employment. Dr. Bowring did not fail to reproduce this argument at the Congress of Economists. But neither did he fail to refute himself. In 1835, Dr. Bowring made a speech in the House of Commons upon the 50,000 hand-loom weavers of London who have been starving without being able to find that new kind of employment which the Free Traders hold out to them in the distance. Let us hear the most striking portion of this speech of Mr. Bowring.[b]

"The misery of the hand-loom weavers," he says, "is the inevitable fate of all kinds of labor which are easily acquired, and which may, at any moment, be replaced by less costly means. As in these cases competition amongst the work-people is very great, the slightest falling-off in demand brings on a crisis. The hand-loom weavers are, in a certain sense, placed on the borders of human existence. One step further, and that existence becomes impossible. The slightest shock is sufficient to throw them on to the road to ruin. By more and more superseding manual labor, the progress of mechanical science must bring on, during the period of transition, a deal of temporary suffering. National well-being cannot be bought except at the price of some individual evils. The advance of industry is achieved at the expense of those who lag behind, and of all discoveries that of the power-loom weighs most heavily upon the hand-loom weavers. In a great many articles formerly made by hand, the weaver has been placed *hors de combat*; but he is sure to be beaten in a good many more stuffs that are now made by hand."

Further on he says,—"I hold in my hand a correspondence of the governor-general with the East India Company. This correspondence is concerning the weavers of the Dacca district. The governor says in his letter,—A few years ago the East India Company received from six to eight million pieces of calico woven upon the looms of

---

[a] The 1848 French edition has: "the more production outstrips consumption, the more supply tries to force demand".—*Ed.*

[b] Marx quotes Dr. Bowring according to *Principles of Political Economy* by W. Atkinson.—*Ed.*

the country. The demand fell off gradually and was reduced to about a million pieces. At this moment it has almost entirely ceased. Moreover, in 1800 North America received from India nearly 800,000 pieces of cotton goods. In 1830 it did not take even 4,000. Finally, in 1800 a million of pieces were shipped for Portugal; in 1830 Portugal did not receive above 20,000.

"The reports on the distress of the Indian weavers are terrible. And what is the origin of that distress? The presence on the market of English manufactures, the production of the same article by means of the power-loom. A great number of the weavers died of starvation; the remainder has gone over to the other employment, and chiefly to field labor. Not to be able to change employment amounted to a sentence of death. And at this moment the Dacca district is crammed with English yarns and calicoes. The Dacca muslin, renowned all over the world for its beauty and firm texture, has also been eclipsed by the competition of English machinery. In the whole history of commerce, it would, perhaps, be difficult to find suffering equal to what these whole classes in India had to submit to" [W. Atkinson, pp. 36-38].

Mr. Bowring's speech is the more remarkable because the facts quoted by him are correct, and the phrases with which he seeks to palliate them are characterized by the hypocrisy common to all Free Trade discourses. He represents the workers as means of production which must be superseded by less expensive means of production, pretends to see in the labor of which he speaks a wholly exceptional kind of labor, and in the machine which has crushed out the weavers an equally exceptional kind of machine. He forgets that there is no kind of manual labor which may not any day share the fate of the hand-loom weavers.

"The constant aim and tendency of every improvement of mechanism is indeed to do entirely without the labor of men, or to reduce its price, by superseding the labor of the adult males by that of women and children, or the work of the skilled by that of the unskilled workman. In most of the throstle mills, spinning is now entirely done by girls of sixteen years and less. The introduction of the self-acting mule has caused the discharge of most of the (adult male) spinners, while the children and young persons have been kept on" [p. 34; Eng. ed., p. 23].

The above words of the most enthusiastic of Free Traders, Dr. Ure,[a] are calculated to complete the confessions of Dr. Bowring. Mr. Bowring speaks of certain individual evils, and, at the same time, says that these individual evils destroy whole classes; he speaks of the temporary sufferings during a transition period, and does not deny that these temporary evils have implied for the majority the transition from life to death, and for the rest a transition from a better to a worse condition. When he asserts, farther on, that the sufferings of the working class[b] are inseparable from the progress of

[a] A. Ure, *Philosophie des manufactures, ou Économie industrielle,* t. I.—*Ed.*

[b] The 1848 French edition has "these workers" instead of "the working class".—*Ed.*

industry, and are necessary to the prosperity of the nation, he simply says that the prosperity of the bourgeois class presupposes as necessary the suffering of the laboring class.

All the comfort which Mr. Bowring offers the workers who perish, and, indeed, the whole doctrine of compensation which the Free Traders propound, amounts to this—

You thousands of workers who are perishing, do not despair! You can die with an easy conscience. Your class will not perish. It will always be numerous enough for the capitalist class to decimate it without fear of annihilating it. Besides, how could capital be usefully applied if it did not take care to keep up its exploitable material, i.e., the workingmen, to be exploited over and over again?

But, then, why propound as a problem still to be solved the question: What influence will the adoption of the Free Trade have upon the condition of the working class? All the laws formulated by the political economists from Quesnay to Ricardo, have been based upon the hypothesis that the trammels which still interfere with commercial freedom have disappeared. These laws are confirmed in proportion as Free Trade is adopted. The first of these laws is that competition reduces the price of every commodity to the minimum cost of production. Thus the minimum of wages is the natural price of labor. And what is the minimum of wages? Just so much as is required for production of the articles absolutely necessary for the maintenance of the worker, for the continuation, by hook or by crook, of his own existence and that of his class.

But do not imagine that the worker receives *only* this minimum wage, and still less that he *always* receives it. No, according to this law, the working class will sometimes be more fortunate, will sometimes receive something above the minimum, but this surplus will merely make up for the deficit which they will have received below the minimum in times of industrial depression. That is to say that within a given time which recurs periodically, in other words, in the cycle[a] which commerce and industry describe while passing through the successive phases of prosperity, overproduction, stagnation, and crisis, when reckoning all that the working class has had above and below mere necessaries, we shall see that, after all, they have received neither more nor less than the minimum; i.e., the working class will have maintained itself as a class after enduring any amount of misery and misfortune, and after leaving many corpses upon the industrial battle-field. But what of that? The class will still exist; nay, more, it will have increased.

[a] The 1848 French edition has "circle" instead of "cycle".—*Ed.*

But this is not all. The progress of industry creates less and less expensive means of subsistence. Thus spirits have taken the place of beer, cotton that of wool and linen, and potatoes that of bread.

Thus, as means are constantly being found for the maintenance of labor on cheaper and more wretched food, the minimum of wages is constantly sinking. If these wages began by letting the man work to live, they end by forcing him to live the life of a machine. His existence has no other value than that of a simple productive force, and the capitalist treats him accordingly. This law of the commodity labor, of the minimum of wages will be confirmed in proportion as the supposition of the economists, Free Trade, becomes an actual fact. Thus, of two things one: either we must reject all political economy based upon the assumption of Free Trade, or we must admit that under this same Free Trade the whole severity of the economic laws will fall upon the workers.

To sum up, what is Free Trade under the present conditions of society? Freedom of Capital. When you have torn down the few national barriers which still restrict the free development[a] of capital, you will merely have given it complete freedom of action. So long as you let the relation of wages-labor to capital exist, no matter how favorable the conditions under which you accomplish the exchange of commodities, there will always be a class which exploits and a class which is exploited. It is really difficult to understand the presumption of the Free Traders who imagine that the more advantageous application of capital will abolish the antagonism between industrial capitalists and wage-workers. On the contrary. The only result will be that the antagonism of these two classes will stand out more clearly.

Let us assume for a moment that there are no more Corn Laws or national and municipal import duties[b]; that in a word all the accidental circumstances which to-day the workingman may look upon as a cause of his miserable condition have vanished, and we shall have removed so many curtains that hide from his eyes his true enemy.

He will see that capital released from all trammels will make him no less a slave than capital trammelled by import duties.

Gentlemen! Do not be deluded by the abstract word Freedom! whose freedom? Not the freedom of one individual in relation to another, but freedom of Capital to crush the worker

---

[a] The 1848 French edition has "advance" instead of "free development".—*Ed.*

[b] The 1848 French edition has "no more customs, no more town dues" (octroi).—*Ed.*

Why should you desire farther to sanction unlimited competition with this idea of freedom, when the idea of freedom itself is only the product of a social condition based upon Free Competition?

We have shown what sort of fraternity Free Trade begets between the different classes of one and the same nation. The fraternity which Free Trade would establish between the nations of the earth would not be more real, to call cosmopolitan exploitation universal brotherhood is an idea that could only be engendered in the brain of the bourgeoisie. Every one of the destructive phenomena to which unlimited competition gives rise within any one nation is reproduced in more gigantic proportions in the market of the world. We need not pause any longer upon Free Trade sophisms on this subject, which are worth just as much as the arguments of our prize essayists Messrs Hope, Morse, and Greg.

For instance, we are told that Free Trade would create an international division of labor, and thereby give to each country those branches of production most in harmony with its natural advantages.

You believe perhaps, gentlemen, that the production of coffee and sugar is the natural destiny of the West Indies.

Two centuries ago, nature, which does not trouble itself about commerce, had planted neither sugar-cane nor coffee trees there. And it may be that in less than half a century you will find there neither coffee nor sugar, for the East Indies, by means of cheaper production, have already successfully broken down this so-called natural destiny of the West Indies.

And the West Indies, with their natural wealth, are as heavy a burden for England as the weavers of Dacca, who also were destined from the beginning of time to weave by hand.

One other circumstance must not be forgotten, namely that, just as everything has become a monopoly, there are also nowadays some branches of industry which prevail over all others, and secure to the nations which especially foster them the command of the market of the world. Thus in the commerce of the world cotton alone has much greater commercial importance than all the other raw materials used in the manufacture of clothing. It is truly ridiculous for the Free Traders to refer to the few specialties in each branch of industry, throwing them into the balance against the product used in everyday consumption, and produced most cheaply in those countries in which manufacture is most highly developed.

If the Free Traders cannot understand how one nation can grow rich at the expense of another, we need not wonder, since these same gentlemen also refuse to understand how in the same country one class can enrich itself at the expense of another.

Do not imagine, gentlemen, that in criticising freedom of commerce we have the least intention of defending Protection.

One may be opposed to constitutionalism without being in favor of absolutism.[a]

Moreover, the Protective system is nothing but a means of establishing manufacture upon a large scale in any given country, that is to say, of making it dependent upon the market of the world; and from the moment that dependence upon the market of the world is established, there is more or less dependence upon Free Trade too. Besides this, the Protective system helps to develop free competition within a nation. Hence we see that in countries where the bourgeoisie is beginning to make itself felt as a class, in Germany for example, it makes great efforts to obtain Protective duties. They serve the bourgeoisie as weapons against feudalism and absolute monarchy,[b] as a means for the concentration of its own powers for the realization of Free Trade within the country.

But, generally speaking, the Protective system in these days is conservative, while the Free Trade system works destructively. It breaks up old nationalities and carries antagonism of proletariat and bourgeoisie to the uttermost point. In a word, the Free Trade system hastens the Social Revolution. In this revolutionary sense alone, gentlemen, I am in favor of Free Trade.

First published in French as a pamphlet at the beginning of February 1848 in Brussels

Printed according to the American edition of 1889, checked with the 1848 French edition

Signed: *Karl Marx*

[a] The 1848 French edition has "ancien régime" instead of "absolutism".—*Ed.*

[b] The 1848 French edition has "government" instead of "monarchy".—*Ed.*

Frederick Engels

THE CHARTIST MOVEMENT

[THE FRATERNAL DEMOCRATS
TO THE WORKING CLASSES OF GREAT BRITAIN AND IRELAND]

The Society of Fraternal Democrats at its last meeting adopted an address to the workers of Great Britain and Ireland. This address, edited by Mr. Harney, of *The Northern Star*, is published in the latest number of this newspaper.[250]

After recalling, in a portrayal as rapid as eloquent, the sufferings of the working class today, this address calls on the workers of the two islands to complete their party organisation:

On all sides the middle class has laid traps for you. In order to divert you from the People's Charter, the only goal important to you, they spawn all sorts of projects for superficial reforms. But within a few years you have twice had to learn the hard lesson that any scheme of reform emanating from the *bourgeoisie* must be for you "like Dead Sea fruits that tempt the eye, but turn to ashes on the lips". Remember the agitation for the Reform Bill, and that for the repeal of the Corn Laws.

...Nonetheless, you are asked to support a "National League for the Reform of Abuses", an "Anti-State Church Association", an "Anti-Bribery Society", and societies for the reform of the currency, and the abolition of certain taxes, etc., etc. The one design of the projectors of these schemes is to perfect the already dominant power of the middle class. They all combine to resist your rightful claim to the privileges of citizenship: they are therefore your enemies. Were they desirous, as they profess to be, of promoting your welfare, they would aid you to obtain sovereign power. They well know that if you controlled the legislature, all the reforms they seek—and reforms of much greater importance—would be forthwith effected. How then can they call themselves your friends, while refusing you the suffrage?

Let this great truth be impressed upon every working man, that it is from the hut and the hovel, the garret and the cellar, that must come the regenerators of his order and the social saviours of the human race. Receive with joy and fraternal love every man who, belonging to the privileged orders, shall renounce class distinctions, and ally himself with you, but look to no class above your own for your emancipation. ...Practically outlawed by the other classes of the state, you must find in your own clear heads, courageous hearts, and powerful arms the means of effecting your regeneration.

...We must call your serious attention to a wicked and abominable conspiracy against your interests, the conspiracy both by the enemies of all reform, and by many of the middle-class sham-reformers. These conspirators seek to revive those national prejudices, now all but extinct, which formerly made the working men of these countries the willing butchers of their fellow men of other lands. They desire to inflame the people of these islands with a dread and hatred of the people of France, under the pretext that the French contemplate the invasion and subjugation of England.

Working men of Great Britain and Ireland, your country is already invaded and subjugated by enemies within—enemies who have reduced you politically and socially to the condition of Helots. You will not dislodge these enemies by increasing the physical power of your rulers. We believe that the veritable people of France—the proletarians—have learnt by experience that, like yourselves, their enemies are not to be found on any foreign shore, but in their own country. In France, as in England, a triumphant moneyocracy rules supreme and grinds the sons of labour to the dust. As in England, the people in France fights against this enemy and for the advent of liberty, equality and fraternity.

Even supposing this country were menaced by aggression from without, England would have nothing to apprehend if her people were freemen. It is not armies, navies or fortresses that constitute the true defence of nations; a nation's best defence consists in a people which is truly free....

Let the privileged classes renounce their unjust usurpations and establish political equality and social justice, and England will have nothing to fear against a world in arms. On the contrary, the people of all countries would hail with joy the march of England's power, if that power were arrayed on the side of the liberty and social emancipation of mankind.

Working men of Great Britain and Ireland, why should you arm yourselves and fight for the preservation of institutions in the privileges of which you have no share? For the maintenance of laws made not to protect, but to constrain you? For the protection of property which you can regard only as the accumulated plunder of the fruits of your labour? You are deprived of the produce of your industry; and then your poverty is made the pretext for withholding from you your citizens' rights! Subjected to plunder, wrong, and insult by the possessors of property, you are asked to pour out your blood in defence of property! Let the privileged and the property-holders fight their own battles! And if they are too weak to do so, let them give the people what belongs to it; let them learn to submit to the popular will; if they do so, the whole nation will form a rampart round these islands which no foreign invader could ever break through!

Your great want is political power as the means to effect your social emancipation; and until that political power is yours, let your resolve be: No vote, no musket! Give us the suffrage, or we will not fight!

Working men of Great Britain and Ireland! Hold in abhorrence the conspirators who would set nation against nation, in the name of that wicked lie, that men of different countries are "natural enemies". Rally round the banner of democracy, with its motto: "All men are brothers!"

Signed on behalf of the Society of Fraternal Democrats: *G. Julian Harney, Ernest Jones, Thomas Clark, Charles Keen* (Great Britain); *J. A. Michelot, H. Bernard* (France); *Carl Schapper, J. Moll* (Germany); *J. Schabelitz, H. Krell* (Switzerland); *Peter Holm, Luntberg* (Scandinavia); *Louis Oborski* (Poland); *C. Pohse, P. Bluhm* (Russia).

Written on January 9, 1848

First published in *La Réforme*, January 10, 1848

Printed according to the newspaper

Translated from the French

Published in English for the first time

Karl Marx

THE SITUATION IN FRANCE

What does the Ministry do?—Nothing.

What does the parliamentary, legal opposition do?—Nothing.

What can France expect from the present Chambers?—Nothing.

What does M. Guizot want?—To remain Minister.

What do Messrs Thiers, Molé and Company want?—To become ministers again.

What does France gain from this *ôte-toi, afin que je m'y mette*[a]?—Nothing.

Ministry and opposition are thus condemned to do nothing.

Who alone will accomplish the coming French revolution?—The proletariat.

What will the bourgeoisie do for this?—Nothing.

Written about January 16, 1848

First published in the *Deutsche-Brüsseler-Zeitung* No. 5, January 16, 1848 and in *La Réforme,* January 19, 1848

Printed according to the *Deutsche-Brüsseler-Zeitung*

Published in English for the first time

[a] Get out so that I can get in.—*Ed.*

Frederick Engels

EXTRAORDINARY REVELATIONS.—ABD-EL-KADER.— GUIZOT'S FOREIGN POLICY

A curious document has just been published and distributed,[a] as if for a New Year's gift to the Chamber of Deputies. It is a statement of facts explaining how a certain M. Petit got the place of a tax collector (*receveur particulier*) at Corbeil, near Paris, and has been published by M. Petit himself. M. Petit has been forced to this act in consequence of a suit for separation pending between himself and his wife, and in which action it had been alleged that he had bought his place by prostituting his wife to a gentleman intimately connected with M. Guizot. He now declares in his publication—

> "Yes, my place was bought, as all places are bought now-a-day; but it was bought not with prostitution, but with hard cash only."

Then he goes on to detail how he first aspired to the office of a Councillor Referendary at the Court of Accounts. How the ministry promised him that place, if he only could procure the resignation of one of the councillors; how the minister's secretary intimated to him, which of the councillors would most likely sell their charge; how he then, for 15,000 francs, procured the wished-for resignation; how then he was told he must procure a resignation of a Councillor Referendary, not of the second, but of the first class, as the government wanted such a one in order to fulfil a promise made by them on their coming into office; how by makeshifts of different sorts, the difference of price of the two resignations was made up; how at last the resignation was procured; how then the ministry wanted not only a resignation like that tendered, but one of a higher

---

[a] "Réponse de M. Petit, ex-receveur des finances à Corbeil, aux calomnies répandues à l'occasion de son procès en séparation."—*Ed.*

degree still, of a Master Councillor; how this new resignation was also procured by the means of "cash down"; how finally it was offered to M. Petit to accept the tax collectorship of Corbeil, rather than the place in the Court of Accounts; how M. Petit accepted this; how then the different resignations were signed and exchanged against the amounts of money stipulated; and how, two days later, the whole of the royal ordinances were published, accepting the resignations, and promoting and naming the several individuals concerned, to the offices stipulated by the transaction.

These are the principal facts of the matter. There are some others of less importance, proving how M. Petit, as soon as he was once hooked by having paid the first sum, was made to pay more and more. But these I pass over. I only mention, that in the publication of M. Petit all the names are given in full.

You will easily imagine what a noise this little pamphlet has made in Paris. All papers are full of it, and the more so, as the Minister of Finance[a] (to which department the Court of Accounts belongs) under whose direction the above transactions took place, had openly denied anything of the sort ever having occurred, when questioned about it in the Chamber by M. Luneau. M. Luneau, at the time, declared the sale of places in the above department to be a matter of public notoriety. Known to the majority, as well as to the opposition. Known to every one, in short, except, it appeared, to the minister himself. M. Lacave met this by a flat denial.[251] Now the matter has come out in a manner which makes all burking impossible. And yet, although all Paris has been full of it for almost a week past, the government has not opened its mouth.

We only repeat the words of M. Dupin the elder, pronounced when M. Luneau brought the matter forward in the Chamber—

> "It was hardly worth while to make a revolution to abolish the venality of places, if this infamous system is suffered to lift up its head again."

The next subject occupying the papers is the capture of Abd-el-Kader,[252] and the resolution which the government will come to as to his future location. There is no doubt they will confirm and execute the Duke D'Aumale's promise, and send the Emir to Egypt.[253] It is curious that almost all the papers of the Opposition, from the *National* to the *Constitutionnel*, demanded the breach of that promise. Now, there is no doubt the promise was granted conditionally, and leaving the government free to confirm, or not to confirm it. The refusal of confirmation would not directly imply, as

---

[a] J. P. J. Lacave-Laplagne.—*Ed.*

the *Sun* has it, an *infamy*. But there is no doubt, either, that a similar act on the part of any other government, particularly the English, would have been treated by those very same papers as the most infamous treason. It is evident, that, it being impossible to replace matters in the same state as they were when Abd-el-Kader conditionally surrendered, it would imply a want of generosity of the first order to refuse to him the confirmation of the conditions of surrender. But in such questions these *national* papers are blind, and would commit the same acts for whose commission they blame others. The only two papers which have spoken in favour of confirming the treaty with Abd-el-Kader, are the *Presse* and the *Réforme*. The first, a monarchical paper, wanted it confirmed, because the government could not give the lie to a son of the king,[a] to a *son of France*; thus reviving the old title of the princes of Royal blood before the revolution.

"No", said the *Réforme*, "the matter is a delicate one—the honour of our country is implied; in such matters we had better be too generous than too narrow, and therefore, confirm the word given, *were it even that of a prince*."[b]

Again, the *Réforme* alone has taken the right view of the matter.

Upon the whole it is, in our opinion, very fortunate that the Arabian chief has been taken. The struggle of the Bedouins was a hopeless one, and though the manner in which brutal soldiers, like Bugeaud, have carried on the war is highly blameable, the conquest of Algeria is an important and fortunate fact for the progress of civilisation. The piracies of the Barbaresque states, never interfered with by the English government as long as they did not disturb their ships, could not be put down but by the conquest of one of these states. And the conquest of Algeria has already forced the Beys of Tunis and Tripoli, and even the Emperor of Morocco,[c] to enter upon the road of civilisation. They were obliged to find other employment for their people than piracy, and other means of filling their exchequer than tributes paid to them by the smaller states of Europe. And if we may regret that the liberty of the Bedouins of the desert has been destroyed, we must not forget that these same Bedouins were a nation of robbers,—whose principal means of living consisted of making excursions either upon each other, or upon the settled villagers, taking what they found, slaughtering all those who resisted, and selling the remaining prisoners as slaves. All these nations of free barbarians look very proud, noble and glorious at a

[a] Duke of Aumale, son of Louis Philippe.—*Ed.*

[b] From articles in *La Réforme*, January 2, 3 and 5, 1848.—*Ed.*

[c] Abd-ur-Rahman.—*Ed.*

distance, but only come near them and you will find that they, as well as the more civilised nations, are ruled by the lust of gain, and only employ ruder and more cruel means. And after all, the modern *bourgeois,* with civilisation, industry, order, and at least relative enlightenment following him, is preferable to the feudal lord or to the marauding robber, with the barbarian state of society to which they belong.

M. Guizot has laid before the Chambers part of the diplomatic correspondence relating to Switzerland and Italy. The first proves again that he has been regularly *done* by Lord Palmerston, and both prove the intimate alliance France has entered into with Austria. That was the last infamy which as yet had been spared to Louis-Philippistic France. The representative of tyranny, of oppression attained by means the most infamous,—the country of stability and reaction, the ally of France, as reconstituted by two revolutions! Deeper she cannot sink. But this is quite well. The deeper the *bourgeoisie* brings down this country, the nearer draws the day of reckoning. And it will come, before the *bourgeoisie* think of it. There is a party they do not take into account, and that party is the noble, the generous, the brave French people.

The dispute between the *Réforme* and the *National*[a] has been submitted to a jury selected by both parties. All hostilities are suspended. By the end of this month the decision will be given. May it be as it will, we hope the *Réforme* will continue in the only course which can save the Democracy of France.

Written in mid-January 1848

Reprinted from the newspaper

First published in *The Northern Star* No. 535, January 22, 1848 with an editorial note: "From Our Paris Correspondent"

---

[a] See this volume, pp. 385-87, 406-08 and 438-44.—*Ed.*

Frederick Engels

THE CHARTIST MOVEMENT

[MEETING IN SUPPORT OF THE NATIONAL PETITION]

The fourth meeting convened for the adoption of the National Petition by the Chartist Council was held in London last Tuesday.[a] Mr. Julian Harney presided. Messrs Clark and Dixon, of the Chartist central committee,[b] West, of Macclesfield, Skelton, Keen, and Fussell spoke in turn. But the orators of the evening were Messrs Harney and Jones. We give extracts of their speeches[c]:

Mr. Ernest Jones.—We are assembled here to assist in passing a *Coercion Bill* against the government, and to produce such a "pressure from without", as shall squeeze poor little Lord John Russell into something like a decent and statesman-like shape. We need this pressure, seeing that of all the parliaments we have had, the present parliament is assuredly the most hostile to working men. (A voice: No! no!) Someone says No. But I repeat that no class has ever proved as hostile to the working class as the middle class of England. (Hear, hear.) It has cast down aristocracy on the left, democracy on the right, and lives on the ruins of both. I do not wish to raise the aristocracy. No! Let the bruised serpent lie, for it would sting the hand that healed it.... Under feudalism, the people were fat slaves; under your rule, Sir defender of the middle class, they are lean slaves. (Loud cheers.)

Seeing then that we never had a more middle class, and therefore a more hostile parliament, it is time to organise resistance. And the people knows this. We too are increasing our army; the Old Guards of Chartism are in the field again. We too are enrolling our militia, the starving millions. We too are strengthening our "national defences", courage in our hearts, discipline in our ranks, and unity in our action. (Applause.)

...But there are some gentlemen here who are not satisfied with this, and who say that millions of determined, well organised and well informed men are insufficient to obtain the Charter. These gentlemen tell the people that they must grow rich and then

---

[a] January 11, 1848.—*Ed.*

[b] The reference is to the Executive Committee of the National Charter Association.—*Ed.*

[c] Quoted from the report: "The People's Charter.—Important Public Meeting" published in *The Northern Star.*—*Ed.*

they will be free. But I tell you, you must become free and then you will be rich! (Applause.)

Become rich! how? In the workhouse or the gaol? Become rich in the deer forests of our nobles? Become rich on six shillings (8 francs)[a] a week? Become rich in the churchyards of famished Ireland? (Applause.) Go tell it to the unemployed in Manchester—to the 20,000 destitute in Bradford. Go tell it to the Irish tenant, dying by the light of his burning cottage set on fire by his landlord. Go tell it to the beggar at the doors of Grosvenor Square! Go tell him once for all to stay a slave; but do not insult his misery by telling him to become rich! I know you will here point to our glorious *Land Company*[254] to prove that the people can become rich.... But do you imagine that the government will let you go on?... This company has succeeded in rescuing 50,000 families from ruin; but rest assured, Parliament will prevent you from forming other companies, unless you obtain political power!... Let the Land Company members remember their forefathers, the *yeomanry* of England, who all owned the land. How did they lose it? Why, by taxation, which ruined them.

...Now then, gentlemen, make money, it will be wanted for the militia, for the increased army. Make money, it will be wanted for fresh palaces, for new bishops, for new royal babies! Make money, become middle class yourselves, and then, as you know, the middle class will no longer fear you! Make money—and this impossible task will be your only salvation. Not one word about our triumph at Nottingham,[b] of our organisation, of our national petition and our National Convention, now being prepared.

...No, my friends, above all we need the vote.... And you, men of London, you have it more in your power to obtain it than your brothers in the rest of England.... Our gallant men of the north are a long way off; their voices will not be heard, for there are hundreds of miles and plenty of barracks between those petitioners and Parliament. But you, men of London, can go in person and knock at the doors of St. Stephen's,[255] knock till your privileged debtors give you back, trembling, what they have owed you for centuries! So knock, and go on knocking until justice has been done. (Thunderous applause.)

Mr. Julian Harney.—We are here to adopt a petition to Parliament.... But we are not asking for mercy or pity. Even were we so degraded as to do such a thing, we know that we have nothing to expect from the pity of our oppressors.... It was not by crying misericordia that our forefathers rescued themselves from the yoke of the traitor Charles I. It was not by begging for mercy that the Americans broke their chains. It was not by crying misericordia that the French people overthrew the tyranny of feudalism, priestcraft and monarchy. (Great cheering.)

No, it would be vain for us to implore Capital for mercy. All our petitions would achieve nothing if they were not followed by other measures. First, we do not ask for pity, we ask for justice. We demand it, not only by the petition, but also by our agitation and our organisation, which is already beginning to terrify the parliamentary middle class. Continue to agitate, then, for when you cease, your petitions are only empty words.

Truly, the prize is worth the struggle. Behold this mighty empire, built up by the strong arms and cemented by the blood of your fathers; this empire of 160 million inhabitants, covering the sixth part of the habitable globe, this empire on which "the sun never sets".[c] How is it that you, owners and conquerors of millions of miles of this

[a] Here and below the French equivalents were inserted by Engels.—*Ed.*

[b] An allusion to O'Connor's election to Parliament.—*Ed.*

[c] A phrase used by contemporaries of king of Spain and German Emperor Charles V about his domains where the "sun never sets".—*Ed.*

fair earth, do not possess a foot of land? That millions of the heirs of this magnificent empire are dying of hunger, that thousands have no shelter from the wintry blast? The natural and manufactured riches of every clime are produced in the limits of the British Empire. Our manufactures are the wonder and envy of the whole world. For skill, industry and heroism our artisans, labourers and sailors are celebrated everywhere. All the elements of greatness and happiness abound, in spite of which you are crushed by misery. This empire is rightfully the property not of an idle, a scheming privileged few, but of the entire people. Is such a prize not worth struggling for? The Charter is the means by which you will win it. (Cheers.) When, therefore, the usurpers ask you to arm in defence of the country, refuse until you have your fair share of its advantages. If you armed yourselves, what would be your fate? Remember the poor soldier who was recently shot in India for insubordination, this is your share; compare it with the share of the Duke of Wellington, who got from the Treasury a sum of two and a half million pounds (60 million francs): So much for the aristocrats.

Well, then! If the aristocrary fears the loss of its broad acres, let it fight for the protection of those acres! If the Church fears the confiscation of its immense revenues, let the parsons and bishops arm themselves! If the Jews and jobbers of 'Change Alley[256] fear the swamping of their funds, let them fight to protect their plunder! If the shopocracy fear the seizure of their tills and their ledgers let them arm and fight to protect their property! But you, men of the people, overworked and ill-paid sons of toil, houseless and shivering serfs of privilege, you who have neither lands, nor revenues, nor rent nor tithes, nor public funds, nor shares, nor profits, nor usury, nor votes, to whom the throne affords no protection and the law no security, fight for something else, or fight not at all! (Great cheering.) If you must fight, fight for yourselves. (Renewed cheering.) When lords and priests and bourgeois ask you to fight, let your answer be: No vote, no musket! Knaves and fools are now rushing into print with talk of national defence; there is only one defence, that of the Chartists: *The land for the people, every man a home, every man a vote, and every man a musket!* (Thunderous applause.)

Written on January 17 and 18, 1848

First published in *La Réforme*, January 19, 1848

Printed according to the newspaper

Translated from the French

Published in English for the first time

Karl Marx
and
Frederick Engels

MANIFESTO OF THE COMMUNIST PARTY[257]

Written in December 1847-January 1848

First published as a separate edition in London in February 1848

Printed according to the text of the English edition of 1888, checked with the German editions of 1848, 1872, 1883 and 1890

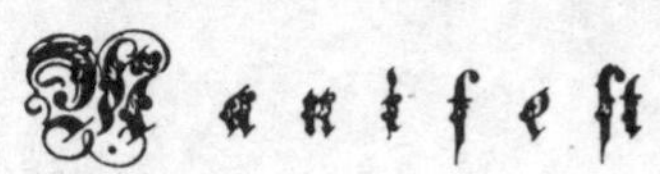

der

Kommunistischen Partei.

Veröffentlicht im Februar 1848.

Proletarier aller Länder vereinigt Euch!

London.

Gedruckt in der Office der „Bildungs-Gesellschaft für Arbeiter"
von J. E. Burghard.

46, LIVERPOOL STREET, BISHOPSGATE.

Cover of the first German 23-page edition of the *Manifesto of the Communist Party*

A spectre is haunting Europe—the spectre of Communism. All the Powers of old Europe have entered into a holy alliance to exorcise this spectre: Pope and Czar, Metternich and Guizot, French Radicals and German police-spies.

Where is the party in opposition that has not been decried as Communistic by its opponents in power? Where the Opposition that has not hurled back the branding reproach of Communism, against the more advanced opposition parties, as well as against its reactionary adversaries?

Two things result from this fact:

I. Communism is already acknowledged by all European Powers to be itself a Power.

II. It is high time that Communists should openly, in the face of the whole world, publish their views, their aims, their tendencies, and meet this nursery tale of the Spectre of Communism with a Manifesto of the party itself.

To this end, Communists of various nationalities have assembled in London, and sketched the following Manifesto, to be published in the English, French, German, Italian, Flemish and Danish languages.

I

BOURGEOIS AND PROLETARIANS*

The history of all hitherto existing society** is the history of class struggles.

Freeman and slave, patrician and plebeian, lord and serf, guild-master*** and journeyman, in a word, oppressor and oppressed, stood in constant opposition to one another, carried on an uninterrupted, now hidden, now open fight, a fight that each time ended, either in a revolutionary re-constitution of society at large, or in the common ruin of the contending classes.

In the earlier epochs of history, we find almost everywhere a complicated arrangement of society into various orders, a manifold

* By bourgeoisie is meant the class of modern Capitalists, owners of the means of social production and employers of wage-labour. By proletariat, the class of modern wage-labourers who, having no means of production of their own, are reduced to selling their labour-power in order to live. [*Note by Engels to the English edition of 1888.*]

** That is, all *written* history. In 1847, the pre-history of society, the social organisation existing previous to recorded history, was all but unknown. Since then, Haxthausen discovered common ownership of land in Russia, Maurer proved it to be the social foundation from which all Teutonic races started in history, and by and by village communities were found to be, or to have been the primitive form of society everywhere from India to Ireland. The inner organisation of this primitive Communistic society was laid bare, in its typical form, by Morgan's crowning discovery of the true nature of the *gens* and its relation to the *tribe*. With the dissolution of these primeval communities society begins to be differentiated into separate and finally antagonistic classes. I have attempted to retrace this process of dissolution in *Der Ursprung der Familie, des Privateigenthums und des Staats*, 2nd edition, Stuttgart, 1886. [*Note by Engels to the English edition of 1888, and—less the last sentence—to the German edition of 1890.*]

*** Guild-master, that is, a full member of a guild, a master within, not a head of a guild. [*Note by Engels to the English edition of 1888.*]

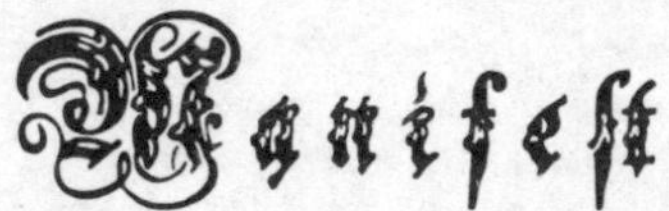

der

Kommunistischen Partei.

Veröffentlicht im Februar 1848.

Proletarier aller Länder vereinigt euch.

London.

Gedruckt in der Office der „Bildungs-Gesellschaft für Arbeiter"

von J. E. Burghard.

46, LIVERPOOL STREET, BISHOPSGATE.

Cover of the 1848 30-page edition of the *Manifesto of the Communist Party*

gradation of social rank. In ancient Rome we have patricians, knights, plebeians, slaves; in the Middle Ages, feudal lords, vassals, guild-masters, journeymen, apprentices,[a] serfs; in almost all of these classes, again, subordinate gradations.

The modern bourgeois society that has sprouted from the ruins of feudal society has not done away with class antagonisms. It has but established new classes, new conditions of oppression, new forms of struggle in place of the old ones.

Our epoch, the epoch of the bourgeoisie, possesses, however, this distinctive feature: it has simplified the class antagonisms. Society as a whole is more and more splitting up into two great hostile camps, into two great classes directly facing each other: Bourgeoisie and Proletariat.

From the serfs of the Middle Ages sprang the chartered burghers of the earliest towns. From these burgesses the first elements of the bourgeoisie were developed.

The discovery of America, the rounding of the Cape, opened up fresh ground for the rising bourgeoisie. The East-Indian and Chinese markets, the colonisation of America, trade with the colonies, the increase in the means of exchange and in commodities generally, gave to commerce, to navigation, to industry, an impulse never before known, and thereby, to the revolutionary element in the tottering feudal society, a rapid development.

The feudal system of industry, under which industrial production was monopolised by closed guilds,[b] now no longer sufficed for the growing wants of the new markets. The manufacturing system took its place. The guild-masters were pushed on one side by the manufacturing middle class;[c] division of labour between the different corporate guilds vanished in the face of division of labour in each single workshop.

Meantime the markets kept ever growing, the demand ever rising. Even manufacture no longer sufficed. Thereupon, steam and machinery revolutionised industrial production. The place of manufacture was taken by the giant, Modern Industry, the place of the industrial middle class, by industrial millionaires, the leaders of whole industrial armies, the modern bourgeois.

---

[a] The German editions of 1848, 1872, 1883 and 1890 have "journeymen" ("Gesellen") instead of "journeymen, apprentices".—*Ed.*

[b] In the German editions the beginning of the phrase is: "The former feudal, or guild, organisation of industry".—*Ed.*

[c] The German editions have here and below "middle estate" ("Mittelstand") instead of "middle class".—*Ed.*

Modern[a] industry has established the world market, for which the discovery of America paved the way. This market has given an immense development to commerce, to navigation, to communication by land. This development has, in its turn, reacted on the extension of industry; and in proportion as industry, commerce, navigation, railways extended, in the same proportion the bourgeoisie developed, increased its capital, and pushed into the background every class handed down from the Middle Ages.

We see, therefore, how the modern bourgeoisie is itself the product of a long course of development, of a series of revolutions in the modes of production and of exchange.

Each step in the development of the bourgeoisie was accompanied by a corresponding political advance of that class.[b] An oppressed class[c] under the sway of the feudal nobility, an armed and self-governing association in the medieval commune*; here independent urban republic (as in Italy and Germany), there taxable "third estate" of the monarchy (as in France),[d] afterwards, in the period of manufacture proper, serving either the semi-feudal[e] or the absolute monarchy as a counterpoise against the nobility, and, in fact, cornerstone of the great monarchies in general, the bourgeoisie has at last, since the establishment of Modern Industry and of the world market, conquered for itself, in the modern representative State, exclusive political sway. The executive of the modern State is but a committee for managing the common affairs of the whole bourgeoisie.

The bourgeoisie, historically, has played a most revolutionary part.

The bourgeoisie, wherever it has got the upper hand, has put an end to all feudal, patriarchal, idyllic relations. It has pitilessly torn

* "Commune" was the name taken, in France, by the nascent towns even before they had conquered from their feudal lords and masters local self-government and political rights as the "Third Estate". Generally speaking, for the economical development of the bourgeoisie, England is here taken as the typical country; for its political development, France. [*Note by Engels to the English edition of 1888.*]

This was the name given their urban communities by the townsmen of Italy and France, after they had purchased or wrested their initial rights of self-government from their feudal lords. [*Note by Engels to the German edition of 1890.*]

---

[a] The German editions have here and below "large-scale" instead of "modern".—*Ed.*

[b] The words "of that class" were added in the English edition of 1888.—*Ed.*

[c] The German editions have "estate" instead of "class".—*Ed.*

[d] The words "medieval", "(as in Italy and Germany)", "(as in France)" were added in the English edition of 1888.—*Ed.*

[e] The German editions have "estate" instead of "semi-feudal".—*Ed.*

asunder the motley feudal ties that bound man to his "natural superiors", and has left remaining no other nexus between man and man than naked self-interest, than callous "cash payment". It has drowned the most heavenly ecstasies of religious fervour, of chivalrous enthusiasm, of philistine sentimentalism, in the icy water of egotistical calculation. It has resolved personal worth into exchange value, and in place of the numberless indefeasible chartered freedoms, has set up that single, unconscionable freedom—Free Trade. In one word, for exploitation, veiled by religious and political illusions, it has substituted naked, shameless, direct, brutal exploitation.

The bourgeoisie has stripped of its halo every occupation hitherto honoured and looked up to with reverent awe. It has converted the physician, the lawyer, the priest, the poet, the man of science, into its paid wage-labourers.

The bourgeoisie has torn away from the family its sentimental veil, and has reduced the family relation to a mere money relation.

The bourgeoisie has disclosed how it came to pass that the brutal display of vigour in the Middle Ages, which Reactionists so much admire, found its fitting complement in the most slothful indolence. It has been the first to show what man's activity can bring about. It has accomplished wonders far surpassing Egyptian pyramids, Roman aqueducts, and Gothic cathedrals; it has conducted expeditions that put in the shade all former Exoduses of nations and crusades.

The bourgeoisie cannot exist without constantly revolutionising the instruments of production, and thereby the relations of production, and with them the whole relations of society. Conservation of the old modes of production in unaltered form, was, on the contrary, the first condition of existence for all earlier industrial classes. Constant revolutionising of production, uninterrupted disturbance of all social conditions, everlasting uncertainty and agitation distinguish the bourgeois epoch from all earlier ones. All fixed, fast-frozen relations, with their train of ancient and venerable prejudices and opinions, are swept away, all new-formed ones become antiquated before they can ossify. All that is solid melts into air, all that is holy is profaned, and man is at last compelled to face with sober senses, his real conditions of life, and his relations with his kind.

The need of a constantly expanding market for its products chases the bourgeoisie over the whole surface of the globe. It must nestle everywhere, settle everywhere, establish connexions everywhere.

The bourgeoisie has through its exploitation of the world market given a cosmopolitan character to production and consumption in every country. To the great chagrin of Reactionists, it has drawn from under the feet of industry the national ground on which it stood. All old-established national industries have been destroyed or are daily being destroyed. They are dislodged by new industries, whose introduction becomes a life and death question for all civilised nations, by industries that no longer work up indigenous raw material, but raw material drawn from the remotest zones; industries whose products are consumed, not only at home, but in every quarter of the globe. In place of the old wants, satisfied by the productions of the country, we find new wants, requiring for their satisfaction the products of distant lands and climes. In place of the old local and national seclusion and self-sufficiency, we have intercourse in every direction, universal inter-dependence of nations. And as in material, so also in intellectual production. The intellectual creations of individual nations become common property. National one-sidedness and narrow-mindedness become more and more impossible, and from the numerous national and local literatures, there arises a world literature.

The bourgeoisie, by the rapid improvement of all instruments of production, by the immensely facilitated means of communication, draws all, even the most barbarian, nations into civilisation. The cheap prices of its commodities are the heavy artillery with which it batters down all Chinese walls, with which it forces the barbarians' intensely obstinate hatred of foreigners to capitulate. It compels all nations, on pain of extinction, to adopt the bourgeois mode of production; it compels them to introduce what it calls civilisation into their midst, i.e., to become bourgeois themselves. In one word, it creates a world after its own image.

The bourgeoisie has subjected the country to the rule of the towns. It has created enormous cities, has greatly increased the urban population as compared with the rural, and has thus rescued a considerable part of the population from the idiocy of rural life. Just as it has made the country dependent on the towns, so it has made barbarian and semi-barbarian countries dependent on the civilised ones, nations of peasants on nations of bourgeois, the East on the West.

The bourgeoisie keeps more and more doing away with the scattered state of the population, of the means of production, and of property. It has agglomerated population, centralised means of production, and has concentrated property in a few hands. The necessary consequence of this was political centralisation. Independent, or but loosely connected provinces with separate interests, laws, governments and systems of taxation, became lumped together into one nation, with one government, one code of laws, one national class-interest, one frontier and one customs-tariff.

The bourgeoisie, during its rule of scarce one hundred years, has created more massive and more colossal productive forces than have all preceding generations together. Subjection of Nature's forces to man, machinery, application of chemistry to industry and agriculture, steam-navigation, railways, electric telegraphs, clearing of whole continents for cultivation, canalisation of rivers, whole populations conjured out of the ground—what earlier century had even a presentiment that such productive forces slumbered in the lap of social labour?

We see then: the means of production and of exchange, on whose foundation the bourgeoisie built itself up, were generated in feudal society. At a certain stage in the development of these means of production and of exchange, the conditions under which feudal society produced and exchanged, the feudal organisation of agriculture and manufacturing industry, in one word, the feudal relations of property became no longer compatible with the already developed productive forces[a]; they became so many fetters. They had to be burst asunder; they were burst asunder.

Into their place stepped free competition, accompanied by a social and political constitution adapted to it, and by the economical and political sway of the bourgeois class.

A similar movement is going on before our own eyes. Modern bourgeois society with its relations of production, of exchange and of property, a society that has conjured up such gigantic means of production and of exchange, is like the sorcerer, who is no longer able to control the powers of the nether world whom he has called up by his spells. For many a decade past the history of industry and commerce is but the history of the revolt of modern productive forces against modern conditions of production, against the property relations that are the conditions for the existence of the bourgeoisie and of its rule. It is enough to mention the commercial crises that by their periodical return put on its trial, each time more threateningly, the existence of the entire bourgeois society. In these crises a great part not only of the existing products, but also of the previously created productive forces, are periodically destroyed. In

[a] The German editions add: "they hindered production instead of developing it".—*Ed.*

these crises there breaks out an epidemic[a] that, in all earlier epochs, would have seemed an absurdity—the epidemic of over-production. Society suddenly finds itself put back into a state of momentary barbarism; it appears as if a famine, a universal war of devastation had cut off the supply of every means of subsistence; industry and commerce seem to be destroyed; and why? Because there is too much civilisation, too much means of subsistence, too much industry, too much commerce. The productive forces at the disposal of society no longer tend to further the development of the conditions of bourgeois property[b]; on the contrary, they have become too powerful for these conditions, by which they are fettered, and so soon as they overcome these fetters, they bring disorder into the whole of bourgeois society, endanger the existence of bourgeois property. The conditions of bourgeois society are too narrow to comprise the wealth created by them. And how does the bourgeoisie get over these crises? On the one hand by enforced destruction of a mass of productive forces; on the other, by the conquest of new markets, and by the more thorough exploitation of the old ones. That is to say, by paving the way for more extensive and more destructive crises, and by diminishing the means whereby crises are prevented.

The weapons with which the bourgeoisie felled feudalism to the ground are now turned against the bourgeoisie itself.

But not only has the bourgeoisie forged the weapons that bring death to itself; it has also called into existence the men who are to wield those weapons—the modern working class—the proletarians.[c]

In proportion as the bourgeoisie, *i.e.*, capital, is developed, in the same proportion is the proletariat, the modern working class, developed—a class of labourers, who live only so long as they find work, and who find work only so long as their labour increases capital. These labourers, who must sell themselves piecemeal, are a commodity, like every other article of commerce, and are consequently exposed to all the vicissitudes of competition, to all the fluctuations of the market.

Owing to the extensive use of machinery and to division of labour, the work of the proletarians has lost all individual character, and, consequently, all charm for the workman. He becomes an append-

---

[a] The German editions have: "a social epidemic".—*Ed.*

[b] The German editions of 1848 have: "bourgeois civilisation and the conditions of bourgeois property".—*Ed.*

[c] The German editions have: "the modern workers, the *proletarians*".—*Ed.*

age of the machine, and it is only the most simple, most monotonous, and most easily acquired knack, that is required of him. Hence, the cost of production of a workman is restricted, almost entirely, to the means of subsistence that he requires for his maintenance, and for the propagation of his race. But the price of a commodity, and therefore also of labour,[258] is equal to its cost of production. In proportion, therefore, as the repulsiveness of the work increases, the wage decreases. Nay more, in proportion as the use of machinery and division of labour increases, in the same proportion the burden of toil[a] also increases, whether by prolongation of the working hours, by increase of the work exacted in a given time or by increased speed of the machinery, etc.

Modern industry has converted the little workshop of the patriarchal master into the great factory of the industrial capitalist. Masses of labourers, crowded into the factory, are organised like soldiers. As privates of the industrial army they are placed under the command of a perfect hierarchy of officers and sergeants. Not only are they slaves of the bourgeois class, and of the bourgeois State; they are daily and hourly enslaved by the machine, by the overlooker, and, above all, by the individual bourgeois manufacturer himself. The more openly this despotism proclaims gain to be its end and aim, the more petty, the more hateful and the more embittering it is.

The less the skill and exertion of strength implied in manual labour, in other words, the more modern industry becomes developed, the more is the labour of men superseded by that of women.[b] Differences of age and sex have no longer any distinctive social validity for the working class. All are instruments of labour, more or less expensive to use, according to their age and sex.

No sooner is the exploitation of the labourer by the manufacturer, so far, at an end, and he receives his wages in cash, than he is set upon by the other portions of the bourgeoisie, the landlord, the shopkeeper, the pawnbroker, etc.

The lower strata of the middle class[c]—the small tradespeople, shopkeepers, and retired tradesmen generally,[d] the handicraftsmen and peasants—all these sink gradually into the proletariat, partly

---

[a] The German editions have: "the quantity of labour".—*Ed.*

[b] The German 23-page edition of 1848 has: "of women and children".—*Ed.*

[c] The German editions have: "The former lower strata of the middle estate".—*Ed.*

[d] The German editions have: "and rentiers" instead of "and retired tradesmen generally".—*Ed.*

because their diminutive capital does not suffice for the scale on which Modern Industry is carried on, and is swamped in the competition with the large capitalists, partly because their specialised skill is rendered worthless by new methods of production. Thus the proletariat is recruited from all classes of the population.

The proletariat goes through various stages of development. With its birth begins its struggle with the bourgeoisie. At first the contest is carried on by individual labourers, then by the workpeople of a factory, then by the operatives of one trade, in one locality, against the individual bourgeois who directly exploits them. They direct their attacks not against the bourgeois conditions of production, but against the instruments of production themselves[a]; they destroy imported wares that compete with their labour, they smash to pieces machinery, they set factories ablaze, they seek to restore by force the vanished status of the workman of the Middle Ages.

At this stage the labourers still form an incoherent[b] mass scattered over the whole country, and broken up by their mutual competition. If anywhere they unite to form more compact bodies, this is not yet the consequence of their own active union, but of the union of the bourgeoisie, which class, in order to attain its own political ends, is compelled to set the whole proletariat in motion, and is moreover yet, for a time, able to do so. At this stage, therefore, the proletarians do not fight their enemies, but the enemies of their enemies, the remnants of absolute monarchy, the landowners, the non-industrial bourgeois, the petty bourgeoisie. Thus the whole historical movement is concentrated in the hands of the bourgeoisie; every victory so obtained is a victory for the bourgeoisie.

But with the development of industry the proletariat not only increases in number; it becomes concentrated in greater masses, its strength grows, and it feels that strength more. The various interests and conditions of life within the ranks of the proletariat are more and more equalised, in proportion as machinery obliterates all distinctions of labour, and nearly everywhere reduces wages to the same low level. The growing competition among the bourgeois, and the resulting commercial crises, make the wages of the workers ever more fluctuating. The unceasing improvement of machinery, ever more rapidly developing, makes their livelihood more and more precarious; the collisions between individual workmen and individu-

---

[a] The German editions have: "They direct their attacks not only against the bourgeois conditions of production, they direct them against the instruments of production themselves."—*Ed.*

[b] This word was inserted in the English edition of 1888.—*Ed.*

al bourgeois take more and more the character of collisions between two classes. Thereupon the workers begin to form combinations (Trades' Unions)[a] against the bourgeois; they club together in order to keep up the rate of wages; they found permanent associations in order to make provision beforehand for these occasional revolts. Here and there the contest breaks out into riots.

Now and then the workers are victorious, but only for a time. The real fruit of their battles lies, not in the immediate result, but in the ever-expanding union of the workers. This union is helped on by the improved means of communication that are created by modern industry and that place the workers of different localities in contact with one another. It was just this contact that was needed to centralise the numerous local struggles, all of the same character, into one national struggle between classes. But every class struggle is a political struggle. And that union, to attain which the burghers of the Middle Ages, with their miserable highways, required centuries, the modern proletarians, thanks to railways, achieve in a few years.

This organisation of the proletarians into a class, and consequently into a political party, is continually being upset again by the competition between the workers themselves. But it ever rises up again, stronger, firmer, mightier. It compels legislative recognition of particular interests of the workers, by taking advantage of the divisions among the bourgeoisie itself. Thus the ten-hours' bill in England was carried.[259]

Altogether collisions between the classes of the old society further, in many ways, the course of development of the proletariat. The bourgeoisie finds itself involved in a constant battle. At first with the aristocracy; later on, with those portions of the bourgeoisie itself, whose interests have become antagonistic to the progress of industry; at all times, with the bourgeoisie of foreign countries. In all these battles it sees itself compelled to appeal to the proletariat, to ask for its help, and thus, to drag it into the political arena. The bourgeoisie itself, therefore, supplies the proletariat with its own elements of political and general[b] education, in other words, it furnishes the proletariat with weapons for fighting the bourgeoisie.

Further, as we have already seen, entire sections of the ruling classes are, by the advance of industry, precipitated into the proletariat, or are at least threatened in their conditions of existence.

---

[a] The words in parentheses were inserted in the English edition of 1888.—*Ed.*

[b] The words "political and general" were added in the English edition of 1888.—*Ed.*

These also supply the proletariat with fresh elements of enlightenment and progress.[a]

Finally, in times when the class struggle nears the decisive hour, the process of dissolution going on within the ruling class, in fact within the whole range of old society, assumes such a violent, glaring character, that a small section of the ruling class cuts itself adrift, and joins the revolutionary class, the class that holds the future in its hands. Just as, therefore, at an earlier period, a section of the nobility went over to the bourgeoisie, so now a portion of the bourgeoisie goes over to the proletariat, and in particular, a portion of the bourgeois ideologists, who have raised themselves to the level of comprehending theoretically the historical movement as a whole.

Of all the classes that stand face to face with the bourgeoisie today, the proletariat alone is a really revolutionary class. The other classes decay and finally disappear in the face of Modern Industry; the proletariat is its special and essential product.

The lower middle class,[b] the small manufacturer, the shopkeeper, the artisan, the peasant, all these fight against the bourgeoisie, to save from extinction their existence as fractions of the middle class. They are therefore not revolutionary, but conservative. Nay more, they are reactionary, for they try to roll back the wheel of history. If by chance they are revolutionary, they are so only in view of their impending transfer into the proletariat, they thus defend not their present, but their future interests, they desert their own standpoint to place themselves at that of the proletariat.

The "dangerous class", the social scum,[c] that passively rotting mass thrown off by the lowest layers of old society may, here and there, be swept into the movement by a proletarian revolution; its conditions of life, however, prepare it far more for the part of a bribed tool of reactionary intrigue.

In the conditions of the proletariat, those of old society at large are already virtually swamped. The proletarian is without property; his relation to his wife and children has no longer anything in common with the bourgeois family relations; modern industrial labour, modern subjection to capital, the same in England as in France, in America as in Germany, has stripped him of every trace of national character. Law, morality, religion, are to him so many bourgeois

[a] The German editions have "elements of education" instead of "elements of enlightenment and progress".—*Ed.*

[b] The German editions have here and below "middle estates" instead of "the lower middle class" and "the middle class".—*Ed.*

[c] The German editions have "lumpen proletariat" instead of "the dangerous class, the social scum".—*Ed.*

prejudices, behind which lurk in ambush just as many bourgeois interests.

All the preceding classes that got the upper hand, sought to fortify their already acquired status by subjecting society at large to their conditions of appropriation. The proletarians cannot become masters of the productive forces of society, except by abolishing their own previous mode of appropriation, and thereby also every other previous mode of appropriation. They have nothing of their own to secure and to fortify; their mission is to destroy all previous securities for, and insurances of, individual property.

All previous historical[a] movements were movements of minorities, or in the interest of minorities. The proletarian movement is the self-conscious,[a] independent movement of the immense majority, in the interest of the immense majority. The proletariat, the lowest stratum of our present society, cannot stir, cannot raise itself up, without the whole superincumbent strata of official society being sprung into the air.

Though not in substance, yet in form, the struggle of the proletariat with the bourgeoisie is at first a national struggle. The proletariat of each country must, of course, first of all settle matters with its own bourgeoisie.

In depicting the most general phases of the development of the proletariat, we traced the more or less veiled civil war, raging within existing society, up to the point where that war breaks out into open revolution, and where the violent overthrow of the bourgeoisie lays the foundation for the sway of the proletariat.

Hitherto, every form of society has been based, as we have already seen, on the antagonism of oppressing and oppressed classes. But in order to oppress a class, certain conditions must be assured to it under which it can, at least, continue its slavish existence. The serf, in the period of serfdom, raised himself to membership in the commune, just as the petty bourgeois, under the yoke of feudal absolutism, managed to develop into a bourgeois. The modern labourer, on the contrary, instead of rising with the progress of industry, sinks deeper and deeper below the conditions of existence of his own class. He becomes a pauper, and pauperism develops more rapidly than population and wealth. And here it becomes evident, that the bourgeoisie is unfit any longer to be the ruling class in society, and to impose its conditions of existence upon society as an over-riding law. It is unfit to rule because it is incompetent to assure an existence to its slave within his slavery, because it cannot help

---

[a] This word was added in the English edition of 1888.—*Ed.*

letting him sink into such a state, that it has to feed him, instead of being fed by him. Society can no longer live under this bourgeoisie, in other words, its existence is no longer compatible with society.

The essential condition for the existence, and for the sway of the bourgeois class, is[a] the formation and augmentation of capital; the condition for capital is wage-labour. Wage-labour rests exclusively on competition between the labourers. The advance of industry, whose involuntary promoter is the bourgeoisie, replaces the isolation of the labourers, due to competition, by their revolutionary combination, due to association. The development of Modern Industry, therefore, cuts from under its feet the very foundation on which the bourgeoisie produces and appropriates products. What the bourgeoisie, therefore, produces, above all, is its own grave-diggers. Its fall and the victory of the proletariat are equally inevitable.

[a] The German editions have here: "The accumulation of wealth in the hands of individuals".—*Ed.*

II

PROLETARIANS AND COMMUNISTS

In what relation do the Communists stand to the proletarians as a whole?

The Communists do not form a separate party opposed to other working-class parties.

They have no interests separate and apart from those of the proletariat as a whole.

They do not set up any sectarian[a] principles of their own, by which to shape and mould the proletarian movement.

The Communists are distinguished from the other working-class parties by this only: 1. In the national struggles of the proletarians of the different countries, they point out and bring to the front the common interests of the entire proletariat, independently of all nationality. 2. In the various stages of development which the struggle of the working class against the bourgeoisie has to pass through, they always and everywhere represent the interests of the movement as a whole.

The Communists, therefore, are on the one hand, practically, the most advanced and[b] resolute section of the working-class parties of every country, that section which pushes forward all others; on the other hand, theoretically, they have over the great mass of the proletariat the advantage of clearly understanding the line of march, the conditions, and the ultimate general results of the proletarian movement.

---

[a] The German editions have "separate" instead of "sectarian".—*Ed.*

[b] The words "the most advanced and" were added in the English edition of 1888.—*Ed.*

The immediate aim of the Communists is the same as that of all the other proletarian parties: formation of the proletariat into a class, overthrow of the bourgeois supremacy, conquest of political power by the proletariat.

The theoretical conclusions of the Communists are in no way based on ideas or principles that have been invented, or discovered by this or that would-be universal reformer.

They merely express, in general terms, actual relations springing from an existing class struggle, from a historical movement going on under our very eyes. The abolition of existing property relations is not at all a distinctive feature of Communism.

All property relations in the past have continually been subject to historical change consequent upon the change in historical conditions.[a]

The French Revolution, for example, abolished feudal property in favour of bourgeois property.

The distinguishing feature of Communism is not the abolition of property generally, but the abolition of bourgeois property. But modern bourgeois private property is the final and most complete expression of the system of producing and appropriating products, that is based on class antagonisms, on the exploitation of the many by the few.[b]

In this sense, the theory of the Communists may be summed up in the single sentence: Abolition of private property.

We Communists have been reproached with the desire of abolishing the right of personally acquiring property as the fruit of a man's own labour, which property is alleged to be the groundwork of all personal freedom, activity and independence.

Hard-won, self-acquired, self-earned property! Do you mean the property of the petty artisan[c] and of the small peasant, a form of property that preceded the bourgeois form? There is no need to abolish that; the development of industry has to a great extent already destroyed it, and is still destroying it daily.

Or do you mean modern bourgeois private property?

But does wage-labour create any property for the labourer? Not a bit. It creates capital, *i.e.*, that kind of property which exploits wage-labour, and which cannot increase except upon condition of begetting a new supply of wage-labour for fresh exploitation.

---

[a] In the German editions this phrase reads: "All property relations have been subject to constant historical replacement, constant historical change."—*Ed.*

[b] The German editions have: "the exploitation of the ones by the others".—*Ed.*

[c] The German editions have: "the property of the petty bourgeois".—*Ed.*

Property, in its present form, is based on the antagonism of capital and wage-labour. Let us examine both sides of this antagonism.

To be a capitalist is to have not only a purely personal, but a social *status* in production. Capital is a collective product, and only by the united action of many members, nay, in the last resort, only by the united action of all members of society, can it be set in motion.

Capital is, therefore, not a personal, it is a social power.

When, therefore, capital is converted into common property, into the property of all members of society, personal property is not thereby transformed into social property. It is only the social character of the property that is changed. It loses its class character.

Let us now take wage-labour.

The average price of wage-labour is the minimum wage, *i.e.*, that quantum of the means of subsistence, which is absolutely requisite to keep the labourer in bare existence as a labourer. What, therefore, the wage-labourer appropriates by means of his labour, merely suffices to prolong and reproduce a bare existence. We by no means intend to abolish this personal appropriation of the products of labour, an appropriation that is made for the maintenance and reproduction of human life, and that leaves no surplus wherewith to command the labour of others. All that we want to do away with is the miserable character of this appropriation, under which the labourer lives merely to increase capital, and is allowed to live only in so far as the interest of the ruling class requires it.

In bourgeois society, living labour is but a means to increase accumulated labour. In Communist society, accumulated labour is but a means to widen, to enrich, to promote the existence of the labourer.

In bourgeois society, therefore, the past dominates the present; in Communist society, the present dominates the past. In bourgeois society capital is independent and has individuality, while the living person is dependent and has no individuality.

And the abolition of this state of things is called by the bourgeois abolition of individuality and freedom! And rightly so. The abolition of bourgeois individuality, bourgeois independence, and bourgeois freedom is undoubtedly aimed at.

By freedom is meant, under the present bourgeois conditions of production, free trade, free selling and buying.

But if selling and buying disappears, free selling and buying disappears also. This talk about free selling and buying, and all the other "brave words" of our bourgeoisie about freedom in general, have a meaning, if any, only in contrast with restricted selling and buying, with the fettered traders of the Middle Ages, but have no meaning when opposed to the Communistic abolition of buying and selling, of the bourgeois conditions of production, and of the bourgeoisie itself.

You are horrified at our intending to do away with private property. But in your existing society, private property is already done away with for nine-tenths of the population; its existence for the few[a] is solely due to its non-existence in the hands of those nine-tenths. You reproach us, therefore, with intending to do away with a form of property, the necessary condition for whose existence is the non-existence of any property for the immense majority of society.

In one word, you reproach us with intending to do away with your property. Precisely so; that is just what we intend.

From the moment when labour can no longer be converted into capital, money, or rent, into a social power capable of being monopolised, *i.e.*, from the moment when individual property can no longer be transformed into bourgeois property, into capital,[b] from that moment, you say, individuality vanishes.

You must, therefore, confess that by "individual" you mean no other person than the bourgeois, than the middle-class owner of property. This person must, indeed, be swept out of the way, and made impossible.[c]

Communism deprives no man of the power to appropriate the products of society; all that it does is to deprive him of the power to subjugate the labour of others by means of such appropriation.

It has been objected that upon the abolition of private property all work will cease, and universal laziness will overtake us.

According to this, bourgeois society ought long ago to have gone to the dogs through sheer idleness; for those of its members who work, acquire nothing, and those who acquire anything, do not work. The whole of this objection is but another expression of the tautology: that there can no longer be any wage-labour when there is no longer any capital.

All objections urged against the Communistic mode of producing and appropriating material products, have, in the same way, been urged against the Communistic modes of producing and appropriating intellectual products. Just as, to the bourgeois, the disap-

---

[a] The words "for the few" were added in the English edition of 1888.—*Ed.*

[b] The words "into capital" were added in the English edition of 1888.—*Ed.*

[c] The words "and made impossible" were added in the English edition of 1888.—*Ed.*

pearance of class property is the disappearance of production itself, so the disappearance of class culture[a] is to him identical with the disappearance of all culture.

That culture, the loss of which he laments, is, for the enormous majority, a mere training to act as a machine.

But don't wrangle with us so long as you apply, to our intended[b] abolition of bourgeois property, the standard of your bourgeois notions of freedom, culture, law, &c. Your very ideas are but the outgrowth of the conditions of your bourgeois production and bourgeois property, just as your jurisprudence is but the will of your class made into a law for all, a will, whose essential character and direction are determined by the economical conditions of existence of your class.[c]

The selfish misconception that induces you to transform into eternal laws of nature and of reason, the social forms springing from your present mode of production and form of property—historical relations that rise and disappear in the progress of production—this misconception you share with every ruling class that has preceded you.[d] What you see clearly in the case of ancient property, what you admit in the case of feudal property, you are of course forbidden to admit in the case of your own bourgeois form of property.

Abolition of the family! Even the most radical flare up at this infamous proposal of the Communists.

On what foundation is the present family, the bourgeois family, based? On capital, on private gain. In its completely developed form this family exists only among the bourgeoisie. But this state of things finds its complement in the practical absence of the family among the proletarians, and in public prostitution.

The bourgeois family will vanish as a matter of course when its complement vanishes, and both will vanish with the vanishing of capital.

Do you charge us with wanting to stop the exploitation of children by their parents? To this crime we plead guilty.

But, you will say, we destroy the most hallowed of relations, when we replace home education by social.

---

[a] The German editions have here and below "education" ["Bildung"] instead of "culture".—*Ed.*

[b] The words "our intended" were inserted in the English edition of 1888.—*Ed.*

[c] In the German editions the end of this sentence reads as follows: "a will, whose content is determined by the material conditions of existence of your class."—*Ed.*

[d] In the German editions this sentence reads as follows: "This selfish conception... you share with all the ruling classes which have perished."—*Ed.*

And your education! Is not that also social, and determined by the social conditions under which you educate, by the intervention, direct or indirect, of society, by means of schools, &c.? The Communists have not invented the intervention of society in education; they do but seek to alter the character of that intervention, and to rescue education from the influence of the ruling class.

The bourgeois clap-trap about the family and education, about the hallowed co-relation of parent and child, becomes all the more disgusting, the more, by the action of Modern Industry, all family ties among the proletarians are torn asunder, and their children transformed into simple articles of commerce and instruments of labour.

But you Communists would introduce community of women, screams the whole bourgeoisie in chorus.

The bourgeois sees in his wife a mere instrument of production. He hears that the instruments of production are to be exploited in common, and, naturally, can come to no other conclusion than that the lot of being common to all will likewise fall to the women.

He has not even a suspicion that the real point aimed at is to do away with the status of women as mere instruments of production.

For the rest, nothing is more ridiculous than the virtuous indignation of our bourgeois at the community of women which, they pretend, is to be openly and officially established by the Communists. The Communists have no need to introduce community of women; it has existed almost from time immemorial.

Our bourgeois, not content with having the wives and daughters of their proletarians at their disposal, not to speak of common prostitutes, take the greatest pleasure in seducing each other's wives.

Bourgeois marriage is in reality a system of wives in common and thus, at the most, what the Communists might possibly be reproached with, is that they desire to introduce, in substitution for a hypocritically concealed, an openly legalised community of women. For the rest, it is self-evident that the abolition of the present system of production must bring with it the abolition of the community of women springing from that system, *i.e.*, of prostitution both public and private.

The Communists are further reproached with desiring to abolish countries and nationality.

The working men have no country. We cannot take from them what they have not got. Since the proletariat must first of all acquire political supremacy, must rise to be the leading class of the nation,[a] must constitute itself *the* nation, it is so far, itself national, though not in the bourgeois sense of the word.

National differences and antagonisms between peoples are daily more and more vanishing, owing to the development of the bourgeoisie, to freedom of commerce, to the world market, to uniformity in the mode of production and in the conditions of life corresponding thereto.

The supremacy of the proletariat will cause them to vanish still faster. United action, of the leading civilised countries at least, is one of the first conditions for the emancipation of the proletariat.

In proportion as the exploitation of one individual by another is put an end to, the exploitation of one nation by another will also be put an end to. In proportion as the antagonism between classes within the nation vanishes, the hostility of one nation to another will come to an end.

The charges against Communism made from a religious, a philosophical, and, generally, from an ideological standpoint, are not deserving of serious examination.

Does it require deep intuition to comprehend that man's ideas, views and conceptions, in one word, man's consciousness, changes with every change in the conditions of his material[b] existence, in his social relations and in his social life?

What else does the history of ideas prove, than that intellectual production changes its character in proportion as material production is changed? The ruling ideas of each age have ever been the ideas of its ruling class.

When people speak of ideas that revolutionise society, they do but express the fact, that within the old society, the elements of a new one have been created, and that the dissolution of the old ideas keeps even pace with the dissolution of the old conditions of existence.

When the ancient world was in its last throes, the ancient religions were overcome by Christianity. When Christian ideas succumbed in the 18th century to rationalist ideas,[c] feudal society fought its death battle with the then revolutionary bourgeoisie. The ideas of religious liberty and freedom of conscience merely gave expression to the sway of free competition within the domain of knowledge.

---

[a] The German editions of 1848 have "the national class" instead of "the leading class of the nation".—*Ed.*

[b] The word "material" was added in the English edition of 1888.—*Ed.*

[c] The German editions have "the ideas of enlightenment" instead of "rationalist ideas".—*Ed.*

"Undoubtedly," it will be said, "religious, moral, philosophical and juridical ideas[a] have been modified in the course of historical development. But religion, morality, philosophy, political science, and law, constantly survived this change.

"There are, besides, eternal truths, such as Freedom, Justice, etc., that are common to all states of society. But Communism abolishes eternal truths, it abolishes all religion and all morality, instead of constituting them on a new basis; it therefore acts in contradiction to all past historical experience."

What does this accusation reduce itself to? The history of all past society has consisted in the development of class antagonisms, antagonisms that assumed different forms at different epochs.

But whatever form they may have taken, one fact is common to all past ages, *viz.*, the exploitation of one part of society by the other. No wonder, then, that the social consciousness of past ages, despite all the multiplicity and variety it displays, moves within certain common forms, or general ideas,[b] which cannot completely vanish except with the total disappearance of class antagonisms.

The Communist revolution is the most radical rupture with traditional property relations; no wonder that its development involves the most radical rupture with traditional ideas.

But let us have done with the bourgeois objections to Communism.

We have seen above, that the first step in the revolution by the working class is to raise the proletariat to the position of ruling class, to win the battle of democracy.

The proletariat will use its political supremacy to wrest, by degrees, all capital from the bourgeoisie, to centralise all instruments of production in the hands of the State, *i.e.*, of the proletariat organised as the ruling class; and to increase the total of productive forces as rapidly as possible.

Of course, in the beginning, this cannot be effected except by means of despotic inroads on the rights of property, and on the conditions of bourgeois production; by means of measures, therefore, which appear economically insufficient and untenable, but which, in the course of the movement, outstrip themselves, necessitate further inroads upon the old social order,[c] and are unavoidable as a means of entirely revolutionising the mode of production.

---

[a] In the German editions the beginning of the sentence reads: "'Undoubtedly,' it will be said, 'religious, moral, philosophical, political, juridical ideas, etc.'"—*Ed.*

[b] The German editions have "in forms of consciousness" instead of "or general ideas".—*Ed.*

[c] The words "necessitate further inroads upon the old social order" were added in the English edition of 1888.—*Ed.*

These measures will of course be different in different countries.[260]

Nevertheless in the most advanced countries, the following will be pretty generally applicable:

1. Abolition[a] of property in land and application of all rents of land to public purposes.
2. A heavy progressive or graduated income tax.[b]
3. Abolition of all right of inheritance.
4. Confiscation of the property of all emigrants and rebels.
5. Centralisation of credit in the hands of the State, by means of a national bank with State capital and an exclusive monopoly.
6. Centralisation of the means of communication and transport[c] in the hands of the State.
7. Extension of factories and instruments of production owned by the State; the bringing into cultivation of waste-lands, and the improvement of the soil generally in accordance with a common plan.
8. Equal liability of all to labour. Establishment of industrial armies, especially for agriculture.
9. Combination of agriculture with manufacturing industries; gradual abolition of the distinction between town and country, by a more equable distribution of the population over the country.[d]
10. Free education for all children in public schools. Abolition of children's factory labour in its present form. Combination of education with industrial production, &c., &c.

When, in the course of development, class distinctions have disappeared, and all production has been concentrated in the hands of a vast association of the whole nation,[e] the public power will lose its political character. Political power, properly so called, is merely the organised power of one class for oppressing another. If the proletariat during its contest with the bourgeoisie is compelled, by the force of circumstances, to organise itself as a class, if, by means of

---

[a] The German editions have here "expropriation".—*Ed.*

[b] The German editions have: "A heavy progressive tax."—*Ed.*

[c] The German editions have "all transport" instead of "the means of communication and transport".—*Ed.*

[d] In the editions of 1848, point 9 reads: "Combination of agriculture with industry, promotion of the gradual elimination of the contradictions between town and countryside." In subsequent German editions the word "contradictions" was replaced by "distinctions".—*Ed.*

[e] The German editions have "associated individuals" instead of "a vast association of the whole nation".—*Ed.*

a revolution, it makes itself the ruling class, and, as such, sweeps away by force the old conditions of production, then it will, along with these conditions, have swept away the conditions for the existence of class antagonisms and of classes generally, and will thereby have abolished its own supremacy as a class.

In place of the old bourgeois society, with its classes and class antagonisms, we shall have an association, in which the free development of each is the condition for the free development of all.

III

SOCIALIST AND COMMUNIST LITERATURE

1. REACTIONARY SOCIALISM

a. Feudal Socialism

Owing to their historical position, it became the vocation of the aristocracies of France and England to write pamphlets against modern bourgeois society. In the French revolution of July 1830, and in the English reform agitation, these aristocracies again succumbed to the hateful upstart. Thenceforth, a serious political contest was altogether out of question. A literary battle alone remained possible. But even in the domain of literature the old cries of the restoration period* had become impossible.

In order to arouse sympathy, the aristocracy were obliged to lose sight, apparently, of their own interests, and to formulate their indictment against the bourgeoisie in the interest of the exploited working class alone. Thus the aristocracy took their revenge by singing lampoons on their new master, and whispering in his ears sinister prophecies of coming catastrophe.[a]

In this way arose feudal Socialism; half lamentation, half lampoon; half echo of the past, half menace of the future; at times, by its bitter, witty and incisive criticism, striking the bourgeoisie to the very heart's core; but always ludicrous in its effect, through total incapacity to comprehend the march of modern history.

The aristocracy, in order to rally the people to them, waved the proletarian alms-bag in front for a banner. But the people, so often as it joined them, saw on their hindquarters the old feudal coats of arms, and deserted with loud and irreverent laughter.

* Not the English Restoration 1660 to 1689, but the French Restoration 1814 to 1830. [*Note by Engels to the English edition of 1888.*]

---

[a] In the German editions the end of this sentence reads: "and whispering in his ears more or less sinister prophecies."—*Ed.*

One section of the French Legitimists and "Young England"[261] exhibited this spectacle.

In pointing out that their mode of exploitation was different to that of the bourgeoisie, the feudalists forget that they exploited under circumstances and conditions that were quite different, and that are now antiquated. In showing that, under their rule, the modern proletariat never existed, they forget that the modern bourgeoisie is the necessary offspring of their own form of society.

For the rest, so little do they conceal the reactionary character of their criticism that their chief accusation against the bourgeoisie amounts to this, that under the bourgeois *régime* a class is being developed, which is destined to cut up root and branch the old order of society.

What they upbraid the bourgeoisie with is not so much that it creates a proletariat, as that it creates a *revolutionary* proletariat.

In political practice, therefore, they join in all coercive measures against the working class; and in ordinary life, despite their high-falutin phrases, they stoop to pick up the golden apples dropped from the tree of industry,[a] and to barter truth, love, and honour for traffic in wool, beetroot-sugar, and potato spirits.*

As the parson has ever gone hand in hand with the landlord,[b] so has Clerical Socialism with Feudal Socialism.

Nothing is easier than to give Christian asceticism a Socialist tinge. Has not Christianity declaimed against private property, against marriage, against the State? Has it not preached in the place of these, charity and poverty, celibacy and mortification of the flesh, monastic life and Mother Church? Christian[c] Socialism is but the holy water with which the priest consecrates the heart-burnings of the aristocrat.

* This applies chiefly to Germany where the landed aristocracy and squirearchy have large portions of their estates cultivated for their own account by stewards, and are, moreover, extensive beetroot-sugar manufacturers and distillers of potato spirits. The wealthier British aristocracy are, as yet, rather above that; but they, too, know how to make up for declining rents by lending their names to floaters of more or less shady joint-stock companies. [*Note by Engels to the English edition of 1888.*]

---

[a] The words "dropped from the tree of industry" were added in the English edition of 1888.—*Ed.*

[b] The German editions have here "feudal lord".—*Ed.*

[c] The German editions of 1848 have "holy" instead of "Christian" (the texts of these editions contain an obvious misprint: "heutige"—of today—for "heilige"—holy).—*Ed.*

b. Petty-Bourgeois Socialism

The feudal aristocracy was not the only class that was ruined by the bourgeoisie, not the only class whose conditions of existence pined and perished in the atmosphere of modern bourgeois society. The medieval burgesses and the small peasant proprietors were the precursors of the modern bourgeoisie. In those countries which are but little developed, industrially and commercially, these two classes still vegetate[a] side by side with the rising bourgeoisie.

In countries where modern civilisation has become fully developed, a new class of petty bourgeois has been formed, fluctuating between proletariat and bourgeoisie and ever renewing itself as a supplementary part of bourgeois society. The individual members of this class, however, are being constantly hurled down into the proletariat by the action of competition, and, as modern industry develops, they even see the moment approaching when they will completely disappear as an independent section of modern society, to be replaced, in manufactures, agriculture and commerce, by overlookers, bailiffs and shopmen.

In countries like France, where the peasants constitute far more than half of the population, it was natural that writers who sided with the proletariat against the bourgeoisie, should use, in their criticism of the bourgeois *régime*, the standard of the peasant and petty bourgeois, and from the standpoint of these intermediate classes[b] should take up the cudgels for the working class. Thus arose petty-bourgeois Socialism. Sismondi was the head of this school, not only in France but also in England.

This school of Socialism dissected with great acuteness the contradictions in the conditions of modern production. It laid bare the hypocritical apologies of economists. It proved, incontrovertibly, the disastrous effects of machinery and division of labour; the concentration of capital and land in a few hands; over-production and crises; it pointed out the inevitable ruin of the petty bourgeois and peasant, the misery of the proletariat, the anarchy in production, the crying inequalities in the distribution of wealth, the industrial war of extermination between nations, the dissolution of old moral bonds, of the old family relations, of the old nationalities.

In its positive aims, however, this form of Socialism aspires either to restoring the old means of production and of exchange, and with

---

[a] The German editions have "this class still vegetates" instead of "these two classes still vegetate".—*Ed.*

[b] The German editions have "the petty bourgeoisie" instead of "these intermediate classes".—*Ed.*

them the old property relations, and the old society, or to cramping the modern means of production and of exchange, within the framework of the old property relations that have been, and were bound to be, exploded by those means. In either case, it is both reactionary and Utopian.

Its last words are: corporate guilds for manufacture; patriarchal relations in agriculture.

Ultimately, when stubborn historical facts had dispersed all intoxicating effects of self-deception, this form of Socialism ended in a miserable fit of the blues.[a]

c. German, or "True", Socialism

The Socialist and Communist literature of France, a literature that originated under the pressure of a bourgeoisie in power, and that was the expression of the struggle against this power, was introduced into Germany at a time when the bourgeoisie, in that country, had just begun its contest with feudal absolutism.

German philosophers, would-be philosophers, and *beaux esprits*,[b] eagerly seized on this literature, only forgetting, that when these writings immigrated from France into Germany, French social conditions had not immigrated along with them. In contact with German social conditions, this French literature lost all its immediate practical significance, and assumed a purely literary aspect.[c] Thus, to the German philosophers of the Eighteenth Century, the demands of the first French Revolution were nothing more than the demands of "Practical Reason"[262] in general, and the utterance of the will of the revolutionary French bourgeoisie signified in their eyes the laws of pure Will, of Will as it was bound to be, of true human Will generally.

The work of the German *literati* consisted solely in bringing the new French ideas into harmony with their ancient philosophical conscience, or rather, in annexing the French ideas without deserting their own philosophic point of view.

---

[a] In the German editions this sentence reads: "In its further development this trend ended in a cowardly fit of the blues."—*Ed.*

[b] In the German editions the beginning of this sentence reads: "German philosophers, semi-philosophers and lovers of fine phrases".—*Ed.*

[c] In the German editions of 1848 there follows: "It must have appeared as idle speculation on true society, on the realisation of humanity." In subsequent German editions the words "on true society" were omitted.—*Ed.*

This annexation took place in the same way in which a foreign language is appropriated, namely, by translation.

It is well known how the monks wrote silly lives of Catholic Saints *over* the manuscripts on which the classical works of ancient heathendom had been written. The German *literati* reversed this process with the profane French literature. They wrote their philosophical nonsense beneath the French original. For instance, beneath the French criticism of the economic functions of money, they wrote "Alienation of Humanity", and beneath the French criticism of the bourgeois State they wrote, "Dethronement of the Category of the General", and so forth.[a]

The introduction of these philosophical phrases at the back of the French historical criticisms[b] they dubbed "Philosophy of Action", "True Socialism", "German Science of Socialism", "Philosophical Foundation of Socialism", and so on.

The French Socialist and Communist literature was thus completely emasculated. And, since it ceased in the hands of the German to express the struggle of one class with the other, he felt conscious of having overcome "French one-sidedness" and of representing, not true requirements, but the requirements of Truth; not the interests of the proletariat, but the interests of Human Nature, of Man in general, who belongs to no class, has no reality, who exists only in the misty realm of philosophical fantasy.

This German Socialism, which took its schoolboy task so seriously and solemnly, and extolled its poor stock-in-trade in such mountebank fashion, meanwhile gradually lost its pedantic innocence.

The fight of the German, and, especially, of the Prussian bourgeoisie, against feudal aristocracy and absolute monarchy, in other words, the liberal movement, became more earnest.

By this, the long wished-for opportunity was offered to "True" Socialism of confronting the political movement with the Socialist demands, of hurling the traditional anathemas against liberalism, against representative government, against bourgeois competition, bourgeois freedom of the press, bourgeois legislation, bourgeois liberty and equality, and of preaching to the masses that they had nothing to gain, and everything to lose, by this bourgeois movement.

---

[a] In the German editions this sentence reads: "For instance, beneath the French criticism of money relations they wrote, 'Alienation of Humanity', and beneath the French criticism of the bourgeois State they wrote, 'Elimination of the domination of the abstractly General', etc."—*Ed.*

[b] The German editions have "French theories" instead of "French historical criticisms".—*Ed.*

German Socialism forgot, in the nick of time, that the French criticism, whose silly echo it was, presupposed the existence of modern bourgeois society, with its corresponding economic[a] conditions of existence, and the political constitution adapted thereto, the very things whose attainment was the object of the pending struggle in Germany.

To the absolute governments,[b] with their following of parsons, professors, country squires and officials, it served as a welcome scarecrow against the threatening bourgeoisie.

It was a sweet finish after the bitter pills of floggings and bullets with which these same governments, just at that time,[c] dosed the German working-class risings.

While this "True" Socialism thus served the governments as a weapon for fighting the German bourgeoisie, it, at the same time, directly represented a reactionary interest, the interest of the German Philistines. In Germany the *petty-bourgeois* class, a relic of the sixteenth century, and since then constantly cropping up again under various forms, is the real social basis of the existing state of things.

To preserve this class is to preserve the existing state of things in Germany. The industrial and political supremacy of the bourgeoisie threatens it with certain destruction; on the one hand, from the concentration of capital; on the other, from the rise of a revolutionary proletariat. "True" Socialism appeared to kill these two birds with one stone. It spread like an epidemic.

The robe of speculative cobwebs, embroidered with flowers of rhetoric, steeped in the dew of sickly sentiment, this transcendental robe in which the German Socialists wrapped their sorry "eternal truths", all skin and bone, served to wonderfully increase the sale of their goods amongst such a public.

And on its part, German Socialism recognised, more and more, its own calling as the bombastic representative of the petty-bourgeois Philistine.

It proclaimed the German nation to be the model nation, and the German petty Philistine to be the typical man. To every villainous meanness of this model man it gave a hidden, higher, Socialistic interpretation, the exact contrary of its real character. It went to the extreme length of directly opposing the "brutally destructive" tendency of Communism, and of proclaiming its supreme and

[a] The German editions have "material" instead of "economic".—*Ed.*

[b] The German editions have "To the German absolute governments".—*Ed.*

[c] The words "just at that time" were added in the English edition of 1888.—*Ed.*

impartial contempt of all class struggles. With very few exceptions, all the so-called Socialist and Communist publications that now (1847) circulate in Germany belong to the domain of this foul and enervating literature.*

2. CONSERVATIVE, OR BOURGEOIS, SOCIALISM

A part of the bourgeoisie is desirous of redressing social grievances, in order to secure the continued existence of bourgeois society.

To this section belong economists, philanthropists, humanitarians, improvers of the condition of the working class, organisers of charity, members of societies for the prevention of cruelty to animals, temperance fanatics, hole-and-corner reformers of every imaginable kind. This form of Socialism has, moreover, been worked out into complete systems.

We may cite Proudhon's *Philosophie de la Misère* as an example of this form.

The Socialistic bourgeois want all the advantages of modern social conditions[a] without the struggles and dangers necessarily resulting therefrom. They desire the existing state of society minus its revolutionary and disintegrating elements. They wish for a bourgeoisie without a proletariat. The bourgeoisie naturally conceives the world in which it is supreme to be the best; and bourgeois Socialism develops this comfortable conception into various more or less complete systems.[b] In requiring the proletariat to carry out such a system, and thereby to march straightway into the social[c] New Jerusalem, it but requires in reality, that the proletariat should remain within the bounds of existing society, but should cast away all its hateful ideas concerning the bourgeoisie.

A second and more practical, but less systematic, form of this Socialism sought to depreciate every revolutionary movement in the eyes of the working class, by showing that no mere political reform, but only a change in the material conditions of existence, in

* The revolutionary storm of 1848 swept away this whole shabby tendency and cured its protagonists of the desire to dabble further in Socialism. The chief representative and classical type of this tendency is Herr Karl Grün. [*Note by Engels to the German edition of 1890.*]

---

[a] The German editions have: "want the living conditions of modern society".—*Ed.*

[b] The German editions have here: "a more or less complete system".—*Ed.*

[c] This word was added in the English edition of 1888.—*Ed.*

economical relations, could be of any advantage to them. By changes in the material conditions of existence, this form of Socialism, however, by no means understands abolition of the bourgeois relations of production, an abolition that can be effected only by a revolution, but administrative reforms, based on the continued existence of these relations; reforms, therefore, that in no respect affect the relations between capital and labour, but, at the best, lessen the cost, and simplify the administrative work, of bourgeois government.

Bourgeois Socialism attains adequate expression, when, and only when, it becomes a mere figure of speech.

Free trade: for the benefit of the working class. Protective duties: for the benefit of the working class. Prison Reform[a]: for the benefit of the working class. This is the last word and the only seriously meant word of bourgeois Socialism.

It is summed up in the phrase: the bourgeois is a bourgeois—for the benefit of the working class.

3. CRITICAL-UTOPIAN SOCIALISM AND COMMUNISM

We do not here refer to that literature which, in every great modern revolution, has always given voice to the demands of the proletariat, such as the writings of Babeuf and others.

The first direct attempts of the proletariat to attain its own ends, made in times of universal excitement, when feudal society was being overthrown, these attempts necessarily failed, owing to the then undeveloped state of the proletariat, as well as to the absence of the economic conditions for its emancipation, conditions that had yet to be produced, and could be produced by the impending bourgeois epoch alone.[b] The revolutionary literature that accompanied these first movements of the proletariat had necessarily a reactionary character. It inculcated universal asceticism and social levelling in its crudest form.

The Socialist and Communist systems properly so called, those of Saint-Simon, Fourier, Owen and others, spring into existence in the early undeveloped period, described above, of the struggle between proletariat and bourgeoisie (see Section I. Bourgeois and Proletarians).

---

[a] The German editions have here: "Solitary confinement".—*Ed.*

[b] The German editions have "material conditions" instead of "economic conditions", and the end of the sentence is: "and could be only the product of the bourgeois epoch".—*Ed.*

The founders of these systems see, indeed, the class antagonisms, as well as the action of the decomposing elements in the prevailing form of society. But the proletariat, as yet in its infancy,[a] offers to them the spectacle of a class without any historical initiative or any independent political movement.

Since the development of class antagonism keeps even pace with the development of industry, the economic situation, as they find it, does not as yet offer to them the material conditions for the emancipation of the proletariat. They therefore search after a new social science, after new[b] social laws, that are to create these conditions.

Historical[c] action is to yield to their personal inventive action, historically created conditions of emancipation to fantastic ones, and the gradual, spontaneous[d] class organisation of the proletariat to an organisation of society specially contrived by these inventors. Future history resolves itself, in their eyes, into the propaganda and the practical carrying out of their social plans.

In the formation of their plans they are conscious of caring chiefly for the interests of the working class, as being the most suffering class. Only from the point of view of being the most suffering class does the proletariat exist for them.

The undeveloped state of the class struggle, as well as their own surroundings, causes Socialists of this kind to consider themselves far superior to all class antagonisms. They want to improve the condition of every member of society, even that of the most favoured. Hence, they habitually appeal to society at large, without distinction of class; nay, by preference, to the ruling class. For how can people, when once they understand their system, fail to see in it the best possible plan of the best possible state of society?

Hence, they reject all political, and especially all revolutionary, action; they wish to attain their ends by peaceful means, and endeavour, by small experiments, necessarily doomed to failure, and by the force of example, to pave the way for the new social Gospel.

Such fantastic pictures of future society, painted at a time when the proletariat is still in a very undeveloped state and has but a fantastic conception of its own position, correspond with the first

---

[a] The words "as yet in its infancy" were added in the English edition of 1888.—*Ed.*
[b] In both cases the word "new" was added in the English edition of 1888.—*Ed.*
[c] The German editions have "Social" instead of "Historical".—*Ed.*
[d] The word "spontaneous" was added in the English edition of 1888.—*Ed.*

instinctive yearnings of that class for a general reconstruction of society.

But these Socialist and Communist publications contain also a critical element. They attack every principle of existing society. Hence they are full of the most valuable materials for the enlightenment of the working class. The practical measures proposed in them—such as the abolition of the distinction between town and country, of the family, of the carrying on of industries for the account of private individuals,[a] and of the wage system, the proclamation of social harmony, the conversion of the functions of the State into a mere superintendence of production, all these proposals point solely to the disappearance of class antagonisms which were, at that time, only just cropping up, and which, in these publications, are recognised in their earliest indistinct and undefined forms only. These proposals, therefore, are of a purely Utopian character.

The significance of Critical-Utopian Socialism and Communism bears an inverse relation to historical development. In proportion as the modern[b] class struggle develops and takes definite shape, this fantastic standing apart from the contest, these fantastic attacks on it, lose all practical value and all theoretical justification. Therefore, although the originators of these systems were, in many respects, revolutionary, their disciples have, in every case, formed mere reactionary sects. They hold fast by the original views of their masters, in opposition to the progressive historical development of the proletariat. They, therefore, endeavour, and that consistently, to deaden the class struggle and to reconcile the class antagonisms. They still dream of experimental realisation of their social Utopias, of founding isolated "phalanstères", of establishing "Home Colonies", of setting up a "Little Icaria"*—duodecimo editions of the New Jerusalem—and to realise all these castles in the air, they are compelled to appeal to the feelings and purses of the bourgeois. By

* *Phalanstères* were Socialist colonies on the plan of Charles Fourier; *Icaria* was the name given by Cabet to his Utopia and, later on, to his American Communist colony. [*Note by Engels to the English edition of 1888.*]

"Home Colonies" were what Owen called his Communist model societies. *Phalanstères* was the name of the public palaces planned by Fourier. *Icaria* was the name given to the Utopian land of fancy, whose Communist institutions Cabet portrayed. [*Note by Engels to the German edition of 1890.*]

---

[a] In the German editions the beginning of this sentence reads as follows: "Their positive propositions concerning the future society, for example, abolition of the contradiction between town and country, of the family, of private profit...".—*Ed.*

[b] This word was added in the English edition of 1888.—*Ed.*

degrees they sink into the category of the reactionary [or][a] conservative Socialists depicted above, differing from these only by more systematic pedantry, and by their fanatical and superstitious belief[b] in the miraculous effects of their social science.

They, therefore, violently oppose all political action on the part of the working class; such action, according to them, can only result from blind unbelief in the new Gospel.

The Owenites in England, and the Fourierists in France, respectively oppose the Chartists and the *Réformistes.*[263]

---

[a] In the English edition of 1888 the word "or" is omitted, but it is given in all other authorised editions.—*Ed.*

[b] The German editions have "fanatical superstition".—*Ed.*

IV

POSITION OF THE COMMUNISTS IN RELATION TO THE VARIOUS EXISTING OPPOSITION PARTIES

Section II has made clear the relations of the Communists to the existing working-class parties, such as the Chartists in England and the Agrarian Reformers in America.[264]

The Communists fight for the attainment of the immediate aims, for the enforcement of the momentary interests of the working class; but in the movement of the present, they also represent and take care of[a] the future of that movement. In France the Communists ally themselves with the Social-Democrats,* against the conservative and radical bourgeoisie, reserving, however, the right to take up a critical position in regard to phrases and illusions traditionally handed down from the great Revolution.

In Switzerland they support the Radicals, without losing sight of the fact that this party consists of antagonistic elements, partly of Democratic Socialists, in the French sense, partly of radical bourgeois.

In Poland they support the party that insists on an agrarian revolution as the prime condition for national emancipation, that party which fomented the insurrection of Cracow in 1846.[265]

* The party then represented in Parliament by Ledru-Rollin, in literature by Louis Blanc, in the daily press by the *Réforme.* The name of Social-Democracy signified, with these its inventors, a section of the Democratic or Republican party more or less tinged with Socialism. [*Note by Engels to the English edition of 1888.*]

The party in France which at that time called itself Socialist-Democratic was represented in political life by Ledru-Rollin and in literature by Louis Blanc; thus it differed immeasurably from present-day German Social-Democracy. [*Note by Engels to the German edition of 1890.*]

[a] The words "and take care of" were added in the English edition of 1888.—*Ed.*

In Germany they fight with the bourgeoisie whenever it acts in a revolutionary way, against the absolute monarchy, the feudal squirearchy, and the petty bourgeoisie.[a]

But they never cease, for a single instant, to instil into the working class the clearest possible recognition of the hostile antagonism between bourgeoisie and proletariat, in order that the German workers may straightway use, as so many weapons against the bourgeoisie, the social and political conditions that the bourgeoisie must necessarily introduce along with its supremacy, and in order that, after the fall of the reactionary classes in Germany, the fight against the bourgeoisie itself may immediately begin.

The Communists turn their attention chiefly to Germany, because that country is on the eve of a bourgeois revolution that is bound to be carried out under more advanced conditions of European civilisation, and with a much more developed proletariat, than that of England was in the seventeenth, and of France in the eighteenth century, and because the bourgeois revolution in Germany will be but the prelude to an immediately following proletarian revolution.

In short, the Communists everywhere support every revolutionary movement against the existing social and political order of things.

In all these movements they bring to the front, as the leading question in each, the property question, no matter what its degree of development at the time.

Finally, they labour everywhere for the union and agreement of the democratic parties of all countries.

The Communists disdain to conceal their views and aims. They openly declare that their ends can be attained only by the forcible overthrow of all existing social conditions. Let the ruling classes tremble at a Communistic revolution. The proletarians have nothing to lose but their chains. They have a world to win.

WORKING MEN OF ALL COUNTRIES, UNITE!

---

[a] In the German editions the end of this sentence reads: "against the absolute monarchy, the feudal landowners and philistinism [Kleinbürgerei]".—*Ed.*

Frederick Engels

THE MOVEMENTS OF 1847[266]

The year 1847 was certainly the most stormy we have experienced for a very long time. A constitution and a United Diet in Prussia[267]; an unexpectedly rapid awakening in political life and a general arming against Austria in Italy; a civil war in Switzerland[268]; a new Parliament of pronounced radical complexion in Britain; in France scandals and Reform banquets; in America the conquest of Mexico by the United States—that is a series of changes and movements such as no other recent year can show.

The last turning point in history was the year 1830. The July revolution in France and the Reform Bill in Britain finally secured the victory of the bourgeoisie; and in Britain this was, indeed, the victory of the industrial bourgeoisie, the manufacturers, over the non-industrial bourgeoisie, the rentiers. Belgium, and to a certain extent Switzerland, followed suit; here again the bourgeoisie triumphed.[269] Poland rose in revolt,[270] Italy chafed under Metternich's heel. Germany was seething. All countries were preparing for a mighty struggle.

But after 1830 there was everywhere a set-back. Poland fell, the insurgents in Romagna were dispersed,[271] the movement in Germany was suppressed. The French bourgeoisie defeated the republicans in France itself, and betrayed the liberals of other countries whom it had spurred on to revolt. The liberal ministry in Britain could accomplish nothing. Finally, in 1840, reaction was in full swing. Poland, Italy, and Germany were politically dead: the *Berliner politisches Wochenblatt*[a] sat enthroned in Prussia; Herr Dahlmann's

---

[a] The allusion is to Frederick William IV, who patronised this reactionary newspaper.—*Ed.*

all-too-clever constitution was repealed in Hanover[272]; the decisions of the Vienna Conference of 1834 were in full force.[273] The Conservatives and the Jesuits were thriving in Switzerland. In Belgium, the Catholics were at the helm. Guizot ruled supreme over France. In Britain, under pressure from the growing power of Peel, the Whig government was in its last throes, and the Chartists were vainly endeavouring to reorganise their ranks after their great defeat of 1839.[274] Everywhere the reactionary party was victorious; everywhere the progressive parties were broken up and dispersed. The arrest of the historical movement—this seemed to be the final result of the mighty struggles of 1830.

1840 was, however, also the peak of reaction just as 1830 had been the peak of the revolutionary movement of the bourgeoisie. From 1840 onward the movements against the existing state of affairs began afresh. Though often defeated, in the long run they gained more and more ground. While in England the Chartists reorganised themselves and became stronger than ever, Peel was forced time and again to betray his party, dealing it a fatal blow by the repeal of the Corn Laws,[275] and finally himself to resign. The radicals gained ground in Switzerland. In Germany, and especially in Prussia, the liberals were pressing their demands more vigorously with every year. The liberals emerged victorious from the Belgian elections of 1847. France was an exception, for there the reactionary ministry secured a triumphant majority in the 1846 elections; and Italy remained dead, until Pius IX mounted the papal throne, and at the end of 1846 attempted a few dubious reforms.

So came the year 1847, and with it a series of victories for the progressive parties of nearly all countries. Even where they sustained defeat, this was more advantageous to them than an immediate victory would have been.

The year 1847 decided nothing, but everywhere it brought the parties into sharp and clear confrontation; it brought no final solution of any questions, but it posed all questions in such a way that now they must be solved.

Among all the movements and changes of the year 1847 the most important were those in Prussia, in Italy and in Switzerland.

In *Prussia*, Frederick William IV was at length forced to grant a constitution. The sterile Don Quixote of Sans-Souci,[276] after long struggles and labour-pains, was delivered of a constitution which was to establish for all time the victory of the feudalist, patriarchal, abolutist, bureaucratic, and clerical reaction. But he had miscalculated. The bourgeoisie was strong enough by then to turn even that constitution into a weapon against the king and all the reactionary classes of society. In Prussia, as everywhere else, the bourgeoisie began by refusing him money. The king was in despair. One could say that in the first days after the refusal of the money Prussia was without a king. The country was in the throes of revolution without knowing it. Then by good luck came the fifteen million from Russia; Frederick William was king again, the bourgeoisie of the Diet crumpled up in alarm, and the revolutionary storm clouds scattered. The Prussian bourgeoisie was, for the time being, defeated. But it had made a great step forward, had won for itself a forum, had given the king a proof of its power, and had worked the country up into a great state of agitation. The question: who shall govern Prussia—the alliance of nobles, bureaucrats, and priests headed by the king, or the bourgeoisie—is now posed in such a way that it must be decided in favour of one side or of the other. In the United Diet a compromise between the two parties was still possible, but today no longer. Now it is a matter of life-and-death struggle between the two. To make matters worse, the committees (those unhappy inventions of the Berlin constitution manufacturers) are now assembling.[277] They will make the already complicated legal issues so enormously more involved, that no man will any longer know where he stands. They will tie matters up into a Gordian knot which will have to be cut with the sword. They will complete the final preparations for the *bourgeois* revolution in Prussia.

We can therefore await the advent of this Prussian revolution with the utmost calm. The United Diet will have to be convened in 1849 whether the king wants it or not. We will give His Majesty a breathing space till then, but not a moment longer. Then he will have to resign his sceptre and his "unimpaired" crown[278] to the Christian and the Jewish bourgeois of his realm.

Thus 1847 was politically a very good year for the Prussian bourgeoisie in spite of their temporary defeat. The bourgeoisie and petty bourgeoisie of the other German states have also noted this and shown the most heartfelt sympathy towards them. They know that the victory of the Prussian bourgeoisie is their own victory.

In *Italy* we have witnessed the amazing spectacle of the man who occupies the most reactionary position in the whole of Europe, who represents the petrified ideology of the Middle Ages, the Pope,[a] taking the lead in a liberal movement. The movement grew to power in a night, carrying along with it the Austrian archduke of Tuscany[b] and the traitor Charles Albert of Sardinia, undermining the throne

---

[a] Pius IX.—*Ed.*
[b] Leopold II, duke of Tuscany.—*Ed.*

of Ferdinand of Naples, its waves sweeping over Lombardy to the Tyrolese and Styrian Alps.

Today the movement in Italy resembles that which took place in Prussia from 1807 to 1812.[279] As in Prussia of those days, there are two issues: external independence and internal reforms. For the moment there is no demand for a constitution, but only for administrative reforms. Any serious conflict with the government is avoided in the meantime so as to maintain as united a front as possible in face of the foreign overlord. What kind of reforms are these? To whose advantage are they? In the first place to that of the bourgeoisie. The press is to be favoured; the bureaucracy to be made to serve the interests of the bourgeoisie (cf. the Sardinian reforms, the Roman consulta,[280] and the reorganisation of the ministries); the bourgeois are to be granted extended influence on communal administration; the *bon plaisir*[a] of the nobles and of the bureaucracy is to be restricted; the bourgeoisie is *to be armed* as *guardia civica.* Hitherto all the reforms have been and could be only in the interests of the bourgeoisie. Compare the Prussian reforms of Napoleonic times. These are exactly the same, only that in many respects they go further: the administration made subservient to the interests of the bourgeoisie; the arbitrary power of the nobility and the bureaucracy broken; municipal self-government established; a militia inaugurated; the corvée abolished. As earlier in Prussia, so today in Italy, the bourgeoisie, owing to its growing wealth and, in particular, to the growing importance of industry and commerce in the life of the people as a whole, has become the class upon which the country's liberation from foreign domination mainly depends.

The movement in Italy is thus a decisively bourgeois movement. All the classes now inspired with a zeal for reform, from the princes and the nobility down to the pifferari and the lazzaroni,[281] appear for the nonce as bourgeois, and the Pope himself is the First Bourgeois in Italy. But once the Austrian yoke has finally been thrown off, all these classes will be greatly disillusioned. Once the bourgeoisie has finished off the foreign enemy, it will start on the separation of the sheep from the goats at home; then the princes and the counts will again call out to Austria for help, but it will be too late, and then the workers of Milan, of Florence, and of Naples will realise that *their* work is only really beginning.

Finally *Switzerland.* For the first time in its history, this country has played a definite part in the European system of states, for the first time it has dared to act decisively and has had the courage to enter

---

[a] Power of arbitrary decision.—*Ed.*

the arena as a federal republic instead of as heretofore an agglomeration of twenty-two antagonistic cantons, utter strangers to one another. By most resolutely putting down the civil war, it has assured the supremacy of the central power—in a word, has become centralised. The *de facto* centralisation will have to be legalised through the impending reform of the Federal Pact.

Who, we again ask, is going to profit by the outcome of the war, by federal reform, by the reorganisation of the Sonderbund cantons? The victorious party, the party which was victorious in the individual cantons from 1830 to 1834, the liberals and radicals, i.e., the bourgeoisie and the peasantry. The rule of the patriciate in the former imperial towns was already overthrown as a result of the July revolution. Where it had been practically restored, as in Berne and Geneva, revolutions followed in 1846. Where it as yet remained intact, as for instance in Basle City, it was shaken to its foundations in the same year. There was little feudal aristocracy in Switzerland, and where it still survived it found its chief strength in an alliance with the herdsmen of the upper Alps. These men were the last, the most obstinate and the most rabid enemies of the bourgeoisie. They were the mainstay of the reactionary elements in the liberal cantons. Aided by the Jesuits and the pietists,[282] they covered the whole of Switzerland with a network of reactionary conspiracies (cf. the canton of Vaud). They thwarted all the plans laid before the Diet by the bourgeoisie, and hindered the final defeat of the philistine patriciate in the former imperial cities.

In 1847[a] these last enemies of the Swiss bourgeoisie were completely broken.

In almost all the cantons the Swiss bourgeoisie had had a pretty free hand in commerce and industry. In so far as the guilds still existed, they did little to hamper bourgeois development. Tolls within the country hardly existed. Wherever the bourgeoisie had developed to any considerable extent, political power was in its hands. But although it had made good progress in the individual cantons and had found support there, the main thing was still lacking, namely centralisation. Whereas feudalism, patriarchalism, and philistinism flourish in separated provinces and individual towns, the bourgeoisie needs for its growth as wide a field as possible; instead of twenty-two small cantons it needed *one* large Switzerland. Cantonal sovereignty, which best suited the conditions in the *old* Switzerland, had become a crushing handicap for the bourgeoisie. The bourgeoisie needed a centralised power, strong enough to

---

[a] The original has by mistake "1846".—*Ed.*

impose a particular course of development on the legislation of the individual cantons and, by sheer weight of influence, to cancel out the differences in their constitutions and laws, to wipe out the vestiges of the feudal, patriarchal and philistine legislation, and energetically to represent the interests of the Swiss bourgeoisie in relation to other countries.

The bourgeoisie has won for itself this centralised power.

But did not the peasants also help in overthrowing the Sonderbund? Certainly they did! So far as the peasants are concerned, they will play the same part towards the bourgeoisie as they played for so long towards the petty bourgeoisie. The peasants will remain the exploited arm of the bourgeoisie, they will fight its battles for it, weave its calico and ribbons, and provide the recruits for its proletariat. What else can they do? They are owners, like the bourgeois, and for the moment their interests are almost identical with those of the bourgeoisie. All the political measures which they are strong enough to put through, are hardly more advantageous to the bourgeoisie than to the peasants themselves. Nevertheless, they are weak in comparison with the bourgeoisie, because the latter are more wealthy and have in their hands the lever of all political power in our century—industry. With the bourgeoisie, the peasantry can achieve much; against the bourgeoisie, nothing.

It is true that a time will come when the fleeced and impoverished section of the peasantry will unite with the proletariat, which by then will be further developed, and will declare war on the bourgeoisie—but that does not concern us here.

Enough that the expulsion of the Jesuits and their associates, those organised opponents of the bourgeoisie, the general introduction of *civil* instead of religious education, the seizure of most of the church estates by the state, benefit above all the bourgeoisie.

Thus the common factor in the three most noteworthy movements of the year 1847 is that all are primarily and chiefly in the interests of the bourgeoisie. The party of progress was, everywhere, the party of the bourgeoisie.

It is indeed the characteristic feature of these movements that those countries which remained backward in 1830 are precisely those which last year took the first decisive steps to raise themselves to the level of 1830—that is, to secure the victory of the bourgeoisie.

So far, then, we have seen that the year 1847 was a brilliant year for the bourgeoisie.

Let us proceed.

In *Britain* a new parliament has assembled, a parliament which, in the words of John Bright the Quaker, is the most bourgeois ever convened. John Bright is the best authority in the matter, seeing that he himself is the most determined bourgeois in the whole of Britain. But the bourgeois John Bright is not the bourgeois who rules in France or who thunders with pathetic bravado against Frederick William IV. When John Bright speaks of a bourgeois he means a manufacturer. Ever since 1688, separate sections of the bourgeois class have been ruling in England. But, in order to facilitate their seizure of power, the bourgeoisie has allowed the aristocrats, its dependent debtors, to retain their rule in name. Whereas, in reality, the struggle in England is between sections of the bourgeoisie, between rentiers and manufacturers, the manufacturers are able to represent it as a struggle between the aristocracy and the bourgeoisie, or, in case of necessity, as a struggle between the aristocracy and the people. The manufacturers have no interest in maintaining the appearance of government by the aristocracy, for the lords, the baronets and the squires do not owe them a farthing. On the other hand they have a great interest in destroying this appearance, for with it the rentiers lose their last sheet-anchor. The present bourgeois or manufacturers' parliament will see to this. It will change the old feudal-looking England into a more or less modern country of bourgeois organisation. It will bring the British constitution nearer to those of France and of Belgium. It will complete the victory of the English industrial bourgeoisie.

Another advance of the bourgeoisie: for an advance within the bourgeoisie is also an extension and a strengthening of bourgeois rule.

France alone appears to be an exception. The power which fell into the hands of the whole of the big bourgeoisie in 1830 is being year by year increasingly limited to the rule of the wealthiest section of this big bourgeoisie, to the rule of the rentiers and the stock exchange speculators. They have made the majority of the big bourgeoisie serve their interest. The minority, which is headed by a section of the manufacturers and shipping owners, is continually diminishing. This minority has now made common cause with the middle and petty bourgeoisie who have no electoral rights and celebrates its alliance at reform banquets. It despairs of ever coming to power with the present electorate. After long hesitation, it has made up its mind to promise a share of political power to the sections of the bourgeoisie next below itself, and especially the bourgeois ideologists, as being the least dangerous—the lawyers, doctors, and so on. It is, of course, still very far from being able to keep its promise.

Thus also in France we see approaching the struggle within the bourgeoisie which in Britain has already been almost ended. But, as always in France, the situation is more sharply defined, more revolutionary than elsewhere. This distinct division into two camps is also an advance for the bourgeoisie.

In *Belgium* the bourgeoisie won a decisive victory in the elections of 1847. The Catholic ministry was forced to resign, and here also the liberal bourgeoisie now rule for the time being.

In *America* we have witnessed the conquest of Mexico and have rejoiced at it.[283] It is also an advance when a country which has hitherto been exclusively wrapped up in its own affairs, perpetually rent with civil wars, and completely hindered in its development, a country whose best prospect had been to become industrially subject to Britain—when such a country is forcibly drawn into the historical process. It is to the interest of its own development that Mexico will in future be placed under the tutelage of the United States. The evolution of the whole of America will profit by the fact that the United States, by the possession of California, obtains command of the Pacific. But again we ask: "Who is going to profit immediately by the war?" The bourgeoisie alone. The North Americans acquire new regions in California and New Mexico for the creation of fresh capital, that is, for calling new bourgeois into being, and enriching those already in existence; for all capital created today flows into the hands of the bourgeoisie. And what about the proposed cut through the Tehuantepec isthmus?[284] Who is likely to gain by that? Who else but the American shipping owners? Rule over the Pacific, who will gain by that but these same shipping owners? The new customers for the products of industry, customers who will come into being in the newly acquired territories—who will supply their needs? None other than the American manufacturers.

Thus also in America the bourgeoisie has made great advances, and if its representatives now oppose the war, that only proves that they fear that these advances have in some ways been bought too dear.

Even in quite barbarous lands the bourgeoisie is advancing. In Russia, industry is developing by leaps and bounds and is succeeding in converting even the boyars into bourgeois. Both in Russia and Poland serfdom is being restricted and the nobility thereby weakened in the interest of the bourgeoisie, and a class of free peasants is being created which the bourgeoisie everywhere needs. The Jews are being persecuted—entirely in the interest of the settled Christian bourgeois, whose business was spoiled by the pedlars.—In Hungary, the feudal magnates are more and more changing into wholesale corn and wool merchants and cattle dealers, and consequently now appear in the Diet as bourgeois.—What of all the glorious advances of "civilisation" in such lands as Turkey, Egypt, Tunis, Persia, and other barbarous countries? They are nothing else but a preparation for the advent of a future bourgeoisie. In these countries the word of the prophet is being fulfilled: "Prepare ye the way of the Lord....[a] Lift up your heads, O ye gates; and be ye lift up, ye everlasting doors; and the King of glory shall come in. Who is this King of glory?"[b] The bourgeois!

Wherever we look, the bourgeoisie are making stupendous progress. They are holding their heads high, and haughtily challenge their enemies. They expect a decisive victory, and their hopes will not be disappointed. They intend to shape the whole world according to their standard; and, on a considerable portion of the earth's surface, they will succeed.

We are no friends of the bourgeoisie. That is common knowledge. But this time we do not grudge the bourgeoisie their triumph. We can chuckle over the haughty looks which the bourgeois deign to bestow (especially in Germany) upon the apparently tiny band of democrats and Communists. We have no objection if everywhere they force through their purposes.

Nay more. We cannot forbear an ironical smile when we observe the terrible earnestness, the pathetic enthusiasm with which the bourgeois strive to achieve their aims. They really believe that they are working on their own behalf! They are so short-sighted as to fancy that through their triumph the world will assume its final configuration. Yet nothing is more clear than that they are everywhere preparing the way for *us*, for the democrats and the Communists; than that they will at most win a few years of troubled enjoyment, only to be then immediately overthrown. Behind them stands everywhere the proletariat, sometimes participating in their endeavours and partly in their illusions, as in Italy and Switzerland, sometimes silent and reserved, but secretly preparing the overthrow of the bourgeoisie, as in France and Germany; finally, in Britain and America, in open rebellion against the ruling bourgeoisie.

We can do still more. We can say all this to the bourgeoisie straight out, we can lay our cards on the table. Let them know in advance that they are working only in our interest. They still cannot for that reason give up their fight against the absolute monarchy, the nobility, and the clergy. They must conquer—or already now go under.

In Germany in a very short time they will even have to ask for our help.

---

[a] Isaiah 40 : 3.—*Ed.*

[b] Psalms 24 : 7, 8.—*Ed.*

So just fight bravely on, most gracious masters of capital! We need you for the present; here and there we even need you as rulers. You have to clear the vestiges of the Middle Ages and of absolute monarchy out of our path; you have to annihilate patriarchalism; you have to carry out centralisation; you have to convert the more or less propertyless classes into genuine proletarians, into recruits for us; by your factories and your commercial relationships you must create for us the basis of the material means which the proletariat needs for the attainment of freedom. In recompense whereof you shall be allowed to rule for a short time. You shall be allowed to dictate your laws, to bask in the rays of the majesty you have created, to spread your banquets in the halls of kings, and to take the beautiful princess to wife—but do not forget that

"The hangman stands at the door!"[a]

Written about January 20, 1848

First published in the *Deutsche-Brüsseler-Zeitung* No. 7, January 23, 1848

Signed: *F. E.*

Printed according to the newspaper

---

[a] Heinrich Heine, "Ritter Olaf".—*Ed.*

Frederick Engels

THE BEGINNING OF THE END IN AUSTRIA

"It will endure Metternich and me," said the late Emperor Franz. If Metternich does not wish to give his emperor the lie, he had better die as soon as possible.

This chequered Austrian monarchy, scraped together by theft and by inheritance, this organised jumble of ten languages and nations, this planless mish-mash of contradictory customs and laws, is at last beginning to disintegrate.

Honest German citizens have for years been fervent admirers of the director of this creaking state machine, the cowardly swindler and assassin—Metternich. Talleyrand, Louis Philippe and Metternich, three most mediocre minds and hence most suitable for our mediocre times, are regarded by German citizens as three gods who for thirty years have manipulated world history as if it were a puppet show. Going by his own daily experience, the honest citizen regards history as a kind of plot hatched in a tavern or as feminine gossip on a somewhat larger scale.

Certainly, there is no country over which the tidal wave of revolution, the triple Napoleonic invasions[285] passed away so completely without trace as Austria. Certainly, there is no country where feudalism, patriarchalism and faint-hearted philistinism defended by the paternal rod, have been maintained so immaculately or harmoniously as in Austria. But is it Metternich's fault?

On what does the might, the tenacity, the stability, of the House of Austria rest?

When Italy, France, England, Belgium, North and West Germany, one after another extricated themselves from feudal barbarism during the latter half of the Middle Ages, when industry was developing, trade expanding, the towns thriving and the burghers acquired political importance, one part of Germany lagged behind West European development. Bourgeois civilisation followed the sea coasts and the course of the big rivers. The inland, especially the barren and impassable mountainous regions, remained the seat of barbarism and of feudalism. This barbarism was especially concentrated in the South German and South Slav inland areas. Protected by the Alps from Italian civilisation and by the mountains of Bohemia and Moravia from that of North Germany, these inland countries had the additional good fortune of being the basin of the only reactionary river in Europe. The Danube, far from linking them with civilisation, brought them into contact with a much more vigorous barbarism.

When the great monarchies developed in Western Europe in the wake of bourgeois civilisation, the inland countries of the Upper Danube likewise had to unite in a great monarchy. This was required if only for the needs of defence. Here, in the centre of Europe, the barbarians of all tongues and of all nations associated under the sceptre of the House of Hapsburg. Here they found in Hungary a mainstay of solid barbarism.

The Danube, the Alps, the rocky breastworks of Bohemia—these are the bases for the existence of Austrian barbarism and of the Austrian monarchy.

The House of Hapsburg supported the burghers against the aristocracy and the towns against the princes because this was the only condition on which a great monarchy was possible. When, later on, it again supported the petty bourgeoisie, this was because the petty bourgeoisie in the rest of Europe had become reactionary themselves with regard to the big bourgeoisie. On both occasions it supported the petty bourgeois for decidedly reactionary purposes. But now this method has miscarried.

The House of Austria was thus from the first the representative of barbarism, of reactionary stability in Europe. Its power rested on the foolishness of the patriarchalism entrenched behind the impassable mountains, on the inaccessible brutality of barbarism. A dozen nations whose customs, character, and institutions were flagrantly opposed to one another clung together on the strength of their common dislike for civilisation.

Hence the House of Austria was invincible as long as the barbarous character of its subjects remained untouched. Hence it was threatened by only one danger—the penetration of bourgeois civilisation.

But this *sole* danger was not to be averted. Bourgeois civilisation could be warded off for a time, it could be temporarily adapted and subordinated to Austrian barbarism. But it was bound to overcome feudal barbarism sooner or later, and shatter the only link which had held the most variegated provinces together.

This explains Austria's passive, hesitant, cowardly, sordid and underhand policy. Austria can no longer act, as before, in an openly brutal, thoroughly barbarous way because it must make concessions to civilisation every year, and because its own subjects become less reliable every year. Every decisive step would lead to a change at home or in the neighbouring countries, every change would mean a breach in the dam behind which Austria laboriously protects itself against the rising tides of modern civilisation. The first victim of any change would be the House of Austria itself which stands or falls with barbarism. Although Austria was still able to disperse the Piedmontese, Neapolitan and Romagnese rebels with cannon fire in 1823 and 1831, it was forced to set in motion a still undeveloped revolutionary element—the peasantry—in 1846 in Galicia; it had to stop the advance of its troops near Ferrara in 1847 and resort to conspiracy in Rome.[286] Counter-revolutionary Austria uses revolutionary means—this is the surest sign that its end is approaching.

Once the Italian insurrections of 1831, and the Polish revolution of 1830 had been suppressed and the French bourgeois had given guarantees of good behaviour, Emperor Franz could go to his grave in peace; the times seemed miserable enough to endure even his feeble-minded offspring.[a]

As yet the realm of the crowned idiot was still safe from revolutions. But who could ensure it against the *causes* of revolutions?

As long as industry remained domestic industry, as long as every peasant family or at least every village produced its own industrial products, without putting much on the market, industry itself remained feudal and excellently suited to Austrian barbarism. As long as it remained mere manufactory, rural industry, few products of the inland countries were made available for export and foreign trade was minimal, industry existed in a few districts only and was easily adaptable to the Austrian status quo. If manufacture could only produce relatively few big bourgeois even in England and France, then it could only produce a modest middle class in thinly-populated and remote Austria, and even this only here and there. As long as hand labour existed, Austria was safe.

[a] Ferdinand I.—*Ed.*

But machinery was invented and machines ruined hand labour. The prices of industrial products fell so swiftly and so low that first of all manufacture and then, gradually, the old feudal domestic industry went under.

Austria fortified itself against the machines by a consistent system of prohibitive tariffs. But in vain, it was precisely the system of prohibitive tariffs which was responsible for bringing machinery into Austria. Bohemia used machinery in the cotton industry; Lombardy for silk spinning; Vienna even started to produce machinery.

The results were quick to follow. The workers in manufacture became destitute. The entire population of the manufacturing districts was torn out of its hereditary mode of life. The former philistines grew into big bourgeois and lorded it over hundreds of workers just as their princely and aristocratic neighbours lorded it over hundreds of peasant serfs. Through the collapse of the old type of industry, these peasant serfs lost their old occupations and acquired new needs as a result of the new industry. It was no longer possible to carry on feudal agriculture alongside modern industry. The abolition of corvée became a necessity. The feudal position of the peasants in relation to the landowners became untenable. The towns became thriving. The guilds were oppressive for the consumers, useless for those who belonged to them and intolerable for those engaged in industry. Competition had to be permitted surreptitiously. The position of all classes in society was radically changed. The old classes withdrew more and more into the background before the two new classes, the bourgeoisie and the proletariat. Agriculture declined in importance compared with industry, the countryside gave way to the towns.

Such were the consequences of machinery in some areas of Austria, especially in Bohemia and Lombardy. They gave rise to a reaction which affected the entire monarchy to a greater or lesser degree; everywhere they undermined the old barbarism, and with it the foundations of the House of Austria.

While in Romagna in 1831 the battered Austrian soldiers replied to cries of *Viva l'Italia* with grape-shot, in England the first railways were built. Like machinery, railways immediately became a necessity for all European countries. Austria *had* to have them, willy-nilly. In order not to give increased power to the already growing bourgeoisie, the Government built them itself; but it went from Scylla to Charybdis. It prevented the establishment of powerful bourgeois joint stock companies only by borrowing from the same bourgeois the money to build the railways, by putting itself in pawn to Rothschild, Arnstein, Eskeles, Sina, etc.

Still less did the House of Austria escape the effects of the railways. The mountain ranges which separated the Austrian monarchy from the outside world, Bohemia from Moravia and Austria, Austria from Styria, Styria from Illyria, Illyria from Lombardy, fell before the railways. The granite walls behind which each province had maintained a separate nationality and a limited local existence, ceased to be a barrier. All of a sudden the products of large-scale industry, of machinery, forced their way, almost free of transport costs, into the most remote corners of the monarchy, destroyed the old hand labour and shattered the feudal barbarism. Trade between the provinces, and with the civilised outside world, acquired an unheard-of importance. The Danube, flowing towards the backward regions, ceased to be the main artery of the Empire; the Alps and the Bohemian forests no longer exist; the new artery now passes from Trieste to Hamburg, Ostend and Le Havre, far beyond the frontiers of the Empire, through the mountain ranges to the remote coasts of the North Sea and the ocean. Participation in the general interests of the State, in what was happening in the outside world became a necessity. The local barbarism began to disappear, particular interests began to diverge here, to merge there. Nationalities separated in one place to link up somewhere else, and out of the confused agglomeration of mutually alien provinces emerged larger and better defined groups with common tendencies and interests.

"It will endure Metternich and me." The French Revolution, Napoleon and the July upheavals had been withstood. But there was no withstanding *steam.* Steam forced its way through the Alps and the Bohemian forests, steam robbed the Danube of its role, steam tore Austrian barbarism to shreds and thereby pulled the ground from under the feet of the House of Hapsburg.

In Europe and America they now have the pleasure of seeing Metternich and the whole House of Hapsburg crushed between the wheels of the steam-driven machines, and the Austrian monarchy being cut to pieces by its own locomotives. It is an exhilarating sight. The vassals rebel in Italy, and Austria dare not utter a word, the liberal pestilence invades Lombardy and Austria hesitates, vacillates, quakes before its own subjects. In Switzerland the oldest rebels against Austria, the *Ur*-Swiss, yield to Austrian suzerainty[287]; they are attacked, but Austria shivers at the bold words of Ochsenbein: If only *one single* Austrian soldier enters Switzerland I will throw twenty thousand men into Lombardy and proclaim the Italian Republic. And Austria goes off to beg in vain for assistance from the despised courts of Munich, Stuttgart and Karlsruhe. In Bohemia, the estates refuse to pay their taxes of fifty thousand guilders; Austria still wants to enforce payment but needs its troops in the Alps so badly that for the first time since the foundation of Austria it has to give way to the estates and do without the fifty thousand guilders. In Hungary, the Diet is preparing revolutionary proposals and is sure of a majority for them. And Austria, which needs the Hungarian Hussars in Milan, Modena and Parma, Austria itself puts forward revolutionary proposals[288] to the Diet although it knows very well that these are its own death warrant. This unshakable Austria, this eternal bulwark of barbarism, no longer knows where to turn. It is suffering from the most terrible rash; if it scratches itself in front then it itches behind, and if it scratches behind, then it itches in front.

And with these comical scratchings, the House of Austria scratches itself out of existence.

If old Metternich does not follow his "upright" Franz pretty quickly he may live to see the imperial monarchy which he held together at the price of such exertions falling apart and most of it into the hands of the bourgeoisie; he may live to have the unspeakable experience of seeing the "burgher tailors" and "burgher grocers" refusing to doff their hats to him in the Prater[289] and calling him plain Herr Metternich. A few more shocks, one or two more costly mobilisations and Charles Rothschild will buy up the whole Austrian monarchy.

We observe the victory of the bourgeois over the Austrian imperial monarchy with real satisfaction. We only wish that it may be the really vile, really dirty, really Jewish bourgeois who buy up this venerable empire. Such a repulsive, flogging, paternal, lousy government deserves to be under the heel of a really lousy, unkempt stinking adversary. Herr Metternich can depend on us to shear this adversary later as ruthlessly as Metternich will soon be shorn by him.

The fall of Austria has a special significance for us Germans. It is Austria which is responsible for our reputation of being the oppressors of foreign nations, the hirelings of reaction in all countries. Under the Austrian flag Germans have held Poland, Bohemia, Italy in bondage. We have to thank the Austrian monarchy for the Germans being hated as vile mercenaries of despotism from Syracuse to Trento, from Genoa to Venice. Anyone who has seen what deadly hatred, the bloody and completely justified thirst for revenge against the *Tedeschi*[a] reign in Italy must be moved to an undying hatred of Austria and applaud when this bulwark of barbarism, this scourge of Germany collapses.

---

[a] Germans.—*Ed.*

We have every reason to hope that the Germans will revenge themselves on Austria for the infamy with which it has covered the German name. We have every reason to hope that it will be Germans who will overthrow Austria and clear away the obstacles in the way of freedom for the Slavs and Italians. Everything is ready: the victim lies there awaiting the knife which will cut its throat. May the Germans not lose their chance this time; may they be bold enough to say the words which Napoleon himself did not dare to utter—

La dynastie de Habsbourg a cessé de régner.[a]

Written about January 25, 1848

First published in the *Deutsche-Brüsseler-Zeitung* No. 8, January 27, 1848

Signed: *F. E.*

Printed according to the newspaper

Published in English for the first time

[a] The Hapsburg dynasty has ceased to reign.—*Ed.*

Karl Marx

THE *DÉBAT SOCIAL* OF FEBRUARY 6 ON THE DEMOCRATIC ASSOCIATION

The *Débat social* of February 6 defends the Brussels Association Démocratique and its branches.[290] We shall permit ourselves a few comments on the character of this defence.

It may well be in the interest of the Belgian radical party to point out to the Catholics that they are acting against their own interest in denouncing the Belgian radical party. It may well be in the interest of the Belgian radical party to distinguish between lower and higher clergy and to compensate the clergy in general with compliments for the truths it addresses to a part of it. We understand nothing of this. We are merely astonished that the *Débat* could overlook the fact that the attacks of the Flemish Catholic papers against the associations démocratiques were printed immediately in the *Indépendance*,[a] and the *Indépendance* is not, as far as we know, a Catholic newspaper.

The *Débat social* declares that the Belgians are demanding political reforms through the democratic associations.

We realise that the *Débat* has forgotten the cosmopolitan[b] character of the Association Démocratique for a moment. Or perhaps it has not even forgotten it. It has merely remembered that a society which strives to promote democracy in all countries will work first on the country in which it resides.

The *Débat social* is not content with saying what the Belgians want of the associations démocratiques; it goes further, it says what the Belgians do not want of them, what one consequently *should* not want if one belongs to the Association, which the Belgians have founded to demand political reforms. *Avis aux étrangers!*[c]

"The political reforms which the Belgians wish to demand through the democratic associations," says the *Débat*, "are not those utopias pursued by certain democrats in

[a] *L'Indépendance belge.—Ed.*

[b] See Note 8.—*Ed.*

[c] Warning to foreigners!—*Ed.*

countries where the social institutions permit no hope of any effective reforms, where it is therefore just as reasonable to think of castles in the air as of the modest well-being of the already free nations. He who possesses nothing does just as well in dreaming of millions at a stroke as of a hundred talers of rent or profit."

Here the *Débat* is evidently speaking of the *Communists.*

We should like to ask it if the "modest well-being" of "free" England manifests itself in the Poor Rate growing faster than the population.

We should like to ask it if by the "modest well-being of the free nations" it understands the destitution in Flanders.

We should like it to let us into the secret whereby it intends to replace wages with a 100 talers of *profit* or *rent.* Or does it understand by the "modest well-being of the free nations" the modest well-being of the free capitalists and landowners?

We should finally like to ask it if it has been charged by the Brussels Association Démocratique to give the lie to those utopians who do not believe in "the modest happiness of the free nations".

However, the *Débat social* is evidently not speaking of Communists in general, but of the *German Communists,* who, because political developments in their homeland do not allow them to found a German alliance or a German association libérale,[291] sink in despair into the arms of communism.

We remind the *Débat* that communism originated in England and France, and not in Germany.

German communism is the most determined opponent of all utopianism, and far from excluding historical development in fact bases itself upon it—for the time being we give this assurance to the *Débat social* in return for its own assurance.

Germany is retarded in its political development, it still has a long political development to undergo. We should be the last to deny this. On the other hand, however, we believe that a country of more than 40 million inhabitants, when it prepares for a revolution, will not seek the model for its movement in the radicalism of small free countries.

Does the *Débat* understand by communism the throwing of class antagonisms and of class struggle into sharp relief? In that case, it is not communism which is communistic, but political economy and bourgeois society.

We know that Robert Peel has prophesied that the class antagonism in modern society must erupt in a terrible crisis.[292] We know that Guizot himself in his *History of Civilisation*[a] believes he is

[a] F.-P.-G. Guizot, *Histoire générale de la civilisation en Europe....—Ed.*

setting forth nothing but particular forms of the class struggle. But Peel and Guizot are utopians. Realists are men who regard the mere statement of social facts as an offence against benevolent worldly wisdom.

The *Débat social* is quite free to admire and to idealise North America and Switzerland.

We ask it whether the political constitution of North America could ever be introduced in Europe without great social upheavals. We believe, for instance, if the *Débat* will pardon our boldness, that the English Charter,[293] if it were to be put forward not by individual enthusiasts for universal suffrage but by a great national party, presupposed a long and arduous unification of the English workers into a class, and that this Charter is being striven for with quite another purpose and must bring about quite different social consequences than the constitution of America or of Switzerland ever strove for or ever brought about. In our eyes those people are utopians who separate political forms from their social foundation and present them as general, abstract dogmas.

The manner in which the *Débat social* attempts to defend the Association Démocratique by simultaneously eliminating "certain democrats" who are dissatisfied with the "modest well-being of the free nations" is demonstrated yet again when it comes to speak of the discussions on free trade held within the Association.[294]

"Six sittings," says the *Débat*, "were devoted to the discussion of this interesting question, and many workers from the various workshops of our city asserted here principles which would not have been out of place at the famous congress of economists held in Brussels in September last." [a]

Before this the *Débat* notes that the Association voted almost unanimously that absolute free trade between all nations should be considered as a goal of democracy.

After this, in the same issue of the *Débat* we find a thoroughly commonplace speech by M. Le Hardy de Beaulieu, scraped together from the most decayed leavings of the English free-trade cookshop.

And to round off, Cobden is glorified.[295]

After this presentation in the *Débat social*, will anyone doubt that the Association voted by a great majority for free trade in the sense of the Congress of Economists and of the bourgeois free traders?

Written about February 10, 1848

First published in the *Deutsche-Brüsseler-Zeitung* No. 13, February 13, 1848

Printed according to the newspaper

Published in English for the first time

---

[a] See F. Engels' articles on the Congress of Economists, this volume, pp. 274-78 and 282-90.—*Ed.*

Frederick Engels

THREE NEW CONSTITUTIONS

Our predictions concerning the imminent triumph of the bourgeoisie[a] are in fact being fulfilled more rapidly than we could have expected. In less than a fortnight three absolute monarchies have been transformed into constitutional states: Denmark, Naples and Sardinia.

The movement in Italy has developed with remarkable rapidity. The Papal State, Tuscany and Sardinia in succession took their place at its head; one country impelled the next further and further, one advance always brought another in its wake. The Italian Customs Union [296] was the first step towards constituting the Italian bourgeoisie, which decisively took the lead in the national movement and came daily more into collision with Austria. The bourgeoisie had achieved almost everything which could be achieved under an absolute monarchy, and a representative constitution daily became a more pressing necessity for it. But the winning of constitutional institutions—this was precisely the difficulty for the Italian bourgeoisie. The princes were reluctant; the bourgeoisie dared not confront them too threateningly as it did not want to throw them into the arms of Austria again. The Italians of the Customs Union might have gone on waiting for a long time, when help suddenly came to them from a quite unexpected quarter—Sicily rebelled; the people of Palermo drove the royal troops out of the city with unprecedented bravery,* the people of Abruzzi, Apulia and Calabria attempted a new insurrection, Naples itself prepared for battle, and Ferdinand

* Palermo with 200,000 inhabitants defeated 13,000 men. Paris with a million inhabitants defeated 7,000 to 8,000 men in the July revolution.

[a] See this volume, pp. 520-29.— *Ed.*

the bloodhound, pressed from all sides, with no hope of obtaining Austrian troops, was the first of all the Italian princes to have to grant a constitution and complete freedom of the press. The news reached Genoa and Turin; both cities demanded that Sardinia should not lag behind Naples; Charles Albert, too involved in the movement to withdraw, and also in need of money on account of armament against Austria—had to yield to the very emphatic representations of Turin and Genoa and similarly grant a constitution. There is no doubt at all that Tuscany must follow, and that Pius IX himself will have to make new concessions.

The Italian bourgeoisie has gained its decisive victory in the streets of Palermo. It is now victorious; what will ensue can only be the exploitation of this victory in all respects and the securing of its results against Austria.

This victory of the Italian bourgeoisie is again a defeat for Austria. How old Metternich must have gnashed his teeth in rage—the man who saw the Neapolitan revolution coming from afar, who again and again begged the Pope and Tuscany for permission to march his troops across their territories, and who nonetheless had to hold back his Pandours and Croats on the Po! One courier after another came to him from Naples; Ferdinand, Cocle and Del Carretto were screaming for help, and Metternich, who in 1823 and 1831[297] had reigned so omnipotently in Italy, could do nothing. He had to look on quietly and see his last, his most reliable ally defeated and humiliated in Italy, and the whole weight of Naples placed on the scales against Austria thanks to a revolution. And he had a hundred and fifty thousand men waiting on the Po! But England was there, and had the Austrians crossed the Po, it would have been the signal for the occupation of Venice and the bombardment of Trieste—and so Metternich's hangmen had to stand still and watch with their rifles in their hands while Naples was snatched from them.

England's conduct in the whole Italian affair has been very proper. While the other great powers, France as much as Russia, have done everything to support Metternich, England has taken its place, quite alone, on the side of the Italian movement. The English bourgeoisie has the greatest interest in thwarting an Austro-Italian protective customs union and conversely in bringing about an anti-Austrian customs union in Italy based on free trade. For this reason it supports the Italian bourgeoisie, which for the time being itself still needs free trade for its development, and which is therefore the natural ally of the English bourgeoisie.

In the meantime Austria is arming. These armaments are completely ruining its finances. Austria has no money, and it has turned to Rothschild for a loan; Rothschild has declared that he does not want a war and will not, therefore, provide any money in support of war. Indeed, is there any banker who will still advance money to the rotten Austrian monarchy for a war in which a country like England may involve itself? Metternich can thus no longer count on the bourgeoisie. He turns to the Emperor of Russia who, in the last few years, has also become a great capitalist, thanks to the mines of the Ural and Altai regions and to the corn trade—to the white Tsar, who has already once helped Frederick William IV with 15 million silver rubles, and who in general seems to be turning into the Rothschild of all declining absolute monarchies. Tsar Nicholas is said to have granted 75 millions—in return for a Russian percentage, it goes without saying, and on good security. All the better. If the Tsar has to cover the expenses of the Prussian and Austrian monarchies in addition to his own, if his money is wasted on arming unsuccessfully against Italy, then his treasure will soon be exhausted.

Will Austria risk a war? We hardly think so. Its finances are chaotic; Hungary is in full ferment, Bohemia is not secure; on the battlefield itself, in Lombardy, guerillas would spring up everywhere. And more than anything else the fear of England will restrain Metternich. At this moment Lord Palmerston is the most powerful man in Europe; his decision determines the issue, and this time his decision has been made known clearly enough.

At quite the other end of Europe, in Denmark, a king[a] dies. His son,[b] a coarse, jovial schnapps-tippler, immediately convokes an assembly of notables, a committee of the estates, in order to deliberate upon a common constitution for the Duchies[c] and Denmark. And so that the Germans shall disgrace themselves everywhere, the Duchies have to declare that they do not want this constitution, because it would mean their being torn away from their common German homeland![298]

It is really too ridiculous. The Duchies have a considerably smaller population than Denmark, and yet the number of their representatives is to be the same. Their language is to have equal rights in the assembly, in the official records, in everything. In short, the Danes make every possible concession to the Germans, and the Germans persist in their absurd national obstinacy. The Germans have never been national-minded where the interests of nationality and the interests of progress have coincided; they were always so where

[a] Christian VIII.—*Ed.*

[b] Frederick VII.—*Ed.*

[c] Schleswig and Holstein.—*Ed.*

nationality has turned against progress. Where it was important to be national-minded, they played the cosmopolitans; where it was important not to be directly national-minded, they were so to the point of absurdity. In every case they made themselves ridiculous.

Either the inhabitants of the Duchies are capable people, and more advanced than the Danes—in which case they will obtain preponderance over the Danes in the chamber of estate deputies and have no reason for complaint; or else they are German sluggards and lag behind the Danes in industrial and political development, in which case it is high time they were taken in tow by the Danes. But it is really too absurd for these upright Schleswig-Holsteiners to beg the 40 million Germans to help them against the Danes and to refuse to take up their positions on a battlefield where they can fight with the same advantages as their opponents; it is too absurd that they should appeal to the police of the German Confederation[299] against a constitution.

The Danish constitution is as much a blow against Prussia as the Neapolitan against Austria, although in itself it is only a reaction to abortive Prussian constitutional experiment of February 3.[300] As a further addition to its many embarrassments the Prussian government now has received a new constitutional state as neighbour; at the same time it loses a faithful protegé and ally.

While Italy and Denmark have thus stepped into the ranks of the constitutional states, Germany lags behind. Every nation is moving forward, the smallest, weakest nations are always able to find a point in the European complications which enables them in spite of their big reactionary neighbours to win for themselves one modern institution after another. Only the 40 million Germans never bestir themselves. It is true that they are no longer asleep, but they still only talk and bluster, they have yet to act.

But if the German governments were to set any great hopes on the bourgeoisie's fear of action, then they would be very much deceiving themselves. The Germans are the last in line because their revolution will be quite different from the Sicilian. The German bourgeois and the philistines know very well that behind them stands a daily growing proletariat which on the day after the revolution will put forward quite different demands than they themselves desire. The German bourgeois and philistines therefore behave in a cowardly, indecisive and vacillating manner—they fear a conflict not less than they fear the government.

A German revolution is far more serious than a Neapolitan revolution. In Naples there is a confrontation only between Austria and England; in a German revolution the whole of the East and the whole of the West will confront each other. A Neapolitan revolution will achieve its aim as soon as downright bourgeois institutions have been won; a German revolution will only really begin when it has got this far.

For this reason the Germans must first of all be thoroughly compromised in the eyes of all other nations, they must become, more than they are already, the laughing-stock of all Europe, they must be *compelled* to make the revolution. But then they will really arise, not the cowardly German burghers but the German workers; they will rise up, put an end to the whole filthy, muddled official German rule and with a radical revolution restore the honour of Germany.

Written in the middle of February 1848

First published in the *Deutsche-Brüsseler-Zeitung* No. 15, February 20, 1848

Printed according to the newspaper

Published in English for the first time

Karl Marx and Frederick Engels

[ON THE POLISH QUESTION]

SPEECHES IN BRUSSELS, ON FEBRUARY 22, 1848
ON THE OCCASION OF THE SECOND ANNIVERSARY
OF THE CRACOW INSURRECTION[301]

SPEECH BY MR. KARL MARX

Gentlemen,

There are striking analogies in history. The Jacobin of 1793 has become the Communist of the present day. In 1793, when Russia, Austria and Prussia divided up Poland, the three powers produced the constitution of 1791,[302] which had been condemned unanimously because of its alleged Jacobin principles.

And what had it proclaimed? The Polish constitution of 1791! Nothing other than a constitutional monarchy: legislation placed in the hands of the representatives of the country, freedom of the press, freedom of conscience, public judicial trial, abolition of serfdom, etc. And all this was then called pure Jacobinism! Thus you see, gentlemen, that history has moved on. The Jacobinism of those days has today become, as far as liberalism goes, the most moderate imaginable.

The three Powers have marched with history. In 1846 when by incorporating Cracow into Austria they confiscated the last remains of Polish nationality, they gave the name *communism* to what they once called Jacobinism.

Now, what is the communism of the Cracow revolution? Was it communism to have wanted to restore Polish nationality? This is as much as to say that the war waged against Napoleon by the European coalition to save nationalities was a communist war, and that the Congress of Vienna[303] was made up of crowned Communists. Or was the Cracow revolution communist because it wanted to set up a democratic government? Nobody will charge the millionaire citizens of Berne and New York with communist leanings.

Communism denies the necessity for the existence of classes; it wants to abolish all classes, all class distinctions. The revolutionaries of Cracow wanted only to abolish political distinctions between the classes; they wanted to give equal rights to the different classes.

But, briefly, to what extent was the Cracow revolution communist?

Was it perhaps that it tried to break the chains of feudalism, to turn tributary property into free property, into modern property?

If one asked French proprietors: "Do you know what Polish democrats want? The Polish democrats want to have the kind of property ownership which you already have", the French proprietors would answer, "They are quite right." But if you say, with M. Guizot, to the French proprietors: "The Poles want to abolish property as you instituted it by the revolution of 1789 and as it still exists in your country." "What!" they will shout, "they are revolutionaries, Communists; these scoundrels must be trampled down!" The abolition of guilds, of corporations, the introduction of free competition, is now called *communism* in Sweden. The *Journal des Débats* went further: to abolish the unearned income constituted by the right of corruption for two hundred thousand electors, is to abolish a source of revenue, to destroy an acquired property, to be communist. Doubtless the Cracow revolution also wanted to abolish one kind of property. But what kind of property? One which could not be destroyed in the rest of Europe any more than the Sonderbund[304] in Switzerland, both having already disappeared.

No one will deny that in Poland the political question is tied to the social question. The one has always been inseparable from the other.

Better ask it of the reactionaries! During the Restoration[305] were they only fighting political liberalism and its inevitable load of Voltairianism?

A very renowned reactionary writer loudly professed that the highest metaphysics of a de Maistre and of a de Bonald was in the end a question of money, and is not every question of money a directly social question? The men of the Restoration did not conceal the fact that to bring back good politics it was necessary to bring back good property rights, feudal property, moral property. Everybody knows that loyalty to monarchy cannot dispense with tithes and corvée labour.

Let us go further back. In 1789 the political question of the rights of man included the social question of free competition.

And what then happened in England? In all questions from the Reform Bill until the abolition of the Corn Laws,[306] did the political parties fight about anything except changes in property rights, questions of property, social questions?

Here, in Belgium itself, is the struggle of liberalism with Catholicism anything but the struggle of industrial capital with large landed property?

CÉLÉBRATION, A BRUXELLES,

DU DEUXIEME ANNIVERSAIRE

DE LA

RÉVOLUTION POLONAISE

du 22 février 1846.

Discours

PRONONCÉS

PAR MM. A. J. SENAULT, KARL MARX, LELEWEL, F. ENGELS
ET LOUIS LUBLINER, AVOCAT.

BRUXELLES.
C. G. VOGLER, LIBRAIRE-EDITEUR.
—
1848

Cover of the pamphlet containing the speeches "On the Polish Question" by Marx and Engels

And the political questions which have been debated for the last seventeen years, are these not basically social questions?

Thus, however you look at it, whether from a liberal, radical, even aristocratic point of view, could you still reproach the Cracow revolution with having joined a social question to a political question?

The men who led the Cracow revolutionary movement were deeply convinced that only a democratic Poland could be independent, and a democratic Poland was impossible without the abolition of feudal rights, without the agrarian movement which would transform the tied peasants into free proprietors, modern proprietors. Replace the Russian autocrat by Polish aristocrats and you will have given despotism naturalisation papers. It was thus that the Germans, in their war against foreign rule, exchanged one Napoleon for thirty-six Metternichs.[307]

If the Polish lord no longer has a Russian lord over him, the Polish peasant will still have a lord over him, but a free lord in place of a slave lord. This political change will have altered nothing in his social position.

The Cracow revolution has given a glorious example to the whole of Europe, by identifying the national cause with the democratic cause and the emancipation of the oppressed class.

If this revolution has been stifled for the moment by the bloody hands of hired assassins it is now rising gloriously and triumphantly in Switzerland and Italy. It sees the confirmation of these principles in Ireland, where the narrowly nationalist party has gone to its grave with O'Connell, and where the new national party is above all reforming and democratic.[308]

It is Poland once again which has taken the initiative, no longer feudal Poland, but democratic Poland; and from this moment its emancipation has become the point of honour for all the democrats of Europe.

SPEECH BY MR. FREDERICK ENGELS

Gentlemen,

The insurrection whose anniversary we are celebrating today has failed. After some days of heroic resistance Cracow fell and the bleeding ghost of Poland, which had risen for a moment before the eyes of its assassins, descended again into its grave.

The Cracow revolution was a defeat, a very deplorable defeat. Let us render the last honours to the fallen heroes, lament their setback and offer our sympathy to the twenty million Polish people whom this failure has again enchained.

But, gentlemen, is that all we have to do? Is it enough to shed a tear on the tomb of an unhappy country and to pledge against its oppressors an implacable hatred, till now not very potent?

No, gentlemen! The anniversary of Cracow is not only a day of mourning, it is a day of rejoicing for us other democrats; for the defeat itself contains a victory, a victory whose fruits are ours to gather, while the results of the defeat are only transitory.

This victory is the victory of young democratic Poland over the old aristocratic Poland.

Yes, the latest struggle of Poland against its foreign oppressors has been preceded by a hidden struggle, concealed but decisive within Poland itself, a struggle of oppressed Poles against Polish oppressors, a struggle of democracy against the Polish aristocracy.

Compare 1830[309] and 1846, compare Warsaw and Cracow. In 1830 the ruling class in Poland was as selfish, narrow-minded and cowardly in the legislative body as it was devoted, enthusiastic and courageous on the field of battle.

What did the Polish aristocracy want in 1830? To safeguard its own acquired rights with regard to the Emperor.[a] It limited the insurrection to the little country which the Congress of Vienna was pleased to call the Kingdom of Poland[310]; it restrained the uprising in the other Polish provinces; it left intact the degrading serfdom of the peasants and the infamous condition of the Jews. If the aristocracy, in the course of the insurrection, had to make concessions to the people, it only made them when it was too late, when the insurrection had failed.

Let it be said clearly: the insurrection of 1830 was neither a national revolution (it excluded three-quarters of Poland) nor a social or a political revolution; it changed nothing in the internal condition of the people; it was a conservative revolution.

But within the conservative revolution, within the national government itself, there was one man who vigorously attacked the narrow views of the ruling class. He proposed really revolutionary measures before whose boldness the aristocrats of the Diet recoiled. By calling the whole of ancient Poland to arms, by thus making the war for Polish independence a European war, by emancipating the Jews and the peasants, by making the latter share in landed property, by reconstructing Poland on the basis of democracy and equality, he wanted to make the national cause the cause of freedom; he wanted to identify the interest of all peoples with that of the Polish people.

---

[a] Nicholas I.—*Ed.*

Need I name the genius who conceived this plan, at once so vast and so simple? It was Lelewel.

In 1830, these proposals were continually rejected by the blind self-interest of the aristocratic majority. But these principles, ripened and developed by the experience of fifteen years of servitude, we saw inscribed on the flag of the Cracow uprising. At Cracow, it was clearly seen that there were no longer men who had much to lose; there were no aristocrats; every step that was taken bore the stamp of that democratic, I might almost say proletarian, boldness which has only its misery to lose and a whole country, a whole world, to gain. There, no hesitation, no scruples; the three foreign powers were attacked together; the freeing of the peasants, agrarian reform, the emancipation of the Jews were proclaimed, without caring for a moment whether this offended certain aristocratic interests.

The Cracow revolution wanted neither to re-establish ancient Poland nor to preserve what the foreign governments had let remain of the old Polish institutions; it was neither reactionary nor conservative.

No, it was even more hostile to Poland itself than to its foreign oppressors, hostile to the ancient Poland, barbarous, feudal and aristocratic, based on the serfdom of the majority of the people. Far from wanting to re-establish the ancient Poland, it aimed to overthrow it utterly, and to found on its ruins, with a wholly new class, with the majority of the people, a new Poland, modern, civilised and democratic, worthy of the nineteenth century, and which might be really the outpost of civilisation.

The difference between 1830 and 1846, the immense progress made within unhappy Poland itself, bleeding and torn; the Polish aristocracy completely separated from the Polish people and thrown into the arms of the oppressors of its country; the Polish people irrevocably committed to the democratic cause; and finally the class struggle, the motive force of all social progress, established in Poland as here, that is the victory of democracy proved by the Cracow revolution, that is the result which will bear fruit when the defeat of the insurgents has been avenged.

Yes, gentlemen, by the Cracow insurrection the Polish cause, from being national, as it was, has become the cause of all peoples; from a question of sympathy, as it was, it has become a question of interest of all democrats. Until 1846 we had a crime to avenge; henceforth we have allies to support, and we shall do it.

And it is above all our Germany which ought to congratulate itself on this explosion of democratic passion in Poland. We are, ourselves, on the eve of a democratic revolution; we shall have to fight barbarian hordes from Austria and Russia. Before 1846 we might have had doubts as to what side Poland would take if there were a democratic revolution in Germany. The Cracow revolution has removed all doubts. Henceforth the German people and the Polish people are irrevocably allied. We have the same enemies, the same oppressors, for the Russian government weighs on us as much as on the Poles. The first condition for the deliverance both of Germany and of Poland is the overturning of the present political state in Germany, the downfall of Prussia and Austria, the driving back of Russia beyond the Dniester and the Dvina.

The alliance of the two nations is therefore not by any means a beautiful dream, a charming illusion; no, gentlemen, it is an inevitable necessity resulting from the common interests of the two nations, and it has become necessary through the Cracow revolution. The German people, which until now had little of its own except words, will now have deeds to offer its Polish brothers; and just as we German democrats present here clasp hands with the Polish democrats, so the whole German people will celebrate its alliance with the Polish people on the very field of the first battle won in common over our common oppressors.

First published in March 1848 in: *Célébration, à Bruxelles, du deuxième anniversaire de la Révolution Polonaise du 22 Février 1846*, Bruxelles, 1848

Printed according to the text in *Célébration...*

Translated from the French

Published in English in full for the first time

Frederick Engels

A WORD TO THE *RIFORMA*

The *Riforma* of Lucca has printed a reply to one of those well-known and vile articles which the *Augsburger Zeitung*[a] is accustomed to publish on instructions from the Imperial Chancellery in Vienna.[311]

That trashy rag from the Lech[b] had not only praised to the skies the loyalty of the 518,000 Austrian soldiers to their feeble-minded Ferdinand, but had also claimed that all these soldiers, Bohemians, Poles, Slovaks, Croats, Heyducks, Wallachians, Hungarians, Italians, etc., were burning with enthusiasm for German unity and would willingly part with their lives for it, *as soon as it should be the will of the Emperor*!

As though this were not precisely the misfortune—that so long as Austria exists Germany has to risk seeing its unity defended by Heyducks, Croats and Wallachians, as though the unity of Germany so long as Austria survives could be anything else but the unity of Germany with Croats, Wallachians, Magyars and Italians!

The *Riforma* replies very aptly to the lying claim of the *All-Gemeine*[c] that Austria is in fact defending the interests of the German nation in Lombardy, and concludes with an appeal to the Germans, drawing a parallel between the Italian movement of 1848 and the German wars of liberation in 1813 and 1815.

The *Riforma* evidently thought that by doing so it was paying a compliment to the Germans, otherwise it would never have equated,

---

[a] *Allgemeine Zeitung* (Augsburg).—*Ed.*

[b] Augsburg is situated on the Lech.—*Ed.*

[c] A pun on the name: *Allgemeine Zeitung*—"All-Gemeine" means thoroughly vile.—*Ed.*

against its better judgment, today's progressive Italian movement with precisely those reactionary wars to which Italy directly owes its subjugation to Austria, to which Germany owes the restoration of as much as possible of the old confusion, fragmentation and tyranny, and to which the whole of Europe owes the infamous treaties of 1815.[312]

The *Riforma* may take our word for it: Germany is fully enlightened as to the wars of liberation, both through the consequences of the wars themselves and through the ignominious end to which the heroes of that "glorious" age have come. Only the hired papers of the government still puff their cheeks and trumpet forth praise for that stupidity-intoxicated period, the public laughs and even the iron cross turns red with shame.

Precisely these newspapers, precisely these enthusiastic French-eaters of 1813, are now raising the same outcry against the Italians as they did before against the French, who sing paeons of praise to Austria, to Christian-Germanic Austria, and who preach crusades against Romance knavery and Romance frippery—for indeed Italians are just as much Romance as the French.

Would the Italians like an example of the sympathy they may expect from the worthy blusterers of the age of liberation, of the kind of ideas these red-headed visionaries entertain about the Italian nation? We shall merely quote the well-known song by A[ugust] A[dolf] L[udwig] Follen[a]:

> Yon land of marvels all may sing,
> Where mandolines and soft guitars do ring
> And, 'neath darkling leaf, the golden orange gleams;
> But I the purple German plum esteem
> And Borsdorf's apple on its leafy beam,

and how these poetic ravings of an ever cool-headed philistine drivel on. Then come the most ludicrous pictures of bandits, daggers, fire-belching mountains, Romance knavery, the infidelity of Italian women, bugs, scorpions, poison, vipers, assassins, etc., seen by this virtuous lover of plums running around in dozens on all the highways of Italy, and finally the gushing philistine thanks his God that he is in the land of Love and Friendship, of shindies with chair-legs, of faithful, blue-eyed pastors' daughters, of probity and cosiness, in short in the land of German Loyalty. Such are the superstitious and novelettish ideas entertained by the heroes of 1813 about Italy, which of course they have never seen.

---

[a] August Follen composed the music and Johann Friedrichsen wrote the words.—*Ed.*

The *Riforma* and the men of the Italian movement in general can rest assured: public opinion in Germany is definitely on the side of the Italians. The German people have just as great an interest in the fall of Austria as the Italian people. They greet with undivided applause every step forward by the Italian people, and, we hope, they will not be missing from the battlefield at the right moment to put an end to all the Austrian magnificence once and for all.

Written about February 22, 1848

First published in the *Deutsche-Brüsseler-Zeitung* No. 16, February 24, 1848

Signed: *F. Engels*

Printed according to the newspaper

Published in English for the first time

Frederick Engels

REVOLUTION IN PARIS

The year 1848 is turning out well. The Sicilian revolution with its long train of constitutions is hardly over before Paris experiences a victorious insurrection.

The opposition deputies had publicly pledged themselves to defend the right of assembly against Guizot, Duchâtel and Hébert by means of a courageous demonstration.

All the preparations had been made. The hall was ready and awaited the banquet guests. Then suddenly, when the time had come to act, the poltroons of the Left, M. Odilon Barrot at their head, beat, as always, a cowardly retreat.

The banquet was called off. But the people of Paris, stirred up by the loud-mouths in the Chamber, raging at the cowardice of these *épiciers*[a] and made discontented at the same time by protracted general unemployment, the people of Paris refused to be called off.

At midday on Tuesday,[b] all Paris was on the streets. The masses were shouting: "Down with Guizot, long live the Reform!" They proceeded to Guizot's residence, which was protected by the troops with difficulty; but the windows were nevertheless broken.

The masses proceeded to Odilon Barrot's house as well, shouted "Down with Barrot!" and broke his windows, too. M. Barrot, the cowardly originator of the whole outbreak, sent to the government and asked for a security guard!

The troops stood by and quietly looked on. Only the Municipal Guard struck out, and that with the greatest brutality. The Municipal Guard is a corps consisting in the main of natives of Alsace and

[a] Grocers, here philistines.—*Ed.*

[b] February 22, 1848.—*Ed.*

Lorraine, that is, men who are half German; they receive three and a half fr[ancs] a day and look very plump and well-nourished. The Municipal Guard is the basest body of soldiers in existence, worse than the Gendarmerie, worse than the old Swiss Guard; if the people win, things will go badly for it.

Towards evening the people began to resist. Barricades were set up, guard posts stormed and set on fire. A police spy was cut down in the Place de la Bastille. Arms shops were looted.

At five o'clock marching orders were sounded for the National Guard. But only a very few turned up, and those who did shouted "Down with Guizot!"

During the night calm was restored. The last barricades were taken and the outbreak appeared to be over.

On Wednesday morning, however, the revolt began again with renewed vigour. A large part of the centre of Paris lying to the east of the Rue Montmartre was strongly barricaded; after eleven o'clock the troops no longer dared venture in there. The National Guard gathered in large numbers, but only to hold the troops back from any attacks on the people and to shout "Down with Guizot, long live the Reform!"

There were 50,000 soldiers in Paris, disposed according to Marshal Gérard's defence plan[313] and holding all strategic points. But these points were so numerous that all of the troops were kept busy with them and were thus already forced into inaction. Apart from the Municipal Guard there were almost no soldiers free for an offensive. Gérard's excellent plan was of infinite help to the outbreak; it paralysed the troops and made it easier for them to maintain the passivity to which they were in any case inclined. The detached forts also proved to be anything but beneficial to the government. They had to be kept manned and thus also withdrew a considerable section of the troops from the battle area. No one thought of a bombardment. In general not a single person gave a thought to the fact that these bastilles even existed. One more proof how fruitless are all defence plans against a mass revolt in a great city!

Towards noon the outcry against the Ministry in the ranks of the National Guard was so strong that several colonels sent word to the Tuileries that they would not hold themselves responsible for their regiments if the Ministry were to remain.

At two o'clock the aged Louis Philippe was forced to drop Guizot and form a new Ministry. Hardly had this been made public when the National Guard went home in jubilation and illuminated their houses.

But the people, the workers, the *only ones* who had erected the barricades, battled with the Municipal Guard and thrown themselves against the bullets, the bayonets and the horses' hoofs, these workers had no desire to fight merely for M. Molé and M. Billault.[314] They continued the struggle. While the Boulevard des Italiens was full of joy and jubilation, there was heavy shooting in the Rue Sainte-Avoie and Rambuteau. The battle lasted long into the night and was continued on Thursday morning. Evidence of the general participation of the workers in the battle was the tearing up of the rails on all the railways around Paris.

The bourgeoisie has made its revolution, it has toppled Guizot and with him the exclusive rule of the Stock Exchange grandees. Now, however, in the second act of the struggle, it is no longer one section of the bourgeoisie confronting another, now the proletariat confronts the bourgeoisie.

News has just arrived that the people have won and proclaimed the Republic. We confess that we had not dared hope for this brilliant success by the Paris proletariat.

Three members of the provisional government belong to the definitely democratic party, whose organ is the *Réforme*. The fourth is *a worker*[a]—for the first time in any country in the world. The others are Lamartine, Dupont de l'Eure and two men from the *National*.[315]

By this glorious revolution the French proletariat has again placed itself at the head of the European movement. All honour to the workers of Paris! They have given the world an impulse which will be felt by every country in turn; for the victory of the Republic in France means the victory of democracy in the whole of Europe.

Our age, the age of democracy, is breaking. The flames of the Tuileries and the Palais Royal are the dawn of the proletariat. Everywhere the rule of the bourgeoisie will now come crashing down, or be dashed to pieces.

Germany, we hope, will follow. Now or never will it raise itself from its degradation. If the Germans have any energy, any pride or any courage, then in a month's time we too shall be able to shout:

"Long live the German Republic!"

Written on February 25-26, 1848

First published in the *Deutsche-Brüsseler-Zeitung* No. 17, February 27, 1848

Printed according to the newspaper

Published in English for the first time

---

[a] Albert.—*Ed.*

Frederick Engels

TO THE EDITOR OF *THE NORTHERN STAR*[316]

Dear Sir,

After the important events accomplished in France, the position taken by the Belgian people and government is of a greater interest than in ordinary times. I hasten, therefore, to inform your readers of what has happened since Friday, 25th of February.

The excitement and inquietude was universal in this town on the evening of that day. All sorts of rumours were spread, but nothing was really believed. The railway station was full of a crowd of people of all classes, anxious for the arrival of news. The French Ambassador, ex-Marquis de Rumigny, himself was there. At half-past twelve at night, the train arrived, with the glorious news of Thursday's revolution, and the whole mass of people shouted, in one sudden outburst of enthusiasm: *Vive la République!* The news spread rapidly all over the town. On Saturday all was quiet. On Sunday, however, the streets were crowded with people, and every one was curious to see what steps would be taken by two societies—the Association Démocratique and the Alliance.[317] Both bodies assembled in the evening. The Alliance, a set of middle-class Radicals, resolved to wait, and thus retired from the movement. The Association Démocratique, however, took a series of most important resolutions, by which this body placed itself at the head of the movement. They resolved to meet daily, instead of weekly; to send a petition to the town-council, reclaiming the arming, not only of the middle-class Civic Guard, but of all citizens in districts. In the evening some rioting took place in the streets. The people cried: *Vive la République,* and assembled in masses around the Town Hall. Several arrests took place, but nothing of any consequence occurred.

Among the individuals arrested, there were two Germans—a political refugee, M. Wolff, and a working man. Now, you must know that there existed here, in Brussels, a German working men's society,[318] in which political and social questions were discussed, and a German democratic newspaper.[a] The Germans, resident in Brussels, were known for being generally very active and uncompromising democrats. They were almost all members of the Democratic Association, and the vice-president of the German society, Dr. Marx, was also vice-president of the Democratic Association.

The government, perfectly aware of the narrow sentiment of nationalism prevalent among a certain class of the population of a small country like Belgium, immediately profited by these circumstances, in order to spread the rumour that the whole agitation for the Republic had been got up by the Germans—men who had nothing to lose, who had been expelled from three or four countries for their turpitudes, and who intended to place themselves at the head of the intended Belgian Republic. This precious piece of news was reported on Monday through the whole town, and in less than a day the whole mass of the shopocracy, who form the body of the Civic Guard, raised one unanimous outcry against the German rebels, who wanted to revolutionise their happy Belgian fatherland.

The Germans had fixed a place of meeting in a coffee-house, where every one of them was to bring the latest news from Paris. But the outcry of the shopocrats was so great, and the rumours of government measures against the Germans were so manifold, that they were obliged to give up even this innocent means of communicating with each other.

On Sunday evening already the police had succeeded in prevailing upon the publican, proprietor of the German society's room, to refuse them the room for any future meeting.

The Germans behaved perfectly well during these times. Exposed to the most petty persecutions of the police, they yet rested at their post. They assisted every evening at the meeting of the Democratic Association. They abstained from all tumultuous crowding in the streets, but they showed, though personally exposing themselves, that in the hour of danger they would not abandon their Belgian brethren.

When, after a few days, the extraordinary agitation of Sunday and Monday had ceased, when the people had returned to their work, when the government had recovered from their first terror, then commenced another series of persecutions against the Germans. The government published orders, according to which all foreign

[a] *Deutsche-Brüsseler-Zeitung.—Ed.*

working men, from the moment they had no work, were to be expelled the country; and all foreigners indiscriminately, whose passports were out of order, were to be treated in the same way. Thus, while they took these measures, they excited, by the rumours they spread, the masters against all foreign working men, and made it impossible to any German to find work. Even those who had work lost it, and were, from that moment, exposed to an order of expulsion.

Not only against working men out of work, but also against women, they commenced their persecution. A young German Democrat, who lives, according to the French and Belgian custom, with a French lady, just as married people live—and whose presence at Brussels appears to have importuned the police—was suddenly exposed to a series of persecutions, directed against his mistress. She having no passport—and who ever before thought in Belgium of asking passports from a woman?—was threatened with immediate expulsion! and the police declared that it was not for her sake, but for the sake of the individual with whom she lived. Seven times in three days, the Commissary of Police was at her house; she had to pass at his office several times, and was sent to the central police office, escorted by an agent—and if an influential Belgian Democrat had not interposed, she would certainly have been obliged to leave.

But all this is nothing. The persecutions against working men,—the spreading of rumours about such and such an individual to be arrested, or about a general chase after the Germans to be made in all public houses of the town on Tuesday evening, all this is nothing compared with what I have now to report.

On Friday evening,[a] Dr. Marx, amongst others, received a royal ordinance, ordering him to quit the country within twenty-four hours. He was engaged in arranging his trunks for the journey, when, at one o'clock in the morning, and in spite of the law which forbids the violation of the dwelling of a citizen from sunset to sunrise, ten police agents, armed, headed by a commissary of police, broke into his house, seized upon him and led him to the Town Hall prison. No reason was given but that his passport was not in order, though he presented them at least three passports, and though he had resided in Brussels for three years! He was led off. His wife, seized with terror, instantly ran to see a Belgian lawyer, who always offered his services to persecuted foreigners—the same whose friendly interposition has been mentioned above,—M. Jottrand, President of the Democratic Association. On her return, she met

---

[a] March 3. *The Northern Star* reported this erroneously as "Saturday".—*Ed.*

with a friend, a Belgian, M. Gigot. He accompanied her home. At the door of Dr. Marx's house, they found two of the policemen who had arrested her husband. Where have you taken my husband? asked she. Why, if you will follow us we will show you where he is. They led her, along with M. Gigot, to the Town Hall, but instead of fulfilling their promise, they delivered up both of them to the police, and *they were put into prison.* Mrs. Marx, who had left her three little children[a] at home, with a servant only, was led into a room where she found a set of prostitutes of the lowest order, with whom she had to pass the night. Next morning she was led into a room where she had to stay three hours without fire, shivering with cold. M. Gigot was also detained. M. Marx had been put into a room with a *raving madman,* whom he was obliged to fight every moment. The most brutal treatment on the part of the jailors was joined to this infamous conduct.

At three o'clock in the afternoon, at last, they were conducted before the judge, who very soon ordered their liberation. And of what had Mrs. Marx and M. Gigot been indicted? Of *vagabondage,* because neither of them had a passport in their pockets!

M. Marx was equally liberated, and ordered to leave the country the same evening. Thus, after having been wantonly imprisoned during eighteen of the twenty-four hours left him to settle his affairs; after having had not only himself, but also his wife, separated for all that time from his three children, the eldest of whom has not attained her fourth year, he was sent away without a minute to put his affairs in order.

M. Gigot, on his arrest, had only left the prison the day before. He had been seized, along with three democrats from Liège, at six o'clock on Monday morning, in an hotel, and arrested for vagabondage, because they had no passports. They were ordered to be liberated on Tuesday, but yet detained till Thursday against all law. One of them, M. Tedesco, is yet in prison, accused of nobody knows what. Both he and M. Wolff will be either liberated or placed before the tribunal in the course of this week.

I must say, however, that the Belgian working men and several other democrats of that nation, particularly M. Jottrand, have behaved exceedingly well towards the persecuted Germans. They have shown themselves quite above all petty sentiments of nationality. They saw in us not foreigners but democrats.

I hear that there is an order of arrest out against a Belgian working man and brave democrat, M. de Guasco. Another, M. Dassy, arrested

[a] Jenny, Laura and Edgar.—*Ed.*

on Sunday last, for rebellion, was before the tribunal yesterday; his judgment is not yet pronounced.

I am daily and hourly expecting my order of expulsion, if not worse, for nobody can foretell what this Belgio-Russian government is about to dare. I hold myself ready to leave at a moment's notice. Such is the position of a German democrat in this *free* country, which, as the papers say, has nothing to envy in the French Republic.

Salutation and Fraternity.

Your old Friend

Brussels, March 5th

First published in *The Northern Star* No. 544, March 25, 1848

Reprinted from the newspaper

Karl Marx

TO THE EDITOR OF *LA RÉFORME*

Dear Sir,

At the present moment the Belgian government is aligning itself entirely with the policy of the Holy Alliance. Its reactionary fury falls on the German democrats with unprecedented brutality. Were we not too distressed by the persecution directed specifically against us, we would openly laugh at the ridiculous attitude assumed by the Rogier ministry when it accuses a few Germans of wishing to impose a republic on the Belgians against their wishes; but it so happens that, in the special case to which we refer, the hateful aspect of it outweighs the absurd.

First of all, Sir, it is as well to know that almost all the Brussels newspapers are edited by Frenchmen, most of whom escaped from France to avoid the ignominious punishments which threatened them in their own country. These Frenchmen now have the utmost interest in protecting the Belgian independence which they all betrayed in 1833.[319] The king,[a] the ministry and their supporters have used these rags to give credibility to the idea that a Belgian revolution, in the republican sense, would merely be an imitation of a *francequillonnerie*,[b] and that all the democratic activity which is now making itself felt in Belgium has only been provoked by some hot-headed Germans.

The Germans do not in the least deny that they openly associated with the Belgian democrats, and this without the slightest degree of

---

[a] Leopold I.—*Ed.*

[b] A scornful expression in Flemish, meaning stupidly copying anything that is French.—*Ed.*

hot-headedness. In the eyes of the King's Prosecutor this means arousing the workers against the bourgeois, making the Belgians suspicious of a *German* king they so dearly love, and opening the gates of Belgium to a French invasion.

Having received, on March 3 at five o'clock in the evening, an order to leave the *kingdom* of Belgium within twenty-four hours, I was busy, that same night, with preparing for the journey when a commissary of police, accompanied by ten municipal guards, burst into the place where I was living, searched the whole house, and ended by putting me under arrest on the pretext that I was without papers. Apart from the quite proper papers sent me by M. Duchâtel in expelling me from France,[320] I had at hand the expulsion papers delivered to me by Belgium only a few hours earlier.

I would not have spoken to you, Sir, about my arrest and the brutalities I suffered, were these not connected with an incident which would be difficult to understand even in Austria.

Immediately after my arrest, my wife went to the home of M. Jottrand, President of the Democratic Association of Belgium, to urge him to take the necessary measures. On returning home she found at her door a policeman who told her, with perfect politeness, that if she should wish to speak to M. Marx, she need only follow him. My wife accepted the offer with alacrity. She was taken to the police station, and the Commissary at first told her that M. Marx was not there; then he brutally demanded who she was, why she had gone to M. Jottrand's house, and whether she had her papers with her. A Belgian democrat, M. Gigot, had followed my wife to the police station with the municipal guard, and when he protested strongly against the Commissary's absurd and insolent questions he was silenced by guards who seized him and threw him into a cell. My wife, under the charge of "vagabondage", was taken to the prison at the Hôtel de Ville and locked up in a dark room with prostitutes. At eleven o'clock in the morning she was taken, under police escort and in broad daylight, to the office of the examining magistrate. For two hours she was held in close custody, despite the most vigorous protests from all sides. She stayed there, in bitter cold, exposed to the most shameless remarks by the gendarmes.

Finally she appeared before the examining magistrate, who was surprised that the police, in their solicitude, had not at the same time arrested the young children. The interrogation was naturally a sham, and my wife's only crime consists in the fact that, although belonging to the Prussian aristocracy, she shares the democratic opinions of her husband.

I have not entered into all the details of this revolting affair. I merely add that, when we were released, the twenty-four hours had just ended, and we had to leave without being able to take even the most essential of our belongings.

Karl Marx,
Vice-President of the Brussels Democratic Association

Written about March 6, 1848

First published in *La Réforme*, March 8, 1848

Printed according to the newspaper

Translated from the French

Published in English for the first time

Karl Marx

[PERSECUTION OF FOREIGNERS IN BRUSSELS][321]

On Sunday, February 27 the Brussels Democratic Association held its first public meeting since the news of the proclamation of the French Republic. It was known in advance that an immense crowd of workers, determined to lend their active help to all measures that the Association would judge it proper to undertake, would be present.

The government, for its part, had spread the rumour that king Leopold was ready to abdicate the moment the people wished it. This was a trap set for the Belgian democrats to make them undertake nothing decisive against such a good king, who asked nothing better than to shed the burden of royalty, provided that he was honourably left a reasonable pension.

At the same time the king's government had ready a list of people whom it considered proper to arrest that very night as disturbers of public order. It had agreed with M. Hody, the chief of public security, to have on this list the foreigners as chief instigators of an artificial riot, as much to cover the arrest of Belgians known as resolute republicans as to awake national susceptibilities. This explains why, later on, his excellency M. Rogier, who is no more Belgian than His Majesty King Leopold is French, had published an ordinance which commanded the authorities to watch carefully the French and the Germans, the former compatriots of M. Rogier, the latter compatriots of Leopold. This ordinance recalls, in its form of wording, the laws on suspects.[322]

This clever plan was executed in a manner the more perfidious and brutal in that the people arrested on the evening of February 27 had abstained from any provocation.

It might be said that pleasure had been taken in arresting these persons in order to maltreat and abuse them at leisure.

Immediately after their arrest they were showered with punches, kicks and sabre-blows; they were spat in the face, these *republicans.* They were maltreated in the presence of the philanthropist Hody, who was delighted to give these foreigners proof of his powers.

As there were no charges against them it only remained to release them. But no! They were kept in the cells for six days! Then the foreign prisoners were separated from the rest and taken directly in Black Marias to the railway station. There they were again put into vans, each in a separate cell, and sent in this way to Quiévrain where Belgian police received them and dragged them to the French frontier.

When at last they were able to collect themselves on the soil of liberty, they found they had in their pockets nothing but expulsion papers, dated the eve of their arrests. One of the expelled persons, M. Allard, is French.

At the same time the government of the Petty King proclaimed, in the Chamber of Representatives, that the Belgian *kingdom,* including the two Flanders,[a] was the best of all possible *republics,* and that it possessed a model police force, directed by a man such as M. Hody, at one and the same time an old republican, a phalansterist and a rejoined Leopoldist. The chamber wept with joy, the Catholic and liberal papers were in ecstasies about the domestic virtues of King Leopold and the public virtues of his servant Rogier.

The Belgian people are republicans. The only Leopoldists are the big bourgeoisie, the landed aristocracy, the Jesuits, the officials and the ex-Frenchmen who, chased out of France, now find themselves at the head of the Belgian administration and the press.

Metternich is delighted to find so opportunely at the French frontier a Coburg, a born enemy of the French revolution. But he forgets that the Coburgs of today no longer count except in questions of marriage.

Written about March 10, 1848

First published in *La Réforme,* March 12, 1848

Printed according to the newspaper

Translated from the French

Published in English for the first time

[a] West and East Flanders—two provinces of the Belgian Kingdom.—*Ed.*

Frederick Engels

[THE SITUATION IN BELGIUM][323]

Brussels, March 18

The Belgian bourgeoisie refused a republic to the people fifteen days ago; now it is preparing itself to take the initiative in the republican movement. It cannot yet be proclaimed out loud, but it is whispered everywhere in Brussels: "Really, Leopold must go; really, only the republic can save us; but what we need is a good solid republic, without organisation of labour, without universal suffrage, without the workers meddling in it!"

This is already some progress. The good bourgeoisie of Brussels who, only a few days ago, desperately denied any intention of wanting to copy the French Republic, have felt the results of the financial crisis in Paris. While still decrying political imitation they submit to financial imitation. While still singing the praises of Belgian independence and neutrality, they found that the Brussels Stock Exchange was completely and most humiliatingly dependent on the Paris Stock Exchange. The cordon of troops which holds the southern frontier has not stopped the lowering of share prices from invading, unimpeded, the guaranteed neutral territory of Belgium.

Indeed, the consternation which reigns in the Brussels market could not be more general. Bankruptcy is decimating the middling and small traders, shares are finding no buyers, quotations are only nominal, money is disappearing more quickly than in Paris, trade is completely stagnant, and most manufacturers have sacked their workmen. Here are a few examples of the general depression: a few days ago a dealer offered to sell one hundred and fifty shares of the Dendre railway at one hundred francs each, which were quoted above par on the London Stock Exchange before the February revolution. The first day he refused 45 francs, the second 35 francs, and the third day he sold them at 10 francs per share! Land sold for six thousand francs two years ago no longer finds buyers for one third this price.

And now, at this moment of general panic, the government demands, firstly, two-thirds of direct taxes in advance, and then a forced loan of fifty to sixty millions, measures which terrify the tax-payers already dissatisfied with an ever-increasing budget!

This is a state of affairs which has not failed to persuade our good bourgeoisie that, in being enthusiastic for the monarchy, they have gained only full and complete participation in the troubles in France without having shared any of the advantages. This is the real cause of the growing republicanism.

Meanwhile, the workers are not quiet. Ghent has had several days of disturbances; here two days ago there were meetings of many workers, ending in a petition to the king, which Leopold in person came to receive from the calloused hands which presented it to him. More serious demonstrations will soon follow. Every day puts more workers out of work. If the industrial crisis continues, if feelings in the working class warm up a little, the Belgian bourgeoisie, like that of Paris, will make its "mariage de raison" with the republic.

Written on March 18, 1848

First published in Marx/Engels, *Gesamtausgabe*, I. Abteilung, Bd. 6, Berlin, 1932

Printed according to the manuscript

Translated from the French

Published in English for the first time

FROM THE PREPARATORY MATERIALS

Karl Marx

PROTECTIONISTS[324]

1) have never protected small industry, only machine industry. Example: the school of List in Germany. Gülich.[a]

2) If we believe what the protectionists say, they merely preserve the status quo. Protection will never effect sales of the protected product on foreign markets. Hence reactionary.[b]

3) The last consolation of the protectionists is that the country is not exploited by foreign but by domestic capitalists.

4) It is said, indeed, that internal reforms must first be made before one can think of free trade.[c] The power to reform the position of the classes is not ascribed to the protective system itself. But they say it would be foolish to reform international relations before domestic relations have been reformed. But what is the protective system? It is proof that the class which carries it into effect has power in its hands. Therefore, given the protective system [...] the capitalists will not concede anything. Moreover, gentlemen, great social and historical reforms are never made by concessions, by the generosity of the ruling classes, but only through the *nécessité des choses.* They must therefore be forced through. It is therefore ridiculous to believe that in a country where the protective system prevails [...] [...] [...] the relations between capital and labour are reformed in any way. I shall say no more of the protectionists [...] of the question....[c]

Written about September 18, 1847

First published in Marx/Engels, *Gesamtausgabe,* I. Abteilung, Bd. 6, Berlin, 1932

Printed according to the manuscript

Published in English for the first time

---

[a] In the original Jülich.—*Ed.*

[b] After "reactionary" the following is written between the lines: "*conservateurs,* and if conserved [?], *conservateurs — hommes réactionnaires.*"—*Ed.*

[c] Marx uses the English term.—*Ed.*

Karl Marx

DEMAND[325]

1) *Demand.* Most economists treat it almost exclusively from the individual standpoint. The world historic development of demand, its first universal development, depends firstly on the products of the various countries of the world becoming known to each other. If in the further course of development demand creates intercourse, initially it is intercourse which creates demand. Demand is the material content of intercourse, the totality of the objects of exchange, of the commodities which come into exchange and trade. Wars, voyages of discovery, etc., all historical events whereby nations are brought into contact, are all so many conditions of expanding demand, of the formation of the world market. The growth of demand consists directly in the first place in the fact that already *existing products* of various countries ⟨in contact, in A⟩ are being exchanged. Demand gradually loses its local etc. character and becomes cosmopolitan. The production of all countries thus enters more and more into the consumption of the individuals of ⟨all regions⟩ of a country.

The *Crusades,* for example, by making known the products of the Orient, greatly increased the demand for such products in Western Europe. (Cf. J., Notebook III, p. 106.) Places where these products stream together for exchange constitute the world market towns; the world market appeared in this form in particular before the discovery of America. In the 14th and 15th centuries Constantinople, the Italian cities, Bruges and London.

Also still at the same time *like fairs,* namely the caravan-like streaming together of merchants. In the 19th century, for example, fairs are of quite subordinate significance. (Cf. J., Notebook III, p. 106.)

How much less these market places depend on their own industry than the latter and its prosperity depend simply on their being the general stores, is proved by the decay of the trade of the Italian cities after 1498, from the moment when *Lisbon* became the chief market for Indian fabrics and spices. *Antwerp*, too, still had the same limited character in the 16th century as Bruges etc. earlier.

Trade supremacy. The first dominant *trading nation* are the Dutch (from end of the 16th to the middle of the 17th century). Until then there were only first *trading towns.* The Spaniards and Portuguese form the transition from dominant trading towns to dominant trading nations. Carrying trade and fisheries nevertheless still form a decisive constituent of Dutch supremacy.

The <agricultural> *European North-East* in the relation of an agricultural country to the European West. In the same measure in which here industry and shipbuilding increase, the demand for the raw products of the North-East increases and with it their production.

Holland as the first trading and industrial nation, from the end of the 16th to the middle of the 17th century, is also the first nation for whom its domestic agriculture is insufficient and where the population is growing in far too great a proportion to domestic agriculture. Therefore carries on the first large-scale trade in grain. *Amsterdam* becomes the chief granary of Western Europe. (Cf. J., Notebook III, p. 107).

Written in December 1847

First published in French in the book Karl Marx, *Œuvres.Économie. II*, [Paris,] 1968

Printed according to the manuscript

Published in English for the first time

Karl Marx

DRAFT PLAN FOR SECTION III OF THE *MANIFESTO OF THE COMMUNIST PARTY*[326]

First draft

1) ⟨Critique⟩ [a] Critical Utopian Systems (Communist).
2)

Second draft

1) Reactionary socialism, feudal, religious petty bourgeois.
2) Bourgeois socialism.
3) German philosophical socialism.[b]
4) Critical utopian systems of literature. Owen, Cabet, Weitling, Fourier, St. Simon, Babeuf.
5) Direct party literature.
6) Communist literature.[327]

Written at the end of December 1847 or the beginning of January 1848

First published in Marx/Engels, *Gesamtausgabe*, I. Abteilung, Bd. 6, Berlin, 1932

Printed according to the manuscript

Published in English for the first time

---

[a] This word is struck out in the manuscript.—*Ed.*

[b] Marx added this point in the left-hand margin and accordingly altered the original numbering from 3 to 4, 4 to 5, 5 to 6.

Karl Marx

PAGE FROM THE ROUGH DRAFT OF THE *MANIFESTO OF THE COMMUNIST PARTY*[328]

13) ...Proletarians, for the Ten-Hour Bill without sharing their illusions about the results of this measure.[a]

We have seen, moreover:

The Communists do not put forward a new theory of private property. They merely state the historical fact that the ⟨means of production⟩ [b] bourgeois production relations and with them bourgeois property relations ⟨and⟩ ⟨eith⟩ ⟨certain⟩ of the ⟨devel⟩ ⟨social⟩ development of the social forces of production no longer ⟨are appropriate⟩ and therefore ⟨to the development of industry itself⟩ ⟨and⟩ in t....

But do not argue with us because you measure ⟨oppose⟩ the abolition of bourgeois property by your bourgeois ideas of freedom, culture, etc.! Your ideas themselves ⟨are only⟩ ⟨prod⟩ ⟨are⟩ ⟨correspond⟩ are products of the ⟨existing⟩ bourgeois production and property relations, as your legal system is merely the will of your class elevated into law. ⟨Your⟩ A will whose content is determined by the material living conditions of your class.

⟨Your⟩ You share with all ruling classes that have perished the biased idea of transforming ⟨the⟩ your ⟨bourgeois⟩ production and property relations from historical, ⟨and merely⟩ transitory relations corresponding only to a certain ⟨stage in the⟩ development of the productive forces, into eternal laws of nature and reason.

---

[a] The first two lines are in Jenny Marx's hand. The rest in Marx's.—*Ed.*

[b] Deletions in the original are given here in angular brackets.—*Ed.*

What you comprehend for feudal property, you no longer comprehend for bourgeois ⟨conditi⟩ property.

And yet, you cannot deny the fact that ⟨in the course⟩ with the development of ⟨bourgeois⟩ industry the one-sided, on....[a]

The Communists do not put forward any new theory of property. They state a fact. You deny the most striking facts. You have to deny them. You are backward looking utopians.

Written in December 1847-January 1848

First published as a facsimile in the journal *Der Wahre Jakob* No. 565 (6), March 17, 1908

Printed according to the manuscript

Published in English for the first time

[a] In the M S. the whole sentence including deleted words is struck out.—*Ed.*

Bottom of the page from Marx's manuscript, "Protectionists", with drawings by Engels

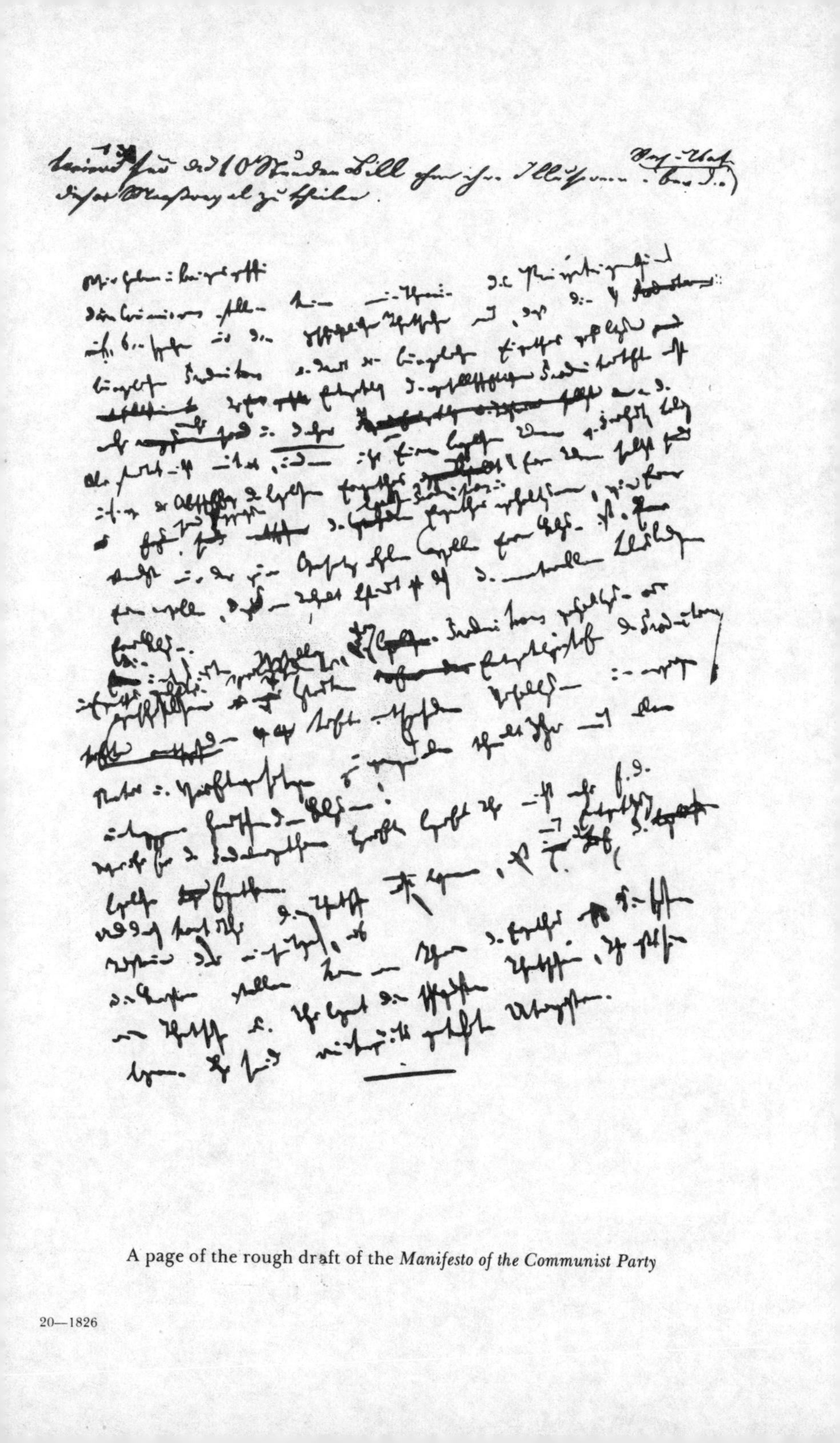

A page of the rough draft of the *Manifesto of the Communist Party*

Karl Marx

NOTES ON THE ARREST, MALTREATMENT AND EXPULSION OF WILHELM WOLFF BY THE BRUSSELS POLICE FEBRUARY 27 TO MARCH 1, 1848[a]

Petits Carmes.[329] 5 étrangers, 34 Belge

Wolff's right eye is so injured it will hardly regain sight.

Sunday February 27, between 10 and 11 o'clock in the evening.

Real maltreatment in the Hôtel de Ville, blows with the fist from all directions. The real maltreatment first in the police station where there were a number of drunken gardes civiques. Police punched Wolff in the right eye so that the sight....

They tore off his glasses, spat in his face, kicked him, punched him, abused him, etc. One of the gardes civiques proved his valour by joining in these manifestations. They tortured him.

In the meantime Hody arrived, chef de la sûreté publique, notorious philanthropist, hypocritical scoundrel.

Wolff had an interview of ⟨1⟩ $^1/_2$ [hours] with him in the presence of the scoundrel who had arrested him amidst frightful maltreatment.

Hody's indignation at Wolff's visiting him. Spoke furiously against the German Workers' Society.[330] "I knew," he said among other things, "that there would be about $^2/_3$ Germans among those arrested tonight." Wolff said ironically: "Oui, insofar as they were already marked in advance for arrest."

Taken from the Permanence to the Amigo.[331] Wolff [..?.] t. evening [...?...]

The whole thing that evening was a provocation organised by the police. The Ministry needed prisoners at any cost, including also Germans.

---

[a] See this volume, pp. 567-68.—*Ed.*

At the Amigo: soon more arrested persons arrived: those who were placed with Wolff: a Belgian. He was so maltreated and injured by the police that he lost at least a quart of blood. A third person see p. 2.

On *Monday* etc. taken to the Petits Carmes.

On Wednesday the 6 arrested foreigners received their expulsion passports. But Wolff's was dated Sunday, February 27, *before* his arrest. In prison horribly maltreated.

Written early in March 1848

First published in Marx/Engels, *Gesamtausgabe*, I. Abteilung, Bd. 6, Berlin, 1932

Printed according to the manuscript

Published in English for the first time

APPENDICES

RULES OF THE COMMUNIST LEAGUE[332]

Working Men of All Countries, Unite!

SECTION I

THE LEAGUE

Art. 1. The League aims at the emancipation of humanity by spreading the theory of the community of property and its speediest possible practical introduction.

Art. 2. The League is divided into *communities* and *circles*; at its head stands the *Central Authority* as the executive organ.

Art. 3. Anyone who wishes to join the League is required:

a. to conduct himself in manly fashion;
b. never to have committed a dishonourable action;
c. to recognise the principles of the League;
d. to have acknowledged means of subsistence;
e. not to belong to any political or national association;
f. to be unanimously admitted into a community, and
g. to give his word of honour to work loyally and to observe secrecy.

Art. 4. All League members are equal and brothers, and as such owe each other assistance in every situation.

Art. 5. All members bear League names.

SECTION II

THE COMMUNITY

Art. 6. A community consists of at least three and at most twelve members. Increase above that number will be prevented by division.

Art. 7. Every community elects a chairman and a deputy chairman. The chairman presides over meetings, the deputy chairman holds the funds, into which the contributions of the members are paid.

Art. 8. The members of communities shall earnestly endeavour to increase the League by attracting capable men and always seek to work in such a way that principles and not persons are taken as guide.

Art. 9. Admission of new members is effected by the chairman of the community and the member who has introduced the applicant to the League.

Art. 10. The communities do not know each other and bear distinctive names which they choose themselves.

SECTION III

THE CIRCLE

Art. 11. A circle comprises at least two and at most ten communities.

Art. 12. The chairmen and deputy chairmen of the communities form the circle authority. They elect a president from among themselves.

Art. 13. The circle authority is the executive organ for all the communities of the circle.

Art. 14. Isolated communities must either join an already existing circle authority or form a new circle with other isolated communities.

SECTION IV

THE CENTRAL AUTHORITY

Art. 15. The Central Authority is the executive organ of the whole League.

Art. 16. It consists of at least five members and is elected by the circle authority of the place where it is to have its seat.

SECTION V

THE CONGRESS

Art. 17. The Congress is the legislative authority of the League.

Art. 18. Every circle sends one delegate.

Art. 19. A Congress is held every year in the month of August. The Central Authority has the right in important cases to call an extraordinary congress.

Art. 20. The Congress in office decides the place where the Central Authority is to have its seat for the current year.

Art. 21. All legislative decisions of the Congress are submitted to the communities for acceptance or rejection.

Art. 22. As the executive organ of the League the Central Authority is responsible to the Congress for its conduct of its office and therefore has a seat in it, but no deciding vote.

SECTION VI

GENERAL REGULATIONS

Art. 23. Anyone who acts dishonourably to the principles of the League is, according to the circumstances, ⟨removed⟩ either removed or expelled. Expulsion precludes re-admission.

Art. 24. Members who commit offences are judged by the ⟨supreme⟩ circle authority, which also sees to the execution of the verdict.

Art. 25. Every community must keep the strictest watch over those who have been removed or expelled; further, it must observe closely any suspect individuals in its locality and report at once to the circle authority anything they may do to the detriment of the League, whereupon the circle authority must take the necessary measures to safeguard the League.

Art. 26. The communities and circle authorities and also the Central Authority shall meet at least once a fortnight.

Art. 27. The communities pay weekly or monthly contributions, the amount of which is determined by the respective circle authorities. These contributions will be used to spread the principles of the community of property and to pay for postage.

Art. 28. The circle authorities must render account of expenditures and income to their communities every six months.

Art. 29. The members of the circle authorities and of the Central Authority are elected for one year and must then either be confirmed anew in their office or replaced by others.

Art. 30. The elections take place in the month of September. The electors can, moreover, recall their officers at any time should they not be satisfied with their conduct of their office.

Art. 31. The circle authorities have to see to it that there is material in their communities for useful and necessary discussions. The Central Authority, on the other hand, must make it its duty to send to all circle authorities such questions whose discussion is important for our principle.

Art. 32. Every circle authority and failing that the community, even every League member, must, if standing alone, maintain regular correspondence with the Central Authority or a circle authority.

Art. 33. Every League member who wishes to change his residence must first inform his chairman.

Art. 34. Every circle authority is free to take any measures which it considers advisable for the security of the circle and its efficient work. These measures must, however, not be contrary to the general Rules.

Art. 35. All proposals for changes in the Rules must be sent to the Central Authority and submitted by it to the Congress for decision.

SECTION VII

ADMISSION

Art. 36. After the Rules have been read to him, the applicant is asked by the two League members mentioned in Art. 9 to reply to the following five questions. If he replies "Yes", he is asked to give his word of honour, and is declared a League member.

These five questions are:

a. Are you convinced of the truth of the principles of the community of property?

b. Do you think a strong League is necessary for the realisation of these principles as soon as possible, and do you wish to join such a League?

c. Do you promise always to work by word and deed for spreading and the practical realisation of the principles of the community of property?

d. Do you promise to observe secrecy about the existence and all affairs of the League?

e. Do you promise to comply with the decisions of the League? Then give us on this your word of honour as guarantee!

In the name and by the order of the Congress

The President,
Karl Schill[b]

Heide,[a]
Secretary

London, June 9, 1847

First published in the book: *Gründungsdokumente des Bundes der Kommunisten (Juni bis September 1847)*, Hamburg, 1969

Printed according to the manuscript

Published in English for the first time

[a] Wilhelm Wolff.—*Ed.*

[b] Karl Schapper.—*Ed.*

[A CIRCULAR OF THE FIRST CONGRESS OF THE COMMUNIST LEAGUE TO THE LEAGUE MEMBERS JUNE 9, 1847][333]

THE CONGRESS TO THE LEAGUE[a]

Dear Brothers!

The First Congress of the League, which was called last February by the Central Authority (*Halle*)[334] and opened on June 2 here in London, has concluded its deliberations. In view of the whole position of our League, its sessions could not be public.[335]

But it is incumbent on us, members of the Congress, to make them public for you in retrospect, by at least giving you a survey of our proceedings.

This is all the more our duty as the Central Authority in office up to now had to render account to us, and *we*, therefore, have to tell you how far the Congress was satisfied with this rendering of account. We must also do so, because we have added an article to the new Rules which makes all legislative decisions of the Congress subject to the vote of the individual communities[b]; hence, for this part of our decisions at least, there are two reasons why we owe you a statement of the grounds for them.

After checking credentials the previous *Halle* had first to give the Congress an account of its conduct of office and to report on the state of the League. The delegates declared themselves completely satisfied with the way in which the *Halle* had looked after the interests of the League and had made a start with its reorganisation. That point was thereby disposed of. We take the following brief summary from the report of the Central Authority and from the original letters submitted to the Congress.

---

[a] Joseph Moll added afterwards in the original: "IN HAMBURG".—*Ed.*

[b] The reference is to Art. 21 of the draft Rules of the Communist League (see this volume, p. 586.)—*Ed.*

In *London* our League is strongest. Freedom of speech and of association immensely facilitates propaganda and gives opportunities to the many able members to use their character and talent for the greatest good of the League and the cause. For this purpose the League uses the German Workers' Educational Society, and also its branch in Whitechapel. Members of the League also take part in the Fraternal Democrats,[336] the French communist discussion clubs,[337] etc.

The previous Paris *Halle* itself realised in how much better a position the London League would be to take over the central leadership of the affairs of the League. The security of all documents and of members of the Central Authority itself is nowhere else as great as here. During its proceedings the Congress had opportunity enough to see that the London communities have a sufficient number of competent people who can be entrusted with the supreme executive authority of the League. It therefore decided that the Central Authority should remain in London.

In *Paris* the League has much declined in recent years.[338] The regional and *Halle* members have for a long time occupied themselves only with quarrels about formalities and alleged breaches of the Rules instead of looking after the affairs of the whole League or of its *Gaus.*[a] In the communities similar time-wasting, superfluous and divisive trifles were dealt with. At most they discussed the old questions which have been talked over again and again, ever since Weitling's *Garantien*,[b] to the point of boredom. In the Paris League itself there was no sign of the slightest progress, not the slightest concern with the development of the principle, or with the movement of the proletariat as it was proceeding in other localities of the League, and *outside the League.* The consequence was that all those who were not satisfied with what they were offered *inside* the League looked outside the League for further enlightenment. This need for enlightenment was made use of by a literary knight of industry and exploiter of workers, the German writer *Karl Grün*. This individual had sided with communism when he noticed that there was money to be made by communist writings. After some time he found that it was dangerous to continue to declare himself a Communist and found occasion to resign in the new book by Proudhon on the economic contradictions[c] which he himself had translated into German. This Grün used the economic statements in this otherwise quite insignificant book as the basis of lectures which

[a] Regions or districts.—*Ed.*
[b] W. Weitling, *Garantien der Harmonie und Freiheit.*—*Ed.*
[c] P.-J. Proudhon, *Système des contradictions économiques.*—*Ed.*

he gave in Paris for League members. These lectures were attended by two kinds of people: 1. those who had already enough of communism in general; 2. those who hoped perhaps to get from this Grün enlightenment on a number of questions and doubts never resolved for them in the community meetings. The latter were fairly numerous and consisted of those members of the Paris communities who were the most useful and the most capable of development. For a time this Grün succeeded in dazzling even a number of these with his phrases and his alleged immense learning. The League was thus split. On one side was the party which had exclusively dominated the *Halle* and the region, the party of the Weitlingians; on the other side were those who still believed one could learn something even from Grün. These soon saw, however, that Grün expressed definite hostility to the Communists and that all his teaching was quite unable to replace communism. Heated discussions took place during which it became clear that almost all League members remained loyal to communism and that only two or three defended this Grün and his Proudhonist system. At the same time it was revealed that this same Grün had defrauded the workers, as was his wont, by using 30 francs, the sum collected for the Polish insurgents,[339] for his private purposes, and had also wheedled several hundred francs out of them for the printing of a miserable pamphlet about the dissolution of the Prussian Provincial Diet.[a] But enough; the majority of Grün's former listeners stayed away and formed a new party which was mainly concerned to develop further the communist principle in all its implications and in its connection with social relations. By this split, however, the organisation of the League fell to pieces. In the course of the winter the Central Authority sent an emissary[b] who restored the organisation as far as possible. But soon the quarrels arose again; the three different parties and principles were irreconcilable. The party of progress succeeded with the aid of the Weitlingians in removing from the League the three or four stubborn Grünians who had declared themselves openly against communism. But then, when it came to the election of a delegate to the Congress, the two parties clashed in the regional meeting. The split became incurable, and in order at least to achieve an election, the three communities in which the party of progress was most strongly represented resolved to separate from the two communities on which the main strength of the Weitlingians rested and to elect a congress delegate for themselves at a general meeting. This was done. The Weitlingians

[a] K. Grün, *Die preussischen Landtags-Abschiede.—Ed.*

[b] Joseph Moll.—*Ed.*

were thereby provisionally removed from the League and the number of League members was reduced by one third. After examining the reasons advanced by both parties, the Congress declared its agreement with the action of the three communities, because the Weitlingian party had everywhere held up the League in its development; this had also been experienced both in London and in Switzerland. The Congress resolved unanimously to remove the Paris Weitlingians from the League and to admit the delegate of the Paris majority[a] to the Congress.

Hence, the number of League members in Paris has been greatly reduced; but, at the same time, obstructive elements have also been removed, and, through the struggle, minds have been quickened to renewed activity. A new spirit is making itself felt, and a completely new energy. The police persecutions seem more or less to have ended; they were in any case not directed against the party which is now victorious and from which only one member was expelled, but struck Grün's party almost alone, proof that information of the Prussian Government was at the bottom of the whole persecution, as will be shown presently. And if the government has dispersed the public meetings at the Barrière, this too mainly hits the Grünians who made loud speeches there and inveighed against the Communists, because here, of course, the Communists could not freely reply to them. Hence, the League is in far better shape in Paris now than at the time when the *Halle* resigned. We are less numerous but we are united and have capable people there.

In *Lyons* the League has regular members who seem to be very active for the cause.

In *Marseilles* we are also established. We have received the following letter about the membership there: "The position of the Marseilles League is not too good. Encouragement by letters would not help much; we shall try to arrange for some of us to go there this autumn and to organise the League anew."

The League has succeeded in gaining a firm footing in Belgium. Brussels has a competent community whose members are Germans and Belgians and who have already founded a second community in Liège among the Walloon factory workers. In that country the prospects for the League are quite encouraging, and we hope that at the next congress Belgium will already be represented by several delegates.

In Germany we had several communities in Berlin which this spring were suddenly dispersed by the police. League members will

[a] Engels.—*Ed.*

have seen from the newspapers that a meeting of workers directed by League members was cancelled by the police, an enquiry was held, and as a result several leading members were arrested. Among the arrested was a certain Friedrich Mentel, a tailor born in Potsdam, about 27 years old, of medium, stocky build, etc. This man, who had formerly been in London and Paris, and in the latter place had belonged to Grün's party and turned out to be a maudlin sentimentalist, and had, by the way, in the course of his travels got to know the situation in the League pretty accurately, was unable to stand up to this little ordeal. This time too it was seen that the weak-mindedness and vagueness of such sentimentalists can find final satisfaction only in religion. Within a few days this Mentel let himself be completely converted by a priest and twice during his arrest took part in the farce of Holy Communion. A Berlin member writes to us as follows: "...he told in court about the communities in Paris, London, Hamburg and Kiel (all of which he had visited himself) and gave the addresses to which Herm. Kriege sent his *Volks-Tribun* to Berlin. To somebody else, he said to his face: 'Did I not sell you these books? Did we not go to meetings at such and such an address? Are you not a member of the League of the Just?' And when the answer to everything was 'No', Mentel said: 'How can you answer for this before God the Almighty and All-knowing?' and other such stupidities." Fortunately, Mentel's baseness did not succeed in confusing the other accused, so the government had no alternative but to let the arrested be acquitted for the time being. Clearly, this Mentel's denunciations are closely connected with the persecutions of the German Communists in Paris. We can only congratulate ourselves that the Grünian Mentel regarded the Grünians themselves as the real leaders of the League and denounced them. Thereby the real Communists were in general protected from the persecutions. Naturally, the entire Berlin circle was disorganised by these events. However, knowing the competence of the members there, we are hopeful that the reorganisation of the League will soon be effected.

Hamburg is also organised. But the members there have let themselves be somewhat intimidated by these persecutions in Berlin. The contacts were not broken for a single moment, however.

The League is also established in Altona, Bremen, Mainz, Munich, Leipzig, Königsberg, Thorn, Kiel, Magdeburg, Stuttgart, Mannheim and Baden-Baden. In Scandinavia it is also already established in Stockholm.

The position of the League in *Switzerland* is not as satisfactory as we might wish. Here the party of the Weitlingians was dominant from the beginning. The lack of development in the communities in Switzerland was particularly evident, on the one hand in their inability to bring the long-standing struggle with the Young Germans[340] to a conclusion, and on the other hand in their religious attitude to the Young Germans and in the fact that they let themselves be exploited in the vilest manner by most despicable knights of industry, such as, for instance, the solemn Georg Kuhlmann of Holstein. As a result of police measures the League was so disorganised in Switzerland that the Congress decided to take extraordinary measures for its reconstitution. The success and the nature of these measures can, of course, only later be made known to the communities.

Concerning *America*, we must wait for more detailed news from the emissary whom the Central Authority has sent there, before a precise report can be given of the final shape of the League's conditions there.[a]

From this report and from the League letters produced two things emerge: firstly, that when the London *Halle* took over the leadership, the League was indeed in a difficult position, that the previous Central Authority[b] had not at all attended to the duties incumbent on it; that it had utterly neglected to hold the whole together, and that in addition to this disorganisation of the League, elements of opposition had gradually germinated even in the individual communities themselves. In these circumstances, which threatened the existence of the League, the London Central Authority at once took the necessary measures: sent out emissaries, removed individual members who were jeopardising the existence of the whole, re-established contacts, called the general congress, and prepared the questions to be discussed there. At the same time it took steps to draw into the League other elements of the communist movement who until then had stood aside from it,[341] steps which were highly successful.

After settling these questions the Congress had to make a review of the Rules. The result of these deliberations lies before the communities in the new Rules, all the articles of which were accepted unanimously, and which the Congress moves should be finally adopted. In justification of the changes made, we make the following observations:

---

[a] Down to here the handwriting is Wolff's, from the following paragraph somebody else's, either J. Moll's or H. Bauer's.—*Ed.*

[b] The *Halle* of the League of the Just, which before its transfer from Paris to London consisted mainly of supporters of Weitling.—*Ed.*

The change of name from League of the Just to Communist League was adopted because, firstly, the old name had become known to the governments through the infamous treachery of that Mentel, and that in itself made a change advisable. Secondly, and chiefly, because the old name had been adopted on a special occasion in view of special events[342] which no longer have the slightest bearing on the present purpose of the League. This name is therefore no longer suited to the time and does not in the least express what we want. How many there are who want justice, that is, what they call justice, without necessarily being Communists! We are not distinguished by wanting justice in general—anyone can claim that for himself—but by our attack on the existing social order and on private property, by wanting community of property, by being Communists. Hence there is only one suitable name for our League, the name which says what we really are, and this name we have chosen. In the same spirit we have altered the traditional names *Gau* and *Halle*, which we took over from the political societies and the German character of which produced a disturbing impression given the nature of our anti-nationalist League which is open to all peoples; these names have been replaced by words which really mean what they should mean. The introduction of such simple, clear names serves also to remove from our propagandist League the conspiratorial character which our enemies are so keen to attach to us.

The necessity to re-call the Congress, now called for the first time, to re-call it *regularly* and to transfer to it the entire legislative power of the League subject to confirmation by the communities, was unanimously recognised without discussion. We hope that in the provisions laid down in this respect we have hit on the points which mattered and through which the effective work of the Congress is ensured in the interest of the whole.

As to the omission of the headings, which insofar as they contained legal provisions are replaced by certain articles of the Rules, and insofar as they contained general communist principles are replaced by the Communist Credo, this gives the Rules a simpler and more uniform shape and has at the same time led to a more precise definition of the position of each particular authority.[343]

After the Rules had been dealt with, various proposals were discussed which had been prepared either by the Central Authority or put forward by individual delegates.

First of all, there was discussion of one delegate's proposal to call a new congress in six months time. The Congress itself felt that, as the First Congress, which has been called and had met at a time when the organisation of the League was flagging, it had to regard itself above all as an organising and constituent assembly. It felt that a new congress was needed to deal thoroughly with the most important questions before it; since at the same time the new Rules had fixed the next congress for the month of August, so that there would be barely two months interval, and since it was also impossible to defer the Second Congress until August 1848, it was decided to call this Second Congress for Monday, November 29 of this year, here in London. We did not let ourselves be deterred by the bad time of the year any more than by the new costs. The League has survived a crisis and must not fight shy of an extraordinary effort for once.—The new League Rules contain the necessary provisions for the election of delegates and so we hope that a large number of circles will send delegates to the Second Congress.

The proposal of the same delegate to set up a special fund for emissaries also found general approval.—The point was made that our League has at its disposal two kinds of emissaries. Firstly, those who are sent out at the expense of the League with special missions to certain localities, either to establish the League in areas where it does not yet exist, or to organise it again where it is in decline. These emissaries must necessarily be under the direct control of the Central Authority.—Secondly, workers who are returning to their own homes or have to make other journeys. Such workers, often very capable men, could be used to the greatest advantage of the League for visits to many communities not far from their travel route, if they are reimbursed on behalf of the League for the additional expenses caused thereby. Such occasional emissaries can, of course, only be under the direct control of the circle authority and only in special cases be placed under the control of the Central Authority. Hence, the Congress decided to instruct the Central Authority to demand from every circle authority a certain financial contribution every three months and from these contributions to set up a fund for sending out emissaries of the first kind. Further, to instruct the circle authorities more than previously to use capable members leaving on journeys as *occasional* emissaries in the manner described and to pay the additional travelling expenses in advance from their own funds. In very special cases the circle authorities can apply to the Central Authority for a contribution for this purpose; whether this financial application is granted, is, of course, decided by the Central Authority. Every emissary is responsible to the authority which has supplied him with funds and must report to it.

All of you will see how necessary it is to organise propaganda through emissaries and to subject it to central leadership. We hope that our decisions, taken after mature consideration, will meet with your approval and that they may be attended by good success for the cause.

The next question was that of the organ of the League; it was recognised without discussion how necessary such a publication is. It was also readily understood that the paper could appear only in London, and that it should not appear more often than weekly and not less often than monthly.—Title, motto and format were agreed and you will be acquainted with them through the specimen number to be published in July. A commission is in existence to act for the editorial board pending the journal's publication; then an editor, who also has already been appointed,[a] will take over the direction in co-operation with the Commission. This considered, the Congress came to the question of costs. Firstly, various things are needed to complete the printing equipment, in particular an iron press, for which the Central Authority was instructed to call for a contribution from the circles. But then the costs were calculated. It was found that at 2 pence,=4 sous,=2 Silbergroschen,=6 Kreuzers for every weekly issue of one sheet the number of subscribers required to cover the costs would be greater than we can rely on with certainty at present. A monthly paper without an editor would be able to exist with fewer subscribers, but would not fulfil the League's requirements. But whether we would be able to get the number of subscribers needed for a weekly paper was, as we have said, too uncertain for us to enter into the necessary engagements. We therefore resolved as follows: To start with, a specimen number will appear in July free of charge. Then the individual communities will have to send word through their circles how many members they have, for the Congress has decided that at least as long as the journal is a monthly, every member pays for *one* copy, but every community receives only *one*, and the remainder are distributed free. League members must, moreover, make enquiries regarding the number of copies which can with certainty be sold in their area, gather subscribers and report on this, too. Then in November, taking account of the notices received by the Central Authority, the Congress will take further decisions and if possible launch the journal before the New Year. In the meantime the London printing press will be used to print pamphlets.[344]

Finally, the question of the Communist Credo. The Congress realised that the public proclamation of the principles of the League was a step of the greatest importance; that a credo which in a few

---

[a] Wilhelm Wolff.—*Ed.*

years, perhaps months, might no longer suit the times and no longer correspond to the spirit of the majority, would be as harmful as a suitable credo would be useful; that this step had to be considered with particular care and must not be taken too hastily. Here, just as on the question of the League organ, the Congress became aware that it could not act definitively but only in a constituent role, that it had to give new food to the re-awakening life in the League by discussion on the *plan* of a credo. Hence, the Congress resolved to draft this plan and to submit it to the communities for discussion, so that proposals could be formulated for amendments and additions to be submitted to the Central Authority. The plan is appended.[a] We recommend it for serious and mature consideration by the communities. We have tried on the one hand to refrain from all system-making and all barrack-room communism, and on the other to avoid the fatuous and vapid sentimentality of the tearful, emotional Communists[345]; we have, on the contrary, tried always to keep firm ground under our feet by the constant consideration of the social relations which alone have given rise to communism. We hope that the Central Authority will receive from you very many proposals for additions and amendments, and we will call on you again to discuss the subject with particular zest.[b]

This, dear Brothers, is the survey, the outcome, of our deliberations. We would very much have liked to have definitively settled the items before us, to have founded the League organ, to have proclaimed the communist principles in a credo. But in the interest of the League, in the interest of the comm[unist] movement, we had to set limits to ourselves here, we had to appeal anew to the majority, and to leave it to the second Congress to carry through what we have prepared.

It is now for you, dear Brothers, to prove that you have the cause of the League, the cause of communism, at heart. The League has emerged victorious from a period of decline. Apathy and laxity have been overcome, the hostile elements which had arisen in the League itself have been eliminated. New elements have joined it. The future of the League is secure. But, dear Brothers, our position is not yet such that we can for one moment relax our efforts; all wounds are not yet healed, all gaps have not yet been filled, many painful effects of the struggle we have gone through can still be felt. Therefore the interest of the League, the communist cause, still demands of you a short period of the most strenuous activity;

[a] See this volume, pp. 96-103.— *Ed.*

[b] From the following paragraph the handwriting is again Wilhelm Wolff's.—*Ed.*

therefore for a few months you must not even for a moment weary in your work. Extraordinary circumstances demand extraordinary effort. A crisis such as our League has gone through, a crisis in which we had first to fight the fatigue caused by the heavy pressure of German and other police harassments and, even more, caused by the hope of an early improvement in social conditions apparently receding ever further from fulfilment; a crisis, furthermore, in which we not only had to fight the persecutions of our enemies, of governments either dominated by or allied to the bourgeoisie against us, but in which we found enemies in our midst who had to be fought and rendered harmless, with regard only for the threatened position of the League, for the menacing disorganisation of the entire German-speaking Communist Party, without any consideration of persons; Brothers, one does not recover from such a crisis overnight. And even if the existence of the League, the strength of the organisation, is re-established, there will have to be months of unceasing work before we can say: We have done our duty as Communists, our duty as League members.

Brothers! In the firm conviction that you will feel the importance of the situation as much as we do; in the firm conviction that you will nevertheless be fully equal to these difficult circumstances, we confidently appeal to you, to your enthusiasm for the cause of the community! We know that the bourgeoisie's infamous lust for gain leaves you hardly a moment to work for the cause; we know that it presses down to the lowest limit even the miserable wage it gives you for your hard work; we know that just now famine and the slump in business weigh on you especially heavily; we know that it persecutes you, imprisons you, ruins your health and endangers your lives if you find time and money despite all to work for the interest of the community; we know all that, and in spite of everything we have not hesitated for one moment to appeal to you for new financial sacrifices, to call on you to redouble your activity. For we ourselves would have to withdraw from the whole movement, blushing and ashamed, if we did not know that the men who elected us to decide on the good of the whole, will vigorously and unhesitatingly put our resolutions into practice; if we did not know that there is no one in our League for whom the interest of the Communist Party, the overthrow of the bourgeoisie, the victory of the community is not his very own, his dearest interest; if we did not know that people with sufficient determination to organise a league which exposes them to great dangers are also determined and steadfast enough to defy these dangers and to make this League great and mighty over the whole of Europe; if we did not know, finally, that such people are the more courageous, the more active, the more enthusiastic, the greater the obstacles they face.

Brothers! We represent a great, a wonderful cause. We proclaim the greatest revolution ever proclaimed in the world, a revolution which for its thoroughness and wealth of consequences has no equal in world history. We do not know how far it will be granted to us to share in the fruits of this revolution. But this we know, that this revolution is drawing near in all its might; this we see, that everywhere, in France as in Germany, in England as in America, the angry masses of the proletariat are in motion and are demanding their liberation from the fetters of money rule, from the fetters of the bourgeoisie, with a voice that is often still confused but is becoming ever louder and clearer. This we see, that the bourgeois class is getting ever richer, that the middle classes are being more and more ruined and that thus historical development itself strives towards a great revolution which will one day burst out, through the distress of the people and the wantonness of the rich. Brothers, we all hope to live to see that day, and even if last spring we did not get the chance to take up arms, as the letter of the *Halle*[a] predicted we might, do not let that disconcert you! The day is coming, and on the day when the masses of the people with their solid ranks scatter the mercenaries of the capitalists: on that day it will be revealed what our League was and how it worked! And even if we should not live to see *all* the fruits of the great struggle, even if hundreds of us fall under the grapeshot of the bourgeoisie, all of us, even the fallen, have lived to be in the *struggle*, and this struggle, this victory alone is worth a life of the most strenuous work.

And so, farewell!

In the name of the Congress,

Heide,[b]
Secretary

The President,
Karl Schill[c]

London, June 9, 1847

First published in the book: *Gründungsdokumente des Bundes der Kommunisten (Juni bis September 1847)*, Hamburg, 1969

Printed according to the manuscript

Published in English for the first time

[a] "Ansprache der Volkshalle des Bundes der Gerechten an den Bund", Februar 1847.—*Ed.*

[b] Wilhelm Wolff.—*Ed.*

[c] Karl Schapper.—*Ed.*

NOTE BY MARX
ON THE FORMATION OF THE BRUSSELS COMMUNITY AND CIRCLE OF THE COMMUNIST LEAGUE
AUGUST 5, 1847

August 5. Constitution of the new Community.
Elected: President—Marx
Secretary and Treasurer: Gigot

Circle Authority: Gigot, Junge, Marx, Wolff.

First published in Russian in the book: Y. P. Kandel, *Marx and Engels—Organisers of the Communist League*, Moscow, 1953

Printed according to the manuscript

Published in English for the first time

THE CENTRAL AUTHORITY TO THE LEAGUE[346]

Working Men of All Countries, Unite!

Brothers:

Three months have now passed since the Congress was held and its Circular[a] was dispatched to you; we therefore now send you another report on our activity since then, and give you a summary of the present state of the League.

We regret that we are unable to send you very encouraging news, but we have resolved to tell you the plain truth, be it encouraging or disheartening. Some of you may well think that emphasis should always be placed on the bright side of the situation so that people should not lose heart; we on the contrary are of the opinion that all should know the enormous and diverse difficulties with which we have to contend. Real men will not be deterred by this, but on the contrary spurred on to new activity.

As long as our League is not strongly and firmly established, as long as it fails to intervene effectively in the course of events, our influence will be insignificant. Admittedly we now have a new basis, and in some places people seem to work with new enthusiasm but on the whole we are still[b] far from the position we should have reached long ago. When the Congress Circular was dispatched we hoped we would receive favourable and definite replies to it from all quarters. The Central Authority had enclosed with it an accompanying letter calling attention once more to the points requiring a response and requesting prompt and definite replies.[347]

---

[a] See this volume, pp. 589-600.—*Ed.*

[b] The original has "noch nicht" (still not).—*Ed.*

So far we have only received a definite reply from the Brussels* circle, other places have only acknowledged receipt of the Circular, thanked us for our efforts, made some general comments, and no more.

What is the cause of this negligence and where is it going to lead us? Many German proletarians are anxious to liberate themselves, but, if they do not set about the task more energetically than they have done so far, they will indeed not make much progress. We can't wait for things to fall into our lap. Many people are hindered in their activity by their mental sluggishness; others talk a great deal but when money contributions are requested they pull long faces, make all manner of excuses and give nothing; others again possess a large share of bourgeois cowardice, see policemen and gendarmes at every turn and never believe it is time to act. It gives one the gripes to see all the goings-on. The majority of the proletarians, and the most active at that—those in Silesia, Saxony, Rhenish Prussia, Westphalia and Hesse have poor or indeed no leadership, at least no communist one.

We therefore call upon all members of our League once more to rise up at last out of their sleep and set to work, and we demand that first of all definite replies to the Congress Circular be sent in so that we can at least know whom we can count upon.

After the Congress was over we sent the Congress Circular, the new Rules,[a] the Communist Credo[b] and an accompanying letter from the Central Authority to ten towns in Switzerland, France, Belgium, Germany and Sweden where we have communities. In addition we sent out from London two authorised emissaries to America, one to Norway, one to Germany and one to Holland.[c] All promised the Central Authority to work to the best of their ability and to set up new communities in the places in which they settled and to put them in touch with us.

In accordance with the resolution adopted at the Congress the League's new newspaper[d] should have begun to appear in August[348] and we had been promised articles and also financial support for it; all League members were moreover requested to give all the help

* Yesterday we received a letter from Leipzig, for details see below.

[a] See this volume, pp. 585-88.—*Ed.*

[b] See this volume, pp. 96-103.—*Ed.*

[c] Johann Dohl.—*Ed.*

[d] *Kommunistische Zeitschrift.*—*Ed.*

they could. Unfortunately here again most promises have been confined to words alone. Apart from the Brussels circle, which for the time being made a monthly allocation of one pound sterling for printing expenses and five francs for propaganda and Brother Heide[a] who sent us an article, we have received nothing so far. The editorial commission, which from one week to the next was being promised the necessary articles, was finally compelled to do everything itself, so as at least to be able to get the specimen issue out. If we do not receive better support in the future than we have received so far, we shall not make any progress here either. In order to set up our printing-press properly, so that besides the League newspaper we can also print leaflets and small pamphlets, we still need another 600 francs. We are not in a position to raise this sum in London alone.

Since the Congress Circular was sent out we have received news from the following places.

Sweden. We received a letter dated Upsala, May 23 from our emissary[b] who travelled to Sweden via Helsingör, crossing the whole country on foot. Here in London, having nothing else, he had filled his kitbag with communist leaflets which he successfully took over the border into Sweden. He writes that in all towns where there are German workers, he called on them in their workshops, distributed our leaflets among them and found their response to our ideas most enthusiastic. Unfortunately, since he did not find any work he was unable to stay in any one place long enough to set up a community. In Stockholm he transmitted to the local community (our communist outpost in the North) the first two circulars from the Central Authority,[349] and his news lent the Brothers there new heart. From Stockholm he went to Upsala, from there on to Gävle, where he worked for a time, and is now on the way to Umeå and Tornea. A communist emissary among the Lapps!

A member of the League who arrived in London from Karlskrona informed us: Brother C., who was previously working in Paris and London, has set up communities in W. and there are already over a hundred League members there now. The Brother from Karlskrona gave us C.'s address and we shall be sending him this Circular together with the New Rules and a special appeal for the League members there. From Stockholm we have received a letter dated July 8 saying that our Brothers there are most zealous supporters of our

---

[a] Wilhelm Wolff.—*Ed.*
[b] Albert August Anders.—*Ed.*

principles. A public attack on communism made by a local priest was countered by a League member, Brother Forsell, in a pamphlet written in Swedish in which he expounded our principles to the people as well.[a] Sweden's biggest newspaper, the *Aftonbladet,* also defends communism against the clerics. We were also told in the letter: "The educational society here in Stockholm, which we were formerly able to regard as a gateway to communism has now unfortunately landed in the clutches of the philistines. On the other hand the democratic element within the local Scandinavian society,[350] of which we are all members and which has one of us as President, is pure and unsullied and it is from this society that we recruit our members." Immediately on receiving this letter we made handwritten copies of the Congress Circular, the Communist Credo and the Rules in Latin characters (since most Swedes cannot read German letters) and then sent them everything by post. We are now waiting for their reply to this dispatch.

Germany. Approximately six weeks ago an emissary from here went to Berlin taking with him letters from us for the Brothers there, and, in order to put new heart into them, exhorting them to be steadfast. He was to spend only about a week there and then travel to Leipzig, from where he was to send us a report. We are expecting news shortly.

The Brothers in Br.[b] acknowledged receipt of our letters and promised to send us a detailed reply in the immediate future, which they have not yet done.

The Brothers in Hamburg acknowledge receipt of our letters and express their regret that the name League of the Just has been changed and wish the former name restored: they also inform us that it is not at all to their liking when the supporters of W. Weitling and Grün are exposed to such hostile criticism, as was the case in the Congress Circular. They call for moderation and unity and write: "Whether someone stands one rung higher or lower as regards the main principle, that is no reason for us to persecute him and cause a split, for how do you think we can make an impact if we take such a one-sided approach. We attract all forces who wish for progress and then seek to win them over to our ideas gradually by persuasion."

We must reply to the Brothers in Hamburg that the reasons for the change in the name notified in the Congress Circular[c] are

---

[a] Carl Daniel Forsell, *Kommunismen och kristendomen...—Ed.*
[b] Probably Breslau or Bremen.—*Ed.*
[c] See this volume, p. 595.—*Ed.*

significant ones and that if no important counter-arguments are put forward, the Central Authority will defend the retention of the name Communist League at the next Congress. This latter name says clearly what we are and what we want, which the previous one did not. League of the Just says everything and nothing, but we must be definite. The Hamburg Brothers would do well to read the reasons given in the Congress Circular once more—if they can refute those arguments then we shall agree with them—we have no right to take mere emotions into consideration.

As regards the second point we stress that we are in no way persecuting Weitling's and Grün's supporters, but purely and simply representing them in their true colours. It is time we came to our senses and therefore we can no longer waste time on dreamers and system-mongers who have no energy for action—we will drag no corpse along behind us. Grün's supporters are people who chatter a great deal about equality without knowing what the word means, who criticise everything except themselves, in other words, opinionated men who talk a great deal, but do nothing. We are no elegant bourgeois and therefore do not beat about the bush but say what we think, i. e., call things by their names.

For over ten years moderation, forbearance and unity have been preached in the League and with all this preaching, with all this brotherly love we have accomplished virtually nothing, and last year the League almost collapsed entirely. We must put an end to this; it is wrong to demand that we should spend our whole life on trifles and idle dreams. Our opinion is that 100 active members are better than 1,000 of whom half are indecisive and lukewarm. Instead of looking back and helping the lame to catch up, we march boldly forward, which will probably get others to their feet somewhat more nimbly as well. The Brothers in Hamburg incidentally do not seem to have got very far with their moderation, for they make no allusion to the dispatch of money for propaganda and printing, and as for the League's newspaper they declare that they are only in a position to take a few copies in view of growing unemployment.

We must make it clear here that every member of the League *is bound* to take a copy of the newspaper; if he is not able to pay for it, then the community he belongs to must do so for him.

Once more, Brothers, let us not allow all our strength to be undermined through untimely moderation, through lumping together opposing forces and thus become a laughing-stock for the other parties. We can make a powerful impact, if we only have the will, and if we do have the will there is only one thing we need: courage! courage! and once again courage! If people are unable or unwilling to go as far as we do—all well and good; if their intentions are honest, we shall not cease to respect them, but when we are called upon to step backwards in order to join up with such people, then we reply: Never!

Not long ago our Brothers in Leipzig wrote that several members who had been intimidated by the somewhat stark terms of the Central Authority's circular had withdrawn their membership. The others promised to remain loyally united and work to the best of their ability. We can only congratulate the Brothers in Leipzig on having rid themselves of people who lacked the courage to behave as men. The letter which we received from Leipzig yesterday was already written in a quite different and more forceful style than previous letters, which shows that the community there is no longer dogged by indecisiveness.

First of all the community in Leipzig believes that it was necessary to phrase the Credo in terms more scientific and more suitable for all social classes. They suggest an almost complete recast and give their reasons for this. We shall put the suggested changes before the next Congress for discussion. The Central Authority agrees with the majority of the points listed in their letter. The community states further that apart from copies of our newspaper for all the members, they wish to take an extra 12 for distribution. If all communities were to follow the example provided in Leipzig, the League's newspaper could appear weekly and at half the price. We request that all contributions for propaganda and printing that have been collected should be sent in as soon as possible. We hope that a second community can soon be set up in Leipzig; if this does not however take place this community could adhere to those in Berlin[351]; we shall take the necessary steps for this.

From Mn[a] we have received no news, nor do we know any address there, for our correspondent in that town is supposed to have left for Paris. We shall try to restore contact with the communities there as soon as possible.

We were unable to send the Congress Circular to Mainz by post. It was not until four weeks ago that a member from here left for that destination with whom we dispatched everything. Thus we could not have received an answer from there yet. In a letter which we received from the Mainz members some time back we were informed that a second community was about to be set up, which means a circle will be formed. Our Brothers in Mainz are being constantly subjected to

[a] Probably Munich or Manheim. The Congress Circular to the Communist League (June 1847) mentions communities in both cities.—*Ed.*

police harassment, but this only serves to spur them on to work all the more energetically for our cause. Credit is due to the gallant proletarians in Mainz; if people were as active as that all over Germany, our prospects would be brilliant.

Holland. In Amsterdam an educational society has been set up which is in touch with us and has competent men. Three weeks ago we sent an authorised emissary there to set up a community.[352]

America. The emissary who this spring set out for New York from here paints us a sad picture of the state of the League in the New World. In New York the League had already made remarkable progress when Weitling arrived[a] and sowed discord there. The meetings were soon the scene of violent disputes and the result was that the whole set-up collapsed. The communities in New York had earlier always been urging us to be moderate and begging us most earnestly to be reconciled with Weitling. After they themselves, a fortnight after Weitling's arrival, entered into a bitter conflict with him, our correspondents there lost heart to such an extent that they no longer wished to write to us any more so as not to have to reveal the sad state of the League there. This is what the emissary sent to New York writes; in this situation he himself was unable to do anything in New York and has now left for the state of Wisconsin, where he promises to promote our cause to the best of his ability.

In Philadelphia there are still several League members whom we have earnestly begged to set up communities there again. We have instructed the two emissaries who left from here for New York and Philadelphia to do their utmost so that the League may be restored in the above-mentioned places, in accordance with the improved Rules.

France. In Marseilles things are as before. A number of members from Lyons have gone there, promising to do their very best to inject new life into the League.

From Lyons we have received word that the League members are sparing no effort in our work and are discussing the Credo. The Lyons circle endorses the new Rules with the exception of Section VII, concerning conditions of membership.[b] The Lyons members believe it to be unnecessary to demand that new members take an oath for there are countless cases of people taking all manner of oaths and not keeping any of them; attention should be paid mainly to conduct. We call the Lyons members' attention to the fact that no oath is demanded, but only the new member's word of honour. The Lyons members also write:

---

[a] Early in 1847.—*Ed.*

[b] See this volume, p. 588.—*Ed.*

"Since now in September we are again in a critical position, we beg you to ask the Parisians if they could not spare a few competent members, who would be ready to make a sacrifice for the common cause and settle in Lyons for a time. The old members all want to leave here and we are therefore short of people who can take over the leadership.

"So try to prevent the possibility of this community breaking up.

"As for the newspaper which you will be putting out, we cannot yet stipulate how many copies we can take, because everything will change."

Not a word about money for printing and propaganda.

We urgently request our Brothers in Paris to send a few competent members to Lyons as soon as possible.

From Paris we have been informed that the Rules have been unanimously endorsed there, that the Credo is being discussed in the various communities and that the membership has increased considerably. We have not yet heard anything about the results of their discussions or any news as to whether money is being collected for printing and propaganda. But it must be said to the credit of the Parisians that they recently made significant money contributions by sending a delegate to the Congress[a] and an emissary to Switzerland.[b]

It unfortunately emerges from a private letter written by a Parisian League member[c] and handed to the Central Authority, that there are still many people in the Paris communities who have not yet shaken themselves free of Grün's nonsense and Proudhon's most strange ideas. Oddly enough, these people, who are members of the Communist League, seem to reject communism; they want equality and nothing else. This inner split also seems to be the reason why we so seldom receive any news from Paris. Proudhon has become such a truly German philosopher that he no longer knows himself what he wants; Grün has made Proudhon's ideas still more obscure,[353] so it is now clearly impossible to demand that the people who follow these two really know where they are going. We urge Proudhon's and Grün's supporters to read Marx's *Misère de la philosophie*, which we have heard has already been translated into German.[354] Then they will see that their state where all are equal and which they demand with a great deal of talk and fuss is no different from that of today. This leads people round and round in circles, chasing false ideas, only to end up where they started.

---

[a] Frederick Engels.—*Ed.*
[b] Stephan Born.—*Ed.*
[c] Probably Frederick Engels.—*Ed.*

We call upon the Communists in Paris to stand firm together and to work to rid their communities of these false ideas. If Grün's and Proudhon's supporters insist on their principles, then, if they wish to remain men of honour, they should leave the League and start working on their own. There is only room for Communists in our League. As long as there are followers of Grün in our communities, neither they nor we can conduct effective propaganda; our forces will be divided and our young people low in spirits; so separation is better than an internal split.[355]

Weitling's expelled supporters have again sent us a long letter in which they inveigh against us and the Paris communities maintaining that it is they who are the real Communists. At the end of their letter they ask for a reliable address for they have further instructions for us. Yet they make no reference to the fact that they, although in the minority, appropriated the whole Paris League's treasury which one of them had in his keeping. Such behaviour most certainly accords with their leader's theory on theft.[a]

We wrote to them in very polite terms saying that we had acted in accordance with our duty and convictions and would also insist on what we considered to be right. Their abuse could not therefore hurt us. We sent them the address they asked for but have not heard anything more from them since.

Switzerland. The Central Authority informed the Brothers in La Chaux-de-Fonds of the imminent arrival of an emissary[b] and urged them to work with all their might towards a reorganisation of the League in Switzerland.

The Berne community has of late appeared in a somewhat dubious light. We were informed that they were planning to bring out a communist newspaper, *Der Wanderer* and our support was requested.

We sent off 25 francs and a remittance for 50 francs to Lausanne and La Chaux-de-Fonds. However, this money was used by the Berne members to print leaflets by Karl Heinzen, who even then had already shown himself to be the bitterest enemy of the Communists. On June 29 we received another letter from Berne which informed us that the Young Germany[356] group were making use of all possible means to work against the Communists in Switzerland and urged us to found a press organ as soon as possible. At the same time they sent us a small leaflet entitled *Der deutsche Hunger und die deutschen Fürsten*

---

[a] An allusion to W. Weitling's book: *Das Evangelium eines armen Sünders* in which he acquits theft as a means of struggle against capitalism (S. 126-33).—*Ed.*

[b] Stephan Born.—*Ed.*

and asked for voluntary contributions so that the "Kriegsartikel",[a] "Vorbereitung", etc., might be more widely distributed. It was stated: "Certain members of the republican party may well have noble intentions, our worthy Heinzen for example, but his hands are tied; he is not the soul of the German republican movement but its right hand for the moment, etc."

Heinzen attacks the Communists most violently; yet the Berne community is printing and circulating his pamphlets and seems to be in close touch with him. This appeared to us suspicious and indeed still does so. We do not want to let ourselves be led by the nose; every honest man must hold up his banner for all to see today. So we wrote a serious letter to the Berne community asking for a prompt explanation, but as yet have received no reply.

Our emissary writes from Geneva that our affairs are progressing in a most heartening way there. Two League members succeeded in setting up a community in Geneva this spring. While the emissary was there a second came into being and a third was planned. In addition there is a public society there which is being used to train efficient Communists. In Geneva our party seems once again to have found a firm footing, and if our Brothers there continue to work as hard as before, then the Communists in Switzerland will soon be stronger than ever. Weitling's expelled supporters, our emissary writes, have already sent to La Chaux-de-Fonds several letters full of the most shameful personal insults to several League members and calling upon the local members to join them. However the communities in La Chaux-de-Fonds have not complied with those people's solicitation and are waiting till our emissary arrives before giving them a final answer. From Geneva the emissary contacted Petersen in Lausanne who still enjoys quite significant influence among the Communists in Switzerland. We hope the former will succeed in winning him over for our movement.

Weitling's followers in Paris have sent a certain Hornschuh as their emissary to Switzerland with the money stolen from our League, in order to bring the communities there over to their side. This Hornschuh is at present in Lausanne. Before that he was in London; we therefore know precisely what he is and can assure you that he is quite incapable of any kind of propaganda work. He is a horribly tedious windbag and in other respects worth precious little as well. When he left London he asked his community for a small advance for the journey promising to pay the money back in the very near

[a] Karl Heinzen, "Dreissig Kriegsartikeln der neuen Zeit für Offiziere und Gemeine".—*Ed.*

future. The community granted him 25 francs. Two years have passed since then and Hornschuh, despite frequent reminders, has not paid anything back yet. It is really sad that people like Hornschuh, whose sole purpose is to indulge their laziness and self-conceit, still find opportunities to squander away the proletarians' hard earned money.

Our emissary is now touring the towns on Lake Geneva and will then visit La Chaux-de-Fonds, etc. He asked us for additional funds to be able to make this journey and we immediately sent him 50 francs, which we were obliged to borrow however, since our resources are exhausted.

Belgium. In Belgium our prospects are good. Since the Congress two circles have been set up in that country; we have not yet established direct contact with the one based in Liège but are expecting letters from them any day.

The Brussels circle is in touch with the Rhenish Prussia people[357] and working most energetically. It has already set up a singing and an educational society[358]; both are led by League members and serve as a preparatory school for the League.

The Rules were adopted in Brussels; however two alterations were proposed for discussion at the next Congress. The first concerns letter (e), Article 3, section I and the second—Article 21, Section V.[a] The Brussels members write: "We hold it for unpolitic to forbid League members to belong to any political or national organisation, since by doing so we deprive ourselves of all opportunities for influencing such organisations." Further on in connection with Article 21, they add: "If the present period were a more revolutionary one, the whole activity of the Congress would be hindered by this restriction. We recall that in 1794 the aristocrats put the same demand before the Convention, in order to paralyse all action."[359]

We request the communities to consider these proposals more closely and to give their delegates to the next Congress appropriate instructions.

As regards the Communist Credo a good number of important alterations were suggested, which we shall put before the Congress for discussion.

As was mentioned above the Brussels circle allocated 25 francs for printing and has agreed to send 5 francs for propaganda work each month. We call upon the other circles to follow this example as soon as possible.

---

[a] See this volume, p. 585 and p. 586.—*Ed.*

London. The new Rules were unanimously adopted in London and lively discussion of the Credo is in progress in all communities. The local circle authority will be sending us all suggestions for amendments and additions as soon as the discussions are over. During the last two months a large number of League members have left London but we shall have filled the resulting gaps soon. The educational societies provide us with preparatory schools, whose great benefit makes itself felt more and more with each passing day.

In the London circle a remarkable sense of unity reigns and members are keen to devote all their energies to our cause. In the last six months we have spent here over 1,000 francs for pamphlets, etc., for the journal,[a] postage and printing costs, Congress expenses, emissaries, etc. In addition, each member has to pay threepence a week into the educational society[360] fund and, besides, hardly a meeting goes by without private collections being made for the needy. Over half our members are out of work and in dire straits, which means it is becoming impossible for us to bear all these expenses alone as we have done hitherto. We are therefore forced to request all circles and communities most earnestly to contribute as much as they can and as soon as possible to the complete installation of the League printing-press, continued publication of our paper and propaganda work: at the present moment our resources are completely exhausted. In the past we always used to send out money as soon as it was requested and so we believe we can rely on you not to leave us in the lurch now.

The specimen number of our League newspaper sells well in London and arouses great interest among the foreigners living here. We have displayed it for sale in several bookshops and newsstands. We have sent copies to all our regular addresses and have another 1,000 still available, so that we shall be able to send off copies wherever they are required.

With this we come to the end of our report on the state of the League and our work; you can judge now for yourselves how things stand and whether the Central Authority has done its duty as the executive body of the League over the last three months.

You will appreciate that although active work is being carried on here and there, as we noted at the beginning of this letter, in general we are still far from the point we should have reached long since. We therefore hope, Brothers, that you will now muster all your strength so that we shall make rapid steps forward and that in the next report

---

[a] *Kommunistische Zeitschrift.—Ed.*

we shall be able to give you more encouraging news than has been the case so far.

However, before closing this letter we must ask you to pay particular attention to the following points. We earnestly request that:

1) All circles and independent communities, if it is at all possible, must elect a delegate to the next congress and see to it that he will be able to come to London on November 29 of this year. You know that we were unable to adopt any definitive decisions at the First Congress[361] and that it was thus considered necessary to hold a second one this year. The Second Congress will be most important because it has not only to formulate the Communist Credo but also to determine the final organisation of the League and its press organ and the future pattern of our propaganda work. It is therefore absolutely essential that as many delegates as possible attend this Congress. Brothers! We hope that you will not shrink from any sacrifices which the fulfilment of your duty may require;

2) All circles and communities, which have not yet made any collections for printing and propaganda work must do so without delay. If everyone contributes *something*, then we shall be in a position to engage in forceful action. Without money we cannot carry on any propaganda work. Those circles and communities which have already made collections should dispatch the same to us as soon as possible;

3) All circles and communities, which have not yet sent in definite replies to the Congress Circular should do so without delay;

4) All circles and communities, which have not yet informed us how many copies of our newspaper they wish to take should do so at once. In addition they should inform us of the best and most reliable ways of dispatching the paper to their respective localities;

5) All circles and communities should inform us whether communist propaganda is being carried on in their particular region and if so what form it takes;

6) All members of the League should send to the editorial office essays and poems. Several members promised essays for the first issue, as observed earlier, but these promises have not been kept: we can only attribute this to negligence, which definitely ought not to be prevalent in our organisation.

Hoping to receive favourable and definite news from you soon, we greet you in the name and on behalf of the Central Authority.

Karl Schapper *Henry Bauer*

Joseph Moll

London, September 14, 1847

P.S. Just as this letter was to be printed, letters arrived from our emissaries in Germany and Switzerland.

From Germany it was reported that the enthusiasm of our Brothers in Berlin is extraordinary, particularly since the important events there.[362] The government has indeed played straight into our hands. Our principles were made public through the uproar about the Communists, and the people, instead of being scared away by these principles, became enthusiastic for them. The emissary concludes his letter with the words: "Brothers, we can look to the future with confidence—there are efficient men on every side who are championing the just cause."

The news from Switzerland also sounds highly favourable. The League is organised there and now established in more than ten different localities. Petersen has been won over. The emissary writes: "In La Chaux-de-Fonds and Le Locle I believe we have the best and most devoted members of our League. Their courage is unshakable." Bravo, Brothers—forward! Weitling's expelled followers have been turned away wherever they went. The misunderstanding with the Berne community has been clarified. We now declare that we were unjust towards the Brothers there. They adhere firmly to our principles. We are extremely happy to be able to announce this.

More details will be supplied in the next report.

The Central Authority

Karl Schapper *Joseph Moll*

Henry Bauer

First published in the book: *Gründungsdokumente des Bundes der Kommunisten (Juni bis September 1847)*, Hamburg, 1969

Printed according to the manuscript

Published in English for the first time

THE NORTHERN STAR ON THE MEETING IN LONDON ON NOVEMBER 29, 1847 TO MARK THE 17TH ANNIVERSARY OF THE POLISH INSURRECTION OF 1830[363]

The anniversary of the Polish Insurrection of 1830 was celebrated on Monday last, the 29th of November, by a public meeting, at the German Society's Hall, Drury Lane.

The meeting had been called by the society of Fraternal Democrats, in conjunction with the Democratic Committee for Poland's Regeneration. The room was crowded with natives of England, Scotland, Ireland, France, Germany, Belgium, and Poland.

Mr. *John Arnott* was elected president. Having stated the object of the meeting, the Chairman called on Mr. Stallwood to move the first resolution.

Mr. *Stallwood*, after recounting the heroism of the brave Poles at Warsaw, and their unbounded devotion to the cause of liberty, and eulogising the "Cracow manifesto"[364] as a model for democratic creeds, moved the first resolution as follows:—

"That we regard the dismemberment of Poland as an atrocious crime worthy of the everlasting execration of the human race. That we remember with grateful admiration the heroic efforts made by the Polish people in 1830-31 for the recovery of their country's independence. That we honour the sacred memories of the martyrs who have perished in the glorious struggle to redeem their nation from slavery; and that we sympathise with all the victims of oppression at present suffering in dungeons, chains, and exile."

The Chairman then introduced

Mr. *Ernest Jones*, to second the resolution. Mr. Jones said: To-night, seventeen years ago, Poland woke from her death-sleep, for her death-struggle; to-night, seventeen years ago, she strained her bleeding limbs on the Russian rack, and burst her cords; to-night, seventeen years ago, she rose from a province into a nation! (Cheers.) Warsaw was silent. Russia never less expected insurrection—when the flame burst forth. Mr. Jones then gave a vivid description of the progress and triumph of the insurrection in Warsaw, particularly dwelling on the circumstance, that until the populace were armed, the issue was doubtful. Then the effect was electrical, and in a few hours, Constantine, the mighty prince, had passed the barrier of Mockstow, with his 11,000 Russians, and spent the night a shivering outcast, beneath a leafless tree. (Applause.) The speaker then alluded to the subsequent course of the insurrection, and expressed his belief that it would have been successful, had it been an insurrection of the people, instead of the aristocracy—had it been based on a manifesto, like the glorious one of Cracow. (Cheers.) But still we need not despond—Poland is ready for a fresh struggle—we have an army of martyrs to canonise—we have an army of heroes to come—and the aspect of Europe forebodes their triumph. The speaker then showed how every country in Europe was on the brink of internal change, analysed the secret weakness of the great powers, and, after a forcible and stirring allusion to Ireland, concluded by calling on his hearers to prepare for the approaching struggle at home and abroad. Mr. Jones' speech was one of great force and eloquence, and excited enthusiastic applause.

M. *Michelot*, in an energetic speech, delivered in the French language, supported the resolution, which was carried unanimously.

Carl Schapper rose, amidst great applause, to move the second resolution, and said: Citizens, when men struggle onwards for truth and liberty in a great cause, though they may not at first succeed, they must ultimately prevail—and such men were worthy of all honour—and hence he said honour to the brave Poles. (Loud cheers.) Honour to those who died before Warsaw—honour to those who died by the hand of the public executioner—honour to those who perished in the mines of Siberia, and to those who fell at Cracow, and to all the martyrs for liberty. (Great applause.) In July 1830, France had her revolution, and in the November following, the cry for universal liberty prevailed, and many wished Poland free from Russia, but did not wish Polish serfdom abolished; and he verily believed, had it not been for this desire on the part of the Polish nobles to perpetuate the slavery of the masses, the revolution would have succeeded, and the whole Slavonic race would now have been free. (Loud cheers.) But the Polish proletarians asked, "What is it to us if Poland be free from Russian domination, whilst I am subject to the knout of the Polish noble?" (Hear, hear.) Well, the revolution failed and Poland's sons emigrated, carrying the seeds of freedom with them to Germany, to France, to England, and other nations, and returned with renewed spirit to the Polish soil in 1845; and issued their famous and ever glorious manifesto of democratic sentiments from the Republic of Cracow. (Great applause.) But, alas, the effort was futile, the bad seed sown in 1830 produced a bad harvest, the tyrants were enabled to employ the peasantry against the patriots,[365] and the revolt was crushed, and the black spirit of Metternich again gloated in the blood of the fallen martyrs of Poland. (Hear, hear.) But happily fraternity was fast spreading, the principles of political and social equality were abroad. (Loud cheers.) Look at Switzerland.[366] (Great applause.) And liberty would progress in spite of the old bloodless spider of the Tuileries. (Groans for "the spider".) The Swiss Radicals had beaten Louis Philippe and Guizot. Then came the beautiful Lord Palmerston, who said, "Let us have the thing settled amicably." "Ay," responded the helpless old spider of Paris, "that's just what I wanted." (Laughter.) And not a single regiment had entered Switzerland, the old spider dared not send them. (Loud cheers.) Well, this was the progress of democracy. Who were the conspirators now? Why, Metternich, the bloodless old spider in France, Lord Palmerston, and the Jesuits. (Loud cheers.) But the people would very quickly put down their conspiracy. (Great cheering.) He had some glorious news for them, a Democratic Society,[367] that is a Society of Fraternal Democrats, had been established in Brussels, and that society had sent a deputy, the learned Dr. Marx, to represent them at this meeting. (Great applause.) Citizen Schapper here read the following document:—

"*To the Members of the Society of Fraternal Democrats*
"*Assembling in London*

"We, the undersigned members of the committee of the Democratic Society, established at Brussels, for advancing the Union and Fraternity of all Nations, have the honour to delegate to you, Dr. Charles Marx, vice-president of this committee, for the purpose of establishing relations of correspondence and sympathy between the two societies. M. Marx has full power to act in the name of this committee for the purposes above mentioned.

"We present to you our fraternal salutations.

"Mellinet (General), honorary president.
"Jottrand, president.
"Imbert, vice-president.
"Picard, secretary.
"George Weerth.
"Lelewel.

"Brussels, Nov. 26th, 1847."

The above address was received with enthusiastic applause. C. Schapper after highly complimenting the great Polish patriot Lelewel, and the grey-haired veteran—"the child of the French Republic"—General Mellinet, concluded by proposing the following resolution:—

"That in pledging all the aid in our power to the Polish patriots, we desire to express our unqualified dissent from the aristocratic spirit which so fatally influenced the struggle of 1830. We recognise in the Cracow Manifesto of 1846 the manifestation of Polish progress, embracing the broad principles of political democracy and social justice, on which alone can be founded veritable liberty and public happiness."

T. Lucas in seconding the resolution, expressed his pleasure in meeting so many of his brother democrats. Certain he was that when the English democrats (the Chartists) obtained their liberty, they would be enabled to say to "the old spider in Paris", and all other tyrants "thus far shall ye go but no farther". (Cheers.) The resolution was then unanimously adopted.

Dr. *Marx*, the delegate from Brussels, then came forward, and was greeted with every demonstration of welcome, and delivered an energetic oration in the German language, the substance of which was as follows—He had been sent by the Democrats of Brussels to speak in their name to the Democrats of London, and through them to the Democrats of Britain, to call on them to cause to be holden a congress of nations—a congress of working men, to establish liberty all over the world. (Loud cheers.) The middle classes, the *Free Traders*, had held a congress, but their fraternity was a one-sided one, and the moment they found that such congresses were likely to benefit working men, that moment their fraternity would cease, and their congresses be dissolved.[368] (Hear, hear.) The Democrats of Belgium felt that the Chartists of England were the real Democrats, and that the moment they carried the six points of their Charter, the road to liberty would be opened to the whole world. "Effect this grand object, then, you working men of England," said the speaker, "and you will be hailed as the saviours of the whole human race." (Tremendous cheering.)

Julian Harney moved the next resolution as follows:—

"That this meeting rejoices to learn of the establishment of a Society of Fraternal Democrats in Brussels, and responding to the alliance offered by that society, receives its delegate, Dr. Marx, with every feeling of fraternal regard; and this meeting hails with exultation the proposition to hold a Democratic Congress of all nations, pledging itself to send delegates to that Congress whenever summoned by the Fraternal Democratic Societies of London and Brussels."

The mover of the resolution then proceeded to address the meeting at considerable length, on the Polish insurrection of 1830, the progress of Chartism; the prospect of an energetic movement in this country for the obtainment of the Charter, the importance of the Society of Fraternal Democrats, and the vast utility of the suggested Democratic Congress of all nations. His remarks were enthusiastically cheered.

Mr. *Stallwood* seconded the resolution, which was carried unanimously.

Three thundering cheers were then given for the glorious Lelewel, three for the heroic General Mellinet, and three for the democrats of Brussels.

Charles Keen moved the fourth resolution as follows:

"That recognising the brotherhood of all men, we consider it our duty to struggle for the triumph of democratic principles in all countries, and believing that the establishment of the 'People's Charter' would enable the people of Great Britain to afford aid to the Polish cause, more effective than the paper 'protests' hitherto employed by the British government, we hail with joy the prospect of an energetic effort on the part of the British people to obtain the legislative recognition and parliamentary enactment of their long-withheld rights and franchises."

The speaker said they taught Universal Brotherhood, because they felt the evils resulting from the want of it. Very true, at churches and chapels on a Sunday, they were told that "we are all brethren", but should it rain on their leaving such churches or chapels, and they were to attempt to get into some of their wealthy brethren's carriages, what a row there would be. (Loud laughter.) Yet, ten minutes before those very same men would have been responding to the sentiment, "All men are brethren." (Hear, hear.) Notwithstanding this, Fraternity was a great truism, and before any great lasting and practical good could be accomplished, it must be universally acknowledged, ay, and practised too. (Loud cheers.) They had met to celebrate the Polish Revolution, and the question was, what could they do to aid Poland? Without power—nothing. Let them get the Charter and they would have power. (Cheers.)

Citizen *Engels* (from Paris), in seconding the resolution said—Fellow Citizens, this commemoration of the Polish Revolution is not only an advantage to Poland, but to the whole world, as it causes the principles of democracy to be spread far and wide. (Hear, hear. He, as a German, had great interest in Polish success, as it would much hasten liberty in Germany, and freedom Germany had resolved to obtain sooner or later. (Loud cheers.) And he firmly believed that no one nation could become free without benefitting all others. He had resided for some time in England, and was proud to boast himself a Chartist "name and all". (Great cheering.) Who were now their chief oppressors? Not the aristocracy, but the wealth takers and scrapers, the middle classes. (Loud cheers.) Hence, it was the duty of the working classes of all nations to unite and establish freedom for all. (Rapturous applause.)

Citizen *Tedesco* (from Brussels, who addressed the meeting in the French language in most eloquent terms, which the following abstract does anything but justice to), said the men of Belgium looked on the English democrats as a leading party, and trusted they would obtain that great measure, the People's Charter. He was delighted with the spirit that prevailed. He should return to Brussels, and relate the good and enthusiastic feeling with which the proletarians of this country were imbued, and their determination to proceed until they had obtained their Charter, and sure he was, that that measure would carry with it a fair day's wages for a fair day's labour. (Hear, hear.) And give such an impulse to the cause of progress, that the whole continent would follow, and universal liberty be established. (Loud cheers.)

Colonel *Oborski*, a Polish exile, said, at the outbreak of the Polish Revolution, two hundred non-commissioned officers had kept three Russian regiments at bay, and when some of the regiments found it was against Poland they were fighting, they turned their arms and fought against their oppressors. Although Old Poland was dead, Young Poland would arise, and become far mightier than her ancestor. (Loud cheers.) He yet hoped to see Poland the first battle-field for liberty. With grateful thanks to the English people he would shout "Hurrah for Democracy!" (Great applause.)

Citizen *Engels* here said, that he had but recently come from Paris, and that the real democrats in that city were in favour of a Congress of Nations. (Loud cheers.) The resolution was then carried unanimously.

Julian Harney again came forward and read extracts from the defence of Louis Mieroslawski, one of the chiefs of the insurrection of 1846, and now lying in the dungeons of Berlin under sentence of death.[369] The reading of the said extracts excited great sensation in the meeting. J. Harney then said, he had been particularly gratified by the remarks of his friend Engels. He was glad to see that the feeling of fraternal sympathy for the Poles was strong amongst the Germans. He was sure that if once the Germans obtained their liberties, they would hasten to perform a great act of national reparation, by undoing the work which the Austrian and Prussian despots helped Catherine to accomplish—the destruction of Poland. He knew that if Frenchmen were free, if they had broken down that disgraceful despotism which had prostrated their country to the lowest depths of shame, their first thought would be the liberation of Poland. (Cheers.) The next time France marched in the direction of Moscow it would not be with an Emperor for her leader. It was a maxim of Napoleon's "that a political blunder was worse than a political crime". He was guilty of both crime and blunder of the worst character; when on reaching Warsaw on his march to Russia, he refused to proclaim the restoration of Poland. Had he proclaimed the republic of Poland to the full extent of its ancient boundaries, he would have re-created the soul of a nation, and twenty millions of people would have formed his army of reserve—an army animated by an unconquerable spirit of enthusiasm and devotion to their emancipator. But no, Napoleon though the scourger of kings was the tyrant of the people; though the most deadly enemy of "divine right", he was not less the enemy of popular sovereignty. He desired to dictate terms to the Northern Autocrat,[a] but for himself, not for Poland, and the other nations trampled under that autocrat's iron heel. His selfishness found the reward it merited. When flying before the avenging lance of the Cossack, and the still more dreadful shafts of the icy tempest and the snow-storm, with their auxiliaries, famine and pestilence; then Napoleon found Poland no rampart of defence, behind which he might have thrown himself to give his stricken hosts time to breathe, and turn upon their pursuers. He had refused to recall Poland to life, and so when he needed her living arm to save him from the blows of the Muscovite, that arm was not. But the coming republic would repair the political crime of the Emperor, and the day was nigh at hand when France would be a Republic and the people of England have their Charter. (Great applause.) The speaker concluded by moving a vote of thanks to the chairman.[b]

Carl Schapper seconded the vote of thanks, which was supported by Mr. Isaac Wilson, who expressed how much more pleased he was with the proceedings he had just witnessed, than he was with those of a meeting held some fortnight since under the presidency of Dr. Bowring, at the Crown and Anchor, at which he was necessitated to

---

[a] Alexander I.—*Ed.*

[b] John Arnott.—*Ed.*

move an amendment. (Cheers.) The vote of thanks was then carried by acclamation.

The chairman having acknowledged the compliment, three cheers were given "for the heroic martyr Mieroslawski"; three for the "*Réforme* and the French Democrats"; three for "*The Northern Star* and the German Brussels Gazette"[a]; and three dreadful groans for the *Times, Journal des Débats,* and *Austrian Observer.*[b] The *Marseillaise Hymn* was then sung in splendid style by Citizen Moll, and closed these interesting proceedings.

First published in *The Northern Star* No. 528, December 4, 1847

Reprinted from the newspaper

---

[a] *Deutsche-Brüsseler-Zeitung.* Reported erroneously in *The Northern Star* as "Universal Gazette".—*Ed.*

[b] *Österreichischer Beobachter.—Ed.*

ADDRESS OF THE DEMOCRATIC ASSOCIATION OF BRUSSELS TO THE SWISS PEOPLE

THE DEMOCRATIC ASSOCIATION, ESTABLISHED IN BRUSSELS (BELGIUM), WHOSE AIM IS THE UNION AND FRATERNITY OF ALL PEOPLES, TO THE SWISS PEOPLE

Swiss Brothers,

An unhappy struggle has just ended for you.[370] All the nations have watched it with the anxiety, blended with sorrow, that generous hearts always feel at the sight of a civil war.

We shall not here discuss the causes of this quarrel. The two parties decided to resolve it alone, without calling for intervention from anyone.

Those who, not having been asked, claimed to set themselves up as the official judges of your domestic quarrels must incur the reproach of a culpable imprudence.

But this imprudence threatens to change in character.

All the friends of liberty have the right to be indignant, if not alarmed by it.

More or less ardent, more or less sincere good wishes, and even offers of service for one or other cause, could be explained without resort to any other motives than those of the diversity of human opinions on political or religious matters.

Today it is a question of something else.

The intervention of a congress of royalty[371] in your affairs can only be understood in the sense of an open or hidden attack on your institutions and above all on the development that you have given them in law during the last fifteen years.

Guardians, for nearly six centuries, of the repository of liberty which was exiled by usurping feudalism successively from nearly all other parts of Europe, you owe it to us, Swiss Brothers, you owe it to yourselves, to defend one last time more this precious heritage, at this supreme hour when all nations are preparing to claim it from you and divide it.

If you let it be seized from your guardianship, the six centuries of persistent vigilance for which we would soon have owed you full gratitude would be lost for you and for the rest of Europe.

Exiled beyond the sea, on the soil of a new world, democratic institutions would have ceased for a long time to be a model for our constant study and imitation.

Government of the State by universally elected leaders;—State administration without crippling financial debts, without the ruin of the worker for the profit of hosts of useless bureaucrats;—the defence of the State without standing armies;—the commercial and industrial prosperity of the State without tariffs;—freedom of belief without theocratic domination;—where shall we find these again, and be able to copy the model of this regime for which all Europe yearns today, if Switzerland allows a concert of kings, bankers, ministers, mercenaries, monopolists, sectarians, to intervene in its affairs?

Their interference can have no other aim but to wipe out once for all from the centre of Europe this example—so fatal for them—of a nation which governs itself without them.

We understand this so well, Swiss Brothers, that, assembled here from all parts of Europe by the political hazards of recent times, and mingling with a small free nation like yours, and rather in your manner, we felt it essential unanimously to express the wish to see you resist the diplomatic intrigues which are contemplated against you.

We urge you therefore not to listen to those treacherous offers of intervention made to you by five Courts (we will not say five peoples) combined to tempt you into a fatal trap.

Fear of their threats, if they carried them out, cannot exist in your hearts. It is only their cunning that you must guard against.

And if their threats were serious, your forces would without boasting be equal to those which the courts in fact control in the midst of the domestic embarrassments increasing for them every day.

Moreover, if they dreamed of constraining you by force, allies would not fail you. Once more, we recommend into your hands, Swiss Brothers, the sacred repository of European democratic liberty which you have guarded so well up to now, and which in recent times you have been able to make flourish to the benefit of the rights and interests of the greatest number.

We offer you, with the future tribute of our gratitude for the firmness which you will show the world,—
the expression of our most sincere sympathy.

On behalf of the above-named Democratic Association, and by virtue of its deliberations in the general assembly of November 29, 1847 after the Polish commemoration celebrated this day at the Hôtel de Ville of Brussels,

The Committee of the Association.

General *Mellinet*, Chief of the civic legions in 1830, Hon. President.

L. Jottrand, barrister, former member of the National Congress of Belgium in 1830, President.

Maynz, barrister at the Court of Appeal at Brussels.

Imbert, Vice-president, former editor of the *Peuple Souverain* of Marseilles.

Karl Marx, former editor of the *Rheinische Zeitung*, Vice-president.[a]

Lelewel, Joachim, member of the National Government.

George Weerth.

The Secretary of the society, *A. Picard*, barrister at the Court of Appeal at Brussels.

Spilthoorn, barrister at the court of Ghent. Leader of the provisional government of Flanders in 1830.

Pellering, shoe-maker.

A. von Bornstedt, editor of the *Deutsche-Brüsseler-Zeitung*.

The German workers assembled in the society at Brussels[372] have joined in the present address. This is attested by the undersigned members of the committee of this society.

Chairman—*Wallau*.
Vice-chairman—*Hess*.
Wolff, secretary.
Riedel, treasurer.

Writen on November 29, 1847
First published in *La Réforme*, December 5, 1847

Printed according to the newspaper

Translated from the French

Published in English for the first time

---

[a] Marx's name was presumably put by proxy for he was in London at that time.—*Ed.*

MINUTES OF ENGELS' LECTURE TO THE LONDON GERMAN WORKERS' EDUCATIONAL SOCIETY ON NOVEMBER 30, 1847[373]

Citizens! When Christopher Columbus discovered America 350 years ago, he certainly did not think that not only would the then existing society in Europe together with its institutions be done away with through his discovery, but that the foundation would be laid for the complete liberation of all nations; and yet, it becomes more and more clear that this is indeed the case. Through the discovery of America a new route by sea to the East Indies was found, whereby the European business traffic of the time was completely transformed; the consequence was that Italian and German commerce were totally ruined and other countries came to the fore; commerce came into the hands of the western countries, and England thus came to the fore of the movement. Before the discovery of America the countries even in Europe were still very much separated from one another and trade was on the whole slight. Only after the new route to the East Indies had been found and an extensive field had been opened in America for exploitation by the Europeans engaged in commerce, did England begin more and more to concentrate trade and to take possession of it, whereby the other European countries were more and more compelled to join together. From all this, big commerce originated, and the so-called world market was opened. The enormous treasures which the Europeans brought from America, and the gains which trade in general yielded, had as a consequence the ruin of the old aristocracy, and so the bourgeoisie came into being. The discovery of America was connected with the advent of machinery, and with that the struggle became necessary which we are conducting today, the struggle of the propertyless against the property owners.

Before machines were invented almost every country produced as much as it needed, and commerce consisted only of such products as one or another country was quite unable to produce; but when machinery came in, so much was produced that in many places it became necessary to stop working and that even people who had previously performed similar work with their own hands bought machine-made goods for their own use. The position of the former workers was thereby completely altered, and the whole of human society, which formerly consisted of four to six different classes, was divided into two mutually hostile classes.

Since the English seized world commerce and raised their manufacturing business to such a height that they could provide almost all the civilised world with their products, and since the bourgeoisie came to political power, they have also succeeded in making further progress in *Asia* and the bourgeoisie has risen there also; through the rise of machinery the barbarian condition of other countries is constantly being done away with. We know that the Spaniards found *East Indies* at the same stage of development as the English did and that the Indians nevertheless went on living in the same way for centuries, i.e., they ate and drank and vegetated, and the grandson worked the land just as his grandfather had done, except that a number of revolutions took place, which, however, were nothing but a struggle of various peoples for domination. Since the English came and spread their manufactures, the livelihood of the Indians was torn from their hands and the consequence was that they abandoned their stable condition. The workers are already emigrating from there and through mixing with other nations they become accessible for the first time to civilisation. The old Indian aristocracy is completely ruined and people are there set against one another just as here.

Later we have seen how *China*, a country which for more than a thousand years has defied development and all history, has now been turned upside down and drawn into civilisation by the English, by machinery.

Austria, the China of Europe, the only country whose internal institutions were not shaken by the French Revolution, and where even Napoleon could do nothing, cannot stand up to steam; everything there has suddenly been changed by machinery; protective tariffs have brought machinery into the country. Thereby the petty bourgeoisie has raised itself up and overthrown the high aristocracy, thereby something has happened to Metternich which he certainly never anticipated; at the last Bohemian Diet 50,000 guilders in taxes were denied him by the bourgeoisie. The classes of society have been changed, the small craftsmen are being ruined and forced to become ordinary workers, whereby an element has entered which can become dangerous to Metternich. In *Italy* also industry has raised itself up, the bourgeoisie everywhere sits on Metternich's neck, so that the government has got into such a dilemma that Metternich has to concede to the Bohemians that they need not pay taxes of 50,000 guilders.

Thus, through the discovery of America all society has been divided into two classes, and without the rise of the world market this would not have happened. The workers of the whole world have everywhere the same interests; everywhere the different classes disappear and the different interests coincide. When, therefore, a revolution breaks out in one country it must necessarily affect the other countries, and only now can real liberation take place.

First published in *Archiv für die Geschichte des Sozialismus und der Arbeiterbewegung*, Jg. 8, Leipzig, 1919

Printed according to the *Archiv...*

Published in English for the first time

MINUTES OF MARX'S REPORT TO THE LONDON GERMAN WORKERS' EDUCATIONAL SOCIETY ON NOVEMBER 30, 1847

From Belgium I have to report that a workers' society has been formed there which at present has 105 members.[374] The German workers in Brussels, who formerly were quite isolated, are now already a power, and whereas formerly they were not asked to take part in anything, this year they have already been requested to send a representative of the society to the celebration of the Polish revolution being arranged in Brussels by the city to speak in the name of this society. Should the government press for the suppression of the society, because it is certainly bound to exercise an influence on the Belgian workers themselves, the society has decided to hand over its library, which consists of *300 volumes*, and other objects to the London society.

I will now add a few remarks on literature. *Louis Blanc* now proves in one of his works[a] that in the French Revolution, at the same moment when the proletariat stormed the Bastille, the prison for the bourgeois, the bourgeoisie took decisions against those who bought the victory for them with their blood. All the leading figures of the revolution are now presented in their true character, a mass of leaflets are being written in the spirit of the proletariat, which are exercising considerable influence on society. The French work more in the interest of a party than for gain. Before the July revolution[b] leaflets circulated in the spirit of the bourgeoisie just as they do now in the spirit of the proletariat.

Of all that has been achieved by German philosophy the critique of religion is the most important thing; this critique, however, has not

---

[a] L. Blanc, *Histoire de la révolution francaise.—Ed.*

[b] Of 1830.—*Ed.*

proceeded from social development. Everything that has been written hitherto against the Christian religion has limited itself to proving that it rests on false principles; how, for example, the authors have used one another; what had not yet been examined was the practical cult of Christianity. We know that the supreme thing in Christianity is human sacrifice. *Daumer* now proves in a recently published work[a] that Christians really slaughtered men and at the Holy Supper ate human flesh and drank human blood. He finds here the explanation why the Romans, who tolerated all religious sects, persecuted the Christians, and why the Christians later destroyed the entire pagan literature directed against Christianity. Paul himself zealously argued against the admission to the Holy Supper of people who were not completely initiated into the mysteries. It is then also easy to explain where, for example, the relics of the 11,000 virgins came from; there is a document dating from the Middle Ages in which the nuns of a French convent made a contract with the Abbess to the effect that without the consent of all no further relics must be found. The occasion for this was given by a monk who was constantly travelling from Cologne to Paris and back and every time left relics behind. Everything that happened in this respect has been regarded as a fraud of the priests, but that would be to attribute to them a skill and cleverness far beyond the time in which they lived. Human sacrifice was sacred and has really existed. Protestantism merely transferred it to the spiritual man and mitigated the thing a little. Hence there are more madmen among Protestants than in any other sect. This story, as presented in *Daumer*'s work, deals Christianity the last blow; the question now is, what significance this has for us. It gives us the certainty that the old society is coming to an end and that the edifice of fraud and prejudice is collapsing.

First published in *Archiv für die Geschichte des Sozialismus und der Arbeiterbewegung*, Jg. 8, Leipzig, 1919

Printed according to the *Archiv...*

Published in English for the first time

[a] G. F. Daumer, *Die Geheimnisse des christlichen Altertums*.—*Ed.*

MINUTES OF ENGELS' LECTURE TO THE LONDON GERMAN WORKERS' EDUCATIONAL SOCIETY ON DECEMBER 7, 1847

Citizen *Engels* gives a lecture in which he proves that commercial crises are caused only by overproduction and that the stock exchanges are the main offices where proletarians are made.

First published in *Archiv für die Geschichte des Sozialismus und der Arbeiterbewegung*, Jg. 8, Leipzig, 1919

Printed according to the *Archiv*...

Published in English for the first time

RULES OF THE COMMUNIST LEAGUE[375]

Working Men of All Countries, Unite!

SECTION I

THE LEAGUE

Art. 1. The aim of the League is the overthrow of the bourgeoisie, the rule of the proletariat, the abolition of the old bourgeois society which rests on the antagonism of classes, and the foundation of a new society without classes and without private property.

Art. 2. The conditions of membership are:

A) A way of life and activity which corresponds to this aim;
B) Revolutionary energy and zeal in propaganda;
C) Acknowledgement of communism;
D) Abstention from participation in any anti-communist political or national association and notification of participation in any kind of association to the superior authority.
E) Subordination to the decisions of the League;
F) Observance of secrecy concerning the existence of all League affairs;
G) Unanimous admission into a community.

Whosoever no longer complies with these conditions is expelled (see Section VIII).

Art. 3. All members are equal and brothers and as such owe each other assistance in every situation.

Art. 4. The members bear League names.

Art. 5. The League is organised in communities, circles, leading circles, Central Authority and congresses.

SECTION II

THE COMMUNITY

Art. 6. The community consists of at least three and at most twenty members.

Art. 7. Every community elects a chairman and deputy chairman. The chairman presides over the meeting, the deputy chairman holds the funds and represents the chairman in case of absence.

Art. 8. The admission of new members is effected by the chairman and the proposing member with previous agreement of the community.

Art. 9. Communities of various kinds do not know each other and do not conduct any correspondence with each other.

Art. 10. Communities bear distinctive names.

Art. 11. Every member who changes his place of residence must first inform his chairman.

SECTION III

THE CIRCLE

Art. 12. The circle comprises at least two and at most ten communities.

Art. 13. The chairmen and deputy chairmen of the communities form the circle authority. The latter elects a president from its midst. It is in correspondence with its communities and the leading circle.

Art. 14. The circle authority is the executive organ for all the communities of the circle.

Art. 15. Isolated communities must either join an already existing circle or form a new circle with other isolated communities.

SECTION IV

THE LEADING CIRCLE

Art. 16. The various circles of a country or province are subordinated to a leading circle.

Art. 17. The division of the circles of the League into provinces and the appointment of the leading circle is effected by the Congress on the proposal of the Central Authority.

Art. 18. The leading circle is the executive authority for all the circles of its province. It is in correspondence with these circles and with the Central Authority.

Art. 19. Newly formed circles join the nearest leading circle.

Art. 20. The leading circles are provisionally responsible to the Central Authority and in the final instance to the Congress.

SECTION V

THE CENTRAL AUTHORITY

Art. 21. The Central Authority is the executive organ of the whole League and as such is responsible to the Congress.

Art. 22. It consists of at least five members and is elected by the circle authority of the place in which the Congress has located its seat.

Art. 23. The Central Authority is in correspondence with the leading circles. Once every three months it gives a report on the state of the whole League.

SECTION VI

COMMON REGULATIONS

Art. 24. The communities, and circle authorities and also the Central Authority meet at least once every fortnight.

Art. 25. The members of the circle authority and of the Central Authority are elected for one year, can be re-elected and recalled by their electors at any time.

Art. 26. The elections take place in the month of September.

Art. 27. The circle authorities have to guide the discussions of the communities in accordance with the purpose of the League.

If the Central Authority deems the discussion of certain questions to be of general and immediate interest it must call on the entire League to discuss them.

Art. 28. Individual members of the League must maintain correspondence with their circle authority at least once every three months, individual communities at least once a month.

Every circle must report on its district to the leading circle at least once every two months, every leading circle to the Central Authority at least once every three months.

Art. 29. Every League authority is obliged to take the measures in accordance with the Rules necessary for the security and efficient work of the League under its responsibility and to notify the superior authority at once of these measures.

SECTION VII

THE CONGRESS

Art. 30. The Congress is the legislative authority of the whole League. All proposals for changes in the Rules are sent to the Central

Authority through the leading circles and submitted by it to the Congress.

Art. 31. Every circle sends one delegate.

Art. 32. Every individual circle with less than 30 members sends one delegate, with less than 60 two, less than 90 three, etc. The circles can have themselves represented by League members who do not belong to their localities.

In this case, however, they must send to their delegate a detailed mandate.

Art. 33. The Congress meets in the month of August of every year. In urgent cases the Central Authority calls an extraordinary congress.

Art. 34. The Congress decides every time the place where the Central Authority is to have its seat for the coming year and the place where the Congress is next to meet.

Art. 35. The Central Authority sits in the Congress, but has no deciding vote.

Art. 36. After every sitting the Congress issues in addition to its circular a manifesto in the name of the Party.

SECTION VIII

OFFENCES AGAINST THE LEAGUE

Art. 37. Whoever violates the conditions of membership (Art. 2) is according to the circumstances removed from the League or expelled.

Expulsion precludes re-admission.

Art. 38. Only the Congress decides on expulsions.

Art. 39. Individual members can be removed by the circle or the isolated community, with immediate notification of the superior authority. Here also the Congress decides in the last instance.

Art. 40. Re-admission of removed members is effected by the Central Authority on the proposal of the circle.

Art. 41. The circle authority passes judgment on offences against the League and also sees to the execution of the verdict.

Art. 42. Removed and expelled members, like suspect individuals in general, are to be watched in the interest of the League, and prevented from doing harm. Intrigues of such individuals are at once to be reported to the community concerned.

SECTION IX

LEAGUE FUNDS

Art. 43. The Congress fixes for every country the minimum contribution to be paid by every member.

Art. 44. Half of this contribution goes to the Central Authority, the other half remains in the funds of the circle or community.

Art. 45. The funds of the Central Authority are used:

1. to cover the costs of correspondence and administration;
2. to print and distribute propaganda leaflets;
3. to send out emissaries of the Central Authority for particular purposes.

Art. 46. The funds of the local authorities are used:

1. to cover the costs of correspondence;
2. to print and distribute propaganda leaflets;
3. to send out occasional emissaries.

Art. 47. Communities and circles which have not paid their contributions for six months are notified by the Central Authority of their removal from the League.

Art. 48. Circle authorities have to render account of their expenditure and income to their communities at least every three months. The Central Authority renders account to the Congress on the administration of League funds and the state of the League finances. Any embezzlement of League funds is subject to the severest punishment.

Art. 49. Extraordinary and Congress costs are met from extraordinary contributions.

SECTION X

ADMISSION

Art. 50. The chairman of the community reads to the applicant Art. 1 to 49, explains them, emphasises particularly in a short speech the obligations which the new member assumes, and then puts to him the question: "Do you now wish to enter this League?" If he replies "Yes", the chairman takes his word of honour to the effect that he will fulfil the obligations of a League member, declares him a member of the League, and introduces him to the community at the next meeting.

London, December 8, 1847

In the name of the Second Congress of the autumn of 1847

The Secretary
Signed *Engels*

The President
Signed *Karl Schapper*

First published in the Appendix to the book: Wermuth und Stieber, *Die Communisten-Verschwörungen des neunzehnten Jahrhunderts*, Erster Theil, Berlin, 1853

Printed according to the book

FROM THE REPORT OF THE *DEUTSCHE-BRÜSSELER-ZEITUNG* ON THE NEW YEAR'S EVE CELEBRATION OF THE GERMAN WORKERS' SOCIETY IN BRUSSELS DECEMBER 31, 1847

...Then *Karl Marx* took the floor and proposed a toast in French to the Brussels Democratic Association, emphasising in an acutely drawn, clear analysis the liberal mission of Belgium in opposition to absolutism, forcefully expressing appreciation of the benefits of a liberal constitution, of a country where there is freedom of discussion, freedom of association, and where a humanitarian seed can flourish to the good of all Europe. (Loud applause.)

First published in the *Deutsche-Brüsseler-Zeitung* No. 2, January 6, 1848

Printed according to the newspaper

Published in English for the first time

THE ASSOCIATION DÉMOCRATIQUE OF BRUSSELS TO THE FRATERNAL DEMOCRATS ASSEMBLING IN LONDON

We received your letter of December last,[a] the proposals contained in which concerning the Democratic Congress of all nations and the establishment of a monthly correspondence between your society and ours were immediately taken into consideration.[376]

The propositions of holding the first Democratic Congress here in Brussels, with a view of calling the second in London; the first Congress to be called by our society for the anniversary of the Belgian revolution in September next, and the programme of business to be prepared by the committee of this society; these propositions were agreed to unanimously and enthusiastically.

The offer of entering into a regular and monthly correspondence with our society was equally hailed with the greatest enthusiasm.

We now proceed to give you an abstract of our progress and general situation.

The state of our society is as prosperous as can possibly be desired. The number of our members is increasing weekly, and the interest taken by the public in general, and by the working classes in particular, in our proceedings is equally on the increase.

The best proof, however, of our progress is the interest excited in the provinces of the country by our movements. From the most important towns of Belgium we have received summons to send delegates for the purpose of establishing democratic societies similar to ours, and keeping up constant relations with the metropolitan association.

---

[a] "The Fraternal Democrats assembling in London to the Democratic Association for promoting the fraternity of all nations, assembling in Brussels."—*Ed.*

We have given to these appeals our immediate attention. We sent a deputation to Ghent to call a public meeting with a view of establishing a branch society.[377] The meeting was exceedingly numerous, and received our deputation, consisting of members belonging to several nations, with an enthusiasm hardly to be described. The foundation of a democratic society was immediately decided upon, and the names of members taken down. Since then we have received from Ghent the news that the society is definitively constituted, and has held a second meeting exceeding the first in numbers and enthusiasm. More than three thousand citizens were present, and, we are happy to say, they mostly consisted of working men.

We consider the ground gained at Ghent as a most important progress of our cause in this country. Ghent is the chief manufacturing town of Belgium, numbering above a hundred thousand inhabitants, and being in a great measure the centre of attraction for the whole labouring population of Flanders. The position taken by Ghent is decisive for all working class movement of the country. Thus we may accept the adhesion of the factory workers of that Belgian Manchester to the revival of a pure democratic movement, as implying and foreboding the adhesion of the generality of the Belgian proletarians.

We hope to report in our next further progress in other towns of the country, thus arriving by-and-by at the reconstitution of a strong, united, and organised democratic party in Belgium.

We entirely share in the view which in your recent address to the working people of Great Britain and Ireland you have taken of the question of "National Defences".[a] We hope that this address will contribute in a great measure to the enlightenment of the people of England as to the question who are their veritable enemies.

We have equally seen with great pleasure the steps taken by the mass of the English Chartists to arrive, at last, at a close alliance between the Irish people and that of Great Britain. We have seen that there is a better chance now than ever before to break down that prejudice which prompted the Irish people to confound in one common hatred the oppressed classes of England with the oppressors of both countries. We hope to see very shortly united in the hands of Feargus O'Connor the direction both of the English and the

---

[a] "The Fraternal Democrats (assembling in London), to the Working Classes of Great Britain and Ireland" (the document is reproduced in Engels' report; see this volume, pp. 466-67).—*Ed.*

Irish popular movement; and we consider this approaching alliance of the oppressed classes of both countries, under the banner of democracy, as a most important progress of our cause in general.

We conclude by offering to you our fraternal salutations.

The Committee of the Association Démocratique

L. Jottrand, Chairman
K. Marx, Vice-President
A. Picard, Avt., Secretary

Brussels, 13th February, 1848

First published in *The Northern Star* No. 541, March 4, 1848

Reprinted from the newspaper

FROM THE *DEUTSCHE-BRÜSSELER-ZEITUNG'S* REPORT ON THE MEETING OF THE DEMOCRATIC ASSOCIATION OF FEBRUARY 20, 1848

Brussels. Meeting of the Democratic Association of February 20. President: Herr Marx.—Frederick Engels first took the floor to reply to an article concerning his expulsion from France, published by the French Government in the *Moniteur Parisien.* He related briefly the circumstances in which his expulsion took place.[378]

The association was completely satisfied with the explanations of Frederick Engels. Several speakers expressed this satisfaction and further added remarks concerning the behaviour of the French Government already on the occasion of earlier expulsions of foreigners.

These proceedings were entered in the official report of the Democratic Association....

First published in the *Deutsche-Brüsseler-Zeitung* No. 16, February 24, 1848

Printed according to the newspaper

Published in English for the first time

FROM THE *DEUTSCHE-BRÜSSELER-ZEITUNG*'S REPORT ON THE BRUSSELS CELEBRATION OF THE SECOND ANNIVERSARY OF THE 1846 CRACOW INSURRECTION[a]

The Cracow revolution was celebrated by a numerous gathering on the evening of the 22nd in the hall of the *Old Court* at Brussels, *rue des soeurs noires,* which was festively illuminated and decorated with Polish and Belgian flags. Several speakers, including Lelewel, Karl Marx, F. Engels, Wallau and Lubliner, the lawyer, took the floor and spoke passionately for the purely democratic character of the Cracow insurrection. We shall report this celebration in detail in our next issue[b] and only remark here that after the public meeting a dinner was held in which about 100 persons took part and at which several toasts were raised by Belgian and German democrats. Nor was the dinner lacking in song.

First published in the *Deutsche-Brüsseler-Zeitung* No. 16, February 24, 1848

Printed according to the newspaper

Published in English for the first time

---

[a] See this volume, pp. 545-52.—*Ed.*

[b] This report was never published in the *Deutsche-Brüsseler-Zeitung*; the seventeenth and last issue of the paper appeared on February 27, 1848.—*Ed.*

TO THE CITIZENS, MEMBERS OF THE PROVISIONAL GOVERNMENT OF THE FRENCH REPUBLIC[379]

Brussels, February 28, 1848

Citizens!

The Democratic Association having as its aim the union and brotherhood of all peoples, established a few months ago at Brussels, and composed of members of several European nations which enjoy with the Belgians on their soil institutions which have long allowed the free and public expression of all political and religious opinions, hereby offers you the homage of its congratulations upon the great task the French nation has just accomplished, and of its gratitude for the immense service which this nation has just rendered the cause of humanity.

We have already had occasion to congratulate the Swiss for having led, as they did not long ago, in the work for the emancipation of the peoples[a] which it has fallen to you to promote with the vigour which the heroic population of Paris always displays when its turn comes. We were counting before long on repeating to the French the message we had addressed to the Swiss. But France has greatly advanced the time when we counted on addressing her.

This is only one reason why all the nations should hasten to follow in your footsteps.

We believe we can be sure in surmising that the nations nearest to France will be the first to follow her in the career on which she has just entered.

This conjecture is all the more certain in that France has just made a revolution destined rather to strengthen the bonds which link it to all nations than to menace the independence of any of them. We

---

[a] See this volume, pp. 624-26.—*Ed.*

salute in the France of February 1848 not the mistress of the peoples but an example for them—France will henceforward look for no other homage.

We already see the great nation whose destinies you direct today, your sole authority the trust of all, we already see it, citizens, forging again, even with peoples whom she has for long regarded as rivals for power, an alliance which the hateful policy of certain men succeeded in shattering.

England and Germany stretch out their hands once more to your great country. Spain, Italy, Switzerland and Belgium are going either to rise or to remain quiet and free under your threefold aegis.

Poland, like Lazarus, will rise again to the appeal you will make in a threefold language.

It is impossible that Russia itself should not join in, with accents as yet only slightly known to the ear of Western and Southern peoples.

Yours, Frenchmen, yours is the honour, yours is the glory to have laid the main foundations of this alliance of peoples so prophetically sung by your immortal Beranger.

We offer you, citizens, in all the flow of feelings of an immutable fraternity, the tribute of our deepest gratitude.

The Committee of the Democratic Association, whose aim is the union and brotherhood of all peoples, at Brussels.

L. Jottrand, barrister, President
Ch. Marx, Vice-president
General *Mellinet*, Honorary president
Spilthoorn, barrister, President of the Democratic Association at Ghent
Maynz, professor at Brussels University
Lelewel
F. Balliu, treasurer
A. Battaille, Vice-secretary
J. Pellering, workman
Labiaux, merchant

First published in the newspapers *Le Débat social*, March 1, 1848 and *La Réforme*, March 4, 1848

Printed according to *La Réforme*

Translated from the French

Published in full in English for the first time

TO MR. JULIAN HARNEY, EDITOR OF *THE NORTHERN STAR*, SECRETARY OF THE FRATERNAL DEMOCRATS SOCIETY, LONDON

Brussels, February 28, 1848

You already know of the glorious revolution which has just been carried out in Paris.

We have to communicate to you that, as a result of this important event, the Democratic Association has initiated here a peaceful but vigorous agitation, to obtain through the ways proper to Belgian political institutions the advantages which the French people have won.

The following resolutions have been passed, with enthusiastic acclaim:

1. The Democratic Association will hold meetings every evening and the public will be admitted;

2. An address will be sent in the name of the Association to the provisional government of France,[a] with the aim of expressing our warm feelings for the revolution of February 24;

3. An address will be presented to the municipal council of Brussels, inviting it to maintain public peace and to avoid all bloodshed by organising the municipal forces generally composed of the civil guard, that is to say, the bourgeois who are armed in normal circumstances, and the artisans who can be armed in abnormal times, according to the laws of the country. Arms will thus be entrusted equally to the middle class and the working class.

We will inform you as often as possible of the measures we shall take later, and of our progress.

We hope that you will soon succeed, on your side, in having the People's Charter passed as a law of your country, and that it will serve you in making further progress.

---

[a] See this volume, pp. 645-46.—*Ed.*

Finally, we invite you; in this important crisis, to keep in frequent communication with us, and to transmit to us all news of your country of a nature to exercise a favourable effect on the Belgian people.

(Signatures of Committee Members follow)

First published in *Le Débat social*, March 1, 1848

Printed according to the newspaper

Translated from the French

Published in English for the first time

FERDINAND FLOCON TO MARX
IN BRUSSELS

Provisional Government	French Republic Liberty, Equality, Fraternity

In the name of the French People

Paris, March 1, 1848

Good and loyal Marx,

The soil of the French Republic is a field of refuge and asylum for all friends of liberty.

Tyranny exiled you, now free France opens its doors to you and to all those who are fighting for the holy cause, the fraternal cause of all the peoples.

Every agent of the French government must interpret his mission in this sense.

Fraternal greetings.

Ferdinand Flocon,
Member of the Provisional Government

First published in the book:
K. Marx, *Herr Vogt*, London, 1860

Printed according to the manuscript

Translated from the French

Published in English for the first time

ORDER OF LEOPOLD I, KING OF THE BELGIANS, FOR MARX'S EXPULSION FROM BELGIUM

Leopold, King of the Belgians,
To all present and to come, Greetings

Considering the laws of September 22, 1835, December 25, 1841 and February 23, 1846
On the proposition of our Minister of Justice,
We have decreed and now decree:

Article One and Only

The here-named Marx, Charles, Doctor of Philosophy, aged about 28 years, born at Trèves (Prussia), is ordered to leave the Kingdom of Belgium within twenty-four hours, and forbidden to return in the future under the penalties contained in Article Six of the afore-cited law of September 22, 1835.

Our Minister of Justice is charged with the execution of the present order.

Done at Brussels on March 2, 1848

[Signed:] *Leopold*

By the royal hand
The Minister of Justice
[Signed:] *De Haussy*

Certified true copy
The Secretary-General
[Signed:] *De Crassier*

Published for the first time

Printed from the original

Translated from the French

DECISION OF THE CENTRAL AUTHORITY OF THE COMMUNIST LEAGUE, MARCH 3, 1848[380]

Working Men of All Countries, Unite!

The Central Authority of the Communist League, meeting in Brussels, in accordance with the decision of the former London Central Authority to move the seat of the Central Authority to Brussels and to dissolve itself as Central Authority, by which decision the circle authority of the Brussels leading circle is therefore constituted the Central Authority, considering:

that in the present circumstances any association of League members, in particular of Germans, is impossible in Brussels;

that the leading League members there have already been either arrested or expelled or are hourly expecting expulsion from Belgium;

that at the present moment Paris is the centre of the entire revolutionary movement;

that present circumstances require a thoroughly energetic leadership of the League, for which temporary discretionary power is indispensable,

decides:

Art. 1. The Central Authority is transferred to Paris.

Art. 2. The Brussels Central Authority confers on League member Karl Marx full discretionary power for the temporary central direction of all League affairs with responsibility to the Central Authority to be newly constituted and to the next Congress.

Art. 3. It instructs Marx, in Paris, as soon as circumstances permit, to constitute a new Central Authority from the most suitable League members selected by him, and for that purpose even to call to Paris League members not resident there.

Art. 4. The Brussels Central Authority dissolves itself.

Resolved at Brussels, March 3, 1848.

The Central Authority

Signed: *Engels, F. Fisher, Gigot, H. Steingens, K. Marx*

First published in the book: Wermuth und Stieber, *Die Communisten-Verschwörungen des neunzehnten Jahrhunderts*, Erster Theil, Berlin, 1853

Printed according to the book

TRAVEL DOCUMENT ISSUED TO MARX ON HIS EXPULSION FROM BELGIUM

Ministry of Justice

Administration of Prisons and Public Security

2nd section
2nd Bureau

No. 73946

TRAVEL DOCUMENT

(Law of Mày 30-June 13, 1790, Decree of May 11, 1815)[a]

DESCRIPTION

AGE	*28* years[b]
HEIGHT 1 METRE	... centimetres
HAIR	*Black*
FOREHEAD	*Average*
EYEBROWS	*Black*
EYES	*Brown*
NOSE	*Average*
MOUTH	*do.*
BEARD	*Black*
SIDE WHISKERS	*Black*
MOUSTACHE	*Black*
CHIN	*Round*
FACE	*do.*
COMPLEXION	*Tanned*
BUILT	*Heavy*
DISTINGUISHING MARKS	

THE ADMINISTRATOR OF PUBLIC SECURITY

invites the civil and military authorities to allow free passage
from *Brussels* to *Quiévrain*
destination *France*
to M. *Marx, Charles*
Profession *Doctor of Philosophy*
born at *Trier, Prussia*
residing at—and to give him aid and protection in case of need.

The present travel document *is valid for exit from the Kingdom today.*

Done at *Brussels, March 4*, 1848

For THE ADMINISTRATOR OF PUBLIC SECURITY

The Head of the Passport Office

Becquet

Signature of bearer

Dr. K. Marx[c]

First published as a facsimile in the book: S. Z. Leviova, *Marx in the German Revolution, 1848-49.* Moscow, 1970

Printed from the original

Translated from the French

Published in English for the first time

---

[a] This is followed by the Belgian national coat of arms.— *Ed.*

[b] Inaccurate: Marx was born in 1818.— *Ed.*

[c] Signature in Marx's hand.— *Ed.*

MINUTES OF THE MEETING OF THE PARIS COMMUNITY OF THE COMMUNIST LEAGUE OF MARCH 8, 1848

MINUTES OF THE COMMUNITY MEETING OF MARCH 8, 1848

Elected *Chairman*: K. Schapper. *Secretary*: K. Marx.

Schapper: proposes to constitute ourselves the Paris Circle, no longer a single community.

Supported by Marx and others. Agreed.

Admitted: *Hermann*.

Discussion on the re-admission of removed community members;

Born gives a report on the meeting in the café l'Europe; so does *Sterbitzki*. Resolved by a large majority not to go into this café, where Decker and Venedey hold a meeting.

Engler, Buchfink and Vogler (Weitlingians) unanimously admitted.

Unanimously resolved: the three above-named League members instructed to admit members of the Weitling community whom they consider suitable.

Schilling unanimously admitted.

Admitted to the public workers' society as:

President: H. Bauer.

Vice-president: Hermann.

2 secretaries: Born and Vogel.

Treasurer: Moll.

3 organisers: Buchfink, Schapper, Horne.

Agreed that the President shall use the form of address: Friends; anybody else as he likes.

Marx to submit draft Rules for the workers' society.

The public society shall be called *German Workers' Club*.[381]

Wilhelm Höger admitted as League member (proposed by Schapper, supported by H. Bauer).

The meeting place of the public society shall be in the centre of the city. Some members are instructed to look for suitable premises.

The League meeting is to be held at No. 6, St. Louis St. Honoré.

Sterbitzki proposes Hermann, who is admitted.

Secretary *K. Marx* Chairman *K. Schapper*

Written by Karl Marx on March 8, 1848

First published in Marx/Engels, *Gesamtausgabe*, I. Abteilung, Bd. 7, 1935

Printed according to the manuscript

Published in English for the first time

MINUTES OF THE MEETING OF THE PARIS CIRCLE OF THE COMMUNIST LEAGUE OF MARCH 9, 1848

MEETING OF MARCH 9, 9 P.M.

Marx submits his draft Rules,[a] which are discussed.

Article 1 adopted with a minority of 2 against. Article 2 adopted unanimously; also Art. 3, Art. 4, Art. 5 and Art. 6.

The draft Rules are therefore adopted without amendments. The Rules of the Communist League are read out by the Secretary. After hearing the Rules the members newly to be admitted declare that they enter the Communist League.

Marx proposes that all members shall give their names and addresses. This is discussed and it is finally resolved that every League member shall give the name by which he is known here, and his address.

Schapper proposes to add another five members to the President and Secretary, so as to form the circle authority of Paris.

One is to be elected from each of the four communities. The elections to be postponed to the next meeting.

Schapper gives a report on the Central Authority. On Schapper's proposal resolved that everybody who speaks rises and removes his hat.

On Marx's proposal the Central Authority will give at the next meeting a report on the situation of the League in general.

Born, who was sent to give a report on the meeting in the *manège*, returns after three-quarters of an hour and describes the miserable state of this society.[382] The next meeting will be held next Saturday at 8 o'clock, café Belge, Rue Grenelle St. Honoré.

---

[a] Draft Rules of the German Workers' Club (see this volume, p. 654).—*Ed.*

At the conclusion of the meeting the members give the Secretary their names together with their addresses. Marx proposes that all League members shall wear a *red* ribbon. Agreed unanimously.

On Schapper's proposal it is agreed that one member shall buy a blood-red ribbon for all. *B. Sax* is instructed to do this.

Written by Karl Marx on March 9, 1848

First published in Marx/Engels, *Gesamtausgabe,* I. Abteilung, Bd. 7, 1935

Printed according to the manuscript

Published in English for the first time

ANNOUNCEMENT BY THE GERMAN WORKERS' CLUB IN PARIS

The committee of the *German Workers' Club* will announce in the newspaper *La Réforme* the arrangements that it considers to make in order to hold its meetings in public.

H. Bauer, shoemaker; Hermann, cabinet-maker; J. Moll, watchmaker; Wallau, printer; Charles Marx; Charles Schapper.

First published in *La Réforme*, March 10, 1848

Printed according to the newspaper

Translated from the French

Published in English for the first time

ANNOUNCEMENT OF THE REGULAR MEETING OF THE GERMAN WORKERS' CLUB IN PARIS

German Workers' Club—Meeting on Tuesday, March 14, at the café Picard, 93, rue Saint-Denis. Those who wish to join the club are asked to give their names to:

Hermann, rue du Faubourg St. Antoine 55, c/o M. Scheuffer;
Stumpf, rue Montorgueil 33, c/o M. Schard;
Seidel, rue Oblin 9, c/o M. Glass;
L. Etrich, rue Saint-Marc 5;
Charles Marx,[a] rue Neuve-Ménilmontant 10;
Charles Schapper, rue Neuve Saint-Augustin 22.

First published in *La Réforme*, March 13, 1848

Printed according to the newspaper

Translated from the French

Published in English for the first time

[a] The original has a misprint: Clarck.—*Ed.*

NOTES AND INDEXES

NOTES

[1] This article deals with a meeting held in London on September 22. 1845 at which an international society of Fraternal Democrats was formed. The society embraced representatives of Left Chartists, German workers and craftsmen—members of the League of the Just—and revolutionary emigrants of other nationalities. During their stay in England in the summer of 1845, Marx and Engels helped in preparing for the meeting but did not attend it as they had by then left London. Later they kept in constant touch with the Fraternal Democrats trying to influence the proletarian core of the society, which joined the Communist League in 1847, and through it the Chartist movement. The society ceased its activities in 1853.

Engels' article, written to show the significance of international unity of the proletarian and revolutionary democratic forces, was directed at the same time against "true socialism"—the petty-bourgeois socialist trend current among German intellectuals and craftsmen from the end of 1844 onwards. This was Engels' second printed article against "true socialism", the first being "A Fragment of Fourier's On Trade" (see present edition, Vol. 4).

Engels describes the meeting of September 22, 1845 and cites speeches delivered at it according to the report published in *The Northern Star* No. 411, September 27, 1845. Excerpts from the article were published in English in *The Plebs Magazine* No. 2, March 1922. p. 3

[2] *Carmagnole*—a song popular at the time of the French Revolution. Subsequent changes made in the words reflected mass sentiments at various stages of the popular movement.

The *maximum laws* and the *law against buying up food supplies* (June 26, 1793) were adopted by the Convention at the time of deepening food crisis under mass pressures and the campaign for fixed prices conducted by the so-called rabid, representatives of the most radical plebeian trend in the revolutionary camp. The first maximum adopted on May 4, 1793, despite opposition on the part of the Girondists introduced fixed prices on grain; the decree of September 11, 1793, fixed a single price for grain, flour and fodder; fixed prices on other staple goods (second maximum) were introduced on September 29. p. 4

[3] The Jacobin revolutionary government headed by Robespierre fell as a result of the coup of 9-10 Thermidor (July 27-28), 1794.

The *conspiracy of equality* organised by Babeuf and his followers aimed at provoking an armed uprising of the plebeian masses against the bourgeois regime of the Directory and establishing a revolutionary dictatorship as a transitional stage to "pure democracy" and "egalitarian communism". The conspiracy was disclosed in May 1796. At the end of May 1797 its leaders were executed. p. 5

4 The period from May 31, 1793 to July 26, 1794 was one of the Jacobin revolutionary democratic dictatorship in France. p. 5

5 The reference is to *associations for improving the conditions of the working classes* set up in a number of Prussian towns in 1844-45 on the initiative of the liberal bourgeoisie who were frightened by the uprising of the Silesian weavers in the summer of 1844. The aim of their founders was to divert the German workers' attention from the struggle for their class interests. p. 6

6 At *Jemappes* (November 6, 1792) and *Fleurus* (June 26, 1794) the French revolutionary army defeated the forces of the first coalition of the European counterrevolutionary monarchies. p. 6

7 *Democratic Association*—a workers' organisation founded in London by the most revolutionary elements among the Chartists (George Julian Harney and others) in 1838; it advocated the revolutionary implementation of the Chartist programme. Many of its members were republicans and supported Babeuf's trend of utopian communism. p. 6

8 *Cosmopolitan*—here and below is to be understood as meaning: free from all national limitations and national prejudices. p. 7

9 The reference is to the meeting of Chartists and heads of the London communities of the League of the Just with the leading figures of the democratic and revolutionary movements in a number of countries; the meeting took place in London in August 1845. Marx and Engels who were in London at the time took an active part in it. According to a report published in *The Northern Star* No. 406, August 23, 1845, the participants adopted the following resolution proposed by Thomas Cooper and supported by Engels: "That a public meeting of the democrats of all nations, residing in London, be called to consider the propriety of forming an Association for the purpose of meeting each other at certain times, and getting by this means a better knowledge of the movements for the common cause going on in their respective countries."

This event marked an important step towards organising the international meeting held on September 22, 1845 and described by Engels in this article. p. 7.

10 The reference is to revolutionary events of August 1842 in England when in conditions of economic crisis and increasing poverty violent working-class disturbances broke out in the industrial regions. In Lancashire and a large part of Cheshire and Yorkshire strikes became general, in some places growing into spontaneous insurrections. The government retaliated with massive arrests of Chartist leaders, who afterwards received severe sentences. p. 8

11 The reference is to the July revolution of 1830 in France which resulted in the overthrow of the Bourbon dynasty. Decisive events took place on July 27-29 in Paris. p. 9

12 *August 10, 1792*—the day when the monarchy in France was overthrown as a result of a popular insurrection. p. 9

13 Julian Harney refers to calls for war against England raised in the French Chamber of Deputies and the French bourgeois press due to strained Anglo-French relations in the mid-forties caused by the colonial rivalry between the two powers in West Indies after the establishment of the French protectorate over Tahiti, the annoyance of the English bourgeoisie at French expansion in North Africa (war against Morocco) and the sharp British reaction against the projected Franco-Belgian-Luxembourg customs union. The planned marriage of the son of Louis Philippe to the Spanish Infanta, opening up the prospects for union of the two monarchies under the Orleans crown, added to the tension. p. 11

14 The *trial of April 1834*—trial of 167 participants in the French workers' and republican movement, accused of high treason in connection with the uprising in Lyons and revolutionary actions in Paris and other towns in April 1834. Among the accused were the leaders of the secret republican *Société des droits de l'homme.* p. 13

15 The *Holy Roman Empire of the German Nation* was founded in 962 and lasted till 1806. At different periods it included the German, Italian, Austrian, Hungarian and Bohemian lands, Switzerland and the Netherlands, forming a motley conglomeration of feudal kingdoms and principalities, church lands and free towns with different political structures, legal standards and customs. p. 15

16 *Imperial Court Chamber* (Reichskammergericht) was the supreme court of the Holy Roman Empire. It was established in 1495 and abolished in 1806; initially it had no fixed seat, but from 1693 to 1806 was permanently located in Wetzlar. p. 16

17 Here the word "metaphysics" is used to denote philosophy as a speculative science transcending practical experience. p. 17

18 *Constitution of 1791,* approved by the Constituent Assembly, established a constitutional monarchy in France, giving the king full executive powers and the right of veto. This constitution was annulled as a result of the popular uprising of August 10, 1792, which brought about the fall of the monarchy. After the Girondist government (Girondists—the party of the big bourgeoisie) had been overthrown by the uprising of May 31-June 2, 1793 and the revolutionary dictatorship of the Jacobins established, the National Convention adopted a new democratic constitution of the French Republic. p. 18

19 The reference is to the Constituent Assembly's decision to repeal feudal services, passed on the night of August 4, 1789 under the impact of peasant uprisings all over the country. p. 18

20 See Note 3. p. 19

21 After the defeat of Austria in 1805 and of Prussia in 1806 by Napoleon and the establishment of the French protectorate over the German states the latter were obliged to declare war on Britain and join the continental blockade proclaimed by the French Emperor in November 1806, which prohibited all trade with Britain. p. 19

22 In his articles "The State of Germany" Engels tried to refute the reactionary nationalistic interpretation of German history and, in particular, the glorification of the role played by the German ruling classes in the wars of 1813-14 and 1815 against Napoleonic France. But he gave a somewhat one-sided appraisal of the war itself. The war to liberate Germany from French domination following the defeat of Napoleon's army in Russia in 1812 was, indeed, of a contradictory nature. Its character was affected by the counter-revolutionary and expansionist aims and

policy of the ruling circles in the feudal monarchical states. But especially in 1813, when the struggle was aimed at liberating German territory from French occupation, it assumed the character of a genuinely popular national liberation war against foreign oppression. Later, when he once again considered that period in the history of Germany, Engels in a series of articles entitled "Notes on the War" (1870) stressed the progressive nature of the people's resistance to Napoleon's rule and in his work *The Role of Force in History* (1888) he wrote: "The peoples' war against Napoleon was the reaction of the national feeling of all the peoples, which Napoleon had trampled on." p. 20

23 The reference is to the Spanish Constitution of 1812 adopted at the time of the national liberation war against Napoleonic rule. Expressing the interests of the liberal nobility and liberal bourgeoisie the constitution limited the king's power by the Cortes, proclaimed the supreme power of the nation and did away with certain survivals of feudalism. The overwhelming power of the feudal and clerical reactionary forces after Napoleon's defeat in 1814 led to the repeal of the constitution, which then became the banner of the liberal-constitutional movement in Spain and other European countries. p. 22

24 The *Holy Alliance*—an association of European monarchs founded on September 26, 1815 on the initiative of the Russian tsar Alexander I and the Austrian Chancellor Metternich to suppress revolutionary movements and preserve feudal monarchies in European countries. p. 22

25 *Peterloo* was the name given at the time (by analogy with the battle of Waterloo) to the massacre by the troops of unarmed participants in a mass meeting for electoral reform at St. Peter's Field near Manchester, on August 16, 1819. p. 23

26 The *Fundamental Federative Act* (Bundesakte)—a part of the Final Act of the Congress of Vienna held by European monarchs and their ministers in 1814-15, which established the political organisation of Europe after the Napoleonic wars. This Act was signed on June 8, 1815 and proclaimed a German Confederation consisting initially of 34 independent states and four free cities. The Act virtually sanctioned the political dismemberment of Germany and the maintenance of the monarchical-estate system in the German states. From 1815 to 1866 the central organ of the German Confederation was the Federal Diet consisting of representatives of the German states.

The promise to introduce constitutions in all the states of the German Confederation, which was stated in Article 13 of the Bundesakte, was never fulfilled. Article 18 of the Act, which vaguely mentioned a forthcoming drafting of uniform instructions providing for "freedom of the press" in the states of the German Confederation, also remained on paper. p. 26

27 *Vendée*—a department in Western France; during the French Revolution a centre of largely peasant-based royalist uprising. The word "Vendée" came to denote counter-revolutionary actions. p. 26

28 The *Corn Laws* (first introduced in the 15th century) imposed high tariffs on agricultural imports in order to maintain high prices on agricultural products on the home market. By the Act of 1815 imports of grain were prohibited as long as grain prices in England remained lower than 80 sh. per quarter. Later further Acts were adopted (1822, 1828 and others) changing the terms for grain imports.

The struggle between the industrial bourgeoisie and the landed aristocracy over the Corn Laws ended in their repeal in June 1846. p. 28

[29] The reference is to the revolution in Spain which began in January 1820, and also to revolutionary actions in Naples and Palermo in July 1820, in Portugal in August 1820 and Piedmont in March 1821 under the slogan of a constitution and bourgeois reforms. The revolutionary movements were suppressed by the Holy Alliance powers which sanctioned the Austrian intervention in Italy and the French intervention in Spain, and by domestic reaction.

The first secret society of carbonari in France was founded in late 1820-early 1821 after the pattern of the Italian societies of the same name. The society included representatives of diverse political trends and sought to overthrow the Bourbon monarchy. It was smashed by the police in 1822. Some carbonari organisations existed till the early 1830s, participated in the July revolution of 1830, and soon afterwards merged with republican societies.

In 1816-19 an upsurge of the democratic movement for an electoral reform took place in England. However, no reform was accomplished until 1832. p. 31

[30] At the first stage of the national liberation uprising of the Greek people in 1821 the European governments were hostile to the insurgents. However, under pressure from public opinion and as a result of rivalries in the Balkans and the Middle East their attitudes changed. In 1827 Britain, France and Russia signed an agreement undertaking to demand jointly that the Turkish government should stop war in Greece and grant the country autonomy. The refusal of the Sultan to meet these demands led to a military conflict between the European powers and Turkey. The defeat of the Turks in the battle of Navarino (1827) was of great importance for the liberation of Greece. Finally the issue was decided by the Russo-Turkish war of 1828-29. The Sultan was compelled to recognise the autonomy of Greece, and soon afterwards its independence. However, the European powers imposed a monarchical form of government on the newly liberated country. p. 31

[31] See Note 11. p. 31

[32] The Polish national liberation uprising of November 1830-October 1831, whose participants belonged mostly to the revolutionary gentry and whose leaders were mainly from aristocratic circles, was crushed by tsarist Russia aided by Prussia and Austria—the states which had taken part in the partition of Poland at the end of the eighteenth century. Despite the defeat the uprising was of a major international significance as it diverted the forces of the counter-revolutionary powers and frustrated their plans to intervene against the bourgeois revolutions of 1830 in France and of 1830-31 in Belgium. As a result of the revolution, Belgium, which had been incorporated into Holland in 1815 by the decision of the Congress of Vienna, became an independent kingdom. For Marx's and Engels' appraisal of the Polish uprising of 1830-31 see pp. 545-52 of this volume. p. 31

[33] The 1832 Reform Act in England granted the franchise to property owners and leaseholders with no less than £10 annual income. The proletariat and the petty bourgeoisie, who were the main force in the struggle for the reform, remained unenfranchised. p. 32

[34] The conference of the representatives of German states held in June 1834 in Vienna passed a decision which obliged the sovereigns to render mutual support in their struggle against liberal and democratic movements. This decision was recorded in the final protocol of the conference of June 12, 1834, the contents of which were long kept secret. p. 32

[35] In 1844 the British Home Secretary, Sir James Graham, to please the Austrian government ordered the post office to let the police inspect the correspondence of Italian revolutionary immigrants. p. 33

[36] The editorial board of *The Northern Star* altered the date from "February 20" to "March 20". Harney gave this explanation to Engels in a letter of March 30, 1846: "On Saturday I received a long letter from you through We[e]rth, or rather two letters. The one for the *Star* I like very much, it will appear this week. I have altered the date from Febr. 20th, to March 20th, it will thereby not look so stale." p. 33

[37] This is a circular of the Brussels Communist Correspondence Committee founded by Marx and Engels early in 1846 for the propaganda of communist ideas and correspondence with advanced workers and revolutionary intellectuals in various countries of Europe (similar committees were founded shortly afterwards in London, Paris, Cologne and some other cities). The Brussels Communist Correspondence Committee made use of such circulars, as Engels stated later, "on particular occasions, when it was a question of internal affairs of the Communist Party in process of formation" (F. Engels, "On the History of the Communist League", 1885).

The "Circular Against Kriege" was directed against "true socialism", a trend followed by the German journalist Hermann Kriege who had emigrated to New York in the autumn of 1845. It was also to a considerable extent directed against the egalitarian communism of Weitling, which had found a number of advocates among the supporters of Kriege and the staff of *Der Volks-Tribun* of which he was editor.

It seems likely that the principal part of the "Circular Against Kriege", which was written by Marx and Engels when they were completing the main part of the work on the manuscript of *The German Ideology* (see present edition, Vol. 5), was originally intended for inclusion in Vol. II of that work.

The document against Kriege was circulated in lithographic copies (in Wilhelm Wolff's hand without title).

A copy was sent to New York with a covering letter written by Edgar von Westphalen: "To Herr Hermann Kriege, Editor of *Der Volks-Tribun.*— On behalf of the local *communist society* and as chairman of the meeting which took place on May 11, I am forwarding to you the decision in which our opinion of *Der Volks-Tribun* is expressed. In case you do not publish the decision together with its motivation in your paper it will nevertheless be published in *the press* of Europe and America. We, however, expect that in the nearest future you will send us the issue of *Der Volks-Tribun* containing our resolution to: M. Gigot, rue de Bodenbroek, No. 8, Brussels, May 16, 1846. *Edgar von Westphalen*." Kriege was compelled to comply with this demand and publish the "Circular" in *Der Volks-Tribun* Nos. 23 and 24 of June 6 and 13, 1846, adding his own insinuations against the authors and the ironical title *Eine Bannbulle*. It was also published in the July issue of *Das Westphälische Dampfboot* under the title of "Der Volkstribun, redigirt von Hermann Kriege in New York" without the authors' name. However, the editor of the journal, the "true socialist" Otto Lüning subjected the document to biased re-editing, adding his own introduction and conclusion, in contradiction to the ideas and spirit of the original document and in some cases changing the text arbitrarily. The original text was for a long time unavailable to scholars; in the book *Aus dem literarischen Nachlass von Karl Marx, Friedrich Engels und Ferdinand Lassalle*, published by Franz Mehring, the document was printed according to the text in *Das Westphälische Dampfboot*. The authentic version was for the first time reproduced according to the lithographic copy of the "Circular" in Marx/Engels, *Gesamtausgabe*, Erste Abteilung, Bd. 6, Berlin, 1932.

In October 1846, the Brussels Communist Correspondence Committee issued a second circular against Kriege written by Marx, the text of which has not yet been found. p. 35

38 *Young America*—an organisation of American craftsmen and workers; it formed the nucleus of the mass National Reform Association founded in 1845. In the second half of the 1840s the Association agitated for land reform, proclaiming as its aim free allotment of a plot of 160 acres to every working man; it came out against slave-owning planters and land profiteers. It also put forward demands for a ten-hour working day, abolition of slavery, of the standing army, etc. Many German emigrant craftsmen, including members of the League of the Just, took part in the movement headed by the National Reform Association. By 1846 the movement among the German workers began to subside. One of the reasons for this was the activity of Kriege's group whose "true socialism" diverted the German emigrants from the struggle for democratic aims. p. 41

39 The reference is to the following passage from Emmanuel Sieyès' *Qu'est-ce que le tiers-état?* published in Paris in 1789 on the eve of the French Revolution: "1. What is the third estate? *Everything*. 2. What was it until now in the political respect? *Nothing*. 3. What is it striving for? To be *something*." p. 48

40 *Essenes*—a religious sect in ancient Judea (2nd century B. C.-3rd century A. D.). p. 50

41 The article was published with an introduction by *The Northern Star* editors informing readers of the supposedly forthcoming publication of the Prussian constitution (the interpretation given in the press to the intention of the King of Prussia to institute a state representative organ on the basis of the united provincial diets) and giving a brief account of the situation in Prussia. The introduction, in particular, stated: "Silesia is in a disordered state, the unhappy people showing every inclination to imitate the Polish peasantry in engaging in an agrarian revolt. Last, not least, financial difficulties add to the embarrassments of the Government and have given rise to a measure involving a further departure from the solemn pledges given by the Crown to the people. On this subject we have been favoured with the following communication from our German correspondent." p. 52

42 According to *Verordnung wegen der künftigen Behandlung des gesammten Staatsschulden-Wesens* (Decree on the future handling of all state debts) issued in Prussia on January 17, 1820, new loans and state debts had to be guaranteed by the forthcoming Prussian assembly of the estates as well as by the government. p. 52

43 The reference is to the *Preussische Seehandlungsgesellschaft* (Prussian sea trade society)—a trade credit society founded in Prussia in 1772 which enjoyed a number of important state privileges. It offered large credits to the government and actually played the part of banker and broker. In 1904 it was officially made the Prussian State Bank. p. 52

44 This letter was written by Marx and Engels on behalf of the Brussels Communist Correspondence Committee in reply to a statement by the Elberfeld socialist G. A. Köttgen, who tried to unite the supporters of socialist and communist views in Wuppertal (the joint name of Barmen and Elberfeld, in the Rhine province, which subsequently merged). Köttgen's statement, written on May 24, 1846 was sent to Brussels only on June 10 with a covering letter to Engels.

Their internal dissension prevented the socialists and Communists of Wuppertal from following Marx's and Engels' advice concerning, in particular, the organisation of a communist correspondence committee. p. 54

45 The article was supplied with an editorial introduction beginning with the following words: "Again, rumours are rife in *Germany*, that the long projected Prussian Constitution is at last framed, and will be immediately published. For ourselves, we will believe when we see. The King of Prussia is such a liar that none but asses would repose faith in his most solemn promises. One thing is certain that, if a Constitution is granted, it will be so worthless as to be utterly inadequate to satisfy the popular demands. From our 'German correspondent' we have received the following brief-but interesting communication which exhibits his Prussian kingship in a new but not very respectable character. He is about to turn swindler on a large scale. He will borrow, and then 'repudiate'." p. 57

46 The address of the Brussels Communist Correspondence Committee to the Chartist leader Feargus O'Connor was written in connection with his victory at the Nottingham election meeting early in July 1846, when he stood for election to the House of Commons. Voting at such meetings (up to 1872) was by show of hands, and all present took part in it. However, only "legitimate" electors (those having property and other qualifications) could take part in subsequent ballot—in which, consequently, candidates who had been outvoted by show of hands could be declared elected. Despite this anti-democratic system, O'Connor was duly elected to Parliament at the August 1847 ballot.

The address of the Brussels Communists was read at a regular meeting of the Fraternal Democrats held on July 20, 1846 and was warmly received there (see *The Northern Star* No. 454, July 25, 1846). p. 58

47 The reference is to the Repeal of the Corn Laws passed in June 1846. (On the Corn Laws see Note 28.) The movement for the repeal of the Corn Laws was led by the Anti-Corn Law League founded in 1838 by the Manchester manufacturers Cobden and Bright. Acting under the slogan of unrestricted free trade the League fought to weaken the economic and political position of the landed aristocracy and at the same time to reduce workers' wages. p. 58

48 The *People's Charter*, which contained the demands of the Chartists, was published on May 8, 1838, in the form of a Bill to be submitted to Parliament. It consisted of six clauses: universal suffrage (for men of 21 years of age), annual elections to Parliament, secret ballot, equal constituencies, abolition of property qualifications for candidates to Parliament, and salaries for M.P.s. In 1839 and 1842 petitions for the Charter were rejected by Parliament. In 1847-48 the Chartists renewed a mass campaign for the Charter. p. 58

49 Early in June 1846 Thomas Cooper started a campaign against O'Connor. In particular he accused him of misusing the funds of the Chartist Cooperative Land Society (later called the National Land Company) founded by the Chartist leader in 1845 (see Note 162).

Cooper set forth his accusations in an open letter "To the London Chartists" (published in June 1846 in *Lloyd's Weekly Newspaper*) and in other statements. In answer to this, O'Connor wrote two letters: "To the Members of the Chartist Cooperative Land Society" and "To the Fustian Jackets, the Blistered Hands, and Unshorn Chins", published in *The Northern Star* Nos. 448 and 449, of June 13 and 20, 1846. The latter issue carried also numerous statements by Chartist organisations expressing confidence in O'Connor. p. 59

50 The Tuileries Palace in Paris was the residence of the French monarchs. p. 61

51 The reference is to the rescripts by Frederick William IV of February 3, 1847 convening the United Diet—a united assembly of the eight provincial diets instituted in 1823. The United Diet as well as the provincial diets consisted of representatives of the estates: the curia of gentry (high aristocracy) and the curia of the other three estates (nobility, representatives of the towns and the peasantry). Its powers were limited to authorising new taxes and loans, to voice without vote during the discussion of Bills, and to the right to present petitions to the King. The dates of its sessions were fixed by the King.

The United Diet opened on April 11, 1847, but it was dissolved as early as June because the majority refused to vote a new loan. p. 64

52 See Note 28. p. 65

53 The *Customs Union* (Zollverein) of the German states (initially including 18 states), which established a common customs frontier, was founded in 1834 and headed by Prussia. By the 1840s the Union embraced most of the German states with the exception of Austria, the Hanseatic towns (Bremen, Lübeck, Hamburg) and some small states. Brought into being by the necessity for an all-German market the Customs Union subsequently promoted Germany's political unification. p. 65

54 *States-general*—a body representing the estates in medieval France. It consisted of representatives of the clergy, nobles and burghers. They met in May 1789—after a 175-year interval—at the time of maturing bourgeois revolution and on June 17 were transformed by the decision of the deputies of the third estate into the National Assembly which proclaimed itself the Constituent Assembly on July 9 and became the supreme organ of revolutionary France. p. 69

55 The reference is to the national liberation uprising in the Cracow republic which by the decision of the Congress of Vienna was controlled jointly by Austria, Russia and Prussia—who had partitioned Poland at the end of the eighteenth century. The seizure of power in Cracow by the insurgents on February 22, 1846 and the establishment of a National Government of the Polish republic, which issued a manifesto abolishing feudal services, were part of the plan for a general uprising in the Polish lands whose main inspirers were the revolutionary democrats (Dembowski and others). In March the Cracow uprising, lacking active support in other parts of Poland, was crushed by the forces of Austria and tsarist Russia; in November 1846, Austria, Prussia and Russia signed a treaty incorporating the "free town of Cracow" into the Austrian Empire. p. 71

56 Karl Grün translated into German Proudhon's work *Système des contradictions économiques, ou Philosophie de la misère.* The book was published in Darmstadt in 1847 under the title *Philosophie der Staatsökonomie oder Nothwendigkeit des Elends.* p. 72

57 The reference is to Proudhon's letter to Marx of May 17, 1846 (published in *Correspondance de P. J. Proudhon* précédée d'une notice sur P. J. Proudhon par J. A. Langlois, T. II, Paris, 1875), which was an answer to Marx's letter to him of May 5, suggesting that he correspond with the Brussels Communist Correspondence Committee in the capacity of a representative of the French proletariat. While in fact rejecting this proposal, Proudhon nevertheless wrote to Marx that he was eager to know Marx's opinion of his latest work. p. 73

58 The review of Marx's work in the *Deutsch-Französische Jahrbücher* quoted here has been taken from Karl Grün's article "Meine Stellung zur Judenfrage" published in the *Neue Anekdota.*

Neue Anekdota—a collection which appeared in Darmstadt late in May 1845 under the editorship of Karl Grün. It contained newspaper articles by Moses Hess, Karl Grün, Otto Lüning and others, written mainly in the first half of 1844 and banned by the censors. Soon after the publication of the collection Marx and Engels, as can be judged from Grün's letters to Hess, made a number of severe critical remarks about its content. p. 74

59 Engels intended to publish this work in 1847 as a pamphlet. In the spring of 1847 he sent the manuscript from Paris (where he arrived in August 1846 to organise communist propaganda) to Marx in Brussels to be forwarded to the publisher C. G. Vogler, who had connections with communist circles. Vogler, however, had meantime been arrested (see Marx's letter to Engels of May 15, 1847). Marx gave a high appraisal of this pamphlet, especially of its first part, but was of the opinion that the other two parts were lacking in precision. The extant manuscript is incomplete. Only seven sheets, each folded in four (28 pages altogether), with the author's paging on the first page of each sheet (1, 5, 9, etc.) have been preserved. Pages 21-24 and the last sheets are missing. There is no title to the manuscript. The extant part was first published in the USSR in 1929 in the first edition of Marx's and Engels' *Works* in Russian under the title "The Constitutional Question in German Socialist Literature" and in 1932 in German in Marx/Engels, *Gesamtausgabe* under the title "Der Status quo in Deutschland".

The present title is given according to Engels' letter to Marx of March 9, 1847, in which this work was called "a pamphlet on the constitutional question". p. 75

60 *Réformistes*—a political party grouped round the Paris newspaper *La Réforme*, which included radical opponents of the July monarchy—republican democrats and petty-bourgeois socialists. The leaders of the *Réforme* party, which also called itself "social-democratic", were Ledru-Rollin, Louis Blanc and others (see K. Marx and F. Engels, *Manifesto of the Communist Party*, this volume, p. 518). p. 76

61 Some of the French *legitimists*, advocates of the Bourbon dynasty overthrown in 1830, who upheld the interests of the big hereditary landowners (Villeneuve-Bargemont and others), resorted to social demagogy in their struggle against the financial and industrial bourgeoisie, passing themselves off as defenders of the working people.

Young England was a group of conservative writers and politicians, including Disraeli and Ferrand, who were close to the Tory philanthropists and founded a separate group in the House of Commons in 1841. Voicing the discontent of the landed aristocracy at the growing economic and political power of the bourgeoisie, they criticised the capitalist system and supported half-hearted philanthropic measures for improving the conditions of the workers. Young England disintegrated as a political group in 1845 and ceased to exist as a literary circle in 1848.

In the *Communist Manifesto* Marx and Engels describe the views of Young England and the above-mentioned ideologists of legitimism as "feudal socialism" (see this volume, pp. 507-08). p. 77

62 See Note 21. p. 80

63 See Note 53. p. 80

64 Apparently, the condition of the working classes of Germany, and primarily the German proletariat, was described in the third, non-extant part of the work. p. 83

[65] See Note 51. p. 92

[66] See Note 53. p. 92

[67] The name of the Spandau fortress near Berlin — a drill hall and a place of imprisonment for "state criminals" in Prussia — is used here as a symbol of the Prussian political system. p. 92

[68] The reference is to the Prussian Government's consent to the incorporation of Cracow into the Austrian Empire after the suppression of the Cracow uprising of 1846 (see Note 55). This act led to the inclusion of Cracow within the Austrian customs frontier and to high import duties there on Prussian goods. p. 93

[69] This document is the draft programme discussed at the First Congress of the Communist League in London on June 2-9, 1847.

The Congress was a final stage in the reorganisation of the League of the Just — an organisation of German workers and craftsmen, which was founded in Paris in 1836-37 and soon acquired an international character, having communities in Germany, France, Switzerland, Britain and Sweden. The activity of Marx and Engels directed towards the ideological and organisational unity of the socialists and advanced workers prompted the leaders of the League (Karl Schapper, Joseph Moll, Heinrich Bauer), who resided in London from November 1846, to ask for their help in reorganising the League and drafting its new programme. When Marx and Engels were convinced that the leaders of the League of the Just were ready to accept the principles of scientific communism as its programme they accepted the offer to join the League made to them late in January 1847.

Engels' active participation in the work of the Congress (Marx was unable to go to London) affected the course and the results of its proceedings. The League was renamed the Communist League, the old motto of the League of the Just "All men are brothers" was replaced by a new, Marxist one: "Working Men of All Countries, Unite!" The draft programme and the draft Rules of the League were approved at the last sitting on June 9, 1847.

The full text of the "Draft of a Communist Confession of Faith" (Credo) became known only in 1968. It was found by the Swiss scholar Bert Andréas together with the draft Rules and the circular of the First Congress to the members of the League (see this volume, pp. 585-600) in the archives of Joachim Friedrich Martens, an active member of the Communist League, which are kept in the State and University Library in Hamburg. This discovery made it possible to ascertain a number of important points in the history of the Communist League and the drafting of its programme documents. It had been previously assumed that the First Congress did no more than adopt a decision to draw up a programme and that the draft itself was made by the London Central Authority of the Communist League (Joseph Moll, Karl Schapper and Heinrich Bauer) after the Congress between June and August 1847. The new documents show that the draft was ready by June 9, 1847 and that its author was Engels (the manuscript found in Martens' archives, with the exception of some inserted words, the concluding sentence and the signatures of the president and the secretary of the Congress, was written in Engels' hand).

The document testifies to Engels' great influence on the discussion of the programme at the Congress — the formulation of the answers to most of the questions is a Marxist one. Besides, while drafting the programme, Engels had to take into account that the members of the League had not yet freed themselves from the influence of utopian ideas and this was reflected in the formulation of the first six questions and answers. The form of a "revolutionary catechism" was also commonly used in the League of the Just and other organisations of workers and craftsmen at the time. It may be assumed that Engels intended to give greater precision to some of the formulations of the programme document in the course of further discussion and revision.

After the First Congress of the Communist League the "Draft of a Communist Confession of Faith" was sent, together with the draft Rules, to the communities for discussion, the results of which were to be taken into account at the time of the final approval of the programme and the Rules at the Second Congress. When working on another, improved draft programme, the *Principles of Communism*, in late October 1847 (see this volume, pp. 341-57), Engels made direct use of the "Confession of Faith", as can be seen from the coincidences of the texts, and also from references in the *Principles* to the earlier document when Engels had apparently decided to leave formulations of some of the answers as they were.

The "Draft of a Communist Confession of Faith" was published in English for the first time in the book: *Birth of the Communist Manifesto*, International Publishers, New York, 1971. p. 96

70 In their works of the 1840s and 1850s, prior to Marx having worked out the theory of surplus value, Marx and Engels used the terms "value of labour", "price of labour", "sale of labour" which, as Engels noted in 1891 in the introduction to Marx's pamphlet *Wage Labour and Capital*, "from the point of view of the later works were inadequate and even wrong". After he had proved that the worker sells to the capitalist not his labour but his labour power Marx used more precise terms. In later works Marx and Engels used the terms "value of labour power", "price of labour power", "sale of labour power" p. 100

71 *The Poverty of Philosophy. Answer to the "Philosophy of Poverty" by M. Proudhon* is one of the most important theoretical works of Marxism and Marx's principal work directed against P.-J. Proudhon, whom he regarded as an ideologist of the petty bourgeoisie. Marx decided that he must criticise Proudhon's economic and philosophical views and at the same time clear up a number of questions relating to the theory and tactics of the revolutionary proletarian movement from the scientific-materialist standpoint at the end of 1846, as a result of his reading Proudhon's *Système des contradictions économiques, ou Philosophie de la misère*, which had appeared a short time earlier. In his letter of December 28, 1846 to the Russian man of letters P. V. Annenkov Marx expounded a number of important ideas which later formed the core of his book against Proudhon. In January 1847, as can be judged from Engels' letter of January 15, 1847 to Marx, the latter was already working on his reply to Proudhon. In writing this book Marx extensively used notes he had made in 1845-47 from works by various authors, primarily economists. (A description of Marx's notebooks was published in Marx/Engels, *Gesamtausgabe*, Erste Abteilung, Bd. 6, Berlin, 1932.) By the beginning of April 1847 Marx's work was completed in the main and had gone to press (see this volume, p. 72). On June 15, 1847 he wrote a short foreword.

The book was published in Brussels and Paris early in July 1847. Marx's followers saw it as a theoretical substantiation of the platform of the proletarian party which was taking shape at the time. While establishing contact on behalf of this party in the autumn of 1847 with the French socialists and democrats grouped around the newspaper *La Réforme*, Engels, speaking to Louis Blanc, one of its editors, called Marx's book against Proudhon "our programme" (see Engels' letter to Marx of October 25-26, 1847). Ferdinand Wolff, a member of the Communist League, published a detailed review of *The Poverty of Philosophy* in *Das Westphälische Dampfboot* for January and February 1848.

The book was not republished in full during Marx's lifetime. Excerpts from §5 ("Strikes and Combinations of Workers") of Ch. II appeared in different years, mostly between 1872 and 1875, in workers' and socialist publications such as *La Emancipacion, Der Volksstaat, Social-Demokrat* (New York) and others. In 1880 Marx attempted to publish his *Poverty of Philosophy* in the French socialist newspaper *L'Égalité*, the organ of the French Workers' Party, but only the foreword and §1 ("The Opposition Between Use Value and Exchange Value") of Ch. I were published.

The first German edition was made in 1885. The translation was edited by Engels, who also wrote a special preface and a number of notes to it. He mentioned in the preface that while editing the translation he had taken into account corrections made in Marx's hand in a copy of the 1847 French edition. (This copy, which contains also numerous underlinings and vertical lines in the margins, is kept in the library of the North-Eastern University at Sendai, Japan; and a photocopy was presented by Japanese scholars to the Institute of Marxism-Leninism in Moscow.) It is still not known when Marx made these corrections and alterations. But it was certainly prior to 1876, as a copy presented by Marx to Natalia Utina, wife of N. I. Utin, a member of the Russian Section of the First International, on January 1, 1876 is extant in which almost all of these corrections and alterations are reproduced in an unknown hand.

In 1886, the Russian Marxist Emancipation of Labour group published the first Russian edition of *The Poverty of Philosophy* in a translation made by Vera Zasulich from the German edition of 1885. In 1892 a second German edition appeared. It was provided with a short preface by Engels, dealing with corrections of certain inaccuracies in the text (see Note 75). Engels planned a second French edition for the mid-eighties. With this aim in view he made a list of necessary corrections to be inserted ("Notes et changements") using for this purpose the copy bearing the corrections in Marx's hand. However, this plan was implemented only after Engels' death by Marx's daughter Laura Lafargue in 1896. The corrections were made in the text according to the list drawn up by Engels.

In the present edition all corrections and changes made by Marx in the copy of the 1847 edition and reproduced in the copy presented to Natalia Utina, as well as the relevant corrections in the German 1885 and 1892 editions and in the French 1896 edition, have been taken into account. The changes affecting meaning and the stylistic improvements made in these copies and editions are introduced in the text itself, the original version being given in a footnote. Where the author's corrections and remarks are intended to revise or give greater precision to the original formulations and terminology, owing to the further development of Marxist economic theory, they are given in footnotes, the original text being left unaltered. This will enable readers to appreciate actual level attained by Marxist economic theory by 1847.

Italics in quotations are as a rule Marx's. In some cases the editors have inserted periods to indicate an omission by Marx in quotations and give in square brackets page references which are not in the original. References in square brackets are made to pages in the following English editions of works of English authors quoted by Marx from French translations: D. Ricardo. *On the Principles of Political Economy, and Taxation.* Third edition. London, 1821; A. Smith. *An Inquiry into the Nature and Causes of the Wealth of Nations.* Vol. I, London, 1835; Ch. Babbage. *On the Economy of Machinery and Manufactures.* Second edition. London, 1832; A. Ferguson. *An Essay on the History of Civil Society.* Edinburgh, 1767; J. M. Lauderdale. *An Inquiry into the Nature and Origin of Public Wealth.* Edinburgh, 1804; J. Steuart. *An Inquiry into the Principles of Political Œconomy...* Vol. I, London, 1767; A. Ure. *The Philosophy of Manufactures...*, Second edition. London, 1835.

The first English edition of *The Poverty of Philosophy* was published in London in 1900 by the Twentieth Century press. The translation was made by Harry Quelch. Since then the work has been republished several times in English. p. 105

72 The reference is to the period which followed the termination of the Napoleonic wars in 1815 and the restoration of the Bourbon dynasty in France. p. 121

73 See present edition, Vol. 3, pp. 424-31, 440-43 and Vol. 4, pp. 375-88. p. 125

74 See Note 70. p. 127

75 The 1847 edition and the German 1885 edition mistakenly have the name of Hopkins, and lower an inexact date of publication of W. Thompson's book (1827 instead of 1824). This served as a pretext for the Austrian economist Anton Menger to reproach Marx with wrong quoting (see A. Menger, *Das Recht auf den vollen Arbeitsertrag in geschichtlicher Darstellung,* Stuttgart, 1886, S. 50). Engels corrected the mistakes by writing in the preface to the second German edition of *The Poverty of Philosophy* in 1892 the following: "For the second edition I have only to remark that the name wrongly written Hopkins in the French text has been replaced by the correct name Hodgskin and that in the same place the date of the work of William Thompson has been corrected to 1824. It is to be hoped that this will appease the bibliographical conscience of Professor Anton Menger. London, March 29, 1892. Frederick Engels." p. 138

76 The *Ten-Hours' Bill* was submitted to Parliament several times. In 1847 after a prolonged struggle the Bill was passed, and applied only to children and women. However, many factory owners ignored it. p. 143

77 *Equitable-labour-exchange bazaars* were organised by Owenites and Ricardian socialists (John Gray, William Thompson, John Bray) in various towns of England in the 1830s for fair exchange without a capitalist intermediary. The products were exchanged for labour notes, or labour money, certificates showing the cost of the products delivered, calculated on the basis of the amount of labour necessary for their production. The organisers considered these bazaars as a means for publicising the advantages of a non-capitalist form of exchange and a peaceful way—together with cooperatives—of transition to socialism. The subsequent and invariable bankruptcy of such enterprises proved their utopian character p. 144

78 The reference is to the following passage from Adam Smith's work, *An Inquiry into the Nature and Causes of the Wealth of Nations*: "In a tribe of hunters or shepherds a particular person makes bows and arrows, for example, with more readiness and dexterity than any other. He frequently exchanges them for cattle or for venison with his companions; and he finds at last that he can in this manner get more cattle and venison, than if he himself went to the field to catch them. From a regard to his own interest, therefore, the making of bows and arrows grows to be his chief business, and he becomes a sort of armourer." (Vol. I, Book I, Chapter II.) p. 147

79 Marx refers to the first edition of Cooper's book. In his notebook dating to July-August 1845, this passage is quoted from a second enlarged edition published in London in 1831. p. 153

80 The full text of the passage from Hegel's *Wissenschaft der Logik* quoted here is as follows: "Die Methode ist deswegen als die ohne Einschränkung allgemeine, innerliche und äußerliche Weise, und als die schlechthin unendliche Kraft anzuerkennen,

welcher kein Objekt, insofern es sich als ein Äußerliches, der Vernunft fernes und von ihr unabhängiges präsentiert—Widerstand leisten, gegen sie von einer besonderen Natur seyn und von ihr nicht durchdrungen werden könnte.... Sie ist darum die höchste *Kraft* oder vielmehr die *einzige* und absolute *Kraft* der Vernunft, nicht nur, sondern auch ihr höchster und *einziger* Trieb, *durch sich selbst in Allem sich selbst zu finden und zu erkennen.*" (Bd. III, Abschnitt 3, Kap. 3). p. 164

81 Marx refers to Chapter VIII "De la responsabilité de l'homme et de dieu, sous la loi de contradiction, ou solution du problème de la providence". p. 173

82 *Le Creusot* (Burgundy)—since the 1830s a big centre of the French metallurgical, machine-building and war industry; at the time referred to, the Creusot works belonged to Schneider and Co. founded in 1836. p. 182

83 The reference is to the first cyclic crisis of overproduction which began in England in 1825. The crisis involved all branches of industry, textiles in particular. It was followed by stagnation in trade, reduction of exports by 16 per cent and imports by 15 per cent and the insolvency of several banks. p. 188

84 *In partibus infidelium*—beyond the realm of reality (literally "in the country of infidels")—an addition to the title of Catholic priests appointed to a purely nominal diocese in non-Christian countries. p. 192

85 Quoting from the French edition of J. Steuart's book published in 1789 (the first English edition: J. Steuart. *An Inquiry into the Principles of Political Œconomy, being an Essay on the Science of Domestic Policy in Free Nations* was published in two volumes in London in 1767), Marx made some explanatory additions and changes. Thus he added the words "impôt sur la production" (taxes on production), "impôts sur la consommation" (taxes on consumption) and the last sentence: "Chacun est imposé à raison de la dépense qu'il fait" (Everyone is taxed according to his expenditure). He changed the place of the sentence "Chacun est imposé à raison du profit qu'il est censé faire" (Everyone is taxed in proportion to the gain he is supposed to make), which Steuart has after "Ainsi le monarque met un impôt sur l'industrie" (Thus the monarch imposes a tax upon industry). Instead of "le gouvernement limité" Marx used "le gouvernement constitutionnel". p. 196

86 See notes 28 and 47. p. 208

87 In 1836-38 a new cyclic crisis of overproduction swept over Britain and other capitalist countries. p. 208

88 In 1824 under mass pressure Parliament repealed the ban on the trade unions. However, in 1825 it passed a Bill on workers' combinations, which confirming the repeal of the ban on the trade unions at the same time greatly restricted their activity. In particular, mere agitation for workers to join unions and take part in strikes was regarded as "compulsion" and "violence" and punished as a crime. p. 209

89 The laws in operation at that time in France—the so-called Le Chapelier law adopted in 1791 during the bourgeois revolution by the Constituent Assembly, and the penal code elaborated under the Napoleonic empire in 1810 (Code pénal)—forbade workers to form labour unions or go on strike under pain of severe punishment. The prohibition of trade unions in France was abolished only in 1884. p. 209

90 The *National Association of United Trades* was established in England in 1845 by trade union delegates from London, Manchester, Sheffield, Norwich, Hull, Bristol, and

other cities. Its activity was limited to the struggle for improved conditions of sale of labour power ("a fair wage for a fair day's work") and for improved factory legislation. The association existed until the early sixties, but it ceased to play any big part in the trade union movement after 1851. p. 210

91 The term "instruments of production" is still used by Marx in a broader sense here than in his later works. Subsequently he drew a more strict distinction between "forces of production" in general and "instruments of production" as a component part of the former. p. 211

92 Engels had in mind first of all Ferdinand Lassalle who widely used the term "workers' estate" in his writings, in particular in his pamphlet *Arbeiterprogramm* (Workers' Programme) published in 1862. The substitution of the terms "workers" or "fourth estate" for "working class" was characteristic of a number of other representatives of petty-bourgeois socialism. p. 212

93 See Note 50. p. 213

94 The reference is to the conservative majority in the French Chamber of Deputies who supported Guizot.

Further on Engels used materials published in *Le Moniteur Universel* for June 4, 18, 23 and 26, 1847. p. 214

95 See Note 47. p. 217

96 This article was written by Marx in reply to the propaganda of feudal and Christian socialism carried on by the conservative Prussian newspaper *Rheinischer Beobachter*. This propaganda was aimed at diverting the popular masses from revolutionary struggle against the absolutist regime and at using them in the struggle against the bourgeois opposition. Such ideas permeated, in particular, the article criticised by Marx, which was published anonymously in the *Rheinischer Beobachter* No. 206, July 25, 1847 as the eighth part in the series *Politische Gänge*. On September 2, 1847 this article was reprinted in the *Deutsche-Brüsseler-Zeitung* without a title but with introductory words quoted by Marx. It is probable that the author of this article was Herr Wagener, a consistorial councillor in Magdeburg, subsequently a conservative leader, who enjoyed the protection of the Prussian Minister of Religious Worship, Education and Medicine, Eichhorn.

Later, in the mid-sixties, while exposing Lassalleans' advances to Bismarck's Government, Marx and Engels referred to this article by Marx as a document demonstrating the firm standpoint of the workers' party in relation to "royal-Prussian government socialism" (see Statement by Marx and Engels to the editorial board of the newspaper *Social-Demokrat*, February 23, 1865).

The article "The Communism of the *Rheinischer Beobachter*" bore the sign instead of a signature. The publication of this article and also of the first part of Engels' essays "German Socialism in Verse and Prose" (see this volume, pp. 220-49) marked the beginning of Marx's and Engels' regular contribution to the newspaper of the German emigrants, the *Deutsche-Brüsseler-Zeitung*. A special editorial note in the preceding issue of the newspaper of September 9, 1847 announced the forthcoming publication of these articles without mentioning, however, the authors' names. Prior to this, Marx and Engels contributed only occasionally to the *Deutsche-Brüsseler-Zeitung* (see this volume, pp. 72-74, 92-95), though they approved their associates—Wilhelm Wolff and Georg Weerth and others—doing so. Prior to their regular contribution the paper followed mainly the line of its editor-in-chief, the petty-bourgeois democrat Adalbert Bornstedt, who tried to combine eclectically various oppositional ideological trends. But by the autumn of 1847 the influence of the proletarian revolutionaries in the paper gained momentum and soon it became a mouthpiece of the proletarian party which was being organised at the time, in fact the organ of the Communist League.

An excerpt from this article was published in English in K. Marx and F. Engels, *On Religion*, Foreign Languages Publishing House, Moscow, 1957. p. 220

97 See Note 51. p. 225

98 In his speech from the throne at the opening of the United Diet in Prussia on April 11, 1847, Frederick William IV declared that he would never let the "natural relations between the monarch and the people" turn into "conditioned, constitutional" relations and a "written sheet of paper" be a substitute for a "genuine sacred loyalty". p. 232

99 Under this common title two essays by Engels were published in the *Deutsche-Brüsseler-Zeitung* in which he analysed the poetry and literary-critical work and also the aesthetic views of representatives of "true socialism". The first essay dealt with Karl Beck's book, *Lieder vom armen Mann* (Songs of the Poor Man), published at the end of November 1845 as a sample of the poetry of "true socialism". There are grounds for assuming that Engels' essay on Beck may initially have been included as Chapter 3, the manuscript of which is not extant, in Volume II of *The German Ideology* (see present edition, Vol. 5). This work was most probably written in the first half of 1846 in Brussels.

The second essay analysed Karl Grün's book, *Über Göthe vom menschlichen Standpunkte* (About Goethe from the Human Point of View), published at the end of April 1846, as a sample of the prose or literary critique of "true socialism". Engels' letter of January 15, 1847 to Marx shows that he intended to revise it for Volume II of *The German Ideology* (judging by its contents it was to follow Chapter 4 devoted to the analysis of Karl Grün's book: *Die soziale Bewegung in Frankreich und Belgien*, Darmstadt, 1845 [The Social Movement in France and Belgium] as a sample of the historiography of "true socialism"). This essay was most probably written by Engels after he had moved from Brussels to Paris, i.e., between August 15, 1846 and January 15, 1847. p. 235

100 The words "Wahrheit und Recht, Freiheit und Gesetz" (Truth and Right, Freedom and Law) were used as an epigraph to the progressive German newspaper *Leipziger Allgemeine Zeitung*, banned in Prussia in 1842, and in Saxony early in 1843. p 236

101 *Restoration*—see Note 72.

Carbonari—see Note 29. The carbonari held their meetings under the guise of charcoal sales (Ventes). p. 237

102 *Ventrus*— representatives of the "belly" of the French Chamber (see Note 94). p. 238

103 An allusion to "Young Germany"—a literary group which appeared in Germany in the 1830s and was under the influence of Heinrich Heine and Ludwig Börne. The group included such writers as Gutzkow, Wienbarg, Mundt, Laube and Jung, whose stories and articles voiced the opposition sentiments of petty-bourgeois and intellectual advocates of freedom of conscience and the press, the introduction of a constitution, emancipation of women, etc. Some of them advocated granting civil

rights to Jews. Their political views were vague and inconsistent; most of them soon became ordinary liberals. p. 243

104 The reference is to a spontaneous rising of textile workers in Prague in the latter half of June 1844. The events in Prague led to workers' uprisings in many other industrial centres of Bohemia. The workers' movement, which was accompanied by factory and machine wrecking, was suppressed by government troops. p. 244

105 The *Friends of Light* was a religious trend opposed to the pietism predominant in the official church and supported by Junker circles. p. 248

106 The first edition of P. H. Holbach's *Système de la nature, ou des loix du monde physique et du monde moral* (London 1770) bore, for conspirational reasons, the name of the Secretary of the French Academy J. B. Mirabaud, who died in 1760, as its author. p. 251

107 Joseph Addison's tragedy *Cato* was written in 1713; Goethe's *Leiden des jungen Werthers* in 1774. p. 252

108 The *Federal Decrees of 1819* (the Karlsbad decisions) were drawn up on the insistence of the Austrian Chancellor Metternich at the conference of the German Confederation in Karlsbad in August 1819 and were endorsed by the Federal Diet on September 20, 1819. These decisions envisaged a number of strict measures against the liberal press, the introduction of preliminary censorship in all German states, strict surveillance over universities, prohibition of students' societies, establishment of an investigation commission for the prosecution of participants in the oppositional movement (so-called demagogues). p. 253

109 *9 Thermidor*—see Note 3.

18 Brumaire—the coup d'état of November 9, 1799 which completed the bourgeois counter-revolution and led to the personal rule of General Napoleon Bonaparte. p. 253

110 In one of the scenes in Goethe's comedy *Der Bürgergeneral* a rural barber who pretended he was a Jacobin general drank a jug of milk and thus angered the master of the house. p. 261

111 See Note 53. p. 266

112 *Ghibellines*—a political party in Italy formed in the 12th century in the period of strife between the popes and the German emperors. It included mostly feudal lords who supported the emperors and furiously opposed the papal party of the *Guelphs*, which represented the upper trade and artisan strata of Italian towns. The parties existed till the 15th century. Dante, who hoped that the emperor's rule would help to overcome the feudal dismemberment of Italy, joined the party of the Ghibellines in 1302. p. 271

113 The International Congress of Economists held in Brussels on September 16-18, 1847 discussed the attitude towards the movement for the repeal of trade restrictions between individual countries started by the British Anti-Corn Law League (see Note 47).

The Communist League members headed by Marx attended the congress, intending to use it for open criticism of bourgeois economics and for defence of working-class interests.

Marx's name was put on the official list of the congress participants (see *Journal des économistes*, t. XVIII, October 1847, p. 275).

During the congress a sharp controversy arose between the bourgeois majority and a group of Brussels Communists, especially after Georg Weerth's speech criticising the free traders' statements about the benefits of free trade to the working class. The organisers of the congress did not let Marx make his speech and closed the discussion. In reply to this Marx and Engels and their followers carried on the polemic with bourgeois economists in the democratic and proletarian press. p. 274

114 An allusion to the fulfilment of Bentham's will by John Bowring (Bentham bequeathed his body for use for scientific purposes). p. 277

115 The report on other sittings of the congress was not published in the *Deutsche-Brüsseler-Zeitung*. On these see Engels' article "The Free Trade Congress at Brussels" (this volume, pp. 282-90). p. 278

116 This work is a part of a speech Marx intended to deliver at the International Congress of Economists in Brussels on September 18, 1847. Not being allowed to do so, Marx rewrote it for the press and sent it to a number of Belgian newspapers. It was published only in the *Atelier Démocratique*, September 29, 1847 in French. Announcing the publication of this article the *Deutsche-Brüsseler-Zeitung* wrote on October 7, 1847: "Unfortunately, not a single big Belgian newspaper had the courage or intelligence to print the speech sent to it." Extant are only a preliminary draft of the speech bearing the author's heading "Protectionists" (see this volume, p. 573) and the German translation of its beginning published in Hamm in 1848 by J. Weydemeyer, a friend of Marx and Engels, together with another speech by Marx on the freedom of trade (see this volume, pp. 450-65). Weydemeyer omitted the end of the speech saying that it was repeated in the speech of January 9.

Engels gives the content of Marx's speech in his article "The Free Trade Congress at Brussels" (see this volume, pp. 282-90). p. 279

117 See Note 47. p. 283

118 The full text of Weerth's speech (Engels quotes parts of it word for word, and gives a free account of others) was published in a number of newspapers, in particular, in French (the language in which it was delivered) in the *Atelier Démocratique* and in German in *Die Ameise* (Grimma) on October 15, 1847. The text published in *Die Ameise* is reproduced in the book: Georg Weerth, *Sämtliche Werke*, Zweiter Band, Berlin, 1956, S. 128-33. In some places the text differs from the passages cited by Engels. Apparently Engels recorded facts more exactly; in particular, in the first passage cited by him he corrected the number of the English proletariat (5 million instead of 3 million as in Weerth), and in the second passage the date on which the Chartists concluded an agreement with the free traders (1845 instead of 1843). p. 283

119 The reference is to provocations on the part of the Anti-Corn Law League which sought to use for its own ends the workers' unrest in the industrial districts of England in August 1842. (On the general strike of 1842 see Note 10.) The free traders encouraged the workers' action during the first stage of the strike hoping to direct their movement towards the struggle for the repeal of the Corn Laws. However, the independent class and political character which this strike assumed as it became general led to the direct and active participation of the free trade bourgeoisie in suppressing the movement. p. 285

120 See Note 46. p. 285

121 This refers to the movement for Parliamentary reform in England in 1830-31, to the July revolution of 1830 in France and the revolution of 1830-31 in Belgium which led to the separation of Belgium from Holland. p. 285

122 The reference is to the brutal suppression of workers' risings in Lyons in 1831 and 1834 and to atrocities perpetrated by government troops against starving workers in Buzançais (Indre Department) who had looted corn shipments and storehouses belonging to profiteers early in 1847. p. 285

123 On the precision subsequently given by Marx and Engels to these terms which express the relations between the worker and the capitalist, see Note 70. p. 289

124 The two articles by Engels against Karl Heinzen were written in reply to this petty-bourgeois democrat's slanderous attacks against the Communists and communism as a social trend. In particular, the Polemik column of the *Deutsche-Brüsseler-Zeitung* No. 77 for September 26, 1847 contained Heinzen's statement in which, among other things, he accused the Communists of seeking to split the German revolutionary movement. Heinzen used as a pretext an editorial note in No. 73 of the *Deutsche-Brüsseler-Zeitung*, September 12, 1847, in which, while refuting the allegation of a certain German newspaper that the article "Der deutsche Hunger und die deutschen Fürsten" published in the *Deutsche-Brüsseler-Zeitung* (No. 49, June 20, 1847) was of a communist character, the editors pointed out that the author of the said article was Heinzen who "as is known ... repeatedly attacked communism". Publishing Heinzen's reply to this note, Adalbert Bornstedt, the paper's editor-in-chief, instead of refuting the insinuations it contained called for appeasement between "various shades of German revolutionaries abroad"; in particular he wrote on behalf of the editors: "We consider it our duty to advise both parties in case polemic arises in some other place to give it up."

As is seen from Engels' letter of September 30, 1847 to Marx the first article with a reply to Heinzen was submitted to the *Deutsche-Brüsseler-Zeitung* on September 27. However, Bornstedt, despite his agreement with Marx and Engels on their regularly contributing to the paper, did not publish Engels' article in the next issue (No. 78) on the pretext of lack of space. Compelled to publish it in No. 79 on October 3, 1847 in the Polemik column he again repeated in the editorial note his appeal to both parties to avoid mutual accusations. p. 291

125 Heinzen visualised the future Germany as a republican federation of autonomous lands, similar to the Swiss Confederation. This was the meaning given by many petty-bourgeois democrats to the slogan of German unity, the symbol of which was the black-red-and-gold banner. Marx and Engels considered such an interpretation of the slogan inconsistent with the struggle against the survivals of medieval seclusion and political disunity. To oppose this they put forward the demand of a single, centralised democratic republic of Germany. p. 293

126 Engels enumerates some major peasant rebellions of the Middle Ages: the rebellions of Wat Tyler (1381) and Jack Cade (1450) in England, the peasant revolt in France in 1358 (Jacquerie) and the peasant war in Germany (1524-25). In later years as a result of studying the history of the peasant struggle against feudalism and drawing on the experience of revolutionary actions of the peasantry during the revolution of 1848-49 Engels changed his estimate of the peasant movements' character. In *The Peasant War in Germany* (1850) and other works he showed the

revolutionary liberation character of peasant revolts and their role in shaking the foundations of feudalism. p. 295

127 The *Illuminati* (from the Latin *illuminatus*)—members of a secret society founded in Bavaria in 1776, a variety of Freemasonry. The society consisted of oppositional elements from the bourgeoisie and nobility, who were dissatisfied with princely despotism. At the same time a characteristic feature of this society was the fear of the democratic movement, reflected in the rules, which made rank-and-file members blind tools of their leaders. In 1785 the society was banned by the Bavarian authorities. Similar societies existed also in Spain and France. p. 303

128 With this article Engels began contributing to the newspaper of the French republican democrats and petty-bourgeois socialists *La Réforme.* Determined to use the French radical press to spread communist ideas and to promote international unity of revolutionary proletarian and democratic circles in the European countries, Engels established close contacts with the editors of *La Réforme* in the autumn of 1847. In his letter to Marx of October [25-]26, 1847 he wrote that he had made arrangements with Ferdinand Flocon, one of the editors, for the weekly publication of an article on the situation in England. Engels intended to popularise in France the Chartist movement and the material from the Chartist press, primarily *The Northern Star.* The article Engels proposed to Flocon (at first it was intended for Flocon's personal information) was published, as Engels himself stated, without any alterations.

After this the newspaper carried almost every week Engels' articles or summaries of *The Northern Star* reports on the Chartist movement which he translated into French. These summaries, as a rule, bore no title. Sometimes they were published in the column "The Chartist Movement", or "The Chartist Agitation", and usually began with the words "They write from London...". Engels contributed to *La Réforme* up to January 1848. Despite differences in views with the editors (in particular Louis Blanc and Alexandre-Auguste Ledru-Rollin), Engels' articles and his propaganda of Chartism helped to overcome to some extent this paper's national exclusiveness and had a revolutionising influence on its readers—the French working class and radical-minded middle sections. p. 307

129 The intended publication of the Chartist daily newspaper *Democrat* did not materialise. p. 308

130 Only a narrow circle of persons with electoral qualifications took part in the ballot (see Note 46). p. 308

131 On the general strike in England in 1842, see Note 10. p. 309

132 The editors of *L'Atelier* prefaced Engels' article with the following note: "A German worker who has been living in England for a long time has sent us a letter we are giving below concerning one of the articles which was published last month. We hasten to print this letter which deserves being printed for a number of reasons."

On his contacts with *L'Atelier* editors who were under the influence of Christian socialism Engels wrote to Marx on October [25-]26, 1847 in connection with the publication of this article: "I was ... at *L'Atelier*. I brought a correction to my article on the English workers in the last issue.... These gentlemen were very cordial.... They kept on suggesting to me to contribute. However, I shall agree only in the last resort...."

This article was published in English in Karl Marx and Frederick Engels, *Articles on Britain*, Progress Publishers, Moscow, 1971. p. 310

[133] The work is a continuation of the polemic with Karl Heinzen. The latter replied to Engels (see this volume, pp. 291-306) with a long article "Ein 'Repräsentant' der Kommunisten" full of rude abuse of his opponent and of the theory of scientific communism in general (Marx ironically called this article "Heinzen's Manifesto Against the Communists"). After the publication of this article in full in the *Deutsche-Brüsseler-Zeitung* (No. 84, October 21, 1847) Bornstedt, the editor of the newspaper, again appealed to the contending parties to take the polemic elsewhere as the newspaper could not afford to publish such long articles. However, the editorial board had to agree to publish Marx's reply to Heinzen in full. When they began to publish the reply in No.86 on October 28, 1847 the editors even censured Heinzen in an editorial note for the harsh tone of his attacks. On November 14, before the whole of Marx's article had appeared, the editors published a special note in answer to Heinzen's attempt to continue the polemic: "We refuse to publish in the *Deutsche-Brüseller-Zeitung* Heinzen's letter of November 1 from Geneva in which he attacks the editorial board of this paper in an infamous way and tries to involve the paper and Karl Marx, for his first article in No. 86, without waiting for the continuation, in a vile private squabble. We declare that this is the way we shall deal with Heinzen's subsequent letters, despite his philistine assertions that he has a right to use our paper to express his views. We shall reply to possible public accusations in the proper time and place if we deem it necessary."

Marx's work was published in the Polemik column in several issues. There were some editorial notes to the first part of it (to the expression "grobian literature", literary personages "Solomon and Marcolph", "goose preacher"). Subsequently, however, author's notes were provided. Nos. 92 and 94 of November 18 and 25, 1847 contained errata. All the corrections, some of which are author's improvements, have been taken into account in the present edition.

This work was published in English abridged in K. Marx, *Selected Essays*, Parsons, London, 1926. p. 312

[134] This note (to the title of the second instalment of the article) published in the *Deutsche-Brüsseler-Zeitung* No. 87, October 31, 1847 was evidently written by Marx in reply to the editorial appeal to the contending parties (see Note 133) to abstain from private polemics. p. 313

[135] Here and below Marx cites Shakespeare from August Schlegel and Ludwig Tieck's edition: *Shakspeare's dramatische Werke*, Th. 1-9, Berlin, 1825-33. p. 313

[136] *Communes*—self-governing urban communities in medieval France and Italy. For their description see Engels' note to the 1888 English edition and the 1890 German edition of the *Manifesto of the Communist Party* (this volume, p. 486). p. 320

[137] By the *German war of liberation* is meant the struggle for liberation from Napoleonic rule in 1813-14 (for more details, see Note 22). In this war as well as in the campaign of 1815, after Napoleon's short-lived restoration, the German states, including Austria and Prussia, which were members of the Holy Alliance (see Note 24), fought against Napoleonic France in the 6th anti-French coalition, the main organiser of which was Britain. p. 320

[138] Marx refers to the "true Levellers" or "Diggers" who broke away from the democratic republican Levellers' movement during the English bourgeois revolution of the mid-17th century. Representing the poorest sections of the population and suffering from feudal and capitalist exploitation in town and countryside, the Diggers, in contrast to the rest of the Levellers, who defended private property,

carried on propaganda for community of property and other ideas of egalitarian communism, attempting to establish common ownership of the land through collective ploughing of communal waste land. p. 321

139 On the struggle of the English bourgeoisie against the Corn Laws, see Note 47. p. 322

140 Marx cites the report of the commission under the chairmanship of William Morris Meredith to investigate the operation of the Poor Law. The report submitted to the Pennsylvania Congress on January 29, 1825 was published in *The Register of Pennsylvania* on August 16, 1828. p. 323

141 Apparently Marx is citing the following edition: Th. Cooper, *Lectures on the Elements of Political Economy*, London, 1831. (The first edition was published in Columbia in 1826.) This is proved by the coincidence of the pages referred to and the relevant passages in the above-mentioned edition, and also by the excerpts copied out by Marx (including the passage cited) in his preparatory notebooks (see *MEGA*, Abt. I, Bd. 6, Berlin 1932, S. 604). p. 324

142 See Note 38. p. 324

143 The reference is to the failure of the Peasant War in Germany (1524-25)p. 326

144 *Thirty Years' War, 1618-48*—a European war, in which the Pope, the Spanish and Austrian Hapsburgs and the Catholic German princes rallied under the banner of Catholicism fought the Protestant countries: Bohemia, Denmark, Sweden, the Republic of the Netherland and a number of German states which had become Protestant. The rulers of Catholic France—rivals of the Hapsburgs—supported the Protestant camp. Germany was the main arena of this struggle, the object of plunder and territorial claims. The Treaty of Westphalia concluded in 1648 sealed the dismemberment of Germany. p. 327

145 The *September laws* promulgated by the French government in September 1835, restricted the rights of jury courts and introduced severe measures against the press. They provided for increased money deposits for periodical publications and introduced imprisonment and large fines for publishing attacks on private property and the existing political system. The enactment of these laws in conditions of the constitutional July monarchy which had formally proclaimed freedom of the press, emphasised the anti-democratic nature of the bourgeois system. p. 331

146 *Fontanel*—an artificial ulcer practised in medieval medicine for the discharge of harmful tumours from the body. p. 331

147 The reference is to the uprising of the Silesian weavers on June 4-6, 1844—the first big class battle between the proletariat and the bourgeoisie in Germany, which assumed the greatest scope in the Silesian villages of Langenbielau and Peterswaldau, and to the uprising of the Bohemian workers in the second half of June 1844. (On this see Note 104.) p. 332

148 The reference is to the appeals for unity of all Germans against the German monarchs in the name of bourgeois freedoms and constitutional reforms, which were advanced by the participants in the Hambach festival—a political event that took place near the castle of Hambach in the Bavarian Palatinate on May 27, 1832. p. 332

149 Movement for the repeal of the Corn Laws—see Note 47. On the election of the Chartist leader Feargus O'Connor to Parliament—see Note 46. p. 333

150 The reference to Mably is not exact: the draft constitution for the Corsicans was drawn up by Rousseau and not by Mably. (J. J. Rousseau, *Lettres sur la législation de la Corse*, Paris, 1765). Mably, as well as Rousseau, drew up the draft constitution for the Poles. (G. Mably, "Du gouvernement et des lois de Pologne" in: *Collection complète des œuvres*, t. 8, Paris, 1794 à 1795.) p. 334

151 An allusion to the conduct of the representatives of the party of the big bourgeoisie—the Girondists—after they had been removed from government and the Jacobins established their dictatorship in France following the popular uprising of May 31-June 2, 1793. In the summer of the same year the Girondists rose in revolt against the Jacobin government to defend the rights of the departments to autonomy and federation. After the revolt had been suppressed many Girondist leaders (Barbaroux among them) were sentenced by the revolutionary tribunal and executed. p. 335

152 *Le Comité de salut public* (The Committee of Public Safety) established by the Convention on April 6, 1793 during the Jacobin dictatorship (June 2, 1793-July 27, 1794) was the leading revolutionary government body in France. It lasted till October 26, 1795. p. 335

153 The reference is to the stories for children written by the German pedagogue J. H. Campe, in particular his book *Die Entdeckung von Amerika*, a section of which was devoted to the Peruvian Incas and the Spanish conquest of Peru. p. 336

154 An allusion to articles which appeared in the *Allgemeine Zeitung*, distorting the ideas of utopian communism and socialism and attempting to ascribe communist views to the radical organs of the German press. Marx exposed this attempt in his article "Communism and the Augsburg *Allgemeine Zeitung*" published in the *Rheinische Zeitung* of October 16, 1842 (see present edition, Vol. 1). p. 337

155 Engels' work *Principles of Communism* reflects the next stage in the elaboration of the programme of the Communist League following the "Draft of a Communist Confession of Faith". This new version of the programme was worked out by Engels on the instructions of the Paris circle authority of the Communist League. The decision was adopted after Engels' sharp criticism at the committee meeting, on October 22, 1847, of the draft programme drawn up by the "true socialist" M. Hess, which was then rejected.

Comparison of the text of the *Principles of Communism* with that of the "Draft of a Communist Confession of Faith" proves that the document written by Engels at the end of October 1847 is a revised version of the Draft discussed at the First Congress of the Communist League. The first six points of the Draft were completely revised. Engels had felt compelled at that time to make some concessions in them to the as yet immature views of the League of the Just leaders. Some of these points were omitted in the *Principles*, others substantially changed and put in a different order. In the rest the arrangement of both documents coincides, though there are several new questions in the *Principles*: 5, 6, 10-14, 19, 20 and 24-26.

The *Principles of Communism* constituted the immediate basis for the preliminary version of the *Communist Manifesto*. In his letter of November 23-24, 1847 to Marx Engels wrote about the advisability of drafting the programme in the form of a communist manifesto, rejecting the old form of a catechism. In writing the *Manifesto* the founders of Marxism used some propositions formulated in the *Principles of Communism*.

The *Principles of Communism* were published for the first time in English in *The Plebs-Magazine,* London, in July 1914-January 1915; a separate edition was put out in Chicago in 1925 (The Daily Workers Publishing C°), in subsequent years they were published several times together with the *Communist Manifesto.* p. 341

156 See Note 70. p. 341

157 The reference is to class-divided societies. Subsequently Engels thought it necessary to make special mention of the fact that in their works written in the 1840s, while touching upon the problem of class antagonisms and class struggle in history, Marx and he made no mention of the primitive classless stage of human development because the history of that stage had as yet been but little studied. (See Engels' note to the English edition of the *Communist Manifesto,* 1888, this volume, p. 482). p. 341

158 In the Appendix to the 1887 American edition of *The Condition of the Working Class in England* (first published in 1845) and also in the Preface to the English edition and in the Preface to the Second German edition (1892), Engels wrote about the recurrence of crises: "The recurring period of the great industrial crisis is stated in the text as five years. This was the period apparently indicated by the course of events from 1825 to 1842. But the industrial history from 1842 to 1868 has shown that the real period is one of ten years; that the intermediate revulsions were secondary, and tended more and more to disappear." p. 347

159 The conclusion that the victory of the proletarian revolution was possible only simultaneously in the advanced capitalist countries, and hence impossible in one country alone, first made by Marx and Engels in *The German Ideology* (see present edition, Vol. 5, Ch. I, 2[5]) and most definitely formulated in the *Principles of Communism,* was arrived at in the period of pre-monopoly capitalism. However, in their later works Marx and Engels found it necessary to give this proposition a more flexible form stressing the fact that a proletarian revolution should be understood as a considerably prolonged and complex process which could develop initially in several main capitalist countries. See, for example, K. Marx, "Revelations about the Cologne Trial" (1853), Marx's letter of February 12, 1870 to Engels and Engels' letter of September 12, 1882 to Kautsky. Under new historical conditions, Lenin, proceeding from the law of the uneven economic and political development of capitalism in the era of imperialism, came to the conclusion that the socialist revolution could first triumph either in only a few countries or even in a single country. This conclusion was first formulated by Lenin in his article "On the Slogan of the United States of Europe" (1915). p. 352

160 See Note 38. p. 356

161 This article, written by Engels for *La Réforme* was reprinted in *The Northern Star* No. 524, November 6, 1847 with the following editorial introduction: "The following article, translated from the *Réforme,* the most able of the French journals, and a consistent supporter of the rights of labour in all countries, will cheer the working classes of England with the proud consolation, that henceforth the battle of universal liberty is not to be confined within the limits of our Sea-bound dungeon". p. 358

162 The reference is to the Chartist Land Cooperative Society founded on the initiative of O'Connor in 1845 (later the National Land Company, it lasted till 1848). The aim of the Society was to buy plots of land with the money collected and to lease them to worker shareholders on easy terms. Among the positive

aspects of the Society's activity were its petitions to Parliament and printed propaganda against the aristocracy's monopoly on land. However, the idea of liberating the workers from exploitation, of reducing unemployment, etc., by returning them to the land proved utopian. The Society's activity had no practical success.

Subsequently, in the "Third International Review" written in autumn 1850 Marx and Engels stressed that the failure of the Land Society was inevitable. They emphasised at the same time that for a while the workers could mistake O'Connor's project for a revolutionary measure only because objectively it was directed against big landownership and thus accorded with the tendency of bourgeois revolutions to break up the big landed estates; only the demand for nationalisation of land put forward somewhat later by the Chartists revolutionary wing (O'Brien, Ernest Jones and others) corresponded to the true interests of the working class (it was included into the Chartist programme of 1851).

Engels thought of sending a detailed report on the activities of the Land Society to *La Réforme* as can be seen from the second part of the article; but apparently he never wrote it, though he reproduced the content of petitions adopted later by this Society in his report "Chartist Agitation" (see this volume, pp. 412-14). p. 358

163 The *banquet in London* on October 25, 1847 was to celebrate the election of the Chartist leader Feargus O'Connor and a number of radicals to Parliament. The elections took place on August 5, 1847 in Nottingham. The account of the banquet used by Engels in this article was published in *The Northern Star* No. 523, October 30, 1847. p. 361

164 The demand for so-called *complete suffrage*, expressed vaguely in a way capable of varying interpretation, was proposed by the representatives of the English radical bourgeoisie in the early 1840s to counter the Chartist social and political programme laid down in the People's Charter and the Chartist petitions. Early in 1842 the radical J. Sturge, who was close to the free traders, tried to found a universal suffrage league in Birmingham with the aim of diverting the workers from revolutionary struggle for the Charter. However, the efforts of Sturge and his adherents to influence the Chartist movement and use it for their own ends were resolutely rebuffed by the Chartist revolutionary wing.

Later, however, the radicals went on trying to replace the Chartists' struggle for universal suffrage and fundamental reform of the parliamentary system with a movement for moderate parliamentary reforms. p. 361

165 The reference is to the July revolution of 1830 in France. p. 362

166 The *National Chartist Association*, founded in July 1840, was the first mass workers' party in the history of the working-class movement. In the years of its upsurge it numbered up to 50,000 members. It was headed by an Executive Committee which was re-elected at congresses and conferences of delegates. The Association initiated many political campaigns and Chartists' conventions. However, its work was hindered by lack of ideological and political unity and a certain organisational vagueness. After the defeat of the Chartists in 1848 and the ensuing split in their ranks the Association lost its mass character, but nevertheless under the leadership of the revolutionary Chartists waged a struggle for the revival of Chartism on a socialist basis. It ceased its activities in 1858. p. 362

167 On the parliamentary reform of 1831-32 in England see Note 33. p. 363

[168] The reference is to the Constitution of the French Republic adopted by the Convention during the Jacobins' revolutionary rule, the most democratic of bourgeois constitutions in the 18th and 19th centuries: it established the republican system, proclaimed freedom of the individual, of conscience, of the press, of petitioning, of legislative initiative, the right to education, social relief in case of inability, resistance to oppression. p. 363

[169] *The Northern Star* No. 523, October 30, 1847, published excerpts from Alphonse Lamartine's article "Déclaration de principes", originally printed in the newspaper *Le Bien Public* in Mâcon. p. 364

[170] See Note 18. p. 364

[171] The reference is to comments of the Paris newspapers *La Démocratie pacifique*, October 25 and 26, 1847, *La Presse*, October 24, 1847 and others on Lamartine's programme. p. 361

[172] This article was occasioned by the civil war in Switzerland unleashed by the seven economically backward Catholic cantons which in 1843 formed a separatist union —the Sonderbund—to resist progressive bourgeois reforms and defend the privileges of the church and the Jesuits. The reactionary actions of the Sonderbund headed by the Catholics and the city patricians were opposed by bourgeois radicals and liberals who in the mid-40s were in the majority in most of the cantons and in the Swiss Diet, the supreme legislative body of the Swiss Confederation. In July 1847 the Diet decreed the dissolution of the Sonderbund, and this served as a pretext for the latter to start hostilities against other cantons early in November. On November 23 the Sonderbund army was defeated by the Federal forces. As a result of this victory and the adoption of a new constitution in 1848, Switzerland, formerly a union of states, became a federal state.

The struggle between radicals on the one side and reactionary patriarchal patricians and clericals on the other attracted Engels' attention as early as 1844, when he described it in his article, "The Civil War in the Valais", published in *The Northern Star* No. 344, June 15, 1844 (see present edition, Vol. 3).

In the present article Engels contrasted modern civilisation to patriarchal backwardness, exposing the Swiss reactionaries and their attempts to link counter-revolutionary separatist aims with the historical traditions of the Swiss people. Engels considered Switzerland's past from this point of view. As a result he presented a somewhat distorted picture of certain periods of its history, particularly the struggle against Austria and Burgundy in the Middle Ages which was anti-feudal on the whole. In his later works of 1856-59 on the history of warfare ("Mountain Warfare", "Infantry", etc.) Engels showed the great historical significance of Switzerland's struggle for independence in the 14th and 15th centuries. Engels also changed his view of the peasants' role in Norway (in the article the stress was laid on their patriarchal traditions). In "Reply to Herr Paul Ernest" (1890) Engels pointed out in particular that the existence of free peasants who had not experienced serfdom had a positive effect on Norway's historical development though it was a backward country due to isolation and natural peculiarities. p 367

[173] In the battle of *Sempach* (Canton of Lucerne) on July 9, 1386 the Swiss defeated the Austrian troops of Prince Leopold III.

At *Murten* (Canton of Freiburg) on June 22, 1476 the Swiss defeated the troops of Carl the Bold, Duke of Burgundy. p. 367

174 Engels uses this term in relation to the mountain cantons which in the 13th and 14th centuries formed the nucleus of the Swiss Confederation. p. 367

175 The battle in the *Teutoburg Forest* (9 A.D.) ended in the rout of the Roman legions by the Germanic tribes who had risen against the Roman conquerors. p. 367

176 The battle of *Morgarten* between the Swiss volunteers and the troops of Leopold of Hapsburg on November 15, 1315 ended in victory for the volunteers.

Marathon, Plataea and *Salamis*—sites of important battles won by the Greeks during the wars between Greece and Persia (500-449 B.C.). p. 368

177 The *Grütli oath*—one of the legends woven round the foundation of the Swiss Confederation, the origin of which dates back to the agreement of the three mountain cantons of Schwyz, Uri and Unterwalden in 1291. According to this legend representatives of the three cantons met in 1307 in the Grütli (Rütli) meadow and took an oath of loyalty in the joint struggle against Austrian rule. p. 369

178 At *Granson* (Canton of Vaud), on March 2, 1476, the Swiss infantry defeated Carl the Bold, Duke of Burgundy. At *Nancy* (Lorraine), on January 5, 1477, the troops of Carl the Bold were routed by the Swiss, the Lorrainians, the Alsatians and the Germans. p. 369

179 The account of the banquet at Château-Rouge was published in *The Northern Star* No. 508, July 17, 1847. p. 376

180 The quotation consists of extracts from the leading articles of the *Journal des Débats*, July 13, 15, 18, 19, and August 7, 1847. p. 376

181 See Note 90. p. 377

182 See Note 11. p. 378

183 The events described here took place in Paris at the end of August and the beginning of September 1847. They were provoked by a conflict between shoemakers at a workshop in the Rue St. Honoré and their master, who tried to defraud one of the workers of part of his pay. p. 381

184 See Note 50. p. 381

185 This article was first published in English in: Karl Marx and Frederick Engels, *On Britain*, Foreign Languages Publishing House, Moscow, 1953. p. 383

186 The session of Parliament opened on November 18, 1847. The democratic forces were represented by the Chartist leader, Feargus O'Connor. p. 383

187 See Note 166. p. 383

188 See Note 1. p. 384

189 The *International League*, or the People's International League, was founded in 1847 by English radicals and free traders. Among its foundation and active members were Thomas Cooper, Sir William Fox, Sir John Bowring and the democratic publicist, poet and engraver William James Linton. The League was also joined by several Italian, Hungarian and Polish emigrants, Giuseppe Mazzini in particular, who was one of its initiators. Its activity was limited to organising meetings and lec-

tures on international problems and distributing pamphlets, and ceased completely in 1848. p. 384

190 In this article Engels used material from *La Réforme*, November 9, 13, 14 and 16, 1847. The banquets of Lille, Avesnes and Valenciennes were held on November 7, 9 and 11, 1847 respectively. p. 385

191 In 1840, under the pretext of fortifying the capital against the external enemy, the French Government began to erect a number of separate forts around Paris. The July monarchy intended them to help safeguard itself against people's revolts. The democratic circles strongly protested against new "Bastilles" being built in Paris. Most of the bourgeois opposition, however, including the followers of the *National*, supported the construction of the forts, justifying it by national defence interests. p. 387

192 Marx's and Engels' participation in the international meeting organised by the Fraternal Democrats to mark the anniversary of the Polish uprising of 1830 showed their eagerness to use their stay in London during the Second Congress of the Communist League (end of November-beginning of December 1847) to strengthen contacts with the democratic and workers' organisations in England. As Vice-President of the Brussels Democratic Association Marx was empowered to establish correspondence between the Association and the Fraternal Democrats and to enter into negotiations on the organisation of an international democratic congress (for details see Note 206).

Concerning the Polish meeting and the reception accorded the German democrats, see this volume, pp. 391-92.

Apart from the *Deutsche-Brüsseler-Zeitung*, the *Deutsche Londoner Zeitung* No. 140, December 3, 1847 and *The Northern Star* No. 528, December 4, 1847 also gave an account of the speeches made by Marx and Engels at the meeting. p. 388

193 This item was in the form of a letter to the editor of *La Réforme*. p. 391

194 The *Democratic Association* (Association démocratique) was founded in Brussels in the autumn of 1847 and united proletarian revolutionaries, mainly German emigrants and advanced bourgeois and petty-bourgeois democrats. Marx and Engels took an active part in setting up the Association. On November 15, 1847 Marx was elected its Vice-President (the President was Lucien Jottrand, a Belgian democrat), and under his influence it became a centre of the international democratic movement. During the February 1848 revolution in France, the proletarian wing of the Brussels Democratic Association sought to arm the Belgian workers and to intensify the struggle for a democratic republic. However, when Marx was banished from Brussels in March 1848 and the most revolutionary elements were repressed by the Belgian authorities its activity assumed a narrower, purely local character and in 1849 the Association ceased to exist.

Fraternal Democrats—see Note 1. p. 391

195 See Note 189. p. 392

196 See Note 145. p. 394

197 The banquet of Dijon, described by Engels, was held on November 21, 1847 and a report on it was given in *La Réforme* on November 24 and 25. Engels repeated his criticism of Louis Blanc's banquet speech somewhat later in the *Deutsche-Brüsseler-Zeitung* (see this volume, pp. 409-11). p. 397

[198] The reference is to the military alliance concluded in 1778 between Louis XVI and the United States of America during the American War of Independence (1775-83) and to the participation of the French expeditionary corps and navy in the hostilities against England—France's trade and colonial rival. p. 398

[199] The reference is to the entry of the French republican army into the Netherlands in January 1795 in support of a local uprising against the aristocratic regime of the Stadholder Wilhelm V. The latter was deposed and the Batavian Republic was established (1795-1806), which soon became dependent on Napoleonic France. p.398

[200] For the meaning in which Engels uses the word "cosmopolitism" see Note 8. p. 398

[201] In his polemic with Blanc Engels made no attempt to disclose the real nature of the bourgeois "civilisation" the capitalist states were spreading in the economically backward countries. He concentrated here on exposing Louis Blanc's nationalistic bombast about France's so-called civilising role. In their later articles and letters devoted to India, Ireland, China and Iran, Marx and Engels showed that these countries were drawn into the orbit of capitalist relations through their colonial enslavement by capitalist states. They were turned into agrarian and raw material appendages of the metropolis, their natural resources were plundered and their peoples cruelly exploited by the colonialists. The disastrous consequences of English rule in India were described by Marx, in particular, in his "Speech on the Question of Free Trade" (see this volume, pp. 460-61 and 464). p. 399

[202] In the latter half of the 16th century the struggle between England and Spain caused by colonial rivalry was closely interwoven with the Netherlands revolution of 1566-1609. The defeat of the Invincible Spanish Armada in 1588 and other victories scored by England over Spain made it easier for the Dutch republic (the United Provinces) to resist the attempts of Spanish absolutism to restore its domination in that region of the Netherlands. In the war against Spain at that period the English and the Dutch often acted as allies. p. 399

[203] The reference is to the English revolution of the mid-17th century which led to the eventual establishment of the bourgeois system in the country. p. 399

[204] This rhyme was popular among the peasant rebels led by Wat Tyler in 1381 in England. It was widely used by John Ball, one of the leaders of the rebel peasants, in his sermons. It is apparently a paraphrase of the verse by the 14th-century English poet, Richard Rolle de Hampole:

When Adam dalfe and Eve spanne
To spire of Hou may spede,
Where was then the pride of man,
That now marres his meed? p. 400

[205] *Covenanters*—the Scottish Calvinists of the 16th and 17th centuries who concluded special agreements and alliances (covenants) to defend their religion against encroachments on the part of the aristocratic circles tending to Catholicism. On the eve of the 17th-century English revolution the Covenant became for the Scots the political and ideological rallying point of struggle against the absolutism of the Stuarts, for their country's independence. p. 400

206 From the autumn of 1847 onwards the Brussels Democratic Association (see Note 194) discussed the question of convening an international democratic congress to rally the European revolutionary forces in view of impending revolutionary events. Marx and Engels took an active part in preparing for that congress. When in London, at the Second Congress of the Communist League, Marx had talks on the subject with the Chartist leaders and representatives of the proletarian and democratic emigrants. Engels apparently had similar talks with French socialists and democrats. In the beginning of 1848 an agreement was reached to convene the congress in Brussels. It was scheduled for August 25, 1848, the 18th anniversary of the Belgian revolution (see this volume, p. 640). These plans did not materialise, however, because in February 1848 a revolution began in Europe. p. 400

207 This item is Marx's reply to an article by a Belgian publicist, Adolph Bartels, published in the *Journal de Charleroi* on December 12, 1847. Bartels distorted the activity of the revolutionary emigrants resident in Belgium and attacked in particular the communist views of the proletarian German emigrants, their *Deutsche-Brüsseler-Zeitung* and the international meeting which they helped to organise in London on November 29, 1847 to mark the 17th anniversary of the Polish uprising of 1830.

Bartels' article reflected bourgeoisie's dissatisfaction at the growing influence of the proletarian revolutionaries in the Belgian democratic movement, particularly in the Brussels Democratic Association (see Note 194; Bartels was a foundation member but soon broke away). The article coincided in time with a campaign of slander launched by the Belgian clerical and conservative press, and primarily by the *Journal de Bruxelles*, against the revolutionary German emigrants. p. 402

208 The *German Workers' Society* was founded by Marx and Engels in Brussels at the end of August 1847, its aim being the political education of the German workers who lived in Belgium and dissemination of the ideas of scientific communism among them. With Marx, Engels and their followers at its head, the Society became the legal centre rallying the revolutionary proletarian forces in Belgium. Its best activists were members of the Communist League. The Society played an important part in founding the Brussels Democratic Association. It ceased to exist soon after the February 1848 revolution in France when the Belgian police arrested and banished many of its members. p. 402

209 The *Journal de Bruxelles* of December 14, 1847, gave a distorted account of Marx's speech at the Polish meeting in London on November 29, 1847. p. 403

210 *Congregatio de propaganda fide*—a Catholic organisation founded by the Pope in 1622 with the aim of spreading Catholicism in all countries and fighting heresies. p. 403

211 Marx refers to the report published in *The Northern Star* of December 4, 1847 on the London meeting of November 29 in support of fighting Poland. Marx's speech was abridged and inaccurately rendered. p. 403

212 Lamartine's letter was published in a number of other papers besides *Le Bien Public*, in particular in *La Presse, L'Union monarchique*, and as a leaflet entitled *Opinion du citoyen Lamartine sur le communisme*. It was a reply to Etienne Cabet who through the newspaper *Populaire* requested Lamartine to give his opinion of Cabet's communist views. p. 404

213 Engels' articles in support of the newspaper *La Réforme* in its dispute with the moderate republicans of *Le National* drew the attention of the staff of *La Réforme* and met with their approval, especially that of Ferdinand Flocon, one of its editors. He praised Engels' articles on this subject in *The Northern Star* (see this volume, pp. 375-82, 385-87, 438-44) and in the *Deutsche-Brüsseler-Zeitung* (this article), as Engels informed Marx in a letter of January 14, 1848 from Paris. p. 406

214 The *dynastic opposition*—an oppositional group in the French Chamber of Deputies during the July monarchy (1830-48). The group headed by Odilon Barrot expressed the sentiments of the liberal industrial and commercial bourgeoisie, and favoured a moderate electoral reform, which they regarded as a means to prevent revolution and preserve the Orleans dynasty. p. 406

215 *Octrois*—city tolls on imported consumer goods, existed in France from the 13th century up to 1949. p. 407

216 The conspiratorial *Society of Materialistic Communists* was founded by French workers in the 1840s. Its members were influenced by the ideas of Théodore Dézamy, a representative of the revolutionary and materialist trend in French utopian communism.

The trial mentioned by Engels took place in July 1847. The members of the Society were sentenced to long terms of imprisonment. p. 407.

217 The article "Louis Blanc's Speech at the Dijon Banquet" is a version of Engels' report "Reform Movement in France.—Banquet of Dijon" published in *The Northern Star* No. 530, December 18, 1847 (see this volume, pp. 397-401). The *Deutsche-Brüsseler-Zeitung* published its own version in the form of extracts from *The Northern Star* report. The introductory lines were written by Engels specially for this version, the rest of the text, including the quotation from Louis Blanc's speech, was a translation into German of the part of the report where this speech was criticised. The translation was made almost word for word with but slight deviations which are reproduced here.

For comments on the text, see notes 197-203. p. 409

218 The translation of the National Petition was not published in *La Réforme*. p. 414

219 In the latter half of December 1847 Marx delivered several lectures on political economy in the German Workers' Society in Brussels and intended to prepare them for publication in pamphlet form. However, as he later pointed out in the preface to *A Contribution to the Critique of Political Economy* (1859), he did not manage to publish his work *Wage-Labour*, written on the basis of these lectures, because of the February 1848 revolution and his subsequent expulsion from Belgium. Marx's intention to publish these lectures in the *Deutsche-Brüsseler-Zeitung* did not materialise either, though on January 6, 1848 the newspaper carried the following note: "At one of the previous meetings of the German Workers' Society Karl Marx made a report on an important subject, 'What Are Wages?' in which the question was presented so clearly, pertinently and comprehensibly, the present situation so sharply criticised and practical arguments cited that we intend soon to make it known to our readers."

Marx's lectures appeared in their final form only in April 1849 in the *Neue Rheinische Zeitung* as the series of articles *Wage-Labour and Capital* (see present edition, Vol. 9). This series was not finished and did not embrace the whole content of Marx's lectures.

Published below is a draft outline of the concluding lectures which Marx had no time to prepare for the press. The manuscript, whose cover bears the words: "Brussels, December 1847", completes *Wage-Labour and Capital.*

The quotations cited in the original in German are either a free translation or paraphrase of writings by various economists and are taken by Marx, as a rule, from his notebooks of 1845-47.

For the use of terms "commodity labour", "value of labour" and "price of labour", see Note 70. p. 415

220 The first four points refer to those of Marx's lectures which were published in the articles entitled *Wage-Labour and Capital.* p. 415

221 The data on the working hours and the number of weavers were taken by Marx from Th. Carlyle's *Chartism*, London, 1840, p. 31, where we read: "Half-a-million handloom weavers, working fifteen hours a day, in perpetual inability to procure thereby enough of the coarsest food...". p. 416

222 An excerpt from Bowring's speech in the House of Commons was used by Marx in his "Speech on the Question of Free Trade" (see this volume, pp. 460-61). p. 416

223 Marx had in mind Carlyle's words about the English Poor Laws: "If paupers are made miserable, paupers will needs decline in multitude. It is a secret known to all rat-catchers: stop up the granary-crevices, afflict with continual mewing, alarm, and going off of traps, your 'chargeable labourers' disappear, and cease from the establishment. A still briefer method is that of arsenic; perhaps even a milder..." (Th. Carlyle, *Chartism*, p. 17). The words "chargeable labourers" are in English in the manuscript. p. 416

224 Marx meant the following passage in J. Wade's *History of the Middle and Working Classes*, p. 252: "The quantity of employment is not uniform in any branch of industry. It may be affected by changes of seasons, the alterations of fashion, or the vicissitudes of commerce." p. 419

225 The reference is to piece-rate wages (see J. Wade, op. cit., p. 267). p. 420

226 Concerning the truck system (Marx used the English term in the manuscript) Babbage wrote: "Wherever the workmen are paid in goods, or are compelled to purchase at the master's shop, much injustice is done to them, and great misery results from it." "...The temptation to the master, in times of depression, to reduce in effect the wages which he pays (by increasing the price of articles at his shop), without altering the nominal rate of payment, is frequently too great to be withstood" (Ch. Babbage, *On the Economy of Machinery and Manufactures*, second edition, Ld., 1832, p. 304). At the time Marx apparently used the French translation of Babbage's book (Paris, 1833). p. 420

227 Marx gave part of this paragraph in a more extended form in his *Wage-Labour and Capital*, Article V. p. 422

228 See Note 225. p. 424

229 In his notes from Th. Carlyle's *Chartism*, Marx quotes the following passage: "Ireland has near seven millions of working people, the third unit of whom, it appears by Statistic Science, has not for thirty weeks each year as many third-rate potatoes as will suffice them" (p. 25). p. 425

230 The reference is to the war waged by the German people against Napoleon's rule in 1813-14. p. 425

231 Later, when Marx had worked out the theory of surplus value and made a more thorough study of the nature of wages, and the laws determining their rate and level, he came to the conclusion that, contrary to bourgeois economists' opinion, the trade union struggle for higher wages and a shorter working day was of great economic importance and could obtain for the workers more favourable terms for the sale of their labour power to the capitalists. Marx set forth his new point of view in *Wages, Price and Profit* (1865) and in Volume I of *Capital* (1867). p. 435

232 In 1846 the Guizot Government managed to arrange the marriage of the Spanish infanta and Louis Philippe's youngest son and thwart England's plans to marry Leopold of Coburg to Isabella II of Spain. In 1847, during the civil war in Switzerland, the British Foreign Secretary Palmerston avenged this failure of English diplomacy. He persuaded Guizot to espouse a project according to which the five powers were to interfere on the side of the Sonderbund but at the same time secretly assisted the latter's defeat. Guizot's diplomatic manoeuvres suffered a complete failure. p. 438

233 The workers were shot at *Lyons* during the weavers' uprisings in 1831 and 1834.

Clashes between workers and troops at *Preston* took place in August 1842, when spontaneous Chartist disturbances swept through industrial England.

Langenbielau (Silesia) was a centre of the weavers' uprising in June 1844. Government troops shot down the rebels.

In *Prague* government troops suppressed the workers' revolt in the summer of 1844. p. 440

234 The reference is to the *Declaration of the Rights of Man and of the Citizen* (Déclaration des droits de l'homme et du citoyen)—the first part of the French republican constitution of 1793 adopted by the National Convention after the overthrow of the monarchy on August 10, 1792. p. 442

235 *Chant du départ* (Marching Song)—one of the most popular songs of the French Revolution (its authors were Chénier and Méhul). It also remained popular later. p. 442

236 See Note 191. p. 443

237 The reference is to the *Constitutional Charter* (Charte constitutionnelle) adopted after the 1830 revolution. It was the fundamental law of the July monarchy. p. 443

238 This article was first published in English in the book, Karl Marx and Frederick Engels, *Ireland and the Irish Question*, Progress Publishers, Moscow, 1971. p. 445

239 *King's County* was the name given by the English conquerors to the county of Offaly (Central Ireland) in honour of Philip II of Spain, husband of Mary Tudor, Queen of England. At the same time the neighbouring county of Laoighis (Leix) was renamed Queen's County. p. 445

240 The *Anglo-Irish Union* was imposed on Ireland by the English Government after the suppression of the Irish rebellion of 1798. The Union, which came into force on January 1, 1801, abrogated the autonomy of the Irish Parliament and made Ireland even more dependent on England. After the 1820s the demand for the repeal of the Union was a mass issue in Ireland, but the Irish liberals who headed the national

movement, O'Connell among them, regarded agitation for the repeal only as a means to wrest concessions from the English Government in favour of the Irish bourgeoisie and landowners. In 1835, O'Connell came to an agreement with the English Whigs and discontinued agitation altogether. Under the pressure of the mass movement, however, the Irish liberals were compelled in 1840 to set up the Repeal Association, which they tried to direct towards compromise with the English ruling classes.

The repeal of the Union was put up for discussion in Parliament on November 18, and the Coercion Bill on November 29, 1847. Accounts of O'Connor's part in the debates, his suggestions and petitions demanding the repeal of the Union and protesting against the Coercion Bill were given in *The Northern Star* Nos. 528 and 529, December 4 and 11, 1847. p. 446

241 This article was first published in English in the book, Karl Marx and Frederick Engels, *Ireland and the Irish Question*, Progress Publishers, Moscow, 1971. p. 448

242 *Repealers* were advocates of the repeal of the Anglo-Irish Union and restoration of the Irish Parliament's autonomy. p. 448

243 See Note 240. p. 448

244 *Conciliation Hall*—a public hall in Dublin where meetings were often organised by the Repeal Association. p. 449

245 The reference is to the second national petition presented to Parliament by the Chartists in May 1842. Together with the demand for the adoption of the People's Charter, the petition contained a number of other demands, including that of the repeal of the Union of 1801. The petition was rejected by Parliament. p. 449

246 The basis of this "Speech on the Question of Free Trade" was the material Marx prepared for a speech he was to have delivered at the Congress of Economists in September 1847 (see this volume, pp. 270-81 and 287-90 and also Note 116), with the addition of new facts and propositions. The *Deutsche-Brüsseler-Zeitung* of January 6 announced in advance that Marx was to speak on free trade. At the same meeting of January 9 at which Marx made his speech, the Brussels Democratic Association decided to have it published in French and Flemish at the Association's expense. On January 16, 1848, the *Deutsche-Brüsseler-Zeitung* published a report on the meeting and a detailed summary of Marx's speech. "Thanks to *Karl Marx's* speech on the question of free trade," the report said, "this meeting turned out to be one of the most interesting of all held by the Association. The report in French took more than an hour, and the audience listened with unflagging attention all the time." *La Réforme* of January 19, 1848, also carried an item by Bornstedt on Marx's speech.

The speech was published as a pamphlet in French (*Discours sur la question du libre échange*. Prononcé à l'Association Démocratique de Bruxelles, dans la séance publique du 9 Janvier 1848, par *Charles Marx*. Imprimé aux frais de l'Association Démocratique) at the end of January 1848. The Flemish edition apparently did not materialise. The *Deutsche-Brüsseler-Zeitung* published its first notification of the publication on February 3. That same year the pamphlet was translated into German and published in Hamm (Germany) by Joseph Weydemeyer together with the beginning of the speech Marx was to have delivered at the Congress of Economists (*Zwei Reden über die Freihandels- und Schutzzollfrage von Karl Marx*. Aus dem Französischen übersetzt und mit einem Vorwort und erläuternden Anmerkungen versehen von J. Weydemeyer. Hamm, 1848). In 1885 this work was republished on

Engels' wish as a supplement to the first German edition of *The Poverty of Philosophy* which he had prepared, and since then it has repeatedly been republished with that work.

"The Speech on the Question of Free Trade" was first published in English in 1888 in Boston (USA) under Engels' supervision. He actually edited the translation made by Florence Kelley-Wischnewetzky, an American socialist. In a letter of May 2, 1888, Engels wrote to her that he had brought her translation, made from the German version of 1885, nearer to the French original and in several places had "for the sake of clearness taken more liberties". Engels wrote a preface for this edition which was published earlier (July 1888) in German in the journal *Die Neue Zeit* as an article entitled "Protectionism and Free Trade". The American edition of the pamphlet appeared in September 1888 (1889 on the title page). Its title was: *Free Trade.* A Speech Delivered before the Democratic Club, Brussels, Belgium, Jan. 9, 1848. With Extract from *La Misère de la Philosophie* by Karl Marx. Engels was satisfied with the edition (see his letter of September 18, 1888 to Kelley-Wischnewetzky). In this volume "The Speech on the Question of Free Trade" is given in the English translation edited by Engels, except for the title which corresponds to the original. Retained are some technical peculiarities of the Boston edition, e.g., paragraphing which somewhat differs in this respect from the French edition of 1848. Where the texts of the 1888 and 1848 editions differ in meaning this is pointed out in a footnote. Pages of sources quoted by Marx are given in brackets. Reference is also made for the reader's convenience to the English editions of Ricardo and Ure (Third Edition, London, 1821 and Second Edition, London, 1835—respectively) which Marx made use of in French translations at that time. p. 450

247 See Note 28. p. 450

248 See Note 47. p. 454

249 See Note 76. p. 456

250 The address "The Fraternal Democrats (assembling in London), to the working classes of Great Britain and Ireland" was adopted at the Society's meeting on January 3, 1848 and published in *The Northern Star* No. 533, January 8, 1848. It is quoted below abridged. p. 466

251 Luneau's interpellation in the Chamber of Deputies concerning the sale of appointments in the Finance Ministry was answered in the negative by the then Minister of Finance, Lacave-Laplagne, on June 13, 1846. The publication of Petit's pamphlet and the sharp reaction to it on the part of the public caused *La Réforme* to publish extracts from the above interchange between Luneau and the Minister of Finance, and also the speech on this subject made by H. M. Dupin, an opposition deputy (quoted by Engels below). p. 470

252 The liberation struggle of the Algerians led by Emir Abd-el-Kader against the French colonialists lasted with short interruptions from 1832 to 1847. Between 1839 and 1844, the French used their considerable military superiority to conquer Abd-el-Kader's state in Western Algeria. However, he continued guerrilla warfare relying on the help of the sultan of Morocco, and when the latter was defeated in the Franco-Moroccan war of 1844, Abd-el-Kader hid in the Sahara oases. The last stage of this struggle was an insurrection in Western Algeria in 1845-47 which was put down by the French colonialists.

In one of his reports published in *The Northern Star* in 1844 Engels commended the resistance of the local population to the French colonisation of Algeria (see present edition, Vol. 3, pp. 528-29). In this article (1847) Engels considered the Algerian movement under Abd-el-Kader from a different angle. As the text below shows, he denounced the barbaric methods used by bourgeois France in the conquest of Algeria, but saw this as the inevitable way in which capitalist relations superseded more backward feudal and patriarchal ones and regarded any opposition to this process as doomed to failure. Engels' judgment was undoubtedly influenced by the ideas he then had of the proximity of a socialist revolution in the developed countries, which was to put an end for ever to all social and national oppression. He thought that favourable preconditions for this revolution were created by backward countries being drawn into the orbit of capitalism with its centralising and levelling tendencies, despite all their negative aspects. This judgment was not final, however. Later, after a deeper study of the history of colonial conquests and the resistance of the oppressed masses to colonial domination, Engels emphasised the liberating and progressive nature of the struggle of oppressed peoples against the capitalist colonial system which helped create favourable conditions for the working class to overthrow the capitalist system. It was from this point of view, in particular, that he described the liberation movement of the Algerians in the article "Algeria" written for the *New American Encyclopaedia* in 1857. p. 470

253 Here the editors of *The Northern Star* gave the following note: "This letter should have reached us last week, but was only delivered to us, by the friend who brought it from Paris, on Tuesday last. Before this time our correspondent will have discovered his error in imagining for a moment the possibility of Louis Philippe, or his man of all work, performing a just or generous action. Abd-el-Kader will not be sent to Egypt; he is to be kept a close prisoner in France. Another specimen of the *honour* of kings!—the *honour* of Philippe the Infamous!"

Abd-el-Kader was held in France as a prisoner for about five years. Only in 1852 was he permitted to move to Damascus, Syria. p. 470

254 See Note 162. p. 474

255 *St. Stephen's Chapel*, where the House of Commons sat since 1547, was destroyed by fire in 1834. p. 474

256 *'Change Alley*—a street in London, where the Board of South Sea Company (founded in the beginning of the 18th century) had its offices; a place where all kinds of money operations and speculative deals were conducted. p. 475

257 The *Manifesto of the Communist Party* was written by Marx and Engels as the Communist League's programme on the instruction of its Second Congress (London, November 29-December 8, 1847), which signified a victory for the followers of the new proletarian doctrine who had upheld its principles during the discussion of the programme questions.

When Congress was still in preparation, Marx and Engels arrived at the conclusion that the final programme document should be in the form of a Party manifesto (see Engels' letter to Marx of November 23-24, 1847). The catechism form usual for the secret societies of the time and retained in the "Draft of a Communist Confession of Faith" and *Principles of Communism* (see this volume, pp. 96-103 and 341-57), was not suitable for a full and substancial exposition of the new revolutionary world outlook, for a comprehensive formulation of the proletarian movement's aims and tasks.

Marx and Engels began working together on the *Manifesto* while they were still in London immediately after the congress, and continued until about December 13 when Marx returned to Brussels; they resumed their work four days later (December 17) when Engels arrived there. After Engels' departure for Paris at the end of December and up to his return on January 31, Marx worked on the *Manifesto* alone.

Hurried by the Central Authority of the Communist League which provided him with certain documents (e. g., addresses of the People's Chamber (*Halle*) of the League of the Just of November 1846 and February 1847, and, apparently, documents of the First Congress of the Communist League pertaining to the discussion of the Party programme), Marx worked intensively on the *Manifesto* through almost the whole of January 1848. At the end of January the manuscript was sent on to London to be printed in the German Workers' Educational Society's printshop owned by a German emigrant J. E. Burghard, a member of the Communist League.

The manuscript of the *Manifesto* has not survived. The only extant materials written in Marx's hand are a draft plan for Section III, showing his efforts to improve the structure of the *Manifesto*, and a page of a rough copy (both are published in this volume in the section "From the Preparatory Materials", pp. 576 and 577-78).

The *Manifesto* came off the press at the end of February 1848. On February 29, the Educational Society decided to cover all the printing expenses.

The first edition of the *Manifesto* was a 23-page pamphlet in a dark green cover. In April-May 1848 another edition was put out. The text took up 30 pages, some misprints of the first edition were corrected, and the punctuation improved. Subsequently this text was used by Marx and Engels as a basis for later authorised editions. Between March and July 1848 the *Manifesto* was printed in the *Deutsche Londoner Zeitung*, a democratic newspaper of the German emigrants. Already that same year numerous efforts were made to publish the *Manifesto* in other European languages. A Danish, a Polish (in Paris) and a Swedish (under a different title: "The Voice of Communism. Declaration of the Communist Party") editions appeared in 1848. The translations into French, Italian and Spanish made at that time remained unpublished. In April 1848, Engels, then in Barmen, was translating the *Manifesto* into English, but he managed to translate only half of it, and the first English translation, made by Helen Macfarlane, was not published until two years later, between June and November 1850, in the Chartist journal *The Red Republican*. Its editor, Julian Harney, named the authors for the first time in the introduction to this publication. All earlier and many subsequent editions of the *Manifesto* were anonymous.

The growing emancipation struggle of the proletariat in the 60s and 70s of the last century led to new editions of the *Manifesto*. The year 1872 saw a new German edition with minor corrections and a preface by Marx and Engels where they drew some conclusions from the experience of the Paris Commune of 1871. This and subsequent German editions (1883 and 1890) were entitled the *Communist Manifesto*. In 1872 the *Manifesto* was first published in America in *Woodhull & Claflin's Weekly*.

The first Russian edition of the *Manifesto*, translated by Mikhail Bakunin with some distortions, appeared in Geneva in 1869. The faults of this edition were removed in the 1882 edition (translation by Georgi Plekhanov), for which Marx and Engels, who attributed great significance to the dissemination of Marxism in Russia, had written a special preface.

After Marx's death, the *Manifesto* ran into several editions. Engels read through them all, wrote prefaces for the 1883 German edition and for the 1888 English edition in Samuel Moore's translation, which he also edited and supplied with notes. This edition served as a basis for many subsequent editions of the *Manifesto* in English—in Britain, the United States and the USSR. In 1890, Engels prepared a further German edition, wrote a new preface to it, and added a number of notes. In 1885, the newspaper *Le Socialiste* published the French translation of the *Manifesto* made by Marx's daughter Laura Lafargue and read by Engels. He also wrote prefaces to the 1892 Polish and 1893 Italian editions.

The 1888 English edition is taken as the basis for the present publication. All the differences in reading between this and the German editions and also Engels' notes to it and to the 1890 German edition are given in footnotes. p. 477

258 See Note 70. p. 491

259 The Ten-Hours' Bill, the struggle for which was carried on a number of years, was passed in 1847 (see Note 76) in the atmosphere of acute contradictions between the landed aristocracy and the industrial bourgeoisie caused by the repeal of the Corn Laws in 1846 (see notes 28 and 47). To avenge themselves on the industrial bourgeoisie some of the Tories supported this Bill. A detailed description of the stand taken by various classes on the problem of limiting the working day was given by Engels in his articles "The Ten Hours Question" and "The English Ten-Hours' Bill" (present edition, Vol. 10). p. 493

260 In the Preface to the 1872 German edition of the *Communist Manifesto* the authors particularly pointed out that "no special stress is laid" on the transitional revolutionary measures proposed at the end of Section II, and that the concrete character and practical application of such measures would always depend on the historical conditions of the time. p. 505

261 See Note 61. p. 508

262 An allusion to Immanuel Kant's *Kritik der praktischen Vernunft* (Critique of Practical Reason), published just before the French Revolution (1788). p. 510

263 *Réformistes* (referred to below as Social-Democrats, this volume, p. 518)—see Note 60. p. 517

264 See Note 38. p. 518

265 See Note 55. p. 518

266 This article was first published in English in the book, K. Marx and F. Engels, *The Communist Manifesto*, Lawrence, London, 1930. p. 520

267 The reference is to the Prussian United Diet convened in April 1847 (see Note 51), which the Prussian ruling circles considered as the maximum constitutional concession to the liberal bourgeoisie. To counter the demands of the opposition the Prussian king and his supporters tried to substitute this assembly representing the estates for a genuinely representative one. The fact that the majority of the Diet refused to vote the new loans and taxes showed, however, how far the conflict between the monarchy and the bourgeoisie had gone. p. 520

268 See Note 172. p. 520

269 The reference is to the bourgeois revolution in Belgium (autumn 1830) which resulted in Belgium's secession from the Kingdom of the Netherlands and the establishment there of the constitutional monarchy of the Coburg dynasty.

After the July 1830 revolution in France, the movement for liberal reforms intensified also in Switzerland. In a number of cantons, the liberals and radicals succeeded in having the local constitutions revised in a liberal spirit. p. 520

270 See Note 32. p. 520

271 In the beginning of February 1831, revolts took place in a number of provinces of the Papal states—Romagna, Marca and Umbria—and also the dukedoms of Modena and Parma. They were instigated by the carbonari, members of bourgeois and aristocratic revolutionary secret societies. In the course of this bourgeois revolution in Central Italy an attempt was made to abolish the absolute monarchy (in Modena and Parma), to deprive the Pope of temporal power (in Romagna) and to form a new, larger state—an Alignment of Italian Provinces. The revolt was suppressed by the Austrian army at the end of March 1831. p. 520

272 From 1833 a moderately liberal constitution was in force in Hanover. A prominent part in drawing it up was played by the historian Dahlmann. In 1837 the King of Hanover, supported by the landowners, abolished the constitution and in 1840 passed a new constitutional Act, which reproduced the main principles of the State Law of 1819 and minimised the rights of the representative institutions. p. 521

273 The *Vienna Conference* of ministers of a number of German states was called in 1834 on the initiative of the Austrian Chancellor Metternich and the ruling circles of Prussia to discuss measures to be taken against the liberal opposition and the democratic movement. The conference decided to restrict the rights of the representative institutions which existed in some German states, to intensify censorship, to introduce more strict control over universities and to repress oppositional students' organisations. p. 521

274 On July 12, 1839, the English Parliament rejected the Chartist petition demanding the adoption of the People's Charter. The Chartists failed in their attempt to organise in reply a general strike and other revolutionary actions, including armed struggle. The miners' revolt in Newport (Wales) in early November 1839, which the Chartists organised, was crushed by troops, and severe repressions followed. p. 521

275 See Note 28. p. 521

276 *Sans-Souci* (literally "Without Care")—a summer residence of the Prussian kings in Potsdam (near Berlin). p. 521

277 The reference is to the so-called United Committees consisting of the representatives of the Provincial Diets which met in January 1848 to discuss the draft of a new criminal code. Convening these committees, the Prussian government hoped that the apparent preparation of reforms would calm down the growing public unrest. The work of the committees was interrupted by the revolutionary outbursts that swept over Germany at the beginning of March. p. 522

278 Engels alludes to the speech of Frederick William IV at the opening of the United Diet on April 11, 1847: "As the heir to an unimpaired crown which I must and will preserve unimpaired for those that shall succeed me...." p. 522

279 The reference is to the patriotic and reform movement among the liberal nobility and bourgeoisie in Prussia during the country's dependence on Napoleonic France. p. 523

280 *Roman consulta*, or Roman State Council—a consultative body inaugurated by Pope Pius IX in the end of 1847. It included representatives of the liberal landowners and the commercial and industrial bourgeoisie. p. 523

281 *Pifferari* (from "piffero"—pipe)—herdsmen in the Apennines in Central Italy; a common name for Italian wandering singers.

Lazzaroni—a contemptuous nickname for declassed proletarians, primarily in the Kingdom of Naples. Lazzaroni were repeatedly used by the absolutist governments in their struggle against the liberal and democratic movements. p. 523

282 *Pietists*—adherents of a mystical Lutheran trend which arose in Germany in the 17th century and placed religious feeling above religious dogmas. Pietism was directed against the rationalist thinking and philosophy of the Enlightenment and in the 19th century was distinguished by extreme mysticism and hypocrisy. p. 524

283 The reference is to the war of 1846-48 between the United States of America and Mexico, as a result of which the USA seized almost half the Mexican territory, including the whole of Texas, Upper California, New Mexico and other regions.

In assessing these events in his article Engels proceeded from the general conception that it was progressive for patriarchal and feudal countries to be drawn into the orbit of capitalist relations because, he thought, this accelerated the creation of preconditions tor a proletarian revolution (see Note 252). In subsequent years however, he and Marx investigated the consequences of colonial conquests and the subjugation of backward countries by large states in all their aspects. In particular, having made a thorough study of the US policy in regard to Mexico and other countries of the American continent, Marx in an article, "The Civil War in the North America" (1861), described it as expansion in the interests of the then dominant slave-owning oligarchy of the Southern States and of the bourgeois elements in the North which supported it, whose overt aim was to seize new territories for spreading slavery. p. 527

284 The project of connecting the Pacific Ocean with the Gulf of Mexico by means of a canal through the Isthmus of Tehuantepec was repeatedly put forward in the USA, which strove to dominate the trade routes and markets in Central America. However, in the 1870s the American capitalists rejected this project, preferring to invest their capital in less expensive railway construction in Mexico. p. 527

285 The reference is to the French army's invasion of Austria during the wars of the European coalitions against the French Republic and Napoleonic France. In March 1797 General Bonaparte's troops defeated the Austrian army in Northern Italy, invaded Austria and launched an offensive on Vienna. This impelled the Austrian government to sign an armistice. In 1805, during the war of England, Austria and Russia against Napoleonic France, most of Austria was occupied by French troops following the capitulation of the Austrian army at Ulm (October 1805). During the Austro-French war of 1809 hostilities took place mainly on Austrian territory and ended in the defeat of the Austrians at Wagram (near Vienna), on July 5 and 6, 1809. p. 530

286 In July 1820 the carbonari, aristocratic and bourgeois revolutionaries, rose in revolt against the absolutist regime in the Kingdom of Naples and succeeded in having a moderate liberal constitution introduced. In March 1821, a revolt took place in the Kingdom of Sardinia (Piedmont). The liberals who headed it proclaimed a constitution and attempted to make use of the anti-Austrian movement in Northern Italy for the unification of the country under the aegis of the Savoy dynasty then in power in Piedmont. Interference by the powers of the Holy Alliance and the occupation of Naples and Piedmont by Austrian troops led to the restoration of absolutist regimes in both states.

For details about the suppression of the revolt in Romagna in 1831 by the Austrians, see Note 271.

During the Polish uprising in the free city of Cracow in 1846 (see Note 55) the Austrian authorities provoked clashes between Ukrainian peasants and detachments of the insurgent nobles in Galicia.

In July 1847, fearing the people's movement in the Papal states, the Austrian authorities brought in troops to the frontier town of Ferrara. In Rome itself they supported the circles which strove to abolish the liberal reforms of Pius IX. However, the general discontent in Italy caused by the occupation of Ferrara forced the Austrians to withdraw their troops. p. 532

287 The Sonderbund, a separatist alliance of patriarchal and aristocratic cantons, which unleashed civil war in Switzerland in November 1847 (see Note 172), received money and armaments from Austria and France, under the pretext that they were guarantors of Switzerland's neutrality (under the Paris Treaty of 1815), and counted on their military interference on its side. p. 534

288 In the atmosphere of growing revolutionary unrest in Hungary the Austrian government attempted to seize from the progressive national opposition the initiative in carrying through a number of bourgeois reforms with the aim of splitting its ranks. In 1843 and 1844 Bills were introduced on the development of credit, road construction, the abolition of customs barriers between Austria and Hungary, the regulation of navigation on the Danube, greater representation of cities in the assemblies of the estates, etc. The manoeuvres of the Austrian government could not, however, halt the national movement or make the opposition renounce its demands for radical changes. p. 535

289 *Prater*—a park in Vienna. p. 535

290 Below Marx gives a critical analysis of the article, "Les Associations démocratiques.—Leur principe.—Leur but" ("Democratic Associations.—Their Principles.—Their Aim"), published in the Belgian radical newspaper *Débat social* (editor-in-chief A. Bartels) on February 6, 1848.

About the Brussels Democratic Association, see Note 194. p. 537

291 *Alliance* (founded in 1841) and *Association libérale* (founded in 1847)—liberal bourgeois political organisations in Belgium. p. 538

292 Marx has in mind Robert Peel's speech in the House of Commons on June 29, 1846, when the government's resignation was discussed. p. 538

293 The reference is to the *People's Charter*—the main programme of political changes proposed by the Chartists (see Note 48). p. 539

294 The reference is to the discussion on free trade held at the meetings of the Brussels Democratic Association in January and early February 1848. It was initiated by Marx's speech on the question of free trade on January 9 (see this volume, pp. 450-65), in which he opposed the tendency of certain bourgeois democrats to idealise free trade. In this speech Marx expressed the opinion not only of the proletarian section but of the majority of the Democratic Association. p. 539

295 Marx refers to the articles published in the *Débat social* of February 6, 1848: "Opinion de M. Cobden, sur les dépenses de la guerre et de la marine" ("M. Cobden's opinion of the Expenses on the War and the Navy") and "Discours prononcé par M. Le Hardy de Beaulieu, à la dernière séance de l'Association Belge pour la liberté commerciale" ("Speech by M. Le Hardy de Beaulieu at the Last Meeting of the Belgian Association in Defence of Free Trade"). p. 539

296 In November 1847 the King of Sardinia, the Pope and the Duke of Tuscany agreed to convene a conference of Italian states to form a Customs Union. The project of a Customs Union met the interests of the bourgeois circles which strove to unite the country "from above" in the form of a federation of states under the Pope or the Savoy dynasty. However, this plan was frustrated by the 1848-49 revolution in Italy and its defeat in 1849. p. 540

297 On the events of 1823 and 1831 in Italy, see notes 271 and 286. p. 541

298 Prior to the 1848 revolution the movement among the German population in the duchies of Schleswig and Holstein against a common constitution with Denmark (the draft constitution was made public on January 28, 1848) was a separatist one and did not go beyond moderate bourgeois opposition. Its aim was to create in the north of Germany yet another small German state dependent on Prussia. During the 1848-49 revolution the situation changed. The events in Germany imparted to the national movement in Schleswig and Holstein a revolutionary, liberation character. The struggle for the secession of these duchies from Denmark became an integral part of the struggle for the national unification of Germany and was resolutely supported by Marx and Engels. p. 542

299 See Note 26. p. 543

300 The reference is to the rescripts of Frederick William IV convening a United Diet in Prussia (see Note 51). p. 543

301 The report on the meeting in Brussels to mark the second anniversary of the Cracow uprising (see Note 55) was published in the *Deutsche-Brüsseler-Zeitung* on February 24, 1848 (see this volume, p. 644). After the meeting a pamphlet in French was issued, containing the reports of the main speakers. The letters of C. G. Vogler, a German publisher in Brussels, member of the Communist League, to Marx, who on March 5, 1848 moved to Paris after his expulsion from Belgium, show that Marx and Engels took a direct part in the publication of this pamphlet. It came out about March 15, 1848 under the title: "*Célébration, à Bruxelles,* du deuxième anniversaire de la *Révolution Polonaise* du 22 février 1846.—Discours prononcés par MM. A. J. Senault, Karl Marx, Lelewel, F. Engels et Louis Lubliner, Avocat, Bruxelles, C. G. Vogler, Libraire-Editeur, 1848." The pamphlet was prefaced with the following short introductory note (possibly written by Marx or Engels):

"Together with the Polish democrats, the Brussels *Democratic Association* consisting of representatives of various nations celebrated at a public meeting the second anniversary of the Polish revolution of 1846. The hall was crowded out, and the public most enthusiastically expressed its sympathy for the event.

"Unfortunately, we were unable to reproduce the ardent speeches in Flemish made by two workers, MM. Kats and Pellering. M. Wallau, President of the German Workers' Society in Brussels, himself a working man, spoke in German. His extemporaneous and highly enthusiastic speech testified that the German workers fully share the sentiments of their brothers in France and in England.

"The speeches are given here in the order they were made. They are preceded by the Manifesto of the Provisional Government formed in Cracow on February 22, 1846."

Extracts from Marx's speech were first published in English in the journal *Labour Monthly*, February 1948, and in the collection, Karl Marx and Frederick Engels, *Ireland and the Irish Question*, Progress Publishers, Moscow, 1971. p. 545

302 The reference is to the constitution of May 3, 1791 adopted by the Four Years' Diet (1788-92). "The Party of Patriots" which constituted a majority in the Diet strove, through a new constitution and reforms, to undermine the rule of feudal anarchy and the domination of the magnates, to strengthen the Polish state (demands to establish a hereditary constitutional monarchy, to abolish the right of every deputy of the nobility to veto the decisions of the Diet) and also to adapt the feudal system to the needs of bourgeois development (the demand to extend the rights of the urban population, and recognise a moderate form of certain bourgeois freedoms). The constitution preserved serfdom, but gave the peasants a certain opportunity to establish state-guaranteed contractual relations with the landowners. The constitution was opposed by the big land magnates, on whose call Prussia and Russia occupied Poland in 1793 and partitioned it for the second time (it was first partitioned by Prussia, Russia and Austria in 1772). After the suppression of the Polish insurrection of 1794 (the insurgents aimed at restoring the 1791 constitution), the Polish state ceased to exist in 1795 as a result of the third partition of Poland by Austria, Prussia and tsarist Russia. p. 545

303 The *Congress of Vienna* (September 1814-June 1815) composed of European monarchs and their ministers established, after the war of the European powers against Napoleonic France, a system of general treaties embracing the whole of Europe (with the exception of Turkey). The Congress decisions helped to restore feudal order and a number of former dynasties in the states previously conquered by Napoleon, sanctioned the political fragmentation of Germany and Italy, the incorporation of Belgium into Holland and the partition of Poland and outlined repressive measures to be taken against the revolutionary movement. p. 545

304 See Note 172. p. 546

305 See Note 72. p. 546

306 On the *Reform Bill of 1832 in England*—see Note 33; on the abolition of the *Corn Laws*—see Note 28. p. 546

307 An allusion to the results of the liberation war of 1813-15 against Napoleon's rule. The victory was taken advantage of by the aristocracy and nobility of the German states to help preserve the political fragmentation of Germany (see Note 26). p. 549

308 The reference is to the *Irish Confederation* founded in January 1847 by the radical and democratic elements in the Irish national movement who had broken away

from the Repeal Association (see Note 240). The majority of them belonged to the Young Ireland group which was formed in 1842 by the Irish bourgeois and petty-bourgeois intellectuals. The Left, revolutionary wing of the Irish Confederation advocated a people's uprising against English rule and tried to combine the struggle for Irish independence with the campaign for democratic reforms. The Irish Confederation ceased to exist in the summer of 1848 after the English authorities crushed the uprising in Ireland. p. 549

309 See note 32. p. 550

310 The Congress of Vienna in 1814-15 liquidated the so-called duchy of Warsaw which depended on Napoleonic France. It was formed by Napoleon in 1807, after the defeat of Prussia, on the Polish territory seized by Prussia as a result of the three partitions of Poland. The Congress repartitioned the duchy between Prussia, Austria and Russia with the exception of the free city of Cracow, which was under the joint protection of the three powers up to 1846. The part incorporated into Russia was called the Kingdom of Poland with Warsaw as its capital. p. 550

311 Engels refers to the editorial in *La Riforma* No. 14, February 11, 1848 in reply to the article "Von der italienischen Gränze" published in the Augsburg *Allgemeine Zeitung* No. 31, January 31, 1848. p. 553

312 *Treaties of 1815*—see Note 303; on the liberation wars against Napoleonic France and Engels' opinion of them in the forties and subsequent years—see Note 22. p. 554

313 The reference is to the plan of deployment and operation of government troops in case of a revolt in Paris. It was adopted in 1840. p. 557

314 When the Guizot government fell on February 23, 1848, the supporters of the House of Orleans attempted to form a ministry consisting of moderate monarchists (the Orleanists) Thiers, Billault, and others and headed by Count Molé. The victorious people's insurrection in Paris, however, thwarted the plan to retain the Orleans monarchy. p. 558

315 The posts in the French Provisional Government formed on February 24, 1848, were held mainly by moderate republicans (Lamartine, Depont de l'Eure, Crémieux, Arago, Marie, and the two men mentioned by Engels from the *National*, Marrast and Garnier-Pagès). There were three representatives of the *Réforme* in the government—Ledru-Rollin, Flocon and Louis Blanc, and a mechanic Albert (real name Martin). p. 558

316 The editor George Julian Harney added the following introductory note when publishing this letter in *The Northern Star*, March 25, 1848: "The following letter was received at the time the editor was in Paris; hence its non-appearance until now. Thank God, the days of the contemptible, 'constitutional' tyranny of Belgium are numbered. Leopold is packing his carpet bag." p. 559

317 The Brussels *Association Démocratique* and the *Alliance*—see notes 194 and 291. p. 559

318 See Note 208. p. 560

319 The reference is to the double-faced policy of the French Orleanists on the Belgian question in the early 1830s. During the period of the 1830-31 revolution they fos-

tered plans of annexing Belgium and incited the Belgians to fight for secession from Holland. Simultaneously, at the London Conference of the five powers (Britain, France, Russia, Austria and Prussia) held with intervals in 1830 and 1831, they colluded, at the expense of Belgium, with the powers supporting Holland. As a result the Belgians had to accept the unfavourable terms of the agreement with the Dutch King (finally signed in May 1833) and cede part of their territory to him. p. 564

320 By order of the French authorities Marx was expelled from France at the beginning of February 1845 together with other editors of the radical newspaper *Vorwärts!* published in Paris. Its closure was demanded by the Prussian ruling circles. For details about Marx's expulsion and his move to Belgium, see present edition, Vol. 4, p. 235. p. 565

321 In this article Marx used notes which he had made at the beginning of March 1848 on the arrest, maltreatment and expulsion of Wilhelm Wolff by the Brussels police (see this volume, pp. 581-82). p. 567

322 The *laws on suspects*—the decree passed by the French Convention on September 17, 1793 and other measures of the Jacobin revolutionary government which declared suspect and subject to arrest all persons who in one way or another supported the overthrown monarchy, including all former aristocrats and royal officials who had not testified their loyalty to the revolution. These laws were drawn up in such a form that even people not involved in counter-revolutionary activity could be placed in the category of "suspects". p. 567

323 This article was written by Engels shortly before he left Brussels for Paris and was apparently intended for *La Réforme.* However, it was never published and survived only as a manuscript. p. 569

324 This is apparently a rough outline of a speech Marx intended to make on September 18, 1847 at the Congress of Economists in Brussels (see this volume, pp. 287-89 and notes 113 and 116). The outline was written on the last page of the tenth notebook containing extracts Marx made in the latter half of 1845 and in 1846. Some places in the manuscript are indecipherable because of ink blots (in the text they are marked by periods in square brackets). At the bottom of the text itself and in the margins there are several drawings by Engels apparently of participants in the Congress (see illustration between p. 578 and p. 579). p. 573

325 This extract is in Marx's notebook which contains his manuscript "Wages" and is dated December 1847. There is no direct indication of its purpose in the extant manuscripts or letters. It might have been a preparatory outline either for the "Speech on the Question of Free Trade" which Marx delivered on January 9, 1848 at the meeting of the Brussels Democratic Association, or for lectures on political economy which he delivered in December 1847 to the German Workers' Society in Brussels (see notes 219 and 246). It may also have been intended for a non-extant economic work by Marx.

Marx made a few references in the text to one of his notebooks of excerpts dating to the summer of 1847. The notebook contains a synopsis of G. Gülich's book, *Geschichtliche Darstellung des Handels, der Gewerbe und des Ackerbaus der bedeutendsten handeltreibenden Staaten unserer Zeit,* Bd. 1-5, Jena, 1830-45. The passages referred to are in Vol. 1. Marx usually wrote the author's name as Jülich and in the manuscript used only the initial letter "J" to denote the author. p. 574

326 The draft plan is written on the cover of Marx's notebook containing the manuscript "Wages" (see this volume, pp. 415-37) and dated "Brussels, December 1847". p. 576

327 In the final version of the *Communist Manifesto* points 5 and 6 were not elaborated. p. 576

328 This is the only extant page of the rough version of the *Communist Manifesto.* The fair copy sent to London at the end of January 1848 to be printed did not survive. The page of the rough copy refers in part to the first and mainly to the second section of the *Manifesto.* p. 577

329 *Petits Carmes*—a prison in Brussels. p. 581

330 See Note 208. p. 581

331 *Permanence*—a police station at the Town Hall in Brussels open all round the clock. *Amigo*—a preliminary detention jail in Brussels, situated near the Town Hall (it derived its name from the Flemish word "vrunte"—a fenced place, interpreted by the Spaniards during their domination in the Netherlands as "vriend"—friend, and rendered in Spanish as "amigo"). p. 581

332 This document is a draft of the Rules of the Communist League adopted at its First Congress in the beginning of June 1847 (see Note 69) and distributed among the circles and communities for discussion. It shows the reorganisation work done by the League of the Just leaders as agreed with Marx and Engels, who consented early in 1847 to join the League on the condition that it would be reorganised on a democratic basis and all elements of conspiracy and sectarianism in its structure and activity would be eliminated. Engels, who was present at the Congress, took a direct part in drawing up the Rules. The draft recorded the change in the League's name, and it is referred to here as the Communist League for the first time. The new motto, "Working Men of All Countries, Unite!" was also used for the first time. The former leading body, the narrow People's Chamber (*Halle*), was replaced by the supreme body—the Congress, composed of delegates from local circles; the executive organ was to be the Central Authority. The relations between all the League organisations were based on principles of democratism and centralism. At the same time a number of points in the draft showed that the reorganisation was not yet complete and that former traditions were still alive, namely: Art. 1 formulating the aims of the League; one of the points in Art. 3, making the sectarian stipulation that members were not to belong to any other political organisation; Art. 21, limiting the powers of the Congress by the right of the communities to accept or reject its decisions, etc. On the insistence of Marx and Engels these points were later deleted or altered. The Second Congress (November 29-December 8, 1847) adopted the Rules in an improved and more perfect form, which finally determined the structure of the Communist League according to the principles of scientific communism.

This document was discovered, together with the "Draft of a Communist Confession of Faith" in 1968 among the papers of Joachim Friedrich Martens, a member of the Communist League in Hamburg. p. 585

333 The Circular, or report of the First Congress of the Communist League to its members, also discovered among Martens' papers, brings to light important details of the convening and proceedings of the Congress and gives an idea of the process of reorganising the League of the Just. p. 589

334 In February 1847 the leading body of the League of the Just—the People's Chamber (in November 1846 its seat was transferred from Paris to London)—called upon

the League's local organisations to elect delegates to the congress which was to assemble in London on June 1. The People's Chamber address also defined the agenda of the congress. London remained the seat of the League's executive body which, however, in accordance with the adopted draft Rules, then began to function as the Central Authority. p. 589

335 Being an illegal organisation, the Communist League could not hold its congresses openly or publish their materials. p. 589

336 The *London German Workers' Educational Society* was founded in February 1840 by Karl Schapper, Joseph Moll and other members of the League of the Just. After the Communist League had been founded the leading role in the Society belonged to the League's local communities. At various periods of its activity the Society had branches in the workers' districts in London. In 1847 and 1849-50 Marx and Engels took an active part in the Society's work. But on September 17, 1850, Marx, Engels and a number of their followers withdrew because the Willich-Schapper sectarian and adventurist faction had increased their influence in the Society. In the late 1850s Marx and Engels resumed work in the Educational Society. It existed up to 1918, when it was closed down by the British Government.

Fraternal Democrats—see Note 1. p. 590

337 The reference is to the French secret workers' societies of the 1840s in which utopian ideas, both socialist and communist, were current. Some of the societies' members were influenced by the pacifist communism of Cabet, some supported the revolutionary utopian Communists Théodore Dézamy and Auguste Blanqui. p. 590

338 The description given below of the situation in the Paris communities of the League of the Just in 1845-46 corresponds to the information which Engels (he had been in Paris since August 15, 1846) sent to Marx and other members of the Communist Correspondence Committee in Brussels (see Engels' letters of August 19, September 18, October 18 and 23, and December 1846 to Marx and of August 19, September 16, October 23, 1846 to the Brussels Communist Correspondence Committee). This part of the report was apparently based on information received from Engels, whose role was decisive in overcoming the ideological confusion within the League's Paris communities and in drawing the demarcation line between their revolutionary wing and the petty-bourgeois elements tending towards "true socialism" and Weitling's egalitarian utopian communism. Possibly this section as a whole was written by Engels. p. 590

339 This refers apparently to the money collected by the Paris members of the League of the Just for the Cracow insurgents of 1846. p. 591

340 The reference is to the revolutionary conspiratorial organisation of German emigrants in Switzerland in the 1830s and 1840s. Initially it consisted mainly of petty-bourgeois intellectuals. Later members of the workers' unions gained influence in Young Germany. In the mid-30s, under pressure from Austria and Prussia, the Swiss government expelled the German revolutionaries and the craftsmen's unions were closed down. Young Germany actually ceased to exist, but its followers remained in the cantons of Geneva and Vaud. In the 1840s Young Germany was resurrected. Influenced by the ideas of Ludwig Feuerbach, its members carried on mainly atheist propaganda among the German emigrants and resolutely opposed communist trends, especially that of Weitling. In 1845 Young Germany was again suppressed. p. 594

341 The reference is apparently to the proposal made to Marx and Engels by the leaders of the League of the Just to join the League and take part in its reorganisation on the basis of the principles of scientific communism. On behalf of the People's Chamber, Joseph Moll had talks with Marx in Brussels and with Engels in Paris at the end of January and the beginning of February 1847. p. 594

342 This reference is apparently to the circumstances which led to the formation of the League of the Just as a result of a split in the Outlaws' League, a secret conspiratorial organisation of German emigrants. The latter was set up in Paris in 1834 and headed by petty-bourgeois democrats (Jakob Venedey and others) and socialists (Theodor Schuster and others). The conflict which arose in the Outlaws' League between the artisan-proletarian elements tending towards utopian communism and the petty-bourgeois republican democrats led to the withdrawal of the supporters of communism, who founded the League of the Just. p. 595

343 The reference is to the changes in the Rules of the League of the Just which were in force prior to the First Congress where it was reorganised into the Communist League. The Rules of the League of the Just have come down to us in the versions of 1838 and 1843, which contained very vague and immature formulations typical of purely conspiratorial organisations. There was possibly yet another, later version of the Rules which is referred to here. p. 595

344 The attempt made by the London Central Authority to arrange for the publication of a regular newspaper or journal of the Communist League failed through lack of funds. It managed to put out only a specimen number of *Kommunistische Zeitschrift*, which appeared in London early in September 1847. It was printed in the print-shop of the London German Workers' Educational Society owned by J. E. Burghard. The influence of Marx and Engels can be traced in its contents. The articles by Wilhelm Wolff, Karl Schapper and others were critical of "true socialism" and various utopian socialist trends, gave a rebuff to Karl Heinzen's attacks on the Communists and expounded a number of points concerning the tactics of the proletarian movement. It was in the specimen number that the motto, "Working Men of All Countries, Unite!", was first used in the press as the epigraph of the journal. When the editing of the *Deutsche-Brüsseler-Zeitung* devolved to a considerable extent upon Marx and Engels (see Note 96), this newspaper became in fact the Communist League's regular organ. p. 597

345 An allusion to the crude egalitarian tendencies in the views of Weitling and his supporters and also utopias of "true socialists". p. 598

346 The Address of the Central Authority of the Communist League dated September 14, 1847 is a quarterly report on the activity of the League after the First Congress (June 1847). It describes the situation in the League in general and the measures taken by the Central Authority to prepare for the Second Congress. Giving important data on the discussion of the draft Rules and the "Draft of a Communist Confession of Faith", the Address reveals the ideological struggle in the local communities between the supporters of Marx and Engels and those of Weitling and Grün. The document testifies to the growing activity of the Brussels circle authority headed by Marx, and to its influence on the affairs of the League as a whole and the elaboration of its programme and organisational principles.

This document, like other documents of the First Congress of the Communist League, was discovered in Hamburg among the papers of J. F. Martens. A note made by Karl Schapper on the last page and addressed to Martens shows that this copy was intended for the Hamburg community, of which he was a member (it is not reproduced in this volume). p. 602

347 The reference is to the letter which the Communist League's Central Authority elected at the First Congress sent with other Congress documents, in particular its Circular (see this volume, pp. 589-600), to the League's communities in various countries in June 1847. Extant is a version of the letter addressed to the Hamburg community and dated June 24. In this letter the Central Authority asked the Communist League members in the localities whether they were satisfied with the decisions of the First Congress, whether they accepted or rejected the new Rules, whether they could allot funds for the general needs of the organisation, whether they had formed circles in compliance with the Rules, how many copies of the *Kommunistische Zeitschrift* then being prepared they could distribute and to what extent they had managed to launch communist propaganda among the masses. The letter also proposed that the League members should discuss the "Draft of a Communist Confession of Faith" and give their opinion of this programme document, and also take steps to appoint delegates to the next congress. p. 602

348 See Note 344. p. 603

349 The reference is to the documents of the leading body of the League of the Just—the People's Chamber—issued prior to its reorganisation as the Communist League at the First Congress in June 1847: the Address of the People's Chamber of the League of the Just to the League, November 1846 and February 1847. p. 604

350 The *Scandinavian Society*—a radical democratic society in the latter half of the 1840s. It was in contact with the Communist League and consisted mainly of workers and craftsmen. Its chairman was the League member Per Görtrek, a translator, publisher and bookseller. p. 605

351 According to the Communist League's Rules adopted at the First Congress, individual communities in a given locality had either to form a circle or, if there were no other communities, join a circle already in existence (see this volume, p. 586). p. 607

352 Johann Dohl, sent to Amsterdam in August 1847, reported to the Central Authority in October on the foundation in Amsterdam of a Communist League community of eight members.

The *Workers' Educational Society* in Amsterdam was set up on February 14, 1847. Members of the Communist League played an active part in its foundation and work. In March 1848 the London German Workers' Educational Society sent its counterpart in Amsterdam a hundred copies of the *Communist Manifesto*. The leaders of the Educational Society in Amsterdam, who were also Communist League members, were subjected to severe police persecution for organising a mass meeting in Amsterdam on March 24, 1848 in support of the revolution in France and Germany. p. 608

353 The reference is to Karl Grün's propaganda of Proudhon's views among German workers in Paris and to his free translation into German of Proudhon's *Système des contradictions économiques, ou Philosophie de la misère*, which he published in Darmstadt in 1847 (see Note 56). p. 609

354 Marx's intention to publish a German translation of *The Poverty of Philosophy* did not materialise. During his lifetime only extracts from Chapter II were published in

German (see Note 71). The first German edition of this work, edited by Engels, appeared in 1885. p. 609

355 By the autumn of 1847 a complicated situation had arisen in the League's communities in Paris. The followers of Weitling, expelled by the First Congress, allied themselves with those of Grün. A split took place in October. One of the communities opposed the communist principles and was expelled from the League by a decision of the Central Authority. Engels, then in Paris, wrote to Marx on October 25-26, 1847: "A few days before my arrival the last Grün followers were thrown out, a whole community, half of which, however, will come back. We are only 30 strong. I have at once organised a propaganda community and have been running around all day and beating the drums. I have at once been elected to the circle authority and entrusted with correspondence. Some 20-30 candidates have been nominated for admission. We shall soon be stronger again." p. 610

356 The reference is to the former members of Young Germany, a secret democratic organisation of German emigrants in Switzerland, suppressed by the police in 1845 (see Note 340). They fought against the adherents of communist ideas. p. 610

357 The reference is to the communist groups in Cologne, Westphalia, Elberfeld, which had earlier been in contact with the Brussels Communist Correspondence Committee founded by Marx and Engels, and set up Communist League communities after the League's First Congress. p. 612

358 The reference is to the German Workers' Society in Brussels (see Note 208). p. 612

359 The amendments made by the Brussels circle authority to the draft Rules of the Communist League were adopted at the League's Second Congress. They revealed Marx's efforts to work out better organisational principles of the proletarian party and overcome survivals of sectarianism in its structure. The article concerning the approval of Congress decisions by the communities was deleted and the ban of League members belonging to other political organisations was restricted to organisations hostile to the League (see this volume, p. 633).

By aristocrats in the Convention are probably meant the counter-revolutionary elements who opposed the Jacobin centralisation measures aimed at strengthening the revolutionary government. p. 612

360 The reference is to the *London German Workers' Educational Society* (see Note 336). p. 613

361 The "Draft of a Communist Confession of Faith" and the Rules adopted by the First Congress were regarded as preliminary drafts to be discussed in the localities, improved and finally approved at the next congress. p. 614

362 The reference is to the trial of the members of the League of the Just arrested in Berlin in the spring of 1847. The main witness, Friedrich Mentel, who betrayed the League, withdrew his previous evidence (see this volume, pp. 593-95) and the court was compelled to pass only light sentences on some of the accused and to acquit others. p. 615

363 The Chartist *Northern Star* published a report on the international meeting in London organised by the Fraternal Democrats at the premises of the London German Workers' Educational Society (about these organisations, see notes 1 and

336). It was entitled "The Polish Revolution. Important Meeting". Speeches by Marx and Engels were reported rather abridged (for the authorised publication of these speeches, see this volume, pp. 388-90). The report gave details about the meeting which supplemented Engels' short correspondence about it published in *La Réforme* (see this volume, pp. 391-92). p. 616

364 The *Manifesto* issued by the National Government set up on February 22, 1846 in the course of the national liberation uprising in the Cracow republic (see Note 55) called upon the people to fight resolutely for national independence, proclaimed democratic rights, the abolition of feudal services, and the transfer of land allotments to the peasants. p. 616

365 See Note 286. p. 618

366 The reference is to the victory of the progressive forces in the civil war in Switzerland (see Note 172) and to the failure of the Sonderbund's attempts to secure military interference by the European powers in its own interests. p. 618

367 See Note 194. p. 618

368 Marx counterposes the proposal to call an international democratic congress (on the preparations for it, see Note 206) to the International Congress of Economists held in Brussels from September 16 to 18, 1847 (see this volume, pp. 274-90 and Note 113). p. 619

369 In 1845 Ludwik Mieroslawski, in his capacity as a member of the "Centralisation" (the governing body of the Polish Democratic Society), was sent to Posen to organise an uprising in the Polish lands. He was arrested by the Prussian authorities shortly before the scheduled time of the uprising (February 1846) and sentenced to death. The sentence was later commuted to life imprisonment. He was set free after the revolution began in Germany in March 1848. p. 621

370 About the *civil war in Switzerland*, see this volume, pp. 367-74 and Note 172. p. 624

371 The reference is to the attempts to organise diplomatic and military interference by the five European powers (France, Britain, Russia, Austria and Prussia) in the civil war in Switzerland in the interests of the Sonderbund. They were initiated by the Austrian Chancellor Metternich and supported by the Guizot government. Metternich and Guizot planned to call a conference of the five great powers on the Swiss question to dictate peace terms to the belligerent parties in Switzerland. However, the speedy rout of the Sonderbund's troops and the negative attitude of the British government thwarted these plans. p. 624

372 The reference is to the *German Workers' Society* in Brussels (see Note 208). p. 626

373 During their stay in London as delegates to the Second Congress of the Communist League in late November and early December 1847, Marx and Engels also took part in the meetings of the London German Workers' Educational Society (see Note 336). They made several reports to the members of the Society. The extant records of their speeches, very laconic and of poor quality, are given here and below in the same sequence as in the Minutes of the Society. p. 627

374 See Note 208. p. 630

375 These Rules of the Communist League are based on the draft Rules elaborated by the League's First Congress (see this volume, pp. 585-88). Marx and Engels, who exerted considerable influence on the elaboration of the League's new organisational principles, greatly contributed to improving the text of the Rules and gave it greater precision. In particular, it was they, in all probability, who drew up the new formulation of Article 1 defining the aim of the League. The Rules in their present version were adopted by the Second Congress of the Communist League.

This document was first published in English in the book: Karl Marx and Frederick Engels, *The Communist Manifesto*, Lawrence, London, 1930. p. 633

376 Proposals to establish more regular contacts between the democrats of different countries and to prepare an international democratic congress were discussed by the representatives of the Fraternal Democrats with Marx acting on behalf of the Committee of the Democratic Association, during his and Engels' stay in London at the end of November and the beginning of December 1847 (see also notes 192 and 206). p. 640

377 The Democratic Association's deputation sent to Ghent for the opening of the Association's local affiliation included Marx. p. 641

378 In mid-December 1847 Engels arrived in Brussels from London, where he had spent some time after the Second Congress of the Communist League, and at the end of December he returned to Paris with the authority of the Brussels Democratic Association to represent it in the capital of France. The French authorities were alarmed by Engels' resumption of revolutionary propaganda among the Paris workers and craftsmen. At the end of January 1848 the Paris police proceeded against Engels under the pretext that his speech at the New Year's Eve banquet of the German revolutionary emigrants on December 31, 1847 contained political allusions hostile to the French government. On January 29, 1848 Engels was ordered to leave France within 24 hours under the threat of extradition to Prussia. Simultaneously with Engels' expulsion and the police breaking into his flat at night, arrests were made among the German emigrant workers. Despite the slander circulated by the governmental press (accusations of defiant behaviour, and of fighting duels), information about the real reasons behind Engels' expulsion filtered into the oppositional newspapers. p. 643

379 The original of this document is kept in the National Archives in Paris among the papers of the Provisional Government of the French Republic of 1848. The Address was published in the Belgian *Le Débat social* on March 1, 1848, and reprinted in *La Réforme* on March 4. The texts differ slightly. In this edition use is made of the text in *La Réforme*.

In English the Address was published with abbreviations in the *Labour Monthly* No. 2, February 1948. p. 645

380 The Second Congress of the Communist League retained the seat of the Central Authority in London. However, in view of the revolution starting in France, Schapper, Bauer, Moll and other members of the London Central Authority intended to move to the Continent and decided to transfer their powers of general guidance of the League to the Brussels circle authority headed by Marx. But the persecution of revolutionaries which had begun in Belgium, the order for Marx's expulsion and the arrest of other activists of the League compelled the Brussels Central Authority that had been formed to adopt the decision (published below) to dissolve itself and to empower Marx to form a new Central Authority in Paris. Marx arrived in Paris on

March 5 and wrote to Engels (he still remained in Brussels for some time) around March 12, 1848 that the new Central Authority had been recently set up and consisted of Marx (chairman), Schapper (secretary), Wallau, Wolff, Moll, Bauer (members). Engels was appointed in his absence.

An abridged version of this document was first published in French in *Annales parlementaires belges*. Session 1847-1848. Chambre des représentants, séance du 31 mars 1848, p. 1203. This document was first published in English in the *Labour Monthly* No. 3, March 1948. p. 651

381 The *German Workers' Club* was founded in Paris on March 8 and 9, 1848 on the initiative of the Communist League's leaders. The leading role in it belonged to Marx. The Club's aim was to unite the German emigrant workers in Paris, explain to them the tactics of the proletariat in a bourgeois-democratic revolution and also to counter the attempts of the bourgeois and petty-bourgeois democrats (among them, Herwegh, Venedey and Decker, the last two being mentioned in the minutes) to stir up the German workers by nationalist propaganda and enlist them into the adventurist march of volunteer legions into Germany. The Club was successful in arranging the return of German workers one by one to their own country to take part in the revolutionary struggle there. p. 654

382 The German Democratic Society, formed in Paris after the February revolution of 1848, held its meetings in a riding school. The Society was headed by petty-bourgeois democrats, Herwegh, Bornstedt, Decker and others who campaigned to raise volunteer legions of German emigrants with the aim of marching into Germany. In this way they hoped to carry out a revolution in Germany and establish a republic there. Marx and Engels resolutely condemned this adventurist plan of "exporting revolution". p. 656

NAME INDEX

B

C

I

J

N

O

P

S

T

INDEX OF LITERARY AND MYTHOLOGICAL NAMES

A

B

C

D

E

F

G

H

I

J

L

M

P

INDEX OF QUOTED AND MENTIONED LITERATURE

WORKS BY KARL MARX AND FREDERICK ENGELS

WORKS BY DIFFERENT AUTHORS

Börne, L. *51. Brief aus Paris vom 8. Oktober 1831.* In: *Gesammelte Schriften. von Ludwig Börne.* 2-te Auflage. Bd. XIII, Hamburg, 1832.—259, 273

Bowring, J. [Speech in the House of Commons, July 1835.] Quoted from: Atkinson, W. *Principles of Political Economy.* London, 1840.—416, 422, 460, 461

— [Speech at the Congress of Economists, September 18, 1847.] Summary in: *Journal des économistes,* t. XVIII, Paris, 1847.—285, 458, 460

Bray, J. Fr. *Labour's Wrongs and Labour's Remedy; or, the Age of Might and the Age of Right.* Leeds, 1839.—138-42, 144, 421

Buchez, P. J. B. et Roux, P. C. *Histoire parlementaire de la Révolution française, ou Journal des Assemblées Nationales, depuis 1789 jusqu'en 1815...,* 40 vols. Paris, 1834-38.—253

Buonarroti, Ph. *Conspiration pour l'égalité dite de Babeuf, suivie du procès auquel elle donna lieu, et des pièces justificatives,* etc., etc. T. I-II, Bruxelles, 1828.—321

Byron, G. *Childe Harold's Pilgrimage.*—8

Cabet, [E.] *Voyage en Icarie, roman philosophique et social.* Paris, 1842.—516

Campe, J. H. *Die Entdeckung von Amerika.* Ein Unterhaltungsbuch für Kinder und junge Leute. 5. Aufl., Th. 1-3, Braunschweig, 1801.—336

Carlyle, Th. *Chartism.* London, 1840.—416

— *The French Revolution: a History.* In three volumes. Vol. III. London, 1837.—10

Carmagnole (a French revolutionary song).—4

Carnot, L.-H. *Les Radicaux et la charte.* Paris, 1847.—443

Chant du départ—see Chénier, Méhul. *Chant du départ.*

Chénier, Méhul. *Chant du départ* (a French revolutionary song).—442

Cherbuliez, A. *Riche ou Pauvre. Exposition succincte des causes et des effets de la distribution actuelle des richesses sociales.* Paris-Genève, 1840.—421

Cooper, Th. *Lectures on the Elements of Political Economy.* Columbia, 1826.—153, 323

— 2nd edition. London, 1831.—153

Cooper, Th. *The Purgatory of Suicides. A Prison-Rhyme.* In ten books. London, 1845.—8

[Dairnvaell, G. M.] *Histoire édifiante et curieuse de Rothschild I-er, roi des juifs.* Paris, 1846.—62

Dante Alighieri. *La Divina commedia.*—271

Daumer, G. F. *Die Geheimnisse des christlichen Altertums.* Bd. 1-2, Hamburg, 1847.—631

Duesberg, F. von. *Denkschrift, betreffend die Aufhebung der Mahl- und Schlachtsteuer, die Beschränkung der Klassensteuer und die Erhebung einer Einkommensteuer.* In: *Der Erste Vereinigte Landtag in Berlin 1847.* Th. I, Berlin, 1847.—230

Dunoyer, Ch. *De la liberté du travail, ou simple exposé des conditions dans lesquelles les forces humaines s'exercent avec le plus de puissance.* T. I-II, Paris, 1845.—278

Edmonds, T. R. *Practical Moral and Political Economy; or the Government, Religion, and Institutions, Most Conducive to Individual Happiness and to National Power.* London, 1828.—138

DOCUMENTS

ANONYMOUS ARTICLES AND REPORTS PUBLISHED IN PERIODIC EDITIONS

INDEX OF PERIODICALS

SUBJECT INDEX

D

E

H

I

J

K

L

M

N